INVERARAY AND
THE DUKES OF ARGYLL

Semper Tibi Pendeat Halec

IAN G. LINDSAY AND MARY COSH

INVERARAY

AND THE DUKES

OF ARGYLL

with a foreword by the Eleventh Duke of Argyll

NE OBLIVISCARIS

EDINBURGH

UNIVERSITY

PRESS

© 1973

EDINBURGH UNIVERSITY PRESS
22 George Square, Edinburgh

ISBN 0 85224 187 9

North America
Aldine Publishing Company
529 South Wabash Avenue,
Chicago

Library of Congress
Catalog Card Number
73–130761

Printed in Great Britain by
The Kynoch Press,
Birmingham
Plates printed by
W & J Mackay Limited,
Chatham

*The Coat of Arms on the title-page is that
of the Dukes of Argyll; the Arms of
the Royal Burgh of Inveraray
are reproduced on
the half-title.*

Foreword

BY THE ELEVENTH DUKE OF ARGYLL

I hope that this book, published by the Edinburgh University Press, will be of the greatest interest to all members of the Clan Diarmid throughout the world, and to many others as well.

It has been long in the making. In 1949 my father's cousin the 10th Duke of Argyll and 24th Mac Cailein Mor died. The Castle had remained exactly as it was when I first knew it in the 1920–27 period—and indeed since my great-grandfather's death in 1900. But the West Coast climate had played havoc with the structure both within and without. The Royal Burgh of Inveraray, known to hundreds of thousands of the Allied Navies, Armies and Air Forces during the last war, was very largely owned by the Estate. There, too, climate and neglect had caused all but irreparable damage.

The crushing burden of Death Duties on my succession made it a question whether or not the restoration of the Castle and Town could be undertaken. Fortunately we decided that one of the most beautiful and original creations of the eighteenth century should not be allowed to perish.

We were doubly fortunate in finding that Ian Lindsay was ready to undertake the task of reparation and restoration of the Castle and later of the Town. For months we shared the frightening experience of finding outbreaks of dry-rot and wet-rot, of stripping floors and walls and ceilings, of tracing Victorian plumbing in the massive walls, of re-wiring a large building which had been the first house 'electrified' in Scotland by my great-grandfather's friend, Lord Kelvin, in the early 1890s. Roof, window frames, doors and floors had to be renewed. It was an apparently endless and expensive job. But in 1953 the Castle was fit to be opened to the public. Now it is visited by some ninety thousand people from all parts of the world each year.

During the course of the restoration and redecoration of the building we had to trace and consult the chaotic mass of eighteenth- and nineteenth-century papers dealing with the Castle and the Town. Miss Mary Cosh, a most indefatigable researcher, took on the task. Not 'little by little', but more and more she became absorbed in the work. Her discoveries were made here, in Edinburgh, in London and in many other likely and unlikely places. The completion and revision of the text of this book is entirely due to her.

Finally my thanks and those both of my Clan and the visitors to Inveraray are due to my contemporary Hugh Molson, now Lord Molson, who as Minister of Works in 1957–59 enabled the restoration of Inveraray Town, which was planned and superintended by Ian Lindsay. Lord Molson was also responsible for the repairs to another old Campbell stronghold, Dunstaffnage Castle on the Firth of Lorne.

Ian Lindsay had an exceptional combination of the gifts of experience, knowledge and curiosity. Many buildings in Scotland, from Iona in the West to our eastern shores of the North Sea, have been saved by him for posterity, some from abandoned ruins, others from the ignorant and tasteless accretions of comparatively recent 'restoration'. The original idea of this book was his own, and we had very many conversations on its form and content.

The restoration of the Castle and the Town of Inveraray posed an infinity of problems, but Ian's enthusiasm and determination conquered all the apparently insurmountable questions. It is tragic that he did not live to see this book in print.

Ne obliviscaris

✤

Contents

Preface

Inveraray, traditional capital of the Dukes of Argyll, and site both of the earliest large mansion built in the Gothick style and the earliest eighteenth-century planned town in Britain, was a place very close to Ian Lindsay's heart. For over five years he directed an inspired restoration and conservation of the town, and it was one of his dearest wishes to complete a history of its remarkable architectural background. At his untimely death in 1966 more than seven years' work had already gone into this book. What had begun as the idea of a small handbook based on new information on the architectural history had, because of the unexpected wealth of material discovered both at the castle and among the Saltoun papers, blossomed into a large and complex volume.

For this as it then stood, Ian Lindsay had written the architectural descriptions and analysis, while I provided the necessary research and wrote the historical and social portions, always with his invaluable guidance and criticism. When he died, however, one chapter (VII) and the Epilogue still unfortunately remained unwritten, while chapter X was incomplete.

With the kind consent of Mrs Lindsay and her family, it was eventually decided that rather than introduce another co-author, I should complete and revise the book with David Walker as architectural adviser. The necessary revision proved, in fact, considerable, as continuing research revealed new and very important information, particularly on the origins of the castle's design (section I of chapter II) and the evolution of the new town (chapters IV and VIII); while the whole book was extensively revised except for chapters III and V, which remain substantially as they had been in the light of our knowledge in 1966.

The completion of the book would have been impossible, at this stage, without David Walker's invaluable expertise and advice, and his noting of my many errors and omissions. I owe him an immense debt of gratitude for his contribution towards finishing the work on the lines that Ian Lindsay would have wished.

The greatest acknowledgment over this book, from the moment of its inception, must undoubtedly go to His Grace The Duke of Argyll, for his deep interest and active encouragement throughout, and his generous hospitality to Ian Lindsay and myself during many visits to the castle, where we had full access to his vast and

Ian Lindsay on Duniquaich

important collection of manuscripts and the value of his own wide knowledge of the place and its history.

I am extremely grateful to Eric Cregeen, of Edinburgh University School of Scottish Studies, who has read the whole work at various stages, and whose detailed knowledge of the social and historical background of the West Highlands in the eighteenth century has been so helpful in placing the subject in perspective.

I am, too, greatly indebted to Arthur Eden, who read the sections dealing with Roger Morris and whose knowledge of that architect's career proved very helpful; to Alistair Rowan, for reading the first two chapters and allowing me to consult his important thesis on the Castle Style in English architecture; to Christopher Hibbert, who also read the whole book at different stages and gave encouragement and advice; to John Reid, now senior partner of Ian G. Lindsay and Partners, for making available his professional expertise on the buildings of Inveraray; to Mrs Marie Draper, for invaluable guidance on finding source material; and to Miss Kitty Cruft, of the National Monuments Record of Scotland, for constant and ready information from her encyclopaedic knowledge of Scottish architects and architecture. I would like to thank virtually the whole staff of the National Library of Scotland, and in particular James Ritchie of the Manuscripts Department and Miss Ann Young and her staff in the Map Room in which I have pursued my researches for so many years. My thanks go to John Imrie, Keeper of the Records, and the staff of the Scottish Record Office; Charles Finlayson of the Edinburgh University Library, Department of Manuscripts; John Harris and the staff of the R.I.B.A. Drawings Collection; and the staffs of the Scottish National Portrait Gallery, the Edinburgh Room of the Edinburgh Public Library, and the British Museum Library, its Department of Manuscripts, and Map Room.

Of those who so generously made their manuscripts, prints and drawings available for consultation, the chief debt of gratitude is, after the Duke of Argyll, to Miss J.M.H. Mylne, of Great Amwell, Hertfordshire, who made her important collection of her ancestor Robert Mylne's papers freely available to us, entertained Ian Lindsay and myself most hospitably, and showed great interest in our researches; and to the Directors of Messrs Coutts & Company for allowing me to consult their Ledgers and Letterbooks, and in particular to their Archivist Miss Veronica Stokes for her unfailing help and interest. For permission to consult and quote from their manuscripts grateful thanks are due to His Grace The Duke of Atholl, His Grace The Duke of Buccleuch, the Most Noble The Marquess of Bute, Sir John Clerk of Penicuik, Captain Charles Adam of Blair Adam, Captain J.T.T. Fletcher of Saltoun, and to John Campbell and the late Donald Clerk, former Provosts, and Peter Monro, former Town Clerk of Inveraray.

Among the many people who kindly gave advice and information at different times are the Misses Catherine and Helen Armet, Geoffrey Beard, C.W. Black of the Mitchell Library, Glasgow, Miss J. Cameron and Miss Grant of Bo'ness Public Library, the late Robert D. Carr, formerly of the Planning Department of Argyll County Council, Anthony Coleridge, Howard Colvin, Edward Croft-Murray,

Angus Davidson, former Head Forester to the Argyll Estates, Richard Dell, City Archivist of Glasgow, John Dunbar, Sir James Fergusson, Bart, John Fleming, Terence Friedman, George Hay, Donald Mackechnie, former Headmaster of the Grammar School at Inveraray, Iain MacIvor, Colin McWilliam, W. H. Makey, Burgh Archivist of Edinburgh, D. G. Moir, Secretary of the Royal Scottish Geographical Society, John Read, of Howard Sant Partnership, Basil Skinner, Sir John Summerson, Dr Alan Tait, Mrs Averil Walker, and Francis Watson. From Paris I had the help of Mme Bouleau Rabaud of the Ecole Nationale Supérieure des Beaux-Arts, Mme Guerin of the Musée des Arts Décoratifs, M. Hébert of the Bibliothèque Nationale (Cabinet des Estampes), and Charles Sterling and the Service d'Etude et de Documentation of the Musée du Louvre; while from Australia information was kindly provided by the staff of the Public Library of New South Wales.

Finally, I should like to express my appreciation to Archie Turnbull, Secretary to the Edinburgh University Press, for taking on the publication of this book against all odds, and to Walter Cairns for his patience and care in seeing an extremely difficult manuscript through the press.

With so much assistance and valued information from so many quarters it remains only to say that any errors are undoubtedly my own.

MARY COSH
London and Edinburgh
December 1971

The death of the 11th Duke of Argyll in April 1973, while this book was in its final stages of production, makes a sad postscript. He had read the whole book in typescript and had made valuable comments and corrections; it is a matter of great regret that he did not live to see it published. The work now stands as a tribute to the memory both of the 11th Duke and of Ian Lindsay.   M.C.

Text Illustrations

Plates

Edwin Smith, who died in December 1971, took these photographs
at the direction of Ian Lindsay in the Spring of 1962

(*overleaf*) Part of Argyll, from Dorret's Map of
Scotland (1750), showing Inveraray's central
but inaccessible position in south-west Scotland

PART ONE

As for the necessity of my being some time in Scotland, its very obvious, & curiosity alone if it were not my Love of laying out Grounds & Gardning would draw me thither, especially considering, that I have now done with Political Ambition, & shall be very unwilling to meddle in such sort of Storms, but content my self merely to satisfie my tasts in things that can occasion no disquiet.

3rd Duke of Argyll to Lord Milton, 12 November 1743, Saltoun 401

Inverary is as singularly beautiful as the road to it is singularly bad, fitt only for Wild Goats to scramble over.

James Smollett of Bonhill to his father-in-law Sir John Clerk,
13 May 1741, Penicuik MSS, SRO, GD 18/5435

I

On 4 October 1743 John Campbell, 'the great Duke of Argyll', died, prematurely worn out at sixty-three. The dukedom which King William III had granted Duke John's father, the 10th Earl of Argyll, passed in the second generation from its direct descent, for Duke John, ambitious, arrogant and erratic, showy as a military commander and as a politician, had married as his second wife a lady of obscure birth, who bore him in disillusioning succession a series of five daughters.

The Duke treated his eldest daughter Caroline, who married the Earl of Dalkeith, as far as possible like a male heir; but he could not will her his titles or his hereditary Scottish estates. Large tracts of Argyll in the Western Highlands, its capital Inveraray with the ancestral castle of the Campbells, far-flung islands some of them many miles off the coast, together with lands in central Scotland and a lodging in the old royal palace or abbey of Holyroodhouse, passed in law to his brother Archibald, Earl of Ilay, a man of almost opposite character to his own. Lady Dalkeith's inheritance included Caroline Park near Edinburgh and Adderbury in Oxfordshire, while the Duchess, still repining her lack of sons, received Sudbrooke at Petersham, the Duke's Bruton Street house, and other London property. The passing of the Argyll estates to her husband's younger brother was a great annoyance to the uncouth Duchess, who used to complain: 'Ay! the estate will go to my Lord Ilay, and he will give it all to his bastard!'[1]

The Earl of Ilay was sixty-one years old, long a widower, and had no legitimate children, so that on his death – which in view of his age his contemporaries supposed not many years distant – the Scottish inheritance would again pass indirectly, to the descendants of John Campbell of Mamore, a younger brother of the 1st Duke.

But the new Duke of Argyll, more phlegmatic than fiery, had immense reserves of energy, and as long as the estates were his he was prepared to undertake a whole series of schemes whose magnitude and difficulty of inception might have deterred a much younger man. Simple to the point of parsimony in his personal tastes and daily life, the new Duke had a comprehensive, even architectonic vision, and a lawyer's shrewd grasp of men and affairs, be they the welfare of tenants, the planning of houses, estates and towns, or the industrialization of a whole country – namely his ancestral Scotland.

To Scotland Duke Archibald now planned to return, almost from the day that he inherited the title and estates from his brother. Both brothers had lived most of their lives in or near London, although their connexions with Scotland were always very close. But whereas the elder had visited his Highland capital of Inveraray comparatively recently, Duke Archibald appears to have been no nearer to it than Edinburgh since his military command during the Jacobite rising of 1715. His journey now took weeks, lengthening into months, to prepare, and long before setting foot in the place he worked out a complete transformation scheme for Inveraray's castle and town, not to mention the lives of its inhabitants – in fact, a remarkably early piece of eighteenth-century town planning.

The Duke's first visit in the capacity of Mac Cailein Mor, Chief of the Campbells, was thus an occasion of historic moment, rendered no less memorable by the physical difficulty of getting there at all. For, as Inveraray could be approached only by a roundabout sea voyage, or a hazardous journey on horseback with guides through wild mountains, considerable preparation was necessary. No carriage road existed nearer than Dumbarton, and a military road between there and Inveraray, though projected, was so far not begun. Characteristically, to the 3rd Duke of Argyll this very inaccessibility was a stimulating challenge.

The man who launched a set of architectural and social changes which were to revolutionize Inveraray, extending over more than half a century, was the fifth successive Archibald Campbell to inherit the peerage, in a family whose political history had been, to say the least, volatile. The second of these men had been his great-grandfather, 8th Earl and only Marquess, the Argyll who, having led the Scottish Covenanters against King Charles I's troops under Montrose (who defeated him), six years later in 1651 placed the crown on the head of King Charles II at Scone; later still engaged himself to support Cromwell's government; and finally, therefore, was repudiated by the restored King, and executed in Edinburgh for High Treason in 1661. The attainted estates and titles (except that of Marquess) were, however, restored to his son the 9th Earl; who in turn was condemned for High Treason on refusing to subscribe to the Test Act of 1681, but escaped from Edinburgh Castle disguised as a page, aided by his step-daughter Lady Sophia Lindsay. The 9th Earl was eventually executed in 1685 on the same spot as his father, after attempting to invade Scotland in an unsuccessful bid to overthrow King James VII and II.

This inherited enmity to the Stewarts reaped a reward for the next generation when in 1701 the fourth of these Archibald Campbells, the 10th Earl, a devoted servant to the Prince of Orange, received from him as King William III a dukedom and a string of other titles, for services during the Revolution of 1688–9.[2] When he received these honours – only two years before his death – his sons John and Archibald, both born at Ham House, Petersham, were already grown men of twenty-one and nineteen. John, 'the great Duke of Argyll', soon became renowned as both soldier and statesman, served with distinction throughout Marlborough's

Low Countries campaigns and effectively directed the forces in Scotland, as Commander-in-Chief, during the rising of 1715. In 1733 he became a Field-Marshal. The younger brother, born in 1682, spent his schooldays at Eton and then studied law at Glasgow University and later at Utrecht, as was common practice among the Scots. He too, however, served briefly under Marlborough, was later appointed Treasurer of Scotland, and in 1706 was one of the Commissioners for drawing up the Act of Union between England and Scotland. For the peerage in his own right which Queen Anne then granted him, Lord Archibald settled on the title of Earl of Ilay ('generally spoken Yela', commented the Earl of Mar, 'tho' it be not so spell'd').[3]*

Lord Ilay became successively a member of the Privy Council, Lord Justice General of Scotland and Keeper of the Privy Seal of Scotland. During the Fifteen he had another short period of soldiering when, under his brother as Commander-in-Chief, he defended Inveraray, and fought at Sheriffmuir, receiving a wound in the arm, and another in the leg which for the rest of his life left him rather lame. In 1734 Ilay resigned the Privy Seal, and from then until his death was Keeper of the Great Seal. Although he made an able soldier when called upon, his interests were more of the intellect. His political and legal ability was demonstrated after the Malt Tax riots in Glasgow and Edinburgh (1725), and in the aftermath of the Porteous Riots of 1736, when Sir Robert Walpole despatched him to Edinburgh to handle the situation for the Government. Ilay's able grasp of Scottish affairs, and his evident skill in these crises persuaded Walpole, while always mistrusting both him and Argyll, to leave Scotland to their control for the remainder of his Ministry; and for nearly twenty years the brothers, with the judges Lord Milton and Duncan Forbes of Culloden (Lord Advocate, later Lord President of the Court of Session), 'managed' the elections, patronage and, in effect, the government of Scotland, until Duke John's political *volte-face* towards the end of his life ended his own public career.[4]* The younger brother still retained his control, to such an extent that he was known as 'King of Scotland'.

In character and temperament Lord Ilay was very different from his elder brother. Duke John, the soldier, was as Lady Louisa Stuart puts it, 'properly speaking, a hero'; politically his fortunes were chequered, ranging from high favour (during one period of which he received the additional United Kingdom dukedom of Greenwich, expiring with him since he had no son) to disgrace, dismissal and royal neglect. At his death he was in his latest period of retirement, having quarrelled with Walpole's most recent policies, and although restored to his position by the Newcastle coalition which succeeded Walpole, he withdrew finally from public life overcome by ill-health, disillusion, and disgust at the new Government's ineptitude.

As his second wife, Duke John married an uncultured lady from Cheshire named Jane Warburton, whose homely appearance and forthright speech – really lack of manners – appealed to the cynical peer, who remained devoted to her throughout their married life, in spite of her failure to bear a son. The Duke left the management of his family to the ignorant, haphazard upbringing of his wife; the bevy of rowdy, undisciplined girls known to society as 'the bawling Campbells' or 'the screaming sisterhood' romped around unchecked at home and filled their parents' public rooms with their dogs and cats. They grew up shrill hoydens, the most spoilt and indulged of them all being Lady Mary, the youngest, whose ungovernable temper was even encouraged by her father for his amusement – with disastrous effects on her married life.[5]*

In public life, the 2nd Duke was held by his contemporaries to have genius, but with a haughty and unpredictable temper. He and Ilay, so widely dissimilar, disagreed over politics as over other things. 'The Duke thought Ilay undignified and time-serving; Lord Ilay thought the Duke wrong-headed and romantic. Yet both were assuredly superior men.' The more subtle and devious Archibald had the lawyer's shrewd penetration and good business sense, unlike his brother's rash but more magnanimous disposition. Indeed, writes their great-niece Lady Louisa, Ilay was, in contrast to his brother, 'altogether a man of this world'.

Lord Ilay had, too, a man of the world's accomplishments which his soldier-brother lacked. Yet his interests were so wide that his associates included men whom his peers considered unsuitably humble; he made a study of 'philosophical experiments, mechanics, natural history', even of the obscure and still barely-developed science of Political Economy. He patronized men who brought him their inventions and aided his scientific pursuits, and was equally at ease with high and low, a gift which brought him the affectionate admiration of those who served him, and the exasperation of his enemies.[6]

When he succeeded his brother, Ilay had been a widower for twenty years, his wife Anne, daughter of Major Walter Whitfield, Paymaster General of the Forces, having died without issue in 1723. The marriage was unsatisfactory and Horace Walpole – who, regarding the Earl of Ilay as a political betrayer of his father Sir Robert, always refers to him with malice and innuendo – hints pretty broadly that Lady Ilay deceived her husband over her financial expectations. In his disappointment Ilay, who had rapidly tired of her, left her to the company of his sharp-tongued mother in the West Highlands, and she died neglected and unreconciled.[7]*

Ilay was not, however, childless, having a son (and apparently also a daughter) by a mistress whom he kept for many years, known impartially as Mrs Ann Williams or Shireburn. Of this lady, who lived partly in a house adjoining his estate at Whitton, and partly in London in one of his Argyll Street houses, there survives no description, and she receives no mention in correspondence during his lifetime. For their son, William Williams, he obtained in 1739 a sinecure as Deputy Auditor of the Exchequer in Scotland, and later a commission in the 3rd Foot Guards (now the Scots Guards).[8] Father and son had a strong affection for one another, and the young man was highly regarded among his father's friends.

In appearance and habits by all accounts Ilay was not attractive. 'His heart was, like his aspect, vile', writes Sir Charles Hanbury Williams in one of his scurrilous verses. 'A pedantic, dirty, shrewd, unbred fellow of a college, with a mean

1. Archibald, 3rd Duke of Argyll, 1682–1761
   From a portrait by Allan Ramsay.

aspect', was how he struck his own political ally Lord Hervey. Although most contemporaries attest his intellect and conversational powers, they also accord with Horace Walpole's description of him as 'slovenly in his person, mysterious, not to say with an air of guilt, in his deportment'.[9] To the present-day observer the face that looks out of the portraits of Ilay in middle life, and of him later as Duke, appears strongly-modelled, secretive, subtle and humorous; but even allowing for the hostile exaggeration of enemies, his person seems to have been anything but elegant, and he was far too interested in cultivating men of intellect and scientific achievement to cut a figure in society.

Not being a lover of ceremony, he was at pains to make the humble – particularly if talented – at home, as well as the aristocratic. A good talker, he 'never harangued or was tedious', writes Dr Alexander Carlyle, 'but listened to you in your turn', and had a collection of good stories which 'he told so neatly, and so frequently repeated them without variation, as to make one believe that he had wrote them down'. Dr Carlyle first met him in 1757, towards the end of the Duke's life, and regarded him as an 'illustrious person, both as a statesman and an accomplished gentleman and scholar'.[10]

Ilay was recognized to have the knack of finding out and employing able men. Chief among these in his political and business exploits was Andrew Fletcher, Lord Milton, who was his associate in Scotland for nearly forty years. Fletcher, nephew of the celebrated Scottish patriot Andrew Fletcher of Saltoun, was nine years younger than Ilay; he became a judge in 1724 with the title of Lord Milton, and through Ilay's influence was appointed Lord Justice Clerk in 1735. He married Elizabeth Kinloch of Gilmerton, an amiable, bustling and rattle-pated woman, and had a large family of sons and daughters; the eldest, another Andrew, was bred up to his father's profession of law and later sent into Parliament. Milton's reputation was not wholly untarnished in that he made use of dubious, time-serving underlings, but he was known as a 'dexterous politician' – indeed his illustrious uncle, who hated politicians, early predicted that he would 'turn out *a corrupt fellow* and a perfect courtier'; and the far less scrupulous Lord Arniston (Robert Dundas the elder), being of a rival faction, referred to him as 'that puppy'. On the other hand, Milton was justly honoured for humanity, and a lack of vengefulness in a vengeful age. His letters breathe kindliness and humanity, even in the administration of the law and manipulation of politics; he continually served his country's economic as well as political interest, and he actively promoted industry and trade, particularly the linen manufacture. Though shrewd in his own canny fashion, Lord Milton was skilled in the way of the world, rather than distinguished for intellect like Ilay.[11]

Among Lord Ilay's own major interests was his library, so important that it gave a name to his London house in Argyll Street. From early youth he was happiest buying and studying 'books and jimcracks', and at the time of his brother's death in October 1743 the new London library, a gallery nearly a hundred feet long and twenty-two feet wide, had been recently completed and was being

2. Andrew Fletcher, Lord Milton, 1692–1766
   Lord Justice Clerk, 1735–48. From the portrait
   by Allan Ramsay of 1748.

stocked. Some ten days after the 2nd Duke's funeral John Maule was describing to
Lord Milton how 'The Peer [the name by which Ilay was facetiously known to his
friends] & I were through every bookseller's Shop in London this forenoon, besides
fifty other places; The Ducal Coronet is not ye least barr upon him & he goes
about & does every thing as usual. I find there will be a new Library purchased for
Inverary, & ye purchases for yt purpose are sett a going already . . .'[12]

One of Ilay's pursuits which did accord with current fashion was his keen
interest in architecture and building, and the attendant art of designing parks and
gardens – with this original distinction, that he preferred the challenge of trans-
forming a piece of barren ground, the more unpromising the better. His estate
known as 'The Whim' in Peeblesshire, cultivated since 1729, was his most extreme
venture of this kind, typical of his eccentricity in the choice of a high, bleak moss.
An earlier experiment was his purchase in 1722 of a tract of waste ground at
Whitton on the wide desert of Hounslow Heath, where he created a nursery and
propagated exotic trees and shrubs; the cedars which he grew there from seed
were to become some of the largest and most famous in the country, and seeds of
many kinds of tree were sent him from abroad – many from friends in North
America – to be raised at Whitton, and their offspring despatched every year to the
nurseries of his friends in Scotland.

Characteristically, before building himself a house at Whitton, Ilay built a con-
servatory – a singular greenhouse designed by James Gibbs and fitted up to accommodate weekend guests. He laid out the estate in a formal contemporary style with
vistas through trees and shrubberies, a canal and other ornamental waters, serpentine paths punctuated by small pavilions, the whole dominated by a high three-
turreted Gothick tower of brick. This tower was very likely also the work of Gibbs,
and the later small Palladian villa, built in or after 1733, was probably designed by
Roger Morris.[13]*

Ilay's passion for the cultivation of 'exoticks', with which he infected his
friends, earned him still deeper contempt from Horace Walpole, to whose opinion,
however, he was oblivious. On the other hand, he had little aesthetic taste and
cared nothing for painting, a singular lack in his family in that age of patronage of
the arts, and indeed Inveraray has never been noted for pictures apart from its fine
collection of portraits.

Such paintings as Duke John possessed in any case passed from the Argyll succession on his death, for the bulk of his personal property was settled on his eldest
daughter Caroline. For the Argyll inheritance itself, however, the 3rd Duke now
had very positive plans. Far from squandering everything on his bastard or on anyone else, as his brother's wife prophesied, he was to turn Inveraray's neglected,
decaying old castle into something entirely new, and begin the transformation of
its gardens, plantations and town into the appearance they have today. To achieve
this purpose, long before he left London for Scotland in July 1744, Duke Archibald
had not only briefed his architect but started negotiations for a competent gardener.

Finding that Walter Paterson, the 2nd Duke's gardener at Caroline Park near

Edinburgh, was able to draw and write a good hand (for 'its very troublesome when a servant cant write to be read'), and was skilled in planting and in 'measuring and taking Levels', he proposed to steal Paterson from that estate before it was handed over to his niece, and employ him at Inveraray. The Inveraray gardener James Halden being 'a favourite of the dutchesses', he saw that he must tread warily; he had no use for Halden, whose ignorance his 'silly letters show sufficiently' – 'I see by his letters that he is a bungler'.[14]*

Plans for garden and gardener took up a large part of Argyll's sporadic correspondence with Lord Milton in the months before his first visit to Inveraray, and of the frequent lively letters of the thirty-eight-year-old John Maule who, since moving to London in 1740 as Member for Montrose, had constituted himself Milton's official news purveyor from the Peer's household, where he acted as confidential secretary. Although the bulk of this voluminous correspondence consists in political news and accounts of law appeals and suits for offices, it also contains much gossip, domestic chitchat, and information on the goods sent up for the Whim and Inveraray, particularly parcels of seeds – for among 'all the new stuff we are busie about', Maule was warned by the Duke not to neglect the Whim : 'he has often told you this winter, yt he never will forget his old friends himself, & you know yt even in ye midst of ye most serious things he must be asking about his Gimcracks'.[15] They obtained from the Whim's former owner Major Tam Cochrane 700 spruce firs to send to Inveraray, and 300 for Rosneath; and from Maule's brother's estate at Panmure, laburnum seed which the Duke intended for a nursery at Inveraray; also slips of yellow rose, from Dalhousie, which meantime Lord Milton was instructed to propagate at Brunstane.[16]

By March 1744 the Duke, having made up his mind to take on Paterson as gardener, warned Lord Milton to 'see that the terms are reasonable, otherwise I had better bring one from hence, I remember I had formerly an old fool at the Whim at a great price'.[17] The necessity of bringing in an able, honest man *from outside* is significant : Paterson, who was thirty-six, 'will by being a stranger be of great service to me in furnishing me with true facts relating to every thing about Inverary, which however necessary for me is very difficult for me to obtain'. The Duke lived at a great distance from his Argyll estates and was to visit them for only two months or so every autumn, and local employees were all too well informed how to make the most out of the place at his Grace's expense. 'I have great reason to believe', he wrote on 3 April, 'that there are many frauds practiced there of various kinds that will take me some time to discover and obviate.'[18] This was, indeed, to be the pattern of labour difficulties at Inveraray for many years.

His inheritance of the Argyll estates opened up, at an age when many men would have been looking forward to a few years of peaceful inactivity, whole new fields of experiment to this versatile Duke; and by his own admission 'curiosity alone if it were not my Love of laying out Grounds & Gardning would draw me thither, especially considering, that I have now done with Political Ambition, & shall be very unwilling to meddle in such sort of Storms, but content my self merely to satisfie my tasts in things that can occasion no disquiet'.[19]

One of his chief projects for Scotland, and particularly for Inveraray, was the encouragement of industry, about which he had already approached the Lord President, Duncan Forbes. 'I am thinking of getting some sort of Manufacture to Inverary,' he wrote to Milton on 29 October 1743, '& will spare nothing to set it up & encourage it. think of it. adieu.'[20]

The party, attended by numerous servants, which eventually reached Inveraray in the second week of August 1744 consisted of the Duke and Lord Milton; Archibald Campbell of Stonefield, Sheriff Depute and Chamberlain of Argyll; the Duke's old friend and physician Dr Charles Stewart, who lived with him in London; and his London architect, Mr Roger Morris.

To assemble these gentlemen, none of them young, in this remote spot at this time had been a feat of organization occupying a number of people's energies for at least eight or nine months beforehand. The Duke, who had begun talking of his visit the previous November, regarded a long stay as a 'very obvious' necessity and was actively planning it from April onwards; although with a French invasion all too possible in the south, and a supporting Jacobite rising imminent in the north, the time seemed hardly propitious for an elderly peer and clan chief, holding high office in the Hanoverian government, to leave London for the disaffected Highlands of Scotland. Furthermore, at the end of June 1744 the Duke celebrated his sixty-second birthday, and by his own admission was likely to make a lengthy business of the journey : 'I travel so slow you will know long before I arrive, the day of getting into Scotland.'[21] Even when all was ready, departure was continually delayed by the Duke's political commitments.

A three-cornered correspondence circulated between the Chamberlain, who was responsible for the Inveraray arrangements, Lord and Lady Milton in Edinburgh, and the Hon. John Maule. Stonefield, an obese, canny man of forty-seven, bred to the law, had been Sheriff Depute of Argyll since 1729,[22]* and for some years past had managed the Argyll estates as Chamberlain. A staunch Whig, he took care of the county's political interests as well.

So long was it since a ducal visit of more than a few days had been paid to Inveraray or Rosneath, the Duke's house on the Gareloch, that conditions for the party's reception at both were, to put it mildly, uncomfortable. The Duke's first intention was to bring 'a great many Company', but when the Chamberlain heard the news he advised Lord Milton that it would be wisest to limit the number to 'but few at this time, till he sees what accommodation there is for him, which I can venture to tell you is none of the best'. 'There is nothing to reckon here', he informed Lady Milton, 'except kitchen furnitur, Peuter, four beds with Blankets Pillows & Coverings, and a dozen of Chairs for the dineing room. In short, there is little else here, but old Remnants The late Good Dutchess of Argyll left here a long time agoe, and your Lap. knows Her Grace was not very modish in things of that kind.'[23]*

3. John Maule of Inverkeillor, 1706–81
  MP for Aberdeen Burghs, 1739–48; Baron of the Exchequer of
  Scotland, 1748–81; the 3rd Duke's confidential aide in London from
  1740–8. From the portrait by Allan Ramsay.

4. Archibald Campbell of Stonefield, 1697–1777
Sheriff Depute of Argyll. From the portrait by an unknown artist.

'The late Good Dutchess', Duke Archibald's formidable mother, had lived for some years before her death in 1735 at Limecraigs, far down the peninsula of Kintyre, and Inveraray Castle had been little occupied. It was from a distant period, Stonefield warned Lord and Lady Milton, that such furnishings as Inveraray now possessed, survived : 'I am apt to think Her Lap. will be Surpriz'd', he wrote, 'to see so litle furnitur in a Duke's house, and that litle so bad.'[24]

Nor were there servants, apart from the cook, 'an old Creature that the Late Dutchess brought here fourty years agoe from Duddistoun, She never knew much of the Nature of the office, and is now so deaf & unfirm, that she is only fit for an Infirmary'.[25]*

The Duke, unperturbed by the prospect of primitive conditions, proposed to rely on the catering of his own servant Peter Ross, not only at Inveraray but at their other stops in Scotland on the way – his house at The Whim, his hereditary lodging at Holyroodhouse, and Rosneath.[26] The actual supply of food was one of the least of the Chamberlain's problems, for meat and poultry were locally plentiful, though he recalled that the former Duke used to bring over a fisherman specially from Fife or Dunbar. Likewise there was abundant game to be had, but no fowler, 'an officer very necessary about a Great man's house', and Stonefield supposed that one must be engaged from Stirling or Dunbartonshire in the Lowlands. In the meantime his wife was fattening poultry for the visitors, the best dairy-women were bespoken for butter and milk, and Lord Milton was consulted about the wine-cellar, for Duke Archibald was a great connoisseur of claret. The bulk of groceries had never been locally obtainable but were ordered from Smith, an Edinburgh merchant : whenever the 2nd Duke was expected, the Deputy Chamberlain had been accustomed to make a visit to Edinburgh and place an order. Even items like candles had to be brought from Hamilton or Glasgow.[27]

The main difficulty was transport. 'As there is no Access of Coming to this place,' wrote Stonefield, 'without rideing a horseback, unless his Grace chuses to make a very long Tour by sea, It is Necessary that I know, if he brings horses along, or if I must send horses from hence to attend his Grace at Lochgoilhead, where the late Duke us'd to take horse.'[28]

For heavy luggage, furniture and equipment there was no alternative to sea transport; and since Britain was now at war with France and Spain this meant sailing in convoy, with the goods despatched far in advance of the travellers' own departure from London. The genial John Maule was responsible for arrangements at the London end, even to the cutlery sent up by sea, and 'I am to trust his Grace's picture in ye same bottom notwithstanding ye war, as she gets a Convoy, so I hope all will arrive safe.'[29]* William Smith, the late Duke's secretary, had drawn up a list of necessaries – to which Duke Archibald made his own additions – with notes on where to obtain them : some at Edinburgh, hams and bacons from Mrs Hill, a Newcastle innkeeper; and the Duke stipulated (Maule told Lord Milton) that 'besides Claret, he must have both strong white wine and french white wine, If a dozen of Champagne or so coud be sent he thinks there woud be no harm in it. . . .'[30]

Besides food and drink 'the Duke is to send down a Compleat Batterie de Cuisine being ye Kitchen Utensils of a Colonel when in ye Camp', and since he was always interested in 'gimcracks' he told Maule to send Lord Milton the pattern of a garden stool 'made out of the wood of some sticks out of a Lawrel Hedg which seems to be finer than any wood we have'.[31] From this, Lord Milton was to have a copy made in Edinburgh, but by a desire for economy, curious in view of the enormous expense of the whole campaign – for this by now it resembled – Maule was advising Lord Milton to save carriage by having the rest of the required dozen made up at Glasgow.[32] They actually spoke of the journey in terms of a field expedition and, learning that on his brother's death the whole contents of Rosneath on the Gareloch had been sold, which though of little value 'will cost me a hantle of siller to replace', the Duke asked Milton to provide 'some coarse common necessaries . . . which will afterwards serve for inferior uses, & will be good enough for me at this first expedition'.[33]

Inventories of the items despatched by sea that June make some odd reading. The *Isabell and May*, which sailed under Captain Haxton for Leith on the 30th, carried twelve chests of goods for the Duke of Argyll, including books, fishing tackle and arms, kitchen furniture, tools and instruments bearing witness to the Duke's scientific interests – a camera obscura, a telescope and a road measure; and trunks whose contents suggest hasty packing: 'Two Boxes of knives & forks, a Coffee Mill a little Alarum Clock, a water Scoop, 6 Stone Pipkins & 2 Basons do.'; and another: '2 Guns, 2 Bullet moulds, some Snuffers, a fork belonging to the Travelling hampers, 2 Canes with Ivory heads, 2 Umbrelloes, a Cruit frame with glasses, a parcell of little wax Candles, a lb Cannister of Tea, & 2 d°. for Lady Milton'.[34] The tea for Lady Milton had been purchased by John Maule, 'one at a Guinea & one at 16 Sh both extraordinary good'.[35]

The smaller luggage was packed in cloakbags, to be stowed in the large, lumbering coach in which the party were to set off for Scotland.

Political events detained the Duke in London longer than he anticipated. In May both Houses debated a bill to make it High Treason to correspond with the sons of the Pretender James Stewart. This over, the Duke began to 'talk of his journey to Scotland in earnest & speaks of setting out towards ye 20th of June'. He told Maule one night at Vauxhall, where the latter had carried him for an evening's entertainment, that he hoped to travel with Doctor Stewart, Roger Morris and Maule himself, so Maule at once set about final details of the journey, baggage and provisions.[36]

On the brink of their departure disquieting news arrived of Prince Charles's movements, and rumours of Dutch negotiations for peace. Argyll delayed once more on being summoned to an audience with the King and (as Maule put it) to 'take leave of all ye Grandees'. 'I believe he is late enough', Maule observed with a touch of impatience, 'if he wants to enjoy Inverary',[37] knowing how slow their progress northwards would be and anticipating an early onset of rainy autumn weather in the Highlands. Thanks to the Royal audience their departure, now

[1] Inveraray Castle and the river Aray, from the east

planned for Wednesday, 4 July, inevitably receded; on the 5th the Duke assured Maule that, after a brief visit to Whitton, 'he would not stir till he steps into ye Coach for Scotland' on Saturday. On Saturday Maule wrote, exasperated, 'We're not away yet, but ye Duke says positively he'll lye at Welling to morrows night, for my part I shall say nothing till we pass Highgate'.[38]

Surprisingly, they actually were past Highgate next day, stayed the night at Welwyn as planned, and so continued their journey by easy stages to Buckden and Stilton, whence Maule wrote that they hoped to stay successive nights at Newark, Doncaster, Wetherby, Northallerton, Durham, Morpeth, Wooler Haughead and Jingle Kirk (now Channelkirk). After ten days on the road they would dine the following Thursday at Dalkeith, 'and lye at ye Whim'.[39]* The stages averaged about 30 miles a day.

The Whim, where the party spent ten days, was appropriately named as a personal enthusiasm of the Duke's, regarded by his contemporaries as eccentric folly. In 1729, as Lord Ilay, he had purchased the land as 'a Comical Bargain' from his friend Major Thomas Cochrane of the neighbouring estate La Manca, a thousand apparently valueless acres on the nominal terms of 999 years at 3d an acre. It was a moorland tract of Peebles-shire fourteen miles from Edinburgh, and some 900 feet above sea-level; the very name, Blair Bogg, testified to its barren character, 'nothing but what they call here Moss', Ilay told his banker George Middleton, 'such ground as the Dutch use for firing'.[40]* He immediately set about improving it out of all recognition – draining, planting, raising a nursery of young trees and forming ornamental lakes, very much in the manner of what he was creating at about the same time on his Middlesex estate at Whitton. Ilay also had Lord Milton build him a house at Blair Bogg, whose execution was supervised by William Adam. This was the core of the rather forbidding mansion which still stands – substantially enlarged later in the century – though scarcely a hint now remains of Lord Ilay's rich landscapes and plantations. He named it 'The Whim' in recognition of the scepticism of his friends who, Major Cochrane claimed, thought Ilay 'madder than himself'.[41]*

In spite of a summary pronouncement that 'as to the famous City of Edenburgh I intend to feed very little there',[42] the Duke nevertheless did, in July 1744, stay in the city, where as Hereditary Master of the Royal Household in Scotland he had a lodging at the Palace of Holyroodhouse. He also stayed with Lord Milton a few miles east of the city at Brunstane, an Argyll property of which Lord Milton was tenant. In Edinburgh the Duke held daily levees, according to Milton 'of Noah's ark in number & kinds'.[43] After a few days John Maule left for his family estates at Panmure in Angus, later joining the party at Inveraray with their mutual friend – who happened also to be a client of Roger Morris – James, 2nd Duke of Atholl.

Early in August the Duke's cavalcade left Edinburgh for the west, together with Lord and Lady Milton. The lady was a great favourite of the Duke's friends because of her vivacity, sociability and (especially valuable on this occasion) her

[2] Inveraray Castle, spiral staircase

capability as a housewife. At Glasgow they were met by John Campbell, Deputy Chamberlain of Argyll, come from Inveraray to attend His Grace and handle the arrangements for the remainder of the journey, which was almost in the nature of a royal progress. At his entry to the city the Duke was received with a grand welcome by the magistrates and crowds of townspeople, followed next day by a levee at the Town House and another at the Lord Provost's.[44]

Their departure from Glasgow was complex and expensive. The numerous boxes and crates sent by sea to Leith and thence by road, were awaiting the Duke's arrival, their contents filling the Customs Shed. The Deputy Chamberlain had to pay the dues, engage working parties, and hire fourteen carts at half-a-crown apiece to carry the baggage to Renfrew. Porters worked until noon loading boxes on to the carts. At Renfrew the horses ridden from Inveraray by John Campbell and his servant were ferried across to Rosneath, while the Duke, the Miltons, Doctor Stewart, Roger Morris and the Deputy Chamberlain sailed down the Clyde, in a barge placed at their disposal by old Sir John Shaw, to Greenock, where they were splendidly entertained for a night or two by Sir John and his redoubtable wife Margaret, at the Mansion close by.[45]* What Roger Morris thought of this non-stop ceremony and public hospitality is not recorded; but judging from the tone of his few surviving letters he felt honoured and gratified to be of the party.

The bulk of the baggage was sent ahead to Inveraray, some of it in a Customs launch, the remainder in a freight boat. Accompanied by Sir John the Duke and his party re-embarked, again in Sir John's barge, and sailed up the entrance of the Gareloch to the Duke's empty castle at Rosneath. This old house, stripped of its furniture by the orders of the Duke's sister-in-law – 'plundered', Lord Milton drily observed, 'by state misunderstandings' – had nothing to offer them and their stay was in the nature of camping. While the Duke and friends sat down to drink, the servants unpacked the tents with which they travelled, and by their exertions and Lady Milton's supervision the camp was pitched before the first bottle was finished.[46]

An express messenger had gone ahead to warn Stonefield to bring servants and horses to Lochgoilhead, and accordingly the Sheriff set off from Inveraray to meet them. The Duke dined at Lochgoilhead next day; after drinking at his expense, Sir John's boatmen took the barge back to Greenock and the Duke's party continued over the only part of their journey which had to be performed on horseback. The way led through the rugged and sombre pass known as Hell's Glen; in the wet August weather of the Highlands the cavalcade picked their way up the pass and then, with Loch Fyne opening to their view below, came down to the ferry at St Catherines, where they were rowed across the loch to the little town of thatched and slated houses clustering round the mouth of the River Aray. On 14 August, some five weeks after leaving London, the 3rd Duke of Argyll at last stepped ashore at Inveraray, below the crumbling walls of his ancient castle.[47]*

The Campbells of Argyll had long shown a remarkable aptitude for acquiring land – perhaps hardly surprising in the chiefs of the most numerous and powerful Highland clan and holders of the Celtic title of Mac Cailein Mor, 'Son of Great Colin'. In 1744 the estates in Argyll alone were about a hundred miles long and eighty across, though it was by no means a solid mass of land. Far across the western sea was the flat, fertile island of Tiree; nearer, the great mountainous island of Mull formerly belonging to the MacLeans, and close by, the sacred isle of Iona with its ruined abbey and the tombs of Duncan and Macbeth. On the mainland were Morvern, the Lordships of Lorn, Nether Lorn, Cowall and so down the long peninsula of Kintyre to the prosperous farms of Southend. The administration of this far-flung province of islands and peninsulas, cut off from Scotland by mountain barriers and long sea lochs, was centred in Inveraray, where the Chamberlain of Argyll has always resided. In Duke Archibald's time, responsible to Campbell of Stonefield were Deputy Chamberlains and factors, at Rosneath and at the distant centres of Campbeltown, Tiree and Morvern.

In spite of its vast extent, by Lowland standards it was not a rich estate. The greater part of the ground was not arable, supporting only that staple export of the Highlands, black cattle, and other parts were poorly cultivated by petty tenants who paid minute rents; but the chiefs in earlier centuries were deemed fortunate since in time of need they could muster a following of hundreds of sturdy clansmen.

The responsibilities of the Chiefs of Argyll led to many hereditary appointments, including those of Sheriff of Argyll, Admiral of the Western Coasts and Isles, Keeper of the royal castles of Dunstaffnage, Dunoon, Carrick and Tarbert (each of which had hereditary Captains). Outside their own territories they were Masters of the Royal Household, and Justiciaries of Scotland.

Their capital, the Royal Burgh of Inveraray, is situated about ten miles down the west side of Loch Fyne, nearly seventy from the open sea, and just south of a shallow bay named Loch Shira, from which the wooded Glenshira leads up to the high, bare hills towards Tyndrum. South of this bay the river Aray runs into Loch Fyne from a glen of the same name, whence a pass gives access to Loch Awe. The mouth of the Aray had for centuries been the headquarters of the Campbells of Argyll; and here in the fifteenth century they had built their castle, round which in the normal manner a town grew up.

The town, which to this day remains very small, was nevertheless the only burgh for many miles around and thus of considerable importance both for its market and port, and as the centre of jurisdiction for a vast area. It had become a burgh of barony in 1472 and a Royal Burgh in 1648, under a charter signed by King Charles I when he was a prisoner in Carisbrooke Castle, only a few months before his execution. By this charter Inveraray was to be the sole market and fair in the sheriffdom of Argyll, excepting Kintyre, and was entitled to a provost, four bailies, a Dean of Gild and twelve councillors, the provost to be elected by the inhabitants and the bailies by the Duke,[48] although in practice the Duke's nomination or leet was frequently not exercised.

5. Old Inveraray from the north, 1747
   On the right is the old castle and the bridge leading to the town, on
   the left the river Aray and Loch Fyne; at the extreme left is Gallows
   Foreland Point, site of the New Town. From a drawing by
   (?) Thomas Sandby.

Although old plans show the town's development to have been haphazard, it
was by no means merely the collection of rude hovels implied by Pennant and
writers who followed him (see p. 185). The majority of the houses were thatched,
like those of most small Scottish towns of the time, but there was a tolbooth containing the court-house and gaol, a Grammar School and an English School, and a
church with a tower. This church, like the one which eventually replaced it in the
new town, was 'double', one half serving the Lowland congregation and the other
the Highland or Gaelic.[49]* Returns made from 1748 onwards show at least twenty-
one houses subject to the Window Tax, which at that time meant a dwelling with
ten or more windows.[50] As capital of a large if thinly populated area, Inveraray
contained the town houses of local lairds, and as a court of justiciary, the houses

of an unusual number of resident lawyers. These were stone-built and slated,
usually of two storeys and garrets; James Fisher, a leading merchant and for some
years past one of the two alternating Provosts of the town, had lately built himself
a stone house three storeys high excluding the garrets, with a street frontage of no
less than 46 feet – wider than most houses in the town today.[51] The Sandby
brothers, Paul and Thomas, who were both stationed in Inveraray during 1746,
left sketches of the town which testify to its quality and charm.

Until the abolition of hereditary jurisdictions in 1748 (an indirect result of the
'45 uprising) this small but busy mercat town was the natural place for the baronial
court of which the Dukes of Argyll, as Hereditary Justiciars, were titular head;
after 1748 it continued to enjoy its legal 'season' twice a year, with the circuit visits
of the judges of the High Court of Justiciary. It so happened that the 3rd Duke of
Argyll was Lord Justice General of Scotland, an office always at that time held by a
layman; but the effective head of the Justiciary Court, supreme criminal court of
Scotland, was the Lord Justice Clerk, Lord Milton. The travelling court, having
lapsed at the end of King Charles II's reign, was revived after the Union of 1707,

making three circuits in Scotland : North, South and West. From 1748 Inveraray was included in the last of these.[52] Every spring and autumn each circuit was made by one or more judges and their train, so that for a few days Inveraray, like the other towns visited, was – irrespective of whether there was any business before the courts – overrun with advocates, writers, clerks and court officials, numerous servants (some judges travelled with as many as five), and the local gentry assembled on business or to serve as assizers.

In addition to its twice-yearly courts of Justiciary, whether baronial or circuit, Inveraray was the scene of a twice-weekly Sheriff's Court, an Admiralty Court, meetings of the Commissioners of Supply (a board of lairds, forerunners of the County Councils), and other gatherings of a semi-legal or political nature. Although the Dukes of Argyll were, again until 1748, hereditary Sheriffs, for centuries the Sheriffs' work had been performed by professionally trained deputies : Archibald Campbell of Stonefield, Chamberlain of Argyll, now held the office, with John Campbell of Danna as his Sheriff Clerk. The Admiralty Court also had its titular head in the Duke of Argyll as Admiral of the Western Coasts and Isles, here represented on the bench by a 'Commissary Substitute'.[53]*

In contrast to all this legal activity, the only industry Inveraray could boast was the herring fishery, for which Loch Fyne was famous. So important was it to the town that herrings figure on its coat of arms, and its motto is 'Semper tibi pendeat halec'. The season lasted from June to January when the herring shoaled up the loch, and during these months a vast fleet of sailing boats plied in and out of the small harbour formed by the mouth of the Aray, and their crews swarmed about the town. Thomas Pennant, visiting Inveraray in 1769 and one of the earliest travellers to publish an account of the place, describes in his first *Tour in Scotland* how 'Every evening some hundreds of boats in a manner covered the surface of Loch-fine . . . on the week-days, the chearful noise of the bagpipe and dance echoes from on board : on the sabbath, each boat approaches the land, and psalmody and devotion divide the day. . . .'[54]*

The fishermen, however, were usually in search of entertainment of a stronger nature than bagpipe music and psalmody; and because of the fishery, and the large gathering of visitors for business and pleasure at the times of the courts, Inveraray possessed a remarkable number of taverns. A survey made in 1748 put the number at forty-three, 'which is surely too many!' – even though many were merely pot-houses keeping a small brewhouse and whisky-still at the back, catering chiefly for the owner's family and friends. Such taverns were often only single-floor huts, not even with garrets above; only three or four could be deemed capable of 'tolerable lodging' to visitors. Unlicensed brewing and distilling was a major problem in the town for many years. In 1731 the late Duke had attempted to deal with the situation by threatening to withhold tacks or leases from those who made no effort to improve their public houses, but in only half a dozen cases had this condition been observed.[55]

The town had long been liable to depression, for its revenues were very small.[56]*

A complaint made in 1706 reveals that there was then neither manse nor school, that only ten men in the parish could speak English, and there were no bridges over the rivers Aray and Shira, which were 'absolutely necessary' even if they consisted only of logs laid across.[57] Three years later the burghers petitioned the 'Manadgers of Argyll' regarding their 'extream poverty' and debts, the ruinous state of harbour, streets 'and other public works', complaining that of late years 'the said noble ffamily have not had so frequently their residence in this place'.[58] The town always depended on the castle, and personal contact whether harsh or mellow was better than none. During the rising of 1715 when the 2nd Duke was commanding the Hanoverian forces, although his brother, then Lord Ilay, defended the town (where his mother was staying at the time), the most lasting result of his passage was that a number of houses were either demolished or gutted and rendered uninhabitable by order, as being outside the defensive earthworks made by the troops.

During the following years, after further piteous appeals, improvements were made. In 1723 the Tolbooth, damaged in the Jacobite siege, was restored; between 1728 and 1737 the ruinous church was repaired and its bells recast at Stonefield's brother's expense; the two schools were set up, a bridge was built and later repaired; and at the time of the 2nd Duke's death trials were being made for a water supply. The 2nd Duke also encouraged private building, and some of the more substantial houses were erected at this time, on tacks of fifty-seven years, three times the traditional length of nineteen years.[59*]

A constant handicap was the lack of public ground. The common grazing was some distance away, since the Duke's parks occupied the whole surrounding area. This led to an established practice of townspeople poaching on the ducal preserves, purloining fences and fallen timber, and breaking into the parks to graze their cattle. Such petty felonies were customarily winked at by the Duke's overseers, usually local men and well aware of the peculiar difficulties.

Yet with all these limitations the town, with virtually no revenue, was held responsible for the maintenance of its own harbour, bridge and streets – a responsibility which put its magistrates to acute financial embarrassment.[60*]

The setting of Inveraray is a superb composition of mountain, river and inland sea. Duke Archibald's cousin and heir, Major-General John Campbell, not the most imaginative of men, when stationed there in 1746 found it 'a charming pretty place'.[61] The surrounding land was well wooded, for in the previous century the Marquess and his son the 9th Earl had been great planters, while in more recent times the late Duke had contributed his share.

The town to which Duke Archibald returned in 1744, after an absence of nearly thirty years, had a nucleus of good houses in its central square round the mercat cross, clustered below the old high tower of the castle and the steepled church and Tolbooth, with rows of low thatched houses straggling towards the river mouth and southwards along the loch. A fine two-arched bridge now

6. Old Inveraray from Loch Fyne, 1746
   From a drawing by Thomas Sandby.

spanned the Aray near the town centre; beside the loch the ground was low and tree-covered, and a series of avenues radiated from the ducal walled parks. The ground ran down to the shallows of the loch destitute of embankment, but at the river mouth, not only the small fishing boats with their creels and nets but two-masted sailing vessels of some size were able to anchor.

to His Grace the Duke of Argyle.

The castle, on the edge of the town, was dominated by a high L-shaped tower of the fifteenth century. Its more recent additions included a small tower with connecting wings, and, built for the 2nd Duke in 1720–2 by Alexander McGill, 'a House of two Storries and Garret having a Jamb [wing] and a small Court . . . wherein he lodged several Times'.[62]* This last house, apparently not joined to the old building, was usually known as 'the pavilion' and had clearly been regarded as temporary accommodation until certain elaborate projects for either restoring or rebuilding the old castle should be carried out. Presumably also in 1720 McGill drew up designs for adapting the old building to contemporary use by the addition of long wings.[62*] Nothing was ever executed, however; and modest though it was, the small 'pavilion' was now the only lodging available for the new Duke and his household, and remained so for all his subsequent visits over nearly twenty years.

The great tower was ruinous and almost uninhabitable; the only people lodging there were a few old servants, pensioners of the Duke's family, while another part of the building was used as a storehouse of the town's arms.[63] The 'new pavilion' stood on one side of the old castle courtyard, on the opposite side of which was a similar building occupied by Sheriff Stonefield; there was also a garden which the late Duke had made in 1721, demolishing several houses for the purpose.

There was great significance in the fact that the English architect Roger Morris arrived at Inveraray in Duke Archibald's train. The Duke intended to launch at once his programme of improvements for Inveraray, regardless of the unsettled times. The most drastic of his proposals was for a wholesale removal of the town from the vicinity of the castle. As early as 9 November 1743, a month after his succession, he had written in confidence to Lord Milton, 'I intend if possible to remove the Town of Inveraray about half a mile lower down the Loch, but' (for he well knew his tenantry) 'it must be a great secret or else the fews [feus] there will stand in my way or be held up at very extravagant prices'.[64]

At the same time he had ordered his resident mason at Inveraray, William Douglas, an Edinburgh man settled at Inveraray since at least 1731, to prepare a report on the state of the old castle, and survey plans including those of his late brother's house, with the idea of reviving the old scheme of restoring and extending the old building. The mason's report, however, completed on 19 January 1744, put this possibility wholly out of count:

'I have Narowly veiw'd the Same Inside and Outside and finde there are few parts of it Sufficent. there are Large Rents in both Side walls And Gevells and run up a Great way from the foundation In most Places it is Greatly Shattered the Rents are not in Strait Lines but for ordinary branching out in severall Slitts or Cracks quite throw the wall to that Degree that the Air Passes sensibly throw.

There are other Cracks or Bulgings in the wall Particularly in the South east Gevell which in Severall Places are half a foot swell'd out from the Perpendicular and Some Stones in a Manner threatning to Drop. The north east side Likewise Swells out from the Perpendicular And in this Side and Gevell the wall has to the Sight of the eye splitt or opened in the heart and the Outside haveing gon from the Inside the foundation has Certianly faill'd Cheefly towards the banck which is Oweing to the buildings being so near it. and the foundation haveing faill'd the Vaults in the Ground Storie by there Pressure Increass the Swelling out of the wall And the Rents have even affected the Vaults themselves . . .'

7. Old Inveraray, the market-place, 1746
   The town bridge can be seen to the right of the Mercat Cross.
   From a drawing by Paul Sandby.

Douglas went on to relate how some years earlier at the late Duke's orders, he had tried to repair the cracks in the walls by filling them and harling over, but the same rents had re-opened. Some of these larger rents had been 'Remembred to be in it So Long as the Oldest people here Remember but I know they Grow wider, And there are Some new Rents Within these four years.' 'Upon the whole,' he concluded, 'I am of Opinion that it Cannot be Repaired for use Except at near the Expence that would build such ane other.'

To Douglas's account the Chamberlain contributed the news that two or three years ago he had ordered the breaches to be tested by means of wedges driven in 'pretty hard'. Within a year the breaches widened so far that the blocks fell out, and at this rate it was only a matter of a few years before the whole fabric collapsed.[65]

Douglas's report decided Duke Archibald to build an entirely new castle and of totally different design.

Neither this decision nor the design he chose were, however, new ideas, for

8. Plan of the policies and old town of Inveraray, *c.* 1722

the 2nd Duke had at least twenty years earlier considered building a new castle as
an alternative to adapting the old, and surviving designs show that Vanbrugh
among others worked on the idea. Why Roger Morris was the architect finally
chosen is not made clear in contemporary correspondence, for over the past
twenty years the Argyll family had patronized several architects, notably James
Gibbs and William Adam; but Morris, who had done more work than the others
for Lord Ilay, seems a natural choice for the latter's greatest undertaking of all.
Not that Morris was given a free hand, for the Duke now reconsidered the old
plans and, approving of several features, ordered Morris to incorporate them in a
new design.

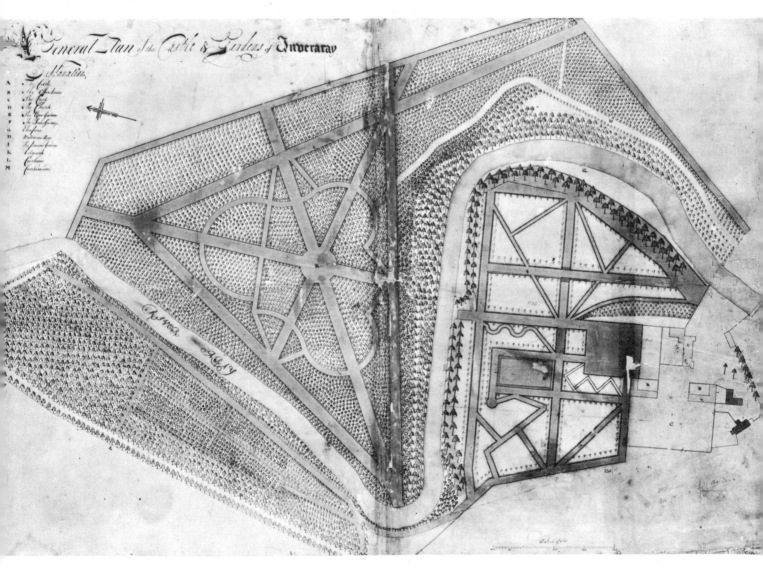

9. Plan of the policies at Inveraray, *c.* 1722
   Showing the additions made by the 2nd Duke in 1720–2.

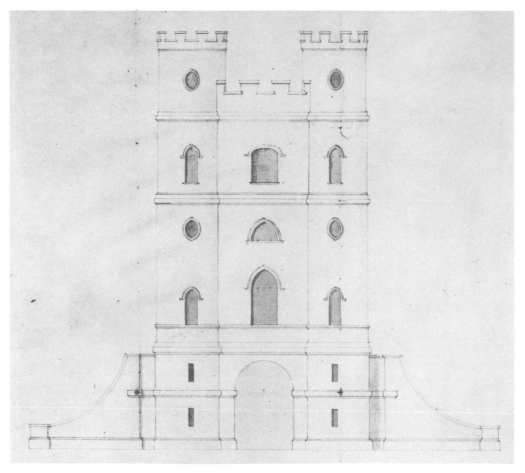

10. Whitton Tower, Middlesex
Triangular brick tower probably designed by James Gibbs
for the Earl of Ilay, c.1730.

    Roger Morris, born on 19 April 1695 and baptized at St Martin's-in-the-Fields, was the son of Owen and Rebecca Morris and of Welsh descent. He was by early training a master carpenter, and his carpenter's expertise and feeling for timber remain evident in his architectural work. Starting as a bricklayer to the Board of Ordnance, whose Master-General from 1725–30 was the 2nd Duke of Argyll, he was later promoted to carpenter and through the Duke obtained the appointment of 'Carpenter and Principal Engineer to the Board of Ordnance'. Morris is well known for his association (from 1724) with Henry Herbert, later 9th Earl of Pembroke, in building the Palladian bridge at Wilton; but more significantly in June 1724 he agreed to build 'the naked Carcass of a house for . . . Lord Illay at Twickenham'–namely, Marble Hill House. Lord Ilay's connexion with Marble Hill is that he was a trustee for its occupant, Mrs Henrietta Howard, later Countess of Suffolk, although it was Lord Herbert who was associated with Morris in supervising the building. Morris also followed Vanbrugh in working at Blenheim and

11. Combe Bank, Kent, from *Vitruvius Britannicus*
    Designed by Roger Morris in the 1720s for Colonel John Campbell,
    later to become the 4th Duke of Argyll.

Eastbury, and fell foul of the old Duchess of Marlborough, again as co-architect
with Lord Herbert, over Wimbledon House (1732–3).

Morris's responsibility for Whitton Place, Lord Ilay's house on Hounslow
Heath, is not proved, but he was at least in part responsible for Combe Bank in
Kent, the home of Ilay's cousin General John Campbell: both were works well
within the mainstream of English Palladianism and spiritually far removed from
the unique, uncharacteristic building now to be put in hand at Inveraray. For
many years Ilay, both as Earl and Duke, and his heir General Campbell, consulted Morris on building problems, and the General in particular regarded him
as a friend and invited him for occasional weekends to his country house.[66]*

The date, January 1744, of William Douglas's report on the condition of the
old castle, shows that Duke Archibald had six months to consider the alternative
before he visited Inveraray; and in view of the short time (less than a week) which
Roger Morris spent at Inveraray on his first visit, and the brief interval of a few
months between that and the start of excavations to his foundation plan, it is
probable that he brought with him sketch plans for the new castle, and that on the
spot he and his patron merely explored likely sites for this and ancillary buildings.
Their task of viewing the ground was not assisted by abominable weather, making
it impossible for them to be out of doors as much as they had wished, for every
project was interrupted by a deluge of rain.[67]*

Morris saw clearly, however, that architectural supervision of the several works, and placing of contracts, could not be carried out by himself from London, so far removed from the site and involving a fortnight's travelling either way. Even by the standards of the time, which required an architect to be on the spot far less often than today, an annual visit, the most that he could achieve, was far from enough. After discussion at Inveraray between the Duke, Lord Milton and Morris, they agreed to appoint a more local representative. The name of William Adam, then the most prominent architect in Scotland, was naturally put forward, as for more than ten years he had undertaken commissions in the Lowlands for both Duke Archibald and Lord Milton (at the Whim and Brunstane), and in 1738 had also visited Inveraray on business for the 2nd Duke.[68] On 17 August 1744 Lord Milton wrote to Robert Brisbane, his factor at Brunstane and a macer of the courts, requesting him to advise Adam in Edinburgh of Morris's impending return. In this way the first meeting was engineered between these architects.

'Accordingly I was at home,' wrote Adam to Lord Milton on 23 August, 'Mr Morris Dind with me on Tuesday and went for Haddingtoun that night when my son [John] attended Him there.' Their meeting was of great significance, with consequences far-reaching for this family which included four potential young architects (John, the eldest, was now twenty-two), and Adam was fully aware of the value of this new patronage by his former clients. 'It is impossible for me to Express in words the sence I have of the obligations I am under to Yo[r] Lop.,' he wrote, 'But cou'd not be altogether Sillent on this occassion.'[69]

The Duke remained in Scotland until October, but Roger Morris now posted south, with instructions to draw up working plans as soon as possible for both Inveraray and Rosneath, for which the Duke also intended substantial alterations. Morris's first visit to Inveraray, however, closed with an event of the greatest sorrow. On his journey south, having arrived without incident as far as Bourne in Lincolnshire, he took up the newspapers at the inn there and glancing through the *St James's Evening Post* saw (so he wrote to Lord Milton in the utmost agitation, from London on 30 August), an account of 'my poor Mrs Morriss Death your Lordship's Humanity will Easey Feel my unhappyness; My Dear Lord Parden your most Dutifull and most obedt. Roger Morris.'[70]

Back in London, overcoming as best he might his distress at this bereavement, to which the blotted and unpunctuated letter testifies, Morris embarked on the working drawings for the excavation and castle foundations : the first of a detailed series of instructions and sketches gathered into a foolscap notebook, together with copies of the letters he sent to Stonefield, William Adam and Lord Milton, and Adam's own memorials on the works. This collection has been preserved at the castle which Morris designed, under the title,

> 'Letters & Instructions for Building Inverera Castle
> for His Grace the Duke of Argyll in Argyllshire
> By R. Morris   1744.5.6.7'[71]*

[3] Inveraray Castle, south front, showing bridge and obelisks

[4] Inveraray Castle, the hall and middle tower roof

D

On ev'ry angle stands a strong round tow'r,
Which adds great elegance; in number four.
And in the midst a *Cupola* there stands,
Which through the whole abundant light commands.
Exalted high upon the roof 'tis fix'd,
For usefulness and ornament commixt.

> James Maxwell *A Descriptive Poem on His Grace the Duke of Argyll's*
> *Noble Palace at Inveraray*, Glasgow 1777

Morris, a minor architect of this country, designed a castle for the duke of Argyll at Inveraray–not a Barons' castle nor even in the Queen Elizabeth Style, but a Gothick one–not what he wished it to be but what he was ignorant how to accomplish.

> John Clerk of Eldin, *c.* 1793. Penicuik MSS, SRO, GD 18/4983;
> quoted by John Fleming in *Concerning Architecture, Essays on Architectural Writers and*
> *Writing presented to Nikolaus Pevsner*, ed. Sir John Summerson, London 1968, p.77

This weather gives but Bade encowragement to take Lands in this deform'd Castaway part of the creation which nature seems to Have quite neglected . . . tho tis much in His Grac's Pour to make this remote Corner of the Shire more happie . . . by erecting Manufacturys fore imploying the younge and a convent to receive the old, then obliging all the Men of the Shire to content them selves with the naturall producte of the Countrie.

> Mrs Jean Cameron, Achairn, to Donald Campbell of Airds, 29 August 1749,
> Saltoun 407 (2)

Take care only that I am not cheated, which in the Highlands they think is fair to do to their cheif.

> 3rd Duke of Argyll to Lord Milton, 31 May 1744, Saltoun 402

II

1. THE DESIGN. Roger Morris produced a design for Inveraray Castle that was uncharacteristic both of his own work and of the times, and until we understand its origin, the style and plan seem equally surprising.

In 1744 'Gothick' as a style barely existed, apart from a few isolated experiments, and Gothic survival, in the form of traditional craftsmanship, was all but dead. Seventy or eighty years later it would become almost unthinkable to house a great Highland chief and duke in anything but a 'baronial' castle, but at the date when Inveraray was built the fact that the client was such a personage evoked none of its later romantic associations. Yet 'Gothick' Inveraray undeniably was, wholly different in plan and conception from mediaeval Gothic, and among the earliest buildings to be designed in this new style. Indeed, no new building approaching its scale had hitherto been attempted in the style, and its predecessors were small and few, whether in execution or merely in design. Among these are notably Vanbrugh's experiments, a few essays by William Kent – mostly remodellings of older houses, as at Esher Place in Surrey (1733) – and the publication in 1742 of Batty Langley's textbook *Gothic Architecture Improved*.

The plan of Inveraray Castle is remarkably simple in outline: a rectangle 118 by 100 feet, with at each corner a tower, 24 feet in diameter, placed as far out as possible on the angle without actually being detached – an un-Scottish feature, for the towers and turrets of sixteenth- and seventeenth-century castles were always subtly integrated. The castle has three floors and garrets, the corner towers four. The main floor containing the public rooms is approached by Gothick bridges on north and south, over a fosse 35 feet wide and some 9 feet deep; above are bedrooms and below, looking out into the fosse, the kitchen offices.

Inside the building, an area of about 60 feet by 38 which might well have been an open courtyard is occupied by a hall, with two flanking staircases in adjoining halls, lit by large Gothick clerestory windows. The hall ceiling is more than 70 feet above the main floor, and the staircase ceilings 65 feet. From the outside this threefold central tower was designed as the castle's main feature, rising above a lean-to roof from the battlemented outer walls. The corner towers were given flat roofs and castellated battlements, and though a storey higher than the bedroom floor, did not compete in height with the importance of the central tower.

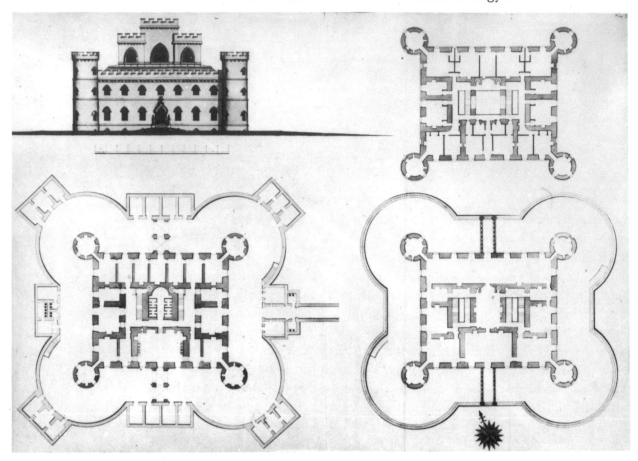

12. Inveraray Castle, plans and elevations by Roger Morris
    Showing original layout, with the main entrance on the south front,
    and the long gallery on the north side of the principal floor.

As originally conceived, the main entrance was on the south front, centred on
an earlier lime avenue. The outer hall (46 ft × 26 ft) was flanked by a drawing-
room or parlour on either side, and opposite the front entrance a door led into the
high central hall with its apsidal northern end, which in turn contained the doorway into a long gallery (111 ft × 22½ ft) running the whole length across the north
side of the house. A sitting-room, bedroom and dressing-room facing east, and a
similar suite facing west, completed the accommodation on the main floor.[1]* The
bedrooms above are entered from an open cantilevered gallery running round the
central and staircase halls.

This apparently simple design of the castle is full of paradoxes. The interior,
except perhaps for the central hall with its high Gothick windows, designed like
that at Blenheim for trophies of arms, was never intended to be other than classical
in treatment. The outside, on the other hand, with Gothick bridges and dry fosse,
suggestive of a water-filled moat, and with every wallhead battlemented, every
window pointed – even though filled with the heavy wooden astragals of the period

– has a very castellated appearance; yet it is meticulously symmetrical, the longer sides with seven windows, the shorter with five. Few houses of its date were so nearly identical on each façade, with each of the four elevations entirely sufficient in itself. The design is so neat and perfect that its general form irresistibly suggests comparison with a vast toy fort rather than a mediaeval castle.

Inveraray, indeed, owes nothing to the mediaeval; nor yet in many of its features to the contemporary. A central hall surrounded by other apartments was in accordance with Palladian practice; and twin staircases, one on each side of the hall, were a not uncommon early eighteenth-century arrangement – for example at Wanstead, Duncombe or Ditchley; yet to combine such twin staircases with a central hall *and* light the whole complex by clerestory windows was rare.

The central hall lighted from above was used by Colen Campbell at Mereworth (1722–5), and Lord Burlington and William Kent at Chiswick House (begun 1725), the first circular, the second octagonal, and both surmounted by a dome. But as neither house had an important upper floor, their staircases were spirals tucked into corners just outside the arc of the circle, in the manner of Inveraray's two service stairs on either side of the apsidal north end of its hall. On the palace scale, however, we do find a top-lit hall combined with double main stairs by Vanbrugh: Castle Howard (1699–1712) and Blenheim (1705–24) each have a great hall lit from high openings, the former in a dome, the latter in the form of clerestory windows, and in each the hall was flanked by staircases very similar in conception to Inveraray's, though more elaborate. But both these halls have one exterior wall.

The immediate inspiration for Inveraray was in fact Vanbrugh's final design for Eastbury, with a clerestory enclosing both central hall and double main stairs, in exactly the same way as Inveraray. A preliminary study of his for Eastbury shows that he developed the idea from one of his favourite features, the roof-top chimney arcade as used at Kings Weston and elsewhere. The fact that this Vanbrugh design for George Bubb Dodington was actually completed by Roger Morris clinches the matter. It is noteworthy that at Eastbury Morris dropped the feature and instead completed the house with a pedimented portico: but the idea obviously appealed to him, so that years later he borrowed it to use for his design for the Duke of Argyll. The Duke himself must have known Eastbury, however, and there may be some significance in his asking Dodington's permission for Robert Adam to visit it in 1758.[2]*

Whereas Vanbrugh seems to have developed the central feature of the house from the idea of a chimney arcade, we may find precedents for Inveraray's design much further back, though they reached similar results by a different process. The most immediately obvious comparison is with Robert Smythson's Wollaton Hall in Nottinghamshire, finished in 1588 and one of the more ostentatious houses of the later Elizabethan magnates. Wollaton, though its plan is more varied, and its predominant shapes are square or rectangular compared with Inveraray's numerous

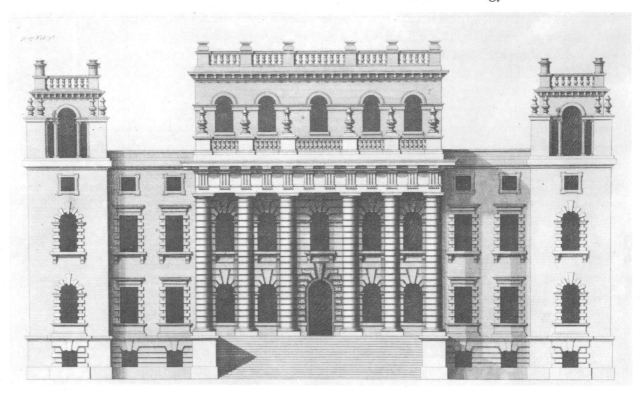

13. Eastbury, Dorset. Vanbrugh's final design, from *Vitruvius Britannicus*

curves and points, has the central hall lighted by clerestory windows, and staircases (not top-lit) on either side; further, at each corner is a square tower rising
one floor above the upper storey.

However, several smaller houses or castles dating from a generation earlier
than Wollaton, resemble Inveraray even more closely. This group develops the
tradition of the late mediaeval fortified house, symmetrical – square or rectangular
– and with corner towers, of which Nunney Castle (fourteenth century) and
Tattershall (fifteenth century) are notable examples. West Wickham Court in
Kent, built as late as 1500, was square with octagonal corner towers and – still
more to the purpose – with an inner courtyard. Nearly half a century after West
Wickham, Mount Edgcumbe (1546), on Plymouth Sound, took the development
of this style yet a further step away from the now archaic fortified house limitations (as Mark Girouard demonstrates) by turning the principal rooms to look
outwards and roofing what would have been the central courtyard to form a high,
clerestoried hall, towering above the long, low fabric of the main building.[3]

Still closer to Inveraray in proportion, and with a larger central tower than the
rest of this group, was Michelgrove in Sussex, built about 1536 for Sir William
Shelley; it has, however, been demolished and its plan is not recorded. Lulworth
Castle (1588– ?1609, gutted in 1929) is almost contemporary with Wollaton, and
resembles it and Inveraray more than does Mount Edgcumbe in being higher and

14. Wollaton Hall, Nottinghamshire
    Designed by Robert Smythson, completed in 1588.

more compact – three storeys and basement, the kitchens being underground – though at Lulworth the 'central tower' is very low, and covers not the hall, but a proportionally smaller area than in the other houses. Like Inveraray, its circular angle towers contain sizeable rooms, and the resemblance appears the more striking from its surrounding raised terrace repeating the castle's plan, in the manner of Inveraray's sunk fosse.

All these buildings were 'follies' in the sense that they were consciously sham-castles, mediaeval in outline, but in detail betraying the Renaissance age to which they belonged. In the same tradition was the (now ruined) Jacobean Ruperra in Glamorgan, apparently inspired by Lulworth to which, as to Inveraray, it has striking similarities. None of these houses, with the possible exception of Michel-grove, had Inveraray's double main staircases, but Lulworth provides another Inveraray feature in that its central 'tower' carried the main flues up the walls.[4*]

Stylistic links between all these houses and Inveraray are obvious; their connexions with the Argyll family and its architects are more tenuous, but not entirely absent. Lulworth, thought to have been built by the brothers Henry and Thomas Howard, 2nd and 3rd Viscounts Bindon, passed in inheritance to their cousins the

15. Michelgrove, Sussex
    Built c.1536 for Sir William Shelley; now demolished.

Earls of Suffolk in 1611 (who sold it again in 1641); it thus provides a possible link
with the Argylls and Inveraray *via* Vanbrugh's connexions with later Howards,
both at Castle Howard and at Audley End – which at one time was the home of
Mrs Henrietta Howard. Ruperra, too, may lead us by tortuous means to Inveraray,
for its builder Sir Thomas Morgan was steward to the Earls of Pembroke, and the
4th Earl's great-grandson, Henry, was the 'architect Earl', acquaintance of both
Lord Ilay and Mrs Howard, and the employer of Roger Morris as clerk of works.
Indeed, it was the 'architect Earl' who recommended Morris to Bubb Dodington
for the completion of Eastbury.

The plan of Inveraray Castle thus stems ultimately from Serlio, *via* the small group
of English Renaissance houses of Mount Edgcumbe type, Wollaton, the Pal-
ladians in whose idiom Roger Morris mainly worked, and Vanbrugh's revival of
the castle form. Morris's combination of standard Palladian with Vanbrughian
features in a house like Inveraray would not, then, be unexpected, particularly as
he knew Blenheim and had very possibly met Vanbrugh (who died in 1726),

through his appointment as Carpenter to the Board of Ordnance; he had, too, worked in the shadow of Vanbrugh for the Duchess of Marlborough, as well as at Eastbury. What is remarkable is the combination with a Gothick exterior in a building of such a size; and for this too the answer is to be found in Vanbrugh, more than twenty years before Inveraray Castle was begun.

The first clue lies in an undated (as are all early drawings of Inveraray) sketch by Vanbrugh of a house intended for 'The Duke of Argyll at Inverary', which though a much smaller building is the germ of the present castle.[5] It seems plausible that this is a rejected proposal for the 2nd Duke's 'pavilion' built at Inveraray in 1720–2. The curious, even fanciful design is a square of over 50 feet outside the walls, with an open court 24 feet square in the centre. At each corner is a round tower, and along the north side a gallery – almost a passage – 49 feet long but only 11 ft 6 in. wide. There are four staircases, all spiral, one in each of the round towers to the north and one on each side of the court but not projecting into it. The south elevation has a central entrance with a round-headed arch, flanked by small, slightly projecting, flat-faced towers pierced by cross-shaped arrow slits on each of the two floors. Only two round-headed windows light each floor between this feature and the round corner towers, which rise no more than parapet height above the main battlemented parapet. The roofs seem to have been intended to be flat except for the towers, where the present castle's Victorian conical caps have been, as it were, oddly forecast. To a very slight extent the high central feature has also

16. Ruperra, Glamorganshire
    A Jacobean house, now ruined, built for Sir Thomas Morgan.

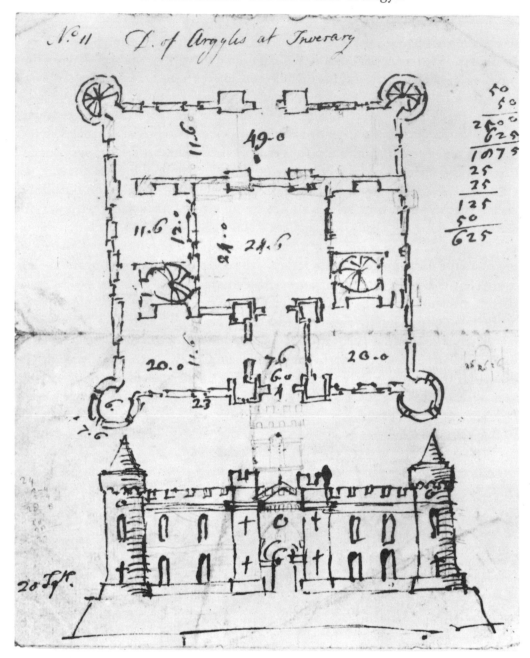

17. Unexecuted design for a house at Inveraray, *c.* 1720
    Plan and elevation by Vanbrugh.

been prophesied in the shape of a great crenellated and arched chimney-stack, similar to those at Kings Weston.

    Variations on this sketch were drawn by Edward Lovett Pearce, a relative and assistant of Vanbrugh's who later practised in Ireland. The elevations are similar, though much higher in proportion to their width.[6]* The Pearce variations give no indication of the person for whom they were intended.

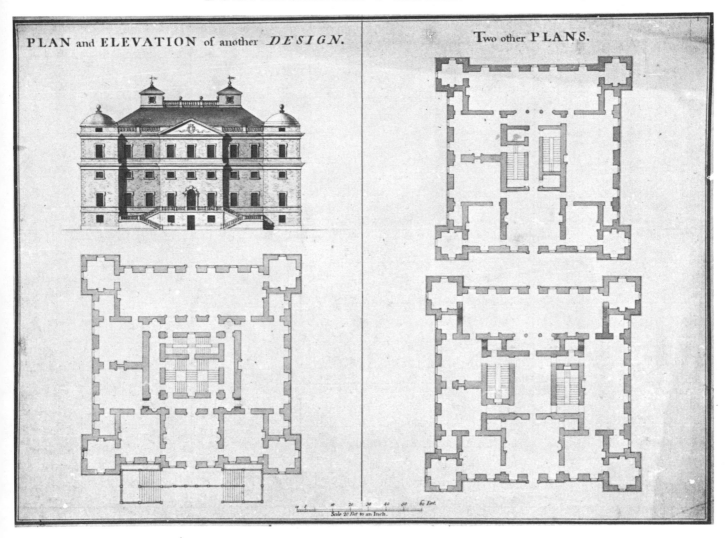

PLAN and ELEVATION of another *DESIGN.*

Two other PLANS.

18. Unexecuted design for (?) Inveraray
      Probably drawn by Roger Morris for the 3rd Duke.

The other clue may be found in two variants of a design (also undated), one for a house 90 feet square, entitled 'Plan of a House of another Design for his Grace the Duke of Argyll', the other 110 feet square having three alternative plans.[7] The elevation shows a four-storeyed house with square corner pavilions, in form though not in style having affinities with William Adam's Duff House in Banff-shire (built in the 1730s for Lord Braco, later Earl of Fife): central pedimented feature – although in the Argyll design the pediment is conventionally at roof level – base storey above ground, double stair to a round-headed first-floor entrance, and cornice running the length of the front between second and third storeys. All three plans of the larger of the Argyll designs resemble Inveraray's, particularly in the central staircase lit from above. One version even has a pair of staircases one at either side of the hall, and in all three there is a long gallery at the rear of the

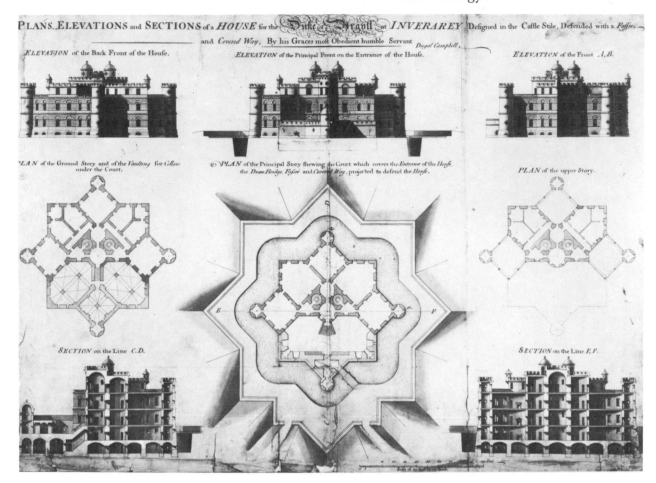

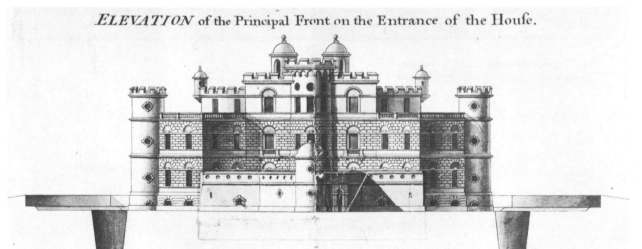

19. (*a*) Unexecuted designs for Inveraray by Dugald Campbell, military engineer. (*b*) Detail from above.

house and, on the entrance front, a hall flanked by two smaller rooms, which was the layout first adopted at Inveraray.

If Roger Morris were responsible for this pair of designs, it may well have been that their orthodoxy did not appeal to his somewhat eccentric patron the 3rd Duke of Argyll who, while approving of the interior planning and the scale, very likely swept aside the proposed unadventurous elevations and told Morris to dress them up on the lines of the bizarre sketch which Vanbrugh had produced for his brother some twenty years earlier. The Gothicized fantasy was thus adapted and translated into fact on a palatial scale.

There remains one other, fantastic, set of drawings which Morris also probably saw, now preserved at Inveraray Castle. Similarly undated, they are signed 'Dugal Campbell' and show a colossal, fortress-like conception with outworks, drawbridges, and innumerable towers and turrets.[8] Dugal Campbell was, appropriately, a military engineer who, starting as Clerk of Works to the Board of Ordnance in 1739, had several rapid promotions and ended his days as a Major.[9*] Some of this extraordinary design's features derive from military architecture, and as a house, even for a Highland chief in the heart of the Campbell country, and elaborately worked out though it is, we can scarcely credit that it was ever more than a flight of fancy. One feature peculiar to this design, however, was adopted by Morris for Inveraray – the fosse or dry moat.

For his English houses at Sudbrooke (*c.* 1716–19) and probably Adderbury (1722–4) the 2nd Duke had employed James Gibbs – himself architect to the Board of Ordnance – who, though a Scot, worked extensively in England. The 2nd Duke's building projects ceased in the late 1720s, but his brother also employed Gibbs for the Whitton 'greenhouse', and later probably Morris for his Palladian-style villa there. Neither brother appears to have employed Colen Campbell in any of their building projects, and although in *Vitruvius Britannicus* he dedicated designs to them both, it was rather to the 2nd Duke as his Chief and to Lord Ilay as his Chief's brother than to either as direct patrons. One 'New Design for the Duke of Argyle' for a large house (Volume I, plates 19 and 20), may be remarked here, for as a central feature Campbell gave it a high coved roof, in the French style, rising over its great galleried saloon.[10*] The 3rd Duke possessed a copy of *Vitruvius Britannicus*, and was obviously familiar with this design; although its raised central feature was different in structure and purpose from the Vanbrughian tower, the idea of such a high feature evidently appealed to him.

About ten years after he had last employed Roger Morris, the Duke now, in 1744, re-commissioned him for Inveraray, and doubtless gave him all the existing and, so far unrealized, drawings to work on; but his own imagination was still exercised by the old Vanbrugh sketch. The carrying into execution of this project occupied the remainder of Duke Archibald's lifetime.

2. THE CASTLE. 1745–49. To embark on the building of a large house in Argyll, in 1745, was a formidable undertaking from a practical point of view – quite apart from the political uncertainty of the times, with the danger of a French invasion in the south supported by a Jacobite rising on the doorstep. Yet the Duke of Argyll, in London, continued his plans unperturbed. In January he was corresponding with Lord Milton in Edinburgh over a cargo of timber, from a Danish ship which had been wrecked the previous autumn off Tiree, an island belonging to the Duke about 200 miles from Inveraray by sea (p. 107). At Roger Morris's orders a thousand fir trees on the Inveraray estate were already being felled for scaffolding,[11] though as yet nothing was started on the castle's site, and William Adam was not due to visit it until the Duke's return the following autumn. Meanwhile household goods, bedding, books and seeds intended for Inveraray and Rosneath were being sent up by sea.

In April Stonefield expressed a hope to Lord Milton that the site of the house might not be fixed until the next visit, recommending 'the ground where the New office stands as the most proper' – although as this meant demolition of a useful building he anticipated objections from the Duke.[12] But he was too late : the site, in the middle of the courtyard, had been agreed; on 3 May Morris sent Adam an excavation plan,[13] and by the following month not only were twenty-six men labouring at the foundation but twenty-two more were carrying timber from the neighbouring Black Hill, and twenty-eight were distributed among three quarries. Masons and labourers also demolished a tower of the old castle, although the bulk of the fabric was left untouched.[14]

Morris's excavation plan provided for digging to a depth of 7 ft 6 in. over an area 170 by 150 feet, and across this, bisecting the long sides, a drain a further five feet deep and three wide with stone walls two and a half feet thick, paved with flags and having at least a three-foot fall to carry away water while the work was going on. This drain was eventually to serve as main sewer to the house. Doubts about the site were settled by an exact description of how to place the excavation in the outer yard of the old castle : in front of the Duke's 'pavilion' and Stonefield's house, the long sides facing the old castle and river on the north and the old lime avenue beyond the great lawn on the south, and the short, the garden avenue and church on west and east. It was within a stone's throw of the town, where the noise and upheaval must have been considerable.

Stonefield had worse problems than siting the castle, for the winter had been difficult. The small army of men engaged, mostly from the Lowlands, had to be paid, but only half the Duke's rental had come in, the country suffered from corn and cattle losses and prices were increasing. Much more disturbing was the prospect that at any moment the Jacobite clans might rise. On 12 June Stonefield, warning the Duke, suggested bringing all boats from Fort William, Morvern and Mull to Dunstaffnage, presumably so that 'the clans' could not make use of them. He hoped that Duncan Campbell of Inverawe, a captain (shortly gazetted Colonel) in Lord John Murray's regiment, would come with his company to protect them as

20. Archibald Campbell of Succoth, w s, ?1704–90
From the portrait by David Martin of 1782.

'we have nobody to execute orders here, till they come, as we have no arms'. In a postscript he added, 'I imagine your Grace will direct all works to be stop'd here.'[15]*

His Grace had no such intention, and signified through Archy Campbell, his lawyer in Edinburgh, that the work should go on with all possible speed. But the lack of provisions held up progress, otherwise the excavation would have been finished by the end of July. 'However the digging of the foundation goes on with all the Vigour we are capable of,' wrote Stonefield on 29 June, 'but it is a very great work, and requires more hands to carry it on speedily than we can imploy in our pinch'd Condition, not one ounce of the provisions from Edinburgh is come here yet.' At last in August some cargoes of meal arrived, so the immediate famine was averted and prices fell.[16]

By then, however, a far greater catastrophe had occurred. At the beginning of August the Duke's seasonal travel programme appeared to be going to plan. He and Lord Milton arrived at Rosneath to be joined by Colonel Jack Campbell, twenty-two-year-old son of his heir apparent, and Member of Parliament since the previous year. Roger Morris had written that he intended to leave London for the north about 10 August, taking in a job at Grantham on the way. Meanwhile William Adam had come to spend a fortnight at Rosneath examining its castle in order to report to Morris on the intended alterations; he also inspected freestone quarries at Greenock, and was seeking out limestone sources elsewhere. The whole party was expecting to proceed to Inveraray where Morris would join them, although as the weather was rainy they were in no hurry to move.[17]

But neither Duke Archibald, Roger Morris nor William Adam got to Inveraray that year, for already on 4 August Prince Charles Edward Stewart had landed in Moidart and the news, when it filtered through, put the whole country in a turmoil. A report of the landing reached Rosneath on 7 August through Stonefield, who had it from the Duke's Morvern factor, Donald Campbell of Airds; from Rosneath Lord Milton relayed it to Sir John Cope, Commander-in-Chief of the forces in North Britain, who was then in Edinburgh. On the day the news arrived William Adam was completing the first of two neat 'memorials' on the proposed additions to Rosneath; but although Adam continued quietly with his survey, the emergency meant that the Duke could not carry on his own intended leisurely pursuits. Messages, despatches and rumours came and went; the Duke sent his account of the news to the Duke of Newcastle in London; Colonel Campbell was despatched to Inveraray with the Duke's instructions, and with a mission to raise troops for the Earl of Loudoun's new Highland regiment of foot.[18]

While engaged in matters of the utmost political importance, the Duke was able to use his building projects at Inveraray to further other purposes. Before leaving Rosneath Lord Milton sent word to Stonefield that work need not be interrupted as the Duke had no intention anyway to build that year, and there was no call to stop the 'diging & carrying earth & raiseing stones &ca'; at the same time he 'sees no reason for dismissing the workmen, it keeps always so many men ready to be better employ'd when it becomes lawful'.[19] The better employment was a general arming, which the Duke thought wiser not to authorize till ordered by the Government; but he approved their cleaning the arms stored in the old castle since the '15, which were unlikely to be in a usable condition.

Writing to the Lord Advocate, Robert Craigie, on 10 August, Argyll was in doubt of his own next move. 'I intend to go to Inveraray next week, if these rumours blow over. If the matter grows serious I shall not be in safety there.'[20] He was now sending the Duke of Newcastle almost daily despatches, not knowing how reliable the Secretary of State (Lord Tweedale)'s information might be. Learning that Sir John Cope urgently wished to see him in Edinburgh, Argyll finally cancelled his visit to Inveraray and left for Edinburgh on 16 August.[21] Here he heard that the Jacobites had threatened to kidnap him as their chief political enemy in Scotland; so he deemed it wisest to return as fast as possible to London where he claimed – not unreasonably in view of the English politicians' vacillating replies to his despatches – that his advice would be of more value. After a few days spent at Brunstane with Lord Milton, issuing orders and advice to the Edinburgh magistrates, his Argyll representatives, the army and the English government, the Duke set off for London on 21 August in company with John Maule, who had joined him at Brunstane.[22]

This apparently precipitate retreat from Scotland drew on him the suspicion and sneers of ill-wishers – such as Horace Walpole, who maintained that on the one occasion when the Duke could have well served the King in Scotland, he posted south for the most equivocal reasons : 'the King was to see that he was not in Rebellion; the Rebels, that he was not in arms.'[23]

On 19 August, two days before Argyll's departure, the Prince's standard was unfurled at Glenfinnan on Loch Shiel by the Marquess of Tullibardine, and the Prince proclaimed Regent in the name of his father King James VIII. That same day Sir John Cope left Edinburgh for Stirling, key point between Lowlands and Highlands, leaving the capital undefended.[24]

By 22 August the Duke and Maule had reached Berwick on their journey south. The Duke, who in addition to frequent pain from the old wound in his leg, was a victim of recurrent migraine ('the vapours') and of malaria or the tertian ague, now had an acute attack of rheumatism. On their stage to Morpeth next day he further complained (writes Maule) of 'a pain in his Guts for which he took three Rhubarb pills'. At Newcastle they lodged with Mother Hill, provider of the hams and bacon for Inveraray,[25*] and by Darlington the Duke though 'troubled wt Stitches yesterday & gripes this day' was temporarily recovered. At Wetherby on the 26th they fell in with General Clayton posting north, and received more news written from Henry Pelham in London, where the prevailing outlook was – incredibly – that 'there is not much in this Invasion'.

As they continued their tedious journey the Duke's indisposition returned, and towards the end they were perpetually expecting the carriage axle-tree to catch fire from friction : as eventually it did, only seventeen miles from London. So they had to hire a post-chaise and arrived home at last on the 31st, the Duke 'much out o' order wt that Inflammation in his side & was very ill of ye vapours, for two days, in so much' (said Maule) 'that I was afraid he must have lyen by for some days but he was easier this day so we proceeded'. On arrival he had himself bled and took to his bed for a month.[26]

His friends and followers, however, were kept on the go as much as ever, with Maule 'quite tired writing letters and running errands, ye Duke's horses are some times as tired as if it was ye time of year of auctions'.[27] For at last, now that the Prince had occupied Edinburgh, the news from the north was taken seriously. On 21 September the Jacobites routed Cope's army at Prestonpans – only a few miles from Lord Milton's house at Brunstane, and almost within sight of the road along which the Duke's coach had passed a month earlier.

In spite of the Duke's strenuous efforts to persuade the dilatory Government to arm local volunteers, and put Scotland into a state of defence, not until towards the end of October were the militia called out and the Duke's heir, Major-General John Campbell, was ordered north 'to command under the Marshal [Wade] in the West of Scotland and Highlands'.[28]

A network of secret information extended between Lord Milton, his shady private agents in Scotland, Sheriff Stonefield, and the Duke and John Maule in London. For letters between the two capitals to receive an answer took at least a fortnight. The Duke communicated not only by his own secret cypher but by an invisible ink made with sugar of lead with which he had years earlier experimented and which yielded its secrets to the heat of a candle flame. He and Maule explained to the Sheriff and Milton the use of this ink, on the blank space at the end of an 'ostensible' or apparently non-confidential letter, and indicated by the word 'Pesta' written like a salutation at the close – or, for the Sheriff, by letting 'two "&c &c" be added to "your humble servant" '.[29]

Eventually on 26 November the Duke of Cumberland set out with his army to intercept the Prince's troops, who were now marching south. But it was confidently expected that the Jacobites would give him the slip, and early in December they were daily expected in the capital. Panic spread, troops were ordered out and camped on Finchley Common, an emergency Council was called and the Government, as Maule drily observed, were all 'in a bleese'.[30]

But although the Prince's army reached Derby without much opposition his generals overrode his earnest plea to advance farther and on 6 December turned the army northwards again; while the Duke of Argyll, who heard the news in London on the 10th, was tiring himself out upbraiding the Government's inattention to the real 'danger from thence threatning this part of ye island'.[31]

At Inveraray meanwhile, well out of the mainstream of these events, work had been quietly proceeding on the great excavation of the castle site, while the Sheriff and Colonel Jack Campbell with some difficulty raised three companies and drilled the militia. Colonel Jack's father the General arrived at last on 22 December, after twice being forced into harbour by storms, to garrison Inveraray with his regiment the Scots Fusiliers.[32]* The handsome, good-hearted General had not visited this place – which he was in time to inherit – for some years. No sooner had he arrived than he was humiliatingly confined with a feverish cold, and had to issue orders from his bed. But he was able to keep the Duke informed about his estate as well as political and military matters. The little town was flooded with troops, besides the labourers and quarriers for the castle. The excavation had been progressing at the rate of – for example – 409, 373 and 241 cubic yards a week, dug out at the cost of 4d a yard; but in winter this was reduced and only seven or eight men were employed in January and February.[33]

With the General's troops now garrisoned about the town in billets and tents, victualling again became an urgent problem. The winter was a hard one and the meal shortage put them into a 'dismall Condition'. Then, too, the General pointed out, '2000 men must have firing', and on 10 January 1746 he warned the Duke that 'Your Grace must expect to suffer in your Timber layd up for building and in your Plantations . . . but I have settl^d such regulations as I hope will preserve what you most value'. He punished those who illicitly felled any of the plantations but accepted, as the lesser evil, their inroads on the 'vast Quantity of Timber laid up for other uses than firing'.

Apart from an inspection of Dumbarton, and an expedition to Perth in February, the General spent this winter at Inveraray, laid out by recurrent attacks of rheumatic fever, raising troops, provisions and money, content to direct operations from a distance – for his command extended from Dumbarton westward, and included many miles of coast and distant castles such as Mingary and Duart, which he reinforced with troops. His son Colonel Jack enjoyed a more active campaign and fought at the Battle of Falkirk on 17 January. In March the General – as his Chief had formerly done when he commanded the troops there during the '15 – organized Inveraray's defence from possible attack by throwing up earthen ramparts to protect the town, the Duke's house and the Sheriff's, with gun emplacements 'at proper stations'. The townspeople, he complained, were 'very curious and suspect that all I am doing is for my own security'.[34]

The Prince's army was decisively defeated at Culloden on 16 April 1746. General Campbell was then given a more active assignment, and set off in pursuit of the Prince around the Highlands and islands – including a fruitless landing on the distant, primitive St Kilda, where he imagined the fugitive might be hidden by the barely-civilized islanders; but they had never even heard of him or the Rising.[35]

Inveraray, quiet again with its last troops withdrawn, was left to the care of the Sheriff. Stonefield still felt the need for military protection; he also asked for money, as the disturbed state of the Highlands had prevented collection of rents, and having laid out more than £600 of his own on the public service and on keeping the Militia, he was now left with only five guineas to pay the Duke's workmen. Besides, he soon had two prisoners on parole on his hands, Macdonald of Glencoe and Cameron of Dungallan, who fortunately expressed themselves 'pleased with the treatment they receive here'.[36]

All this while parcels of seeds and young trees had continued to arrive at Inveraray for planting. Major Tam Cochrane presented the Duke with a thousand four-year-old spruce from La Manca, for which Lord Milton arranged transport, but articles sent up from London met with more difficulty because of a Government embargo on shipping. However, at the Duke's representation Henry Pelham removed the embargo from 'all ships going to the Clyde & to Campbelton Dumfries & ye South parts of Scotland' (reported Maule to Lord Milton), '& as to ye north as far as ye Rebells are not in possession'.[37]

There was no question of the Duke visiting this summer, for he was detained in London by the treason trials at Westminster of the attainted rebels, Lords

Kilmarnock, Cromartie and Balmerino. He was, too, again unwell with attacks of the vapours and the ague, and kept going only by 'ye help of a terrible deal of pills'. But since the castle excavation at Inveraray had now been completed, the Duke ordered that its foundation should proceed regardless of his absence, 'wch is all yt is necessary as nothing more is to be done this year'.[38]

Roger Morris had on 19 June sent Adam his foundation plan, with instructions for building in 'common Rough stone . . . filld with Morter' to a level of three feet, equivalent to the bottom of the base-storey rooms; which would put the work into 'great forwardness for ye next year'.[39] The Duke sent a copy of this plan to Stonefield, who expressed his pleasure at the move but went on to sound a warning against embarking on the work without an overseer. His proposed solution was to engage what he was pleased to call an 'Intendant General' (a name never applied to any person employed at Inveraray before or since), who would 'direct the Execution of the work, engage the Tradesmen Settle their prices, and Draw their pay, and keep accots. of the different branches of the work'. This Intendant or Director General should visit the works monthly between March and November, and 'stay as long as necessary'. The name he suggested was William Adam.[40*]

It may be that Stonefield did not know of Adam's previous appointment as Roger Morris's representative, for the Jacobite rising had prevented Adam from reaching Inveraray in 1745. These proposals were in any case detailed and specific, and after consideration the Duke asked Lord Milton (as Maule put it) to 'order what is proper wt regard to ye building at Inveraray, that its impossible yt can go on without some body to overlook it'.[41]

But the suggestion of employing a general semi-resident overseer was not adopted, a neglect which did shortly lead to just the sort of chaos which Stonefield predicted. Although William Adam came to supervise working arrangements, as a busy architect with his own practice he obviously could not undertake monthly visits to Inveraray. Besides, although not yet fifty-seven he was in declining health, and at the beginning of the year had been confined to bed with a severe quinsy and for some weeks had been obliged to let his son John – who, born in 1721, was seven years older than his next son Robert – deputise in his architectural business.[42]

General Campbell returned to Inveraray on 18 August from his unsuccessful pursuit of Prince Charles. He called in and disbanded the outlying troops, and next day again succumbed to rheumatic fever. But in spite of his health and his military commitments, he found time to think about the plans for the new castle, which he fancied he could improve upon. In the middle of September William Adam arrived, the General talked him into his idea, and as a result on the 20th sent his kinsman the Duke some suggestions so tiresomely ill-timed that he soon found himself under a cloud:

> 'If I should take upon me to alter the Front of your House, I am persuaded you'll forgive me . . . Adams is here you know He is slow but sure He seems very clear as to the Front & positive as to the breadth of the Gallery which He says should be 26 feet wide.'

21. Inveraray Castle, foundation plan
Probably made in William Adam's office.

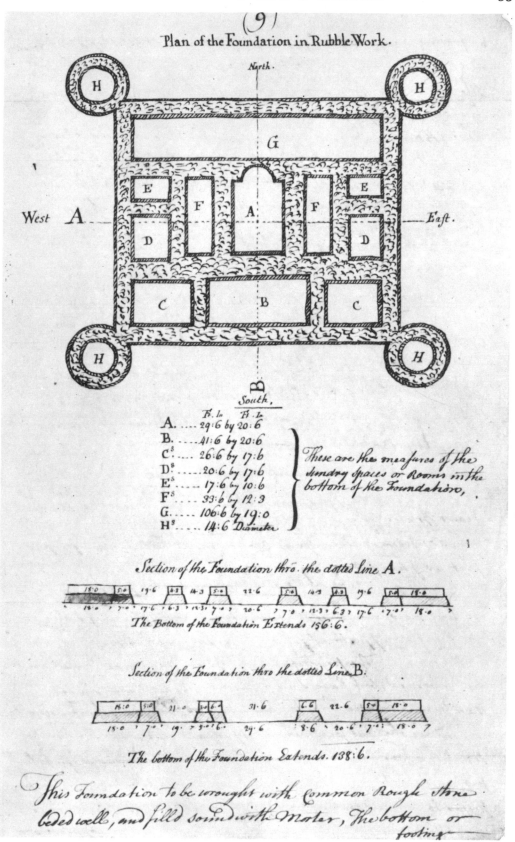

(9)

Plan of the Foundation in Rubble Work.

North.

West   A

East.

B

South.

	Ft. In.	Ft. In.
A.	29:6 by	20:6
B.	41:6 by	20:6
Cˢ	26:6 by	17:6
Dˢ	20:6 by	17:6
Eˢ	17:6 by	10:6
Fˢ	33:6 by	12:3
G	106:6 by	19:0
Hˢ	14:6 Diameter	

These are the measures of the sundry spaces or Rooms in the bottom of the Foundation,

Section of the Foundation thro' the dotted Line A.

The Bottom of the Foundation Extends 156:6.

Section of the Foundation thro the dotted Line B.

The bottom of the Foundation Extends. 138:6.

This Foundation to be wrought with Common Rough Stone bedded well, and filld sound with Moter, The bottom or footing

The General's idea was, no doubt for aesthetic reasons, to alter the castle's front by 90 degrees so that it faced the loch rather than the old avenue on the south side. However, his suggestion was also partly based on miscalculation of the dimensions of the long gallery planned for the north front, and such an unasked-for alteration, just when everything was ready to begin, irritated the Duke extremely. Lord Milton, whom the General had taken the precaution of sounding first, replied tactfully:

> 'I do not know if his Grace will take time to reconsider the Situation when he is not upon the Spot however I have transmitted your Letter, I suspect if it was altered nothing could be done this year, a point perhaps more material, than ye other, in one of his time of day.'

But the General had put his foot in it, and the Duke's reply was sharp and to the point. John Maule did his best to minimize the unfortunate blunder:

> 'I am sorrie the D: was so peevish about your proposal about altering ye fronting of the house at Inveraray, which has been entirely owing to his Grace's misunderstanding your words, & as if you had given orders about it without waiting for his approbation, which you certainly never intended ... If you had given orders for such an alteration it wou'd have put him out of humour, but as you only meant to lay your thoughts about it before him, & if he had understood it so, he was rather oblidged to you, for it, than any thing else. – I have been very concerned that this mistake shou'd have occasion'd vexation to either of you. But as its between friends who like each other, it may be easily forgot.'

To Lord Milton Maule was more forthright:

> 'The Duke bids me tell you he ... has wrote to ye Sheriff, that he's displeased wt ye Alterations G. Campbell & Adams proposed about ye house at Inverary that he has expressly discharged them, & that they proceeded upon a mistake in one of ye Alterations viz about ye breadth of ye Gallery as they have only ye plan of ye foundation where the walls are thicker than they will be above, & that ye Gallery by making ye party wall thinner as it mounts will be 22½ wide, wch is ½ a foot wider than his Library at London, which is a better vidimus of what is right than any thing else.'[43*]

A Latin inscription for the foundation stone also caused some argument, since the combined scholarship of the General, Lord Milton and John Maule was too weak for accuracy. Maule produced the original draft at Lord Milton's request: 'Gulielmus Dux Cumberlandiae nobis haec otia fecit. 1746. A.D.A.' (Archibaldus Dux Argatheliae). Three weeks later Lord Milton was explaining a correction to the General: 'Instead of Cumberlandiae it must be Cumbriae the Latin name. Jo Maule made use of the former, I objected & the Duke gave it for mee in point of Latin.' To posterity the invocation of the Duke of Cumberland in connexion with such a house may seem in curious taste, but to a group of staunch Hanoverians and Whigs the gesture was of calculated diplomacy. The General was delighted with the motto, 'so proper and well chose' that he proposed to 'borrow the thought and

22. William Adam, 1689–1748
    From the portrait by William Aikman.

place it upon one of the work Houses in Glasgow or Edinburgh'.[44]

The foundation stone was laid in the presence of William Adam on 1 October 1746. Its inscription as finally agreed, laid face to the ground, was certainly apposite to the time and place:

CAL. OCT. ANNO DOM. MDCCXLVI POSUIT A. A. DUX
GULIELMUS CUMBRIAE DUX NOBIS HAEC OTIA FECIT.

According to Adam's directions the stone measured 'from 4 to 5 foot long, from two to three foot broad or more . . . & from 6 to 8 Ins or more in the thickness'. At John Maule's suggestion a notice was sent to the Edinburgh papers and appeared in the *Scots Magazine*.[45]*

After a couple of months of changeable weather the autumn took a turn for the better. Adam stayed in Inveraray a month, inspecting the 'very good freestone quarry' four miles down the loch at Creggans, comparing alternative sites for a sand-pit (inland would be dryer, he concluded, and thus more suitable for the extra thick mortar the castle walls required), reckoning the cartage requirements, and already noting the easy-going, feckless attitude of local labourers. He decided that carters from the Lothians would be 'much better than the men here who seem not so proper for work of that kind nor for the management of the Horses'. Adam's on-the-spot study also revealed the need for a full-time smith. Morris approved most of his suggestions, but was too cautious to authorize the purchase, without the Duke's consent, of a gabart or working-barge, and hire of a crew to bring materials like coals from Clydeside for the kilns, or lime from the loch-shore.[46]

Early in December Adam was able to report (from Edinburgh) that

'the foundations of the House with the Common Sewer, have been carried on as fast as the Nature of the Season would admitt and in everything agreable to Mr Morriss Plan & Directions . . . and if frosts do not prevent the foundations of the whole outer walls, and Towers, will be compleated to the height directed [3 feet] before a final Stop for ye Season.'[47]

Adam habitually gave a copy of his recommendations to Lord Milton in Edinburgh and sent another to the Duke in London, who passed it to Roger Morris for comment. Up to five weeks could pass before a reply filtered back to Adam, who was 'a good deall imploy'd when at home, in corresponding with Mr Morris at Lond⁰, & with the Sherriff, & Foreman, about any difficultys that occurred in the execution'. His task also included 'engaging & sending all the Trades people to Inveraray; And making agreem^ts with different persons, such as the Wheeller, the Smith, the Brickmaker, & the Lyme burner, all which, particularly the last, required a good many Computations, to bring them to a certainty'.[48]

Inveraray now presented a scene of industry such as it had not known for many years, excepting the hectic days when the General's troops had been quartered there. Besides the masons and labourers at the castle, a host of wrights with their own labourers were making sheds to house men, tools, carts and barrows; the smith and his men at the forge turned out quarry-tools and other iron-work, and there were a wheelwright's shop, a shed full of sawyers making planks and scaffolding, lime-burners at the kilns, carters hauling up stone from the quarries, not to mention the increased staff of gardener's men improving the parks. Further, military parties were now working on the King's Road, and some of them were quartered near at hand. Another road had to be made to Creggans quarry down the loch, where a hut was built from its stone for the quarriers to live in and a stable for their work-horses. The stone itself, however, was carted only the quarter mile to the loch-side and then ferried up to the town by water.

This curious blue-grey stone, of which Inveraray Castle is built and which rouses very varied emotions in the observer, is geologically described as a chloritic schist, or 'chlorite slate passing into talc'.[49] It is hard, micaceous, but in its newly-quarried state of a soapy texture and thus easy to work – a valuable quality since one-third of the stones quarried had to be dressed with a curved face, this being the proportion of round tower to flat wall-surface in the building. It is capable of a smooth polish but soon hardens in the air, and though it turns black in rain it is subject to no visible weathering, an advantage Adam had already noted for 'there is full proof of its being durable, as many stones of the old Castle are from that Quarry'.[50]* The St Catherines quarry on the opposite side of the loch, which provided the stone from 1751 onwards, yields a very similar but more greenish-brown stone, whose colour may be seen in the tall central tower of the castle. Alexander Cumming described it to Bishop Pococke in 1760 as 'soft when dugg, and may be cut with a knife; hardens in the air; if burnt in a moderate fire it becomes almost impenetrable, and loses near a third of its weight . . . serpentine'. Cumming compared it to Cornish soapstone. Pococke, who saw it as new, found it 'a lightish green'. Many visitors commented on its curiosity. Pennant in 1769 referred to it as 'a coarse lapis ollaris . . . the same kind with that found in Norway, of which the King of Denmark's palace at Copenhagen is built'. John Mawe, who appended some Scottish notes to his *Mineralogy of Derbyshire*, published in 1802, found it 'a singular kind of stone, I scarcely know what name to call it; it appears a species of argillaceous pot stone; the magnesian earth seems predominant from its soap like feel'.[51]

All writers describe it as coming from across the loch, and Inveraray Castle is always referred to as being of St Catherines stone; yet in point of fact for at least the first four years of its building the quarry was Creggans, and the distinction between the two stones can be seen to this day.

Winter suspended activities, and considerably reduced the throng; Lowland workmen were paid off and given their travelling expenses (a matter of shillings), and went home. By March 1747 masons and labourers were back and the new season began. 'They are just now Employd in Building the sides and Arch of the Main draine,' Adam reported, 'Northwards from the House, till it lands on ye Low ground at the River side near the Bridge.' He sent Morris sketches of 'a window, an inner door and a chimney, in the way we commonly do them in the ground storys of good houses here', as suggested occupations for the craftsmen in bad weather.[52]

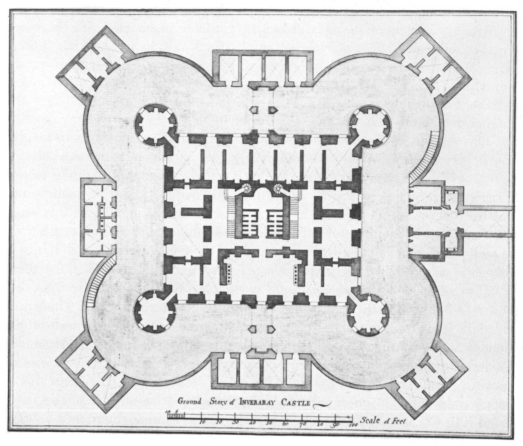

Ground Story of INVERARAY CASTLE

Scale of Feet

23. Inveraray Castle, ground plan by Roger Morris

But at this stage, apart from buying the wrecked cargo from Tiree, there was no question of providing timber other than by thinnings from the Duke's woods for scaffolding boards. Another suggestion of General Campbell's, to lay in a timber supply and season it ready for use, had received no notice from Morris, who as long ago as August 1745 had informed Lord Milton that he would require none 'this 3 years' – 'for I dow not purpos to put in one piece of timber Till the whole Building is up, Battlment wall finnishd, and the scafold are taken downe'.[53]

William Adam paid two more visits to Inveraray, the first of a fortnight in the early summer of 1747, when he reported some unhappy discoveries: lack of efficient supervision, slack workmanship, fraud and embezzlement of materials – problems which no matter what remedies were tried, bedevilled the works at Inveraray from beginning to end. Finally he spent a month there at the end of August, joining the Duke and Morris there on their first visit since 1744.[54]

'The Duke of Argyll & his Company Came here in good health upon Munday 17th Cur^t.', wrote Stonefield to Lord Milton on 20 August, 'all in high Spirits, They had a very quick & good passage from Roseneath.'[55]

The occasion was of some social splendour and the Duke's small house over-

24. Inveraray Castle, plan of the principal storey by Roger Morris
Probably drawn by William Adam.

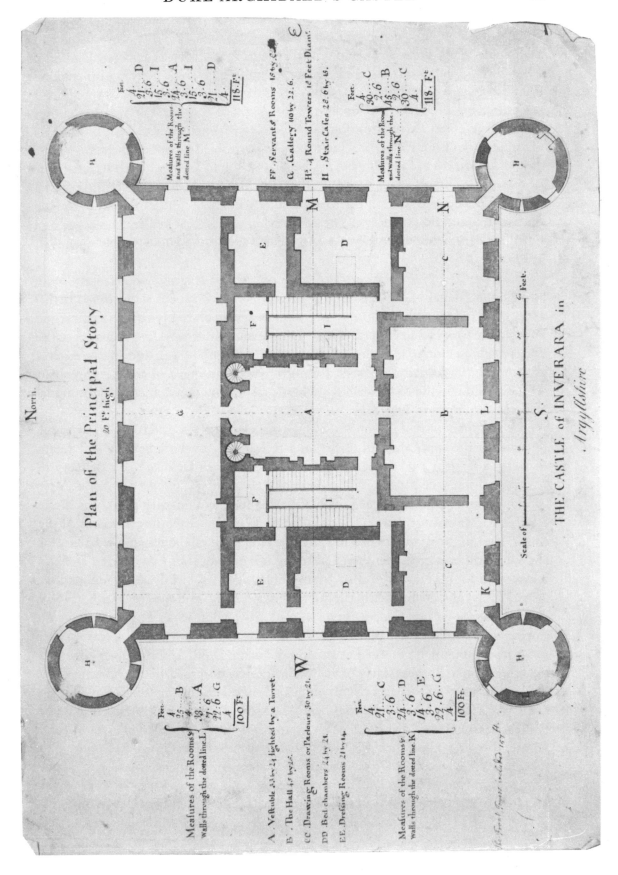

North.

Plan of the Principal Story
20 Ft. high.

Measures of the Rooms and walls through the dotted line M

	Feet.
D	21
I	3.6
A	15.6
A	14
I	3.6
D	21
	4
	118 Ft.

FF. Servants Rooms 14 by 5.
G. Gallery 110 by 22.6.
H. 4 Round Towers 12 Feet Diamr.
II. Stair Cases 22.6 by 15.

Measures of the Rooms and walls through the dotted line N

	Feet.
C	30
B	22.6
B	45
C	22.6
	30
	4
	118 Ft.

A. Vestible 33 by 24 lighted by a Turret.
B. The Hall 45 by 26.
CC. Drawing Rooms or Parlours 30 by 21.
DD. Bed chambers 24 by 21.
EE. Dressing Rooms 21 by 14.

Measures of the Rooms & walls through the dotted line L

	Feet.
B	25
A	48
G	7.6
	22.6
	4
	100 Ft.

Measures of the Rooms & walls through the dotted line K

	Feet.
C	21
D	24
E	14
G	22.6
	4
	100 Ft.

Scale of Feet.

THE CASTLE of INVERARA in
Argyllshire

flowed with visitors and retainers. Lord Milton, who had been seriously ill, was unable to make the journey, and his absence was much felt; but John Maule had accompanied the Duke to Scotland in July, and after a visit to his own Panmure, where he was emulating his noble friend in 'pulling down & building up, making Ponds & Canals & building ruins', he and his friend Fothringham of Powrie joined the others for a few weeks at Inveraray at the end of August. The weather at first was very fine and (Maule told Milton) they 'reconnoitred all ye beauties of this place, a work of some time, & which we have performed wt much pleasure, & this day wt a good deal of fatigue, having been at ye top of Dunniequech to finish our labours. The Duke is in very good health & you may easily believe very busie, as he has Morris Adams & the Gardner for his aid de Camps.' The gardener, following the Duke round his policies on a heavy cart-horse, was that Walter Paterson from Caroline Park, installed at Inveraray since 1744; and the Duke greatly approved of his works.[56]*

The parties of soldiers were also busy on the last stages of the military road, and Commissioner Colin Campbell of Prestonpans, who spent six weeks at Inveraray, reported that 'the buildings goe on likeways much to his Graces satisfaction and Morrice says he never saw so fine a Stone nor better work'.[57]* A model of the castle made in Morris's London office was on its way up by sea, and was so eagerly awaited that eventually 'We sent a Cantire wherry in quest of the Glasgow boat which found it in the Kyles of Bute', where presumably they transferred the model to bring it at once to Inveraray.[58]

Morris spent part of his time examining sites for bridges, and roughed out some designs on the spot. Mindful of his long-term policy over timber, he and Adam drew up a lengthy timber scantling to be ordered from Denmark, for delivery in two years' time (see p. 110).

The visitors had their relaxations. Catering for the numerous party was in the capable hands of Lord Milton's factor Robert Brisbane, attending as macer of the court; he, too, was well pleased in spite of a later spell of abominable weather, for (he said) 'there is great plenty of Charming fair ones hear, if I were not a Domine I woud be Lightheadded'.[59] But John Maule, of more bawdy and rumbustious tastes, sadly missed his featherbrained 'gossip' Lady Milton: 'My Lady Sheriff does not agree wt our Constitutions so well as we coud wish, & we can have no riot wt the females of this place.'[60]

A tradition much observed at Inveraray during Duke Archibald's regime was the admission to burgess status of visitors whom the burgh wished to honour, from noblemen, army officers and circuit judges, to their servants, masons employed on the Duke's works (mostly Lowlanders), merchants, drovers, craftsmen and the Duke's personal staff. On the Duke's first visit in 1744 the Duke of Atholl, John Maule, the judges and their staff were among those admitted burgess, along with the Duke's butler James Fleeming and his valet James Dorret. Next year Major Caulfield in charge of the military road was so honoured, and now in 1747 Roger Morris, 'Mr Carpenter to the Ordnance' and his servant David Barclay, along with

Lord Deskford (heir to the Earl of Findlater and Seafield), the judge Lord Tin-wald, several more ducal servants and, later, Robert Brisbane.[61]*

Before leaving, Morris discussed his plans for the improvements at Rosneath, and at Major Caulfield's suggestion he returned to the Lowlands by the new military road which took him along Loch Lomond, 'that he may see and make a report of his operation'. It is probable that at William Adam's introduction, on his way he also visited the Duke of Montrose, who had 'something to do' for him at Buchanan.[62]

Towards the end of the Duke's stay the weather deteriorated, and at the start of his return journey *via* Rosneath, in the first week of October, he was storm-bound at Lochgoilhead: 'His Grace Cou'd not Stir from thence, nay I had it not in my power' (wrote Stonefield) 'to send to know how they all were, no boat Cou'd Cross Lochfine all that day, Thursday being but tollerable, they sett out & I hope got safe to Roseneath.'[63]

This was the only occasion when all three principals were on the site together. Neither Morris nor Adam were ever to see Inveraray again, for within eighteen months both architects were dead. But Duke Archibald, responding eagerly to Inveraray's challenge, was pronounced by all to be in better health than ever. While directing operations, and marking trees to be felled for 'vistos' through his woods he was, said the Sheriff 'in good spirits ever since he came here, & makes every body about him happy'.[64]

Behind the gay activity it was plain from Adam's reports, Stonefield's advice, and the Duke and Morris's own observation, that for lack of authoritative super-vision the building works and estate were grossly mismanaged. The Duke agreed with Stonefield on the need for a full-time, resident Clerk of Works, such as the busy William Adam could not be : 'not only for paying the Tradesmen & Labourers Wages, & keeping the Accompts in order, but likeways as a General Inspector of the fidelity & diligence of the Overseers & men'.

Stonefield's Deputy Chamberlain John Campbell had hinted at such an em-ployment for himself, but Stonefield, who had doubts of his deputy's integrity, answered evasively that he 'judged it Incompatable with his other office'.[65] Adam warned Lord Milton that a qualified Edinburgh accountant would cost them £50 a year, and further would lack the required knowledge of measuring timber and stone. For a time they considered offering the job to Walter Paterson, who was trained in accountancy, and allowing him a bonus though not an increase in salary, 'wch once raised', Lord Milton cannily observed, 'is not so easyly reduced'.[66] In the end the administration was divided between two Argyll gentlemen : general responsibility for the works was given to Archibald Campbell of Knockbuy, a Commissioner of Supply and Deputy Lieutenant of the county; while Robert Campbell of Asknish, a young advocate trained in the office of Alexander McMillan, Deputy Keeper of the Signet, became the estate accountant.[67]*

Adam's proposals for more efficient organization were also put into effect, and during the winter he drew up contracts for provision of building materials : lime by

William Douglas the mason, bricks by John Innes, a Carlisle brickmaker now in business in the Canongate in Edinburgh, who was to work at Loch Gair, twelve miles below Inveraray. An attempt was made to recruit more Lowland labour for the Creggans quarry, in the hope of reducing the 'excessive and Extravagant drinking of Spirits which happened there last summer'.[68] In February, when the new season's work was ready to start, Stonefield reminded Lord Milton that the Duke had suggested employing an agent to supply 'Coals, Nails, Iron, ropes, Tar, Horse funitur, pouder for blasting, & Tools for Labourers'.[69] Hitherto these had been purchased in Glasgow by the Rosneath factor, Colin Campbell, and sent over on specially freighted boats; but from now on they were commissioned direct from 'a kind of fac totum', a Glasgow merchant named Robert Lang.[70]*

The Duke was highly satisfied with Adam's contracts, and Morris informed him that 'his Grace observed in the one Article of Lime that know [sic] it wont Cost more then one half what it Did last year'.[71]

Adam, who suffered from kidney disease, was seriously ill during the winter – so seriously that malicious rumours of his death began to circulate. On 29 January 1748, he wrote ironically to Lord Milton,

'I have on many occasions had good reason to be thankfull to your Lo^p. for your concern about me, And I had a fresh proof of it this morning, by one of Your Serv^ts calling to know if I was alive. I was indeed at first a little surpriz'd at the message, but sometime after a Gentleman came to see me, who also said he had heard I was dead. My son had also a Letter from another Gentleman on the same subject, & we find this news took its rise in my Freind Lord Braco's. This in appearance to me is but a poor peice of revenge. But I thank God I am yet alive, & some stronger than when I had the honour to see Your Lop last . . . Many many thanks for all the prooffs of Your goodness, & while I am, I shall always be with the utmost sence of Gratitude & Esteem', etc.[72]

For some years past Lord Braco, heir to the Earldom of Fife, had harried the architect in revenge for (not unjustifiable) expense the latter had caused him in the building of Duff House.

John Adam, deputising for his father during his illness, had left home in December on a business visit to England, partly on Ordnance work, partly no doubt to discuss Inveraray with the Duke. With him John carried a notebook which he filled with drawings made on his travels, including a chimney-piece and other features at Combe Bank – the Kent house built in the 1720s by Morris for General Campbell – and the Gothick brick tower at Whitton, which John visited in January. He was back in Edinburgh by 2 February, when his father wrote to Morris of his, John's, pride in being entrusted with supervising the Garron Bridge near Inveraray on the King's road.[73]

Soon after this Morris, too, became seriously ill, and in March, when the Duke was beginning to plan next summer's northern expedition, Morris informed Adam that 'I have begg'd to be excused coming down this Summer; but have promised next Summer please God I live'. He shortly moved to the Bath, to try the effect of its waters on his sickness, but with little success.[74]

Nor did William Adam's health improve as spring passed, and at last his chronic nephritis brought his life to an end in the inevitable coma; he died after some hours' unconsciousness on Friday 24 June 1748. He was under fifty-nine; his death was due, Lord Milton told the Duke, to 'a Suppression of Urine, ye last he passed was black like Ink – he was affected with a Swelling not only in his belly, but his right hand, when ye Swelling abated'.[75]

Lord Milton learned of this sad loss the following day. As John was again away on business, the duty of informing their father's patron fell to his younger brother Robert, now within a month of his twentieth birthday.

'As you was long pleased to honor my Father with your Countenance & regard And As I have often heard him mention your Name with the greatest respect & gratitude I thought it my duty to inform your Lordship That yesternight we were deprived of him for ever . . .'[76]

This was probably the first approach to a client that Robert had made in his life, and even on this occasion of a family tragedy one can sense a certain flattery and opportunism in approaching the rich and powerful, which is never displayed by his less gifted and ambitious brother John.

John's absence obliged the family to delay the funeral for a few days, and Lord Milton attended the ceremony at Greyfriars. The friend who composed William Adam's obituary notice for the *Edinburgh Evening Courant* and the *Caledonian Mercury* recalled how his genius had

'push'd him out of Obscurity, into a high Degree of Reputation: And his Activity of Spirit, not to be confin'd within Narrow Bounds, diffus'd itself into many Branches of Business; not more to his own Benefit than that of his native Country'.

The writer praised the qualities of those 'Promising Young Men' his sons, whose 'Regard for so Worthy a Man their Parent would be to them a more than ordinary Incitement to trade in his Steps'.[77] John Adam, at the age of twenty-seven, inherited his father's work at Inveraray, Fort George and elsewhere.

Soon after Adam's death Harry Barclay of Colairny, an eccentric old friend of the family and of Lord Milton, and a director of the British Linen Company, seeing the family's 'very moving distress' and 'Disconsolate condition', appealed to Milton for John to succeed his father as Master Mason to the Scottish Board of Works; particularly since, should an outsider secure the post, William Adam's outlay for materials at his own expense would be lost, and then 'how fatall the consequences woud prove, was the son to be laid aside'.[78]*

Between Lord Milton and the Duke of Argyll, with whom he discussed his future that autumn (1748) at Brunstane, John obtained his father's Government post, and succeeded to the ordnance work at Fort George near Inverness which occupied him and Robert for several years. For the next ten years, the firm was carried on almost entirely by John; for as eldest of a large family it was sensible, less imaginative John who ran his father's large and flourishing practice, made the

25. John Adam, 1721–92
   From the portrait by Francis Cotes.

decisions, and later rendered possible the departure of first the obviously gifted Robert, and then James, to study in Italy, while he carried the burden at home – with his own wished-for studies abroad receding year by year like a will-o'-the-wisp.[79]*

Inveraray devolved on John more completely than anyone had anticipated, for Morris continued too ill to leave Bath and by November his disease was seen to be fatal. Three months later, on 4 February 1749, he too died, 'which is a great loss to His Grace' (wrote Lord Milton's prosy son Andrew).[80] He was equally a loss to the Adam brothers, for as Lord Milton had earlier remarked to the Duke, 'I belive Mr Morris had such a real Kindness for poor Mr Adams yt he would act a Kind part to his family'.[81]

John's inheritance of the assignment from his father, and Roger Morris's death so soon after, ends the first phase in Inveraray's building history. Morris's designs were complete; their execution remained for the next thirteen years in John Adam's hands.

1748 was significant for several reasons. After months of ducal manœuvring Lord Milton, resigning his office of Lord Justice Clerk, was created Keeper of the Signet for life as a belated reward for his services during the Forty-Five, and was granted the reversion of the Auditorship of the Exchequer for his eldest son Andrew, who the year before had become Member of Parliament for the Haddington Burghs. Changes also took place in the Duke's household. In June John Maule, now forty-two and still an irrepressible, hard-drinking bachelor, obtained through Argyll's influence a Barony of the Exchequer, which being a specifically Scottish office removed him from the Duke's London circle to live in Edinburgh. Maule's place as the Duke's confidential secretary was taken by young Andrew Fletcher, some fifteen years his junior and generally admired for having remarkable ability. Unfortunately for posterity he had not a spark of humour or imagination, and his political letters to his father are a poor substitute for John Maule's. In place of Maule's earthy asides Andrew lards his reports with Latin tags, comments of heavy pomposity and monotonously uninformative bulletins that 'His Grace continues hearty and well'.

Before dropping out of the Inveraray picture Mr Baron Maule, as he was known from now on, left an account of the place in the busy days of the Duke's visit in September 1748. The Duke had left London early in August with Andrew, and with his nephew the Hon. Stuart Mackenzie, Member for Bute. At the end of the month he and his retinue, increased by Maule, the advocate Henry Home and Maule's friend Fothringham of Powrie, set off from Edinburgh on their protracted journey to Inveraray. They spent a night at Falkirk, another at Glasgow and a few days at Rosneath; from there (reported Andrew) 'row'd up the GareLoch in the Dukes Boat', took horse across the narrow strip to Loch Long, 'and saild from Portenkaple to Loch Goyles head in the Custom house boat, There was just wind enough to stretch our foresail, which made it agreeable.' On this, his first visit, Andrew was shocked by the standard of local roads : that from Lochgoilhead to

F

St Catherines, praised by their guides as 'a good highland road', he thought so abominable that their safe arrival at last on 5 September, 'per varios casus, et tot discrimina rerum, I reckon no small Blessing'.[82]* They might have found it easier to travel by the new military road from Dumbarton, for a month earlier Stonefield, traversing it on a visit to his own estate of Levenside near Balloch, reported it practically finished, and that Caulfield anticipated 'a Coach may go the length of Ardkinlass in a fourthnight at furthest'.[83]

Again the weather was at first fine, again the Duke was in good health and spirits. On their first day 'Mr Dobs who went in quest of the North west Passage and three Irish Gentlemen arrived here . . . from Dublin'.[84]* John Adam came from Edinburgh for about a week, noted the need of further administrative improvements, drew up the usual memorial full of recommendations for preventing fraud and slack work, and made a contract with another Lowlander, William Cowan, to take over the working of Creggans quarry; so that now the three articles of stone, lime and bricks were set by bargain.[85]

'This house was like a cryed fair ye first five or six days,' wrote Maule to Lord Milton, 'but Powrie, Tuder, Mcleod & Castle Stuart are gone, Harie Home, Shawfield Allan Ramsay & Succoth are still here. Tell my Gossip [Lady Milton] every thing is in ye froth . . . The Great work of Reformation goes on here & ye other works I mean buildings &c advances apace, & new things dailly projected.' The crowd was so great that even the circuit judges, Lords Minto and Tinwald, had to lodge where they could, Minto 'in ye Sheriffs & his son in ye Duke's', while Tinwald must 'get his own bed', but both were invited to dine and sup with the Duke at any time.[86]* When the court opened on 15 September the Duke took the place of honour in his role of Justice-General, as he was often to do in later years, and (reported the *Edinburgh Evening Courant*), 'there is a splendid company of Gentlemen & Ladies in that Town at present . . . it is so crowded, that it is difficult to get Lodging'.[87]

There was good reason for the crowd of notabilities, for this was the Duke's first appearance on the bench at Inveraray since the abolition, in May, of the Scottish heritable jurisdictions, regarded by Lord Campbell as the most beneficial legislative measure ever passed in Scotland.[88]* No longer, after the cessation of that 'cruel, remorseless, and arbitrary tribunal', could a single chief or laird impose on his vassals without interference from Government or from an impartial legal authority. The removal, long overdue, of this feudal survival by Act of Parliament had been achieved in the teeth of Jacobite opposition the previous year by the Lord Chancellor, Lord Hardwicke – thanks in great measure to the Duke of Argyll, who recognized the inevitability of this abrogation of traditional privilege, and brought to reason the numerous Scottish judges who, as landowners, stood to lose these powers as he did himself. From now on justice was dispensed locally by the circuit judges and sheriffs appointed by the Crown.

The autumn sessions over, the crowd dispersed from Inveraray, and Lady Milton came for a few days. The Duke, who had been harassed by 'some of the Old

Administration at Inveraray who woud Impose upon him if they coud', rode out daily inspecting progress 'with the adjutants Messieurs Campbel and Paterson', wrote Andrew, 'and seems inclined to strengthen the hands of that Ministry'.[89] This particular Campbell was probably Baillie Peter or Patrick (the names were interchangeable), wig-maker and Dean of Gild, 'a diligent active man', employed during the '45 as a confidential messenger and in 1747 as escort to London of witnesses for Lord Lovat's trial. He now acted in Inveraray as a kind of informer to the Duke's friends, particularly of scandals such as unauthorized sale of liquor by the overseers.[90]* A brisk guerrilla campaign was waged between town and castle, in later years sometimes breaking out into open hostilities. As a result of the Duke's tours of inspection, John Adam's warnings against dishonesty and mismanagement, and Baillie Peter's confidential reports, fresh attempts were made to regulate the works, by the empirical methods always used at Inveraray. From lack of proper supervision, fraud and slackness were the norm, and the quarriers tippled on home-distilled whisky while the Duke's tools were stolen, reported lost or damaged, and then sold back to his overseers. Therefore, in October 1749, the apparently easy-going Deputy Chamberlain retired and was, confusingly, replaced by another John Campbell (of Danna), the Sheriff Clerk. Meanwhile, in 1748 the commissions were renewed of two subsidiary Chamberlains, Donald Campbell of Airds for the Mull and Morvern estates, at a salary of £100 a year, and John Campbell of Clenamacrie for the rest at £40.[91]*

With autumn's onset the weather deteriorated, and Maule, who had carried Andrew away with him to visit Panmure, soon wrote that his guest had been 'detained days, nay weeks by storms of wind & rain at Inveraray & here'.[92] Not till the second half of October did Andrew rejoin his father and his patron, at Brunstane, where John Adam waited on the Duke with his reports and was instructed to hand over to Lord Milton Morris's 'last designs for Rosneath'. It was then, too, that the Duke promised his interest in John's career, and the reversion of his father's Ordnance post.[93]

Argyll's own patronage, however, kept John Adam busy supervising the execution of Morris's designs at Rosneath and Inveraray, and later as the projected new town began slowly to take shape, it was John who advised the Duke and Milton on its plan, and designed its modest public buildings.

Every autumn, from 1747 to 1760, Duke Archibald visited his Argyll possessions, travelling from London to Edinburgh with Andrew Fletcher and spending a few days at his 'old friend' the Whim, or at Brunstane with Lord Milton, before continuing westwards 'with a great retinue'. In Glasgow, as at Edinburgh, Provost and councillors, followed by a crowd of friends and place-seekers, waited on the great man, and usually entertained him at a ceremonial dinner. In 1751 the Duke bought a yacht, the *Princess Augusta* (master Josiah Corthine), and sailed in her up the lochs; but after two or three seasons he disposed of the boat.[94] He normally spent a few days at Rosneath and about six weeks at Inveraray, often accompanied by Lord and Lady Milton (except when the former, who had poor health, was unable to join him), and in later years by their young daughters Mally and Betty. There was always a vast number of visitors, and during the few days of the autumn circuit courts in September, the Duke frequently presided at the opening as Justice-General, although as often as not the court had little or no business. In October the annual estate accounts were drawn up by Lord Milton, audited by the accountant, Robert Campbell of Asknish, and usually witnessed by the Duke, who also transacted an enormous quantity of estate business, such as the granting of tacks or leases, the hearing of petitions, and the legalities of his purchases of land with the compensation money for his loss of the Argyll jurisdictions. Meanwhile his detailed directions for the coming year's work were written down and circulated among the Chamberlains and the building and farm overseers. John Adam regularly attended the Duke at Inveraray, occasionally made a further supervisory visit in the spring, and during the rest of the year took his instructions from Lord Milton in Edinburgh.

3. THE CASTLE. 1749–56. A tradition has long existed that on the death of Roger Morris the supervision of Inveraray was continued by his kinsman Robert, until his own death in 1754. For many years Robert Morris was actually credited with the design of the castle, until this was disproved by re-discovery of the *Letter-Book* containing correspondence and signed drawings of the then little-known Roger.[95] The 3rd Duke of Argyll indeed possessed, among the works of architecture in his library, a copy of both Robert Morris's *Essay in defence of ancient architecture*, published in 1728, and his *Lectures in Architecture* of 1734; but there is no evidence that Robert had any hand in the work at Inveraray.[96]

The Duke's bank account confirms this, for whereas he paid Roger Morris large sums (usually in units of £200) regularly from 1731 until shortly before Morris's death, there is not a single payment to Robert. On the other hand the bank records reveal that Roger's son James inherited his practice, and occasional large payments by the Duke to James succeed the more frequent ones to Roger. For example, in March 1750 the Duke paid James Morris £400, in May £489; in June 1751 £500, and so on until September 1756, about which time the younger Morris appears to have gone out of business.[97*]

These large payments to James Morris must also have covered commissions for the Duke in England, since the materials used at Inveraray were locally paid for, and there is no record that James visited the place. References to 'Mr Morris' in correspondence indicate little more than occasional advice. John Adam may well have consulted him during another visit he made to the south early in 1750; when the timbers were to be laid Morris sent up by Andrew Fletcher a plan of 'the best method of piecing of Timbers' (December 1752), and there is talk of a model to follow.[98*] Early in 1754 Morris also provided a list of duties payable on Norway deals, and in 1756 advised on window sashes.[99*]

The only other evidence is a waspish remark of Robert Adam's, written in Rome in September 1755 to one of his sisters, and hitherto taken to refer to Robert

Morris. As Robert Morris appears to have died in November 1754, had he appeared a potential rival it seems very unlikely that the news of his death should not have filtered through to Adam, even in Rome, during the following nine months. The Morris whose competition Adam here dreads, however, is his own contemporary James, whom he jealously feels that the Duke retains for the sake of his dead father. Remarking that the Duke may have recommended him, Adam, to Lord Home ('and I should like that Channel much'), he continues:

'You know the Duke's attachment to Morris, so that in case of an English Scheme He might be difficulted, how to Act between freindship & Merit . . . Had the Duke less Constancy & friendship, I should not att all dread my Rival.'[100]*

If the connexion of James Morris with the 3rd Duke of Argyll is obscure, with Robert Adam it is a different story. Twenty years old when his father died, and already revealing his original talent, powerful *amour propre* and overweening ambition, the younger Adam was soon accompanying his brother John to Fort George and later to Inveraray, Hopetoun and Dumfries House. In August 1754 he spent some time at Inveraray with John, and it was from there that he departed on his Italian travels towards the end of September. The architect's fees, which had been exercising the brothers for some time, were only now under discussion with the Duke. Six months earlier John had written to his kindly old friend Harry Barclay admitting anxiety over the amount he might reasonably ask the Duke to pay:

'. . . the conducting of so great a Work, has cost a good deall of trouble, & the journeys have been some expence; yet I would not on any consideration have The Duke or My Lord Milton think that we are covetous, & declare we'd rather never see a farthing for it.

I think I told You that on a former occasion My Lord pressed me very much to know what would satisfie on this Score, when I assured His Lop that whatever The Duke or He should think it deserved, would be acceptable. He then pressed to know the Custome in the like cases, & I told Him that a Surveyor in Lond° or England has 5 p C^t of the Sum expended, And in Scotland a Master Mason has $3\frac{1}{3}$d p day of profite allow'd on each Man, But that we neither desired nor expected so much. In short a penny a day (or less if that is thought too much) we shall reckon fully sufficient, And if possible I should wish that this matter could be determined by My Lord himself without our being at all seen in it. It would have been lucky if this matter had been settled at the beginning & the payments made annually, as the Gratification that this deserves will appear high in the Lump, & would not have done so in parcels; But there is no help for it now . . .'[101]

We may doubt whether Robert would have rated their deserts so modestly, and their firm must have suffered financial loss at Inveraray for the want of a fee agreed by their father in advance. But they must have been embarrassed by their position as architects by devolution, not by commission; and in John at least the tone of responsibility and sober deference never varies. With Robert the mask of humility towards superiors in rank is thrown off when he addresses his own family, and his comments on the fancied slights of the Fletcher girls when staying at Inveraray are uncharitable, even crude. A letter written to his sisters from Inveraray on the eve of his departure for his studies in Italy suggests that his attentions had been snubbed by the girls:

'Miss Betty Fletcher told me to day that Her great Taste was for Painting, that she envy'd my Happiness & wish'd she cou'd accompany me. This from the Stinkingest of Mortals I look'd on as no small compliment till next disdainful look from her Nizzety Gabb, wipt entirely away all impression of it. Mally with as much pride as can dwell in one Carcase, As much overbearing as, as plague on't . . . as the Bitch her Mother, I nevertheless give the preference, on account of Her speaking what vice she utters, with greater virulence . . . By these anecdotes says my good pretty, witty Girls, My Brothers infected. Well, you can't say its with Love however, no danger that way I'll assure you.'[102]

But even Robert was satisfied with the Duke's interim settlement of their account.

'We are to receive Three Hundred pounds for all trouble at this place from the very beginning to this day. Though it comes to but about £30 p Annum Yet it is so much that we never expected, & The Duke was extreamly pleased with the settling it, which Tinwald & Milton did, and as Johnie told that if it was but £50, that we wou'd take it with chearfulness, The Duke say'd that we had behaved vastly genteely & that he was obliged to us.'[103]

This first payment settled the Adam family's account to date, from William's appointment some ten years previously.

With this satisfactory conclusion to his own share in the work Robert set off for Hopetoun, then Edinburgh and thence for Italy; two days afterwards John also left, to meet Colonel William Skinner, Chief Engineer for North Britain, and his assistants on Ordnance business at Dumbarton.[104]

The appearance of the unique Gothick castle which he had just left, in which he was concerned at this early stage of his career, undoubtedly impressed Robert Adam deeply, and can be seen to have influenced his own ideas, regardless of how much they were to expand during his next years in Italy. He had already experimented with sketches for Gothick follies and towers, and the numerous alternative designs for the ornamental dairy at Tombreac on the Duke's estate resemble (in simpler form) some of Robert's fanciful sketches, and may even have been designed by him, or adapted by John from one of his ideas.[105]

In September 1754, when Robert Adam went abroad, the walls of Inveraray Castle were built up to battlement level, the main roof was slating and work on the high middle tower had begun – slow progress, perhaps, by modern standards; for seven years had passed since his father and Morris had last visited the place, when the great drain across the foundation excavation was being lined and arched. But considering what was involved in building to that scale, in that area and at that time, it was much to the credit of young John Adam that he maintained continuity.

26. Inveraray Castle, part elevation
Working drawing by William Adam.

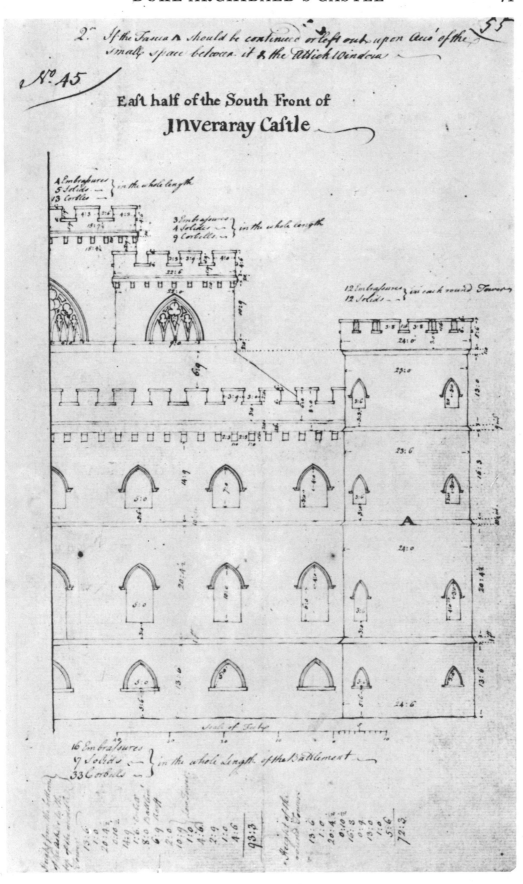

East half of the South Front of
Jnveraray Castle

Soon after his father's death he had introduced changes. Until then it was assumed that nothing would happen between November and March, but, at John's suggestion, during the winter of 1748/9 thirty masons were kept after the normal autumn pay-off 'very bussie . . . in providing Matterials for the Building next sumer and a great number of Massons have been employed . . . in hewing stons qch will graitly forward the work.'[106] Observing this progress in his spring visit John was so well pleased by the experiment that next winter he repeated it. However, the labourers (he reported in September 1749) were

'so excessively bad that nothing can be made of them, And at the same time so scarce that there is no change to be had, when any of them is turn'd off for a trespass, So that the Foreman has sometimes been oblig'd to imploy these people again in order to get the building Masons served'.

He drew up a list dividing the labourers into twelve 'good', six 'indeferent' and ten downright 'bad'. From experience at Fort George and from the building of the military road John observed that 'soldiers make by far the best labourers'– and because of their low rates of pay were more economic to employ.[107]

The first timber cargo was at that time (September 1749) daily, and for long in vain, expected, but there was no intention of departing from Morris's original instructions to lay no joists until the roof was on; instead, John executed Morris's scheme of binding the walls with temporary girders at various heights, cut from trees which the Duke personally marked out in his grounds: 'For tho' the outside Walls are thick & Substantial, [Mr Morris] was afraid they might be subject to be damaged & thrown out of an upright unless this precaution was taken.' Six girders were required for the long gallery on the north side, two for the hall, '1 in each Parlour, & 1 in each Bed Chamber, in all 12 Girders, to be put in when the building should be as high as the Springs of the Arches of the Principal Story Windows',[108] a point reached early in December, just before John left for his second visit to London. But the little timber roofs to protect the wall-heads remained only half made for lack of sawyers, until Lord Milton authorized engaging two more men from Glasgow.[109]

The same autumn John had to interpret Roger Morris's written instructions for building the chimney vents. Morris had carefully designed them to avoid smoking or 'Lodgements for Smoak & dust', but had not anticipated the effect of the West Highland rainfall, and his recommended internal finish of plaster and horse-dung, whose smooth surface was meant to aid 'the passing of the Smoak', was washed away before it could even dry. John recommended casing the chimneys with the flagstones now being quarried across the loch at St Catherines, 'which as they harden by heat, will answer extreamly well for that purpose'. He also had to calculate the rate of diminution of size for the various chimneys, and their points of emission through the battlements.[110]*

Adam's deputy on the site was not the Duke's mason William Douglas, but George Hunter, another Lowlander engaged 'to see things done as they are ordered & make true reports'.[111] Douglas, whom Stonefield regarded as 'soe peevish & unsettled a Creature that I am very unwilling to have any thing to do with him',[112] was not employed on building the castle itself, though he was under contract to supply and sour lime for all the works; but he was responsible for the ornamental additions to the Duke's policies, and later for the new town's inn. The chief mason at the castle, under Hunter, was James Calder.

George Hunter, like Douglas before him, settled with his family in Inveraray, and in Adam's absence in the south proved a responsible foreman, sending Lord Milton the necessary clearly written reports.

The best castle masons were paid 2s 6d a day, their labourers 6d.[113] By 1749 their numbers had so increased that the hewing-sheds, designed to take only one row of men, had to hold two, so that the back row had not enough light, and their labourers hindered the front row as they carried out the hewn stone. Meanwhile the gabart laden with new stone from the quarry rowed daily up the loch to unload at the quayside, from where a string of carts rattled over the stone causeways through the town to the castle site, breaking up the surfaces, which in turn by their roughness shook the carts to pieces. On Sundays and after working hours the townspeople curiously wandered about the site, and for want of better occupation chipped at the stones lying ready for the masons. At night cows ambled into the hewing-sheds and found what must have been an uncomfortable resting-place among the stones. Adam, rather exasperated, suggested by-passing the town with a road through the Wintertown park, and the building there of an additional masons' shed, so that carts could avoid the rough town road and all access be closed to 'idle People' and cows.[114]

At the same time Adam issued a warning that a great many scaffolding boards would now be required (Hunter estimated 500), but although at this stage efforts to obtain a good timber supply were abortive, and although lack of supervision caused the wrights to be 'very Dillatory In geteing what is Necesscary for the Building don', Hunter anticipated that the 1750 season would bring the height of the castle 'to the Cills of the window of the uper Story'. In June Knockbuy reported good progress, as 'the front nixt the old Castle is now up to where the 2d belt is fixd on the model'. At this, the busiest time of the year, seventy-eight masons and sixty labourers were employed, and their weekly wage bill was £34 14s 8d. The shortage of labourers hampered the work as the masons could not be 'propperly served', and early in November only thirty-four labourers remained to sixty-two masons.[115]

A number of the masons also now returned to the Lowlands (with five shillings apiece for travelling expenses), and 'haveing got Employmt in ye Low Country decline to return to Inveraray'. On top of this William Cowan, one of the contractors at Creggans quarry, had to give up work through ill health, and Hunter, whom Adam now found so valuable a subordinate that he contrived to have his wages raised, found it necessary to go to Edinburgh in December to recruit more men. He then suggested to Lord Milton that they could save '20 £ p an:' by employing an overseer at the quarry instead of putting it out to contract;[116] but in the

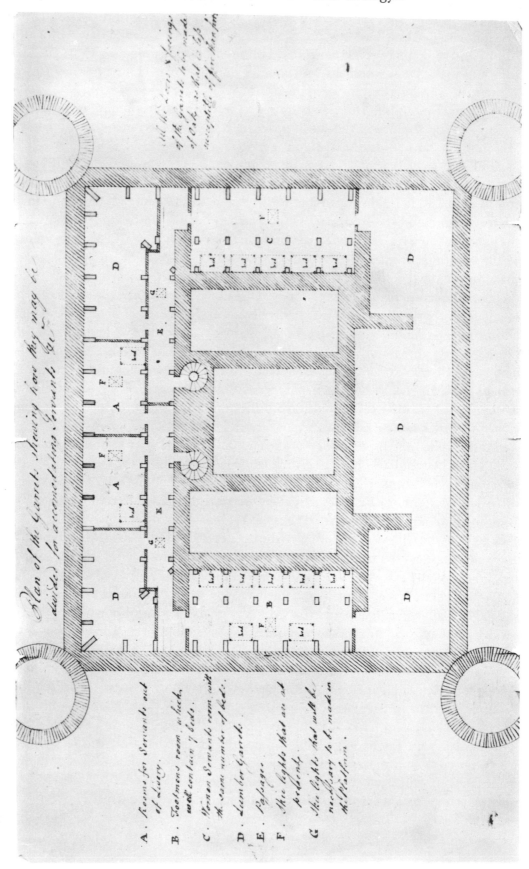

Plan of the Garrets shewing how they may be divided for accomodating Servants &c

A . Rooms for Servants out of Livery.

B . Footmens room which will contain 7 beds.

C . Women Servants room with the same number of beds.

D . Lumber Garrets.

E . Passage.

F . The lights that are at present.

G . The lights that will be necessary to be made in the Platform.

event Creggans was shortly run down once the flags and other stones already cut had been removed. From 1751 the chief quarry was St Catherines on the opposite side of Loch Fyne.

The shortage of scaffolding continued, although George Haswell, the chief wright, had been warned always to have enough 'timeously prepared', and the small quantity available had constantly to be dismantled and shifted where most urgently required. Adam reckoned in 1751 that 'near a fourth of the building Masons time is taken up in carrying the dealls from one part of the building to another', and he calculated a need for between 700 and 1000 deals for scaffolding boards alone.[117]

They were now working at battlement level, and a crane on wheels or castors was ordered for hoisting large stones up to the parapets.[118] More important, they were now nearly at the stage where six years earlier Roger Morris had ordained that the first joists be laid in the castle : when 'the whole Building is up, Battlment wall finnishd, and the scafold are taken downe'. The usual method of buying timber in Scotland was to go to a Clydeside or Leith merchant, or better, to commission cargoes direct from Scandinavia. Both these sources were freely used in the building of Inveraray, and as far back as September 1747 Roger Morris and William Adam on their last visit had ordered a consignment of timber and iron from Peter Frelsen, a visiting Danish captain from Holstein, for delivery in 1749. But the order did not materialize, and eventually the first large timber cargo direct from Norway was procured after great difficulty and embarrassment, in 1752 (see p. 112 and note 252).

In 1751, modifications were made to the castle's roof design, and John Adam drew a new plan for the attic floor and revised the scantling of timber required for roof and joists. His list included 40 principal rafters 21 feet long and 13 inches square; 44 timbers for diagonals and tie-beams between 25 and 36 feet, the same number of king-posts 14 feet long, and 12 by 18 inches in section; and 35 for principal girders over the hall, parlours, bedchambers, gallery and round towers. There were also 300 tons of baulks 'for purloins, Springs, Hows, Spars; Rafters over the middle Tower & Staircases, Collar beams; Runtrees, Sleepers &c.', all in 'the best upland red firr, as Square as possible, & free of Sapwood & Shakes'. Finally, 2,000 deals were required between 10 and 12 feet long and $1\frac{1}{2}$ inches thick for roof sarking, and for lining the lead platforms and gutters.[119]

At this advanced stage of the building other new trades and materials were also required. In 1749 Tam Cochrane had recommended a plumber, John Graham, as both skilled and cheap, and Lord Milton employed him for the Duke's house at the Whim.[120] In March 1752, Graham – equivalent in rank to the overseers, and therefore addressed as 'Mr' – set off for Inveraray with Adam's instructions 'to direct the propper breadths & drips of the Gutters behind the battlements, and the method of bringing through the Rain water pipes, All which we talked over with him fully before he went'. He was also to cast and cut lengths of sheet lead ready to be raggled into the backs of the battlements. Graham's bill for 1753 was £189 11s 9d, and in

27. Inveraray Castle, attic storey
   Plan by John Adam, 1751

1754, £153 18s 7d. By the time he completed his task in November 1754, he had earned the hatred of everyone he worked with, for a report very soon reached the Duke that 'altho' he is a good workman yet he is so illnatur'd, that wherever he works, he is ready to set People by the ears'.[121]*

To supply Graham, lead bars now began to arrive by sea from the lead mines at Strontian, on Loch Sunart in Morvern,[122]* and, since by midsummer 1752 the castle roof was ready to be put on, slates were now required as well. On the Duke's instructions Knockbuy applied for these to Colin Campbell of Carwhin, heir-presumptive to the Earldom of Breadalbane, who lived at Ardmaddy Castle on the Firth of Lorne, opposite the 'Slate Islands' of Easdale, Luing and Seil.[123]* Here slate had been worked since mediaeval times, and as late as 1845 the quarries employed up to 200 men.[124]* Knockbuy asked Carwhin to order '10 or 12000 of the best slate' from the Easdale quarries, for which the Campbeltown factor was to send up a small coaling vessel when they were ready.[125]*

Carwhin was also asked to find a skilled marble quarrier from the works in Nether Lorne, for a marble quarry had now been opened within a mile of Inveraray Castle, on a hill beyond Duniquaich known as Tombreac or Tombreck. Here, since 1750, William Douglas's men had been building a park wall, and a little ornamental Gothick dairy, designed as an eye-catcher, was shortly built nearby. The marble was required for the castle's two great staircases in the subsidiary halls flanking the great hall, and when the Duke arrived in September 1752 four quarriers began working under Hunter's supervision, on an order for nearly 140 tons of marble, 134 of the pieces being six feet long.[126] Carwhin agreed to supply the special tools, and recommended Alexander Campbell 'who was under greive att the marble works here, & is well skilled in raising blocks of marble & sawing likewise, & well known to Wm. Douglas mason'. Alexander Campbell came to inspect the Tombreac quarry the following December (1752); after a disappointing start, by the end of 1753 Hunter and Douglas were satisfied with its output.[127]

In 1752 the Duke travelled to Scotland early in July having a number of political and legal matters to attend to in Edinburgh, notably the elections. A month later he travelled west, taking in Rosneath as usual on his way, and was for some days prevented by severe storms from visiting his new yacht, bought the previous year but not yet seen. But the weather soon changed completely, and Lady Milton, who preceded him to Inveraray, suffered on the ascent of Glen Croe from a combination of acute toothache and 'violent heat, . . . beyond Mount Etna for if it had not been for some Spirmont Water I had fainted away in the Chaise'. She was forced to stay an extra night on the way at Sir James Campbell's at Ardkinglas, drowning her toothache with opium. A day later the Duke and Andrew followed in the *Princess Augusta*, delayed by the lack of wind and phenomenally calm, hot weather.[128]

That autumn Inveraray had many distinguished visitors, including the Minister to London from the Republic of Genoa, Signor Gastaldi 'l'Illustrissimo' – who like so many others was honoured with burgess-ship of Inveraray. 'A very entertaining

28. Slate quarrying in 1803. Etching by W. H. Pyne after a drawing by J. H. Nattes.

good Naturd body', thought Lady Milton, and very anxious to meet her husband before setting off again for Stirling and a visit to the Earl of Traquair.[129] The gentleman on his side was quite 'in love with Lady Milton, she being he says, the politest finest Lady ever he met with, he thinks likeways his Grace is turned very religious, as a proof of which he notices the Dukes going so regularly to church' – an ironic allusion to the Appin Murder trial which had just opened in the church at Inveraray. [130]

Next they were joined by the Duke's nephew Stuart Mackenzie and his wife Lady Betty (daughter of the late Duke), arriving from Stonefield's house at Levenside. The weather continued brilliant; by the time Lord Milton followed, a few days after his wife, not a drop of rain had fallen for over ten days and on the new road the sun still beat down in the glens with near-tropical intensity. Another September visitor was Corbyn Morris, Secretary to the Customs, politically a dubious ally but expressing himself much impressed by the Duke's 'condescending civilities' and the hospitable entertainment of Lord and Lady Milton, their daughters and Colonel Jack Campbell.[131]

But the sensation of 1752 was neither the visitors, the extraordinary weather, nor the progress of Inveraray Castle, but an event of dramatic political significance concerning the Duke, as Chief of the Campbells, very closely : the notorious trial of James Stewart for complicity in the shooting, on 14 May, of Colin Campbell of Glenure. Justly or unjustly the Appin Murder was pinned on Stewart, a natural brother of Ardshiel, whose forfeited estate had been in process of inspection by the murdered man. For the past four months the case had occupied everyone's attention. The scene of the murder was within the jurisdiction of Inveraray, and when Stewart's trial opened there on 21 September the Duke naturally presided in his official capacity – although on other occasions he usually retired after the first ceremonial opening of the court. This was Campbell country and the jury, as always, numbered a large proportion of Campbells (eleven out of the fifteen), one of whom was Carwhin.[132]*

The one aspect of the trial which concerns us here is the scene of the proceedings. For four years the Sheriff had been pressing for a new Court House and prison, now a public responsibility since the abolition of the heritable jurisdictions; the existing Court House, built many years earlier at the expense of the Argyll estate, was in serious disrepair. An account of the trial by Lord Milton shows that the old building was so inadequate that it could not possibly accommodate so important and crowded a trial, and so the sessions were held in the church.[133]*

After the trial, at which the jury sat for over forty-eight hours without adjournment, the unfortunate Stewart being found guilty was committed back to the old gaol for a further fortnight. He was then transferred to the prison at Inverness and finally handed back to Sheriff Stonefield for execution on 8 November at Ballachulish Ferry, and his body hung in chains.

The excitement of the Appin trial did not interrupt Inveraray's building progress or estate business. Among the numerous memorials, petitions and complaints presented to the Duke that autumn was one from William Douglas, who had run into difficulties as supplier of lime from the works, and now surrendered the contract to James Potter, another mason.[134]* A more difficult customer was Donald Campbell, feuar of St Catherines where the main quarry was now being worked. 'Ignorance or avarice or bad advise' made this intransigent character resist offers to buy him out, nor would he grant the Duke a tack until the Chamberlain had argued with him many times. At last Donald grudgingly agreed to terms, but would allow only 'grass for two horses', not three (always an important clause in this district, where the land was all appropriated). The Chamberlain begged the Duke to confirm the deal at once, for 'the person to be dealt with is weak & fickle and possibly may change his mind before we see him again'.[135]

A third claim was made by some masons whose 'guildhalls' on the site, where they slept, ate and kept their tools, had been destroyed by fire that spring. The fire, probably caused by a spark in a wooden chimney vent, began at about seven in the morning of 13 March and in a short time burnt to a cinder 'not only Your Grace's houses, but all our provisions, Clothes and every thing else we had therein … Extending in all to £39 14s 5d Sterling'. The masons had to remove to lodgings in the old castle and the town, while new guildhalls were converted from the wrights' sheds. Adam directed that to avoid future accidents they must have dry stone gavels above roof level, which would effectively cut them off from the hewing-sheds adjoining. But the fifteen masons concerned – regular employees at the works almost from the beginning, six of them with families – had to wait for their money for eighteen months, for claims at Inveraray were usually deferred from season to season, and this one was not settled until autumn 1753.[136]

Dilatory settlement of debts and obligations was not due to an aristocratic contempt for business, but to the heavy drain which the building works caused on the Duke's income. The first rumblings of anxiety were heard in March 1752 when Knockbuy warned Lord Milton that 'their Treasury is so low att Inverara, that we should apply your Lo/' – who was a not uncommon source of funds. Asknish was soon also appealing to the Campbeltown Chamberlain, when timber and slates were on order : 'If you have any cash by you I wish you woud send it me as we have at present great demands & not much of the ready'.[137] Whereas in October 1751 the annual accounts showed an outlay of little over £8,000, including over £1,000 left in Asknish's hands, in 1752 expenditure rose to nearly £10,000. The main increases were not in payments to the castle masons (which rose only £50 to £1,511) or quarriers, but for a series of park walls now being built all over the estate, costing nearly £700 that year alone, and for the modest start now made on building the new town. Outlay on materials had also soared, the major expenditure of the year being on timber (£1,684), and many cargoes were still to come.[138]

Annual payments continued to rise. In 1753 the total was £10,017, in 1754 £11,926. Of this, the masons' bill in 1753 was £1,742; payments to wrights and for St Catherines stone were some £800 each; Henry Roy's bill was £919; for roofing the castle, the lead, slates and workmen's wages together came to over £1,000. At the height of the season eighty masons were employed, and nearly fifty quarriers at St Catherines. In 1754, although the masons' bill fell slightly (to £1,569), timber cost over £1,000, the quarry about £650, and slating and plumbing much the same.[139] Items like lead often had to be paid for in spot cash, of which there was embarrassingly little; timber cargoes might have to be snapped up at a steep price for the sake of their quality. Not only Lord Milton but the Kintyre Chamberlain at Campbeltown, whose receipts were agreeably high thanks to the prosperous farms in that district, was often called on for an advance. In April 1754 Asknish, awaiting a shipload of lead for which he would have to pay, remarks to Lord Milton, 'Our ffinances are very low and unless Providence supply us we shall be distressed next pay day. I wrote to the Baillie Kintyre … My greatest dependance for some time to come is upon him …' In November, when Graham the plumber had finished the lead roofs and had to be paid off, Asknish ingeniously gave him 'the odd £53 18s 7½d, to pay the whole [another £100] was beyond my present ability as Martinmass brings many demands with it'.[140] That autumn, too, the Adam brothers were paid to date.

Fraud and negligence increased the bills. Henry Roy the smith, always a slight grievance to Asknish because of the promptitude with which he presented his account, was (Asknish suspected) profiting by careless supervision at the quarries and buying up tools reported lost or damaged, to sell back to the overseers.[141]

The *ad hoc* methods employed resulted in an ill co-ordinated labour organization, and Asknish proved an inept economist. As for labour relations and output, when hard-won experience showed their deficiency, what would now seem the obvious solution was then only slowly and painfully evolved after prolonged correspondence with Edinburgh and London, and waiting for orders from John Adam, Lord Milton and ultimately the Duke.

The Duke lost patience with his improvident managers. A slipshod agreement made by Knockbuy with some Inveraray merchants in February 1754, with 'an exotick clause' committing the Duke to pay £470 for meal and oats before they were even delivered, so incensed him that he stopped payment: 'I never saw such a bawdy house agreement in my life, some measures or other must be taken about my Inveraray affairs . . .[142] Six weeks earlier he had written to Lord Milton on the situation at some length:

'I observe what you say as to Rob. Campbells getting sums of money from you & demanding more, I must of necessity put an end to that manner of going on, or I shall break, the last Year it was necessary to hurry on the Roof at any expence & I was sensible of it, this Year I knew I should have the lead to pay for, but its high time I should have some rest, for if most part of my Rents are to be laid out at Inveraray & when I come here I can not have the income of my Offices, I must in one shape or other diminish those expences which bring these evils upon me; I have now these 2 or 3 Years together been forced to sell out great Sums of my funds in the Stocks & after this Year I can go no farther that way.'[143]

In 1756 the crisis came to a head. Not only was this an extremely bad year for public relations, with every overseer complaining bitterly of the rest, but the money shortage was acute. An attempt had been made to reduce expenditure, and in Asknish's absence (he was staying the winter in Edinburgh) his deputy paymaster the Chamberlain, John Campbell, carefully checked his accounts against those of the astronomical year 1755. But although it was winter, with fewer men employed, in the last week of February the Chamberlain found himself in the embarrassing position of having to feign illness on pay day because his treasury was completely empty.

'Want of Cash hindered actual payment, & a few fair words procured a delay till next Munday, when every body was assured they shoud be cleared to a farthing. – This & a feigned Indisposition on the pay day made them & me pretty easy since that time – But unluckily Munday next is too near & if I have just now £5 in the world I have £50,000 – All my Stock of Rents Feu duties Cess & part of my Credit (for I have really borrowed £50) is gone.'

His accounts were so seriously in arrears that with the numerous other calls on the estate in addition to building costs, even if all the rents due were by some miracle paid before Whitsun it still 'woud not long answer the monstruous outlay in this place . . . Rari, in gurgite vasto – There is scarce the Shadow of money thro' this Country before that time.' After raising advances from his usual allies Lord Milton and the Baillie of Kintyre, he was reduced to borrowing from his own neighbours.[144]

The weekly wage bill even in February was £60 17s, a sum the Chamberlain found ludicrous,

> 'in my own private opinion a great deal more than it ought to be; Especially upon three articles – The Shoals at St Catherins quarry – no less than 62 Masons besides George Hunter employd to very little visible advantage & above 40 men on the ffisherland whose work makes but a sorry figure to my unskilful Eye; that is, in proportion to their numbers.'

So frayed were the Chamberlain's nerves that he issued an ultimatum to Asknish:

> 'Let me tell you seriously that no consideration, other than incurring the displeasure of My Lord Duke or my Lord Milton, shall for another year induce me to be the paymaster here unless ffunds are first put in my hands to answer the occasions we may have – If that is not done you shall stay at home & I go to Edr. next winter.'[145]

At first Asknish was inclined to dismiss this as a temporary crisis due to his deputy's inefficiency, but he informed Lord Milton and they instructed Campbell to order Walter Paterson and Robert Bathgate, the new farm overseer, to cut down on labour, and Lord Milton sent the Chamberlain £100 for his immediate needs. 'After I shall have paid the Demands of tomorrow', replied Campbell bitterly, 'double that Sum will scarce clear the Debt I have contracted in my office of deputy paymaster.' Asknish hurried back to Inveraray at once.[146]

But his supposition that he could put matters right was soon shattered. The spring rush was about to begin – masons building park walls, canalizing the river Shira, making a road to the inn:

> 'How much I have been deceiv'd your Lop will see from the enclosed two Bills which instead of diminishing are encreas'd and yet I foresee the worst is not yet come . . . Legions will be employ'd . . . and when to all these is added the Smiths Accots. ffreights from St Cathrines – coals oats seeds &c from Glasgow & their freights with numberless other incidents that one cannot think of I confess I cannot see where it is to end Nothing under a Royal income can support such a constant high outlay.'

There were now sixty masons, whose work directly depended on the quarriers, whose output in turn incurred huge freight charges. Then there was excavation of the fosse round the castle, occupying fifty labourers – but although this had been one-third excavated last autumn before Lord Milton left Inveraray not a single stone had yet been laid: 'One wou'd think that considering how much digging

is now necessary and how rainy the Climate is that one half of the Masons might hew & Build as fast as at least 100 Labourers wou'd dig but this is under correction.' As for money, 'there is no such thing to be had here, the only times that there is money is after Whitsunday and after Criefe and all the rest of the year they are as poor as rats.'[147]*

It proved almost impossible to dismiss any masons, for consultation with George Hunter soon showed that even when the castle was finished, they would still be needed to build the Town House, whose foundation had been laid the year before (1755). Even if the 'present standing army' were disbanded no money would come in for months unless Lord Milton continued his subsidies.[148]

Following Milton's orders, Asknish now kept strict comparative accounts. The bills started at £79 and next week shot up to £109. Then Asknish caught William Paull, quarry overseer at St Catherines, in dishonest dealing, and his dismissal with twenty workmen reduced expenses a trifle, but 'still very high'. Henry Roy stepped up the pressure by presenting an account for £30 with his usual smartness; Bathgate the farm overseer reported that they were out of oats, and their Glasgow agent Robert Lang warned Asknish that he could supply no more goods until his overdue bill of £80 was settled. Next week the expenditure was £110.

So it went on. 'From what corner a supply is to come for tomorrows pay I know not but at present ffinances are quite Ebb'd.' This time it was Donald Campbell of Airds, the Morvern factor, who came to their rescue. Then Hunter discharged a few masons, and the new iron-works at Furnace on Loch Fyne offered jobs to half a dozen more (page 136). Payments dropped to £50, then went up again – but never quite so steeply, and the immediate crisis seemed to be weathered.[149] To implement the financial reforms, next autumn at the Duke's order all but twelve masons were dismissed for the winter and the wrights were similarly reduced.[150]

This campaign brought to an end the days of an army of workmen idling through the winter months, drawing the Duke's pay to the tune of £50 a week, pilfering his equipment to sell to the smith, and getting drunk on illicitly distilled whisky. A legal inquiry by a kind of committee including Lord Milton, Asknish and two Lincoln's Inn lawyers, Alexander Forrester and George Ross, uncovered 'a reel in his Grace's ministry . . . from several frauds',[151] and more effective, if belated measures were taken to stop the rot. Robert Bathgate, a young man from Saltoun (of a family long trusted tenants of Lord Milton) whose unimpeachable Lowland morals made him a natural target for the unscrupulous, was ordered to obtain a signed inventory from the quarry overseers of all tools in use, and to give out no more except on receipt. No tools were even to be made by the smith without an order signed by the Chamberlain or Asknish. An advertisement was posted at the kirk doors one Sunday that all keys to the Duke's parks (by which the townspeople used to sneak in to graze their cattle and steal firewood) must be handed to Bathgate at once, anyone found concealing one to be prosecuted.[152]

Much of the trouble had been caused by drunkenness. Boatmen and checkers

29. An iron foundry in 1802
    Etching by W. H. Pyne after a drawing by J. H. Nattes.

unloading supplies at the shore were so often drunk that many frauds had passed unnoticed; the whisky was dispensed by the gardener – the ingenious Walter Paterson–and James Gibson the new groom. Even after exposure these two managed to continue trafficking in liquor, and as for unsuspecting Bathgate, he was soon the victim of a conspiracy headed by Gibson, the schoolmaster (a vengeful man named John Fallowsdale) and others, who tried as ingeniously as unsuccessfully to pin on the young overseer charges of gross dishonesty.[153]*

4. THE COMPLETION. 1753–60. From 1752, when Inveraray Castle reached roof level, the town quay was a scene of busy activity as ships unloaded Easdale slates, Strontian lead, and timber from Clydeside or direct from the Baltic. The local customs official checked the cargoes and collected their dues before the loaded carts lumbered off to the building sites – for some of the timber and slates were now needed for houses in the new town. Competition soon arose between the men, and George Hunter in charge of the castle and William Douglas in charge of the new inn both wanted sole access to St Catherines quarry. Douglas particularly would listen to neither Hunter nor Knockbuy, swearing that unless he could take over he would be fobbed off with inferior stones improperly blocked. Eventually Knockbuy sought Lord Milton's arbitration and Douglas was allowed his own men at the quarry, but to work under the overseer William Paull (who was shortly discharged for fraud).[154]

At the castle, critics from the Duke downward repeatedly complained of slow progress. James Potter, another Lowland mason, was in 1753 cutting stone for the windows of the high middle tower, and when he took over as builder of the great kitchen garden wall it was understood to be strictly secondary to the castle.[155] By spring 1753, when they were slating the last side of the main roof, John Paterson, a wright from Queensferry who had been employed by the Duke at Holyrood and the Whim and who also worked at Hopetoun House, was brought over to make the garret skylights and the roofs for the various towers. Paterson was soon clamouring for timber, otherwise 'I am affraid I shall be obliged to lett most of the hands go'.[156]

The huge edifice now rivalling the height of the decaying old castle, and towering over the clustered houses of Inveraray, was a mere shell of masonry containing its main internal walls, but no floors or stairs. The timber caps protecting its wall-heads were removed when the permanent roof was put on. In 1754 the arched vaults supporting the principal floor were begun under the long gallery on the north side.[157] Marble quarrying for the stairs continued at Tombreac, with saws specially brought from London, but at Adam's orders the basement stairs were built of the lapis ollaris from St Catherines. This stone, as it hardened excessively on exposure, was already becoming more difficult to win and heavier on tools, and a forge had to be built at the quarry for the Ardkinglas smith to keep them constantly tempered.[158]

In March 1754, the masons began on the last external feature, the great middle tower, finishing its eastern quarter towards the end of May;[159] and from now on

30. Inveraray Castle, the staircases
Instructions by Roger Morris.

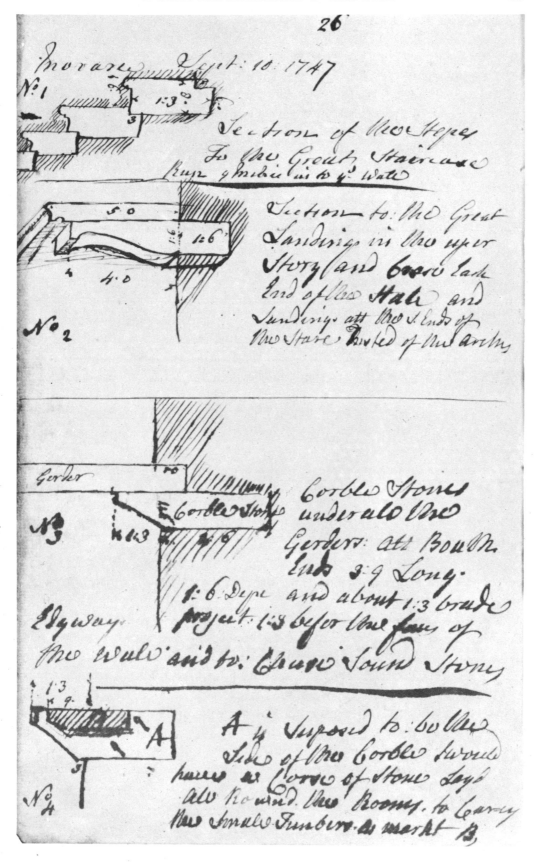

26

Inverary Sept: 10: 1747

N.º 1

1:3

3

Section of the Steps
For the Great Staircase
Runs 9 inches in to y.º Wall

5 0

1:6

4. 0

N.º 2

Section to: the Great
Landings in the upper
Story and 6 are each
End of the Stair and
Landings att the 2 Ends of
the Stair insted of the arches

Girder

Corble Stone

N.º 3

Corble Stones
under all the
Girders: att Both
Ends 3: 9 Long.
1: 6 Depe and about 1: 3 brade
project 1: 3 befor the faice of
the Wall and to: be of Sound Stone

Edgeway

1:3
9

A

3

A is Supposed to: be the
Side of the Corble which
have a Corse of Stone Layd
all Round the Rooms. to Carry
the Small Timbers as markt B,

N.º 4

the castle was at that agreeable stage where the client can actually appreciate the progress. Floors and pavements were laid in 1755 and 1756, the basement mostly with brick tiles made at Rosneath.[160] The basement staircases were built by May 1755, and the main flights to the upper landings by June 1756; in September iron arrived from the Argyll Furnace Company for the upper gallery railings and for the two spiral service staircases running from basement to attics.[161] Bedroom floors were laid, and the walls plastered. John Paterson made twenty window-frames at Queensferry for the base story, as well as windows for the Court House in the new town, which were picked up in September by the Duke's yacht and brought to Inveraray, and for which Paterson charged £148 10s 7d including the crates. But thirty-four windows still lacked glass, and no sashes were ready for the upper floors.[162] In March 1756 the Duke had consulted James Morris who advised buying the glass in London, although 'Upon comparing the estimates of Sashes', observed the Duke on 1 April, 'I think Morris allows that they will be cheaper in Scotland'.[163]

As the gaping holes in the façade began to be closed with window-frames, at ground level another great work was begun : excavation of the fosse or dry moat surrounding the castle, and the construction of casemates round that again. The contractor for digging out the fosse, at 5d a cubic yard, was a mason named John Wardrop. By the end of September 1756 fosse and casemates on the northern or old castle side were finished to the point beyond which they would encroach on the Duke's house and stables, and digging then had to wait until the Duke had left for the winter in London. On the south side, with no such impediment, the casemates were complete but for the stone copings, and the ground sloped away beyond them.[164]

On north and south George Hunter's men now built a pair of ornamental bridges over the fosse, with open stone parapets; in June 1755 Hunter reported 'the Bridge over to the Gallaray Door and front wall of the Casmets is pretty well advanc'd',[165*] and a year later the south bridge reached a similar stage. For bridges and casemates they worked from a scale model, probably made by the noted Glasgow millwright Robert Mackell, and kept with other models in a shed used by John Adam as his site office. The office was later burnt and this particular model was unfortunately destroyed.[166*]

The fosse bridges terminated in pairs of squat obelisks, carved by William Templeton between November 1756 and 1758 at a total cost of £48 16s 9d.[167*] They are square on plan, but set diagonally to the parapet, the angles adorned with meagre crockets and the flat surfaces with hard, rather un-Gothic rosettes.

At the end of autumn 1756, when the Duke left for London, they were working at lowest and highest levels – the middle tower was not quite complete and its upper windows were boarded against the weather – and were so far advanced as to be able to list the work outstanding and the materials still required : more timber for floors and finishings, glass, more windows, and locks and hinges for the upper stories. In the next six months the ground immediately round the new castle, become very uneven after ten years of building and dumping, was levelled under

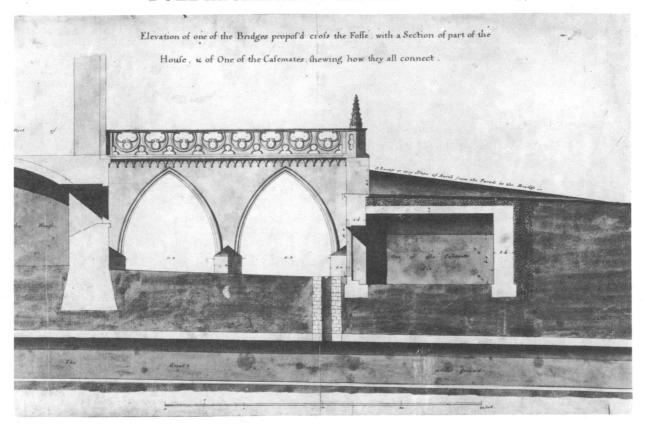

Elevation of one of the Bridges propos'd cross the Fosse, with a Section of part of the
House, & of One of the Casemates, shewing how they all connect.

31. Inveraray Castle, fosse bridge

Walter Paterson's supervision, to result in the flat and featureless lawn which forms the extensive foreground in many contemporary prints.[168]

1757 began inauspiciously with eight days of 'the Greatest Snow that has fallen since the year 1740', and a corn and meal shortage, for the previous year's harvests had been damaged by heavy storms, and supplies did not improve until the late spring.[169] In the autumn the Duke ordered partial demolition of his old stable pavilion, which still blocked the fosse on the north side. The freestone finishings of this building were to be carried down to the new town site and used for the two manses.[170]

The important stage of plumbing installation had now arrived. Wardrop's men were ordered to excavate in the fosse for a pair of servants' necessary houses on the side next the old castle, where by diverting a small rivulet which ran near the wrights' shed (on the way to the White Barns), a natural water supply could be made to serve the drains.[171] Privies flushed by running water appear to have been rare enough at this period, and indoor water closets rarer still. Inveraray Castle must have been among the few great houses then to instal them, which considering its situation remote from the more sophisticated parts of the country is perhaps remarkable. References to them appear in accounts and memoranda of 1756, when John Graham the plumber supplied 7 yards of $3\frac{1}{2}$-inch and 7 yards of $1\frac{1}{2}$-inch bore pipe for the closets;[172] but no mention is made of an adviser on sanitary fittings.

By an odd coincidence, however, the Duke had since 1752 employed at Inveraray a talented young man (then nineteen) named Alexander Cumming, who eventually removed to London and established a reputation not only as a clock-maker and inventor of mechanical devices, but in 1775 was the first person in Britain to patent a w.c. since Sir John Harington's of 1596.[173]* If it was not Cumming who actually designed Inveraray's water-closets in 1756, it must certainly have been there that he learned about their construction.

Cumming, assisted by his brother John, was employed by the Duke to build an organ, first mentioned in 1757 as being assembled in the great dining-room of the castle, for which a temporary floor, windows and doors were hastily made up to protect it. The walls were roughly plastered, but the doors and windows were not weather-proof, and Cumming was impatient for the permanent fittings which John Paterson was making at Queensferry. On 28 August, when the Duke was staying at Holyrood after brief visits to the Whim and Saltoun, Cumming wrote to Lord Milton,

> 'I have now got up most part of the Organ, without the least difficulty; but most of the Pipes are so much out of tune, that I despair of adjusting them to my mind, in less than three or four weeks (working from six in the morning till eight at night). I have got a good number of Overseers, but I think, that good Doors & Windows for the Room, wou'd be of greater service than all of them: as all the alterations of weather, tend to drive out of tune, those pipes which I, with all manner of care have adjusted.'[174]

Cumming's organ was erected in the apse of the gallery above the great hall, and in later generations was played on by the ladies of the Argyll family to the great admiration of guests. It unfortunately perished in the fire of 1877 – but the bedroom behind the apse is still known as the Organ Room.

At the time of the assembling of this organ its maker would be about twenty-four years old. In later years he was to make an astronomical clock for King George III and a machine organ for Lord Bute, and experimented in hydraulics and electricity; but we are given hints that his versatility and inventiveness went hand-in-hand with a perhaps obsessional petty-mindedness, and at Inveraray he appears to have been one of the trouble-makers.

As the castle neared completion it gained in interest, and the increased ease of access by the new military road brought still more visitors. The Duke had first travelled by the road in 1750, as far as Loch Long-side, where he transferred to his own boat;[175] in 1755 he bought a chaise, a new kind of vehicle, far speedier than the old lumbering coach, and in which as he posted up the Great North Road now being improved by turnpikes, he cut his travelling time to Scotland by half – that is to five or six days.[176] The ducal retinue clattered up and down the length of the country, through Buckden, Tuxford, Boroughbridge and Northallerton, over Yorkshire roads cut up and 'broke with the Coal Carriages', and along the two-day stint between Newcastle and Peeblesshire. Roads near the Whim were par-

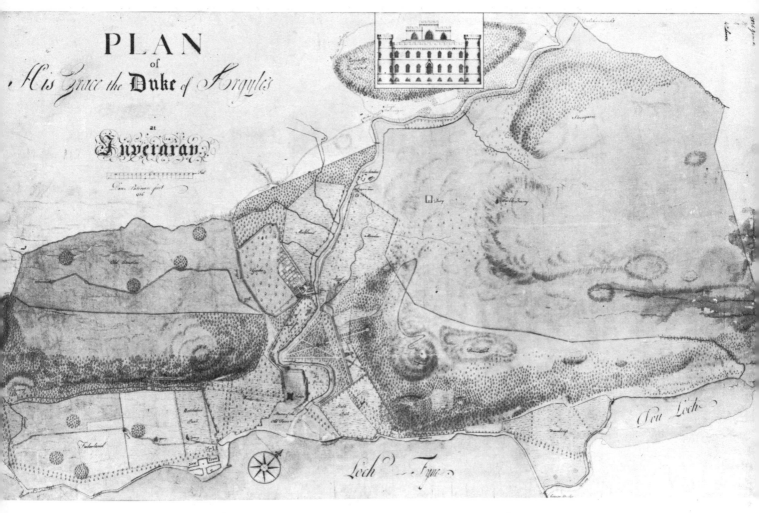

32. Inveraray, the Duke of Argyll's estate, 1756
    Plan by Daniel Paterson.

ticularly bad, and the Duke caught a heavy cold sitting in his new chaise with the
window-glasses down, while they were held up on an impassable stretch.[177] His
'cavalry' of servants in 1755 included 'Professor Couture, the Black, and two
Valets'. 'The Black' was a young East Indian whom the Duke had added to his clan
in 1754 by having him baptized at Inveraray old kirk, with the name of William
Campbell: the witnesses at that unique ceremony included the schoolmaster Fallowsdale, Alexander Cumming and James Dorret.[178]*

James Dorret, the Duke's personal servant, who first accompanied him to
Inveraray in 1744 (when he was among those admitted burgess), was like Cumming one of the able men whose talents the Duke encouraged. Finding him apt as a
map-maker, the Duke employed Dorret on an exact survey of the county of Argyll;
he also made a complete map of Scotland, published by Act of Parliament in April
1750. The Duke kept Dorret's maps in a roll at Inveraray or at his lodging at Holy-

roodhouse. But although he worked as a land surveyor his place in the hierarchy entitled him only to a cart-horse in their travels, and officially he was 'a genteel Servant who may attend his Grace to Scotland and is Qualifyd for taking care of a Table, &c . . . extremely useful about His Grace at Inveraray'.[179]*

The Duke's protégés also included Archibald Campbell, son of Commissary James Campbell who in 1756 became Chamberlain of Argyll; and Walter Paterson's son Daniel. The Duke commissioned Archy to make a landscape view of his policies, and a drawing at Inveraray Castle showing a proposed 'belvedere' on the spur below Duniquaich is signed 'Arch[dus] Campbell delnt. 1757'. Also in 1757 the eighteen-year-old Dan Paterson produced an elevation of the castle entrance, showing the traceried parapet and obelisks then being carved by William Templeton. Dan Paterson later became assistant to George Morrison, Q.M.G. of the Forces, and published a couple of those characteristic traveller's vade-mecums of the later eighteenth century.[180]*

While Daniel, in 1757, was at the outset of a successful career, his father the gardener narrowly saved his own from disaster : he was detected selling produce from the Duke's gardens, and with the groom Gibson persisted in selling unlicensed liquor against express instructions. The Duke made Lord Milton warn Paterson that 'if he does not like his place, to acquaint the Chamberlain that he may look out for another Gardener'. A few months later the Duke was outraged to learn that Paterson had taken out a licence to sell drink in accordance with the Act of Parliament, and swore to dismiss him at once if only a new gardener could be found. But none could. Paterson survived in his job long after his master's death, dying in 1770 at the age of about sixty-two.[181]*

The complaints against Paterson were only part of an enormous, all-embracing row that had broken out between almost everyone of any authority in Inveraray. While the Duke's representatives were struggling to check fraud and reduce expenses, the venomous John Fallowsdale had sent the Duke (anonymously – though his identity was obvious) such a formidably comprehensive list of accusations involving Bathgate, Paterson, Patrick Campbell (now Customs riding-officer), and anyone else against whom he had a grudge, that his malice over-reached itself. But a good deal of mud was thrown on either side, culminating in an exhaustive public inquiry held in June by the Duke's doers, Archibald Campbell of Succoth and Colin Campbell, the Rosneath baillie, who diplomatically reported that Fallowsdale's charges 'Do not Come out in the proof near so strong as hinted at in the Letter and Queries'. In 1758 this trouble-maker was dismissed by the magistrates.[182]

Meanwhile Commissary James Campbell, appointed Chamberlain in 1756, fell out with Bathgate, who had some time earlier caught him illicitly grazing cattle in the Duke's grounds, and he joined with Fallowsdale and John Corssar, a wright, to victimize the incorruptible young farm overseer. He openly overrode Bathgate's orders to damage his authority with the herdsmen and carters, and they ended by having a violent quarrel. The Chamberlain threatened Bathgate with a thrashing, and Bathgate appealed to the Duke.

33. Rosneath Castle, proposed alterations, 1744,
Elevation and plan by Roger Morris,
with annotations by the 3rd Duke.

N:W.

fronts up the Gare Loch.

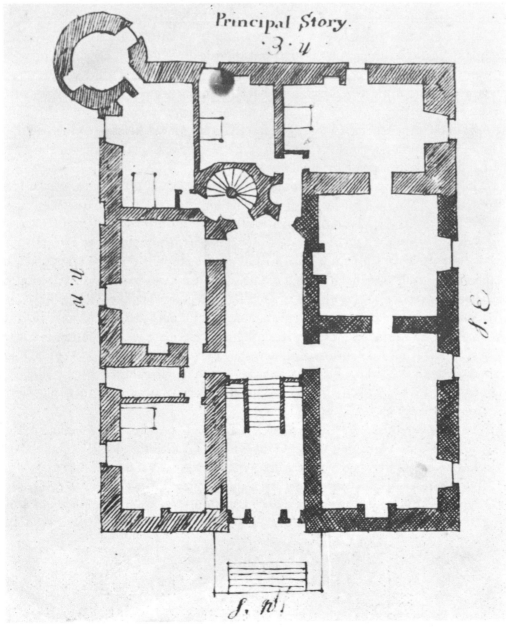

Principal Story.
·3·4·

But James Campbell, who had begun by earning golden opinions for his clear and sensible reports on the works, soon lost them by this tyranny. 'He seems to be very clever and alert,' commented Andrew Fletcher, 'but wants common prudence and discretion . . . in all probability he will fall, by meddling wt things wherein he had no concern.'[183] Two months later the Duke, back at Inveraray, reorganized his administration, dividing the Chamberlain's authority into three factorships. On 11 November 1757, he signed commissions for Dugald McTavish of Dunardry to be his Baron Baillie in Argyll, with authority to hold courts, remove tenants and oversee all works at and near Inveraray; Commissary James Campbell in future to deal with his revenues in Argyll, Inverness and Bute; and Colin Campbell, the Rosneath baillie, to manage the Inveraray parks with Bathgate under him in charge of cattle. For their numerous duties the Duke allotted these three gentlemen salaries of £20 a year, and a room each with coal and candles.[184]

Inveraray in 1757 was a hotbed of intrigue and malice, and the Duke's castle there was still far from complete; but that season he had the satisfaction of occupying for the first time his newly-enlarged castle at Rosneath. This building was then about 150 years old, three storeys high and of typically Scottish L-shaped plan, with a round tower at one corner. Roger Morris's original alteration, designed in 1744, envisaged filling in the re-entrant angle of the L to form a rectangular house, with three new circular corner towers to match the existing one, which would have made its elevations rather similar to those conceived for Inveraray, although much smaller in scale. It is unlikely, however, that all three new towers were built, for the 1747 plan shows only the single original tower.[185]

These extensive alterations should have been finished in time for the Duke's reception in 1756, but although crates of china, linen, kitchen equipment and (wrote Andrew to his mother) 'a great deal of fine Furniture . . . Chairs, Glasses and Tables', were bought and crated for transport, the house was after all not ready, and the party once more had to stay in the adjoining house known as the Clachan.[186] But during the following months Rosneath was papered and decorated with hangings sent from London, and since no grates were yet fixed, its damp rooms dried out by moving those grates they possessed from room to room. More furniture was made on the spot, and more crates of china, chocolate, tea and other luxuries were shipped from London to Leith and sent over. In September 1757 the Duke arrived with all the ladies of the Fletcher family, to be taken agreeably by surprise at the sight of Rosneath completed and looking, Miss Mally approvingly declared, 'in Great Beauty'.[187]

They were joined here by Frederick Campbell, General Campbell's second son, and by Major Tam Cochrane, and the Duke was understandably in no hurry to leave his beautiful new house for Inveraray. Sir Harry Bellenden next arrived; the weather was fine and they idled their time away agreeably. Only at the end of the month did they go on to Inveraray, where Lord Milton now awaited them : most of the party went by boat, and the Duke with the ladies by road, staying overnight with Sir James Colquhoun at Luss. The Duke remained at Inveraray until early November.[188]

While Cumming was assembling the great organ that spring, three of the castle's main rooms had been prepared for decoration; sections of the two dining-rooms had been drawn for George Haswell, windows and doors for the larger of the two being made at Queensferry, and plasterers arrived from Edinburgh. The only plasterer named in payments is Philip Robertson,[189*] but in September 1756 Thomas Clayton of Hamilton – who had worked for the Adam brothers at Hopetoun and Dumfries, and was now employed at Blair Castle by the Duke of Atholl – had sent the Duke a detailed estimate for stucco-work,[190*] and we may reasonably assume that Clayton was responsible for, or at least supervised, such of the work as was completed in the Duke's lifetime.

The Duke now gave Adam detailed instructions for finishings and decorations: wainscoting for his bedroom, lining for tapestries, plaster mouldings and architraves for the other chief rooms (a Corinthian entablature for the drawing-room, with 'some genteel Ornaments of Stucco' on the ceiling, and Ionic for the hall), and appropriate finishings for lesser rooms and attics. The masons were ordered to make the attic chimney-pieces of St Catherines stone. The staircase rails, the galleries above and, outside, the fosse, its bridges and the casemates, were all to be completed. However, although to this end orders were several times given to demolish the west side of the 'Stable Pavilion', this was never finished in the Duke's lifetime. The Duke ordered marble chimney-pieces for his bedroom, dressing-room and adjoining turret in the castle's west angle. The Adam brothers' account presented for 1757/8 includes £10 5s 2d and £10 7s 10d for two chimney-pieces, one in white and veined marble, the other dove-coloured; they were finished by Mr Mathie in 'plain workmanship' and ornamented with copper balls for a further £13 5s 4d, bringing the total to £33 18s 4d, including packing.[191*]

Glazing the vast amount of window-space now became a major item. Inveraray Castle contains twenty-one windows on each of its long sides, fifteen on the short, not counting the attic story which at the time of building was lit by skylights; each of the four turrets had twelve window-openings (some of them left blind), besides six 'arrow-slits', and the great central tower was lighted by twelve large windows. In considering alternative proportions for frames and panes, the Duke had unhesitatingly chosen a breadth of four panes: the only debate was between Newcastle glass and the more expensive glass from London. The Adams finally obtained the latter, their first order being for '59 Square panes of best London Crown Glass' at 1s 4d a foot, and forty-five 'arched' panes, in two sizes, at 1s 6d a foot. The total cost of this, £16 8s 5$\frac{1}{4}$d, was made up of £13 9s 8d for the 2,104$\frac{1}{4}$ feet of glass, a small cutting charge, 64 lb. of glazier's putty at 4d a pound, and 11s for packing. Next year a further £25 worth of glass was ordered, 78$\frac{1}{4}$ feet 'for supplying part of the Gothick windows', and thirty panes to replace breakages in transit.[192]

The glazier was Robert Dewar from Edinburgh (probably recommended by John Paterson, the Queensferry wright), who, with two assistants, spent 'six days

34. Imaginary view of Inveraray, 1759
    From the painting attributed to Agostino Brunias.

going & coming & 8 days waiting at Inveraray before the Glass came to hand', and twenty-eight working days when they fitted 594 panes of glass into forty windows. The most costly windows were, of course, those in the middle tower, whose sashes Adam estimated would cost £45 less if the 'great Springs' were finished in timber but the smaller spaces filled with lead. John Paterson protested when Lord Milton told Adam that 'I charge over mutch for my atendance at inverarrie', explaining that he had his best men on the job for six months together, and had to keep up an expensive correspondence with George Haswell at fivepence a letter. Adam allowed him 234 working days at 3s 6d, 260 days for his horse at a shilling, 24½ weeks' board at five shillings, and 63 days' travelling at five shillings – or £75 16s 6d, including expenses.[193]

1758 saw the castle structurally complete, though not habitable. By midsummer the last consignment of glass was shipped, and few materials remained to seek save mahogany and oak for the remaining doors and windows. Unfinished items included plaster-work for some of the principal rooms, and the main and turnpike stair railings.[194] Three ornamental chimney-pieces were carved for the hall, dining-room and Duke's dressing-room, with the pedestal for Cumming's organ, by a visiting craftsman George Jamieson and his son, paid £71 for 284 days.[195]*

'I have finish'd every thing here this Season,' wrote Adam to Lord Milton (who was ill and unable to visit Inveraray) on 1 November 1758, '& have deliver'd to His Grace all the Drawings I have made' – with notes on the few outstanding details.[196] Next February there was a mild panic when the fabric sprang a few leaks round some of the Gothick windows on the south front, over some of the projecting 'belts', and at the join of leading and the battlements. Adam quickly reassured Lord

Milton that all could be mended by 'squeezing a paste into the places complained of that shall grow harder than the Stone itself'. Andrew Fletcher complained censoriously to his father that he wondered Mr Adam 'did not propriis sumptibus voluntarily go there to examine this defect, which if they cannot cure must throw a vast Ridicule upon His Graces Masons'. Adam's protective measures were successful, and the following winter caused 'not the smallest appearance of wet';[197*] but meanwhile the leak had Lord Milton, Chamberlain, overseers and all running round in circles for a week or two, and seemed likely to delay occupation of the new castle and force the Duke to remain in his old 'pavilion' for another season.

Andrew Fletcher perhaps also disapproved of Adam's next move, which was to go not to Inveraray but to London, to see his brother Robert who in 1757 had returned from his Italian travels. John's trip lasted two months, and he visited several country houses in the north of England, in Norfolk and in the London neighbourhood. Before returning to Scotland at the beginning of June he waited on the Duke and Andrew, to discuss the remaining Crown glass needed for Inveraray, and wood for wainscoting.[198]

While in London John probably saw a remarkable painting by Agostino Brunias, the draughtsman whom Robert had brought back with him from Italy, and of which Robert wrote to James Adam in June with pride and pleasure. Robert's attempts to launch himself as a fashionable London architect had so far not had much success, though he cultivated all the aristocrats he knew, prominent among them, of course, the old Duke of Argyll. He wrote discontentedly to James that he wished Baron Maule would remind the Duke of an earlier promise to get him into the Board of Works – 'though its best not to be too pushing incase of disgusting him'. Robert had, however, thought of an ingenious means of flattering his intended patron :

> 'I have fast hold of His G—— at present as I have Brunias busy making out a large view of Inveraray in Oil Colours which·if it succeeds well, will surely lay him under obligations to me, on a favourite subject. I intend not to take anything for it . . .'[199*]

In the end Robert accepted £20, supposedly for Brunias, though he kept most of it himself. But his object was attained : His Grace was delighted with the picture, and it hangs today in the gallery at Inveraray Castle, a highly fanciful landscape (for Brunias knew nothing of the place beyond Robert Adam's sketches and descriptions) showing the new castle, Duniquaich with its watch-tower, and the new inn and Court House on Gallows Foreland Point in the Fisherland. But – and this was the great compliment aimed at the Duke – Inveraray's old castle and town are completely imagined away, and a stretch of green sward substituted in their place. It need hardly be mentioned that never at any stage did Inveraray look as it appears in this rather wooden, artificial painting; but that was the beauty of the idea.

Meanwhile the stream of Inveraray's visitors did not slacken. In 1755 they had included Argyll's old friend the Duke of Atholl,[200] and in 1756 'Parson' John Home, shortly before he presented his highly successful play *Douglas* in Edinburgh and earned the censure of his presbytery.[201]* In 1758 came Lady Milton and the young ladies, Baron Maule, General Jack Campbell and Sir Harry Bellenden; Stonefield's son John Campbell with his wife Lady Grace Stuart, daughter of the Earl of Bute and hence Argyll's niece; Dr Alexander Carlyle, and Harry Barclay, who came in a borrowed chaise with John Adam.[202] Next year again included the Fletchers (and Lady Milton again in agony with toothache), and several more who stayed only at Rosneath – probably because, being now fully habitable, it was very pleasant and spacious, whereas Inveraray remained disappointingly unfinished and its accommodation as limited as ever. But the Duke was joined at Inveraray by his two young kinsmen Jack and Frederick Campbell,[203]* and shortly afterwards by General Jack's newly-married wife the beautiful Elizabeth Gunning, Duchess of Hamilton, the latest addition to the family.

Elizabeth Gunning, daughter of a penniless Irish gentleman, had burst upon London society half a dozen years earlier with her even lovelier sister Maria and become legendary almost overnight. Within two years Elizabeth had married the rakish, arrogant Duke of Hamilton and the slightly older Maria hastened to follow with a lesser prize in the Earl of Coventry. Neither marriage was happy. Maria died in 1760 at the age of twenty-seven from white lead poisoning, through daubing cosmetics on her silly, pretty face, and Elizabeth, far Maria's superior in character and wit, was left a widow when her young Duke died of a chill taken after hunting. The Duchess Elizabeth, mother of two sons and a daughter, quickly captured the affections of Colonel Jack Campbell, at thirty-five still a bachelor, and Jack soon obtained the blessing of his Chief, who (he enthusiastically told his old friend Lord Milton) 'approved of it from the first moment I mentioned it'. The Colonel and the twenty-five-year-old widow were married early in 1759 and spent their honeymoon at the house of the bridegroom's uncle Sir Harry Bellenden at Petersham – a stone's-throw from the Duke of Argyll's birthplace at Ham.[204]

For the next ten years the former Miss Gunning continued to be known as the Duchess of Hamilton. It was well known that eventually her husband – who this same year was promoted Major-General – must succeed his father as 5th Duke of Argyll, and meanwhile she did not choose to surrender her title. They moved that spring into 'the Clachan', the small house by Rosneath which had served the Duke until the castle there was completed, and which they proposed to do up for themselves. Part of the Duchess's time, however, was spent at Hamilton Palace in Lanarkshire, her late husband's house, and during her son's minority she controlled (through her advisers) the Parliamentary elections for the Hamilton seats.

Elizabeth Gunning's first visit to Inveraray must have been in autumn 1759, soon after the Argyll party moved there from Rosneath. Of this visit no record remains, nor from beginning to end of her connexion with it is there a word of what the beautiful Duchess thought of Inveraray, or how much her taste influenced her husband's own later alterations. But from now on we have a series of visitors' accounts which provide valuable evidence of the appearance and progress of Inveraray's castle, town and parks.

H

The earliest detailed account is in the manuscript journal of the twenty-six-year-old William Burrell, on tour with a friend named John Symonds.[205*] This was in 1758, a fairly early date for such a tour in Scotland and not without pioneering qualities. Burrell's solemn observations on the country, in parts as rude and wild as Captain Burt had found it more than thirty years earlier, are historically of great value.

They must have arrived at Inveraray at the beginning of September, and the Burgh records note that they and their servants received the customary Freedom on 2 September.[206*] In the Duke's absence they were received politely and hospitably by Asknish and Provost John Richardson who (Burrell recorded), 'shewed us every Thing, that could afford us Entertainment, of wch the Castle of Inverary was the chief Subject'. Burrell is the first to leave us a description of this odd, uncharacteristic 'castle', and in noting its dimensions and shape he observed that it was 'built in the Manner of the Old Castles in the Time of Henry 2d, & in some particulars is said to bear a strong Resemblance to Solomon's Temple'. Far less flattering things have been said about it since. The fosse, then being dug out by Wardrop and his men, struck him with its usefulness and 'good Effects', in particular that 'no Servants appear except those who must necessarily attend, nor are any of the Transactions or Business of the Family apparent above Stairs . . . Loaded Carts pass through a Subterraneous Passage, to the Fosse'.[207*] He admired equally the 'beautyfull Gothic Arches', Templeton's obelisks on the entrance bridges, and the unusual building stone which, they told him, was weather-proof.

The two young men were shown all the castle's principal rooms, its long gallery on the north front, the dining-room (now the Saloon) on the south, the drawing-room adjoining and the large central hall, then called Saloon. In a room in the Duke's old house they saw Roger Morris's model of the new castle and several of the Duke's scientific models, including one of Marshal Saxe's 'travelling house', a campaign caravan 'ingeniously & mechanically contrived', with a reception room and a semi-circular bedroom, which could be drawn by six horses like a wagon and dismantled when required. The original had been captured in battle by the British a few years earlier. From the model – presumably, like most of the others, made by Robert Mackell – the Duke of Argyll had a full-sized copy made at a cost of £500, which was unfortunately blown over and smashed in a violent storm on 7 October 1756, and never repaired.[208*]

A month after Burrell, John Wilkes, Member of Parliament for Aylesbury, then about thirty years old and little known, at the Duke's invitation rode over from Edinburgh, where he had been staying, for a short visit. Having many tastes in common with his host he is recorded as having passed an agreeable visit, but neither host nor guest left any account to posterity.[209*] However, another visitor who came about the middle of October has left a lively and vivid description of Inveraray during Duke Archibald's later years.

This was Dr Alexander Carlyle, minister since 1747 at Inveresk near Brunstane, a few miles from Edinburgh, a sound Hanoverian who at the age of twenty-

35. Marshal Saxe's 'Travelling House' in 1780
    Engraved after a painting by Paul Sandby.

four had served as a volunteer against the Jacobites during the Forty-Five. His
friend John Grant, son of the judge Lord Elchies, had in 1753 married Lord
Milton's eldest daughter, and it was through Lord Milton that Carlyle first met the
Duke of Argyll at Brunstane in the late autumn of 1757.[210]

Carlyle had already visited Inveraray in 1754, when he refers to a good inn –
presumably in the old town, since the new one did not open until 1755. In 1758 he
again put up at the inn, arriving very late on horseback from Loch Long over the
steep, rough track facetiously known as Argyll's Bowling Green, where early frosts

forced him to dismount and walk six miles so that he almost missed the last ferry from St Catherines. He writes :

'I did not go that night to the Duke's house, as I knew I could not have a bed there (as he had not yet got into the Castle), but I went in the morning, and was very politely received, not only by the Milton family, but by the Duke and his two cousins . . . who were there. His Grace told me immediately that Miss Fletcher had made him expect my visit, and that he was sorry he could not offer me lodging, but that he would hope to see me every day to breakfast, dinner, and supper . . .

I was told that he was a great humorist at Inverary, and that you could neither drink his health nor ask him how he did without disobliging; but this was exaggerated. To be sure, he waived ceremony very much, and took no trouble at table, and would not let himself be waited for, and came in when he pleased, and sat down on the chair that was left, which was neither at the head nor foot of the table. But he cured me of all constraint the first day, for in his first or second glass of wine he drank my health and welcomed me to Inverary, and hoped that as long as I stayed, which he wished to be all the week at least, I would think myself at home. Though he never drank to me again, I was much more gratified by his directing much of his conversation to me. His colloquial talent was very remarkable, for he never harangued or was tedious, but listened to you in your turn.

We sat down every day fifteen or sixteen to dinner; for besides his two cousins and the Fletcher family, there were always seven or eight Argyleshire gentlemen, or factors on the estate, at dinner . . . After the ladies were withdrawn and he had drunk his bottle of claret, he retired to an easy-chair set hard by the fireplace : drawing a black silk nightcap over his eyes, he slept, or seemed to sleep, for an hour and a half. In the mean time, Sandie M'Millan, who was toast-master, pushed about the bottle, and a more noisy or regardless company could hardly be.

Milton retired soon after the ladies, and about six o'clock M'Millan and the gentlemen drew off (for at that time dinner was always served at two o'clock) when the ladies returned, and his Grace awoke and called for his tea, which he made himself at a little table apart from that of the company. Tea being over, he played two rubbers at sixpenny whist, as he did in London. He had always some of the ladies of his party, while the rest amused themselves at another table. Supper was served soon after nine, and there being nobody left but those with whom he was familiar, he drank another bottle of claret, and could not be got to go to bed till one in the morning . . . I may add that the provisions for the table were at least equal to the conversation; for we had sea and river fish in perfection, the best beef and mutton and fowls and wild game and venison of both kinds in abundance. The wines, too, were excellent.

I stayed over Sunday and preached to his Grace, who always attended the church at Inverary. The ladies told me that I had pleased his Grace, which gratified me not a little, as without him no preferment could be obtained in Scotland.'[211]*

During the Duke's long absences regular arrangements were made for the reception of distinguished visitors; a party splendidly entertained by Asknish and Provost Richardson early in June 1758 was Lord George Beauclerk, Commander-in-Chief of the forces in Scotland, with his family and a great number of officers. The officers, and Lord George's five servants, were made honorary burgesses; Asknish, Richardson, Alexander Cumming and Mrs Robertson the Duke's housekeeper showed them round, and Hawkesley, the innkeeper, had been warned to lay in an enormous stock of mutton, veal, lamb, poultry and a daily supply of fish, with more poultry provided by Mrs Robertson and even 'a few green peas & strawberrys' – then still a great delicacy in Scottish households – from Walter Paterson's kitchen garden.[212]

In 1759, shortly before the Duke's arrival his tempestuous niece Lady Mary Coke made a brief 'jaunt' to Inveraray. The marriage of this wayward, undisciplined young woman – one of those 'bawling Campbells' fathered by the 2nd Duke of Argyll – had come rapidly to grief as much through her own temperament as that of her execrable husband, and her visit to Inveraray was expected with some trepidation by the Sheriff's son John Campbell, who was detailed to escort her and was 'a little apprehensive that it wou'd not turn out a party of pleasure'.

But John Campbell was 'very agreeably disappointed'. The pair reached Inveraray on 19 August after visiting Mountstuart and Rosneath, and stayed about four days before going on to Stonefield's Levenside estate and then to Edinburgh. Lady Mary's escort was fairly astounded by her fortitude and good humour from the moment when, as they sailed up Loch Fyne in 'a very smart gale', she alone felt no sea-sickness :

> 'When the boat we were in was like to be dashed to pieces by running foul of a ship, Lady Mary sat unmoved; when the winds blew high, she was not afraid; when they were cross, she was not uneasy; when the seas run high, and the ship was tossed from side to side, she was not sick; when it rained she was pleased, and when she was wett, she was not dissatisfied.'

This remarkable woman confounded expectation by displaying 'so much sense and spirit, attended with such gentleness and condescension, I have never observed in woman'.[213]* One wonders how pleased Campbell's wife Lady Grace was to hear his praise of the paragon. Lady Mary appears to have left no account of her visit, and her sole reference to Inveraray in extant letters is a spiteful reflection that on his own estates the Duke of Argyll could live very cheaply off the country – fine gratitude for the battery of hospitality she received from Mrs Robertson and the rest.[214]*

The Duke's relatives and most favoured visitors were often brought by barge, but the flow of other travellers was now swelling to a flood thanks to the completion of the military road. In 1758 work on the road culminated in the building of a Gothick bridge across the mouth of the Aray, superseding the old town bridge

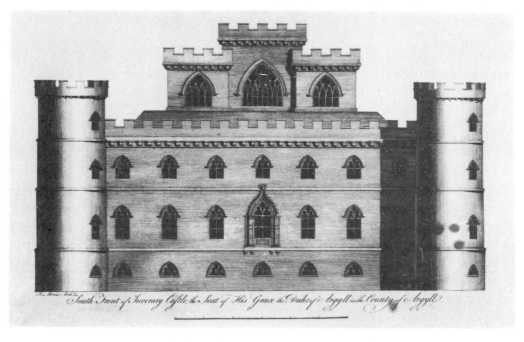

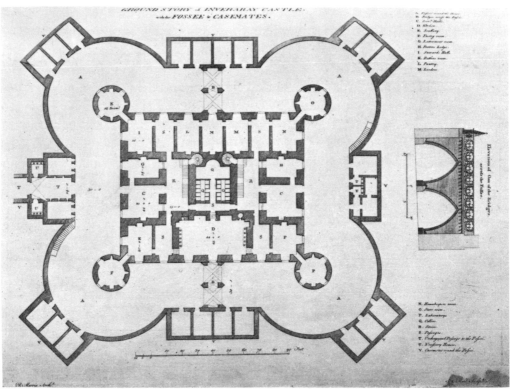

36. Inveraray Castle, elevation and plan from *Vitruvius Scoticus*

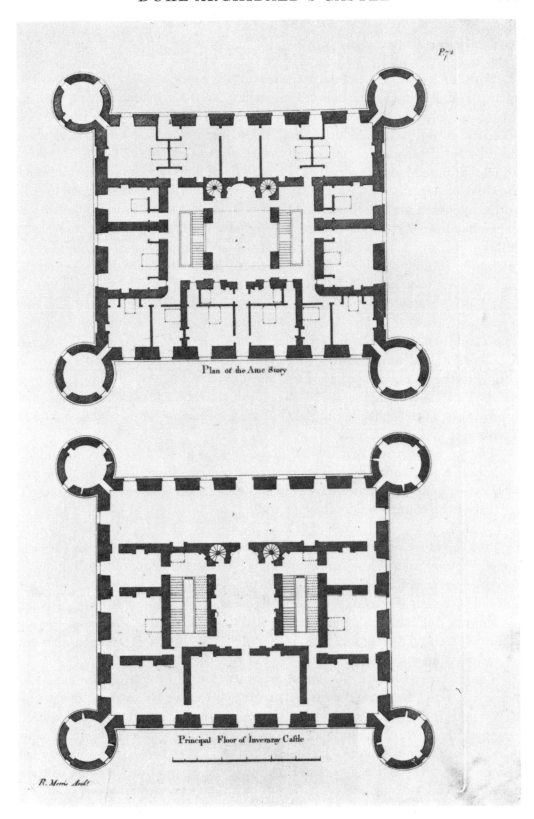

37. Inveraray Castle, plans from *Vitruvius Scoticus*

upstream nearer the castle. More and more visitors now came by carriage or on horseback, for the new road opened up the Western Highlands to the world, even if the journey was still accompanied by an exhilarating sense of adventure. In 1759 the Duke of Bedford's heir, the Marquess of Tavistock, made a brief visit with a friend, and shortly before him came the first Lord Lyttelton, touring with his fifteen-year-old son in excellent weather. Lord Lyttelton wrote from Inveraray to his friend Mrs Elizabeth Montagu that 'the House deserves to be call'd, as it was stil'd by Lord Leicester, "the Royall Palace of the King of the Goths" '; and he urged that noted lady to grace 'her northern dominions' and honour her admirer, the Duke of Argyll, with a visit.[215]* But it was six years before she deigned to come north, by which time there was no longer a Duke Archibald to welcome her, and then – like Lord Lyttelton – she was too self-absorbed in extravagant communion with nature, and praise of the vastness of the landscape, to spare interest for the works of man it contained.[216]* In October 1759 Benjamin Franklin and his son on their first visit to Scotland, having already dined with the Duke in Edinburgh, stayed at Inveraray during a round tour in which Franklin also visited Glasgow, stayed with another of Mrs Montagu's friends, Lord Kames, at his Stirlingshire house and then, 'extreamly happy' after seeing Inveraray, went on to the Duke of Atholl's.[217]* Lord Kames himself, who was to become renowned as an arbiter of taste with the publication of his *Elements of Criticism* in 1762, had in his days as an advocate visited Inveraray with the circuit courts. In his book he commented approvingly on the suitability of the Gothick form to Inveraray, in the chapter on 'Gardening and Architecture':

> 'The profuse variety of wild and grand objects about Inverary, demanded a house in the Gothic form; and every one must approve the taste of the proprietor, in adjusting so finely, as he has done, the appearance of his house to that of the country where it is placed.'[218]*

By 1759 the Duke of Argyll was seventy-seven years old, and was feeling his age. For some years past he had abandoned active participation in politics, but he kept control – some said a stranglehold – of Scottish elections and appointments, and showed little sign of relaxing either in business or in entertaining friends. Although his handwriting had become noticeably shaky, in constitution he was sound and vigorous; it was rather Lord Milton who was constantly ill and confined for weeks to his house, or taking goat's-whey cures at Dunkeld.

The Fletcher family had suffered many troubles. In the late autumn of 1758 Francis, a frail, melancholy young man, always a cause for anxiety, died; Lady Milton and Andrew were also both in poor health; and finally Betty, Lord Milton's youngest and favourite daughter, who in February had made a blissfully happy marriage to Captain John Wedderburn, died in December, shortly after Francis, of a child-bed fever. Her husband unhappily was at the time away on overseas duty, and Andrew, who earlier had sent him a pompous request to break to Lord Milton the 'melancholy Account' of Francis's death, after this sad Christmas now stiffly condoled with his father on his new loss, 'infinitely severe' – 'never surely was there a more agreeable and more amiable young Person'. Andrew himself remained a bachelor until he was well over forty.[219]*

Following this year of tragedies, during the next two summers Lord Milton's vain and frivolous daughter Mally accompanied him to Dunkeld for his now customary cure; but his gout and other ills continued, and Andrew, in Scotland both for elections and to superintend the Saltoun estate, also remained unwell. In Andrew's absence John Maule for some months resumed his old employment as the Duke's confidential secretary.[220]

Until 1758 the Duke, still lively and active, pronounced himself 'as able for travelling this year as I was the last'. That winter, however, he was much troubled with an unhealed sore on his leg, and in 1759 agreed to take his Highland travels more slowly, 'not being able to hurry through in a day', in a season of abominable weather, preferring to wait for a better day before moving on. In 1760 he did not reach Scotland until mid-September, after which the usual 'gang' – as Maule called them – appeared at Inveraray.[221]

Building progress and personal relationships had taken a better turn. Asknish, although foreseeing that funds would remain low and 'the Expence this year will run very high', in April reported 'great concord and Unanimity here at present'.[222] The new expense was partly due to a heavy building programme about the Duke's policies and in the new town of Inveraray, particularly of bridges, and a new court of offices and stables in the Cherry Park, a short distance from the castle. Several hundred pounds' worth of timber cargoes had also to be paid for, and nearly £400 for lead for plumbing, and water-pipes for the castle and office houses. In the summer the central hall's chimneys were completed, and the middle tower windows, installed in 1759, appear to have been fitted (by the glazier Robert Dewar) with coloured leaded panes.[223]* After protracted discussion on grates and fenders the Duke eventually agreed with Lady Milton on polished grates for the principal rooms, and 'as I have only 2 bedchambers in the principal Appartment, I believe I must have in the 4 best Bed chambers in the Atticks, bright Grates'.[224]

Hundreds of thousands of nails had been ordered for 'single' and 'double' flooring, about 500 bars of lead for the plumbing, and 15,000 more slates for the new town, so that in 1760 the cost of materials remained as high as ever.[225]*

The last description of Inveraray before the death of Duke Archibald was written in June 1760 by the notable Richard Pococke, Bishop of Ossory in County Leix, who was already renowned as a traveller. The Bishop spent two nights at Inveraray and was received in the customary manner by Asknish and shown all the sights before departing for Iona, or Icolmkill as it was called, and Skye. He sent his sister Elisabeth in Ireland a full description of the surrounding landscape, parks and buildings, 'most agreeably surprized with the sight of Inveraray, the grand castle built by the Duke of Argyll, and the beautiful hill to the north ...' The 'magnificent Gothick building', he described in detail, adding that 'some of the rooms are finished, and all the others are going on with the utmost expedition'.

Pococke also had an interesting talk on the mineralogical qualities of St Catherines stone with Alexander Cumming, who impressed him by his ingenuity and skill in 'experimental philosophy and mechanics' (as he had already impressed the Duke by his rare ability to render clear and informative progress reports). Cumming also described a clock he was making 'to regulate time by the stars as well as sun'.[226]*

Having satisfied his antiquarian, geological and social curiosity at Inveraray, Bishop Pococke left on 4 June for Loch Awe by the new extension to the military road, through the Duke's estates round which James Potter and his men were building dry-stone walls covered with turf. Only five miles of this section of the road were yet completed, and for the rest of the Bishop's trip the going was as abominable as ever.[227]*

Bishop Pococke's account clearly shows that at the age of seventy-eight Duke Archibald was planning for years ahead. But although at that time no one was aware of it, the Duke was never to occupy his new castle; the clutter of old castle and town still remained at his very doorstep, and of his new town he lived to see only a few buildings erected.

Some 2,000 miles away the young architect who was eventually to complete the castle, transform its interior, and build Inveraray town in a style undreamed of by the 3rd Duke of Argyll, had already begun to make his mark. At Rome in October 1758, Robert Mylne, one of the two architect sons of Deacon Thomas Mylne of Edinburgh and descendant of a noted family of King's Master Masons, had been awarded – to Robert Adam's chagrin – 'the prize in the highest class, given by the academy of St Luke, for drawing in architecture'. In the Grand Salle of the Senatorial Palace on the Capitol, before an audience of sixteen cardinals, the nobility, ambassadors and 'ladies and gentlemen of the first distinction', the twenty-five-year-old Mylne with his fellow prize-winners was honoured by a suitable oration, and personally complimented by Cardinal Sacropanti as he received his two large silver medals. 'This piece of distinction' (wrote an admiring friend to the Edinburgh papers) 'so justly conferred on Mr Milne, gives great pleasure to every body here, as it is an instance of the uncommon merit for so young a man, to gain a prize, which the greatest architects in this country with keenness aspire after.'[228]

5. THE TIMBER CARGOES. The most local building material for Inveraray Castle, the stone, had to be ferried several miles up the loch in gabarts. All other materials came from far afield, and the shiploads of lead from Strontian, glass from Newcastle and London, slates from Easdale, and iron from Clydeside put in at Inveraray's quayside, while larger cargoes first went to Campbeltown to be unloaded into smaller ships; the Duke's annual accounts were swelled by sums spent on freights. By far the most expensive of these items was timber, and the variety of ways this arrived at Inveraray makes a saga in itself.

The usual source of supply for the building of great houses was Baltic timber, and in Scotland this was generally ordered from merchants at Clydeside or Leith.

At Inveraray, where building methods were empirical, not to say hit-and-miss, the first cargo was obtained by the merest chance : from a wreck – a not uncommon occurrence off the west coast of Scotland, where salvaged cargoes were frequently put up for roup or auction.

Roger Morris's programme for the castle deferred any serious efforts to lay in a stock of building timber for the first few years. But even before the castle's foundations were dug, a wreck off Tiree was the subject of complex negotiation.

Tiree, the most remote and westerly of the Inner Hebrides, was a fertile part of the Argyll possessions but so flat and sandy that no ships could put in except on its eastern coast. On 9 July 1744, just after the Duke of Argyll set off from London on his first visit to Inveraray, a drifting ship was sighted off the island's west coast by a visitor, Dugald Campbell, son of Archibald Campbell of Ballamore, the Duke's factor in Mull. Rowing out with some islanders he found her abandoned, 'Her Masts broake, no Rudder, Her Sailes and Rigging much damag'd, Three Anchors on her Bow, & one Cable cut away'.

Another Mull laird, Donald McLean of Torloisk, wrote to his son in Edinburgh an account of this curious affair of

'. . . a Three Masted Ship reckon'd 500 Tuns burden . . . She's loaded with jeasts and firr plank, There was not a Living Soul Aboard, when she came ashore. There were no papers found that could Discover, whence she came, or to whom she Belongs. I hear there where some books found which the Minister, the most learned man in the Island, could not read ; by which I conclude she is foreign. All the chests aboard had the Keys in the Locks. Her masts and Rigging are greatly shatter'd, with Cannon and small shot But her Bottom is not much hurt . . . We Belive her to be Dutch.'

However, McLean over-stated the mystery. Dugald Campbell, who had the ship towed to shore, while helping himself to a few items (like one of the eight cannon on board) found a tin deed-box in the Captain's cabin which showed her to be the *Maria-Elizabeth* of 300 tons, a Danish three-masted galiot, built in 1742, from Appenrade (now Aabenraa) in Schleswig-Holstein.[229]*

To the Tiree islanders who swarmed aboard, salvaging wrecked vessels was a commonplace. More than fifty men found employment, some for as much as a month, in rescuing the ship, anchor and cable, mainsail and the rest, and many of the tons of drifting logs from her hold which they pulled in to the western shore – whence nobody could get them off, as there were no anchorages on this side. Dugald sent word to Sheriff Stonefield, and finding the *Maria-Elizabeth* totally unseaworthy he accompanied his father, the factor Ballamore, to Inveraray and asked the Duke's permission to break her up and sell her cargo and materials.

One month later the mystery was solved. A passenger in a ship from Liverpool, forced ashore on the Isle of Lewis by storms, announced himself as her master and part owner, Peter Frelsen of Appenrade. He explained how in a fearful gale the *Maria-Elizabeth* had sprung a leak, lost her boats, capsized, then miraculously righted herself again but with the loss of two of her masts ; all her crew save two managed to hang on miserably for twenty-four hours, soaked, waterlogged and nearly starving, till they were eventually rescued by another Danish vessel. There seemed no chance of bringing her to land, so Frelsen regretfully abandoned ship and was taken with his men to Liverpool. The supposed signs of enemy powder and shot in the rigging proved merely a product of the Tiree islanders' ingenious imagination.

Frelsen now turned back and journeyed the 200-odd miles to Inveraray, to apply to the Admiralty Court for compensation for the loss of his ship and cargo of 'Square firr Timber . . . 500 Loggs, 200 Deals Eight ffathom Lath Wood and about 500 Powlls [poles] of betwixt 20 and 28 feet long . . . all markt thus A–H and designed for Mr Samuel Seel Merchant in Liverpool'.

Mr Seel never got his cargo from the *Maria-Elizabeth* : being declared salvage it was put up to roup on 27 September, ship and cargo raising between them £390, which the Sheriff awarded Frelsen on the latter's petition – less £123 'necessary charges' to Dugald Campbell for the hire, meals and whisky supply of his fifty-odd helpers. Dugald generously renounced his due award of one-eighth of the salvage value, and also returned to Frelsen the cannon which he had appropriated, accepting only his expenses 'in respect of the losses already sustained by the owners of the ship and cargo thro' the misfortune that had happened them'.[230]

The cargo of timber was earmarked by the Duke as soon as he heard of the affair : 'Pray what is a Scotch Tunn, and I should be glad to know the dimensions of the pieces of Timber in order to make Morris consider it.'[231] Acting on his instructions, passed on by Stonefield, Dugald attended the roup and secured 255 tons of the timber for £191 5s, or fifteen shillings a ton. The immediate purpose was for a house intended to be built for the Duke on Tiree; but the rest the Duke proposed to have shipped down to Inveraray and laid in store for the works there.

The story of the Tiree timber, however, is protracted, and at least two years were to pass before it reached Inveraray. The logs were floated round the island to the east coast ready for loading as soon as a ship was available,[232] and meantime Frelsen, fêted up and down the coast and islands and delighted at the hospitality he had received, wished to demonstrate his gratitude to the Campbells by some gesture towards their Chief and Admiral. The most profitable demonstration of gratitude would be to bring over another timber cargo for Inveraray, which he suggested to Stonefield as worth the Duke's consideration since it would cut out dealings with middle-men in Clydeside or Liverpool. 'The Timber of that Countrey is reputed very good,' Stonefield noted to Lord Milton, and he gave Frelsen a letter of recommendation to carry to Lord Milton in Edinburgh.[233]

In London, Roger Morris, who had asked for 1000 fir-trees to be felled on the Argyll estate for scaffolding poles,[234*] discussed Frelsen's offer with the Duke and advised laying up the Tiree timber to season, though some would also be needed for the castle at Rosneath. In short, more was required. 'I incline to think,' concluded the Duke in January 1745, 'that I cant do better than to employ the danish Skipper to bring me timber.'[235]

The Tiree cargo, stacked at Dugald Campbell's orders, lay waiting for spring weather to be shipped to Inveraray. Stonefield wrote several times for the Duke's instructions, and the sizes required, for (he noted on 25 March 1745) 'It will be mighty costly to put it aboard again if it is not cut to less dimensions.'[236] But not until late summer did Lord Milton obtain Morris's sardonic warning on what would happen if they cut it:

'. . . I must have 8 of the Largest piece of timber 29 foot long and 40 peices of the Larges^t 26 foot Long. Every pece of timber has 2 Ends and If you Cutt a piece in the Middle it will Make four Ends which will make sum wast in the Timber. Know If the timber is taken Care It may as well Lay wheare it is as be brought to Invrarey this 3 years, for I dow not purpos to put in one piece of timber Till the whole building is up Battlment wall finnished and the scafold are taken downe and as I shall make a modell of the Building this winter then I Can Give you Every perticular Dimention of Every Single piece of timber in the whole Building . . .'[237]

The Jacobite rising prevented hopes of bringing off the Tiree timber for a further year, but at the end of June 1746, when the Prince's army had been finally defeated at Culloden and the Prince was on the run, with General Campbell somewhat ineptly searching for him in H.M.S. *Furnace*, Stonefield evolved a neat scheme to kill two birds with one stone.

'The Duke of Argyll has a parcell of Timber in the Isle of Tirij for his house. He will find it very troublesome to get it put aboard there, without a great force of men, Nor is it easie to get it transported from thence.

He never can have so good an opportunity as when the Fleet the General has along with him, is upon their Return from their Expedition, That they make a Start there, and take in the Timber, & bring it all at once. The Duke may afford to give them £120 for their Trouble. The Wherrys will be necessary as well as the Large ships, As the last cannot get closs to the Shoar, The Wherrys will do rarely for bringing the Timber to the Large ships. – and now is the proper Seasone for this business . . . The Duke may afford to give 10 sh per Tun for bringing it here.'

He wanted Colonel Jack to get his father to instruct Archibald Campbell of Barnecary, the lieutenant 'charg'd with the timber' (that is, charged with supervising its removal to build the Tiree house) to undertake its loading on to the boats.[238] Colonel Campbell certainly despatched Barnecary to Tiree with thirty men, but his orders were to disarm rebel sympathizers and there is no suggestion that he brought off the timber. But by one means or another, probably in more than a single voyage, the bulk of it did reach Inveraray before August 1747, when freight charges of £178 15s appear in the accounts for 'timber from Tiree'.[239]* This payment would include not only unloading and customs charges at Inveraray but the cost of manhandling the timber from island to ship.

Through the early history of the Inveraray timber the shadowy figure of Captain Peter Frelsen flits like a will-o'-the-wisp, never wholly materializing. On

7 September 1747, Morris and William Adam drew up the commission for a cargo (see page 60) – two and a half years after the Duke first agreed to employ Frelsen – ordering the Dane to produce square timbers, red fir planks, and twenty tons of iron bars, 'for his Grace's works here & to be deliver'd . . . against Summer 1749'. At the date of this contract Frelsen had been long back in Holstein, and it was despatched to Liverpool to await his return, to the care of a firm of merchants, Thomas Steel & Company. Frelsen was to be paid Liverpool prices, for the square timbers 'by the Cubical foot or Ton, the Dealls or planks by the hundred & Twenty, And the Iron by the Stone weight'.[240]

There were abortive attempts to get the cargoes of another wreck off Stranraer and later, one off Barra ;[241]* while an offer to import came from an enterprising young Inveraray tradesman Angus Fisher, son of the Provost, who at one blow gained the Duke's good graces for his initiative and the jealous enmity of his townsmen for his business flair and ducal favour. Angus, at twenty-five saddled with a growing family, ran a string of projects ranging from a small tannery, a brewery and a tobacco factory, to a scheme for killing beef throughout the winter to supply the town with fresh meat. His suggestions for importing iron and timber for the Duke's 'House and Works', made in October 1747 during the Duke's second visit to Inveraray, are worth attention as indicating the means of supply then open to builders. The 'proper ports for buying Firr timber in dales planks or squair loggs' (he reported), were Christiania, Fredrikstad and Fredrikhal in Norway. He also recommended Gothenburg in Sweden for 'as good a market as in the North Sea for all sorts of Rough Iron and Red firr timber, Loggs, planks and dales of all kinds'. In the 'proper seasons', March to September, Scandinavian timber was moderate in price and, for Scottish importers, easy of access. Further-more, it was economic to charter vessels registered at West of Scotland ports where freight charges were lowest, and to avoid waste freight by loading outgoing ships with butter, cheese, 'or in particular Leaf tobacco' (a shrewd fellow, Angus). He also suggested importing cargoes of equal timber and iron, for 'a Ship cannot be loaded or made well Stiff enough with timber, and with Iron, the Ship may have on[e] half of hir Hould unemployed or empty . . .'[242]

Scaffolding timber soon ran short, and the problem was more urgent because Frelsen did not reappear and their expected Danish cargo did not materialize. Roger Morris's illness and death deprived the builders of his expert advice. At first fir trees from the grounds and from Duniquaich had kept the sawyers busy making planks, gangways, poles and putlogs. But as the walls rose higher and (as Morris had directed) were bound with temporary girders, in the autumn of 1749 when they reached window-arch level neither poles nor the protective wooden roofs could any longer be locally supplied. The idea of avoiding the Clydeside middle-men was popular, and John Adam recommended chartering a small ship to bring Norway timber next spring, 'by which means the work would be well supplied & at an easier rate than at present'. But by February the shortage was serious, and while Adam was away in London, George Hunter informed Lord

Milton that if he were to fulfil his orders to build as far as the upper storey cills that year, he needed at least 500 more scaffolding boards.[243]

Meanwhile James Campbell, the Inveraray lawyer – who with his wife had launched the spinning industry among the local girls – had learned of another source of timber through a Dane named Captain Bees, whom he put in touch with Lord Milton with the object 'that his Grace might have a Cheap Bargain of wood'. The arrangement must have been rather uncertain, for Lord Milton, sceptical both of the elusive Frelsen and the unknown Bees, was negotiating with old friends of his own, the merchants and entrepreneurs Charles and Robert Fall of Dunbar – although he did not close with their offers because at the end of October 1749 Knockbuy assured him that Bees' cargo of deals was expected at Inveraray 'by the first fair wind'.[244]

When after another month Captain Bees failed to appear the Duke bowed to Milton's persuasion. 'You certainly guessed right about the Danish Timber Merchant. I am willing to employ Mr Fall in such manner as you think right.'[245]

By the turn of the year Captain Bees' credit was very low. A Larne merchant who came to Inveraray reported that Bees and his ship had come to Larne 'the Latter end of Octr last, where he sold his Cargo of Dails planks &c to Larn Merch^ts but at what price he could not tell'; the merchant, who had seen a lot of Bees, 'heard him tell that he was under promise to go to Inveraray with his cargo, but that he had made no posotive bargan, but thereafter that he was informed that there was no water to carry his Ship to Inveraray, which oblidged him not to go'.

This perfidy caused James Campbell, who felt morally responsible for the fiasco, deep mortification. 'The Dains conduct,' he told Lord Milton, 'now discovers him to be a disingenuous Bold Knave in giving The D such a disappointment, and am Greatly Vext I shou'd have Introduced him to your Lop'; as for the ludicrous excuse of 'no water to carry his Ship to Inveraray', 'I conclude That the Offerr of a Larger price is What Tempted him to Break Bargain'.

The Kintyre factor suggested that, as some compensation, 'if there be any reall agrement or writes between my Lord Milton and Captain Bee, so as to fix the Bargain, I beleive some of Bees Effects might be still found at Learn to make up Damages as there is ane Admirall Depute at Carickfergus near hand'.[246*] But the disingenuous Bold Knave appears to have got away, having advantageously sold his cargo without the trouble of the long voyage round Kintyre and up Loch Fyne. He is heard of no more; and one of his customers lost no time in making a profit out of his purchase.

'Last Thursday evening,' wrote Knockbuy to Lord Milton on 11 March 1750, a Larne merchant named Shutter was 'forc'd up this loch, as he says himself, with a Cargoe of plank 18 and 14 feet long, a part of your ffriend the Danes loading.' Knockbuy was put in the position of having to strike a bargain with the aptly named Shutter at a price much above what they would have had to pay Captain Bees direct – 'after all the caution, prigging, & pingling, sometimes absolutely necessary with such gentry ... The want of Scaffolding, the expences of Shifting what of that kind is here, so frequently, and the high prices of dales just now in Clyde, with the opinion of George Hunter, and all the Dukes servants here, made me venture upon the bargain.' 'The exact number,' he reported later, '. . . was 648 whereof 238 @ 18 feet long', for which he paid £10 per 100 and for the shorter £7, including duty, which would 'serve all the Scaffolding the Castle will need for this Season.' Better still Shutter, bound now for Norway, promised Knockbuy to bring over another cargo in June to Horseshoe Bay in Lorne and 'step over here himself, in order to make a bargain'.[247]

The disillusioned James Campbell fell back on trying to renew contact with Peter Frelsen. Getting in touch with Seels, Frelsen's Liverpool agents, he learned that Frelsen might return to Liverpool in July 1751, and 'He may be write to at Apenrade, by way of London, or Letters may be sent to the Harbours of Tobbermory in Mull, The Sound of Ilay, & the horseshoe in Lorn, at Either of which places He will surely stope on his way to Liverpole.'[248]

Lord Milton, however, was more interested in an offer from the Falls, who (they told him) had

'been at all imaginable Pains, in Learning where the best Plank are to be had . . . & we find Dantsick is the Place, where they may be got of any size ; what you seem to fix on is 20 feet long & 7 Inches thick : as to the quality of the wood, its Red, & Pretty full of Rozin, generaly free of Knotes, but where they happen are large : the very lowest we can engage for, is 12D p Cubical foot deliverable free at the mast at Inverera, the Charges at landing & Duty, to the Buyer . . . The wood in Norway may be had some Cheaper, but then its inferiour in quality, & unless bespoke a long time before, can not be had of the exact dimensions, the Gothenburg Deals are the best wood of any, but there is none of such size . . .'[249]

By now the fame of 'the House of Inverera' was such that at least three Clyde-side merchants were offering bargains to Asknish: 'a parcell of Oak timber . . . which is indeed the best that ever I saw of the Kind', a cargo of redwood deals, and a third at a bargain price, 'for the owner is oblig'd to part with 'em, being straiten'd for money'.[250*]

But the scaffolding shortage continued, although Haswell was warned to keep enough poles 'timeously prepared' ; and if they were to prevent the waste of time in shifting scaffolding from place to place as required, as many as a thousand deals were needed. To meet the immediate emergency two or three hundred were ordered from Clydeside.[251]

From now on orders were chiefly for wood for the fabric itself. In October 1751 Adam drew up a list of 'Timbers necessary for the Roof & Joisting', which had to be altered at least once due to changes in the roof design. Such orders usually specify timbers 'of the best upland firr, as Square as possible, & free of Sapwood & Shakes', or 'of the Clossest Grain, as Square and free of Knotts as possible . . .'[252*]

James Campbell, still hoping that Captain Frelsen might reappear, in November sent Frelsen the scantling of roof timbers, reminding him that since he had 'frequently signified to me, your Anxiety of having an Opportunity of Furnishing the Duke of Argyle with both better and Cheaper Wood than any Other cou'd provide him, In return of the Civilitys Shown you, When your Ship was Wreck't in his Bounds', it would be 'Extreamly right in you, & Greatly your Interest', to bring an appropriate cargo to Horseshoe Bay next spring.[253] But Frelsen's gratitude appears to have evaporated, and nothing more is heard of him at Inveraray ; nor indeed of the obliging Mr Shutter who had promised to 'step over' again.

Lord Milton, while confessing that he had little acquaintance with this kind of business, finally got things moving with the help of yet other friends ; and by March 1752 three ships had been chartered and an agent found to go to Norway. First the *Annabella*, or *Anne Belle*, master Thomas Knox, was chartered at Saltcoats in Ayrshire by William Fullarton of that Ilk, near Irvine, and recommended as 'much the biggest ship belonging to any of our Ports', yet with low freight charges ; her size would enable her to carry large timber without cutting. Then George Cheap, Collector of Customs at Prestonpans and like Lord Milton a director of the British Linen Company, engaged the *Betty* of Airth, a ship of 140 tons with master John Conachie. The third ship, whose name is never quoted, was chartered by Richard Tod of Leith, by agreement with William Douglas, to bring a cargo of timber for the new inn.[254]*

Cheap also provided an agent in the merchant James Hay, who was to sail from Leith in the *Betty* and, when the *Betty* and *Annabella* made their rendezvous at Moss in Norway, or at the neighbouring port of Langesund (from which Cheap had obtained a price list), was to buy a suitable cargo. The price quoted for redwood logs from 14–20 feet long and up to 14 inches square was $14\frac{1}{2}$ 'Rex Dollars' a dozen, and of 16-foot redwood deals two inches thick 34 dollars a hundred.[255]*

From the moment he arrived in Norway James Hay began to wish he had never undertaken his commission. He quickly learned that no timber at all was to be found : spring was late, the rivers still frozen, and the ports already crammed with ships waiting for cargoes. 'The Country was allmost emptied last year,' he wrote to Cheap from Brevik, '& what remained was bought on Comission in the winter.' He had come two months too soon, the merchants told him, urging him to wait till the middle of June when the new season's timber would float down to the fjords with the melting snows ; but rather than give in so tamely (and at such expense to his employers) Hay occupied himself in sending out expresses in all directions, combing the country for miles around, all to no purpose. At last he secured a single cargo at a very high price, but there was simply no hope of fulfilling Lord Milton's specific order – and to add to his chagrin, he learned that only last year prices had been very low.

'I dont know what can be made of it at Inveraray', he wrote, 'but I have no choice.' To Archy Campbell of Succoth he confessed ; 'They are all of the ordinary kind ... Deals are not to be got for any money. I could not procure as many as stow up the ship which has obliged me to buy for that end a good deale of ramble,' but he sent 18 dozen red wood and 11½ dozen white wood logs and a number of deals. Price and quality were not what he had hoped; 'all this considered has given me so much pain, as make me heartily wish I had not engadged in this affair'.

Hay wrote on 12 May and gave his letters to Conachie, master of the *Betty*, as the latter set sail for the west coast of Scotland. The *Annabella*, which had been bound first for France with a cargo of tobacco, had not yet arrived in Norway. Meanwhile Hay went on to try his luck at Fredrikstad, but found it no better. A fortnight later he was writing to Cheap of 'price rising dayly, the people here themselves acknowledge they have never seen it so before which causes me maney uneasy reflections that I shoud fall in with such an unlucky Junctur'. The samples of long deals he was shown ('what they call here high country wood') though good quality were excessively dear, and even here not available till mid-June. Besides, they were sold not by quantity but 'by measur, I pay six dollars for the lod of 50 feet besides duty & charges', and on top of this 'my stay here & my travelling the country all . . . are much more expensive than I coud have imagined in this part of the world'.

Even when he at last succeeded in obtaining a cargo for the *Annabella*, which arrived on 2 June, Hay's troubles were far from over.

> 'I sett imediatly about squaring & Shiping the timber & had shiped about two thirds of the pices contained in my Lord Miltons note when I observed the timber come out too smale for the demsions required & I doubt shall have verey great difficulty to make up the remainder. this was impossible for me to forsee for all this timber lyes in the water till it is called for & when taken ashoar & squared most be for the buyers account & I could be in no doubt of geting my full number from amonge five or six hundred pices.'

However, he did his best to make up his full consignment, and they were put aboard the *Annabella* which sailed on 8 July.

Hay stayed on in Norway to complete his third commission, for timber for the great inn at Inveraray, faced with a choice between Fredrikstad, where the only 'long logs' were to be bought, and Langesund where prices were lower. Eventually he succeeded (though at what port is not stated); and the cargo, despatched on behalf of Richard Tod, reached Campbeltown early in August.[256]*

The *Betty* and her cargo, meanwhile, had arrived at Inveraray on 20 May, and Conachie reported to the Chamberlain John Campbell that Hay had ordered him to await the Duke's further instructions before undertaking a second voyage. The cargo was cleared by the Customs and unloaded. 'As your Lordship directed', wrote the Chamberlain to Lord Milton on 16 June, 'the white-wood Logs are a sawing out for scaffolding, and particular care is taken that none of the small wood be embezled which is piled up within the Close hard by the Wrights Sheds.' No orders came (possibly because Lord Milton was ill) and they had to let the *Betty* sail without commissioning a new cargo.[257]

When the wrights had taken stock of the purchase George Haswell reported to the Chamberlain on its possibilities.

'Ther is 15 Dozen of sizabel Red wood Loogs, of which 10 Dozen of them will
Serve the Towers, the Rest of them will answer for the Scantling of the Principall
Roof: ther is about on Dozen that will serv for Rafters to the Principall Roof.'
The Tiree timber would provide 'the Beams of on of the Short frounts', and if ap-
proved they could be going ahead with the roof until the second cargo arrived.

Haswell had also written about the dimensions to John Paterson, the Queensferry wright – whom Lord Milton had now briefed to undertake the roof at Inveraray – but, he wrote reproachfully to Paterson on 16 June, 'you have not Returned
me no answer'.[258]

In the middle of July the *Annabella* arrived at Inveraray, and James Hay followed soon after. To complete Hay's misfortunes he had had the humiliation of the
bank's returning his cheques. Before leaving for Norway he had received permission from the Duke to draw on the banker George Campbell in London, but confirmation of this must have been forgotten. On ordering his first cargo Hay drew
three bills to the value of £155; by the time he had drawn £321 15s 6d towards the
second cargo, the first three bills were 'returned by Mr Campbell as not knowing
the drawer and oblidged to redraw for £175 which includes £20 of Charges'.
Eventually Lord Milton instructed the bank to honour Hay's bills, but the agent's
amour propre had been deeply wounded.[259]

The expense of bringing over a timber cargo was enormous. For example, the
£321 15s 6d needed by Hay for the *Annabella*'s cargo, equivalent to 1506.33 Norwegian dollars, included 96.11 dollars for Captain Knox's fee (about £30) and 62.51
dollars (about £20) for Hay's own expenses in Norway. Hay also incurred expenses
of £11 3s 7d in Scotland at either end of his journey; the remaining 1375.42 dollars
was the actual value of timber, duty and freight charges. For this outlay he had
obtained 2,517 deals of different dimensions, a few hundred quarter- and half-deals
and battens, and 400 paling boards. The duty paid on these at Inveraray was
£37 6s 10½d, and on all three cargoes, £126 14s 11½d. The cost of 'leading up' the
timber from quay to site, starting at the end of July and still going on in October,
had to be added to the total. Much the most expensive of the three cargoes, as it
happened, was for the inn (it included 10,000 deals), for which in September
Richard Tod received a total of £1,130 2s 3d, accounting for duty, commission, and
'sundries for Will Douglass'. The annual accounts made up in October show the
season's total outlay on 'timber delivered to George Haswell' as £1,684 16s 4d.[260*]

This was only the beginning. James Campbell, besides trying to locate Frelsen, had
also been corresponding with a John McCulloch of Kirkcudbright, who proposed
that his ship the *Friendship* of 260 tons (master James Brown) pick up a fir timber
cargo in Norway, and land it at Horseshoe Bay, whence an express could ride to
Inveraray with a tender. But the chance was missed, the *Friendship* sailed to Virginia instead. Campbell's third contact was Baillie John Wilson of Edinburgh and
his son, 'a Considerable Timber Mercht.' in touch with Thomas & Richard
Spencer & Co., a British firm in Riga.[261]

Wilson informed Lord Milton in August 1752, in a very frail and shaky hand, of the prices of a cargo obtainable next summer. His advice is interesting, recommending Stettin or Riga logs as better and generally cheaper than Norway timber, 'But will run all Hazards on Swedish Dealls & Russian Logs giving ample satisfaction' –

> 'most of the Norway Logs has a great deall of blew wood upon them, & Tapers so much that before they are brought to a sqr a fourth part of the wood must be hewen off, wheras the Other is all squard from end to end and nothing left but reed wood, and the Factors in Sweden & Russia are men of greater Character & Stocks than the Norwegians genrally are, for wee can allwayes depend upon a good Cargo from the former, but verry rarely from the latter.'

The reason was that in Norway there were two kinds of log,

> 'the best they call upland and the worst Lowland which are all Blinded togither for the most part when sent to us, so that your Lop will plainly see how easy it is for them to impose upon us unless they are men of Strict integrity which they cannot greatly boast off more than owr selves.'[262]

No doubt James Hay would have heartily endorsed this verdict.

The remaining timbers needed for the castle roof, joists and floors were re-reckoned several times; by the spring of 1753 both central and corner towers were ready for their roofs, and seasoned oak was required for the windows. Adam's first scantling (50 beams, and as much square timber in addition as would load a ship of 300 tons), bearing Wilson's warning in mind stipulated wood 'of good upland red firr, & not of the Nerva or lowland kind'.[263]

But this year's attempts to secure a cargo direct were even less successful than James Hay's. Hay either refused or was not asked to undertake the commission again; instead Robert Cormack, an Edinburgh merchant who had served Lord Milton before, wrote to Norway on Adam's order for timber at 11d or 12d a foot. But he had no better luck, and by 20 August word arrived that not before next April (1754) could he find 'the best of wood & of any Dementions wanted'.[264*]

In an effort to save time it was decided to order from Clydeside or the Forth, but in September John Paterson drew a blank at both places. In his carpenter's hand, ham-fisted with a pen, he scrawled to his colleague Haswell,

> 'Gorg. you may aquent my Lord milton that thear is no timbr neather at Glasgou nor grinok that is fit for the tours for tho thear is a great quentit it is uors [worse] then that you have is all from your frind
>
> John Paterson'[265]

Back in Edinburgh Duncan Glassford, a Bo'ness merchant, warned him that the season was too late: by late October, the earliest a cargo could be got ready, few ship-masters were willing to brave Cape Wrath:

> '. . . if they should goe the freight would at least amount to 4d p foot besid^s the Extravagant Charges in Shipping &c: and its not every ship that heath a port that will recive timber 15 inch sq^r 25 foot long . . .'

Several merchants promised cargoes, usually at rather a high price, but none before spring, and the best offer would be Glassford's at 14d a foot, deliverable in June. Paterson wrote to Lord Milton in September :

> 'There is Scarce a possibility of getting any vessell all this season to Carry it to Inveraray, Besides the time it would take in Loading, the Charges thereof & freight would bring the timber to a very high price, Because they ask no less than 5d p foot of freight & will not venture about with it till the month of March att soonest.'[266]

1754 soon produced happier results. In January, Greenfield, a Dalkeith merchant and another of John Paterson's contacts, offered a cargo of 175 tons of Copenhagen timber, whose logs 'generally run' (reported Adam) 'from 30 ft. to 54 ft. & from 10 to 13 Ins Sqr, And there is no shorter lengths than 30 ft. except what is cut for stowage'.[267] But at the same time Robert Cormack was writing anxiously to re-establish his reputation, arguing that 'it was not my Fault' and that he had worked incessantly for his clients. He had laid out £700 'purely to Secure a good Cargo Loggs . . . & the Cargos now Lying by me all to oblidge your Lordship which I much at Heart'; it would be too unjust if he were now 'afronted' by losing the commission to another. 'I am told his Grace will not hear of my Name but I hope its not so; for that would be hard to make An Innocent Man Suffer.' (To get over that little difficulty he naïvely proposed the cargo might be made out in the name of his clerk.)

Cormack's appeal had its effect, and he was authorized to buy fifty beams to Adam's specification of the previous summer. After protesting that, while he appreciated the honour, 'I must be a Loser or at best can be no Gainer; there is no Doubt your Lo/ will make the best bargain for his Grace thats possible but I perswade my selfe that your Lo/ would not incline that I should be a Loser', Cormack accepted the commission and chartered a couple of ships to carry the order.[268]

Unfortunately he was forestalled by an unexpected shipment of Norway timber which arrived at Campbeltown in the *Hibernia*, from a Christiansand merchant named Edward Smyth; and her captain, Sven Olsen Flink, travelled up to Inveraray on 1 June and offered the cargo to Asknish. This was a very unlucky chance for Cormack, for Smyth's despatch of the cargo had been purely speculative : 'both the Owner and Capt. are Strangers to this Country but having heard of the Works My Lord Duke is carrying on they have Judg'd that a mercat might be had for Timber here'. It was a shrewd business stroke, the result of a chance meeting between Asknish and the owner's son in Edinburgh the previous summer, and even if the Duke did not need it the cargo of 300 tons would be equally useful in the new town. Alternatively, the skipper could find a ready market on Clydeside. Asknish hastened to get Lord Milton's instructions, 'since I fear the Capt. will soon grow impatient'. Flink prudently travelled to Clydeside to seek a provisional alternative offer, and a few days later the unsuspecting Cormack, who in his over-anxiety had ordered more timber than his commission warranted, left his office at Leith, boarded the Edinburgh stage-coach at six in the morning, and journeyed to Inveraray as fast as he could.[269]

But his timber ships did not arrive, and for several weeks he was kicking his heels at Inveraray, nearly distracted with uncertainty. To complete his fury Asknish, comparing his prices with the Dane's suggested that Cormack was charging too much, and Cormack was beside himself. His irate reply, vilely written and vilely spelt, Asknish tactfully forwarded to Lord Milton for a decision.

'I never will tye my self down to a dains praice I know be [i.e. by] sade experience at Leith that they bring nothing to Scotland but bade wood . . . to be at al this charge that I might hav honner of a good cargo and for that to tak dains praice wood be hard, to Give Good Logs the praice of bade is not Reasonale but I shal ask no mor then the worth of my Logs as in Goodness to be Judged by any honest men that my Lord milton pleas to nam – but for any thing I can sie I wil not be fond to com this way again . . .'

And so forth.

At last the ships arrived, the consignment was approved, and on 27 August Cormack was paid for his cargoes, amounting to 9,802 feet (827 pieces) of Norway fir logs, 128 dozen deals, and 7,527½ feet (307 pieces) of Copenhagen fir. As the bill came to £993 17s 9¼d, his anxiety is understandable. Captain Flink was presumably allowed to sell his cargo in Glasgow (though some of his logs may have been taken to Rosneath). Much of Cormack's timber was handed over to William Douglas for finishing the great inn.[270]

A fair amount of timber was now in hand at Inveraray, but although Adam reckoned it would suffice for partitions and for lathing the ceilings, 'as most of it is extremely course, it will not answer for Doors, Window Shutters, Floors, or any other good Work'. He therefore, in 1755, recommended importing 'Wanscot Loggs of 9 feet long from Holland (called Pipe Hault)', because of their lower duty, for the doors and deal floors; and wainscot for window-sashes direct from Leith, 'as that will be better Season'd than what can be imported from Holland'. James Morris had agreed on Scotland as a cheaper source for the window-sashes, and accordingly in 1756 they were ordered from Edinburgh and shipped to Inveraray with deals, wainscots and paving tiles on board the *Margaret* of Leith.[271]

Most of the necessary timber was now supplied, except for deals for flooring the main rooms, and mahogany for fine work such as 'Architraves & Breast Linings for doors & Windows'. In December 1757 George Haswell obtained in Glasgow '17 pices Jamaice mahogany' from Crawford & Craig, amounting to 1,053 feet superficial at 7¼d a foot, and 14 similar pieces from Quentin Leitch at Greenock, 1,051¼ feet superficial at 8d. The Clydeside deals, however, he considered of insufficient quality and not well seasoned, 'which made it necessary to take it off at Leith where Mr Adams luckily had great Store of well seasoned good Timber'. The Adam brothers supplied, in fact, '16,000 superficial feet of fine seasoned single Gothenburg deals free of sap & knots @ 4d p. ft' (£266 13s 4d), and others of 2 and 2½-inch section; in spring 1758 this was brought by ship to Inveraray and used 'for flooring the 3 Rooms on the East side of the house upon the first floor viz the Drawing Room Bed-Chamber & Closet'.[272]

Three thousand feet of Jamaica mahogany were still required for the sashes of the six middle tower windows, half of it at least $9\frac{1}{2}$ to 10 feet long, and at least 11 or 12 inches in breadth, 'the ouldest Imported that Can be Got', requested Haswell, 'as it is for present ouse'. The usual difficulties were suffered by the agent – this time Graham Strathearn, the Rosneath carpenter – who could not persuade the merchant to 'break' the cargo and allow him to select, although he could see that rotten wood was hidden under the best pieces cunningly laid on top.[273] Some of the last timber ordered, in 1759, was for the new court of offices then building at the Cherry Park, '200 Tun of Copenhagen Logs wch will require one ship and about 150 Tun of Deals wch will require anoyr ship', ballasted for economy's sake with iron; '& they assure me', wrote Lord Milton, 'there can be no loss rather profite on this article, as yr own works will require some part of it . . .'[274]

Finally, in 1760, timber 'fitt for joisting houses' for the new town was ordered by John Watson, an Edinburgh lawyer, from Riga, 'the properest place for Goods of that kind'. The *Young Tobias* and the *Concordia*, both of Gothenburg, arrived at Campbeltown in the autumn with the warning that 'the freights on Swedish Ships have been high for some time bypast, on account of Prussian Privateers &c. but the Duties here [i.e. Gothenburg] are much lower than in British Ships'. The Gothenburg agent, George Carnegie, added a warning that 'the Loggs must be pass'd for Swedish Timber, otherwise they are not alowed to be imported to Brittain in a Swedish Veshell'.[275]*

'The cargow I think is the best that we ever had heir', noted Haswell approvingly as they unloaded the *Concordia* cargo in November.[276] This, so auspiciously named, was probably the last to arrive in Duke Archibald's lifetime – the last of many ship-loads of deals, lead, iron, nails and slates that had sailed from Scandinavia and from other parts of Scotland, unloaded their freights at Campbeltown or Inveraray, gone through the customs, and been carted off and stored for the building of Inveraray Castle and the first houses of the new town.

This country is far from being so bad an one as English prejudice and English ignorance represent it. A great part of it is barren, because they want hands to cultivate it . . . but now they begin to improve their lands, and to plant. The whole face of the country will be totally changed in fifty years more.

Lady Hervey to Rev. Edmund Morris, from Mellerstain, 11 September 1756,
Letters of Lady Mary Lepel, Lady Hervey, London 1821, p. 221

III

At the time of Duke Archibald's succession the vicinity of Inveraray was already well wooded, for his ancestors the Marquess and the 9th Earl of Argyll had been great planters. A seventeenth-century account shows Inveraray in the latter's day to have been a 'very faire and pleasant' place with 'sundrie zeairds [gardens], some of them with divers kynd of herbs growing and sett thereintill. And other zairds planted with sundrie fruit trees verie prettilie sett, and planted, and there faire greens to walk upon.' Both Glen Aray and Glen Shira were described as 'verie fertill' and rich.[1]

The lime avenue on which the south front of the castle was centred probably dates from soon after 1650, and although largely replanted in the nineteenth century it still contains a few of the original trees. The great beech avenue – later known as the Town Avenue – on the seaward side of the Fisherland, then an open park, dates from about the same period; but at the age of about 300 years the remaining trees were over-mature, and in 1955–7 the avenue was felled. The original intention, never carried out, was that the large 180-acre tract of the Fisherland should form a great plantation, with this avenue forming its boundary on the loch-side.

Another contemporary beech avenue still survives, somewhat depleted, at the entrance to Glen Shira. Sycamore, Spanish chestnut and larix were planted as early as 1674, and Scots pine even earlier, in 1661.[2]* Estate maps of the early eighteenth century show numerous vistas radiating through the woods from circular glades, but whether all these elaborate layouts were in fact carried out is impossible to say.

Outside the town and castle area no buildings of note then existed in the policies, and if proposals for any were made during Duke Archibald's first visit in 1744, nothing was done to implement them, for the two immediate issues were the founding of the new castle and the making of the military road from Dumbarton.

Although the road was an army operation, it was one in which the Duke naturally took a great interest, not only on account of the future ease it promised in getting to Inveraray, but because he wished to be sure of the road's line of approach to his parks, and to have a say in the design of the bridge at the head of Loch Shira.

Within a month of the Duke's succession John Maule was asking Lord Milton to approach General Guest, senior officer in the Lowlands (who was stationed in Edinburgh), as the Duke was 'endeavoring to learn the best way of Penetrating to Inveraray'.[3] On 31 December the Duke wrote to Milton from London: 'I wish Guest would apply to the Marq. Tweeddale, & to Sr Will. Young for the making a road from Dumbarton by land to Inveraray, I shall apply here.' Nearly three weeks later he reported: 'I shall get the Road ordered from hence, so that Guest need not be at all concerned but in the execution'.[4] As he well knew, General Guest, who was in his eighties, was fully occupied since an invasion by the French was then commonly expected.

Because the Duke was in a position to further the plans for the road and because it was 'both very convenient for me & highly necessary for the publick',[5] by 1 May 1744 Stonefield, in his capacity as Sheriff and Chamberlain of Argyll, was able to meet the engineers, Mr Dugal Campbell (see p. 45, n. 9*), and Mr Brereton from Fort Augustus. Together they began the survey along the River Leven from Dumbarton, skirted Stonefield's own estate, continued up Loch Lomondside and so across to Loch Long and Loch Fyne via Glen Croe and Glen Kinglas. After reaching Inveraray Stonefield, this time accompanied by engineer Campbell and the Duke's mason William Douglas, resumed the survey back to Loch Fyne-head and once more to Dumbarton, with 'Three Men that Carry'd the Line & pinns'. The total preliminary survey of forty-five miles for the road, most of it over very difficult country, took only about a fortnight.[6]

'I believe there will be 1000[11]', wrote the Duke at the end of May, 'ordered to Account for beginning the work of the Roads from Dumbarton to Inveraray, let them begin at Dumbarton where they will have little to do till they come to the end of Loch Lomond, being all a flat Country.' He added: 'Make my Compliments to Sr John Cope, I received his letter about the Roads & shall write to him by next post.'[7] Cope had in January been appointed Commander-in-Chief of the Scottish troops and was now in Edinburgh.

The Duke had personal reasons for wanting the road-works to begin at Dumbarton because, he told Lord Milton,

'I have a project of varying the road near to Inveraray which I must consider of when I am upon the place, as for example, there are at present 3 Roads to Inveraray which cut my Parks or projected Gardens most miserably to pieces ... I wish there is not at present even a 4th Road.'[8]

It is hardly necessary to add that the work did begin at Dumbarton, and that in the meantime it was routed not to cut across his parks.

Early in 1745 300 men of Lascelles' Regiment (the 23rd) were labouring under the supervision of Major William Caulfield, Inspector of Roads and Bridges in North Britain. Following the methods of General Wade, who had begun the military roads in Scotland in 1725, Caulfield divided his men into working parties of not more than 100 under a sergeant or subaltern, and employed artificers at 1s 6d a day for the bridges and other mason-work.[9*] Officially a dozen 'wives' were allowed with the troops, to cook for and serve them in their messes, but by degrees more drifted in to swell this curious throng cutting its slow, laborious way over the

38. Inveraray and its environs
From General Roy's military map of the West Highlands.

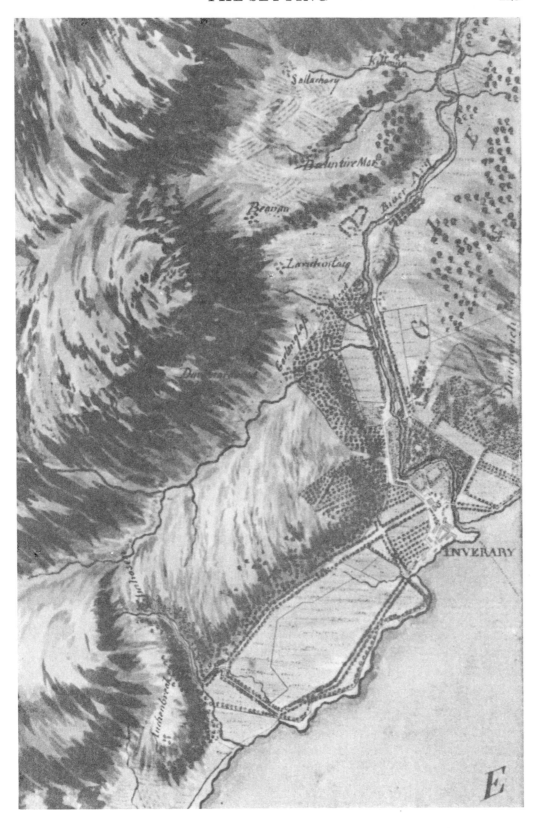

wild glens, until there were almost as many women as men; the women brought their children, the children ate up all the provisions, and the wives 'steal from and quarrel with the Inhabitants, and bring their Husbands into perpetual Broils with the Country People'.

Major Caulfield's task was anything but a sinecure. The turnover in officers was increasingly rapid and their replacements were inexperienced in the peculiar difficulties of the work. As for the men, most were in debt to their captains and regarded their day's output as 'only working for a dead Horse' – pay being docked towards the debts – so their speed of working was sluggish at best. Then came the Jacobite rising when Caulfield, as Quartermaster to General Cope, was occupied far away. Progress on the road was dramatically halted when 'a Party of Rebels' under McGregor of Glengyle swooped down from the hills,

> 'took the Masons and Men at the Bridges, Prisoners, carried off the Tools, Timber, Dale Boards and Materials, by which some of the unfinished Bridges were destroyed by the Winter Floods, and all necessarys were to be bought again'.

When they resumed, as the working-parties approached Argyll, the county's Commissioners of Supply called on the tenantry to provide the soldiers with blankets and to bring carts for loading gravel and take a share of the work.

Round the wild lochs and across the rough pathless slopes of the hills was hard going. The stretch from the Water of Douglas (Inverbeg) to the point where the road was to leave Loch Lomond and cut across to Loch Long occupied 500 soldiers, hacking and blasting through solid rock faces as their route wound round the jutting headlands. They had to build supporting walls between the road and the water below as a protection in every foot of progress, and in bad weather, which was frequent, the miners worked under 'little Hulls of Hurdles thatched with Heather'.

Once across the glen and round the head of Loch Long, above Ardgartan they made a diversion to avoid two streams and cut the distance by two miles. Now the road again left the waterside, and foot by foot was dug and blasted up the valley-bottom of Glen Croe. A final effort carried it in a steep zigzag up to the head of the pass, meeting place of three valleys, whence an even wilder pass, treeless, uncharted and all but pathless, wound down southwards to Loch Goil, while their own way lay ahead, past the black and sullen waters of Loch Restal. At this desolate spot the soldiers, miners and engineers commemorated their achievement in reaching the highest point of these wastes and lonely rocks by setting up an inscribed stone:

REST AND BE THANKFUL

During the summer of 1747 the troops built no less than eighteen bridges, some with arches of up to fifty feet. Caulfield calculated that he ought to achieve the eight miles of rough going down Glen Kinglas to Loch Fyne-head by June 1748; after that came six miles through grass and cornland which need take only a month or six weeks. But his progress was less smooth than expected, for by trying to re-site the Loch Fyne-head bridge he fell foul of the Member of Argyll, Sir James Campbell of Ardkinglas. Sir James, 'all fire and fury' that the Major wished to 'Carry the road four miles about through the best of his arrable ground', took his complaint to the Sheriff and forced Caulfield to keep to the original route.[10]*

Along Loch Fyne the road cut between Dunderave, the old stronghold of the MacNaughtons on its little promontory, and the wooded, craggy mountainside only a few yards from the shore. Then, round the point at Stron, the town of Inveraray came suddenly in sight less than two miles away. The road was to end at the town, which had its own old bridge over the Aray inland from its mouth; but before the town, at the head of the deep inlet where the Garron water ran out from the Dhu Loch in Glen Shira, preliminary work on a bridge with a 60-foot arch had begun in 1744.[11] Since this lay within the policies of the Duke of Argyll, the Duke's own architect provided its design.

Caulfield already had centring available for a bridge, and the design was probably drafted in the autumn of 1747 when the Duke, Roger Morris and William Adam met at Inveraray. On his way to Clydeside after leaving Inveraray, at Caulfield's suggestion Morris returned over the line of the new road, to look at the bridges and sites, and, either then or in Edinburgh later, he proposed that young John Adam should supervise the building of the bridge over the Garron Water.[12]

During that summer 38 dozen oak piles, cut from the Duke's woods, had been taken up the loch to the site, and by February 1748 the responds were built on these piles. Only now did William Adam receive Morris's completed design, and on the 5th wrote in reply:

'It is Exceedingly neat and well done, And you may believe my son and I will take care to order the Execution corresponding thereto, wch. when finishd must have a very fine appearance, John is not a Little vain of the confidence you Repose in him, as to the fixing the proportitions [sic] and if any doubts arise will communicate his thoughts to you.'[13]

For the next eighteen months John Adam supervised this military bridge, and in September 1749 Major Caulfield informed Lord Milton that

'It would be well if Mr Adam gave our Master Mason Mr Christie, orders to finish as soon as possible, and shoud he want a few more Hewers for a week or so, I submit it to your Lordsp whether it woud not be right to have them lent us'.[14]

Caulfield was at this time in trouble with no less a person than the Duke of Cumberland on account of his outlay on the military road; Henry Fox, the Secretary at War, in a bitter complaint of the estimates which he regarded as both extravagant and sketchy, remarked to General Churchill that 'HRH would have the Bridges on the Inverara Road let alone till next year, those to Brae Mar and Fort-William being more necessary'. But Caulfield succeeded in representing to the C.-in-C. that all would be 'ruined by Stopping the work at present', and the bridge appears to have been finished that same year.[15]

This completed the stretch of military road between Dumbarton and Inveraray.

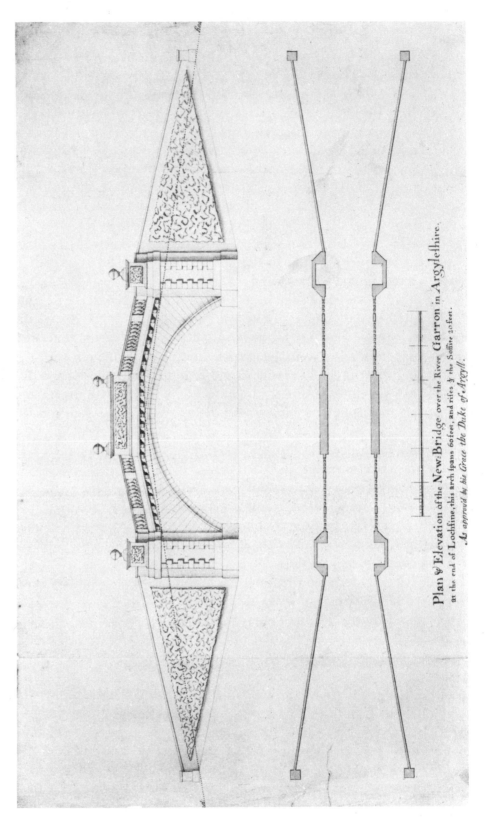

Plan & Elevation of the New-Bridge over the River Garron in Argyleshire. at the end of Lochfine, this arch spans 60 feet, and rises & the Soffite 20 feet. As approved by his Grace the Duke of Argyll.

39. The Garron Bridge, by Roger Morris
Plan and elevation probably drawn by William Adam.

[5] The Garron Bridge

The Duke travelled by it in August 1750, although only over the section between Luss and the house of Ardkinglas at Cairndow; his letter written from Rosneath to Lord Milton, who had preceded him to Inveraray, shows how complex the journey still remained:

> 'I am very glad the Roads are so well. I intend to set out to morrow & lie at Luss ... You need not send your Coachman, for Colquhoun lay here last night & assures me that the Road from Arncaple to Luss is very passable, he will be here to morrow morning to conduct us & will bring some men to assist in case of accidents. Spare horses will probably be of use. The Boat should I think be at Arkinlass on tuesday afternoon.'[16]

On that journey, therefore, the new bridge at Garron would be seen by the Duke only in the distance, as he sailed or was rowed past Stron Point and the inlet of Loch Shira. Viewed either from the water or by the land approach, as the road swings round the point to give the first sight of Inveraray, the Garron Bridge makes a spectacular introductory flourish to the Duke's policies. Built at high-water mark with a tidal river beneath, it has a single 60-foot arch with steep approaches on either side, and is surmounted by balustrades and terminated by ornamental stone balls on the central parapet and flanking piers.

An anonymous manuscript account compiled in the 1770s, of the genealogy of the Argyll Campbells, contains a summary (slightly inaccurate) of the building works sponsored by Duke Archibald:

> 'Quarries set to work at St Catherine Quarry and Creggan's Quarry and the hewing and building carried on vigorously in 1747 and a number of Masons – Quarriers – Wrights – and Service Men employed and several vessels from Denmark or Sweden, came with wood from time to time. ... The new roads brought forward in 1747 & 1748, to the point of Strone Shira by Royals and the Garran Bridge rebuilt [i.e. built] the well in the Black hill built and the new Garden at the White Barns begun
>
> ... a fine Physic well built in the Meadow and a Pigeon house built in the North end of the Meadow – the Townbreck Court for Dairy built Carlunin Milln built and slated the Square Court in the Cherry Park built the High Garden Wall surrounding the Garden and the Barns built the New Bridge upon the Water foot begun the Bulwark upon the Shore begun a Spire built on Dunequech ...'[17]*

The contract for the erection of the first two small ornamental buildings in the policies was drawn up between Roger Morris, William Adam and William Douglas on 2 October 1747. One was the dovecot a mile from the castle, centred on the oak walk and the old castle, across the point where the Garden Bridge was later built; the other was the so-called Watch Tower (the 'spire' named above) which crowns the sheer and rugged hill of Duniquaich.

The wording of this contract, witnessed by John Adam and typical of many which followed, gives an interesting glimpse of the building methods employed.

[6] The Garron Bridge

'Mr Douglas mason agrees to build & finish the two above buildings by the 1st of July next, according to the sign'd plans giv'n him by Mr Morris, for His Grace the Duke of Argyll, & to be done to the Approbation & liking of Willm Adams Architect. The pidgeon house to be built at the end of the Oak walk being a Circular building 20 f^t Diam^r & 42 f^t high, to stand upon a Slope of 3 f^t high, For which, he is to be paid Fourty Eight pounds Ster.

Also to build a Tower upon Duniquaich 20 f^t Sq^r & 45 f^t high, the inside a Circle (And to find all Materials for both buildings, except Doors, Wind.^s Iron work, Glass & plaistering) for the Sum of Fourty Six pounds Ster.

His Grace is to find Carts & horses. And as it may not be propper for Mr Douglas's Labourers to drive His Graces teams, he will supply a Labourer to go into the Dukes works instead of the Carter that drives the teams.

And what scaffolding may be wanting at each building, Douglas shall be obleig'd to give a Receipt for the same, & return the Scaffolding back to prevent waste or embezzlement.'[18]

In preparation for these jobs Douglas travelled to Edinburgh for masons, quarried the stone at Carlundon on the Aray, and obtained his lime from Ardkinglas at the head of Loch Fyne. Morris sent to ask for a progress report on 1 January 1748, to which Douglas replied two months later that the stone for Duniquaich was quarried and would be taken up as soon as the road they were making there was ready. Stones for the pigeon house were already loading, and work would start that week.[19]

The tower on Duniquaich was cleverly sited on the verge of the steep hill face, but not quite on top, and thus when seen from the castle and the town is silhouetted against the sky. The steep slope on which it is set caused it to be made two stories high on one side and only one on the other. The lower floor, in the original drawings termed 'the cave', is a small semi-circular vaulted chamber entered through a rough pointed arch. The upper floor entered from the higher ground is circular, with a high conical vault. It is lit by two more or less pointed windows commanding a superb view down Loch Fyne with the castle immediately below, the River Aray winding through its parks to join the loch, and the town on the headland. The building is of rough rubble, roofed in four receding stages by stone slabs; but its isolated position, 813 feet above the loch, rendered it vulnerable in thunderstorms. In May 1752, only a few years after it was completed, the roof was damaged by lightning, but was repaired by Douglas by 1 July at a cost of £7.[20]*

Duniquaich formed a natural climax to any tour of the policies, and the watch tower was soon a goal for visitors who struggled up the hillside by its steep zigzag road. Horses were frequently ridden up it, and at a later stage even carriages, but it was usually regarded as a journey whose magnificent view at the end, on top of what seemed like a small mountain, was the climber's reward for his effort. The tower itself, 'in Imitation of a Ruin',[21] more than fulfilled what was surely its designer's intention, to deceive the visitor into supposing it historical and antique. 'The corrosions, which the stone of this tower has experienced,' noted Mr Bailey from Yorkshire with perfect seriousness in 1787, 'should fix it of a date very much

40. The Watch Tower on Duniquaich, 1748
Drawings probably by Roger Morris,
with annotations by William Adam.

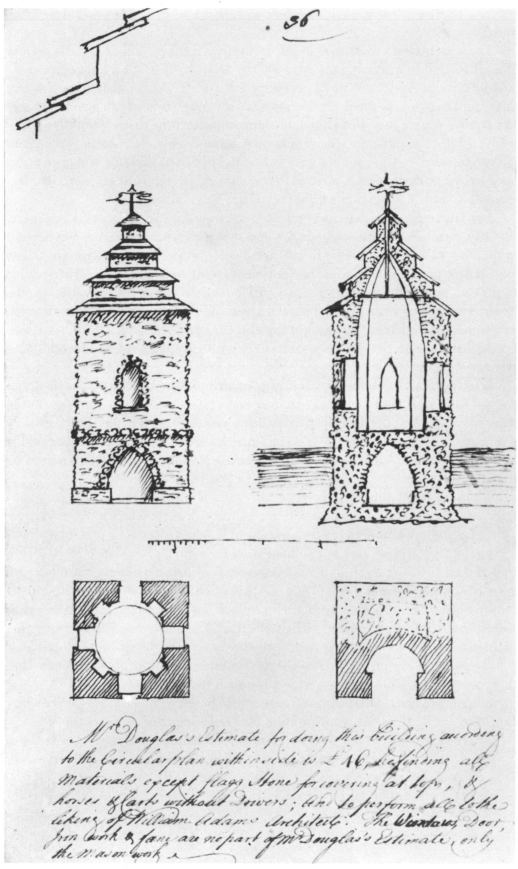

Mr Douglas's Estimate for doing this building according to the Circular plan within side is £16, he finding all materials except flagg stone for covering at top, & horses & carts without drivers; And to perform all to the likeing of William Adams Architect. The Windows, Door, Iron work & fane are no part of Mr Douglas's Estimate, only the mason work.

anterior to that of the present mansion, and, perhaps, it may be co-eval with the antient one . . .'[22]

The watch-tower cost £46 to build, as estimated; the pigeon-house was slightly altered in building, costing an extra £4 19s 10d,[23] and is of an altogether more urbane design. A 'doocot' was a necessary feature of most Scottish estates, where doves and pigeons, particularly the 'squabs' or young birds were a prized delicacy to vary the winter diet. But although commonplace in the eastern counties, especially in Fife, doocots were almost unknown in the Highlands because of the rarity of corn or other feeding-stuffs for the birds. In 1617 their building had been regulated by Act of Parliament, restricted to persons paying 'yearly Rent to ten Chalders victual . . . at the least lying within two miles of the same'.[24]

The Inveraray doocot is among the few ever built in Argyll, and because of its site, in a meadow terminating a vista, it was designed with a certain sophistication in the form of a circular tower. It has harled walls, a doorway with wrought rebats and, at first-floor level, the usual precaution of a wide well-projecting string-course to prevent access by climbing rodents. Above are two sets of plain windows, the lower designed as blank, the upper shuttered. The pigeons' entrance is through an elegant domed lantern surmounting the conical slated roof. Within are two floors, the ground a circular vaulted chamber with a fireplace, the upper containing stone nesting-boxes.

After completing these two pleasing small buildings William Douglas contracted for a new water-mill, 40 feet long and 17 feet wide, at Carlundon on the Aray quite close to the dovecot. His estimate was £79 18s 6d, and the machinery was made by Robert Mackell.[25] The mill had no architectural significance and is now a picturesque ruin, though an unexecuted plan made in 1757 visualized its transformation into an ambitious Gothick structure.

One building of this period whose history is obscure is the rusticated grotto referred to in the genealogy quoted above as 'the well in the Black hill'; entered by a circular arch, it is built over the spring-head known as Bealachanuaran. A drawing among a set captioned by William Adam[26] is further evidence of its being undertaken at this date, although not necessarily to Adam's design, but otherwise it is inexplicably missing from plans and instructions, notably from the Morris Letter Book. The only conceivably relevant references in Inveraray papers are to a mysterious building known as 'the Countess'. On 8 March 1748, reporting his preparations for the watch-tower and the dovecot, Douglas informs Morris that 'I have men casting the Foundation of the Countess', and the accounts show that this cost £55 2s 4½d to build – a little more than the pigeon-house.[27]

But an explanation of the name 'Countess' is found eighteen years earlier when Lord Ilay, as he then was, was planning his newly acquired estate at the Whim:

'There is one part of our Architecture which I believe we have forgot to think of, viz The Countess of Pigburgs Appartment (as we call it here from her having used it more than usual) Anglice A House of Office.'[28]

The name stuck, and was used as a slang term by all his friends, and even 'officially'

[7] The Watch Tower on Duniquaich

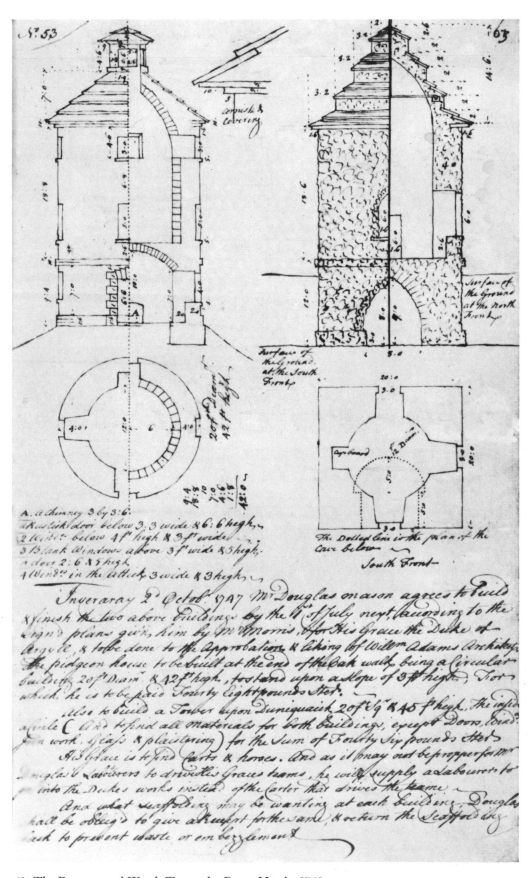

41. The Dovecot and Watch Tower, by Roger Morris, 1748
    Working drawings and annotations by William Adam.

[8] The Dovecot

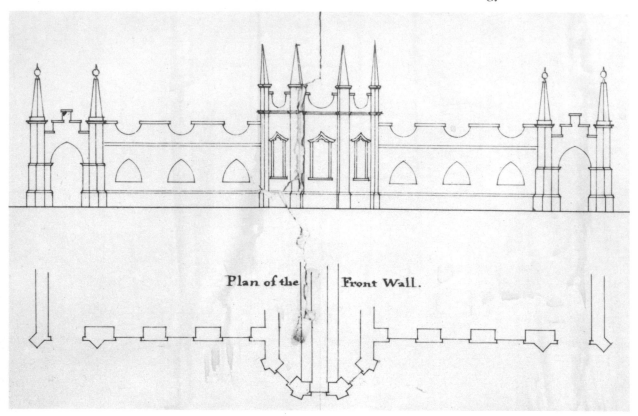

Plan of the   Front Wall.

42. Carlundon Mill
    Proposed new elevation, 1757, probably by John Adam.

in building accounts, as at the Whim in 1733.[29]

If 'The Countess' at Inveraray were really no more than 'the necessary house in the garden', its cost shows that it was a sizable, even elaborate affair, accounts including 'Iron work for the pump' and more than £8-worth of ashlar and flags;[30] but there is no sign today of such a building's existence. Nor, on the other hand, do contemporary references specifically fit the building of Bealachanuaran's well-head. Yet identification of the two seems highly unlikely, unless in this context the name 'Countess' has some other forgotten topical meaning. But whoever designed the well-head, which shelters a spring of pure water later piped downhill to serve the town of Inveraray, it remains an attractive addition to the policies.

Douglas, although he never worked on Inveraray Castle itself, was kept well employed in these days. He supplied stone and lime for the building from St Catherines, and his account for £376 13s 4¾d, dated 5 October 1749, included £192 11s 1¾d for those items, and his charge for the tower on Duniquaich, the dovecote and the Countess.[31]

In 1751 Douglas produced an estimate for a bridge over the River Aray just above the mill:

[9] The bridge over the Aray at Carlundon,
built by William Douglas, 1755–7

43. Bealachanuaran, the springhead
    Design, c.1747, attributed to William Adam.

'Imprs.	To quarrying wall-stones and fflaggs for said bridge	£15 : 10 : 0
Itt.	To 26 Chalder Lyme for Do. at 10s 6 a Chalder	£13 : 13 : 0
Itt	To Building and Lay the Cassway of Do. bridg	£24 : 00 : 0
Itt.	To Sawing and Binding the timber for Centers of Said bridg wt. Nails &c	£ 7 : 00 : 0
		£60 : 3 : 0

N.B. the Arch 40 feet wide the Leading to be furnished by the Employer and timber for Centers and Scoffolding and all workmanship & other materialls to be furnished by the Undertaker.'[32]

[10] The springhead at Bealachanuaran

The situation of Douglas's bridge is romantically contrived and the single rubble-built arch spanning a rocky, tree-clad ravine strikes an appropriately rustic note. It was begun in the winter of 1751/2, but temporarily abandoned when Douglas secured his largest commission, for building the Great Inn in the new town. However, in April 1755 he wrote to Lord Milton that 'the mason work of the Inn being now Done : I am ready to Sett about the Bridge, which will not be Long a building if I can get the materials Lead up to the place.' Permission was at once given, and the first of Robert Bathgate's carts arrived on the site with stone and lime on 12 May. On 21 October 1757 it was inspected by the mason George Hunter, who reported it 'intirely finish'd'.[33]

The other chief mason employed about the policies and the new town was James Potter, who built the great walls of the kitchen garden, several small bridges – for example at Cromalt beyond the Fisherland – and the boathouse on the Dhu Loch, finished in 1752 at a cost of £39 10s 3d.[34*]

Old Inveraray Castle's kitchen garden was on the west side of the building, but Duke Archibald ordered a new one to be laid out nearly half a mile beyond at the White Barns. Its area was later increased by the 5th Duke, but even at the beginning, in 1752, Potter's task was formidable enough, his wall being more than 500 yards long overall, and at its highest point 19 feet; it included 1006 holes 'for fixing timber frames to the walls' for growing fruit trees. Not surprisingly the wall took over three years to build, and cost (with the addition of a tool shed) £486 18s 0d although merely of common rubble with a freestone cope.[35]

These were only a few of the many works going on in the policies. A network of estate roads was constructed, with small bridges to carry them over burns, and miles of dry stone dyking were built to enclose the parks. The huge tract of the Fisherland was drained by Robert Bathgate and labourers, and to prevent flooding the Aray banks were canalized, and a series of 'cascades' – shallow paved rapids – made in its bed for some distance up from the river mouth. In charge of this was Walter Paterson.[36]

A salt-water pond controlled by a sluice, made on the loch side near the mouth of the Aray took up a quite disproportionate amount of labour. The idea – one of Duke Archibald's experiments – was excellent, for on 11 December 1752 it was stocked with 400 oysters sent by Captain Archibald Campbell of Craignish, General Bland's aide-de-camp, and another 500 from the same source were put in on Christmas Day. But alas, towards the end of February it was found that they were all 'covered pretty deep with mud', so 'we're afraid to venture puting in any more, till we discover, whether their mudding, be hurtfull to them or not'.[37] What became of the mudded oysters is not recorded, but a lot of work went on during 1753, mainly shoring up the bank against the sea, and in June 1755 the merchant Richardson warned Lord Milton that there must be a fault in the outlet for barely two tons of water remained in the pond, 'nor was there a fish to be seen larger than my ffinger'.[38] The pond was vulnerable because of the high spring tides, and the bulwark along the loch side was continually being strengthened. An exceptionally

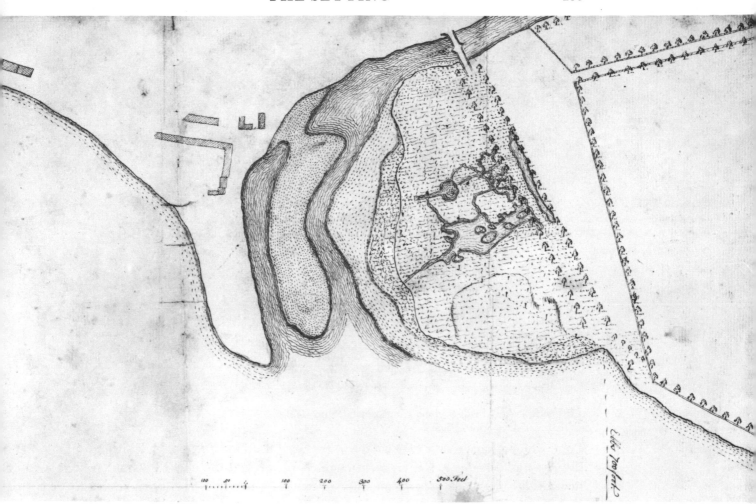

44. Site of the Salt Water Pond
    'The Mouth of the River of Aray and the Shoar on both sides',
    c.1750, showing the marshy site used for the pond on the north
    bank and part of the old town on the south bank.

high tide on 23 March 1757 – the worst since 30 January 1750 – broke through
bulwarks and park walls and carried away whole trees and road surfaces, flooding
the salt water pond to wash its banks two feet lower than before.[39]* The pond's
productive days were ended when in the same year it was decided to bring the
military road along the shore of Loch Fyne and to build a 'King's' bridge across
the mouth of the Aray, which had the effect of cutting off the pond from its sea
sluice.

The military road had terminated at the old town bridge of Inveraray, 250 yards
up from the river mouth, but was now about to be extended towards Loch Awe.
Meanwhile building the new town had begun, and the Duke was already wanting to
clear the site of the old, leaving the town bridge as a potential ornamental feature
of his parks. With the altered site of Inveraray town, on the Gallows Foreland

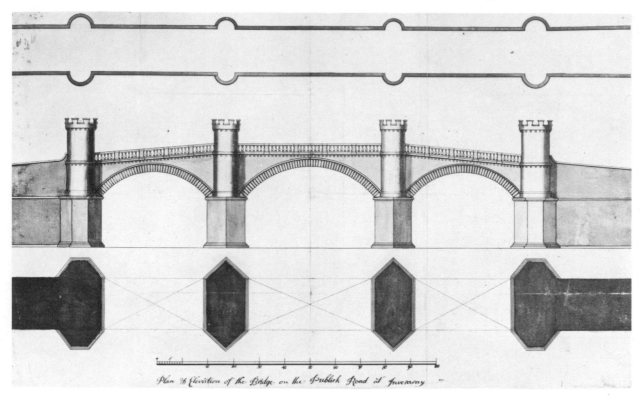

Plan & Elevation of the Bridge on the Publick Road at Inveraray

45. The first Aray bridge on the King's road, begun 1758
Attributed to John Adam.

Point, the military road's extension was required to follow the loch-side, bridging the Aray at its mouth. Government engineers surveyed the new line, but as the new bridge must feature prominently in the view from the castle windows the Duke undoubtedly had some say in its design to harmonize with the prevailing Gothick effect. In *Vitruvius Scoticus* the bridge is attributed to John Adam[40] which, in view of his being in charge of everything else at Inveraray at this time is very likely, particularly since he had supervised the building of the Garron Bridge, and had now been appointed to his father's office of King's Mason.[41]

The new three-arched 'Sea Bridge' accordingly had a distinctly Gothick air: small crenellated bastions with dummy cross-shaped arrow slits terminated the piers, and the parapet was battlemented. The undertaker for the bridge was John Brown, a Master Mason from Dumbarton who in 1754 had built the road bridge at Loch Fyne-head. The Duke provided the usual facilities (listed in detailed memoranda drawn up in the autumn of 1757): access to St Catherines, Creggans and the rubble quarries; a shed and hay for three cart-horses in winter, grazing for six in summer, and accommodation in the town for Deacon Brown and his men. A thousand feet of oak for the piles were bought for £25, or 6d a foot, from an English firm of iron smelters who since 1754 had held a concession on the Duke's Loch Fyne woods; and 360 feet of fir logs at 14d a foot 'for the framing of the piers' were supplied by John Richardson.[42]*

By July 1758 the piers of the Aray Bridge were built up to 14 feet which, considering they stood in tidal water, seems fair progress, aided by a spell of good weather. The road between bridge and new town skirted the Wintertown Park, and on the Duke's instructions the park boundaries were secured in the winter of 1758 by a sunk wall six feet high.[43] The wall still stands, but Deacon Brown's handsome bridge was swept away by an autumn flood in 1772, after a life of little more than a dozen years.

Another sizable bridge was also building in the late 1750s. The Duke had long considered a higher crossing of the Aray, from the site of the old castle gardens, to centre on the Oak Walk with the dovecot at the far end of its axis. The 'Vew to the Pidgeon house' had been widened in March 1756, and in the October he received an offer from another mason named Brown to execute a bridge of 60-foot span designed by himself, for the sum of £250 of which 'fiftie pound I alow . . . for ornaments'; he also proposed to build a 60-foot span bridge 'at the head of New intended deer park in the glen', for which the same centring would serve, for £170. This Thomas Brown is probably the same who built a bridge at Irvine between 1748 and 1753.[44]*

46. Inveraray bridges built in the 1750s, from *Vitruvius Scoticus*

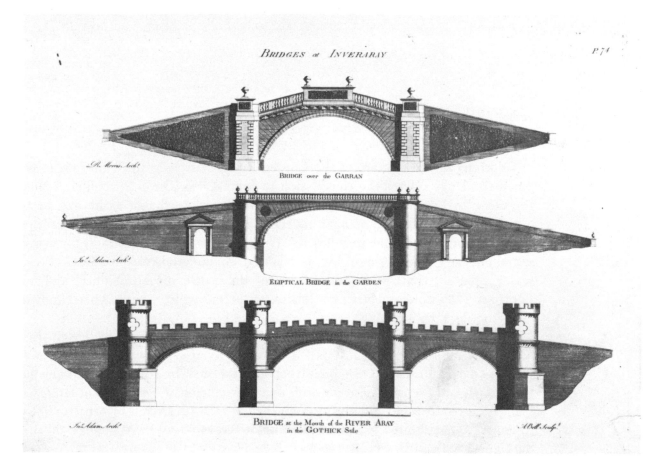

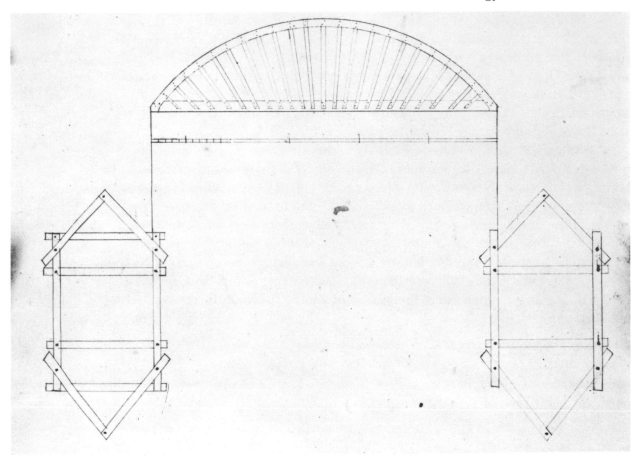

47. Centring for the 'Sea Bridge', 1757

Nothing further is heard of the Garden Bridge, however, until autumn 1758, when the Duke offered the commission to John Adam. On 1 November Adam, reporting to Lord Milton on his season's work, proposed that as he had been appointed for the bridge, he might at the same time conveniently embark on the intended churches for the new town.[45] The churches remained unbuilt for many years, but the Garden Bridge now materialized. An undertaker named David Frew was appointed, smith work and cutting of the centres began at once, and by February 1759 stone and other materials were preparing for what has been known ever since as Frew's Bridge.

For the centring, 'Most of the Timber came from the great Bridge on the Kings way', this being the third time it was used. Even so Haswell had an account of £20, £6 of it for nails. The stone, from St Catherines, by June 1760 had mostly been hewn and prepared, and the arch was 'more then half over'. A year later the bridge was to all intents and purposes finished, for the 4th Duke's first instructions in August 1761 desired that it be filled up at the ends and 'layd Smooth on the Surface with Small Gravel'.[46]

48. Proposed dairy at Tombreac
Designs of 1753, probably by John Adam.

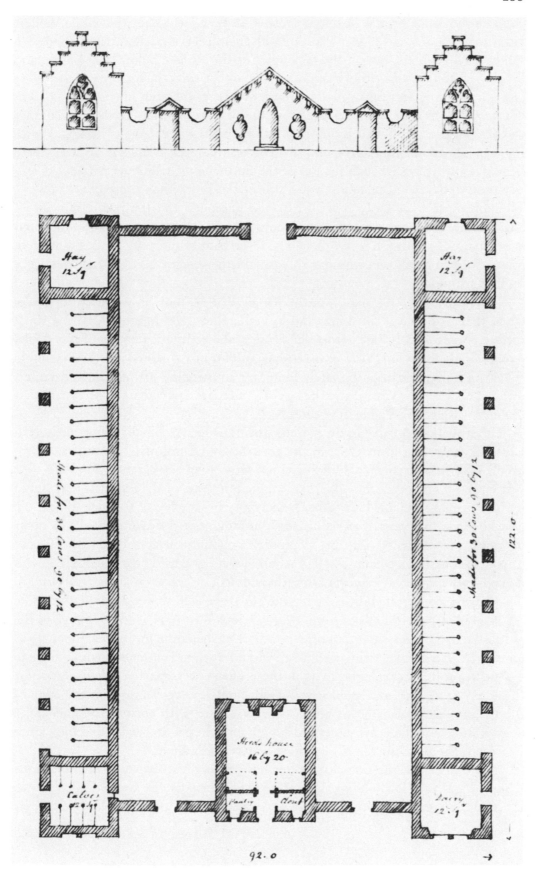

The design of Frew's Bridge is unusual in that it consists of a single shallow elliptical arch of some 60 feet span. In each spandrel is a circular panel filled with ashlar on level beds, but on the remainder of the surface below the cornice, and butting on to the semi-circular abutments on either side, the masonry is treated as gigantically long and thin voussoirs, radiating from the arch line at right angles. The parapets of the abutments and above the arch are level and open, with circular classical balusters : though John Adam shows that it was originally designed 'with Battlements and Embrassures, and the Towers upon the Peers and abuttments to be rais'd a little higher than the top of the Battlements, which would have a very airy pretty effect, and be more in the Stile of the Work than the Ballustrades'.[47*] The approaches are fairly steep, with solid parapets, and the retaining walls of heavy, almost cyclopean rubble. Each approach is pierced by a classical pedimented doorway giving through access along the river banks under the road. From these passages open small semi-circular rooms, and there is a tradition that they were built as privies.

John Brown, master mason of the King's Bridge, took on work for the Duke when that bridge was finishing, and in September 1760 began to build a small rubble two-arched bridge across the Shira a short distance above Maam. Duke Archibald died not long after it was begun, and for no explained reason this simple structure took a disproportionately long time to complete (it may have been left unfinished for a few years), and the last of a number of payments to Brown on that account was only settled in May 1768.[48]

Other works executed in the policies during Duke Archibald's time included a Gothick dairy, begun in 1752, in the park beyond Duniquaich known as Tombreck, where an ornamental building could serve as an eye-catcher. The dairy was substantially altered in the 5th Duke's time, but some of the alternative sketches by John Adam resemble his brother Robert's early sketches of Gothick follies; the underlying principle is of a small central building joined by screen walls to a pair of flanking pavilions.[49*] The 'pretty physick well in the meadow', another piece of ornamental Gothick over a so-called 'mineral well' in a field near the dovecot, was demolished about twenty years after it was built.

The last major item begun during the 5th Duke's lifetime was the stables. The old stables or court of offices, forming a spacious forecourt at the entrance to the old castle, had by the mid-1750s become a mere obstruction, for its west block stood on the site of a corner of the new fosse and underground casemates which were to extend from it. Accordingly, in 1758 these offices were partly pulled down (for the sum of £8), and new stables and coach-houses were planned on the edge of the Cherry Park, near the wrights' shed, as a court with corner pavilions and a central pend for the coach entry. Although any cherry orchards have long since vanished, the building has always been named after them.[50*]

The timber specifications for roofing and joisting 'the Offices to be built in the Cherry Park' and 'for Roofing the Stables to be erected at the Garden' were drawn up in December 1759, and quarriers were cutting the stone at St Catherines. By

[11] The Garden or Frew's Bridge, 1759–61

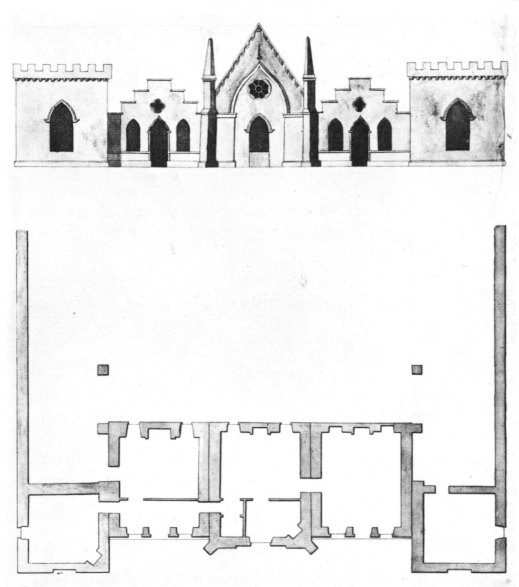

49. Tombreac Dairy in 1771
    From a water-colour by John Campbell.

April 1760 the walls had begun to rise, and in June Hunter reported that the elevation facing the castle had reached eight feet 'except that part of the wall where the Venetian Windows are plast which is owing to the want of proper Stones for that purpose and is not yeat Come to hand from St Catherins Quarry'.[51] In the year ending October 1760, £541 12s $0\frac{1}{4}$d was spent on its mason work alone. In August 1761, the window-sashes being finished, Haswell put in a request for the glass, '591 Peens in wholl which will take 10 Creats of Glass the materials for the Putty is all got'; but he was looking too far ahead, for John Adam's report in June had showed the building by no means complete. Parts of the walls were still unbuilt

[12] Detail of the Garden Bridge

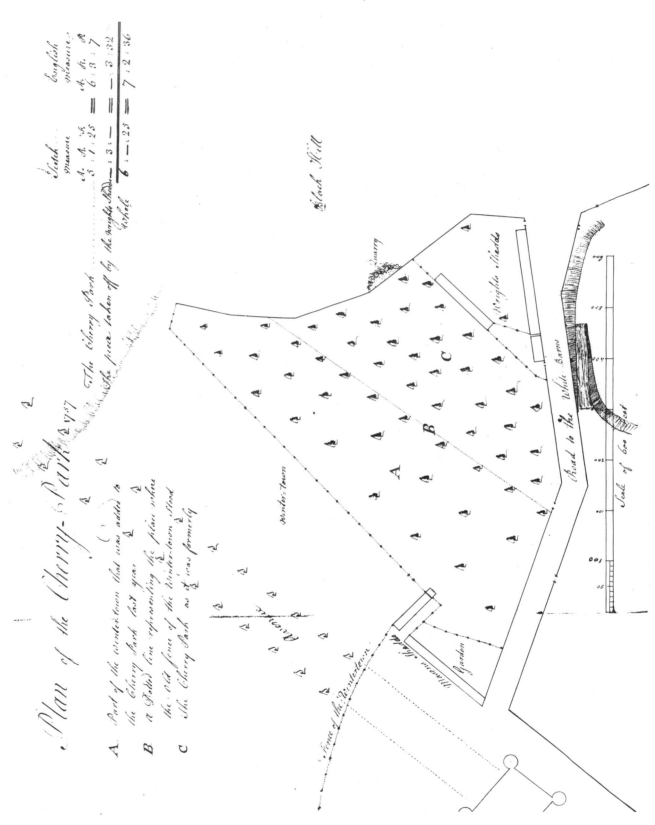

50. Inveraray Castle and Cherry Park, 1757
Plan by John Adam, showing the wrights' and masons' sheds.

[13] The Cherry Park court of offices, begun 1760

for lack of stone, and the roof was ready on only one side, with timber available for another.[52]

At the time when the Cherry Park offices were begun, further stables and coach-houses were started at the White Barns – now the Maltland – by the kitchen gardens. Although limited to lean-to buildings against the north side of Potter's great garden wall, here too work progressed only slowly. The foundations were laid in June 1760 to the instructions of John Adam, who in his report of 1761 noted that six stable-spaces were roofed and the piers of the coach-house built, but not the arches – again for lack of stone – and no fittings were ready.[53] Ten years later, when work was resumed, the buildings were substantially altered and added to by Robert Mylne.

The list of the Duke's building in the policies catalogues his later achievements as follows:

'The new Garden at the Barns and Garden walls surrounding it finished. – The fine Bridge in the low Garden called Mr Frews Bridge finished – and the water brought in lead Pipes from the fountain head west side of Dunequech alongst that Bridge to the Duke's House, and to the Cherry Park Court – the improvements in the Fisherland Park with sunk fences betwixt the plots carrying on, and Hedges planted, he caused raise a great number of exotics and had many of different kinds planted out on the Strone Hill, and through the Parks and enclosures every where in vacancies and Clumps of Trees in sundry places.

The enclosures of Dry Stone Dykes begun at Garran Bridge runs along the Strone Hill to Kilblane . . . and end at Douglass Water. . . .'[54]*

Bishop Pococke, writing in 1760, gives a fuller account. After describing the approach by the new military bridge with its 'circular piers', he continues,

'The D . . . designs to adorn an old bridge which is a little higher, and is building a third bridge above this. . . .

. . . The Duke is building the farm offices round a court some way off to the south-west, and designs the stable offices half a mile to the west to be built to the kitchen garden wall. To the north of that is a Gothick building on 4 arches over a mineral well of steel and sulphur, and this is near the hill on which the turret is built, round which there is a coach way up to the top, and from it the castle appears very grand. The D designs to make some additional buildings to it. To the west on an eminence is a building made to appear like a ruin, which is the dairy. All the ground to the west is finely planted, the Aray running through it. . . .

The old town which is to the east of the castle, is to be pulled down, and a new town built to the south of a little bay, where the townhouse and the Inn now are, between which there is to be a street to the south, and another will be built to the east of them along the Lough. . . .

There are large woods to the south, with ridings cut through them, and a Gothick arch is built over a well in one part of the wood where a spring of fine water runs out of the rock.'[55]*

[14] Another view of the Dovecot

Here the Duke of Argyle has built a stately Palace, on purpose to indicate what, in so advantageous a Situation, Posterity may do for enlarging and embellishing the Town, when Industry shall have improved the Country round about; and the Inhabitants, from its Produce and its Fishery, for which it is already very justly famous, have made it, what Nature seems to have designed it, the Centre of the Commerce of the Western Coast, and of the Isles.

Daniel Defoe *A Tour Thro' the Whole Island of Great Britain, by A Gentleman,* IV, London 1761, p. 211

IV

When Thomas Sandby was stationed at Inveraray with General Campbell's troops in 1746, he made a sketch of the town from the end of Gallows Foreland or Fisherland Point. Sandby's view of the old town clustered round its castle and Tolbooth also shows, well to the south, a scattering of thatched cottages, facing the bay which ends in the point whence he made his drawing. These cottages stood on the fringe of the site intended for Duke Archibald's new town.

The project of the 3rd Duke of Argyll in 1744 was to launch, in this out-of-the-way part of the west Highlands, a building plan of a kind never before known in Scotland, though he had witnessed such plans on a larger scale in London and Bath; and also a development of the linen and fishery industries, hitherto attempted without much success in Scotland by the 'Trustees for the Manufacturers'. Already, at Lord Milton's instigation, the Duke had subscribed £3000 and brought in other influential backers to establish the British Linen Company in Edinburgh, of which he was Governor and Lord Milton Deputy Governor.[1]* Although the design which he initiated at Inveraray was only completed long after his death, with his schemes for that and Campbeltown[2]* Duke Archibald became the father of the planned town in his native country. Neither his nor subsequent attempts to introduce industry to Inveraray met with more than temporary success, but his experiment in town planning, a generation earlier than similar creations elsewhere, remains as a testimony to the peculiar genius of the 3rd Duke of Argyll.

The great beech avenue at Inveraray, extending nearly a mile southward across the Fisherland Meadow, effectively cut off the flat headland from the rest of the castle parks; and this small area, though cramped, was from the Duke's point of view an ideal building site, as the windswept point was neatly out of the way and could not interfere with agricultural activities. The avenue itself was strictly private, and would form a barrier between the townspeople and the rest of the estate. Further, a town built on a headland offers scope for picturesque composition from a distance, and in this respect new Inveraray was advanced for its time; or rather, was happily placed in that its potentialities could be realized by a later generation.

The main axis of the site is obviously north and south, parallel to the beech

avenue, but the town plan went through several radical changes before finally
evolving a generation later in the form it is today. That the Duke and Lord Milton
originally recognized its natural orientation is seen in their 'First Draught New
Town of Inverary 1744'[3] which they sketched, with notes in their own handwriting, during their first visit. As an initial piece of planning – in some ways more
successful than subsequent designs of the Adams, father and son – this provisional
sketch repays study.

All round Inveraray the public ways were kept as close as possible to high-
water mark, a fact which was often to endanger property in the storms and flood-
tides of succeeding decades. The boundary wall of this appendix to the Fisherland
as shown on the plan roughly follows the shore line, allowing just enough width
for the public track leading south. The main 'Argyll Street' traverses the headland
parallel to the avenue or 'Mall'; this main axis is, indeed closer to the avenue (166
feet centre to centre) than the present street (235 feet centres), leaving room for a
second parallel, 'Kintyre Street', a cul-de-sac with a sketchily indicated kirk closing
its vista to the south. The site of the Tolbooth and Court House, the second major
public building, is presumably indicated by the word 'Provost' in the centre of
Kintyre Street, looking west down 'Lorn Street' which opens at right angles and
intersects with Argyll Street (approximately on the present church site) to make
a market place 120 feet square.

This new town, built on the Duke's own land, was sophisticated to the extent
of being planned, not left to haphazard growth; the initial draft further shows a
hint of zoning, in that industry and commerce are grouped – albeit in a scrappy,
unarchitectural fashion – in 'Cowall Street', proposed forerunner of the present
Front Street or northern terrace-façade. The space between Argyll Street and the
'Mall' (later dignified by the Court House and Chamberlain's House), the Duke
and Lord Milton allotted to 'Granarys', and west of the avenue (site of the Great
Inn) to 'Warehouses'. The 'Great Inn' itself is here banished to a small cul-de-sac
at right angles to the warehouses, its outlook confined to backyards of adjoining
'Brewery' and 'Tannery' in Cowall Street.

Beyond the tannery they assigned a site for Mrs Margaret Anderson, a cottage
stocking-manufacturer whom they hoped to entice to Inveraray, and alongside her
house they proposed an open space for a 'Bletchfield for thread & Stockings'. Mrs
Anderson had waited on the Duke at Rosneath at his first arrival, seen Lord Milton
in Edinburgh, and received an advance of £50 for looms. She set up her small
industry at Rosneath, but eventually her friends persuaded her against 'going out
of the world' so far as Inveraray, and that particular venture failed to be established.[4]

As Inveraray was also historically the seat of the courts, the bringing of the
road from the Lowlands thus had commercial and legal purposes as well as military.
In November 1744 Lord Milton, attending the levée of Duncan Forbes of Culloden, the Lord President, found Forbes 'most Gracious, in high raptures wt
the fame of yr Graces intentions of doing so much good in the Highlands'. The
President also expressed approval of the military road to Inveraray, observing

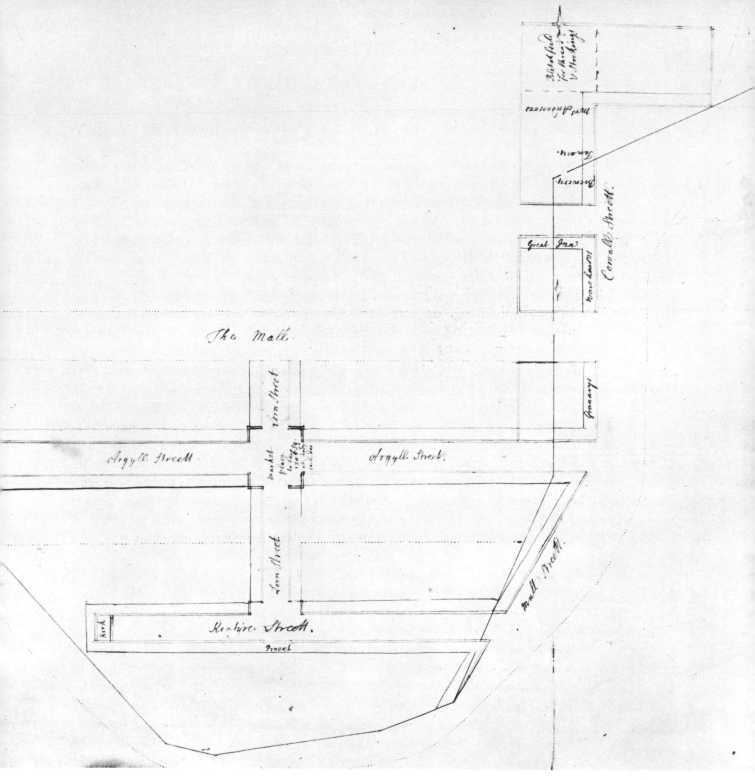

51. Inveraray New Town, first draft of 1744
Sketch as proposed by the 3rd Duke and Lord Milton, showing the grouping of industry on the north-west side and the church to the south-east by the shore of Loch Fyne.

'how much in the wrong some people were who endeavord to oppose the new
Road, a thing absolutely necessary & usefull both for the Crown & the Subjects'.[5]

During the Jacobite rising these projects lapsed, and when eventually the castle
foundation was laid and the military road resumed, plans for the new town were
still deferred. But the inhabitants of Inveraray were uneasy about their town's
future, and the more discerning – or more self-interested – applied for building
plots on the empty Fisherland site. One application had indeed been made by
James Campbell during the Duke's first visit in 1744;[6] but the next requests were,
by implication, for reward of services rendered during the Forty-Five. Thus the
first man actually to obtain a tack of ground and build himself a house in the new
town was John Richardson, a local merchant, who in 1746 served the Duke without
fee under Archibald Campbell of Ballamore, at Duart Castle in Mull, and later was
to become Provost of Inveraray.[7]* Richardson's tack was granted as early as 1748,
though his house was not finished – 'in a more expensive manner than at first
proposed' – until 1753, and in recognition of his enterprise his tack duty for the
first year was fixed at sixpence and he was exempted from 'all Cess Schoolmasters
Sallaries and other Publick Burdens'.[8]* The house has always remained free-
standing because of subsequent changes in the town-plan, and this and Richardson's second house (see p. 170) are the only ones in Inveraray with the feature,
elsewhere common in Scotland, of a circular turnpike stair. Another faithful political supporter, the wig-maker Baillie Peter Campbell, was rewarded with the post
of Riding Officer or Surveyor of the Customs at Inveraray and (at his own suggestion) a grant of ground at Dalchenna, two miles down Loch Fyne. By the Duke's
order in 1753 James Potter built two small houses here for Baillie Peter and
Provost Alexander Duncanson.[9]

Persuading others to move to the new town site proved less easy. In 1749 old
Provost Duncanson was asked by the Duke to exhort the inhabitants to make
building proposals, but he was met without enthusiasm.

> 'Some said they wanted to know what your G proposed to do with them. Others
> said they would build in the New Town if the houses they built in the Old
> Town were Comprised and full value was paid them. . . . Others again who
> have no houses and cannot built without wronging their Trade . . . propose to
> build if yr Grace let them have the loan of money at Three per Cent Intrest.'[10]

Duncanson himself showed a natural reluctance to remove from a house which 'he
& his Predicessors have had for these Two Hundred years bygone' unless compensated by money, equivalent ground, and materials from the old house for building the new. Thanks to the townspeople's not surprising caution, Inveraray's new
town got off to a slow start.

Meanwhile the castle masons and labourers had swelled its population, and
since there was no point in building further in the condemned old town, and
building in the new could not begin until a plan was determined, in 1749 a development of cottages or 'hutts', mostly built by James Potter, was started south of the

new site, on the road between the Fisherland park and the sea. At first referred to simply as 'the houses in the New Town', or 'the new houses in the Fisherland', they soon came to be known as the Gallowgate, corresponding with the Newton Row of the present day; indeed, a few smaller, older houses in the Newton survive from this period. Sixteen were eventually built, most of them divided into two, and housed employees of the Duke and townspeople removed there by his order. In October 1751, for example, the Duke instructed his Chamberlain that 'When the Two Houses now a building in the Gallowgate are finished, I desire that four of the Families now possessing the Houses next the East end of the Bridge [in the old town] may be removed thither and the old Houses pull'd down.' Later in the same instructions he adds : 'I have allowed James Gilmor Mason to possess one of the Houses in the Gallowgate rent free and that he be employed in building the new Houses there and the Wall which is to divide their Gardens from my Inclosures, and that the Wall be sufficiently built seven foot high.'[11]

Behind these new cottages ran the great avenue or 'Mall', on no account available to their occupiers; but the seven-foot extension to the avenue wall here spoken of appears not to have been built, for in 1760 the Chamberlain was warned 'To take care from time to time to see that no Windows be struck out in the Back of Houses in the new toun Unless agreeable to the directions formerly given Viz^t. where it can be done that they be reduced to Six Inches Breadth & when larger Windows are Absolutely necessary to be secured so that people cannot get through them.'[12] Thus until the end of his life the Duke continued the battle to exclude his tenantry from trespassing in the parks, grazing their animals there and stealing his timber.

If little was yet visible on the ground, plenty took place on paper, and two elaborate town plans were evolved by William Adam,[13] far removed from the Duke's and Lord Milton's first tentative draft. The main difference between these two Adam plans is that one is surrounded by a masonry sea-wall with pairs of semi-circular and polygonal bastions, and the form is of a square set within an (incomplete) octagon, an idea which seems to derive from military origins. The southernmost street, as comparison with the non-bastioned plan shows, is shortened to give the town a symmetrical frontage of five sides or part-sides of the octagon. It is interesting, too, to see that the idea of a circular church appears at this early stage, focal point – as is Mylne's later church – of the town but nearer the centre of the small promontory than Mylne's; it was sited in the 200-foot wide 'Great Square' on the axis of two main streets running east and south. The back (west) of the square was left open to the 'Mall' with a railing and gateway, giving an effect of a three-sided court opening on the avenue. In the centre of the square's north side is the Tolbooth, evidently raised over a piazza allowing access from the Great Square to the market place on the north – an arrangement similar in some ways to that of the Tolbooth at, for example, Peebles, or Montrose in its original form. A zigzag of side-lanes, concentric to the Great Square, threads between back gardens of

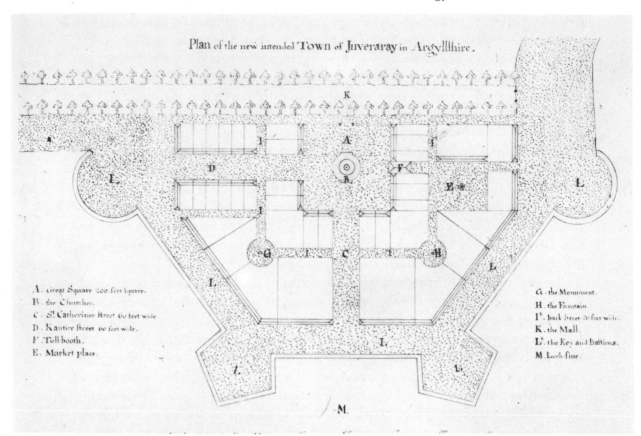

Plan of the new intended Town of Inveraray in Argyllshire.

A. Great Square 200 feet square.
B. the Churches.
C. St Catherines Street 60 feet wide
D. Kantire street 60 feet wide.
F. Toll booth.
E. Market place.

G. the Monument.
H. the Fountain.
Iˢ. back Street 30 feet wide.
K. the Mall.
Lˢ. the Key and Bastions.
M. Loch fine.

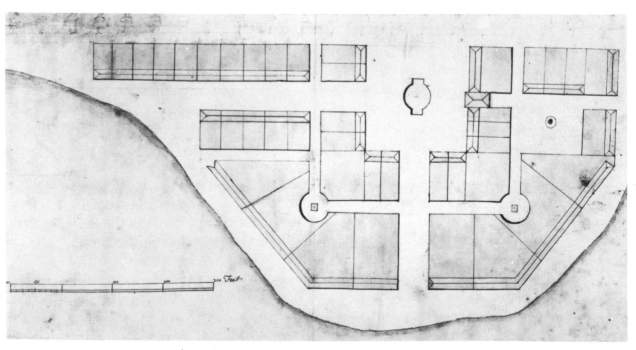

52. Proposals for Inveraray New Town, c. 1747
William Adam's plans, showing a central church and the main street
orientated east-west: (a) with bastions, (b) without bastions.

houses facing to the square and outwards to the loch. At their right-angled corners were small circular piazzas, one containing a monument, the other a fountain. Two other noteworthy features are the quantity of garden ground allowed for in the plan, and the width of the main streets, 50 feet (the present main street is 60 feet including the pavements). In execution this intricate layout would have appeared exotic, to say the least, for a small West Highland town, but it was a good deal more interesting than John Adam's revised drafts, dated 3 September 1750.

By contrast the 1750 designs (both drawn by John Adam, but one marked 'as propos'd by His Grace')[14] were very dull. Based this time on an incomplete hexagon, they simply ranged houses round the promontory. The chief difference between them is one of axis: the Duke's version has, like the William Adam plans, an east-west axis, leading to a circular church in the town centre, while in John's a dotted line indicates a street parallel to the avenue. Evidently the Duke had been influenced by William Adam's ideas into dropping the avenue axis; but the alignment of Richardson's house suggests that John's plan, not the Duke's, was adopted. However, the William Adam/ducal siting of the church was theoretically retained. The inn is now placed near its present position, though closer to the avenue; the clerk's house occupies the present Court House site. In John Adam's version the Court or Town House is shown flanked by private houses much as eventually built, though sited farther east.

A detailed plan on which each house-plot was numbered, or else identified by the tackman's initials, was later drawn up, apparently in 1758 – a year in which the town seemed about to make great advances; but this has unfortunately disappeared, and only plans and elevations by James Potter for a few individual houses (and those differing from houses actually built) survive.[15]* Meanwhile everybody appears to have worked from versions of John Adam's 1750 plan. In 1754 the turf was removed to mark the line of the streets,[16]* and by 1756 (when Richardson's house was complete and he was planning to build another north of the first), the tack granted to Alexander McPherson, merchant, the second private builder in the new town, shows that house bounded on the east by an 'intended street' parallel to the avenue, in fact on the line of Inveraray's Main Street today.[17] In October 1755 James Whyte, a house-wright, had been granted a 140-foot frontage to build three houses along this line, though presumably for financial reasons he never did so, and McPherson took over and built on the southernmost of the three plots. The tack's wording also shows that the plot marked the corner of the square intended for the church – at least 100 feet north of the present church site.[18]

By 1755, then, the town plans had been modified to incorporate part of two earlier layouts: the 'Great Inn' had been sited west of the avenue entrance, as in 1750, and the main street was parallel to the avenue, as in the 1744 draft and John's version. But the church was still visualized as central, and facing east.

1749 saw in the town – besides the sole tangible result of the first Gallowgate cottages – a succession of schemes for the inn, for a new Court House and Tolbooth, and industrial enterprise. The first two were connected with the Circuit Courts,

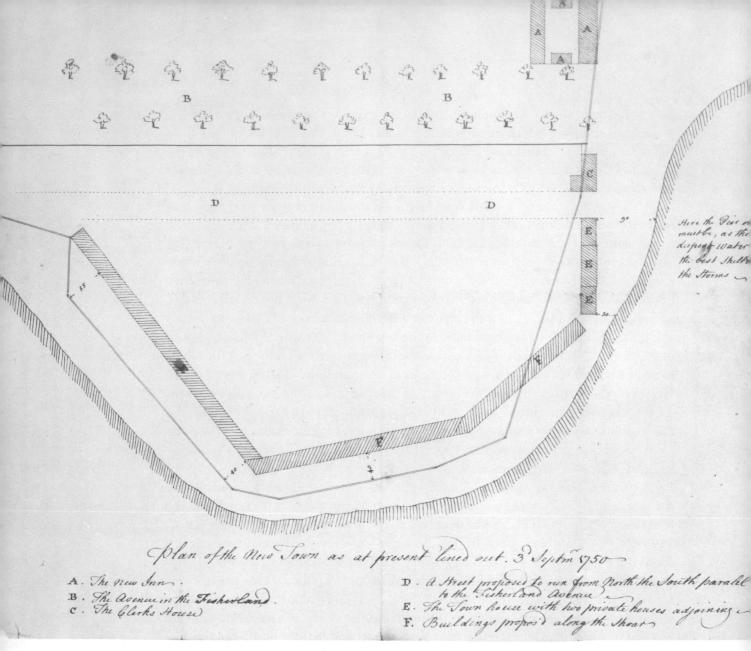

Plan of the New Town as at present lined out. 3ᵈ Septᵐ 1750

A. The new Inn.
B. The Avenue in the Fisherland.
C. The Clerks House

D. A Street proposed to run from North the South paralel to the Fisherland Avenue
E. The Town house with two private houses adjoining
F. Buildings propos'd along the Shoar

53. Proposals for Inveraray New Town, 1750
John Adam's plans of the town: (a) above, 'as at present lined out',
showing a north-south street axis, (b) opposite, 'as proposed by His
Grace'.

since with the abolition of Heritable Jurisdictions in 1748 the new order of judicial proceedings throughout Scotland meant a corresponding need for increased facilities for judges, lawyers and court officials. A new Court House and an inn were in any case long overdue. Stonefield, who under the new system was confirmed by Royal commission in his office of Sheriff Depute of Argyll and the Isles, had (he claimed) 'had it in his head' to rebuild Inveraray's Court and prison long before the abolition of the Argyll Jurisdiction, 'in acknowledgment of my Regard for the family, & the favours I had received off the shire'; and he had spoken of it to William Adam as early as spring 1743.[19]

This early attempt proved abortive because he gave Adam no precise dimensions; shortly afterwards the 2nd Duke died, and the resulting pressure of business occupied Stonefield until, as he put it, in summer 1745 'the world was turn'd upside down'. Now with the reversion of the jurisdictions to the Crown the situation was again changed, for the building replacing the semi-ruinous prison must be 'modelled in Terms of the late Act of Parliament' and, what is more, at the expense of the County, not the Duke. Further, its site must now be transferred to a still non-existent new town.[20]

Stonefield's interest in the building was not wholly public-spirited. Some years earlier he had been jointly responsible with his half-brother James for collecting the cess (an early form of rates) in Kintyre, and was accused with some justification of levying a 'superplus'. This excess sum had remained in his possession, and although he never ceased to minimize the extent of the 'superplus', or to justify himself, he was now prepared to end what he claimed to be misrepresentation by putting up some £400 for rebuilding Inveraray's Court House, and £200 for one at Campbeltown.[21]*

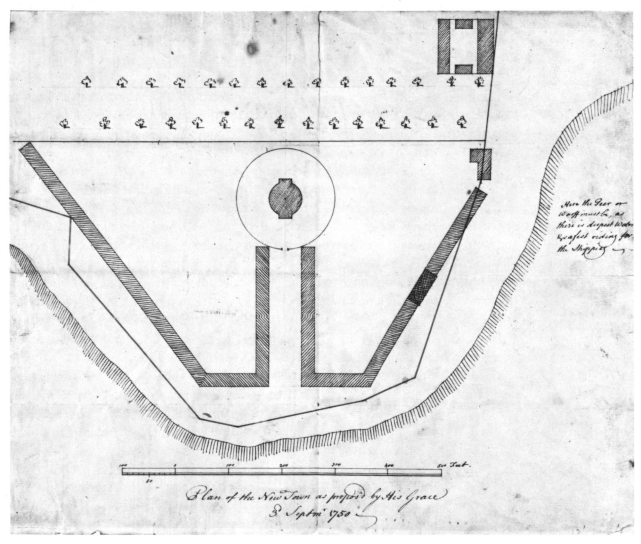

As for the need for a good inn, although old Inveraray had almost sixty 'Change houses . . . who do little if any thing els than to Retail liquors, cheifly spirits', it could provide little accommodation for travellers,[22] let alone the twice-yearly hordes of the legal profession attending the circuit courts. In 1750 John Adam produced plans for both a new Court House and 'a magnificent Inn', the latter to be paid for by the Duke, who also financed an inn beside Loch Long at what is now Arrochar, on land acquired from the Laird of McFarlane.[23] Certain unspecified revisions to the Inveraray inn plan were proposed by Harry Barclay of Colairny, who had a taste for amateur architecture. Early in 1751 the Duke received Barclay's revised plan in London and sat in judgment with his friends. Andrew Fletcher wrote to his father on 23 January: 'His Grace is pleased wt Mr Barclays alterations, as they seem to be very judicious, and well founded.'[24] The building contract for £1400 18s 3d was given to William Douglas, who was also building a new mill and roofing the Gallowgate cottages, and by April Douglas had laid a road from the Fisherland quarry to the inn site and was leading up materials.[25] In March 1752 he was sufficiently advanced in building to be specifying the timber required, including 80 23-foot logs for joists and 120 10-foot for sarking; the first order of 627 logs, totalling 6,625 feet, bought in Frederikstad by James Hay on behalf of Richard Tod of Leith, arrived at the end of August (see p. 114).[26]

William Douglas, however, quickly ran into trouble. For the past five years he had been supplying lime for the Duke's works and at Adam's advice had invested twenty guineas in building a draw-kiln near the Fisherland quarry, and four guineas in a lime-kiln at Carlundon; but in October 1752 he gave up his contract to James Potter, complaining of his heavy expenses and the rising price of coals (due to the closing of several mines on Clydeside) and limestone freightage, and of shortage of labour because of increasing competition from the many other works about Inveraray.[27] Douglas was dissatisfied, too, with progress on the inn, especially the delay in bringing up materials. In February 1753, in Edinburgh, he complained to Lord Milton, who proposed doubling the number of quarriers, with a commonsense division of carts so that the small carts carried sand and lime from the shore, leaving the larger to bring up stones for the castle and inn.[28] Organization methods which may seem elementary by today's standards took years to establish at Inveraray, whose building from beginning to end was by *ad hoc* methods, with no reserve of local experience or precedent on which to draw.

Even with these suggested improvements the inn showed little advance, and a year later Baillie Peter Campbell, returning to Inveraray after an absence, 'made it his Business . . . to know what has been a Doing about the Works', and reported to Lord Milton (28 February 1754) that as Douglas was again away in Edinburgh and Knockbuy also absent,

'things go very Sloly on, as there is only four Joiners Employed at present, And [the writer] has been well Assured, that they have not Timber for the Windows as yet, And in observing the Mason Work finds that there is Nine of the Lintles of the Doors & Windows quite broke through, and what is more Surprising

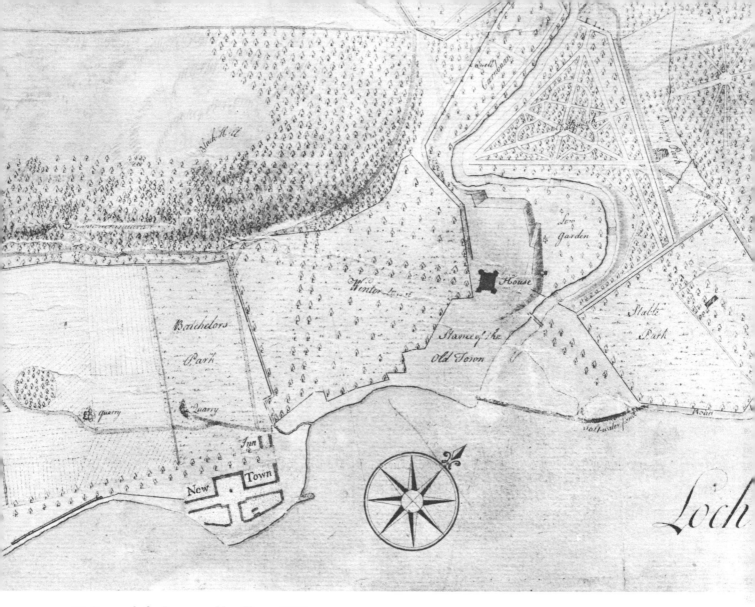

54. Proposals for Inveraray New Town, 1756
   Detail from Daniel Paterson's plan (figure 32). Richardson's house
   is marked on the line of the town's east front.

there is no Safe Lintle for a Suport in the whole House; And if this gross Error
is not soon helped the wall cannot stand, as by the Like fault a good Dale of the
Inner wall fell Last year which he was obliged to rebuild Archways. . . . Such a
gross Mistake in Such a Building Cannot Miss to be observed by Strangers
when Viewing it.'[29]

Whatever Lord Milton's reply to this indictment, an improvement followed in
speed if not in quality. In September, 15,000 of the 218,000 slates commissioned
from Carwhin were assigned to the inn; in October, when the latest timber cargo
was unloading, Douglas requested 'for ffinishing the Inn about Six tons of Timber
. . . the Loggs twixt 12 to 20 foot'.[30] The building's completion was now urgent
since the Duke, anxious to introduce some superior competition to the old town's
many change-houses, engaged an inn-keeper, John Hawkesley – possibly an
Englishman, 'whose skill and obliging Behaviour, in his way, had recommended

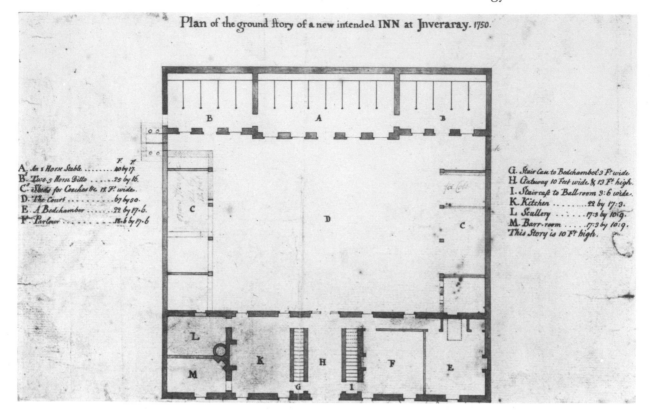

Plan of the ground ftory of a new intended INN at Jnveraray. 1750.

A. An s Horse Stable .... 40 by 17.
B. Two 5 Horse Ditto ..... 25 by 16.
C. Sheds for Coaches &c. 12 Ft. wide.
D. The Court .... 67 by 50.
E. A Bedchamber .... 22 by 17:6.
F. Parlour .... 18:6 by 17:6

G. Stair Cafe to Bedchamber 3 Ft wide
H. Gateway 10 Feet wide & 13 Ft. high.
I. Staircafe to Ball-room 3:6 wide.
K. Kitchen .... 22 by 17:3.
L. Scullery ...... 17:3 by 10:9.
M. Barr-room ..... 17:3 by 10:9.
This Story is 10 Ft high.

55. The Great Inn at Inveraray
     John Adam's plan of 1750.

him'[31] – to come to Inveraray the following March (1755). Douglas was ordered
'That the Ten Chimneys in the ordinary size of Rooms . . . be done up with
Ribbs let into Stone Jambs according to a Sketch to be given to you by George
Hunter and also the Dining Room with the three principal Bed Chambers . . .
all finished before Mr Haxlay's arrival at Inveraray . . . and particularly to have
the Kitchen and the Rooms in the Lower Story first Finished.'
George Haswell, engaged for the wright work of the chimney-pieces, proposed to
Lord Milton in December that six of these 'should be good in the best Rooms',
while in the ten 'ordinary' rooms stone grates would serve.[32]

    The pressure put on Douglas may have been detrimental to his work, for
although the inn (still unfinished) was able to open its doors for the great celebra-
tion party after laying the Town House foundation stone, six months afterwards
the cellars and inn-yard, undrained, unpaved and unprotected, were flooding; the
well and brewhouse pump were out of order, and for lack of water-spouts rain lay
on the roofs and seeped under the slates, and through other weak spots. On 9
October, John Adam carried out a detailed inspection and drew up a formidable
list of remedial works. Some of these appear to have been done next year by George
Hunter,[33] not Douglas; but the inn was still reported so un-weatherproof that for
the spring circuit in 1756 the Duke arranged for the judges to lodge at his own

house. 'They say the Inn is in a terrible condition', he wrote to Lord Milton on 1 April, 'by the Rain driving through the walls. The Whim I think was never dry till it was cast on the out side, & lath'd & plaistered within.'[34] But while Douglas was not to blame for the weather, he had certainly been lax: 'The Road betwixt the new Inn and the foot of the Town is not as yet begun,' reported the indefatigable Baillie Peter on 14 February, 'notwithstanding of my frequent applications to Mr Douglass agreeable to your Lordsh's orders to me at parting.'[35]

There were, of course, extras to Douglas's estimate – a well in the court, a necessary house, fifteen additional stone chimneys, partitions in the attic storey, and so on. They amounted to £136 7s 5½d, but £50 was withheld from Douglas until the building was deemed water-tight and Adam's list of 'Reparations' had been carried out.[36]

Much of the inn's furniture was made on the spot by George Haswell, and when Hawkesley and his family moved in Asknish noted that 'there is six doz. Chairs half a doz. Tables and some Bed Steads quite ready'. The old castle's kitchen grate was installed there, and an Edinburgh smith, William Richardson, supplied £6 15s 0d worth of fenders, pokers and tongs. By October 1756 the Duke had provided four 'posted bedsteads', six press beds, two box beds, 4½ dozen leather-bottomed and 9½ dozen timber-bottomed chairs, five chests of drawers, six square folding tables and eighteen small tables, four joint-stools, two presses, two kitchen dressers and fifteen fenders.[37] Whatever the deficiencies of the building, Hawkesley's catering at once filled a great demand, and less than two months after the inn opened Mr Henry Kendall, director of the Loch Fyne smelting company, wrote ingratiatingly to Lord Milton,

> 'I know your Lordship will be pleased to hear that at Inveraray there is as good and as cheap accomodation for Travelers as any where in Britain, and I think it would be great injustice to Mr Hawkesley & not less ingratitude to His Grace for any man who knew Inverary before not to make due acknowledgments now.'[38]

Hawkesley was, strictly speaking, a concessionaire, and until 1761 (when the annual rent was reduced to £30) paid the Duke £360 a year for the privilege of running the inn and entertaining the judges.[39]*

John Adam's great inn at Inveraray is extremely simple in design and remarkable chiefly for its size, having nine window-bays facing the loch, and three main storeys with cellars and, originally, servants' attics. As designed, it had a central pend leading through to the stable court, but this common eighteenth-century feature has, as in so many other cases, been built up to form a hall. Since its opening both hotel and stables have had numerous alterations and some additions, but the street front, apart from the Victorian glass vestibule and the unfortunate removal of the astragals, is practically as William Douglas left it.

The Inveraray inn first received the public on the day when the foundation was laid of the second chief building in Duke Archibald's new town, the Court House.

For this building, also, John Adam produced his plan in 1750, probably immediately after designing the inn, and it was discussed during the Duke's autumn
visit. Stonefield, smarting over the amount he had had to settle on his son for the
marriage with Lady Grace Stuart, was beginning to regret his offer to finance the
Tolbooth. The Duke had proposed a payment of £600 spread over six years, but
now that the building seemed likely to materialize Stonefield began to prevaricate,
and wrote nervously to Lord Milton : 'If the work goes any higher, I think the
Shire shou'd bear the Expense . . . Had I taken the Advice of my Lawiers, before I
made the offer, I shou'd not have gon so high, but I was over anxious to stem the
Torrent of the invidious Clamour then made.'[40]

For whatever reason, four more years passed before the new Tolbooth was put
out to contract. Although by 1753 nearly 600 men were working for the Duke
about Inveraray, few were concerned with his new town except for William Douglas's halting progress on the inn, Richardson's house, and a weaver's house and
other cottages in the Gallowgate. Yet the town's need for a new tolbooth was
shown to be acute in September 1752 when the old building proved too small for
the hundreds of people attending the Appin murder trial, which had to be held in
the church.

Either Stonefield or the magistrates demurred at the cost of the new building;
and the burgh council, although since 1750 their income had been increased by
the Duke's annuity of £20 in compensation for annexing their town muir, and by
harbour dues from the many cargoes now unloading, were further embarrassed at
the prospect of financing a new town quay. However, beyond the quarrying of a
few stones in 1755, the latter scheme made no progress either.[41]*

In May 1754 Stonefield again brought before the Commissioners of Supply the
question of a modern Town House and gaol, representing 'the Great Inconven-
iency The Shire lys under' for lack of it; reasserting his gratitude for the county's
employment of himself and his late brother as collectors of cess, he reminded them
of his offer. The Commissioners at their next meeting diplomatically exonerated
the brothers from any charge of extortion, and accepted Stonefield's bond for the
money.[42] The Duke's final approval of the design was sought, and that summer
foundations were dug on the site John Adam had fixed four years earlier, east of
the avenue and in line with the inn, for a group of buildings comprising a Tolbooth,
prison and two flanking houses.

The undertaker for this group was George Hunter, whose estimate of
£630 17s 2d for Town House alone (the two private houses were paid for by the
Duke) was confirmed by a contract dated 25 October 1754 with Donald Campbell
of Airds, a Commissioner of Supply and co-trustee for the building – witnessed by
the Duke, Lord Milton and Asknish.[43]

Building was to start in 1755, and meanwhile Hunter had the timber sawn and
seasoned, stone was ordered from St Catherines, and of the vast stack of Easdale
slates lying in the Fisherland 11,000 were allotted to the Town House and 8,000
for each wing. Hunter also asked for two Gallowgate houses for his masons, and

56. Inveraray Town House and the two adjoining houses
John Adam's plans, c.1755.

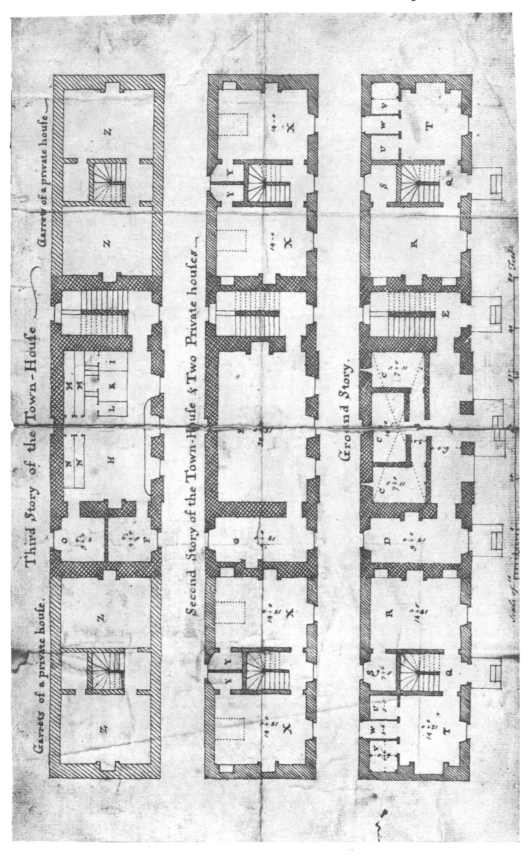

(not least important) for coal, 'as I am obledged to find them in fireing for Makeing Ready there Vitalls'.[44] John Campbell, chamberlain, wrote to Lord Milton in February:

> 'Tho' the works about this place were far from standing still during the winter, yet they are now pushed on with vigour every where – Mr Bathgate is very busy upon the Fisherland-Moss – Mr Douglas in finishing the New Inn, Mr Hunter preparing for the Town:house, the foundation-stone whereof is to be laid to morrow – Mr Paterson has several parties at work, making the new road at the back of the Winter:town, the serpentine course for the water thro' the Meadow, Salt water pond &c And the wrights are mostly employed making Tables, Chairs & beds for the Inn.'[45]

This rosy picture of humming industry proved not wholly accurate, for a remarkable eye-witness account published a few weeks later in the *Glasgow Courant* shows that the foundation-stone ceremony was deferred until 26 March. At the author's identity of this uniquely documented episode in Inveraray's building history we can no more than guess, but his tale is well worth reading.

> 'Inveraray, March 27
>
> As you desire to know when anything new occurs here, I am glad it is in my Power to gratify you by what follows, which I believe you will consider in that Light. It is a procession I was an eye-witness to yesterday, at laying the South-East Corner Stone of our Town House, the Plan of which is allowed to be done in fine taste.
>
> The Free Masons were warned to conveen by ringing the bells between 11 and 12 o'clock in the forenoon. Those of the Town Lodge of Inverary, Kilwinning, being 90 in number, at Mrs St Clair's, near the Cross, and the Operative Brethern in the Duke of Argyll's new castle; these last were 150 in number, and members of 37 different Lodges, each distinguished by its proper Livery, and precisely at 12 they began to march from the Castle in the following Order:
>
> Musick
> 3 Stewards with white Rods
> Foremen of the Masons
> Entered 'Prentices and Fellows of Craft, according to their
> Seniority, in Ranks of 3 each at proper distances
> Musick
> 2 Master Masons, Overseers of Out Work
> Mr Hunter, Overseer and Director of the Duke of Argyll's
> Buildings, and Undertaker for the Town House
> 3 Stewards with white Rods
>
> At the Cross they were received by the Members of the Town Lodge, with the Magistrates, Ministers, and Town Council, drawn up in two lines, at one end of which stood Masters and Wardens, and at the other the Duke of Argyll's and Town's Colours. The Operative Brethern passing between the Lines, were properly saluted by the Officers of the Lodge and Standard Bearers, and in their

rear, the Town Lodge marched in this order:

Musick

3 Stewards with white Rods

2 Pair of Colours

Entered 'Prentices, Fellows, &c. in Ranks of 3 each at a
suitable distance

Musick

Treasurer of the Lodge carrying the Purse in a cover of
Crimson Velvet, with the Keys of the Strong Box

Secretary ⎤
Wardens ⎬ with their Jewels
Master   ⎦

3 Wardens with white Rods

2 Operative Masons with Tools

Town Officers and Halberts

Magistrates, Ministers, and Town-Council

9 Operative Masons with white Rods,
to keep off the Crowd

The whole being marched (with the utmost Regularity) in this Manner, to the
Foundation, the Master of the Town Lodge, with the accustomed Ceremonies,
laid the Corner Stone, upon which was this Inscription:

VII. Cal. Ap. A.D. MDCCLV

'Positum et Justitiae Publicae Dedicatum'.

After a short Prayer by the Master, and a Speech addressed to the Magistrates,
Undertakers, and operative Masons, all suited to the occasion, a Glass went
round, and with PROSPERITY to the NEWTOWN and TOWN-HOUSE of
INVERARY, followed by three Huzzas from a multitude of joyful Spectators.
The rest of the Liquor was left with the operative Bretheren at the Foundation,
who afterwards returned in the same Order in which they had first marched.
But the Ministers, Town-Council, and other Gentlemen present, together with
Mr Hunter and the other Overseers, by invitation from the Magistrates, accompanied them to the New Inn, which was then opened for the first time; and
which in point of Elegance and Variety of Accommodation, is not exceeded by
any Thing of this Kind in North Britain.

Here we all sat down at one Table, by 3 o'clock, to the Number of 50, to an
elegant and plentiful Entertainment prepared for us by the Innkeeper, Mr
Hawkesly, whose skill and obliging Behaviour, in his way, had recommended
him to the Duke of Argyll, who at a great Expense encouraged him to come and
live among us.

After dinner, Bumpers were drank to the health of the KING, Prince of
Wales, Princess Dowager of Wales, Prince Edward, and the rest of the Royal
Family, the Duke and the Army, the Admiralty and Fleet, Prosperity to Great
Britain, Prosperity to all true Friends of our present happy Establishment,

M

good news from Virginia, the Duke of Argyll, &c., &c., &c. – with variety of other toasts expressive of the warmest Affection for our invaluable Constitution, and of the sincerest and most dutiful Gratitude and Attachment to the best of Princes.

I know not what you may think of all this Detail of public Edifices, Free Masons, Entertainments, and Mirth, etc. – for my own Part, as some years ago I did not hope to see such a Day at Inverary, I was once and again tempted to think there was some Magick in the case, but on second thought found it to be that sort of Entertainment only which is the Effect of a Free and happy Government, conducted by an excellent KING, and of the Bounty of a generous and discerning PATRON, possesst of a great Estate, pursuing with unwearied Constancy every Measure that tends to beautify and improve his Native Country. Yours, &c., &c. –'46*

Once this colourful conviviality was over, Hunter ran into troubles very like those of his fellow-mason Douglas. During those same rain-storms that were now revealing the new inn's weak points, the Court House timber, sawn and stacked out of doors, deteriorated, and the carpenters had no work-place under cover. Unable to get the wood made up, Hunter asked Lord Milton for use of a room in the new castle. But for lack of carts to bring up materials work went on 'But Sloly', and likelihood of finishing the building by the contract date (May 1756) receded. 'I do not Blame Mr Bathgete for it,' Hunter assured Lord Milton, 'as he Dos all in his Powre to keep all the Deferent works going one and the Town House in particular . . .'47 George Hunter was one of Bathgate's few allies at Inveraray, and before long became his father-in-law.

As usual, there were extras to the building contract. The main joinery was done by Haswell, but all the front windows were made by the Duke's new wright John Paterson and the glazier James Veitch, at an additional cost of £37 16s 10½d for the Tolbooth (13 windows), and £37 0s 6d for the adjoining houses (12). Both men, as skilled artisans brought seasonally from the Lowlands, had their expenses paid by the Duke. On his own contract Hunter incurred an extra £11 19s for mason work on the piazza and front stair, £14 17s 3d for the inner stair, and £12 11s 0d for plasterwork and cornices. Because Hunter had made insufficient allowance for the site slope, the eastern house proved to require deeper foundations than the western, and its total cost was £363 12s 8d against £342 – 'a considerable expense . . . which did not occur at making the estimate'. So it went on.

Not surprisingly, the buildings were not complete until Whitsun 1757, a year after the due date, although Hunter had long ago been paid the contract fee both by the Duke and the County. He now presented the Commissioners with an account of £77 18s 11¾d for the extras.48

The Commissioners and magistrates objected strongly, pointing out that – like Douglas with the inn – Hunter had failed to make the building watertight, that in his original estimate 'some things very material were entirely omitted' (including

[15] The old Town House at Inveraray, 1755–7,
showing Gillies' house at the far left

the piling of the foundation), that other tradesmen found the original sum 'fully adequate to the undertaking', and finally that they had already punctually paid him, whereas he on his side had finished the job a year late. Hunter submitted a protest, and appeared before the Commissioners. A majority rejected his petition. He then appealed to John Adam, who had earlier attested his account with the Duke; Adam pointed out to Lord Milton that 'the Gentlemen of the County' were divided over the case's merits, and that for Hunter £70-odd was 'a very great Sum ... & must go hard with him if he is cut off'. The Duke was inclined on the whole to support the Commissioners and ordered Hunter to make the Town House roof watertight, but foreseeing further trouble he warned the Commissioners to 'take care that no insinuation be made that any part of the load should be laid upon the Sherif'.[49]

For yet more expenses now followed. Having engaged a young mathematics teacher in Glasgow, Robert Dobson, for Inveraray, the Duke had earmarked the new western house or 'pavilion' for the master, with use of an upper room in the Town House for a temporary school. But Dobson, who arrived at Whitsun 1758 bringing some boarding pupils with him, did not think much of his accommodation. He complained particularly that the schoolroom (probably an attic with skylights) was too dark, indeed 'so ill lighted that its thought necessary there be two windows Struck out in the South Side'. He also demanded garden ground for a byre and 'little house'—reasonable requests but 'very inconvenient' for the magistrates, and slow to be granted. Before long he was such a popular teacher that he found the schoolroom too small altogether and asked for another.[50*]

Meanwhile, prompted by Adam, Lord Milton had persuaded the Commissioners to relent and pay Hunter's claim, although (Hunter remarked) 'if Stonefield had Got his will I had never toched a farthing of it'. Only Asknish and one other Commissioner had defended his right to the money, for Stonefield's hostility influenced the rest, including the Sheriff Depute John Campbell (now of Clochombie), who after promising to stand by Hunter 'Neaver opened his Mouth, but I expected no feavour from him as it is well known in this place that he is at the Sheriefs Devoition'.[51] Hunter had particular need of that money now, for Robert Bathgate had barely been married to his daughter long enough to father two children on her before he died, and Hunter had to take the bereaved family into his own household.

But although the Duke, Lord Milton and John Adam were still willing to employ Hunter, and Adam secured him as undertaker for his next intended building, the church; and although Hunter could scarcely be blamed for the Tolbooth's unsuitability as a schoolroom, Stonefield and through him the other Commissioners were now his declared enemies. They were affronted to find yet another essential omitted from Hunter's contract – ironwork for the prison doors and windows, for which a fresh sum had to be voted to Henry Roy.[52]

So that when Hunter, who had been trying not very successfully to buy timber from Glasgow for the schoolroom windows (now increased to three), was next

[16] Front Street, Inveraray

57. Inveraray Town House
    Alternative elevations by John Adam.

called to a meeting of the Commissioners in June 1759, it was to hear Stonefield announce that they had obtained other estimates and were engaging a new mason. In vain Hunter argued that he had been employed at the Duke's desire, and that he had the Chamberlain's order for the new windows : 'They would have nothing to do with me.' Letting Stonefield do the dirty work, the gentlemen of the county sat 'al Silent' while the Sheriff told Hunter that he was no longer employed.[53]

Hunter imputed Stonefield's hostility to jealousy at his recommendation to the Duke by Lord Milton. Airds, when he challenged him on the subject, was lamely evasive; but as Hunter observed to Lord Milton when reporting his dismissal, 'Your Lordship will see . . . that Stonefield has Explain'd that matter himself.' The Commissioners remained dissatisfied with the Tolbooth, and as late as April 1761 were complaining that it had never been harled, its windows were in disrepair, and the debtors' room and criminal cells were 'insufficient'.[54]*

This building over which such political and financial battles raged has a very pleasing exterior, three storeys high (balancing the inn) with a Palladian touch in its slightly projecting central feature with three rusticated ground-floor arches, at that time forming an open piazza leading to the prison. It has a simple pediment adorned only by a recessed roundel; an alternative version which John Adam designed shows a plain slated roof between skews running up to the inner chimney stacks, which would have more monotonously repeated the style of the inn. The two flanking houses are much lower, but the composition is drawn together by a dressed stone band at first-floor sill level, finishing the rustication above the central arches. The two house porches, both later additions, are good in scale, and appear more or less essential to the composition.[55]*

Little of the interior of the Court House remains in its original arrangement. The vaulted cells on the ground floor have long been swept away, and on the removal of the court and prisons early the next century the loggia was unfortunately filled in and converted into a Town Clerk's office. The large Court room above, now used for Town Council meetings, is featureless, and the top floor, once Dobson's schoolroom, is now a flat.

While the arguments over Town House and school were at their height John Adam had been quietly arranging with Lord Milton to undertake the building of his own church. When Adam first designed this curious building is not known, but on 1 November 1758 he offered to supervise it along with the building of the Garden Bridge: 'I would imploy George Hunter as foreman, but as the Church is a matter of considerable moment, & in several parts will need a good deal of attention in the execution, I should willingly contribute all in my power to its being done to purpose.' By the 13th he had produced a detailed estimate 'for Building a Circlear Church in the New Town of Inveraray', for a cost of £2,958 0s 9d, excluding pulpit and seats, the bulk of this expense being for the mason-work; the undertaker as usual was to provide materials and the Duke carriage and scaffolding timber, with use of masons' sheds and lodgings.[56]

Adam's application for the contract followed a rumour that James Ewing from Greenock, the Duke's Rosneath mason, had already applied,[57]* and Adam probably fancied that if the contract were withheld from Hunter, he could get round this by asking for it himself and giving Hunter a good share of the work.

When Adam produced his design the Duke certainly envisaged carrying it out, and a small quantity of stone was quarried both from the rubblestone and St Catherines quarries, the latter ($150\frac{1}{2}$ cubic feet) amounting to three boat-loads. But between them Adam and Hunter had forced the pace, and in January 1759 Hunter suggested diverting the St Catherines stone 'laid Doun for Building the New Church' for use at the castle – where a hiatus in delivery was feared because (Adam reported in February) Potter had 'failed a good deal in his Circumstances' and could no longer pay his quarriers.[58] This suggested diversion implies that there was then no serious intention to build Adam's church; and by the following season the idea seems to have sunk without trace. Adam made a further set of drawings, with alternatives of rectangular or turnpike stairs to the gallery, in 1760, but in any case the Duke's death the following spring prevented any hopes he still cherished of the building's execution; so that the plans, elevations and detailed estimates seem to have remained little more than a darling project – unfortunately, for it could have been a most interesting building.

As the early town plans show, John Adam evidently took over the idea of a circular church from his father, and William Adam himself appears to have derived the curious design from his own Hamilton church, built twenty-six years before John produced his drawings (1732).

But whereas Hamilton was internally a centrally planned church, John Adam had to adopt the traditional Inveraray pattern of containing both a Gaelic and

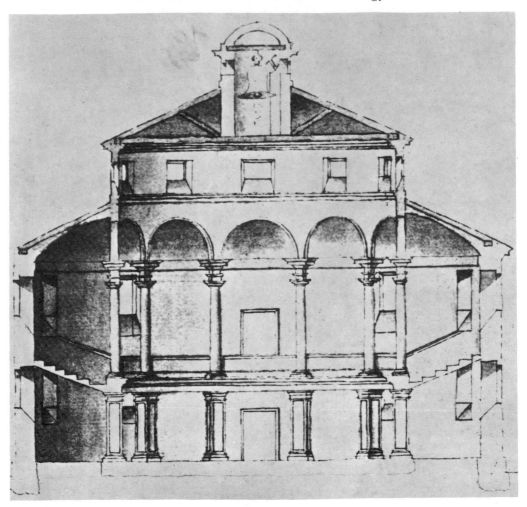

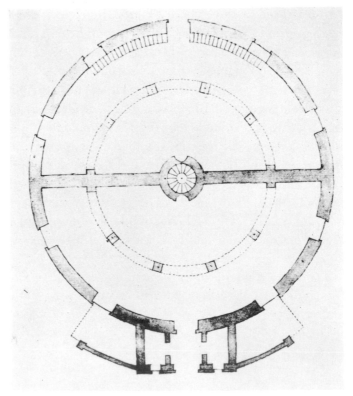

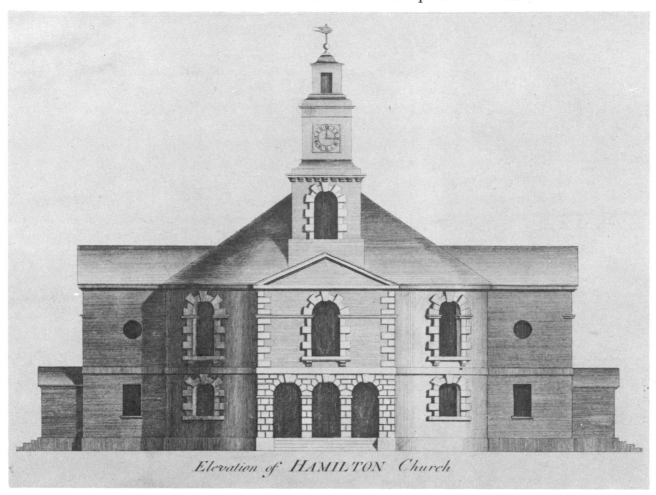

Elevation of HAMILTON Church

59. Hamilton Parish Church, from *Vitruvius Scoticus*
   Elevation by William Adam, 1732, from which John Adam's
   unexecuted design for Inveraray church was derived.

Lowland church under one roof. Hence his interior is of two semi-circular churches – a perfectly sound and reasonable plan for the Presbyterian usage of the time, involving merely a central pulpit in an auditorium with a tiered gallery round the circumference. This gallery Adam planned to be supported by square panelled piers with simple Roman Doric caps and bases. Above these are shown Doric columns carrying arches, and a clerestory with rather squat square-headed openings. The lower part of the exterior has two storeys of near-square windows, a lean-to roof to the central clerestory rotunda, and above, a small domed structure with a large bell hanging within. From the central axis of the Lowland church projected a pedimented porch with a circular window above a large rusticated doorway; this is flanked by a pair of sweeping stone balustraded staircases leading to the ducal and magistrates' seats in the loft. By contrast the Hamilton church has four projections, so that its external plan resembled the outline of a disc-headed

58. Proposed circular church at Inveraray, *c.*1758
   Section and ground plan by John Adam.

Celtic cross, and there the main porch facing the town is surmounted by a steeple rising above three rusticated arches, remarkably like John's arches at Inveraray Court House.[59]

New manses materialized no more than did the kirk, beyond putting aside some wrought stone, and by the 1760s the two ministers had ended up in 'temporary' accommodation, one of them (the Reverend Peter Campbell) in the Gallowgate.[60] The new town's harbour, however, was at last built to Adam's design after being discussed and abortively budgeted for in 1754. 'We began the building our new Harbour about ten days ago', writes John Richardson to Lord Milton on 29 May 1759 – not a gratuitous piece of information, but a heavy hint that the Duke, having helped them so far, should supply them with not only a cart for leading the stones, but a horse for leading the cart. Between 1758 and 1760 the Duke allowed £30 annually towards the work, and in 1761 his successor the 4th Duke gave a further £30.[61]

This modest jetty, only 100 feet in length, designed by John Adam for a fee of ten-and-sixpence, was built in a leisurely fashion by James Potter. It was still unfinished when the Duke died, raised in height in 1765, and by 1771 was found to be ruinous owing to 'the repeated violent storms of last harvest'. The shabby thatched cottages, which had stood for a generation or so before the new inn and Court House sites, had been demolished over the winter of 1756 so that by the time of the spring circuit in 1757 they were removed. By the Duke's order the stones were given to the magistrates to be used in the new quay.[62]

One result of designing and siting the church had been that the line of the town street, parallel with the avenue, had been fixed, and in 1756 Adam produced the only surviving elevation of its appearance as projected. Plans and elevations of single houses were being drawn at about the same time, none of them executed as designed; but had the 1756 street-scheme materialized Inveraray would have con-sisted, not very happily, either of a row of four identical detached houses or (for the two elevations were presumably meant as alternatives) of three pairs of semi-detached, all of them with single-storey lean-to outbuildings at the side terminating in pillars with stone balls. These would presumably have formed decorative entries to the backs.[63] It is not difficult to imagine that had the proposed street ever been built the outbuildings would before long have been demolished and the spaces filled in with other houses of varying quality, and that the original idea, such as it was, would early have been lost.

Early in 1757 James Potter built the town's boundary wall 25 feet from the avenue; thus, although nothing else was built between the elements of a front and the Gallowgate row beyond the far end of the headland, something approaching the town of the future could at last be visualized. No street was yet laid out although the turf had been removed; by the autumn of 1758 the necessity for paving and draining was seen, as a stagnant pool had formed behind the Town House which could only be removed by digging a proper drain under the street and paving it at a higher level. However, this was deferred so long as the church was expected to be

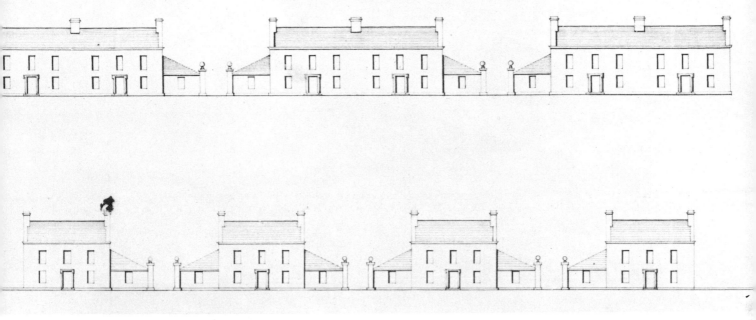

60. Proposed main street at Inveraray, 1756
    Elevations probably by John Adam.
    Compare fig. 61 for a treatment possibly derived from this design.

built, for the paradoxical reason that 'Carriages for building the Churches &c will
come alongst this Street' and break up the paved surface. Meanwhile it was roughly
raised above flood-level with 'rubbish' from the Fisherland quarries.[64]

One single house of the new main street plan did materialize, Alexander
McPherson's, built in 1756 on the southern end of the triple plot formerly allotted
to James Whyte. This house, still easily distinguishable from the rest of the street
by its dressed stone quoins and keystones above its doorway and central window,
was more elaborately finished than most of the later houses, but conformed to
requirements stipulated by the Duke in his grant to Whyte:

'The South end of your building To be at that End of the Square which is next
to the Town house, on the west side of the street, and from thence in a straight
Line towards that private house which Is Contiguous to the East End of the
Town house, so that the front of your houses and the East Gavel of that private
house shall be in one Line, and make so much of the Buildings on that Side of
the Street . . . the Entry to your houses [to] Be on a Levell with the Entry to that
private house . . . and to Enter two steps above the Levell of the Ground. . . .'[65]

McPherson's tack was granted from Whitsun 1757 for the usual 57 years, at a rent
of five shillings. The terms of all tacks granted show that thatch was never allowed
in the new town; all the specifications were for houses stone-built and slated, and
concessions were normally granted to use the Duke's quarries.

Meanwhile Provost John Richardson, whose house had also been finished in
1756, let it to John Campbell of Clochombie and, while he himself apparently did

61. Lowther, Westmorland
   A planned village built in the 1760s by a distant connexion
   of the 3rd Duke and possibly designed by James Adam.
   See chapter 4 note 2.

not wish to live in the town but was angling for the tenancy of a small farm called
Barvrack, observing the general resistance to remove to the new town he piously
offered to continue his good example by building another house – provided he
received certain rewards, such as the title to Barvrack.[66] The foundation for
Richardson's second house appears to have been dug as early as 1756, and in
October 1758 he sought permission to build

> 'On that piece of Ground where he formerly dug a foundation, on the other Side
> of the Street in a Line with the House adjoining to the Town House.
>
> He intends to Ornament the Doors and windows with Hewen Stone, and
> hopes his Grace will upon these conditions grant him a Lease of three nineteen
> years. . . .'

A month later permission was granted 'conform to the division on Mr Adams plan
1758', with a four shilling tack duty.[67] This house, built in 1759–60 with the usual
forty-foot frontage, remains one of the finest in Inveraray. At that time it was the
sole building at the east or quay end of the front to balance the Town House and
attendant buildings west of the street. Besides the dressed quoins to its angles and
door surround, it has a short flight of steps to the front door, and its façade,

crowded with four windows below and five above, imparts a more prosperous and sophisticated air to the street than the simpler houses which followed it. Richardson apparently disposed of the house at once to a sea captain named Neil Gillies, whose tack ran from 1759, and Richardson's name is not heard again in this connexion.[68]

Thus by 1761 Duke Archibald's new town of Inveraray had a real existence, if only as a façade. Its fine public buildings, inn, Court House and gaol, were functioning in spite of their history of mismanagement, ill-feeling and frustrating delay. The houses adjoining the Court House were occupied (Stonefield had moved from his old house beside the castle courtyard into the easternmost of the group); and three privately-built houses stood in isolation in different parts of the town. At the Gallows Foreland Point a harbour and quay were taking shape. A new wall divided the town area from the Duke's avenue and parks, a street was marked out parallel to that wall, and a church, facing east down another hypothetical street, had been at least visualized, to occupy the very centre of the area.

Beyond the sparsely occupied main town site on the headland was the Gallowgate, extraneous but by far the busiest and most populated part of it. It was now occupied by a number of the Duke's wrights, carters and masons (including James Potter), and other approved persons for whom no better houses were available, such as the schoolmasters and one of the ministers. The Gallowgate also had some stables and barns; and, more interestingly, the first rudiments of the new town's industry.

The 3rd Duke's attempts to establish industry in Inveraray were, in the event, connected more with the old town than the new, but their history is worth recounting here.

Mrs Anderson and her stocking factory having failed to remove to what her friends regarded as this desolate part of Scotland, the next industrial proposal came in 1749 from Mr David Campbell of Dunloskin who, supported by many of the Argyll lairds, was hoping for the British Linen Company's sponsorship of the osnaburg or coarse linen industry in the county. Campbell wanted to establish factories in both Inveraray and Campbeltown; but William Tod of the British Linen Company, sceptical that 'some of the Gentlemen of Argylshire would only make use of the Company to introduce the Manufacture and then set up in opposition to it', would only promise a supply of flax to employ the local people in spinning.[69] David Campbell in the event set up his factory at Dunoon, and also had a share in the abortive Campbeltown Whale Fishing Company, which wound up in 1753.

At Inveraray the first move was made in 1751 by Mrs Elizabeth Campbell, wife of James Campbell, who subject to the Linen Company's advice 'bespoke some skilful spinners' as instructors to the local women and girls. By November she had obtained from the Duke use of an empty building next door to her own house in the old town, collected forty pupils and opened a spinning school. Within a month she worked up so competitive a spirit among the girls that she was busy from morning till night, and constantly applying to the Edinburgh Trustees for 'wheels and reels'. As an official encouragement, the revised 'set' of the town in April 1752 made it a condition that rents up to 20s be paid in spun flax;[70] so the school's prosperity was for the time being assured, and new spinners joined so fast that an unfamiliar prosperity appeared in the town: 'The little idle girls . . .who were naked and starveing now go to church well clad wt ribbons in yr heir.'[71] Spurred on with prizes, their output rocketed. The school's fame spread, and a wheelwright named Alexander McArthur with fifteen years' service for the Duke of Montrose, arrived from Buchanan with a recommendation to maintain the spinning-wheels.[72]

By April 1753 a dramatic change was visible:

'the Spining Buissieness is now so successfull that there's 112 Wheels kept going by Females Besides Three more Occupy'd these 10 days by Boys That my Wife has prevaild on with no Smal Trouble to apply to the Spining To Whom for their Incouragement I've given Frocks, Shirts, Treusars, Bonats and Combs, and They're Besides Well fed in my kitchen, and Now they begin to like the Buissieness and think themselves much happier than by their former Stroaling Idle Life. . . .

My Wife has made a Convert of One of these Boys who was Remarkable for his Idleness & Wickedness, he being Captain General of all the Idle Boys in this place, and as his Old Companions now see him become so Virtuous that he gives Closs application to Industry, They Snake about with a Seeming desire of being Imployed could their Silly Gentle Spirit, & the common prejudice against such New Work allow them. . . .'[73]

But trouble was brewing. To avoid constant passing in and out of the school's back door and the yard, the husband and wife re-opened a disused close between the school and their house; the close ran through Baillie Peter Campbell's property, and when Baillie Peter found out he 'came in a Ferocious manner and with a Bundance of abusive Insulting Languag to the Respondent [James Campbell]'s Wife, Stopt the Works'. For the sake of peace they returned to using the school's back door, but in winter this made the room so cold and draughty that several girls fell ill and others left.[74] The quarrel seems to have died down when Baillie Peter removed to Dalchenna, and Mrs Campbell's successes continued; in 1755 she received a £5 and in 1756 a £10 prize from the Trustees for teaching the most spinners and producing the most yarn for the year. Her husband, too, was rewarded by the legal appointment for which he had long wished, as Commissary of the Isles.[75]* In 1756 he was appointed Chamberlain of Argyll, where, as we have seen, he was less successful (see p. 92).

Meanwhile the spun yarn must be woven, and weavers were imported to Inveraray. A weaver's house built by Potter in 1753 for Hugh Mories or Morris, to a plan approved by the Duke, was actually known as 'the factory' and appears to have been a substantial two-storeyed affair with five vents; the mason-work cost £47 10s. By 1753 two more weavers and a wheelwright were living in the Gallowgate, and the coarse linen industry seemed set for a prosperous future.[76]

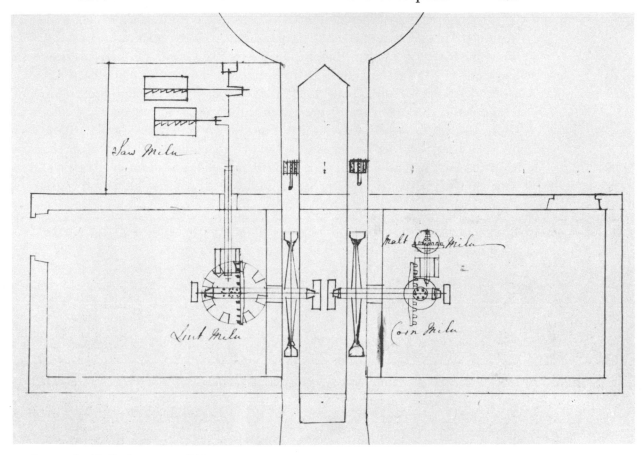

62. Proposed mills for Inveraray, 1750
   Design by Robert Mackell for saw, malt, lint, and corn mills.

The next developments are difficult to reconcile. Weavers were still being encouraged to settle and the town rental of 1757 shows four in the Gallowgate; yet Hugh Mories' house, no. 13, was by then occupied by Robert Bathgate. There was rumour of demolition of both James Campbell's old-town house and Baillie Peter's next door, and early in 1758 Baillie Peter, now living at Dalchenna, applied for lodging for his children while at school in the old house 'in which the Spinning School was keept and which . . . is now as good as given up . . . and if the Spinning School revived there's a house . . . wou'd answer for that purpose . . . not above 30 yards distance from the house call'd the Spinning house.'[77]

The immediate reason for the closure of the school was, simply, that Mrs Betty Campbell had worked herself out of a job: in 1758 she informed the Trustees' Riding Officer that she had had no scholars at all the previous year, because she had already taught everyone in the district who was able to learn, and that a school was no longer necessary. The Trustees therefore discontinued her salary and the bounty, and Mrs Campbell's job came to an end.[78] Yet in 1760 there was still a 'Sewing Mistress', Mrs Catherine Wright, who was permitted by the Duke 'to possess a part of the house Called the ffactory house'.[79]

Although the Trustees now tried to encourage the raising of flax and local weaving of linen, there appears to have been little more organization of this briefly flourishing cottage industry before Duke Archibald died, and with his death the encouragement of manufactures in Inveraray lapsed, along with other activities, for a decade. Some of the 'Hutts' and 'little houses' built by Potter for spinners, weavers and ducal servants, were improved by 'striking out doors, windows & Chimneys' for the schoolmasters and the minister;[80] others now housed the masons building Frew's garden bridge. These Gallowgate cottages, the humble precursors of Inveraray's new town, had a varied history, not the least interesting chapter of which was their temporary association with the town's first industrial venture.

[17] 'Neil Gillies' House' (Richardson's second house),
1759–60, Front Street

[18] The bow windows of the Argyll Arms, 1793–4

This place will in time be very magnificent . . . The founder of the castle designed to have built a new town on the west side of the little bay the house stands on: he finished a few houses, a custom-house, and an excellent inn: his death interrupted the completion of the plan, which, when brought to perfection, will give the place a very different appearance to what it now bears.

Thomas Pennant *A Tour in Scotland, 1769*, London 1776, p.238

His ideas seem to have been so grand; that it is probable he would have struck out something beyond the taste of the times, in the improvements around it, if he had lived to complete his designs . . . The Duke proceeded so far in his plan, as to build a noble row of houses.

Rev. William Gilpin *Observations relative Chiefly to Picturesque Beauty*, London 1779

A cold climate, rude inhabitants, a soil uncultivated, and all the accomplishments of savage greatness may please surly and solitary pride, but I think his Grace of Argyle is much in the right to rule there by a viceroy, the greatest part of the year, and enjoy the comforts of being a subject of England for the rest.

Mrs Elizabeth Montagu to Lord Lyttelton, 16 September 1759, in *Letters of Mrs Elizabeth Montagu,* ed. Matthew Montagu, Esq., IV, London 1813, p. 238

V

After Duke Archibald's departure from Inveraray in 1760 John Maule remained in Scotland for the first part of the winter, travelling to London in February 1761 to be with the Duke. He found his old friend, now in his seventy-ninth year, in good health, and although his pace was much slower, with his hands still on the reins. Maule returned temporarily to his old position *vis-à-vis* the Duke, for in March Andrew Fletcher went north with Lord Adam Gordon to canvass for the forthcoming Parliamentary elections and to visit the Saltoun estate.[1]

The Duke himself intended to be in Edinburgh by the beginning of May, for there was fierce opposition to his candidate, an Englishman, and the contest was likely to be sharp. Meanwhile his political letters to Lord Milton still flowed, written in that unmistakable round, ugly but clear hand, now enfeebled by age. In March he asked Milton to tell the Inveraray overseers – Andrew Bathgate, George Hunter and Walter Paterson – to defer their regular reports until 6 May, by which time he expected to be in Scotland.[2]* Lord Milton warned Asknish that suspension of work returns was not to be a signal for laxity. Milton also enquired about the duty on the last timber cargo, for which he had left Asknish £5, but by the time he received a reply he was laid up with another attack of gout. On 4 April he wrote a note to London, mentioning his illness.[3]

This letter had only just reached London when on the 15th John Maule, hardly able to guide his pen for grief, and covering his ill-written, incoherent missive with blots – surely from his tears – sat down to tell his old friend Lord Milton of the Duke's sudden and unexpected death:

'My Dear Lord

Its wt ye greatest grief at heart I write you this scrawl by ye express to give you ye melancholy account of ye D: of Argyll's death wch happened this afternoon about five. He was taken ill at Mr Couttss at 2, came home, satt down to dinner wt ye Dr & Colonel Williams, he eat none, said he woud take a Camomile puke, They dined, he fell into a little slumber, & soon after had a convulsive motion over his body, & died in a minute, Middleton ye Surgeon and Dr Taylor were immediately sent for, ye former tryed to blood him but not above a tea spoon full came from him. Notice was soon brought to me where I was at dinner, I got here as fast as I coud be brought, but alas all was over. God pity us all who have lost such a friend, & ye Countrey who has lost such a protector, I can say no more so my Dr Lord Adeiu.

J: M:

Mr Wm Campbell has wrote to his Brother ye General by ye express.'[4]*
This quiet, unspectacular death came as the greater shock to Argyll's friends because, although he had since his youth contended against ill health, and by contemporary standards he was already an old man when he succeeded to the dukedom twenty years earlier, they had become accustomed to his unflagging energy. Year after year he endured the long-drawn-out journey to the Western Highlands, maintained his tight control of Scottish politics, continually launched new projects, and by taking life more easily of late years, had kept in remarkably good health.

Maule sent his letter by express. That night, hardly knowing what to do with himself, he stayed on at Argyll House, 'and I think it was ye most melancholy night I ever past.'[5] But we may feel it the intervention of providence that Maule was at hand—though too late by a few minutes—when his friend died instead of being hundreds of miles away; and for posterity's sake it was lucky that the account of the Duke's death fell to his pen and not that of prim, colourless Andrew Fletcher, at that moment away attending to his affairs in Scotland.

The morning after the Duke's collapse a sad little party gathered at his house to hear his English will read by the banker Coutts. Maule, the Dukes's nephew Lord Bute, his son Colonel Williams and his niece Lady Dalkeith's second husband Charles Townshend, all learned that the whole estate in England, 'real and personal', was settled on his old mistress Mrs Williams, 'wt full power' (wrote Maule) 'to her to dispose of every thing as she shall think fit'; in default of such disposal to Colonel Williams, and after him to Williams's sister Ann. The only personal bequests were to the Duke's servants.[6]*

That same afternoon the body was opened by the surgeons. Maule felt that he had endured enough. After the shock of his friend's death, the sorrow of the long night, and the miserable aftermath of death, he had no wish to stay in the house longer than he could help. The formal observances were too much for him; he told Lord Bute and the others that 'if they did not think it was want of regard for his Grace's memory, which I hoped they coud not believe me capable of, I woud choose to go out o' ye house, as it was a constant scene of melancholy to me'.

The gentlemen signified their agreement and sympathy, and Maule departed into lodgings, arranging with Williams to take over his room, and seeing that Andrew Fletcher's effects were locked up and taken care of.[7]

Outside the news had spread, and for the moment little else was spoken of. Lord Bute, 'thoroughly affected', declared it 'one of the greatest losses, which cou'd have befallen him'. 'There is justly an universal lamentation for him, & every body speaks of it, as a event of ye greatest consequence yt coud have happened in this Kingdom.'[8]

Much as John Maule chafed to escape from the associations of London and the dead Duke's household and solace himself by a visit to Lord Milton, it was some time before he could be off. He was distressed, too, as the days passed to hear no word from Milton, not even a message through a third party to tell him how he did. There was no rest for Maule – whatever his sorrow he had to bestir himself about business matters arising from the Duke's death, and worse still, write a great number of letters – 'tho every letter costs me a heavier heart,' he told Milton on the 25th, 'especially if Im oblidged to mention the cause of our sorrow'.[9]

Further search among the Duke's papers had revealed a codicil, specifying safeguards to Mrs Williams's inheritance, also papers dealing with the reversion of his judge's salary and British Linen Company stock. Despite the wording of the codicil old Mrs Williams became alarmed when it was explained to her that, now that the Duke was dead and she was to inherit his personal estate, unless she now formally bequeathed it to her two illegitimate children, on her own death everything would go to her heirs at law. The old lady sent to ask John Maule's advice, who urged her at once to make a will in favour of her son William, and within twenty-four hours the thing was done.[10*]

The dismal completion of affairs left unfinished by a death now fell to the executors. The usual spring consignment of goods for Scotland was in train of despatch, some of them already on board. It was decided to let these go ahead; Henry Pujolas, the major-domo, dealt with the bills of lading and direction of the boxes, while Maule agreed to take with him the inventory of their contents, whenever he finally achieved departure. He was anxious to be back in Scotland in time for the elections, in which his brother Lord Panmure was a candidate, but duty forced him to prolong his stay. He wished to write to his young friends Andrew and Mally Fletcher, yet knew it would only renew his grief. One comfort he found in the behaviour of Lord Bute, who was 'extremely attentive to every thing yt can do honour to ye memory of his uncle'.[11*]

Colonel Williams, between whom and his father a powerful affection had existed, appears to have been physically struck down by his loss. Not until the end of May was he well enough to write to Lord Milton, expressing his sorrow and his friendship for the Fletchers:

> 'Your Lordship well knows the Loss Mankind in general must suffer, but what his nearer Friends have felt, is more than I can describe. I can only say that all future troubles, it may please God to afflict me with, will be light to loosing so good a Parent.'[12]

Meanwhile, the embalmed body of the Duke had travelled slowly in state up the Great North Road he had known so well, and on reaching Edinburgh lay in state at Holyroodhouse, where a vast crowd of people filed past paying their last tribute to the dead chief of the Campbells. Then the solemn procession went on its way to Glasgow, and so to Greenock and across the Clyde to the Holy Loch, where the corpse was laid to rest with the Duke's forebears in the family vault, beside the mediaeval church of Kilmun.[13]

About the funeral arrangements the new Duke, General John Campbell, piqued

63. John Campbell, 4th Duke of Argyll, 1694–1770
Detail from the painting by Gainsborough.

that no one had consulted him throughout, displayed offended dignity : since he had not been consulted, was he obliged to defray the expenses? He came weightily to the conclusion – and was at pains to inform Lord Milton so – that to avoid any 'indecency' he was willing to foot the bill, on the understanding that the legal liability be gone into, when it would surely (he felt) prove that the expenses should come from the late Duke's estate.[14]

The Duke's papers and valuables at Rosneath and Inveraray were carefully sealed up in the presence of the local ministers; the servants, labourers and tradesmen were told of their master's death, and continued in their posts until their future should be decided by the new head of the clan.

An obituary among Lord Milton's papers – unsigned, but by the handwriting evidently compiled by the Reverend Patrick Cuming – summed up Duke Archibald's character as follows:

'In private Life he was easie and affable; his conversation was pleasant, entertaining, and instructive. He allways expressed himself in the most elegant &
correct Manner, and made every body about him happie. His Temper was even,
and he had allways a full comand of his passions. He had a Noble contempt of
pride and false State. He could talk with every man in his own profession, from
the deepest philosopher to the Meanest but ingenious Mechanick.'[15]*

The 'King of Scotland' was a man subtle, shrewd, even wise; an autocrat who yet
knew how to put people at their ease and maintained his balanced temper, caring
little for his enemies. While forgoing grandeur and ceremony, and indulging foibles
which ill-wishers considered whimsical and ridiculous, he had the foresight to
realize that his experiments – whether in chemistry, arboriculture or economics –
would be important for his own country's future; and as for his great building
venture at Inveraray, it remained for years unparalleled either in Scotland or in
England.

So passed Archibald Campbell, 3rd Duke of Argyll: patron of learning and
supporter of universities, owner of the most valuable private library in the country,
promoter of Scottish industry, pioneer in cultivation, founder of the planned town
in Scotland, and experimenter in new architectural forms. With his death the first
great period of the rebuilding of Inveraray's castle, estate and town comes to an
abrupt end.

In the seventeen years since he first came to Inveraray as Duke of Argyll, Archibald
Campbell had gone far towards achieving the transformation he visualized, though
the magnitude of his conception prevented its completion during his lifetime.
That he should never have spent a night in his great new castle seems ironic, after
nearly two decades of work and planning; its interior was far from finished, much
of the principal storey had no floors, the long gallery walls were not yet lathed and
the hall and other rooms were only first-coated with plaster. One of the main and
one of the small spiral stairs still lacked a hand-rail, the north bridge was not paved,
the old 'pavilion' still stood, obstructing completion of the casemates at the north-
west corner of the fosse, and the Duke's recent order to lower the kitchen window-
sills to admit more light, had not been carried out.

At the Cherry Park court of offices, the elevation facing the castle was complete
and now being slated, but its other sides were only begun. The Garden Bridge's
stone-work was complete, but the roadway not formed. At the Maltland by the
kitchen garden some stables were finished, but coach-houses were only partly
built. The Gothick dairy at Tombreac was still in the builders' hands, and John
Brown's bridge at the head of Glen Shira built only to the spring of the arches.[16]

Inveraray's new town in 1761 was still less an entity than a pious hope for the
future. Nearby the past was still dominant : the old castle in its disrepair stood close
to the new, providing a tenement for a few ducal pensioners and employees, and
the old town, save for the few houses demolished by the shore, squatted in increasing shabbiness beneath the new palace's light blue walls.

64. Inveraray old town and the two castles, *c.* 1760
From the painting attributed to John Clerk of Eldin.

In June John Adam travelled over to report on the situation, and the new Duke
followed in August, when he gave orders to George Haswell for completion of
certain minor works, like the hand-rails of the castle stairs, and minimal finishings
at the Cherry Park.[17]

Although he had intervened years ago on the siting of the castle and the dimensions of its long gallery, Duke John was not now very interested in Inveraray. Yet
he did have some experience as an amateur in architecture. Some thirty years
earlier he had been actively interested in the building of his house at Combe Bank
in Kent, for which either he or Lord Ilay (to whom it belonged) employed Roger
Morris,[18]* and he was fond of giving advice to friends like Lord Milton on how to
plan their houses.

The 4th Duke's main interest, however, was the army. He had been made a
colonel in his twenty-first year, when serving at Dunkirk in 1713. During the 1715
rising he was aide-de-camp to his kinsman the 2nd Duke, fought at Dettingen in
1741 as brigadier-general, became a major-general in 1744, and (as already related)
in 1746 was based at Inveraray commanding the King's troops in the west of Scot-

land. For politics, he and his father, John Campbell of Mamore, between them represented Dunbartonshire in Parliament continuously since the Union, the General having held the seat from 1727 and last being re-elected in 1761 only a few days before his cousin Duke Archibald died; on succeeding then to the peerage, he had to relinquish the seat. In May 1761 he further succeeded to Duke Archibald's vacant place in the House of Lords as one of the sixteen representative Scottish peers. More locally, he had for some years been an honorary member of Inveraray's burgh council, and visited the town fairly frequently during the 3rd Duke's life-time; this office he now surrendered to his sons John and Frederick.

The General was a handsome, kindly man, if not particularly gifted or quick-witted, and he had been a good husband and father. In 1720 as a young colonel and groom of the bedchamber to the then Prince of Wales, he fell in love with and married the lively, beautiful and rattle-pated Mary Bellenden, daughter to the 2nd Lord Bellenden and maid of honour to Princess Caroline. They had four sons and a daughter before his adored wife died in childbirth in 1736 at the age of forty-one; so that on succession the 4th Duke, like his predecessor, had been a widower for many years. His heir General Jack now became Marquess of Lorne. Lorne's wife Elizabeth Gunning, however, until Lorne himself succeeded, was still known as the Duchess of Hamilton.

The new Marquess and his wife were abroad at Aix-la-Chapelle when the 3rd Duke died in April 1761, and during the summer of 1763 they spent some weeks in Paris. It was presumably on one of these trips that they ordered furniture and tapestries which were later installed at Inveraray Castle. Lorne from the first took a keen interest in Inveraray and its future, and that future after some years of anxiety, in which the Duchess's first son by Lorne died an infant and another was born dead, seemed reasonably secure: for a son George was born in London in September 1768.[19]*

The 4th Duke of Argyll, with Lorne and his wife, often came to stay at Rosneath, but seldom to Inveraray, and as far as the place's building history is concerned very little now went on. The few trifling accounts for work show merely maintenance of the estate, and a gap of several years' inactivity now occurs, save for one or two houses built by feuars in the new town.

Lorne, bearing in mind his father's advanced age and present indifferent health, was probably responsible for what little did happen there. In 1762 it was proposed that he take possession of the family house and estates at Inveraray as part of his annuity, but this was not implemented, for in 1767 he suggested to his father (from whom he seems at the time to have been estranged) that if he were allowed to manage the estates on his father's behalf they could be run to greater profit.[20] Evidently his suggestion was at least partially adopted, and from then onwards occasional masons' accounts begin again to appear. In 1768 and 1769 some half-dozen (probably ruinous) houses were pulled down at the Old Town Head[21] and – far more significant – in September 1769 at Rosneath, where Lorne and his duchess were in residence, a new architect arrived.

This was Robert Mylne, the same brilliant young man who eleven years before had received the Papal medal of St Luke in Rome and who, to the jealous fury of Robert Adam, on his return to London won the competition for Blackfriars Bridge. Adam, who regarded his contemporary as a dangerous rival, was always ready to slight his work. The nickname 'Blackfriars' used among his family and friends was loaded with contempt. However, in spite of Robert Adam's earlier attempts to put the old Duke of Argyll under an obligation to himself, Robert Mylne had come to stay, and until long after Adam's death.

The 4th Duke died in 1770, and this with Robert Mylne's advent in 1769 started an entirely new era at Inveraray. After 1761 John Adam is never heard of again there; and it is doubtful whether Lord Milton, on whose shoulders all the administration originally fell, ever returned to it before his own death in December 1766. The old judge's powers, both mental and physical, failed sadly in his last years, and with the loss of his old friend Duke Archibald his hold on communications with London and Westminster slackened and probably his zest for living as well. It is said that towards the end his faculties so deteriorated that he used to amuse himself with children's toys, a melancholy sight in one who not many years earlier had held his country's political fortunes in the palm of his hand.[22]

John Maule and Andrew Fletcher also drop completely out of the Inveraray picture. Andrew retired to Saltoun, while Maule continued to live chiefly at Edinburgh in his office of a Baron of the Exchequer; in his old age Maule was to serve as a kind of pattern of elegance to the young James Boswell who admired him enormously. 'He was always very civil to me,' noted Boswell in 1776, 'and is exceedingly entertaining, being full of anecdotes, and having the true old Scotch gentleman's manners, with a picturesque peculiarity of humour.' A month later Maule, at a dinner party at which Boswell was present, was keeping 'all merry with his forcible humour and variety of anecdotes'. Admiration did not prevent Boswell from trying – unsuccessfully – to snatch from the aging Maule his post of Clerk to the Court of Sasines. Maule lived for twenty years after the death of Duke Archibald and died in Edinburgh, still a bachelor, in 1781 at the age of seventy-five.[23*]

By the time the 4th Duke died, in November 1770, many of the familiar faces in Inveraray were already gone. Commissary James Campbell had died in 1760, and the Chamberlain of Argyll was now Donald Campbell of Sonachan. Both Walter Paterson and Henry Roy also died in 1770;[24*] as for the former overseers of Duke Archibald's works, it appears that they returned to the Lowlands when building at Inveraray came to a standstill. Only George Haswell now remained.

Archibald Campbell of Stonefield served as sheriff for forty-seven years and did not retire from office until he was eighty, in 1776; he died in 1777. His son, who had married the Duke's niece Lady Grace Stuart, in 1763 became a judge with the title of Lord Stonefield. The Sheriff's daughter Elizabeth in 1758 had married Carwhin, that 'sencible pretty fellow' who provided the Easdale slates for Inveraray and who at the time of the marriage was fifty-four years old; and their son John eventually succeeded collaterally to the Earldom of Breadalbane.

A new figure in the town was Lachlan Campbell, a lawyer who became Provost and Stonefield's Sheriff Substitute. Provost James Fisher had died in 1757 and although his son Angus, once so full of business initiative, lived on at his small estate of Pennymore on Loch Fyne, the old pattern of Fisher and Duncanson alternating as Provost came to an end, and towards the end of the 3rd Duke's life John Richardson was the first of a new series.[25*] In 1765 the Reverend John Macaulay – grandfather to Lord Macaulay – was appointed to the Inveraray or Lowland church; but for lack of new manses he had to remain in his old house, while his fellow-minister of the Gaelic church, the Reverend Patrick Campbell, was still obliged to live in the Gallowgate.[26]

The Duke's legal representatives had also changed. Archie Campbell of Succoth had been Duke Archibald's Edinburgh lawyer since 1743, although his abominable handwriting so enraged his chief that at first he swore he could not employ him unless he wrote more legibly.[27] As he grew older Campbell delegated much of the work to James Ferrier, who became his apprentice, aged fourteen, in 1758.[28*]

So the old figures passed, and their sons or newcomers took their places – lawyers, town officials, overseers, craftsmen, and architects.

Although in September 1769 Lord Lorne went on from Rosneath to Inveraray, Robert Mylne on his first visit to the west did not get so far. But between 5 and 7 September Inveraray was visited by the noted traveller Thomas Pennant, whose first Scottish tour, published in 1771, contains an interesting impression of the town in this transitional period. The fame of Inveraray had spread widely in the polite world, but nothing had yet been published on it or its appearance, and as the first real travel book on Scotland Pennant's work was to become the classic guide for at least a generation.

Pennant did not care for the castle's exterior, whose unusual design with its high central tower, filled on each side with Gothick windows, he regarded as 'a most disagreeable effect'. As for the interior, 'in the attic story are eighteen good bed-chambers : the ground-floor was at this time in a manner unfurnished, but will have several good apartments'. The crumbling masonry of the old tower still stood alongside. For the surroundings, he allowed that

> 'This place will in time be very magnificent : but at present the space between the front and the water is disgraced with the old town, composed of the most wretched hovels that can be imagined.'[29*]

To such a condition had the formerly attractive little capital deteriorated, that 'charming pretty place' which the 4th Duke, as General Campbell, had admired a quarter of a century earlier, its sorry existence perpetuated merely because during his lifetime no new projects were undertaken. Nor could repairs be carried out in a place whose future was so problematical.

But it was only little over a year after Pennant's visit that the old Duke died, and immediately Inveraray's future burgeoned with promise.

PART TWO

The splendour of the French nobles is confined to their town residence; that of the English is more usefully distributed in their country seats; and we should be astonished at our own riches, if the labours of architecture, the spoils of Italy and Greece, which are now scattered from Inverary to Wilton, were accumulated in a few streets between Marybone and Westminster.

> Edward Gibbon, 1763, when travelling in France; from *The Memoirs of the Life of Edward Gibbon*, ed. George Birkbeck Hill, London 1900, p. 150

The Arabesque painting on the pannels of some rooms, and French papering in others, seem to indicate that foreigners were employed in the fitting up of the interior.

> Northern Tour journal of Rev. John Skinner of Camerton, Somerset, 1825, vol. 5, p. 247, BM Add. 33687

What I admire here is the total defiance of all expense.

> Dr Johnson at Inveraray, 1773; James Boswell, *Journal of a Tour to the Hebrides*, ed. Pottle & Bennett, London 1963, p. 353

Inverary promises a gentle Reception, and its Interior cherishes every Hope.

> Mrs Thrale at Inveraray, 1789; Thrale MSS, John Rylands Library, Ryl. Eng. MS. 623, f.13v.

VI

John, 5th Duke of Argyll, inherited his estates in a country which had notably progressed in the generation since the great Archibald succeeded. During these years Scotland, even the Highlands, had moved away from semi-feudal inaccessibility, while politically, socially and aesthetically England, the 3rd Duke's adopted country, had equally entered a new age. The 1770s were removed by more than political change and stability from the days of the Forty-Five: that stability, and the increased opportunities and improved communications which it brought about, introduced a new social era of elegance and aristocratic privilege never before enjoyed in Britain.

In Scotland, a generation of politically more settled times had shown results in the development of some of civilization's more agreeable benefits, such as the building of new houses and the improvement of agriculture. Travel to the Highlands, though not yet commonplace, had lost many of its terrors. The military roads were an accepted part of the countryside, the industries sponsored earlier were established and flourishing. The age of the Industrial Revolution had begun.

Duke John was truly representative of his family – and indeed of the most outstanding men of his period – in one very important aspect: where his country was concerned his vision was broad and his attitude constructive. With the opening up of the Highlands he foresaw a great future in new industries, modernization of agricultural methods and development of natural resources. What Duke Archibald had had to attempt under enormous difficulties, overcoming all the obstacles of lack of communications, untrained labour and the necessity of experimenting at every step, Duke John could embark on with the advantage of his predecessors' experience. Living in a general climate of expansion, he was eager to develop his own estates, to increase prosperity and trade, and to create a town – indeed towns, for besides Inveraray he was also interested in planting fishing ports round the north and west coasts – which should be a model of enlightened planning. It is hardly necessary to add that he set about beautifying Inveraray Castle in accordance with the most modern and elegant taste.

In the long run the Duke's ambitious philanthropic efforts mostly came to grief, as indeed did the majority of those of the best-intentioned landlords in Scotland at that period. His schemes for establishing industry and for improving the lot of the

65. John Campbell, 5th Duke of Argyll, 1723–1806
   From the painting by Gainsborough.

small tenantry eventually failed, partly at least because of the vast sums of money required, which outran his rents (he was less rich than Duke Archibald, who had enjoyed the emoluments of numerous offices, and the cost of labour had increased), partly because of the economic difficulties resulting from the prolonged wars with France, and partly because of the ingrained apathy of the people whose lot he was trying to change. But for a generation a new wind was blowing through the West Highlands in the areas watched over by the 5th Duke of Argyll.

At the time of his father's death, the 5th Duke, born in 1723, was forty-seven years old. He had early entered the army, was a Lieutenant-Colonel at the age of twenty-two, commanded various regiments and from 1755 to 1759 was ADC to King George II; at the time of his succession he had been Colonel of the 1st Foot (now the Royal Regiment) for five years with the rank of Lieutenant-General. In 1767 he was appointed Commander-in-Chief of Scotland, and his annual visits to his country – considerably longer than those of Duke Archibald – were generally prefaced by a review of the troops, on the links at Musselburgh and elsewhere.

Like the 3rd and 4th Dukes, Argyll now became a representative peer of Scotland, but he was in any case entitled to sit in the Lords by virtue of an English peerage: Lord Chatham, whose 'great point' in so doing was 'to destroy faction', in 1766 had him created Baron Sundridge of Combe Bank. Politically he served his country neither more nor less efficiently than many of his contemporaries who represented pocket boroughs. In Duke Archibald's time he sat for the Glasgow burghs, and later (1765–6, before he became an English peer) for Dover.[1] If he at all resembled his father who, representing Dunbartonshire for over thirty years, admitted ingenuously that he understood nothing of politics, General Jack is likely to have made a Parliamentary Member more conventional than skilled.

Though handsome, the new Duke was not a great figure in society and when in London entertained little; by the fashionable world he was probably considered rather a dull dog, and like Duke Archibald was more keenly interested in the sciences and his improvements than in the social scene. How he had captured the affections of the beauty Elizabeth Gunning is something of a puzzle, but they remained a devoted husband and wife during the thirty years of their married life.

By her first marriage the Duchess of Hamilton had had two sons, and a daughter, Betty, born in 1753. In 1769 her elder son George, 7th Duke of Hamilton, died at the age of fourteen and was succeeded by his younger brother Douglas; and so by the end of 1770, when her second husband became the Duke of Argyll, Elizabeth Gunning had become wife to two Dukes and mother to two more.

The Duchess, a woman of great charm and fascination, was possibly a better politician than her husband, and seems to have had almost as good a business head. She managed the Hamilton elections, corresponded shrewdly with her agent Andrew Stuart and through him kept a grasp of the tangled legal details of the notorious 'Douglas Cause'; altogether she displayed far more commonsense (some even said *solidity*) than her unfortunate feather-brained sister the Countess of Coventry, whose gaffes had been the talk of dinner-tables and the chitchat of letter-writers. While of less celebrated beauty than Maria's, Elizabeth Gunning's features were deservedly among the most frequently reproduced in the country.[2]*

Although the Duchess accompanied her husband to Scotland every summer, except on the rare occasions when the health of either prevented, nothing is known of her personal opinion of Inveraray. Her surviving letters record not a line on the subject of its taste or decoration, let alone the architect or progress of work; and except for a tradition that on a visit to Paris early in their marriage she and her husband commissioned the Beauvais tapestries, later hung in the state rooms at Inveraray Castle, nothing can safely be said of her personal influence in the alterations and modernization initiated by the 5th Duke. It would be ridiculous to suppose that Elizabeth Gunning did not have considerable say in the new designs,

66. Elizabeth Gunning, Duchess of Hamilton and Duchess of Argyll,
   1734–1790. From the painting by Gavin Hamilton.

but all instructions to the Chamberlain and the wrights – barring one reference to
looking-glasses which she ordered – are phrased as the Duke's own wish.[3]* In fact
the Duchess's taste, rather than her husband's, is more likely to have been responsible for the strong French influence seen in the tapestry, furniture and carpets
installed at Inveraray during the 1770s and 1780s – a taste no doubt formed by
her years as mistress at Hamilton Palace.

Inveraray possesses scarcely any estate accounts for the period 1763 to 1767, and a large ledger begun in the latter year is the first to record resumption of even minimal building work.[4]* Since 1761 Elizabeth Gunning and her husband had divided their summers between Hamilton and a house on the Gareloch called the Clachan, a stone's-throw from Rosneath Castle and long the property of her husband's family. In 1771 the pair took up residence at Inveraray, where there seems little doubt that, though still unfinished, the new castle was ready for occupation, and that the necessary work to make it at least habitable had been completed during the last two or three years.

After reviewing the troops on Musselburgh Links during the first days of June the Duke, with his young step-son Douglas, 8th Duke of Hamilton, set off for Inveraray where his wife had already arrived.[5] This first visit in their new role was, in number and brilliance of the company, well in the tradition of Duke Archibald. The modest ducal pavilion, the inn and probably the new castle as well, were so crammed with people that ceremony was abandoned.

> 'So fine a Duke and so fine a Duchess, there, opening house after so long an *Interregnum*, drew all the country – and though fifty beds were made, they were so crowded that even *David Hume*, for all his great figure as a Philosopher, and Historian, or his greater as a fat man, was obliged . . . to make one of three in a bed.'[6]

Hume, long since an admirer and protégé of Duke Archibald's, had recently been employed by the new Duke's brother-in-law General Henry Seymour Conway as an Under-Secretary of State; General Conway and his wife, Lady Caroline Ailesbury, were therefore almost certainly among that festive first party at Inveraray.

The dramatis personae was thus of a new generation, but it was as lively and and varied, and probably more elegant than in Duke Archibald's day. There were more relatives now: the Argylls' own children; the Seymour Conways, and the Duchess's nineteen-year-old daughter Lady Betty Hamilton (who in 1774 made an imprudent marriage to the ugly young Lord Stanley). Occasionally there were Andrew Stuart, and Baron Mure of Caldwell and his wife,[7]* great friends of Hume's; and of course Hume himself, coy as a girl and having to be wooed to come by his friends, never sure till the last minute whether he would turn up or not. In September 1775 Mure tried to entice him to Inveraray with promises of non-stop whist with Lady Betty, and a guarantee that since Lord and Lady Eglintoun had left there was 'no Body there but Miss Sempill. You dont call that Company sure . . . How can I give your strange Reason to the Duke and Duchess, in an empty House, that because it was full, you would not keep your Promise.'[8]

A notable visit in these early years was that of Dr Johnson and James Boswell in October 1773, during the Argylls' third season at the Castle.[9]* The two travellers, fresh from the Hebrides and thankful after weeks of hard journeying, and rough living in wild places, to reach Inveraray's 'most excellent inn' – seeming by contrast on the threshold of civilization – discussed Boswell's scruples at waiting on the Duke and Duchess. The latter was known to be displeased at Boswell's

o

'zeal in the Douglas Cause', for he had represented the other side. On Johnson's advice Boswell next day went up to the castle alone, strategically at the time when the ladies might be expected to have left the dinner table. Luck was with him. The Duke, sitting over the claret with Airds[10]* and other gentlemen, civilly invited both travellers (as Johnson had anticipated) to dine next day, and pressed Boswell to take tea with the ladies there and then.

The sooner to get over the embarrassing business Boswell 'respectfully agreed ... But the Duchess took not the least notice of me'; nor, for fear of offending her, did Miss Sempill; but Lady Betty offered him tea, and the Duke was courteous as always. So were Mr David Campbell, a lawyer who escorted Boswell back to the inn and conversed with him and Dr Johnson; and the Reverend John Macaulay, who breakfasted with them next morning.

After breakfast the minister accompanied them to the castle, round which they were shown, but Boswell made note of nothing more edifying than the neatly turned-out ladies'-maids tripping about the rooms; Boswell then drove Dr Johnson about the estate (omitting the steep ascent to Duniquaich) in 'a little low one-horse chair', with Macaulay riding ahead. 'Mr Johnson was much pleased with the remarkable grandeur and improvements about Inveraray. He said, "What I admire here is the total defiance of expense." He thought the castle too low, and wished it had been a storey higher. . . .' Two days earlier, while they were drying their wet clothes in a smoky hut by Loch Awe, Johnson had argued with Boswell that Duke Archibald, in spite of his great building achievement at Inveraray, was 'a narrow man'. 'Sir,' said he, 'when a narrow man has resolved to build a house, he builds it like another man. But Archibald, Duke of Argyll, was narrow in his ordinary expenses, in his quotidian expenses.'

They returned to the castle to dinner. The Duchess continued glacial, but the Duke placed Johnson by his side and Boswell, taking a middle place, dispensed the soup 'with all imaginable ease, though conscious of the Duchess's peevish resentment. I was in fine spirits, and offered her grace some. . . . I was the Duke of Argyll's guest, and we had nothing to do with the Duchess of Hamilton's foolish anger.'

In bravado he even dared rise to his feet and (defying the local custom, which eschewed personal toasts) raise his glass to the unresponsive Duchess and drink her health. The Duchess revenged herself by being very attentive to Dr Johnson, acknowledging Boswell's presence only once: when he spoke of the second sight she frigidly remarked 'I fancy you will be a Methodist' ('a good hit on my credulity in the Douglas Cause'). Johnson, in an agreeable and expansive mood, drew Lady Betty irresistibly to his side, where she listened eagerly to everything he said, and when they went to the drawing-room for tea, the Duchess in turn brought the Doctor to her side, who paid her all possible attention, while the Duke walked up and down talking to Boswell. Boswell overheard the Duchess remark on the late date of their Hebrides journey, and the Doctor explain that this was, of course, because Mr Boswell had had to attend the Court of Session until 12 August.

67. Inveraray Castle in the 1770s
Engraved after a drawing by Moses Griffith.

'I know *nothing* of Mr Boswell,' retorted the Duchess freezingly, and the morti-fied gentleman reflected (though probably not until long afterwards and in a cooler mood) 'that my punishment was inflicted by so dignified a beauty, I had that kind of consolation which a man would feel who is strangled by a silken cord.'

After an evening at the inn with Mr Macaulay, who again breakfasted with them next day, the two travellers set off on 26 October for Tarbet and Rossdhu, Dr Johnson mounted on a horse of the Duke's. The Duchess never forgave Boswell, and four years later when the pair met her and the Duke passing through Ash-bourne, although the Duke was as civil as ever the Duchess still ignored Boswell with haughty disdain.

Boswell's references to Inveraray Castle, descriptively uninformative though they are, convey at least the unmistakable basic fact that in the autumn of 1773 it was fully occupied. A visitor six months earlier who left a more detailed, if far less entertaining description of the castle as it then appeared was a romantic young lady of eighteen.[11]* Anne McVicar's father, Duncan McVicar of Craignish, after living for some years in Glasgow was now appointed Barrack-Master of Fort Augustus; he and his family visited Inveraray on their way north, on an April day in heavy rain.

Miss McVicar's account reveals several interesting facts. First, that the castle's interior was already in its then form complete and something of a show place (she was impressed by 'the Gothic grandeur of the hall' with its central 'cupola' and gallery, whose originality she thought 'not like any thing you ever saw before'). Secondly, she remarked on a point noted disapprovingly by many later visitors: there were scarcely any pictures. Never at any time was there that collection of old masters which enriched so many great houses in Britain, for the Argyll family had little taste for fine painting and never amassed any, other than their own superb family portraits; in 1773 there were comparatively few even of these.[12]*

Finally, Miss McVicar's is the first account we have of the castle after a most important alteration had been effected in its main floor rooms. The greatest moment of their visit, she writes, was when they were 'suddenly ushered into a beautiful summer parlour, which had a sashed door that opened into a beautiful lawn'. It was hung with the fine Aubusson tapestries (which Miss Anne, like many later writers, took to be Gobelins), and so life-like were their designs that, she naïvely confessed, at first she thought they had stepped among real hay-makers and rural sports. The significance of this description is that the room admired by the McVicars was newly created by reversing the castle's fronts; the architect responsible for this alteration was not Robert Mylne, but his younger brother William.

Details of how the Mylne brothers were introduced to the family of Argyll have not survived, and the earliest references to Robert's work for the 5th Duke as Marquess of Lorne occur in his diary entries for 1764 and 1765, when he carried out alterations, including the building of stables, for Lorne's London house.[13] He also gave Lorne 'outlines for tapestry for a house in Scotland'. He was then already well known and his high reputation, and his being a Scot, would be recommendation enough to a Scottish client.

William Mylne, a year younger than Robert, had studied with him in Rome and was now practising in Edinburgh, where plans for the intended New Town were taking shape. William Mylne was the architect for the new North Bridge to link the new site to the old city, but unfortunately part of it collapsed with loss of life shortly before it was completed in 1769.[14]

This was the same year in which Robert Mylne visited Rosneath. For the next three years it was William Mylne, however, who went to Inveraray, and between March 1770 and July 1772 he stayed there three times, in each case for at least a week.[15] His account of £48 7s 4d gives no details of work at the castle, but the Chamberlain's accounts show that much of his supervision was of a routine nature, preparing sections of the main state rooms and making them ready for the plasterers. His reversing of the two castle fronts, however – whether at his own or the Argyll family's suggestion is not known – was of major importance. By this the main entrance to the castle was made on the north side and the former hall on the south became the parlour admired by Miss McVicar – possibly the one in which the Duchess so cruelly snubbed Boswell.

The creation of a new entrance meant a division of the 3rd Duke's and Roger

Morris's original long gallery into a central vestibule, with partition walls separating it from a new dining-room and drawing-room on either side. In February 1771 the order was given 'To Build the two divisions in the Gallarie to the Plan given, the walls to drawing Room to have a Arch in Midd for a Stove'.[16] Further, the new rooms were to have their windows 'bayed', not in the modern sense, but by hollowing out the inner window-reveals into shallow arcs. In the event only the drawing-room windows took this form, but both rooms eventually had their window ingoes and shutters rounded (though this may have been the work of Robert Mylne a dozen years later).

Traditionally the Duke's bedroom (now the Brown Library) was on the west side of the castle, but the state bedroom was, and remained until 1951 (when it became the private dining-room), the middle room on the east front; the Duke and Duchess's dressing-rooms were the two small rooms north of it. The Duke's turret on the east corner adjoining his dressing-room was also completed for his first ducal visit in 1771, 'to be ready for his Grace about the Middel of May'. Whether they could fully occupy the suite that summer, however, is doubtful, for next winter orders were given to 'finish' and paint the rooms; even the 'Mocke door' in one corner was not yet installed, and a press was therefore to stand in the aperture. Meanwhile, the Duke had been sent sections of the smaller rooms for tapestries with which their walls were later hung.

A stair was built against the wall of the west ('Print') turret to the cook's room below, probably so that servants could pass up and down without having to be seen in the main body of the house, where were the only existing stairs to the basement.[17]* Improvements were made to the servants' necessary houses in the vaults. For the benefit of 'principal servants', too, five garret rooms originally designed by John Adam were fitted up 'to the plan agreed on by his Grace', and another was created on the main floor by partitioning the 'waiting room' on the east front. Otherwise, apart from garret bedrooms, personal servants' bedrooms at Inveraray were in the form of large cupboards with borrowed lights, contrived by partitioning off corners of main bedrooms, or under the stairs.

Servants' rooms may also account for the mysterious references at this period to entresols above the two chief dressing-rooms in the north-east corner. In December 1771 a doorway on the staircase was ordered to be cut to serve the 'Intersole' above the small (Duke's) dressing-room. Presumably a similar room existed on the other side; for although no further mention is made in instructions, nor is there any sign of them now, in 1806 Joseph Bonomi, on his plans for proposed alterations, marked the dressing-rooms on both sides of the house 'No Intersol'. This suggests that for at least 35 years (for they may have been built even earlier than 1770) poky entresols existed above the three smallest rooms on the main floor.

This was the extent of William Mylne's work at Inveraray. After July 1772 he disappears without explanation; in September his elder brother Robert makes his first visit, and 11 years after Duke Archibald's death, the second great period of Inveraray Castle begins.

68. Robert Mylne, 1733–1814
   Engraved after a drawing made by Miss Maria Mylne in 1785.

In 1772 Robert Mylne, at thirty-nine, was, as his notebooks demonstrate, a busy and successful London architect with connexions all over the country. In the years since his return from Italy he had become established as an engineer as well as an architect of repute, by his success in the Blackfriars Bridge competition (although his design with elliptical arches evoked violent controversy), by private commissions for bridges on the estates of the Duke of Portland and the Earl of Warwick, and by alterations to town bridges in Newcastle-upon-Tyne, Glasgow and Yarrow. One of his earliest Scottish commissions was the design (1762) of an oval music-room, St Cecilia's Hall in Edinburgh. In 1767 Mylne was elected a Fellow of the Royal Society and six months later was appointed Surveyor to the New River Company, a post which he held till his death. He also became Surveyor to Canterbury Cathedral, designed the new Almack's Rooms in King Street, St James's, and among other private undertakings began Tusmore House in Oxfordshire for William Fermor, and the transformation of Wormleybury in Hertfordshire for Sir Abraham Hume.[18]*

[19] Inveraray Castle, ceiling of the north turret
designed by Robert Mylne in 1773

Robert Mylne, a man of singular personal attractions, also had to his own misfortune a highly individual, indeed choleric temperament. John Nichols remarks in his *Literary Anecdotes* (1815) that he 'had peculiarities in his character; but they were chiefly connected with a high independence of spirit, and an inflexible sense of duty and justice'.[19] Mylne's remarkable ingenuity, originality and professional patience as an engineer, testified by laconic journal entries about the problems presented by his numerous bridges, was balanced by an equal lack of patience in human relationships, and the brisk turnover in servants – particularly his footman and hard-worked coachman – recorded with equal brevity, suggests frequent irascible domestic scenes. His wife Mary, daughter of the surgeon Robert Home, bore him ten children and died in 1797, fourteen years before her husband, who appears during his lonely last years to have become more intractable.

But in spite of his thorny individualism Mylne was associated with the 5th Duke of Argyll, and later with Argyll's eldest son George, as Lord Lorne, for well over thirty years; without reckoning his sporadic early commissions this association occupied him almost continuously from 1772 to 1793. His dealings with the family terminated rather unhappily after some stormy differences of opinion and, after prolonged discussions over Inveraray church in 1800 and 1801, patronage by the Duke and his son came to an end. Soon afterwards the Duke, at least, began to feel powerful regret for his quarrels with 'old Mylne'.

In 1772, however, Mylne, still comparatively young, was setting off on a lengthy trip to Scotland in his chaise, taking as he customarily did four days to reach Edinburgh (where he was then engaged on St Cecilia's Hall), and another six days to Inveraray via Perth, Blair Atholl and Tyndrum. He reached Inveraray on 6 September, and next day the Duke and Duchess initiated their scheme for the castle's complete interior transformation when Mylne made his first survey of 'the Castle and Apartements from top to bottom'.[20]

A strange coincidence now brought Mylne a new responsibility. While he was viewing the castle a fearful storm blew up, rain fell in torrents for some hours and Inveraray, which over the past twenty years had experienced some disastrous weather, suffered the most catastrophic damage its inhabitants could recall:

> 'Large trees that had stood a hundred years, were torn up, numbers of bridges were swept away, and the military roads were rendered impassable. The great bridge over the water of Aray, and three smaller ones in Glenary, were entirely carried away; and both the great bridges at the head of Loch fine were greatly damaged. In the Duke of Argyll's policy all his Grace's cascades, bridges, and bulwarks, were entirely destroyed.'[21]*

Next day the weather had subsided enough for the damage to be surveyed, and Robert Mylne went out and inspected the ruins of Major Caulfield's fine three-arched military bridge, destroyed after only a dozen years of existence. He also examined the old town bridge and the garden bridge, and gave advice on shoring up the banks and treatment of the abutment. Two days later, as he drove away to Dumbarton through the shattered countryside, Mylne paused on the road to look

[20] Inveraray Castle, arch over the north entrance designed by
    Robert Mylne, probably in 1780

at Roger Morris's Garron Bridge and the damaged bridge at Loch Fyne-head.[22] He already had a commission lasting several years for building bridges on the military road, in conjunction with Colonel Robert Skene, Adjutant General to the Scottish Forces and Major Caulfield's successor as Inspector of Roads; the rebuilding of the Aray Bridge at Inveraray was now added to his list – in this case with suggestions on its design from the Duke of Argyll in whose lands it lay.

During the next two years Mylne sent the Duke of Argyll a number of designs. His first task at the castle was to alter the windows on the main floor, as a preliminary to fitting up the principal rooms in a magnificent style with which Morris's Gothick design would not be in keeping. First, the pointed arches were to be masked from the inside, and Mylne designed circular-headed top sashes which would leave the external window-openings in their Gothick form. At this stage only the south 'saloon' was altered, but eventually the windows of all the main rooms were so treated. Even more important, the lowering of the windows to floor level was also suggested this early, either by the Duke or by Mylne, who among other Inveraray jottings noted at the end of his pocket-book, relating to his first visit: 'Cutting down the Windows of Saloon the height of 2 Panes & leving a Course of Stones outside.' The details, however, he did not work out until 1777.

Mylne was also asked to design ceiling mouldings for four of the main floor rooms, including the north turret circular dressing-room whose drawing he sent the Duke in June 1773 with 'the papier maché for the same', for a fee of five guineas.[23] The mention of papier maché, which he ordered in London, suggests that this turret ceiling was finished in raised paper stucco, made of pulped paper and gum arabic cast in a mould. This form of ceiling-treatment, almost indistinguishable from stucco proper, was especially popular in Ireland for about two decades and was also used at Bulstrode, Dunster Castle and elsewhere in the 1750s; its use at Inveraray at so late a date is perhaps unusual.[24*]

The remainder of the decoration for the principal rooms appears at this stage to have been kept simple. The present (south) Saloon, a 'summer parlour', was as we have seen hung with tapestries, and after Mylne's visit the Duke ordered the north dining-room to be prepared for painting 'so as to serve to dine in Next Summer', and himself sent its chimney-piece from London.[25] Here, then, Johnson and Boswell must have dined with the family in October 1773.

No *petits-maîtres* of interior decorating were yet required, and the first artist recorded as working in the castle is a gilder. Leonard Dupasquier's first commission began as early as May 1771 and lasted until February 1775, when he appears to have worked chiefly on picture-frames: those for the state bedroom, for example, are mentioned in November 1773. His wages recorded for irregular periods over nearly four years totalled £69 13s 3d, of which his half-yearly wages proper were £18 7s 6d; a guinea and a half per month may be calculated as board wages and five guineas were travelling charges. The amount of travelling expenses suggests that Dupasquier ranked fairly high in the social hierarchy of employees. He reappears with other artists from August 1782, when the grand decoration of the main castle

69. Design for enlarged window at Inveraray Castle
Robert Mylne's adaptation of the drawing- and dining-room
windows for the principal floor.

All between the Semicircular and gothick Arches
is made of sold Plank over the Back, cut out into
Pannells such as they dip, & the Pannells painted Black.—

Outside of New Sashes.
The Windows cut down to the Floor.

rooms was begun and when he was gilding the furniture specially made at Inveraray for the Duke.[26]*

Externally, in these first half-dozen years under the 5th Duke, Inveraray Castle still appeared in an unaesthetic and ill-organized setting, a nude, razed area within a clutter of building works and remnants of a town now increasingly being abandoned. A positive move towards its final appearance was made when in 1775 the ruinous fifteenth-century high tower, which for twenty years had stood side by side with the new, and the 2nd Duke's 'pavilion' and offices of 1720–1, were finally demolished.[27]*

At the same time the new town was at last taking shape, and Mylne's next visits in 1775 and 1776 were largely concerned with this and the policies. Like the castle's interior, the town's style and layout were revised to suit contemporary taste, and as its buildings began to rise the old town was by degrees vacated and demolished.

Mylne's only work for the castle at this time was a design for a post-and-chain fence for the fosse which, after what seems to have been an abortive enquiry at the Carron works, was eventually wrought by the Inveraray smith; and a proposal (not executed) for 'a new Covered Way from the Castle to the Offices', presumably for reaching the casemate privies without crossing the open fosse.[28]*

Between 1776 and 1783 Mylne did not revisit Inveraray,[29]* but he produced a number of designs for his patron; although only one of these concerned the castle, it was of great importance.

When Mylne first saw the castle its main-floor windows were only four rectangular panes deep, ending two masonry courses above floor-level, as built to Roger Morris's design more than twenty years earlier. Having first 'un-Gothicized' the state drawing-room and dining-room windows, and altering their astragals accordingly, Mylne in April 1777 executed his design 'for altering, fitting up and finishing all the windows of the principall floor', a plan, section and elevation presented to the Duke in London at a fee of ten guineas. By this their opening was to be enlarged by the length of two masonry courses, to lower the sills to floor-level. This major alteration, however, was not ordered until 1782, and as it involved every window-opening on the principal floor, room by room it took several years to complete.[30]

Otherwise little of significance was taking place to change the appearance of the castle. The long pause which now followed Mylne's new design for the windows and its execution must have been the result, at least in part, of a serious illness of the Duke's which nearly killed him.

In May 1777 the Duke set off as usual for his annual review of Scotland's troops and fortifications. The Duchess was again pregnant and did not travel until the 9th of June,[31]* and Argyll's stepson, the Duke of Hamilton, was celebrating his coming-of-age that summer and expected to travel nearer the time to Hamilton Palace, where great preparations were making for his birthday on 24 July. At Musselburgh the Duke reviewed the 3rd (Prince of Wales's) Regiment of Dragoons

70. Design for enlarged window at Inveraray Castle
   Robert Mylne's drawing for the principal floor, 1777.

and on 23 May went on for a short stay at Rosneath and Inveraray before his annual inspection of the garrison at Fort George, where the officers customarily entertained him to a grand dinner. On 23 June he reviewed the 2nd Battalion of his own regiment, the Royal Scots or 1st Regiment of Foot. Coming south again a fortnight later, on reaching the inn at Taymouth he was suddenly taken ill with so violent a fever that a rumour soon got about that he was dead.[32]

Young Hamilton was urgently sent for from London and hurried up to Taymouth Castle, seat of the Duke of Argyll's distant kinsman the Earl of Breadalbane, to where the Duke had been removed from the inn. The Duke was attended by the famous Dr Cullen (of whom Duke Archibald had formerly been the patron), and later in London by Dr Wood. But although by the end of July the invalid was out of danger and soon able to travel south, the illness left its mark and another rumour, equally wild, had it that he was forced to resign his military command on health grounds. However, for several months the Duke was unable to continue at his usual pace, and he and his family did not return to Inveraray until the summer of 1779.

His illness was a financial as well as a physical setback. An interesting set of accounts reveals that 'fruits, expresses, horse and chaise hyres, board wages to servants &ca during your Grace's illness, and stay at Kenmore and Taymouth' cost over £200, the fees to Dr Cullen £365 and Dr Wood 400 guineas, making the cost of this almost fatal illness no less than £1,009 8s 6½d.[33]*

It may have been this sobering expense which made the Duke feel the need for economies :'I have wrote to Sonachan [the Chamberlain] to form a Plan for the farther Reduction of the Expences at Inveraray,' he told his Edinburgh lawyer in June 1778, admitting that his London tradesmen's bills came to nearly £1,800, 'which gives me some uneasiness & discomposes me to the prejudice of my health'.[34] To raise funds Sonachan was instructed to sell part of the woods to the Argyll Furnace Company, and to lessen expenses. As part of a policy 'to reduce the works as low as possible' twenty carthorses were sold at Glasgow fair, leaving Inveraray with an establishment of 24 carriage and coach horses, and half a dozen more were soon declared redundant ; but Sonachan confessed—echoing the cry of Asknish and a former Chamberlain—that he found it 'Difficult to bring the Establishment to £100 per month'.[35]

During the Duke's enforced absence Inveraray affairs were entrusted to his younger brother Lord Frederick Campbell. Lord Frederick had just been made Colonel of the Argyll Fencible Regiment, and spent much of that summer recruiting at Greenock, for during the war with the American colonies the west coasts were threatened by an American naval expedition commanded by the famous Captain John Paul Jones.[36]* From Greenock it was a simple matter to visit Inveraray from time to time, where Lady Frederick and two of their daughters were staying.

Meanwhile the improvement in Scotland's roads drew more English visitors to view the country's increasingly fashionable savage splendours. Their comments were not without criticism. For example, in August 1775, shortly before Baron Mure of Caldwell wooed the reluctant David Hume to join the castle party, Inveraray was visited by an ingenuous lady who described it as 'the seat of the present Duke of Argyll, but ... originally the property of the Campbel family'. Mrs. Hanway admired the castle, 'this superb modern building ... genteelly furnished in the present taste', but thought its ample accommodation for 'a numerous train' probably very necessary, since it was said that rain fell for eleven months in the year. Indeed the weather was so bad that she left Inveraray with little regret after one night at the inn, reflecting that the castle's situation 'in a Bottom' was 'the great fault of all their houses in this country, for you do not know you are near any inhabited place, till you find your chaise at their gates'.⁰⁷

A more professional judgment was passed when the Reverend William Gilpin, Prebend of Salisbury and authority on the picturesque, arrived in 1776. Gilpin was an arbiter of taste, but after him and Pennant every traveller who visited Inveraray (or indeed anywhere else) was inclined to rush into print with aesthetic observations – many of them lifted wholesale from either of these writers.

Gilpin was fortunate in seeing Inveraray at an improved stage, since much of the old town had already been demolished, and the new could boast, besides Duke Archibald's town front, a 'noble row of houses' now built by Duke John. The castle he admired:

> 'Yet there are two very disgusting parts about it. These are the square appendages, which are tacked to each side of the middle tower.... The contrivance is awkward; and greatly injures a noble pile. The inside seems to be admirably divided into grand and convenient rooms.... At the entrance is a guard chamber; which in most private houses would be ridiculous; but in a Highland castle is characteristic, and gives an uncommon dignity.'

Of Duke Archibald's total conception for the surroundings Gilpin condescendingly added that

> 'it is probable he would have struck out something beyond the taste of the times, in the improvements round it, if he had lived to complete his designs.'

Taking his cue from the sad and neglected remains of the old town, he fell into the trap of supposing it always 'a dirty, ill-built hamlet ... a disgrace to the scene'; but viewing together the grandly conceived new town, splendid castle, and landscaped scenery with the approach over Frew's garden bridge and the fine walk up to Duniquaich, Gilpin concluded that nowhere in Scotland except Hopetoun even bore comparison: 'It will probably in a few years, be as well worth visiting, as any place in Britain.'³⁸

Lord and Lady Frederick during their residence in May 1778 received an interesting visitor in David Loch, a Leith merchant and Inspector-General of both Woollen Manufactures and Fisheries in Scotland, who for the past few years had been a vigorous campaigner for development of the woollen industry, which he

regarded as the 'staple' of the country, whereas other promoters had always favoured linen. Loch was therefore particularly interested in the Duke's recent establishment of the woollen industry in his new town of Inveraray. Being at present on
a journey of inspection of the western coasts and islands, Loch arrived on horseback from Lochgilphead at five o'clock one evening, and 'immediately went to the
castle, and waited on Lord Frederick Campbell, who received me in the politest
and most friendly manner, giving me a hearty welcome'; while he found the ladies,
at tea, 'as affable and complaisant as they are amiable and accomplished'. His business with the Chamberlain obliged Loch to refuse his hosts' kind invitation to stay
the night, but he dined at the castle next day after visiting the Duke's new carpet
factory and the town.

Loch was as pleased with Lord Frederick's conversation as with the policy of
enlightened benevolence to which town and estates bore witness. They discussed
Scotland's trade, fisheries and manufactures, and he secured Lord Frederick's
support for the proposed canal at Crinan. The ladies, on lighter topics, 'conversed
with ease, dignity, and propriety, and [their] politeness and dégagé manner contributed not a little to render this visit the more pleasing'.[39*]

Yet not even Loch could equal the enthusiasm for Inveraray of an impoverished
poet called James Maxwell, one of those humourless but amiable wandering pedants
whom the eighteenth and early nineteenth centuries spawned in such numbers.
Maxwell, who visited Inveraray in September 1777, was bitterly disappointed to
find the Duke away in London recovering from his illness; however, 'some learned
Gentlemen' later encouraged him to print a few copies of the eulogy he composed
upon the place, and the result was a slim volume of verses of stupendous imbecility.
The Duke himself may have accepted a copy, but if so it has not survived.

Maxwell's verses are among the earliest extant of streams of doggerel which
Inveraray inspired over the next half century or so – some of it never published at
all. His magnificently McGonagalesque composition is also a valuable picture of
Inveraray during its temporary standstill in 1777 and 1778; it is garnished with
copious notes such as explaining that 'Through many a rugged step, and stormy
blast' means 'I set out from Gourock, Sept. 1st, and it proved very stormy weather
by the way, most part of my journey'. 'Flow'rs and fruits . . . In such a cold, and so
remote a clime', are identified as 'The Duke's gardens', and Michael Waterstone,
apostrophized, as 'The Gardiner'. Again, having rather infelicitously compared
his own reluctant departure to Lot's wife leaving Sodom, he tactfully notes: 'my
looking back was to a place which the Lord hath blessed, and I hope will bless'.

To select from Maxwell's gems on Inveraray is almost impossible, but a few
passages, reluctantly abridged, will illustrate his style:

> There's *Blenheim*, *Woburn*, *Ragley*, these fam'd three,
> Suppos'd the noblest that in *England* be,
> Are none of them to be compar'd with thee;
> Thou stand'st on such a lovely rising green,
> The best design'd that ever I have seen . . .

Four square it stands, fronted on ev'ry side,
Spacious and lofty like a stately bride.
Built on a rock, it stands both firm and sound,
With the first story underneath the ground ...
A courteous Lady, to whose faithful care
All was committed, shew'd me every where.
Up the majestic stairs we softly walk'd,
And of the wonders in the Palace talk'd ...

Such lofty rooms, all arch'd with costly stone,
For paltry beams and joists, lo, here are none.
The carvings, paintings, pictures, and such things,
Are fit t'adorn the Palaces of Kings.
Rich tapestry, with borders deck'd with gold,
Adorn the walls, most glorious to behold ...

So far as finish'd, all is more than neat,
Though yet the whole is but in infant state;
But when compleated, I can hardly tell
If any House on earth can it excel.

But to describe the Furniture, so grand,
I must confess is far above my hand.
The Organs, Instruments, and golden Chairs,
Can never fully be describ'd to ears ...

Upon the leaden Roof I walk'd all round,
Where I a most delightful prospect found ...

And now before I left the splendid Hall,
I din'd, and drank the owner's healths withal.
A bottle of their ale I drank, so fine,
As in my judgment, ev'n excelled wine ...

I thought this sight had all my toil repaid,
And with myself communing thus I said,
Here's nothing wanting in this noble Dome,
But the more noble Owners not at home ...

POSTSCRIPT
Howe'er the Critics may these lines despise,
They cannot say I've crammed my page with lies.
Yet some may say, they're void of life and spirit,
And therefore destitute of real merit;
But let them say so, ev'n as they think fit,
They are as void of flatt'ry as of wit. 40*

'Yet the whole is but in infant state.' When Maxwell in his 'habit mean, which speaks the Poet poor', explored Inveraray with such admiration and thoroughness, the last vestiges of old castle and old town had been utterly swept away, and the site so smoothed and levelled that the bald new castle towered naked, with nothing either to soften or overshadow it, above an equally bald green sward. Away from the raw newness of its immediate vicinity, however, Walter Paterson's successor Waterstone[41]* maintained his walks, flower-borders, hedges, fruit-trees, water-courses and cascades in a style to rival the most elegant and famous gardens of the south.

Indoors the central hall was adorned with its armoury of guns, swords and pistols, in a manner probably similar to that of today, and in the gallery above, Alexander Cumming's organ-case provided a handsome focal point; the present pavement had not been laid. The large south saloon was then hung with tapestries, their surrounds gilded by Dupasquier, who may also have finished the furniture Maxwell mentions, but the most important suites were not yet made (see p. 219). Maxwell's description suggests that the paintings were now noticeably increased in number. It is interesting to note that some visitors, at least, were admitted to the leads,[42]* and finally refreshed with traditional hospitality. But Maxwell, perhaps, was treated with particular indulgence.

James Maxwell's descriptions of the castle interior are more glowing than exact, but the room decorations which he saw had all been executed during the 1770s, and were before long to be discarded in favour of Robert Mylne's series of grand designs in the height of contemporary taste. This transformation of Inveraray's interior began in 1782. Meanwhile, on the Duke's return following his illness, the most notable changes undertaken were no more exotic than a new subsidiary stairway and a water-closet. One such closet was made east of the kitchen and another in a vault adjoining the old 'covered way' off the fosse, while an old water-closet of the 1750s was removed from the basement of the south turret to accommodate a staircase made in the wall of 'The Dutches round Tour'. This adjoined the Duke and Duchess's private drawing-room, and the service staircase matched the one built in the opposite turret in 1771–2.[43]*

In the autumn of 1780 Mylne, who was then also designing the Duke's farm buildings at Maltland, executed his drawings for the complete decoration of ceilings and walls of all the castle's main rooms, 'Saloon, Drawing Room, Dining Room & Small Hall'. They were despatched in three parcels 'by the Post Coach', either to the Duke or to his lawyer Ferrier, for a fee of £30 for the ceiling designs, ten guineas for 'finishings' and twenty-four guineas for the walls, with a further guinea for carriage.

The finishings consisted of
'Drawing of doors – how framed, finished, and carved.
Do. of deal dressing round doors of architraves, freezes, and cornices to do.
Do. of corner flowers of hall ceiling.

71. Design for a door at Inveraray Castle
Robert Mylne's drawing of 1780.

Profile

Base & Surbase Mouldin[g]
to stop against edge of[d]
Pilaster.

Doors of Principal Rooms.

Plan of Doors & Jaumbs.   *Projection of Mouldings.*

P

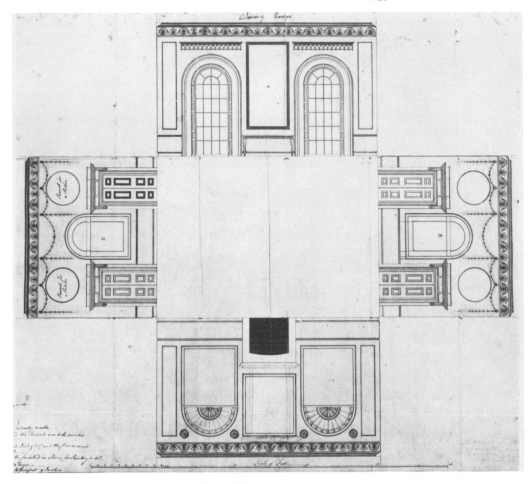

72. Section of the dining-room at Inveraray Castle
    Robert Mylne's working drawing of 1780.

Do. of base and impost mouldings for saloon, dining-room, drawing-room,
    and hall';
and the walls:
    '1. Section of saloon, four sides fairly drawn.
    2. Entablature and freeze of do. at large on brown paper.
    3. Section of dining-room, four sides, in lines, the sides with pannells, richly
        ornamented, &c.
    4. The mouldings at large for do. on brown paper.
    5. Entablature and ornaments of freeze at large on brown paper.'[44]
These drawings are now in the collection at the castle. Mylne produced no other
interior designs before his next visit in 1783, but meanwhile arranged the contracts
with artists and craftsmen.

The ceiling moulds were executed by John Papworth (1750–99), Master
Plasterer to the Office of Works and father to J. B. Papworth, the architect of many
buildings in Cheltenham. Entablatures and friezes were the work of Mr Clayton,

presumably John, also presumably son to the Thomas Clayton consulted by the 3rd Duke in 1756.[45]* Casts and moulds were prepared in London and sent up to Inveraray, and Mylne settled the artists' accounts. His own accounts show that in 1781 and 1782 he drew a 5 per cent commission on the following:

'Plaster work in casts, models, and moulds for ornamented ceilings and walls of hall and the dining-room, by Mr Papworth	£150	0	6
Metal sashes, by Mr Underwood & Co.	5	11	9
Carved trusses for door, by Mr Bower,	21	0	7
A quantity of artificial enrichments for bases and surbases for various rooms,	9	18	11
Artificial ornaments, by Mr Jacques	6	15	8
Carving, by Mr Lawrence,	4	12	6
	£197	19	11.'[46]*

The reference to metal window sashes at this early period is interesting. Sonachan corresponded with Ambrose Tibbets of the Carron Iron Works, sending him 'an Exact model in wood . . . to see if the Iron part of the Windows can be made there'; but the 'iron part' here referred to may mean the simple wrought iron balconies which were integral to Mylne's design. A note in the Chamberlain's instructions shows that in the event the windows were made at Inveraray.[47]*

Orders for the new windows' installation were first given for the dining-room in the autumn of 1782, for the drawing-room and its adjoining turret in 1783, the Duke's closet on the north front and the saloon or billiard-room in 1784 (leaving its glass door to the garden to be altered next year 'in the manner directed by Mr Milne'), and the two dressing-rooms in 1785.[48] So year by year the main windows were enlarged by cutting down their masonry to floor level, and on one or two of them traces may still be seen of where the stones were cut away from their sides. The change in balance of the castle's four façades by thus increasing the height of the main-floor windows in proportion to the rest, is undoubtedly an improvement in its appearance. The job was completed in 1787, and an order by the Duke that October runs

> 'All the new Windows and Balconies in the Castle to be painted over early in the spring, and Wm McEwan the painter to be got from Glasgow to do that work paint the Gates and Railing round the Castle'.[49]

Between 1782 and 1789 the state rooms and hall were undergoing their transformation, though Clayton seems to have come to instal the plasterwork by October 1781. In September 1783 Mylne spent five days at Inveraray, probably to supervise installation of his designs, and made a brief stay at Rosneath, where he was designing an addition to the castle. His journey to the west also included visits to Sir James Colquhoun at Luss, and to Gargunnock in Stirlingshire. On Mylne's next and last visit to Inveraray, from 18 to 25 September 1785, he was chiefly concerned with the town, the Dubh Loch bridge and other features, but he inspected the castle's public rooms and advised on finishing the door into the saloon and on an alteration to a chimney-piece.[50]

Further designs for the new town followed his visit in 1785, but Mylne never returned to Inveraray again. He had by then been associated with the 5th Duke of Argyll for over twenty years, and in later years, apart from his design for the church at Inveraray in the 1790s, his major work for the Duke was his alteration of Rosneath Castle.[51*]

The last link with Duke Archibald's days was broken in 1784 with the death of George Haswell on 24 March. The latest instructions for that Duke's carpenter, dated 19 December 1783, include orders for the new drawing-room windows, for putting up the arms in the hall, and for flooring the turret-room with larch-wood. A few months earlier Haswell had been sent, as in the old days, to Glasgow to buy timber – fir, oak plank, and Swedish oak for the new window-casings.[52*]

For many particulars of the progress of Mylne's interior finishings we are again indebted to the numerous contemporary descriptions, of which almost a score survive of visits made in the 1770s and 1780s – a small number in comparison with the later flood, but of greater value, for they describe the castle's unfinished state during the lifetime of the famous Duchess Elizabeth. Some of these accounts are still in manuscript, like those of John Inglis and Mr Bailey, some are to be found in family letters or memoirs; others form part of published tours, and their tone ranges from sycophantic to pompously dismissive.

Among the most interesting is, first, that of John Inglis, a farmer of Holm (near Douglas in Lanarkshire), who in July 1784 made a journey through the Highlands on horseback, spending several days at Inveraray. Although he was naturally more interested in agriculture and gardens, he describes in some detail what he saw at the castle.[53] Next, in September of the same year came a French geologist, Barthélemy Faujas de Saint-Fond, with a party of friends, who were automatically invited to stay at the castle; Saint-Fond's account of life there is of the greatest interest, although he says comparatively little about the decorative works then in progress.[54*] In 1786 a rather snobbish sportsman, Colonel Thomas Thornton, arrived with a vast retinue, but again his social descriptions are worth more than his architectural observations, for he wrote up his experiences afterwards in tranquillity, apparently telescoping several visits, and did not publish them until 1804[55], leaning heavily on the accounts of Pennant and of Thomas Newte, another gentleman who had visited in 1785 and published his Tour in 1791.[56] Then in 1787 came Mr J. Bailey from Otley in Yorkshire, a person of some substance, who in his voluminous travel journal praised Inveraray extravagantly, although his reliability in point of detail sometimes appears questionable.[57] Nevertheless, from these and other accounts a picture of the progress and appearance of the castle's main rooms can be deduced.

The first to be completed was the great hall in 1783. Indeed, by June 1782 its floor was 'paved in the same manner as the Vestibles' for £23 4s 6d, or 6d a foot,[58] and Mr Bailey in 1787 found its polished black marble surface – as it still is today – 'so slippery as not to be very pleasant to the tread'. Its ceiling, 70 feet above in the great central tower, was (Bailey tells us) 'divided into compartments by cross beams, and the interior of each of these is a deep concave ornamented with carving in the highest style of elegance'. He further describes the balustrades 'of iron, extremely massy and full of scroll-work, the main supporters in the form of dolphins, double, or treble, fourched, and richly gilded and burnished'.[59*]

The hall had, if St-Fond is to be believed, heating arrangements as curious as they were attractive:

> 'This vestibule was ornamented with large bronze vases, of antique shape, placed on their pedestals, between the columns. These vases served at the same time as stoves to warm the air of the vestibule and the staircase.'

By 'columns' St-Fond would appear to mean the archways between the central and subsidiary halls at first floor level, except that these usually displayed sculpture. Perhaps St-Fond had merely misunderstood his guide, for Colonel Thornton more prosaically notes that chimneys running from top to bottom as flues make the house 'the warmest imaginable'. 'So much has good sense been exercised,' adds Thornton in a dubious compliment, 'in making the *useful* the first object, the *beautiful* the second, which has not been always attended to in houses of such consequence.' We appreciate what he means, in comparing houses like Houghton and Blenheim Palace; yet Thornton sounds grudging beside the enchantment of Mr Bailey, who puzzlingly writes of 'innumerable relievos ... most of them copies of the chastest, and most classical subjects of the Vatican, Portici and Naples'. (We may, however, doubt the accuracy of a man who describes Inveraray's central tower windows as 'Egyptian'.)

The other chief adornments of the hall were the gallery organ, the arrangements of armour, and some sculpture. St-Fond describes Alexander Cumming's organ in its apse as 'ornamented with groups of Gothic columns', and, if the magnificent barometric clock in Buckingham Palace which Cumming made for King George III in 1766 is any guide, the Inveraray casing must have been of some splendour.

In 1784, the Duke's large collection of swords, guns and pistols was arranged on the hall walls 'in the manner directed by Mr Miln'[60*] – 'most nobly hung with armour', Mr Bailey tells us, 'in stars, and every other species of pile'. Included were arms and colours of the West Fencible Regiment, whose last four companies were disbanded in 1783 and the colours carried to Inveraray 'in Grand Military Procession'. Inglis, who saw them soon afterwards, remarked on their 'very neat' arrangement round the base of the side walls.

The few pieces of sculpture owned by the Duke were displayed particularly in the open upper arches flanking the two staircases. In the hall, too, were specimens of Tiree marble (*Marmor hebridianum*) first discovered on the island in 1764, and much admired by the Duke. Dr John Walker, a contemporary professor of Natural History, describes it as of a carnation ground with 'concretions of green chrystalized schorl',[61] and Bailey considered the examples he saw 'not unlike, and little

73. Inveraray Castle, the saloon or south drawing-room
   Showing the girandoles designed by Robert Mylne and gilded by
   Maitland Bogg in 1788–9.

inferior to those of Sienna'. Chimney-pieces of this marble were put up in the
'Billiard Room' or saloon in 1782,[62] but were removed in the nineteenth century.
It would be a specimen of the Tiree marble which, during Boswell's visit, the Duke
asked Colonel Livingstone to fetch for him to show the company; the Colonel
having brought a wrong piece was sent back again, and 'conscious of an appearance of servility . . . as he walked away, he whistled, to show his independency.
Mr Johnson thought this a nice trait of character.'[63]*

   The saloon was the biggest room in the house and the only one to contain two
fireplaces. Between 1782 and 1784 it served various purposes – for billiards, dining,
music, and, when the party was large, for breakfast as well. Faujas de Saint-Fond,
staying at the castle in September 1784 when the guests were numerous, mentions
that they took breakfast in 'a large room, ornamented with historic pictures of the
family' – including the Batoni of the Duchess's son, the young Duke of Hamilton –
and that besides 'several tables' laid with an elegant breakfast were 'a billiard-table,
pianos, and other musical instruments': in fact, the present saloon. Ordinarily,
the breakfast-room appears to have been the south turret opening off 'the Dutchesses room' (the present private drawing-room); both were hung with tapestries:

   'The billiard room is the largest in the house and is adorned with several good
   paintings. The Dutchesses room and breakfast room are finished with tapesting
   in which are wrought many ingenious devices.'[64]*
Descriptions at different dates show that the tapestries were moved from room to

[21] Inveraray Castle, east end of the dining-room

room more than once, but the private drawing-room and the state bedroom (now the private dining-room) remained hung with tapestries until redecorated by the present Duke in the 1950s.

The billiard-room/saloon was then hung with silk, and in 1788–9 a set of four finely carved gilt wood girandoles were put up on its east and west walls, each pair flanking a large portrait. They are in the form of decorated lyres suspended from ribbons with knots and bows, intertwined with floral garlands. Within the topmost garlands are framed cartouches containing the carved ducal letter A, and behind the lyres are crossed sprays of laurel leaves. Otherwise, apart from its gilded plaster cornice, this room, while of the greatest elegance in proportions and with splendid doors, has remained a relatively simple setting for some of the castle's largest and most sumptuous portraits; since the silk hangings, having deteriorated, were removed in recent years, the white walls now provide a very happy background for the large paintings and the rich gold girandoles. The Victorian fireplaces which replaced the originals of Tiree marble were themselves removed by the present Duke in 1952, when he re-installed chimney-pieces recovered from Rosneath House before its demolition; they are typical of the 'Adam' style with sphinxes, vases linked with ribands, pendants and, on the uprights, tapering pedestals twined with garlands. The saloon ceiling is entirely plain since, for whatever reason, Mylne did not produce any design for it, and a rich Victorian plaster ceiling brought to Inveraray some eighty years later has remained ever since in its packing cases in the Cherry Park.

The ceilings of the other main rooms, and the friezes, were erected by the plasterer Clayton between September 1781 and October 1782 for a total of £308 4s 1d – which included 'finishing the Stucco work of Dining Room, Drawing Room Saloon and vestibule', and 'finishing the Turret off the dining Room'.[65*] Clayton supervised the fitting of ceilings from the moulds made by Papworth in London, and other decorations he presumably executed on the spot.

John Inglis describes the dining-room as 'just finishing' in July 1784, 'and though very small will be the finest room in Scotland, it is painted and gilded very elegantly by two foreigners who were at work in it'. Thomas Newte, in July 1785, also remarks on the castle's 'many good rooms . . . the ceilings beautifully painted and gilded. Several of [the rooms] are not yet finished.' The drawing-room, under-taken last of all, was completed only in 1789.

The dining-room, though the smallest of the three main rooms (in dividing the old Long Gallery a dressing-room, today used as a butler's pantry, was contrived in the end bay of this side, so that the dining-room has only two windows to the drawing-room's three), is perhaps the most splendid in the whole house. Every surface is covered with painting, gilding and plaster-work of the most exquisite kind. Mylne's round-headed window-frames, the deep splays adorned with pan-elled and partly gilded double shutters, are echoed by round-headed looking-glasses above console tables at either end of the room, each between two doors; a rectangular glass surmounts the fireplace. These glasses are framed by borders of

[22] Inveraray Castle, south side of the dining-room, one of the
     painted panels with grisailles

delicately painted feathers and leaves. Above the doors are circular grisailles repre-senting bodily pleasures – food, drink, warmth and scent – and oval grisailles flank the chimney-piece. All these panels are in painted settings, their frames and span-drels exquisitely decorated with vases, peacock feathers, cornucopias and floral arabesques. Above the plaster frieze of acanthus leaves Mylne's ceiling design of a large circle between spandrels is most harmoniously integrated, the gilded border and the central patera, surrounded by a vine in grisaille, being of raised plaster-work, the remainder painted with the feather, vase and floral motifs.

The equally elaborate drawing-room ceiling is more geometrical, in sections of paterae and fans, adorned with painted garlands and vases. Here Mylne designed the walls to take the set of seven Beauvais tapestries by Jean Baptiste Huet and made by Sieur de Menou which are the room's most splendid adornment,[66]* but there is still space for two painted floral panels bordering the glass over the marble chimney-piece, and three painted overdoors of classical ruins. Further, the window-casings, whose inner splays are hollowed out into arcs, are painted in panels of floral arabesques. The drawing-room is completed by three resplendent hanging lustres.

In this room's adjoining turret, whose bookcases of a later date contain a display of Crown Derby, Meissen and other china and porcelain, is another ceiling designed by Robert Mylne – in fact papier maché – by contrast very restrained, its circular border of vases and feathers repeating, with a slight modification, the painted border of the dining-room ceiling.

Who, then, were the artists who created these splendidly decorated rooms? For the false sculptures and arabesques in the dining-room Biagio Rebecca has been suggested, but although this may seem plausible, it is in no way substantiated by the documentary evidence. Stylistically, too, the feathery brushwork and softer colours are in keeping with the French *petits-maîtres* who worked in England before and during the Revolution, in the characteristic *grotesque* manner, rather than with the harder Italian outlines and colourings of Rebecca's Etruscan and other rooms at Heveningham or Heaton Hall. The parallels are, perhaps, the painted canvases at Ashburnham Place, now at the Victoria and Albert Museum; or Delabrière's painted boudoir (1796–1800) at Southill Park; or even, in spite of the neo-classical subject, the painted room of about 1795 from Kempshott Park now at the City Art Museum in St Louis.[67]*

The names of the Inveraray painters have, in fact, been established, and in view of the quality of the work they are surprisingly obscure. The most exact infor-mation is contained in a note concealed by one of the artists behind the tapestry when it was first hung, and discovered a few years ago during cleaning:

'touttes Les peintures de de [i.e. ce] Salon on E'ter Compassez Et peint par Irrouard Le Girardy En Lannée 1788 Cette artiste Neé a paris, Esttet de Lacad-emie de peinture de Cette ville Et de Celle de Londres.'

In confirmation of this is one of the 'Instructions' of 1788 which specifically orders execution of

74. Design for a window at Inveraray Castle
An alternative design of ?1777 by Robert Mylne,
subsequently altered.

A . is the Lath = Board
from whence the
Curtains are to hang.

B.B. The Circular part
may be finished plain.
But the whole to be
executed in plaister.
some small Mouldings
may be formed into
pannels, if this is
thought too rich.

'three small Cornesses for the Tops of the doors large drawing Room Castle a draught of which was drawen by Mr Girardy and also one draught for the Tope of the glass in said Room'.[68]*
(The Chamberlain's note, 'Done', beside this instruction testifies that it was completed by 1789.)

Of all the many visitors at that period, the only one to make a precise record is Stebbing Shaw, a young clergyman travelling with his charge Francis Burdett in August 1787, who relates how they saw

'on the left hand . . . an excellent dining room elegantly fitted up, the ceiling and ovals richly finished by Guinon and Gerardi; but the former died during this undertaking, and the latter is now at work in the opposite drawing-room, which, when complete, will be most elegant; the modern French tapestry is here as beautiful as fancy can design, and art execute.'[69]*

The best that can be said of the other documentary evidence available is that it does not contradict this statement. The castle accounts mention carriage of 'Guinard's' trunk in August 1784, after which he is not mentioned again. A painter named 'Mr Gerrard', 'Girardi', 'Le Gerardy' and 'Gerardy' is employed between October 1786 and October 1789, and Leonard Dupasquier reappears between 1782 and December 1787.[70] These artists were employed seasonally and paid wages, board wages and expenses, so that details of their work are never quoted. However, the evidence of date and Stebbing Shaw's description shows that the 'two foreigners' whom John Inglis saw working in the dining-room in July 1784 must have been Guinard and Dupasquier, the former executing the grisailles and the grotesques, and the latter all the gilding that embellished the ceiling and walls. It would, too, be Guinard or possibly Dupasquier who carried a note to the inn inviting St-Fond and his friends to become the Duke's guests in September of the same year, described as 'a French painter, who was working at the Castle'.

These, then, were the names of the foreign masters: but who *were* they? Of Guinard or Guinand nothing appears to be recorded. The oddly named Irrouard le Girardy, paid far more highly than Dupasquier, appears to have worked in London, and perhaps was introduced by Mylne. No 'Le Girard', 'Le Gerard' or 'Le Girardy' is named by Bénézit, but the various Girards of the eighteenth-century Ecole Française include one who executed paintings for the ceiling of the Cabinet de la Reine at Versailles, one who exhibited architectural views at Paris in 1774, and a porcelain painter who worked in arabesques and chinoiserie at the Sèvres factory between 1771 and 1800. A Jean-Baptiste Girard, painter and sculptor, was working in Paris in 1771. More likely candidates are, perhaps, Romain Girard, born in Paris about 1751, a stipple-engraver who studied in England, and later in Paris published a number of 'English'-looking engravings after William Hamilton, Greuze and others, and also a series of decorative ornaments; and finally, a certain 'J. de Girardy'. This de Girardy, quoted in the *Dictionary of Royal Academy Contributors* as exhibiting two flower pictures (nos. 181 and 197) at the Academy in 1784, lived in London at 10 Great Pulteney Street. He may not impossibly be

[23] Inveraray Castle, the drawing-room,
showing painted overdoors by Irrouard le Girardy

connected with yet another Girard of the French School named by Bénézit as a still life painter and Member of the Académie de Saint-Luc, who exhibited there in 1774 such subjects as 'Légumes sur une table' and 'Pêches dans un panier'.[71]*

Dupasquier, who during his second commission at Inveraray worked for five successive seasons, also gilded a great deal of the Duke's new furniture; but another gilder from Edinburgh, known as Maitland Bogg, worked only in 1788-9 and his chief assignment was the decoration of the four girandoles adorning the billiard-room walls for a fee of £17 19s.[72]

Other enrichments for the billiard-room – mahogany, marble for the fireplaces, grates, and crown glass for Mylne's new windows – arrived during the years 1781-5; the large looking-glasses were delivered in the spring of 1786. The fine doors for the main rooms, beginning with a set of ten in 1782, were made by two wrights, Hugh Alexander and John Johnstone. Upholstery was made on the spot by William Grievar, and the Duke's own weaver Daniel Campbell – presumably at his new factory near the town – between 1786 and 1789 wove dornick and other cotton cloth for chair covers, and new table linen.[73]*

As for the furniture itself, great quantities of it were made at Inveraray by a pair of Edinburgh cabinet-makers, Peter Traill and his son Douglas, who worked together between June 1782 and May 1784, while Douglas appears to have returned alone between October 1787 and September 1788. The suites and other items they made were from the pattern books, or from prototypes sent or brought by the Duke from London: such as four tables for the 'Great Vestible' in 1782, and in 1787 four small tables

'for the use of the Bed Chambers, two of Planetree & two of Geentree, two square and two round according to the patterns of those which have been sent from London, they must all have drawers'.

Other pieces included four dressing-tables 'like the one in the duchess' small dressing room with two drawers to each of Mahogany' (1787), and six oval tables and six 'corner Bason Stands' (1788).[74]

More important, however, were the fine sets of chairs, many of them in the French taste, in the dining-room and the drawing-rooms – two French-style settees, and a set of Hepplewhite armchairs, all covered with Aubusson tapestry, and a set of heavy mahogany chairs, gilded and covered in Beauvais tapestry, to name only a few. The Beauvais tapestry chairs, of Régence or early Louis XV design, were possibly bought by the Duke and Duchess in Paris in the early days of their marriage, and of the others, it cannot be said with certainty which suites were made by the Traills to French prototypes and which ordered from France. One important suite de salon (now in the south-west drawing-room or 'saloon'), of giltwood and covered in tapestry, was evidently made by the Traills for it was gilded by Dupasquier in 1782, who then stencilled his name and the year on the underpart of one of the chairs. Whatever their origin, the splendidly carved, upholstered and gilded suites completed the effect of the castle's richly painted, tapestry-hung and glittering interior.[75]

[24] The private dining-room, originally the Duke's bedroom
    The portrait is of Mary Bellenden, wife of the 4th Duke

The castle was, in all important respects, finished. By 1789 Douglas Traill had been paid for his last items, Maitland Bogg and his apprentice had ridden off from Inveraray for the last time, and Le Girardy, with his trunk and brushes, had finally departed for London.

For eighteen years, except for the season when the Duke had been so dangerously ill, he and his Duchess had lavishly entertained friends and strangers at their castle while, year by year, it was being transformed under their very eyes. Dozens every season arrived by invitation, but many more came as strangers, or provided with an introductory letter, and the normal process for such gentlemen travellers was (writes John Knox in 1785)

> 'to leave the servants, horses and carriages at the inns, while the company pay their respects to the noblemen or gentlemen in the neighbourhood'.[76]

Those less privileged might find themselves out of luck. Robert Burns, making a short tour of the Highlands in June 1787, found the castle full to overflowing and the innkeeper at the Argyll Arms 'too much occupied with the surplus to have any attention to spare for passing travellers'. Burns supposedly scratched an exasperated epigram on one of the inn windows:

> *On Incivility Shewn him at Inveraray*
> Who'er he be that sojourns here
>   I pity much his case,
> Unless he comes to wait upon
>   The Lord their God—his Grace.
> There's naething here but Highland pride,
>   And Highland scab and hunger;
> If Providence has sent me here,
>   'Twas surely in an anger.

In a letter to a friend after his inhospitable reception Burns described some of the miseries to be found in Argyll, where

> 'savage streams tumble over savage mountains, thinly overspread with savage flocks, which starvingly support its savage inhabitants'.[77]*

Burns's unlucky experience at Inveraray was probably due to the visit of the British Fishery Society's Committee, of which the Duke had been elected President, on the eve of departure for the Hebrides to select a site for a new fishing town.[78]* Surprisingly, perhaps, after his bitter complaint, the names of the Duke and Duchess of Argyll headed the list of subscribers to the next edition of Burns's poems.

Even accommodation at the castle, however, might not be a guarantee of comfort. In 1788 slates were off the roofs and rain was coming through the turrets' walls, but the Duke was obliged to press even these top rooms into use and to have them 'white washed in the inside and fitted up so that Gentlemen may Sleep in them if needfull'.[79] He may have found himself regretting, with Doctor Johnson, that the castle had not been built with another storey.[80]

Johnson's strictures on the height were, however, aesthetic. Another feature criticized by such different visitors as the farmer Inglis and the snobbish sportsman Thornton was the castle's sunk storey in the fosse – which Inglis thought 'much against its appearance', with its surrounding casemate cellars. Colonel Thornton in his published account proposed to the world that the castle, being diminished by its grand natural surroundings, would have appeared more handsome, though less convenient,

> 'had the whole of the offices, which, on the present plan, are sunk, been added to it as wings, with a handsome colonnade'.[81]

In thus missing the entire significance of the castle's design, Thornton was not less patronizing than an anonymous young man, probably a Cambridge scholar, who visited Inveraray with friends in July 1789 and recorded his pompous and jejune impressions in a diary of his Scottish travels. Here as elsewhere the writer appears to have had little understanding of what he saw, dismissing the castle in one line as 'a handsome modern building' which 'contains some fine Paintings with Furniture by far too rich'. Of Duniquaich he wrote, inaccurately, that the Duke's father

> 'was at the expence of making a good *Horse* Road to the top . . . but the present Duke (owing I suppose to a Depravity of Taste) has not only suffered the weeds etc to grow, but Permits with a disgraceful neglect the water to run down the path. N.B. Do not forget (if after Rain) to hire a fisherman's Boots.'[82*]

Henry Skrine, LL.B., in 1787 had similarly thought that most rooms in the castle were 'fitted up in a taste far too spruce and gaudy for the simplicity and magnificence of the scene around'; while as for the architecture itself,

> 'being a bad imitation of the Gothic, [it] is not pleasing : and an enormous tower placed in the centre, to give light to the staircase, encumbers the whole pile disagreeably.'

Thomas Newte, who found the exterior 'very monastic', also thought the central tower had 'a rather heavy appearance on the outside, and is by no means pleasing within'. On the other hand Faujas de Saint-Fond was delighted in all respects, praising equally the fresh, neat look of the dressed masonry, the 'clean and perfect' angles, and the skilful lighting of the 'magnificent, tastefully decorated' hall and staircases.[83]

Visitors during the 1780s whose opinions must have been of value, though they appear not to have survived, include George, Lord Herbert (1781), heir to the 10th Earl of Pembroke (who was himself son of the 'architect Earl' and had visited Inveraray in earlier years); Edmund Burke and William Windham, the latter then principal secretary to Lord Northington, Lord Lieutenant of Ireland (September 1785); and Rudolf Raspe the Swiss geologist and author of the *Adventures of Baron Munchausen*. In 1789 Raspe, at the instigation of the Duke and Lord Breadalbane, was engaged on a mineral survey of the Highlands, and was trying without much success to set up a rather dubious mining company. This adventurous gentleman was soon accused of planting in Sir John Sinclair of Ulbster's land the mineral deposits he then pretended to discover, and it was lucky for the

Duke that Raspe's passing through Inveraray had no worse results for the Argyll fortunes and estates.[84]*

1789 in Inveraray also saw Mrs Thrale, on a Scottish tour with her second husband, Piozzi. Mrs Thrale was, like Mrs Montagu some twenty years earlier, enraptured with the surroundings' romantic natural beauties:

'. . . an Idea of simple Grandeur, & solitary Dignity, not of sullen haughtiness tho' or inhospitable Pride . . . Inveraray promises a gentle Reception, and its Interior cherishes every Hope . . . In short, Inveraray is princely but Alnwick is Tyrranical.'[85]*

The most absorbing of the contemporary accounts are those which describe family life at the castle, and here again for the 1780s we must turn to Faujas de Saint-Fond, Colonel Thornton and Mr Bailey. St-Fond's record is by far the liveliest, starting with his relation of how he and his friends on 15 September 1784, at the outset of their journey through Scotland, found themselves unable to stay at the inn because the circuit judge (Lord Braxfield) was every moment expected. The innkeeper advised St-Fond to send a note to the Duke mentioning the letter of introduction which he carried, and sure enough a pressing invitation to dine and stay at the castle arrived by the hand of the French painter. The party at once accompanied Guinard (or Dupasquier, as the case may be) up the drive, while their carriages were driven to the stables by the Duke's servants.

The others in the party were Count Paul Andreani of Milan, a keen amateur scientist whom St-Fond had met in Paris; William Thornton, 'a very worthy and intelligent American' educated both in Edinburgh and Paris, and M. de Mecies, a studious young naturalist and mineralogist recently met in London (see n. 86*).

On their way to the castle they were met by the Duke's eighteen-year-old heir George, Lord Lorne, 'who came to meet us with manifestations of the frankest politeness and the most gracious affability'. Then, once arrived, they were greeted 'with every mark of friendship in the midst of a numerous company and an amiable family, who joined to the most polished manners these prepossessing dispositions which are the natural dowry of sensitive and well-born minds'.

They went in to dinner. St-Fond for one was much gratified to find that 'French was spoken at this table with as much purity as in the most polished circles of Paris'.

The Duke, characteristically, pressed his new guests to stay at the castle 'at least a few weeks'. But alas, time was limited, as St-Fond was anxious to reach Staffa, so the weeks had to be compressed into three days, a time which they spent in unalloyed pleasure.

Life at Inveraray was easy and informal. Rising when they pleased, everyone amused himself—riding, shooting, or in St-Fond's case pursuing natural history—until breakfast, which as we have seen took place in the large south room now known as the Saloon.

'Here we find several tables, covered with tea-kettles, fresh cream, excellent butter, rolls of several kinds, and in the midst of all, bouquets of flowers, newspapers, and books.'

Again they please themselves until the dinner-hour at 4.30, when they find the
table laid with 25 to 30 covers:

> 'When every one is seated, the chaplain, according to custom, makes a short
> prayer, and blesses the food, which is eaten with pleasure, for the dishes are
> prepared after the manner of an excellent French cook; every thing is served
> here as in Paris, except some courses in the English style, for which a certain
> predilection is preserved; but this makes a variety . . .
>
> I was particularly pleased to see napkins on the table, as well as forks of the
> same kind as those used in France. I do not like to prick my mouth, or my
> tongue with those little sharp steel tridents which are generally used in England
> . . . the English knives being very large and rounded at the point, serve the same
> purpose to which forks in France are applied; that is, to carry food to the
> mouth . . . The manoeuvres at an English dinner are founded upon the same
> principle as the Prussian tactics – not a moment is lost . . .
>
> The entrées, the rôti, the entremets are all served as in France with the same
> variety and abundance . . . hazel-hens, and above all moorfowl, delicious fish,
> and vegetables, the quality of which maintain the reputation of the Scottish
> gardeners who grow them.'

Similarly the hothouse fruits of chilly Scotland in mid-September – 'beautiful
peaches, very good grapes, apricots, prunes, figs, cherries, and raspberries', took
St-Fond by surprise, not to mention the magnificence of the mahogany table once
the cloth was removed, the excellent wines, fine decanters and porcelain dishes.

> 'Towards the end of the dessert, the ladies withdrew to a room destined for the
> tea-table. I admit that they were left alone a little too long; but the Duke of
> Argyll informed me, that he had preserved this custom in the country' –

to avoid offending the gentlemen of Argyll, who still liked to sit long over their
drink as in the generation earlier. For some three-quarters of an hour they drank
toasts and also freely as they wished, of fine French and Portuguese wines,

> 'and if the lively champagne should make its diuretic influence felt, the case is
> foreseen, and in the pretty corners of the room the necessary convenience is to
> be found. This is applied to with so little ceremony, that the person who has
> occasion to use it, does not even interrupt his talk during the operation. I sup-
> pose this is one of the reasons why the English ladies, who are exceedingly
> modest and reserved, always leave the company before the toasts begin.
>
> At last we proceed to the drawing-room, where tea and coffee abound, and
> where the ladies do the honours of the table with much grace and ceremony;
> the tea is always excellent, but it is not so with the coffee . . . I imagine that the
> English attach no importance to the perfume and flavour of good coffee . . .
>
> After tea those who wished retired to their rooms; those who preferred
> converse or music remained in the drawing-room; others went out to talk. At
> 10 o'clock supper was served, and those attended it who pleased. I find that as
> a rule people eat a great deal more in England than in France. I do not know
> that they are more healthy for it; I doubt if they are . . .'

Such was the tenor of life at Inveraray in summer and autumn during the 1780s. St-Fond is equally informative about the characters whom he met:

'There were staying in the castle, at this time, the Duke of Argyll, one of the best of men, who had travelled in Italy and in France; the Duchess . . . she passes, and justly, for having been one of the most beautiful women in Great Britain: she is certainly one of the best informed; the Countess of Derby, the Duchess' daughter, by her first marriage: this lady had travelled a great deal, and speaks French with so much ease and so little accent, that she might be taken for a native of Paris . . . The children of the Duke were at home. The eldest daughter sings exceedingly well, and plays admirably upon the piano-forte, and she, as well as her younger sister, has the sweetest and most lovely expression. The Duke's son . . . has the courtesy and kindness of his father, and already shows much skill in drawing. A physician and chaplain formed the rest of the family circle. There were also several visitors in the house, among whom was a member of Parliament, a man of much intelligence, who had travelled, with advantage, in almost every part of Europe.'[86]*

On the second day of their stay the elderly Lord Braxfield, several times the cause of their finding no beds at inns, arrived – with whom they rapidly made peace when over a bottle he assured them, in the broad Scots accent for which he was notorious, that 'he would have shared his lodgings with us, if he had known what passed'.[87]*

Colonel Thornton, who passed through Inveraray in 1786, travelled not only with a friend (Mr Parkhurst), but with a 'complete camp equipage, guns, fishing-tackle' and 'a valet, groom, waggoner, falconer, boy and other servants', and brought his own boat for part of the journey, with a gig, change of horses, and baggage wagons for the rest. Also in his train was the painter George Garrard, a pupil of Dr Gilpin's recommended by the master himself, whom Thornton had engaged to 'take some views' for him. This throng of people arrived one October day at Inveraray Castle to find it crowded with company, including another judge, this time Lord Stonefield (John Campbell, the old Sheriff's son). While Thornton went off to the moors with young Lorne, 'a very keen shot', Garrard spent the day sketching, so much to the Duke's approval that he persuaded the young man to stay on and take some sketches for himself after the sporting party had moved on.[88]

Mr Bailey, from Otley, also travelled in style; and although he had no introduction to the Duke, he had been advised that in order to visit the castle in comfort

'it would be right in me to send my name, and additions, to the Duchess of Argyle, and also to signify to her Grace, on the same card, the objects of my journey. I was, moreover, instructed to point out the route I had taken, and to mention the names of the principal towns, islands, ruins, and other remarkable objects I had visited. This, I was informed, would secure to me a marked attention. . . . The result was, a person was immediately dispatched to me, who had orders to attend me during my stay, and who was not to quit me so long as I might think him useful.'

Having successfully acquitted himself in this catechism Mr Bailey spent an agreeable morning wandering in the grounds with his escort, rhapsodizing over the layout, taste and fashionably picturesque landscaping (Chinese, he fancied) of the policies. He returned to the castle by one o'clock, 'the hour which had been recommended to me as the most proper for surveying the interior of that princely edifice'.

Not only did he view that interior with gratifying admiration, but

'on my entrance into the Castle I was met on the terrace by the Duke and Duchess, with the Ladies Augusta and Charlotte Campbell, who very condescendingly asked me some questions on the subject of my tour, and desired I would amuse myself'.

Perhaps they had approved of the list of remarkable objects he had already visited before Inveraray.[89]

Not merely Mr Bailey, but everyone else who met the Duke and Duchess was enchanted. The Duke's improvements to his estate filled all with admiration, even those who criticized the taste of his buildings, and among gentry and tenantry his reputation was impeccable. 'He is rever'd as a prince in this country,' wrote another young scholar, Jacob Pattison, who made a horseback tour of the Highlands with a friend in 1780. 'By what we can learn of his Character, he is a just & an honest man.'[90]* Anne McVicar, a few years earlier, had been given a similar impression:

'A model of manly grace in his day, though now a little jaundiced with stomach complaints . . . One hears so little about him, he is so quietly passed over to make room for dashers, and feasters, and fighters, and talkers. He does not wish to be talked of, 'tis certain . . . I have a whole volume to write of this good Duke's worth, and wisdom, which improves and blesses the whole country . . . this modest and amiable benefactor of mankind.'[91]

John Knox, the noted bookseller, praised Argyll as 'a noble example to the gentlemen of the Highlands, whose efforts, if assisted by government, may do wonders in their hitherto useless country'.[92]*

The beautiful Duchess, however, was in failing health, and even by the time of St-Fond's visit had been giving cause for alarm. That year (1784) she had, for health reasons, to resign her post as Lady of the Bedchamber,[93]* as she was suffering an aggravation of the tuberculosis which had seemed to threaten both her life and beauty even in her twenties. Little more than a month after St-Fond and his friends saw the united family in such gaiety at Inveraray, the Duke accompanied his wife back to London, and having there taken formal leave of the King and Queen, escorted her and Lady Derby to the south of France where they remained, chiefly in Marseille, until the following June.

The Duchess, then fifty-one, was so frail that she appeared only once at a public hall in Marseille. Yet her beauty must still have been remarkable, for Joseph Cradock relates how on that occasion 'the Lieutenant of Police, rather too loudly, exclaimed, "I have never seen any one so completely beautiful before".' Cradock was himself moved to remark to the Duke 'that I thought her Grace really looked as well as when I first saw her in the Court-room in England, as Duchess of Hamilton';

to which the ungallant husband replied with a smile, 'Less aided then, perhaps, than now, Sir!'[94]

Somewhat recovered in health by her stay abroad the Duchess returned to England with the Duke in the summer of 1785, and spent the next few summers at Inveraray as usual. In September 1789, for the sake of the health of both, they again travelled abroad, visiting Flanders and Italy and returning in July 1790. The Duchess seems not to have accompanied the Duke to Inveraray the following autumn, for her strength was rapidly deteriorating; on 20 December 1790, she died at their house in Argyll Street among her anguished family, having 'never utter'd a groan, nor made a single complaint, she preserv'd her senses & speech to the very last', and also the fortitude to beg her husband to leave the room that she might spare him the sorrow of seeing her die.

General Seymour Conway, who wrote this account of the death to his cousin Horace Walpole, was connected with the Duchess only by marriage, yet 'having much regard, & love for her' felt her loss keenly; how much more then, her adoring husband, 'from his constant attachment, and perpetual habit of living with, and in appearance for her, & his family alone'. But although the Duke's affliction was so great he 'bear's the stroke with all the fortitude possible; & instead of yielding to it, makes every effort to comfort his family'.[95]

On Wednesday, 12 January 1791, the Duchess's embalmed corpse was borne through Edinburgh

> 'in a hearse drawn by six horses, attended by several other carriages, and accompanied by every appendage of the highest funeral pomp, which was justly due to the remains of such a distinguished personage'.[96]

Two days later the cortège slowly traversed the streets of Glasgow on the way to the family burial place at Kilmun. Among those following the hearse was her own coach and six; 'The Hearse, and all the horses were decorated with Escutcheons of her rank and title, in all the Funeral pomp becoming her Elevated station'.[97]

Elevated indeed she was: 'the Duchess with two tails', as Dr Johnson termed her, had married two Dukes and already seen two of her sons succeed to the title; but in addition she had since 1776 been Baroness Hamilton of Hameldon (Leicestershire) in her own right, and she was reputed to hold nearly sixty titles. She was almost universally loved, a happiness rarely the lot of a famous beauty. 'If her fortune is singular' (wrote Walpole, years earlier), 'so is her merit.'[98]

At Inveraray, during the Duchess's last declining years, although the final stages of the castle's interior decorations were not brought to a halt, great changes already began to be seen. If more adornments had ever been envisaged none were undertaken, and in 1789, in preparation for the family's long absence abroad, the Duke left special instructions for the castle's supervision.

Mrs Alexander, the housekeeper, was dismissed, an inventory was made, and the resident tailor (Archibald Macintyre) given charge of 'the standing furniture and keys of all the Rooms in the two principal Stories'. His duties as caretaker included 'to show the Castle to all Strangers . . . take care of the ffurniture and keep the Rooms properly aired'. For this responsibility he was paid two and sixpence a week, and the Duke authoritatively ordered that 'he is on no account to take vails from any Person whatever he shows the Castle to'. Pictures and tapestries were shrouded, as was customary, in green linen coverings to protect them from the sun (the tapestry covers alone, made by Macintyre, cost over £20).

The enormous staff was reduced to skeleton numbers and the base storey left to the sole charge of two chambermaids, 'spinning constantly' when they were not washing and airing the many rooms. Outside work was reduced to routine and maintenance; even poultry and rabbits were killed off and sold.[99]

Whereas by 1788 the castle, at last completed, was at its zenith in beauty, splendour and lively society, afterwards it probably never recovered quite the same state. Although after his wife's death the Duke lived more and more at the castle until his own death in 1806, and although his son George, Lord Lorne and his other children still filled the house with friends and it was visited more than ever, as the interest of the ageing Duke slackened a running-down became increasingly noticeable, until in his last years the house became – as Lady Louisa Stuart found – 'Confusion Castle with a witness'.

Upon a place so elegantly sweet,
I ne'er before set my Poetic feet.
O! what a lovely view I hence command,
While on the Nation's Glory, here I stand! . . .
The pleasant Parks and Plantings round the Town,
Are also worthy to be noted down.
The charming Woods, and Fir-trees rising high
Salute the clouds, and kiss them as they fly . . .
For Providence Divine I see doth smile,
On ev'rything belonging to ARGYLE!
Nothing is base, contemptible, or mean,
In all his territories to be seen.

James Maxwell *A Descriptive Poem on His Grace the Duke of Argyle's
Noble Palace at Inveraray*, Glasgow 1777

The chief amusement of the Duke seems the improvement of his Palace &
Environs, nothing fancyful appeares in his plan, all is Bold & Natural therefore
will last.

Thomas Wilkinson *Tour to the British Mountains* [1787], London 1824

The Castle stands on a verdant lawn encompassed by groves of the largest trees I
have seen in the country, the domain is deservedly accounted one of the richest
gems in the northern diadem.

Northern Tour journal of Rev. John Skinner of Camerton, Somerset, 1825,
vol. 5, p. 247, BM Add. 33687

VII

The surroundings of Inverarary Castle struck eighteenth-century visitors with their magnificence and natural beauty, and particularly the contrast between the richness and sophistication of this ducal domain and the barren moorland beyond. In 1780, the scholar Jacob Pattison, leaving Inveraray and journeying to Loch Awe, observed when he reached Port Sonachan that 'we had not seen a tree for 8 miles, since we had left the Duke of Argyles'.[1] Earlier, Thomas Pennant wrote of the splendid view 'from the top of the great rock Duniquaich ... the lawn sprinkled with fine trees, the hills covered with extensive plantations, a country fertile in corn, bordering on the Loch, and the Loch itself covered with boats'.[2]

Pennant in 1769, however, remains revealingly silent on any works of man in this landscape, for Duke Archibald's building in his policies was on a very small scale in comparison with what the 5th Duke was to execute between 1771 and 1790. The 5th Duke, unlike his father, had no intention of marking time or even merely consolidating. Rich, privileged, inheriting while still comparatively young, he was a product of the new age, and the age by comparison with the recent past was one of progress and enlightenment. In attempting to plant industries and modernize the Highlands Duke Archibald had been well ahead of his times; Duke John was in tune with his, encouraging not only industry but advanced farming methods, and wishing his own estates to demonstrate the superiority and civilized progress of man. His chief interests being agricultural and scientific, like his forebear Duke Archibald he cared little for fashionable society, and when at home amused himself in his workshop with mechanical devices, and with the study of improvements. The experiments which he introduced locally were, indeed, to become renowned throughout Scotland and beyond. Even when he was over eighty he could impress the poet James Hogg by showing him tools and implements he had made in his own workroom.

The first outdoor changes made by the 5th Duke, then, were more practical than ornamental. On taking over the management of Inveraray during the last years of his father's lifetime he had consulted William Mylne over the Court of Offices at the Cherry Park, which had then stood unfinished for several years, and Mylne submitted a plan for its alteration and completion. William Mylne visited Inveraray when the Duke and Duchess were there in August 1771, and shortly afterwards he drew three plans (of which only the second has survived) for a church, a bridge, and the court of offices.[3] The church was perhaps the first 'temporary' building put up in 1772 in the new town (see p. 258); the plan for completing the Cherry Park was partly executed in the spring of 1772, finishing with the brewhouse, ale-house and cellar the following winter and spring. In April 1773 Miss Anne McVicar, while morally disapproving the stateliness of great houses like ⁻ Inveraray, was able to admire the magnificence of this now complete office-court of St Catherines stone, with its pedimented gateway and glistening Bristol glass panes, even to the very roads laid to serve it : 'but what I greatly wonder at is, that they should place the offices at such a distance as to require such roads'.[4]

The appearance of the Cherry Park square has a hint of the *foresteria* of some Italian Palladian villa, with corner pavilions connected along north and south sides by heavy stone arches (subsequently filled in), and in front by a range of rooms with a central pedimented carriage entrance. The pavilions have high Venetian windows on their external sides, six-paned windows above, and sloping roofs rising to a central louvre-like chimney-stack. The rear range was occupied by cottages.[5]*

The stables and coach-houses at the old White Barns half a mile away, largely built under John Adam's direction between 1760 and 1762, were also completed.[6] A row of rubble-stone sheds, cottages and a hay-barn was added against the great kitchen-garden wall, and in 1775–6 a hot-house was made, where before long Waterstone the gardener was growing 'a great deal of nectarines, peaches, many grapes, cucumbers &c.'[7] According to Samuel Rogers, who visited as a young man in 1789, this was created 'for Lady Augusta, who is particularly fond of plants'. The cottages were built for those of the Duke's servants removed from the old town.[8]

Most of this row was probably supervised by William Mylne, but as his brother Robert makes his first appearance at Inveraray in 1772, it is reasonable to assume that the 'great shade' or barn built at right angles to it in 1774–5 was the first stage of Robert Mylne's design to complete the Maltland Court. Three storeys high and with a double pitched roof, this was really a two-aisled hall divided by an arcade along its internal length. The façade had five great open arches rising its full height, and at this stage the barn was fitted with a forge and a water-driven saw-mill and used by the Duke's wrights, smiths and other craftsmen.[9]

As an initial step in his agricultural experiments, in the autumn of 1771 the Duke inspected the large Fisherland meadow, beyond the new town site – now fully drained and reclaimed, its woodland clumps and quarries tidily fenced, and yielding an annual corn crop. On the loch-side adjoining the Gallowgate row the Duke chose the site for a large barn, begun the following year, to serve at present both for himself and for the town, and designed to prevent the havoc wrought on crops by the West Highland climate. Being of experimental design it proved unexpectedly difficult to complete, and in 1772 Robert Mylne must have been invited to include it in his first survey, for in 1774 he sent the Duke a drawing of alterations

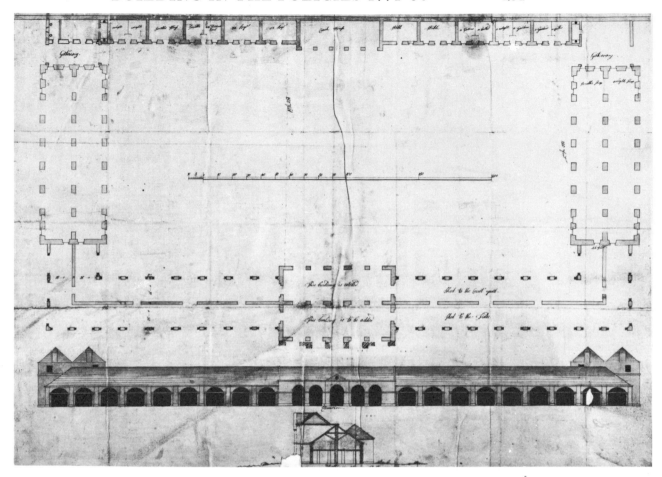

75. Design for the Maltland square
   Robert Mylne's drawing of 1776, with notes by George Haswell.

to its upper storey and roof;[10] in 1775 it was still unfinished, and that autumn the
Duke ordered the upper floor both here and at the Maltland hay-barn to be laid
with slats nailed to the joists 'so that there may be a ffree passage for wind & air to
Dry the Corn'.

The principle of the great Fisherland or Newtown Barn, and of the later barns
at Maltland and Glenshira, was ingenious and, before long, famous. A constant
current of air, admitted through a series of louvres, circulated round the sheaves
hung on pegs along the walls, allowing them gradually to dry under cover; in this
way corn and hay could be harvested even in bad weather, and stored in this
'perfect model for a west country barn' without danger of rotting. A contemporary
description of Maltland will serve equally for all:

'about 300 feet long, supported on wooden posts, the floor is raised 6 or 7 feet
above the ground, between the floor and the ground the hay is carried as soon
as cut, and there it is turned over till dry, and then stacked. The corn is carried
into the barn in the same condition; each sheaf is hung upon a separate peg.
The barn is full of latticed wooden windows which admit of the air freely.'[11]

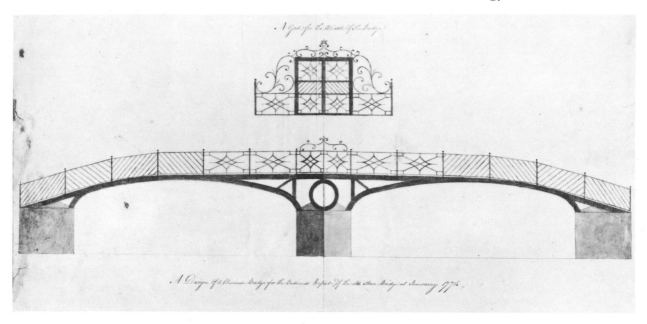

76. Proposed alterations to the old Town Bridge
    Unexecuted design in the Chinese taste, 1774.

For Mr Richard Sulivan, unfortunate enough to visit Inveraray during a very wet
spell in 1778, the sight of the Newtown barn merely confirmed his prejudice:
'Deluged with rain almost the whole year round, his grace of Argyle . . . is obliged
to strew some of his meadows with tarpaulins to dry his hay; and in harvest time to
range his sheaves of corn upon pegs, in granaries erected on purpose, and there to
let them ripen with air, instead of sunshine'.[12]

Between 1772 and 1777 the great work of demolition, starting with the removal
of houses nearest the castle, was carried out by companies of soldiers of the 15th,
43rd and later the 22nd Regiments, all billeted in the town. Most of the old houses
were razed in 1774 and 1775, and as the dust settled from stones and plaster, slate
roofs and thatch, the dung and rubbish was shovelled up, carted away and laid on
the Wintertown meadow. Forty or fifty soldiers were employed on digging out the
castle bank alone.[13] Under the direction of the Duke's overseer Thomas Hall they
cleared fallen rubble, drained and gravelled the area until the ground north of the
old tower, instead of rising as before, fell gently towards the river bank to create a
vista from the principal windows of the new castle. At length the stark, fortress-
like building rose in the midst of a large devastated area bare of trees, shrubs or
even grass. Only the castle green was yet covered with lawns, barbered to a fine
sward in summer by rolling with a horse-drawn roller, and 'sworded' by 'half a
dozen of old two edged Broad Swords . . . to Cutt down daizys, windlestraws &c'.

Much of the soldiers' digging was purely utilitarian, for the ground between
castle and Cherry Park was full of standing water and choked with rushes, and the
great storm of 1772 which destroyed the Aray and other bridges left a trail of general
devastation. Overseers and their parties built and repaired dykes, made a breast-

work to secure the river, and repaired the garden 'cascades'.[14]* The river bank, henceforth considered 'secure against any Risque of ffurther Encroachmts. from the winter floods', was finally banked up in a spell of brilliant late summer weather in 1778[15] (which Richard Sulivan, had he only known, missed by only a few days). No repetition seems to have occurred of the disaster of 1772, or of the earlier storms in 1750 and 1757.

Mrs Thrale, who saw Inveraray in this unsoftened state in 1789, claimed to admire the bare setting, for 'being insulated [it] looks ancient and being unadorned with Flouring Shrubs or other frivolities gives the Mind an Idea of simple Grandeur, & solitary Dignity . . .'[16] The Wordsworths on the other hand, in 1803, while praising the castle deplored the appearance of the river 'stripped of its natural ornaments, after the fashion of Mr Brown, and left to tell its tale . . . to naked fields and the planted trees on the hills'.[17]

During his first visit as landlord, in 1771, the Duke commissioned from John Campbell a set of water-colour drawings of Duke Archibald's ornamental buildings in the policies. This architectural draughtsman, of whom nothing otherwise is known, produced plans and elevations of the Gothick dairy at Tombreac, William Adam's well-head at Bealachanuaran, the Garron Bridge and the Gothick physic well in the meadow beyond Maltland. The first of these drawings is interesting as showing the dairy before later elaboration, and the last as the only surviving picture of a now vanished feature; for in the early years of Duke John this creation of Roger Morris was swept away, for reasons unexplained. Possibly it had dried up, as the meadow now shows no sign of a spring. The well-head was demolished in 1775 and its blocks of hewn St Catherines stone re-used, under George Haswell's direction, in doorways and window-surrounds for the manses in the new town.

Another darling project of Duke Archibald's to disappear about the same time was the salt water pond, made nearly thirty years earlier by the mouth of the River Aray. The pond had probably ceased to function when the military bridge on the King's road cut it off from its sluice; but when Robert Mylne was supervising the building of the new Aray bridge and the river bank was dammed against further flooding, the salt water pond was gradually filled in, and the ground newly planned.[18]

A single feature of the old town – the old bridge, long superseded by the military bridge – was almost given a reprieve. A charming sketch (anonymous) dated 1774 shows how it would have looked if ornamented in the Chinese taste. But although the fall of the military bridge must have given it a further lease of life while Mylne's bridge was being built, the removal of the old town rendered it superfluous and it was after all demolished in 1777,[19] leaving us to regret that this folly was not indulged. Two years later a 'floating plank bridge' was ordered on the site, and a set of stepping-stones, which still exist today.

77. The old Aray Bridge, shortly before its collapse in 1772
From the engraving by Moses Griffith.

The strange coincidence of the Aray Bridge's destruction on 7 September 1772, two nights after his arrival at Inveraray, presented Robert Mylne with the un-expected chance to rebuild it. 'Surveyed military bridge fallen', he recorded on 8 September, and on his departure by the Dumbarton road he also inspected the condition of the bridges over the Garron and at the head of Loch Fyne.[20]

Between 1773 and 1776 Mylne was several times consulted about the Aray bridge by the Duke and by Major Caulfield's successor Colonel Robert Skene. In April 1773 Mylne sent the Duke his designs to forward to the Colonel – elevation, section, drawings in wash, and rough plans; and a month later sent Skene a tech-nical description of his method, along with plans for the Colonel's own house which he had been commissioned to design at Pitlour in Fife.[21] Mylne at this time was working on several bridges – one at least (Dumbarton) in conjunction with Skene – including the building of Jamaica Bridge, Glasgow, and rebuilding at Newcastle, whose great bridge over the Tyne had been destroyed by a gale.[22]

The mason for the new Aray Bridge was John Brown, possibly son of the John Brown who had built the old, and the Duke provided timber for the centring. Although this was a public enterprise, the Duke took a personal share in the design, and on 25 September 1775 he wrote to Mylne, who had just returned to London from Scotland,

'I am much inclined to have some more Balustrades on the Bridge here, as it appears to me that so long an extent of solid parapet looks a little dead and heavy. I think they may be placed either on the Crown or Centre of the Arches,

[25] The Aray Bridge, begun 1775

or on the top of the Pillar which forms the abuttment. Let me know whether you approve of either of these alterations, which, I think, would make the Bridge look lighter and better.'[23]*

This change was adopted with successful results, and in view of Mylne's noted pride and reluctance to compromise, one must assume that he personally approved the Duke's suggestion. We know from his diary that, while at Inveraray in August that year, Mylne made a detailed inspection of the bridge's construction and meticulously compared it with his plans, sending his comments to Colonel Skene in 'a long letter of observations and alterations', which he shortly afterwards discussed with him in person. A year later almost to the day he again visited the bridge, whose structure had developed a crack, and his last note on the subject is that he 'surveyed the New Bridge – examined the fracture of it – advised some works to be done'.[24]

Robert Mylne's two-arched bridge over the Aray, partly built of St Catherines stone, combines lightness with strength, for the massive spandrel above the abutment is pierced by a large circular opening, the diameter of whose moulding equals the height of the balustrade above the abutment. Of the Duke's two alternatives, Mylne adopted that of introducing balustrades above the bridge's centre as well as on either side of the arches, with happy effect. The large circular opening to reduce spandrel weight was a feature notably employed by Smeaton in the Perth and Coldstream bridges, both begun in 1766, which Mylne certainly knew.[25]* It is,

78. Design for the new Aray Bridge by Robert Mylne
    Section and elevation of 1773.

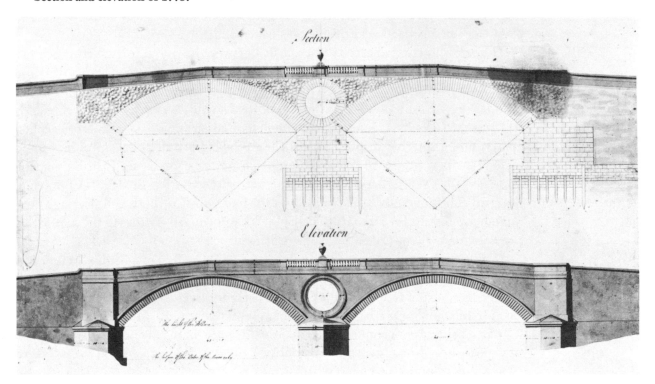

[26] Another view of the Aray Bridge

too, with variations, a favourite feature in Mylne's Inveraray buildings, used particularly in his screen walls and as a simple finish to pediments. As used in the
bridge, the opening is a satisfying solution to the problem of how to unify a composition in two parts, and prevent the large spandrel from looking (to borrow the
Duke's phrase) 'a little dead and heavy'.

Early in 1774 Mylne produced his first design for the new town front, followed
by suggestions for altering the Fisherland barn. Other commissions followed his
visit in August 1775:

> 'Gave the D. of Argyll a design of an Elevation, section, 2 plans for a Dairy farm
> house with a large room over it, proposed to be erected on the side of Loch
> Fyne, Inverary. – 16 [£]
> 'Gave him also a design of 2 elevations, plan and section of a lodge and gate
> for the entrance into the park at Inverary near the Bridge [Garron, see p. 237]
> and fronting the Loch – all washed neatly – 8.'[26]

His accounts mention a fee of 18 guineas for his four-day stay in Inveraray and
'various consultations . . . on the scite of dairy farm, a lodge at Garron Bridge, and
many other matters in the Castle and offices'.[27]

'Many other matters in the offices' evidently included the Maltland farm buildings, for which in February 1776 Mylne gave the Duke 'a plan with elevations and
sections, on the same sheet, of making the buildings behind the garden into a compleat farm yard', fee £5. His unexecuted design of a small domed, four-apsed
house with lower wings for the Kilbryde dairy, three miles down Loch Fyne, was
as elegant as one might expect; occasional references to this dairy occur in later
instructions, including alterations made in accordance with Mylne's plan in
1785–6, but this particular design was never built.[28*]

The new lodge and gate at Garron Bridge were intended for the entrance to a
new private approach to the castle, begun in 1775 under the steep slopes of Duniquaich, as an alternative to the Wintertown gate entrance near the town. This new
road leaves the military road at the end of the Garron Bridge by a gate centred on
it, skirts the Deer Park along a fine (though now much depleted) avenue of beeches,
and, running roughly parallel with the high road above the burial ground of Kilmalew, swings westward under Duniquaich to circle the bend in the river and
approach the castle from the north-west, across the Garden Bridge.[29] A branch of
the road continued north-eastwards past the fountain-head and, still skirting Duniquaich, up the slope to the 'High Dairy' at Tombreac. All visitors to the castle used
the new road, as described by Henry Skrine in 1787:

> 'The grand approach . . . is through a gateway at the foot of a bridge, before you
> reach the town, from whence it immediately crosses a magnificent avenue of old
> beeches, near a fresh-water lake in the park, and ascends the side of a consider-
> able hill, through a range of pleasing plantations; here all the beauties of the
> place break at once upon the sight; the little town, in several neat and regular
> fronts, lies spread over the extremity of the bay . . . surrounded every where
> with mountains, and filled with vessels.'[30]

79. Proposed alterations to the pigeon house, 1776
   Robert Mylne's unexecuted design in the style of a round temple.

To keep the entrance to this new and extremely picturesque approach a porter
was required, whose lodge, sited close to Morris's Garron Bridge, was architecturally integrated with it in Mylne's design. The plan was not fully executed, and
because of the Duke's illness was not even begun for several years.

   Mylne also advised on additions later made to the Gothick dairy at Tombreac,
begun in the 1750s but not completed, and fixed the line of several new roads about
the farm buildings, presumably including the new private entrance from Garron
Bridge to the Castle.

   In 1776 (if not earlier) Mylne – now in such high favour that he was presented
with a portrait of the Duchess – was invited to advise how to elaborate Roger
Morris's dovecot, and on 26 August produced 'a design of 4 drawings, washed, for
altering the Pidgeon House into a Round Temple'.[31] The result would have been
a total transformation, adding a dome, with a smaller dome surmounting the
original central lantern, and a colonnade encircling the original simple cylindrical
building. This transformation materialized only as far as an order by Sonachan

in December 1780 for pillars, to be 'cutt and Bor'd in order to make the intended alteration of the Pigeon House in the course of the Summer if it can be over-taken'; but we hear no more of the change, and Morris's dovecot stands as he built it (though now disused) to this day.

The abandonment, delay or modification of this and other schemes coincided with the Duke's serious illness in 1777 and 1778. Apart from nearly ending his life it prevented him from visiting Inveraray for two seasons, and proved cripplingly expensive. But the need for retrenchment went far deeper than this, for a report drawn up by his lawyer, James Ferrier, at the time shows that the Duke's expendi-ture on Inveraray – policies, improvements and upkeep included – since 1770 had averaged £4,500 a year,[32]* about half of his net income from the Scottish estates, and it was more than they could bear. An imposition of heavy rent increases had produced not more revenue, but merely an increase in unpaid arrears. Further-more, the economic background in the 1770s was not a healthy one, and the out-break of the American War in 1776, in its effect on markets and cattle prices, further aggravated the situation.

During the Duke's illness and absence, when the Chamberlain, Donald Campbell of Sonachan, had instructions to practise economies, outside work at Inveraray was limited to maintenance and to making some of the estate roads fixed by Mylne. A sale of the product of the Duke's woodlands, for a price eventually settled at £2,500, was negotiated by Lord Frederick Campbell with Mr Kendal, director of the Furnace Company.[33] Lord Frederick, who stayed with his family at the Castle for some months while his Fencible Regiment was stationed at Greenock, super-vised the works and estate, and in the Duke's absence it was he who received David Loch, General Inspector of Fisheries in Scotland, to discuss local industry and the future of the herring fishery. Loch, although viewing all that he saw at Inveraray with a business man's eye, spared time to admire 'the ground about the castle . . . laid out with the greatest taste into a *policy* or plantation'.[34]

In February 1779 the Duke sent James Ferrier detailed instructions for putting his financial affairs in order,[35] and after Lord Frederick's departure tried, more or less frustratedly, to control his affairs by correspondence. He met with the same obstruction or incompetence as had Duke Archibald. Sonachan and the overseers, Thomas Hall for the estate and Michael Waterstone for the garden, were supposed to render weekly reports on fixed days, but the Duke considered Sonachan irregular in writing and dilatory in executing his orders. His tone becomes increasingly exasperated: why is the Chamberlain not more informative? – 'otherwise your letters are for very litle use or amusement to me, for Example as to the Dalbuy road what is the length of it, what Bargain was made for the working it, is the Gravell good . . .' And this new road from Bealachanuaran to Esachosan, 'I never ordered and can see very little use for it, in proportion to the Expence . . . for the future never undertake such a work without consulting me.' Hall, too, had made 'a tedious job' of levelling the ground near the smith's shop, 'it was begun on the

17th March and on the third of Aprile it was still to Cover with Earth and Sow'd, as well as I remember there is not much more than two hundred yards Square of it'.

The 5th Duke, like the 3rd, had an eye that missed no detail, and was like a gimlet to his aides; he further resembled Duke Archibald in short patience for muddled reports : 'Hall, send me a Skeetch upon paper of the improvement on the Maltland in the most minute manner . . . I do not precisely understand your last Discription . . .'; and again, 'If you had wrote me Distinct and Minute Letters as I desired some time since, it would have saved me the trouble of asking those questions.' No one could for long have preserved any illusion that life at Inveraray might be easier with the Duke away.

At the end of July 1779 the Duke returned to both Inveraray and Rosneath, and normal progress was gradually resumed. His first orders were for consolidation and repairs, for example at the dairy at Tombreac, and the 'great shade' at Maltland; but in 1780 he authorized the making of several more roads, and even approved the disputed route past Bealachanuaran, now to be made sufficient 'So that Carriages may Go up & Down Without the least difficulty'.

Between the years 1779 and 1790 were made the most important contributions to the policies : the Garron Lodge and screen wall, completion of the Maltland, the Dubh Loch Bridge, and the important farm buildings at Maam in Glenshira. The Gothick dairy at Tombreac was also completed, under Mylne's guidance, 'according to the Original plan', although as this pretty little eye-catcher was unfortunately demolished in the late nineteenth century it may be dealt with very briefly.

In January 1787, after consulting with Mylne in London,[36] the Duke dictated an elaborate order for his wrights:

'The front of Tombreck Dairy to be finished the mock windows to be plaistered
& painted to show as a window, one of the Turret windows that is in the Castle
to be put in the middle part and the wall to be straighted about it . . .'

An order the same winter to make a new carriage entry there shows that the Gothick Dairy was intended to form part of the round of pleasure excursions now made possible by the numerous carriage roads laid about the estates and ornamental policies. Much of the dairy's façade was only of wood which soon rotted or 'failed', so that in the 1790s further alterations had to be made; but a suggestion approved by the Duke in November 1794, to raise the central gable to match the sides, with battlements in more durable materials, was slow to be executed because all masons were then diverted to building the new church in the town. Surviving drawings make us regret the loss of this decorative though un-durably built little folly, commended by visitors such as Thomas Newte and Colonel Thornton, for, surprisingly enough, its 'neatness' and, as termination of a romantic vista from the castle, for thriftily combining the picturesque with practical use.

Transformation of the cottages and barns at Maltland into an architecturally harmonized whole must have been discussed at least as early as Mylne's 1775 visit; his plans for 'a compleat farm yard' there were dated February 1776 (see p. 236). The scheme was then laid aside until after the Duke's illness, and in November

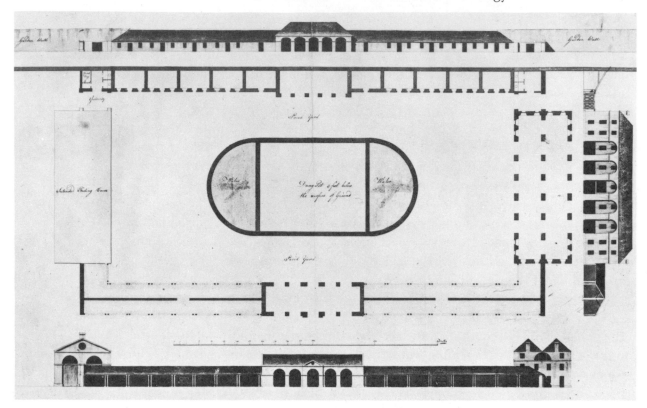

80. Amended design for the Maltland square
    Robert Mylne's plan and elevation of 1780.

1780 Mylne sent him, as a modification of his original design, 'a drawing of the plan, elevation and section of a shed, to be built at the Great Square of farm offices at Inverary, in room of one intended by great drawing formerly', followed by written descriptions sent to the Duke and Haswell. Other working drawings and details were given to the Duke or sent to Inveraray in 1781 and 1782.[37]

Meanwhile, in 1779 on his first return visit the Duke had ordered the brickwork of the 'Great Shade' to be harled, and the making of storm windows. This large building was continually being reorganized, the north end altered for carts below and hay above, and later (1783) converted into a girnel; while the sawpits for two pairs of sawyers were removed to a separate work-place at the other end. The smithy was arched with brick to prevent fire, and an internal wooden stair was built (for though in places open to the roof, the great shade was equivalent to three storeys high) its timber hoisted by a crane set up outside.

The Maltland square was completed in 1781 and 1782 by building a long row of 'new shades' on its north side, and on its east the great Riding House facing the 'great shade'. John Tavish was the mason for the shades, and built the upper part of the Riding House. In the early autumn of 1782 the two ranges were slated and shaped timber columns were erected along the north side, making a series of open sheds.[38] They were completed and painted in 1784 and, like the Fisherland barn, fitted with 'pins' or pegs for the sheaves, and similar pins made for all floors of the Riding House. In fact, in 1787 the Duke demanded 'many more pins', particularly in the Riding House.

The courtyard thus formed in the centre was levelled, drained and gravelled by the masons, who at the same time were arching the smith's forge; the Riding House was harled and plastered.[39] Apart from a few extras like the making of strong oaken gates pierced with air-slits for the coach-houses, and (early in the 1790s) a set of ten gates for the great barn by the new wright, Simpson, Maltland was complete.

So were created 'the magnificent Drying Barns of the Duke of Argyle, so far famed, and the only ones of the kind in Scotland'. Mr Bailey of Otley, inspecting the Maltland in the early autumn of 1787, enquired minutely about the ventilation principle which enabled them to dry such huge quantities of crops.

> 'Excepting at the angles, and at intervals, where the roofs and beams require support, the sides and ends are wholly composed of boards regularly cut, and disposed with the lower edges declining outwards, in the manner of Venetian blinds. The coverings are of a beautiful blue slate, which is brought from Cowal; . . . The interior is furnished with joists, at proper intervals, over which the sheaves, being loaded two by two, are suspended; and four or five days are, in general, found sufficient to render them fit for the mow. The successive dryings are, oftentimes, continued until near Christmas.'[40]*

The only noteworthy later addition was a new gardener's house on the garden-wall range, to which the masons were directed as soon as they finished the shades in Glenshira. This house was completed and occupied by Whitsun, 1791, its chief point of interest being an economical attempt to contrive its flues so as to make a hot wall for the hot-house on the other side of the wall—but without success.

All visitors remark on the rural setting of Maltland, hidden from the house and bowered in trees. But not all approved. William and Dorothy Wordsworth, who found much to dispraise at Inveraray, were 'disgusted with the stables, outhouses, or farm-houses . . . behind the Castle: they were broad, out-spreading, fantastic, and unintelligible buildings'.[41]

'Fantastic' and 'unintelligible' are puzzling verdicts, for Mylne's design brings an urbane symmetry and scale to a set of simple farm buildings. The earlier sheds and cottages on the south side are balanced by the long northern series, whose open-fronted sheds flank a higher five-arched central arcade with a slightly projecting pedimented feature. This north range is divided longways by an internal wall, with an identical front on its outer side, and its central loggia repeats in miniature the five giant arches of the 'Great Shade' on the western side. The large Riding House which completed the square was the scene of the amateur theatricals of the Duke's children and their friends, particularly Monk Lewis. It was unfortunately burnt down in 1817, but the 'Jubilee Hall', rebuilt on the same site in 1897, is more or less a copy of Mylne's original. Having become ruinous, much of the north range was demolished in 1967, but the remainder, though now badly in need of restoration, retains a hint of the refinements of Mylne's conception.

To farmers Maltland was of especial interest, and John Inglis, who saw it in 1784, was full of praise, as of the policies generally:

'All round the house is walks in every direction with very large single trees, clumps and avenues . . . Here are some of the finest beeches limes and chesnut trees in Scotland. The River Erra . . . is beautifully banked and levelled through all the policies and has some fine bridges over it . . .

The garden is a little behind the house, is well furnished with flowers and kitchen stuff and has a variety of exotick plants and trees in it . . . and here a great range of farm houses viz. stables smithy wrights' shops, and besides the Duke has several dairies in which are many cattle. The policies extend along the loch full 6 miles and two miles back. A vast deal has lately been planted.

The wood in the whole policies . . . is valued at fifty thousand pounds sterling.'[42]

The timber especially was always admired, though as a farmer Inglis viewed the splendour with a prosaic eye. Most visitors were more extravagant – 'Thousands of the gloomy fir are weeded out, and trees pleasing to the eye rise from the vale to the lofty summit, in all the sublime magnificence of nature'.[43]* Even more enthusiastic was Mrs Thrale:

'Never were so many – I might say so many Thousand Trees disposed with so much Taste, Two long lines of enormous Beeches fill the Base of the principal Mountain, up the sides of which Pale Ash, and gloomy Pines, and Sycamores . . . diversify the Tints.'[44]

The porter's lodge at Garron Bridge, deferred until after the Duke's recovery, took shape as slowly as did most buildings at Inveraray. Whinstones were quarried as early as 1778, and later hewn and dressed at Carlundon, but although winter instructions were twice issued to build next spring, the foundation was only cast in June 1782. Even then, while materials were prepared, the building was not done until the Duke's visit of 1783, and was then finished quickly and harled the following spring (1784), with 'the building adjoining' – that is the screen wall: 'the arch part is to be of dark Collour like the Inveraray stone and the pillars and other parts to be white and done with the Irish lime stone'. During his last, and longest visit to Inveraray in 1785 Robert Mylne further advised on the lodge and wall, and on landscaping the ground about them.[45]

Mylne intended a terminating lodge for either end of Garron Bridge, linked to its abutments by two seven-arched screen walls, whose central arches were raised into embellished pedimented features. A 'long drawing' which he gave the Duke in January 1777, 'wherein Garron Bridge, the 2 Lodges, and fence-wall, etc. are introduced',[46] demonstrates what has been lost by not executing the full plan. The drawing shows a small, plain-pedimented house with short wings gabled at each end, a front door in a round-headed frame, set between a pair of windows surmounted by circular openings in the upper storey; and a lower window in each wing in a round-headed frame like the door. The back elevation was apsidal. The single lodge built was less happily designed; the horizontal emphasis has been lost

[27] Garron Lodge, 1783–4, designed by Robert Mylne

by abandoning the pediment for a plain gable broken only by a small solid oval, and by removing the entrance to the back and omitting the wing windows, leaving three shallow insets in the harled wall-surfaces to maintain the continuity of the arched screen wall. The round windows, placed so far apart as to leave a large blank area in the centre, give the façade a disturbingly staring appearance. The blank space, and lack of a pediment, impart a sense of emptiness not apparent in the drawing.

Mylne's journal entries, at best merely allusive, often omit whole sites which he must have inspected at Inveraray; and one visit about which he recorded no details at all was of five days spent there in September 1783, 'giving much and varied advice on subjects'.[47] Two of the subjects may, however, be deduced as the Dubh Loch bridge and the farm in Glenshira – both in the neighbourhood of the Garron Lodge – for in 1784 Mylne sent a small plan of the farm buildings, and in November 1783 compiled, for the large single-arched stone bridge by the Dubh Loch, the only detailed specification to have survived of any of his Inveraray designs.[48]

These works were both connected with the great agricultural improvements now in hand for Glenshira, the rich and beautiful valley running down to Loch Fyne at the point where Garron Bridge, on the military road, spans the short tidal water of that name. Garron Water drains from the small, rather forbidding Dubh Loch, north of the Deer Park, into Loch Shira, a bay of Loch Fyne; Dubh Loch was well stocked with salmon and trout, and herring were netted in shoals from Loch Shira. Better roads were now to be laid through this glen, and in order to give access to the fertile fields beyond the east side of Dubh Loch it was necessary to build a second bridge over the Garron Water – which, though now always known as the Dubh Loch bridge, was in contemporary accounts sometimes confusingly referred to as the 'Garron' or 'new Garron' bridge.

As well as advising on the Garron lodge, then building, Mylne in 1783 must have fixed the position of the new bridge, which was centred on the great lime avenue in the Deer Park, through which a proper road was now laid. The Duke had already (December 1782) required estimates from the mason (? Duand) who had built two other Argyll bridges, over the Awe and the Orchy. In December 1783, however, a month after Mylne made up his specification, an estimate of £312 10s was accepted from John Tavish, mason of the new Maltland sheds and Riding House, with his guarantee to maintain the bridge for seven years.[49]

True to the Inveraray tradition, first the work was delayed and then progress was slow. The order to build was eventually given in October 1784, but cannot have been implemented, for the contract drawings were not signed by Tavish and the Chamberlain until 10 August 1785. However, that September Mylne set out the lines of the approach banks and ordered that the river-bed under the bridge should be paved in the spring;[50] by 1787 the gravel was being laid on the deck, and in the following year John Tavish received his final payment.

Mrs Murray, of Kensington, considered the Dubh Loch bridge 'somewhat in the style of Wade's bridge in Appneydow [Aberfeldy] but without its spires'.[51]

[28] The Dubh Loch Bridge, 1786–7, designed by Robert Mylne

It is in great contrast to Inveraray's two military bridges, whose classical balustrades and enrichments Mylne here eschewed; he further, by means of a shallow segmental arch springing from the heavily splayed base of the abutments, produced a comparatively level road with a horizontal parapet line. The style hints at the castellated, with abutments incorporating corbelled and battlemented quarter-circle towers, while on the parapet are blind cross-shaped loopholes – hardly showing up today, as the blackened background originally ordered has worn off. The mediaeval conception was to have been further strengthened by a pointed archway across the road on the abutment at either end, but these were never built. Hence, while this bridge has not the elegance of its predecessors, its strong, simple line and sparse use of ornament anticipates some of the fine bridges of the early railway age.

For his long visit in 1785, Mylne's summaries of his professional tasks at Inveraray are unusually full, perhaps because having a lengthy and complex programme it was necessary to jot down his activities every day, whereas the fewer matters considered in a short visit could be easily remembered. Some of the references are, however, extremely obscure, particularly to a 'New Lodge & Gates staked out' at a site (according to his drawings of the following spring) 'at Entrance going to the Deer Park'[52] – unless this refers to the second Garron lodge, later countermanded. Plans and elevations, undated like most of Mylne's drawings, exist for a lochside lodge with spire, dome and battlements, and a note on one of these drawings shows it to be intended for Hugh Main, the Duke's fisherman. But no references appear to this intended lodge, whose site cannot now be determined, although nineteenth-century estate plans show a lodge under the wooded slopes of Duniquaich near the south-west corner of the Deer Park.

Mylne's tasks this season also included the siting of road crossings in the 'Pleasure Grounds', landscaping round the spring-head at Bealachanuaran, the alteration of Tombreac dairy, and his elaborate frontage for the New Town, to which his screen wall at the Garron Bridge forms a kind of preliminary foretaste. Another small problem solved this autumn was that of the ice-house.

Recorded references to the ice-house show an anomaly which can be only tentatively explained. In December 1781 the Duke ordered the Chamberlain to try one of the vaults in the fosse casements round the castle as an ice-store, but the expedient 'did not answer'. The idea was not abandoned, for in September 1785 Mylne was consulted on it, and on 10 November sent the Duke a drawing of 'an Ice House, adapted to the ground under the Fosse, of the Castle at Inverary'.[53] Yet in October an expert named William Stothard had been brought to Inveraray from Arrochar to advise how to build a detached ice-house in the grounds, and in a short time the little domed building now to be seen by the roadside north of Cherry Park, was completed. It was stocked with ice in January 1786, and the total cost, including the ice and a fee of two guineas to Stothard, was £25 5s 7½d.[54] Whether this, too, was under Mylne's direction is not stated, or whether he reached his solution for an ice-house in the vaults unaware that the Duke had already acted on other advice.

The last of Mylne's contributions to the policies at Inveraray also marked the end of their architectural development, apart from a few later trifles by Nasmyth and others. It marked, too, the last stage in the Duke's experimental farms : the important and indeed probably unique group of buildings at Maam in Glenshira.

This valley, now a luxuriant backwater whose narrow roads wind only to a scattering of farms and, since the 1950s, eventually to a large power dam and reservoirs at the head of the River Shira, was in the seventeenth century a populous place occupied by families of McKellars and McVicars. Even as late as 1760 the population was 260. The McKellars were in ancient times chief musicians to the Argyll family, and (wrote a descendant, Patrick McVicar, in the less thriving days of 1802),

> 'I have seen myself in my grand father McKellars house . . . the Harp & Case with Quiver & Case . . . The Harpers Foord on Sheera, between Stuckscarden & Kilblaan, has been pointed out to me, where sat on each side the River, the two musicians of Stuckscarden & Kilblaan, playing in concert.'[55]

'My grand father McKellars house' may well have been the very farm at Maam which now, transformed by its ingenious outbuildings and made accessible by a new road from Dubh Loch, was to complete the list of celebrated sights which no visitor to Inveraray was expected to miss.[56] Maam was certainly the birthplace of the military engineer Patrick McKellar, who served under General Wolfe at Quebec and built the forts at Ontario and Oswego.[57]*

The change in Glenshira's fortunes was part of the farming policy of Duke Archibald, who from about 1750 onwards began to take over the valley's farms from their owners for cattle grazing, and the change-over from corn to cattle was sign-posted by his suppression of the Glenshira mill in the 1750s. Thirty years later, although ripe for development, the valley was already well known for its beauty and fertility. Even the farm gates were worthy of comment, made to a quasi-Gothick design by the Duke's wright Graham Strathearn. The poetaster James Maxwell, describing his visit in 1777, long before either the bridge or other improvements were made, writes:

> 'First to *Glenshiray* I my course did steer,
> To see some wonders that had reach'd mine ear . . .
> The very gates that leadeth thereunto,
> Do almost all that I have seen out-do.
> Thy works *Strathern*, shall celebrate thy name,
> And like a Monument exalt thy fame . . .
>   On one hand lies a Park of Fallow Deer
> Of noble brood, which finds rich pasture here.
> And on the other grows such lofty woods,
> Upon a bank, whose tops salute the clouds.
> Again a Fish-pond, border'd all with green,
> One of the best and richest I have seen . . .
> And farther up the valley still doth lie

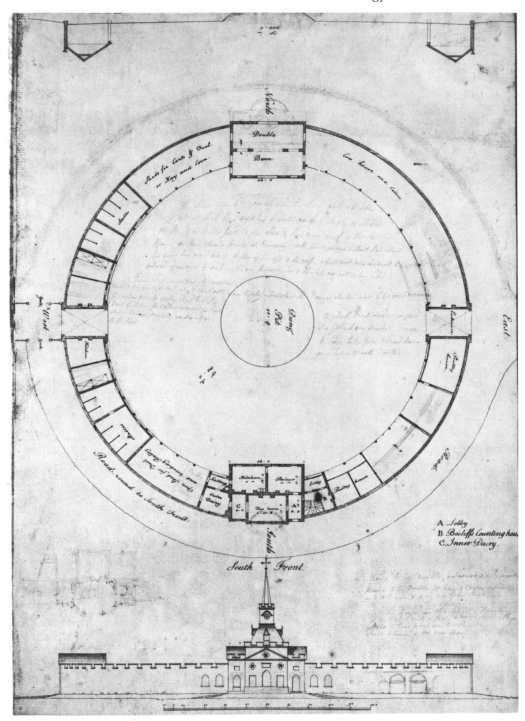

81. Maam, Glenshira
    Robert Mylne's working drawing of ?1785.

[29] Maam, Glenshira, the incomplete circle of farm buildings

Delightful *meadows*, pleasing to the eye.
And, O what loads of Hay from hence are brought,
Such as could hardly be believ'd or thought.'[58]

To these most far-flung of his valley farms the Duke now brought the benefits of his improved method of corn drying. Mylne evidently inspected the Maam site in 1783, producing in July 1784 'a small plan for farm buildings in Glenshira' with an explanatory letter. The Duke returned this, presumably for alteration, and exactly a year later a second plan followed.[59] The obscurity of Mylne's references during his visit in 1785 sometimes defies interpretation, but his drawing of a 'Circle and 4 Cross Roads', and a subsequent conference at the Duke's house at Ealing in May 1786 on (among other matters) the 'Drying Ground', probably refer to Glenshira and its farm. The Maam house was extended between 1784 and 1786, and between 1787 and 1789 was built the great 'circle' – actually only a semicircle – of the barn and outbuildings, in principle if not at all in appearance following the tradition of the Fisherland and Maltland barns, in architectural ingenuity outstripping either. The stone was quarried in Glenshira itself by William Lessly, and a neighbouring house turned into a 'guildhall' for the masons. For the considerable amount of woodwork – staircase, gates for the arches, and the 'open floor' of peculiar construction – two pairs of sawyers were required. The 'ambrasures' were made by Peter Gardner, a stone-cutter who later worked at Inveraray church; but the chief mason work, including pointing and pinning the cornice, was done by John Tavish, who in 1789 received £85 7s 4d for his work. Sir Archibald Campbell advised on finishing the gavels terminating the east and west ends, and the roof was originally finished with wooden ornaments or pinnacles, which have not survived. When, in 1790, the new building was harled 'not quite white', it was complete except for fitting up the stables and stalls and laying a pavement outside and inside.[60]

Although the intended circle was never completed, so impressive are the barns that we may even prefer them as they stand, with their effect of a central 'villa' with pillared wings, curving forward to plain harled façades whose castellated parapets mask the gable-ends. (These façades were of course regarded as temporary, and would have been removed had the full circle ever been built.) The openings between the pillars supporting the steeply-pitched roofs of the wings were closed with wooden gates, but have since been haphazardly filled in.

The main building, double-roofed like Maltland, is surrounded by an embattled parapet matching the ends of the wings, but with a small central gable in front, below which are large pointed openings flanked by narrow pilaster-buttresses. At either side are small pointed-arched doorways on the ground floor, and circular perforated openings above. The rear elevation is almost identical except that the centre openings are contained in a shallow bow which emphasizes the circumference of the building's circle; and a string course carries on the line of the barns level with the spring of the roof.

This group of buildings, and the Dubh Loch bridge, are Mylne's sole ventures into the Gothick at Inveraray. The satisfying sweep of their curve is enhanced by

[30] Maam, Glenshira

their situation on the valley floor, where they can be viewed at full extent from the road above on the eastern slope of Glenshira. The Honourable Mrs Murray thought them 'like so many noble castles . . . with Gothic exteriors', for 'those parts of the barns which could not be built castle-like, are painted so as to complete the resemblance'. Indeed, Mrs Murray privately christened Glenshira barns 'Hay Castle'[61] – while Lord Palmerston's father, in 1800, thought that at a distance they resembled 'great monasteries'![62]

The situation, romantic though it was, was not chosen for aesthetic reasons. Lying across the middle of the valley, the barn with openings on either side created a constant through draught, and the corn sheaves hung in the upper storey from sharp pegs fixed at an angle, on wooden frames suspended from the roof, jointed for lowering to stack the corn and raising to dry it. As the floor was made of battens set two inches apart, a draught was created through this as well. Openings at the appropriate level enabled hay and corn to be unloaded directly from the carts. The barn also had a closed floor for threshing above, and a flagged ground floor where potatoes were stored, kept constantly turned until dry, when they were removed to cellars.[63] The closed yard encircled by the wings was intended for a 5-foot deep dung-pit, eventually dug and paved in 1799 by Robert Lemon (who also made the Newtown middenstead in 1798). If built, the other semicircle would have contained stables, and its central feature, in appearance like the other, was to have held a dairy, henhouse and servants' rooms.[64]*

In October 1793 Thomas Hall told a visiting agriculturist, James Robson, that the barn held the corn crop of thirty acres, and that here and in the 'Glenaray' barn (presumably Maltland) 45,000 stones of hay had been dried that season. The crop was, Robson noted, 'remarkably green and fresh, and better than what is generally dried out of doors'.[65]

Glenshira contained several other farms, such as Stuckscarden and Stuckagoy; the most distant was Elrickmore a mile beyond Maam, where another large barn was first adapted and shortly rebuilt.[66]* To link all these, from 1791 onwards a road was carried by degrees up the valley, but as the River Shira was subject to flooding its course had to be diverted in several places and new bridges were built – one of them, at Stuckagoy, by John Tavish (1798). William Hervey, making a return visit in 1794 after nearly thirty years, rode out with the Duke and the surveyor Mr Langlands to visit the Glenshira drying-barns, and saw labourers there 'driving piles into the ground to prevent the encroaching floods destroying the banks'.[67] But in 1798 the River Shira again seriously encroached on the surrounding fields and the Duke complained of the 'partial repairs . . . ignorantly & expensively carried on of a sudden by David Greig' (the assistant overseer employed to alter Elrickmore barn). Colonel Graham, the then Chamberlain, was obliged to summon contractors from the new Crinan Canal to help in a survey of the flood area and a scheme for its protection. By 1802 a large 'bulwark' of eight or nine feet high had been built.[68]

The road up Glenshira was intended eventually to be extended northward

82. Maam, Glenshira
Plan and elevation of 1796, showing Robert Mylne's original
intentions for a completely circular farm building.

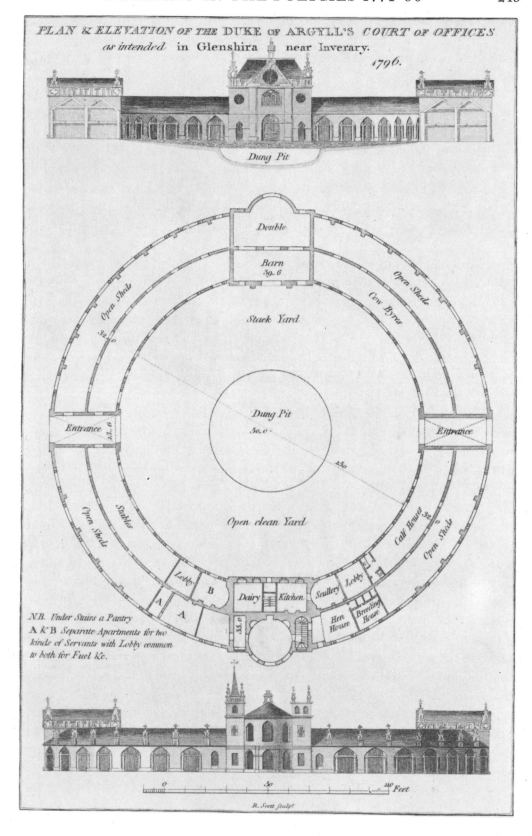

PLAN & ELEVATION OF THE DUKE OF ARGYLL'S COURT OF OFFICES as intended in Glenshira near Inverary.

1796.

Dung Pit

Double

Barn
39. 6

Open Sheds

Cow Byres

Open Sheds

Stack Yard

Entrance

Dung Pit
50. 0

Entrance

Open clean Yard

Stables

Open Sheds

Calf House

Open Sheds

Lobby

B

Dairy

Kitchen

Scullery

Lobby

A A

Hen House

Breeding House

N.B. Under Stairs a Pantry
A & B Separate Apartments for two
kinds of Servants with Lobby common
to both for Fuel &c.

0   50   110 Feet

R. Scott sculpt

through the mountains in order to join the King's road that now linked Dalmally and Tyndrum. An interesting account exists of a survey made about 1796, of the line of the intended road and the bridges it would require; though to this day it has never been built:

'From the Garron Bridge to Elirick More Wood is Four Miles all a Good Bottom. From thence to the Herds House of Ben Buie is three Quarters of an English Mile is mostly Rough Rocky Ground. From thence to the Sheil of Pollion is two Miles and an half all a Fine Bottom at this place the Publick House is Propos'd to be Built from thence for a Mile something Mossy which may be thrown off with little Trouble under which is Fine Gravell from thence for nine Miles to where it joins the Kings High Road through Glen Urchy at the Stron is a Good Bottom.'[69]

The time when Glenshira barns were completed was probably the period of greatest achievement and prosperity at Inveraray. The chief buildings were now erected, agricultural improvements were showing their effects, and the fame of the Duke's achievements had spread far and wide. Early in the history of tourism it was remarked of Inveraray that 'in 1790, a hundred have viewed it in the space of one week, and in 1792 that number has been doubled in the same space of time'.[70] English travellers who, along their road, had been shocked at the country's poverty, the limitation and infertility of crops, and the general backwardness and lack of initiative of the natives, invariably exclaimed with astonishment at the contrast when they reached the Duke's parks and plantations. Five hundred labourers were employed about the estate, and during the season sixty or seventy people might be seen making hay in the meadows round the castle.[71] Since the beginning of the century more than two million trees had been planted, chiefly on hilly or rocky ground unfit for cultivation, and measured in money terms alone the improvement was staggering. An early valuation of the woodlands at £100,000 trebled or quadrupled itself by the century's end, and the annual thinnings were worth £1,500.[72] In 1794 William Hervey noted that Benbuy, above Glenshira, let for £30 thirty-five years before, now brought in £300 for sheep pastures, and as much as £400 had been offered.[73] The Duke's celebrated breed of Highland cattle, reckoned the finest in Scotland, in 1794 numbered more than 600 head;[74] so late as 1799 he was considering dividing Glenshira into three or four farms in order to maintain them (for which he proposed 'small neat Houses in the Cottage Stile' in suitable places for the herdsmen). Another of his unexecuted projects was a model scheme for the south side of Inveraray round the farm of Achnagoul, whose land in 1788 was ordered to be enclosed and laid out 'like a village'. George Langlands, the agricultural surveyor, drew up a plan by which the tenants were to continue in possession and half a dozen houses to be rebuilt in 'a handsome regular Front . . . towards the Public road' (1792).[75]*

But the many ducal improvements were not matched by a corresponding uplift among local farmers and workpeople. 'It was with pleasure I learned that the present Duke of Argyle is peculiarly attentive to every thing that can tend to improve the practice of agriculture or the breed and management of cattle', observed Robert Heron in 1793;[76] but on the other side of the coin, only a year later James Robson remarks that 'the people do not seem to have any particular turn for improvement'.[77] They did not take to the enclosure system, and their primitive tillage contrasted with the advanced (and very expensive) ducal farms. Except immediately round the castle, and in Glenshira, the soil needed constant enrichment by lime, a commodity beyond the means of most farmers because of the high cost of fuel to burn it.[78] Oats, a little barley and coarse potatoes made up the usual range of crops, and in spite of the Duke's example local tenant-farmers made no use of fallow or dunghills, and their tools were clumsy and ill-fashioned.[79]

Meanwhile, the comparative failure of the woollen factory left little to tempt the population, temporarily swelled by building and estate work for the Dukes of Argyll, and between Duke Archibald's day and the 1790s it fell by more than 900 to 1,832.[80]

A few years after the death of the Duchess in 1790, the estate accounts and instructions begin to testify to the gradual decline of prosperity and efficiency during the Duke's last years, and the laxity or inability of his servants to arrest it. Repeated instructions to attend to leaking roofs, failing gates, rotten woodwork, and references to diseased cattle, moss and reeds choking the pastures, and crops spoiling from lack of expert tillage, tell their own tale. The Duke, indeed, to the last kept up his interest in his estate and farms, maintaining an autocratic correspondence with his Rosneath manager, Robert Campbell, with as much regularity as ever; and he now lived chiefly at Inveraray, removing to Edinburgh in winter; but his horizon had narrowed and his grasp was less sure. Yet such warnings as this to his farm overseer in 1800 show that his intolerance of slackness, when he was aware of it, never decreased:

'Your Crops of Potatoes considering the immense quantity of dung laid out, and the time and expense employed are very bad and far inferior to those of Glenshira and Roseneath, and I give you notice that if the Crops of next yeare are not better I shall discharge you at the end of it.'

From time to time stricter rules were issued, the estate plans put in order, or overseers warned to render better accounts to the pay office. A new gardener in 1798 started vigorously by exposing the corrupt habits of his predecessor (Bruce), and at his suggestion the Duke hired a journeyman gardener from the Lowlands (always the answer to inefficiency at Inveraray); and in 1800 the huge kitchen garden was reduced by a quarter by building a new wall along its west and south sides.

For some of the deterioration Colonel Graham, ageing like his master, must be held responsible; but more to blame was the Marquess of Lorne, always ready to amuse himself at the castle with parties of friends, and (as Lady Louisa Stuart noticed) capable of rousing himself to action if his own comfort suffered, but generally lazy and more interested in his own building schemes at Rosneath. Here Robert Mylne's years of advice and supervision went up in smoke when the castle was burnt down in May 1802; and Bonomi, not Mylne, was commissioned to rebuild it.

Yet in view of his patronage of younger and more modish architects it was probably Lorne who was behind the otherwise surprising spate of building at the century's end. The first, and today the most obvious, was a porter's lodge built in 1795–6 at the Wintertown Gate, now the main entrance to the castle : a low, square house, the work of visiting masons Thomas Black and Robert Young. A pair of granite gateposts was made for the widened entrance by the stone-cutter Peter Gardner, and finished with caps of Fisherland flags; the gate itself, cast from Carron iron, has long been replaced.[81]

Several thatched, miniature Gothick lodges with latticed windows sprang up round the policies. In 1797 and 1798 Duncan McNuir and Charles McArthur were building one 'at the end of the Douloch' at a cost of only £9 0s 2½d – no doubt the small house near the north-west edge of the Deer Park, then centred on another radial avenue running towards the new bridge.[82] In 1799 the lochside cottage at the salmon draught, near Kilmalew burial ground, was either built or altered by Dugald McKellar, and Donald McPhederan built two cottages for the miller at Carlundon, and for a gate-keeper at Kilbryde Bridge.[83] Between 1800 and 1802 McPhederan also built two lodges on the Dalmally road in the Balantyre plantations.[84]

At Cromalt, the southern end of the Fisherland meadow, where one lodge had stood since before 1790, another, a Gothicized, latticed affair, was built in 1801. At the other end of the policies, above the falls of Aray at Carlundon, in 1802–3 Tavish built a summer-house known as the 'Hexagon'. This little building was harled and equipped with a stove, and thatched by McPhederan, who also built a protective breastwork round it, fulfilling an intention the Duke had had at least since 1798, to enable visitors to view the 'cascade' in comfort from above – although it is more modest than the 'temple or grotto' first envisaged.[85] In both of these pretty trifles one may perhaps detect the hand of another of Lorne's protégés, Alexander Nasmyth.

Nasmyth, son of a noted Edinburgh builder and now in his early forties, had for over twenty years been established as a portrait painter, extending his field by degrees to landscape and architecture. He visited Inveraray in 1800 and in 1801, probably at Lord Lorne's invitation, and a letter he wrote the Duke on 7 November 1801 from his house in York Place, Edinburgh, also shows that he was the architect of the tiny 'Beehive Cottage' in the woods opposite the castle at the foot of Duniquaich.

The design for this 'Circular Cotage for one family' was nothing if not original, foreshadowing the 'open plan' house with a single room built round its central chimney, one segment being cut out to serve for kitchen and offices.

'The fire place is in the centre and the chimney suposed to be of sheet iron', wrote Nasmyth, 'which from an experiment I have made would give a very

83. Proposed lighthouse for the pier at Inveraray
An unexecuted design by Alexander Nasmyth, 1801, from the architect's own water-colour. Note the borrowing of detail from Inveraray Castle.

Goound Plan

general and wholsome heat to all the Coatage and without smoke. Cooking &a
might be carried on in an easy and cleanly manner, by this kind of fire place,
as it is nearly on the same construction as the old cradle chimney. the Country
Peapole would soon be accustomed to it.'[86]*

In August 1802, Nasmyth is known to have spent a further fortnight at Inveraray
'to draw for the Duke' on the evidence of one of his Edinburgh pupils who saw
him both before and after this 'Jaunt'.[87] The water-colour drawings at the castle
of the romantic fancies he evolved on his visit in 1801 are all in the Gothick style:
some 'ruined castles' or follies, one apparently proposed for the top of Duniquaich
and another for Stron Point at the mouth of Loch Shira, where it would have
formed an attractive eye-catcher from the grounds and the town; another was for
a lighthouse nearly 140 feet high, on a heavily rusticated square base, with an
octagonal lower floor and a circular five-storey tower.[88]* None of these fantasies
was ever carried out, and on this prettily decadent note the grand building history
of Inveraray parks and policies may be said to come to an end.

[31] Hexagonal summer-house at Carlundon, above the Aray,
possibly designed by Alexander Nasmyth. Built 1802–3

[32] Looking south from Inveraray pier, the old courthouse on the right

The town is new and the houses good and looks very well... It never can increase much, being confined to the point by the Duke's policy which comes close to their houses and obstructs the light from some of their windows. . . The inhabitants are very gay, having mostly estates in the neighbourhood.

Diary of John Inglis, 1784; Inglis MSS, SRO, GD 1/46/16

. . . a commodious, elegant plan, becoming the dignity of the capital of Argyle-shire, a country most admirably situated for fisheries and navigation. The town hath been rebuilt agreeable to the original design. The inhabitants are well lodged in houses of stone, lime and slate. They are fully employed in arts and manufactures.

John Knox *A View of the British Empire, More Especially Scotland*, II, London 1785, *A Short Tour of Scotland*, p.597

. . . all the beauties of the place break at once upon the sight; the little town, in several neat and regular fronts, lies spread over the extremity of the bay, beyond which the water swells into an amazing expanse, surrounded every where with mountains, and filled with vessels.

Henry Skrine, *Three Successive Tours in the North of England*, 2nd edn, London 1813, p.46

Inveraray, to me, is the noblest place in Scotland; but the climate of it is dreadful. I asked a lady if the streets were ever perfectly dry? She answered me, *never* . . .

The Hon. Mrs Sarah Murray, of Kensington, *A Companion and Useful Guide to the Beauties of Scotland*, I, London 1799, p.358

VIII

At the time when the 5th Duke succeeded in 1770, Duke Archibald's grandly conceived New Town had begun to look very forlorn; the gap between its visionary plan and the small part so far realized remained depressingly wide, while ten years of inactivity under the 4th Duke had left the expanding new site with an appearance of being abandoned, and turned the once flourishing old town into a gradually run-down village with no prospects of improvement.

Now all was to be changed. Of the many transformations wrought during the 5th Duke's regime, that of the town was visually the most striking, for the buildings erected in his policies were scattered over a wide area, and the castle, though internally totally changed, remained outwardly much the same. Almost our sole glimpse of how old Inveraray must have looked during the first summer visit of the Duke and Duchess in 1771 is a painting, ascribed to Lord Eldin,[1*] showing old and new castles as they stood side by side for twenty-five years, along with the Duke's old 'pavilion', the church, town bridge, and group of houses and cottages beside the Aray. There, all was crowding and clutter; but half a mile down the loch on Gallows Foreland Point, the sparse houses of the New Town stood isolated on the Fisherland's flat, windswept expanse softened only by the avenue of beeches dividing Town House and Great Inn.

Neil Gillies' house on the front was still in the same hands, but Richardson's had now become Carwhin's, while McPherson's up the 'street' had passed to a lawyer named John McNeill; next to that was a new house built by Mrs Elizabeth Campbell, widow of Colin Campbell of Bragleenmore, and opposite was another, little more than a cottage, built by the new Sheriff-Substitute and Provost, Lachlan Campbell. Beyond was nothing – except, perhaps, in the place intended for the town centre, the monument to the Campbells who were executed in 1685. On the front 'street', the western house of the Town House group was now occupied by Archibald Campbell of Danna, Sheriff-Clerk of Argyll, and the eastern by the Chamberlain, Sonachan.[2*]

Beyond the far end of the town the irregular row of Gallowgate 'hutts' provided rent-free homes for some of the Duke's dependents, including the 'Highland' minister, Mr Patrick Campbell, and both schoolmasters, Mr John Watson and Mr James Wright. Two miles south, Baillie Peter Campbell's house at Dalchenna had in 1768 been made over to James Campbell of Silvercraigs.[3*]

Some changes had already been made since the Duke, as Marquess of Lorne, took over the administration in 1768. By 1770 a water-supply had been led to the town in wooden pipes from Bealachanuaran, the spring-head on the Black Hill;[4] and a tiny model fishing village was begun at Kenmore five miles down the loch. In this compact fishermen's community of cottages built round a green, the earliest tenants shown in the Inveraray rental of 1771 included four families of McVicars.[5]

As part of the process of making his great new castle ready for himself and the Duchess to live in, the Duke needed to remove the now unsightly old town crowding below its walls, and before he could do this he had to rehouse his servants and tenants, and persuade the more substantial inhabitants to take out new tacks and rebuild for themselves. But even before this, consistent with his first strictly practical measures elsewhere, his first orders for the town (December 1771) were to build a new smithy and granary, and a stable in the neighbourhood of the intended Fisherland barn. The smithy adjoined the bakery built by the Wintertown entrance in the 3rd Duke's time, and to it was removed the new Duke's smith, John Roy, son and successor to Henry Roy.[6] The Duke also ordered the town plan to be 'extended at each end' in order to accommodate the tenement blocks shortly to be built;[7] and finally, he proposed to follow up Duke Archibald's encouragement of local industry on a larger scale, by founding a woollen mill to spin the wool from an improved breed of sheep, which he and other far-sighted land-owners introduced into Argyll.

At this early stage the Duke's architect was William Mylne, who, during the week he spent at Inveraray in August, must have inspected the town site with him and was, we may reasonably assume, his adviser about the Fisherland Barn. In December 1771 one of three plans submitted by William Mylne was for a church, which may (for the plan has not survived) have been the 'temporary' building erected in 1772 between the present church and the beech avenue:

> 'A House of 60 ffeet longe & 2 storrys High to be built in New Town where Marked out by the Duke the lofts and Seats to be removed from English Church and to be put up in ditto house so as to serve for the Church.'[8*]

William Mylne's name is not mentioned in this connexion in the annual Instructions, but George Haswell was at least partly concerned, for as Mylne's final account settled in 1772 includes a fee 'for giving directions to Haswell',[9] he may be at least tentatively associated with this hastily erected building, of proportions large enough to contain the existing magistrates' seats and lofts from the old town kirk. This last and most complicated part of the operation had to have the magistrates' approval, 'observing', ordered the Duke, 'to reserve Seats for all my Servts'.[10*] The old kirk bell, the same one recast in 1728 by Robert Maxwell in Edinburgh, was also brought over, hung on a tree for lack of a belfry and eventually rehung in the present church.

In September 1772, when Robert Mylne first came to Inveraray, he too must have made a tour of the town with the Duke, with one long-term result in a drawing

[33] Arkland (1774–5), looking south

84. The 'temporary' Lowland Church at Inveraray
Probably designed by William Mylne, 1772; demolished early this
century. From a photograph of about 1900, when the building was
used as a school.

produced in 1774 'for front of new town of Inveraray'[11]* – a project not executed
until 1787, and then with modifications.

New Inveraray is substantially Robert Mylne's town, and the stamp of his
architectural personality is visible in the design of Arkland, Relief Land, and
succeeding tenement blocks; yet apart from the 1774 drawing Mylne does not refer
to the town until 1776. But although he remains tantalizingly silent, and no correspondence or working drawings (which were probably made by Marr and other
masons) survive, Mylne's name is inevitably linked with its layout and building.

All town plans subsequent to John Adam's projects of 1750 have disappeared,
but plainly Mylne advised on that finally adopted, which, while retaining a central
church site, would reorientate the church to face north and south along the main
street, parallel to the beech avenue – instead of east and west as Adam originally
proposed. The result was far simpler than any earlier plan: a main street, a short
cross street eastwards from the still imaginary side wall of the church to the loch;
and parallel to this a straightened Front Street, from the Dalmally road bordering
the Duke's policies to the small headland near Adam's pier. This layout removed
all the obtuse angles of Adam's plan, which would have continued Front Street
round the headland as four sides of an (incomplete) hexagon; thus it happened
that Richardson's or Carwhin's house, sited in accordance with the old plan, was
left out of alignment with the strict angles of the new.

This particular part of the town has stayed comparatively empty of buildings,

[34] Arkland and Relief Land (1775–6), looking north

partly perhaps because it was regarded as being the industrial quarter. A small slaughter-house had been built in the 4th Duke's time about 80 yards south of Carwhin's;[12]* now came the 5th Duke's woollen factory. This 'House Built for the workmen in the New toun', a large upper-floor workroom over a series of tenement dwellings, was erected in 1774, facing the loch between Carwhin's and the slaughter-house. The mason was John Marr, who came from Cullen in 1772 and at first had been put in charge of demolition work, particularly the pulling down of the old church and steeple in 1773–4. With this contract Marr moved on to new houses.[13]* By the date of the annual rental at Martinmas 1774 the 'Eight New Houses below the ffactory', providing homes for its workmen, were also complete and the 1776 rental shows that its 'houses' were by then eleven – some of them probably of only one room.[14]* In 1777 when the factory removed to Clunary, a three-storey tenement, later known as Ferry Land from its traditionally housing the ferryman, was built against its north end.[15]

Mylne's chief tenements were built at the south end of the town. Arkland – as the first row of five 'Great Houses', three-storeyed and flat-fronted, later came to be called – dates from 1774 – 5 and fills most of the south-west side of the extended street, alongside the Great Avenue; the contractor was again John Marr.

> 'All the front Windows and Doors to have hewen Stone, a great part of which you are to order from Clyde. The side walls to be $2\frac{1}{2}$ foot thick in the foundation & only two foot Thick above the first Joists, the gavels when Joined to other Houses to be only $2\frac{1}{2}$ foot Thick.'[16]

The sole adornment of this white-harled row of tenements with its five entries, is the finishing of windows and doorways with the dressed stone surrounds from Dumbarton quarries,[17] and the regular chimney-stacks rising above the roofs of Easdale slate. The block's dour but impressive quality, enhanced by placing the top storey windows immediately below the eaves, appears positively ornamental in comparison with Relief Land, built opposite in 1775–6: although the elevation of this second row is almost identical with Arkland, its effect, lacking the other's stone surrounds, is one of gaunt simplicity.

Relief Land's wholly functional appearance was dictated by the status of the tenantry it housed, 'workmen, & others of the low people', whom the Duke regarded as so irresponsible that he ordered the row to be internally arched with brick 'in order to secure them from fire, as well as to make the upper floor fitt for such people, who would soon Destroy any wooden floor'.[18]* Relief Land was built by John Brown, mason of the new Aray Bridge, with a hint that the Duke was dissatisfied with Marr and anxious in future to employ Brown as much as possible; for it was Brown who soon obtained contracts for later tenements and the manses, aided by junior masons, the more quickly to complete this large commission.[19]

By 1776 the town was taking shape, with a water-front of elegant public buildings (Duke Archibald's Town House and inn, and Duke John's manses, built in 1776), from which a main street of tacksmen's private houses led to the still empty central square. Eastward was the 'industrial' end, and south of the square the large houses of the tenantry. In that area was only one privately-built house, that of Neil McCallum, the Duke's wright, who in 1775 as a tacksman built the small house beyond Arkland,[20]* set at a slight angle to the row because of the curving shore. But now, with Arkland finished and Relief Land building, the Duke ordered total demolition of the old town to be completed by Whitsun 1777, and for accommodation of the rest of his tenantry he authorized a third block for 24 families 'if the Buildings already planned are not Sufficient' – a statistical vagueness which reads rather oddly. Accordingly in the winter of 1776 John Brown embarked on the last series of tenements, completing them the following year. Since McCallum's little house now occupied the corner beyond Arkland, these new tenements had to go beyond that again, where the street was so close to the shore that they had to run inland in two rows at right angles to the earlier blocks; for which reason they later came to be called Cross Houses. McCallum's was so intrusive on the site that for years to come all rentals identified neighbouring houses *vis-à-vis* his.[21]*

On 5 February 1776, the Duke found it prudent to take out an insurance policy with the Edinburgh Friendly Insurance Society for his Inveraray possessions. For the sum of £11 3s he succeeded in insuring his new castle for £4,000, its furnishings for £1,000, the Cherry Park offices for £1,000, and in the new town the following buildings so far completed:

> 'Five Tenements newly built lying on the South West side of the street of Inverary [i.e. Arkland] one of said Tenements occupied as an Inn – and the other four possest by private Families all stone and slated and not exceeding Two hundred pounds sterling on each Tenement, Inde One thousand pounds. – Five Tenements also newly built lying on the North side of the said street and fronting the Sea – the upper part of which Tenements is occupied as a Factory for the spinning of Wool – and the under floors possest by private Families all stone and slated and not exceeding One hundred pounds sterling on each Tenement – Five hundred pounds. The new Inn at Inverary being a Tenement of three stories and Cellars belonging thereto possest by John Buchanan all stone and slated not exceeding Five hundred pounds. – Stables and Offices belonging thereto lying at the back of said house all stone and slated not exceeding Two hundred pounds all Sterling.'[22]*

To ensure the old town's removal by Whitsun 1777 the Duke ordered Sonachan to press ahead with the new, and employed another mason, Thomas Muckle, under John Brown for building 'so many of the workmens Houses, or Ministers Offices as he ffinds hands to Execute'.[23]

The town's removal operation followed a well-regulated pattern. First of all the Duke's servants had been transferred to the Cherry Park and the Maltland; then the tenantry were evacuated in series as their new flats were completed, and finally, over a period of years, the more substantial private inhabitants were building and moving into their own houses, mostly on tacks granted for 57 years.[24] Besides the industrial buildings, the wholesale accommodation of his 'workmen & others of the low people of the Town', and a few houses he built for dependents and certain tacksmen to whom he owed compensation for their old houses, the Duke was further responsible for erecting two manses, and for fitting up two more churches.

The manses, designed by Mylne, were built by John Brown in 1776 at the north-east corner of the town, one on either side of Gillies' large Front Street house, thus forming a small row between Main Street and quay and creating an entity out of the town front there. These two identical houses, of two storeys and attics, were finished with dressings of St Catherines stone brought from the dismantled 'physic well' in the meadow. Smaller and lower than Gillies' house, from which they are slightly set back, they conform with it and the other Front Street houses in having round-headed doorways.[25]*

The following year (1777) we find, a little unexpectedly, that at the Duke's order John Brown built 'two Large Houses at the End of P. L. Campbells the one intended for a Highland Church'.[26]

The history of Inveraray's churches is a curious one of plans changed, deferred or abandoned. Had Duke Archibald lived a year or two longer, John Adam's circular church would almost certainly have been begun, and once begun its position and orientation would have determined the eventual lay-out of the town. But on the Duke's death Adam's drawings, along with many other papers, had disappeared from sight as Lord Milton declined into senility and the elderly 4th Duke showed no interest in Inveraray. The 5th Duke quite possibly never even knew of their existence. However, his new town had to have a church, and the temporary church had been one of the very first buildings he erected. But Inveraray, as a Highland capital, required two churches, 'Highland' or Gaelic and 'Lowland' or 'English', and these the old town had possessed. By 1776, as the old Highland church demolished along with the Lowland had to be replaced, the Duke rather surprisingly ordered one to be made in the ground-floor flat of the latest pair of private houses he was building. Still more surprisingly, perhaps, these houses are identifiable as the present George Hotel.

In addition to designing the large tenement blocks of the new town Robert Mylne must also have been responsible – at least to the extent of supervising the masons' drawings – for other buildings erected to the Duke's orders, which included several private houses in the main street. The church's clue lies in his diary entry for 27 August 1776:

'Fixed on a situation for a New Kirk – a new aproach from the new Town, and advised a new Covered Way from the Castle to the Offices.'[27]

Here, Mylne was not, as has sometimes been supposed, revising the town plan by siting his own intended church – which indeed was not built or even designed until the 1790s. As the bulk of the town was already built, it would have been rather late for its architect to determine a town plan. Mylne was simply doing what he says: fixing a site for 'a New Kirk' – 'a' is the operative word. When he did design Inveraray's present kirk in 1792 it was a double one, and he referred to it as such.

[35] The town front, from the Aray Bridge, showing, on the left, the two original manses (1776), one on either side of 'Gillies' House'

Once Mylne had approved the site, this Highland kirk was built; its conceal-ment inside a double house has hitherto obscured its identity. Yet the double house is itself significant – for in 1783, at the Duke's further order, the existing 'temporary' Lowland Kirk was removed to the ground floor of the other half, so that the two churches now served their purpose side by side, a stone's-throw from the site of their permanent successor. In 1784 John Inglis notes, 'The church is not yet built, divine service is performed in a house and the bell hangs on a tree'.[28]

'P. L. Campbells', next door, means Provost Lachlan Campbell's, the small house built opposite McPherson's in 1768, when houses in the new town had conformed to a less exacting standard than was later set.[29*] The new pair of ducal church tene-ments, by comparison fairly towering above the cottages next door, are further dis-tinguished by a string-course below the second-storey sills. In other respects they more resemble the Arkland houses, hinting at the hand of Robert Mylne, whose touch is also evident in the circular sunk panel on their large south gavel facing the square. The Highland church was placed in the house adjoining Lachlan Camp-bell's, and the Lowland, fitted up in 1783, in the corner house (now the George Hotel entrance). The reason for the Lowland kirk's removal here is not explained: it may simply have been that the Duke wished the two kirks to be side by side; or that the 'temporary' building of 1772 was already seen as suitable for a school.[30*]

Between 1774 and 1777, what with building the new town and knocking down the old, Inveraray's thriving activity recalled the great years of Duke Archibald. Huge cargoes of materials sailed in weekly from Clydeside, Ayr and Campbeltown to be 'livered' at the quay and loaded on to carts. At the factory and new tenements workmen slated, harled and plastered, while masons' wages ran into hundreds of pounds. In the summer of 1774 alone, cargoes totalling some 100,000 bricks arrived from Wilson's of Glasgow and other Clydeside firms, ferried up the loch from the intermediate port of Campbeltown, and followed by an equivalent number of slates from Easdale. Later, the increased demand for bricks to arch Relief Land kept a brickfield working at Limecraigs near Campbeltown, while thousands more were shipped from Ayr, Gourock and Glasgow; then came timber from Lindsay and Company, Greenock lead, Dumbarton freestone, Irish limestone for harling the new houses ('it being much whiter than Carlunnand lime'), and Newcastle glass.[31]

By the time of the Duke's illness in 1777 the town's building programme was so far ahead that the pause after this climax of activity was no obstacle. 'There being more houses finished at present than are wanted,' dictated Lord Frederick on his brother's behalf in 1778, 'no more houses are to be finished during the next year.'[32]

The face of new Inveraray had completely changed and suddenly, at last, taken on the appearance of a town, with the last large tenements all but finished and Front Street filled with substantial houses; though on Main Street numerous gaps still remained. Yet it was still a town without a centre, for between the new tem-porary church and the large tenements was a broad open space; and the various elements of Front Street remained unconnected.

[36] East side of Main Street, looking south. Left to right: gable of manse (1776), Patrick Brown's (1773–4), Baillie John Colquhoun's (1774–5), James Campbell of Silvercraigs' (c. 1773–80, tall house, centre), Lachlan Campbell's (1767–8 and lower addition of 1775), Highland and Lowland churches with tenements above (1777)

'The Town is now remov'd from where it was,
Unto another, more convenient place :
The antient rubbish now is all thrown down,
And now behold a neat, new lovely Town.
The houses here are stately, strong and neat,
Three stories high : all cover'd with blue slate.'

So wrote James Maxwell in 1777. Demolition of the buildings nearest the castle – stables and houses occupied by the Duke's servants – had started as early as May 1772; cottages at the old bridge end followed,[33] and then the old town came tumbling down in a gathering momentum of destruction rivalled only by the speed at which, on Gallows Foreland Point, the new was rising. In its last years the now ramshackle place must have been crammed to overflowing, for all evicted inhabitants who were considered worthy and industrious were unceremoniously squeezed into the remaining houses, strictly rationed for space (though the Duke's ominous order to choose, even among the worthy, 'by lote Promisquisly' proved unnecessary);[34] a sinister silence reigns about those inhabitants *not* so considered. The vacated houses were temporarily used before demolition as billets for the hordes of soldiers, Lowland masons and labourers employed on the works; a little space was forcibly created when the herring-fishers were banished to their new village down the loch at Kenmore, where more cottages were now being built.[35]

'A very *Czarish* plan', complained the idealistic Miss McVicar, who in 1773 saw the decaying old town and the site of the new, much as they had looked for the past dozen years. Old Inveraray was then still 'a mean-looking yet chearful and populous place . . . one street facing the water; and beyond it a fine road, surrounded by a beautiful lawn, sprinkled with prodigious beech-trees'. Miss McVicar admitted, however, to a certain sentimentality, 'being no friend to alterations'.[36] The removal was not a continuous operation; in 1776 the Rev. William Gilpin observed that the Duke had 'already removed as much of the old town, as was a nuisance to himself; but whether he means to carry his predecessor's full intention into execution does not yet appear.'[37] However, by 1778 David Loch found the old town 'so totally annihilated, as not to have the smallest vestige remaining'.[38] Its houses were razed, the rubble carted away wholesale and the ground broken up and levelled ; all that remained was a nude bank from the fosse's edge down to the Aray shore and along to Loch Fyne. A great part of the 3rd Duke's intention had been realized at last.

An interesting account of the building achievements of the 2nd to the 5th Dukes of Argyll, compiled in 1776 by an anonymous genealogist and amateur historian, lists the works of the 5th Duke as follows :

'He caused throw down the large old high Tower built in Anno 1440 and all the office houses and Little Tower which were contiguous to the Palace, the Physick Well in the Meadow, the Lowland Kirk, the Old Tolbooth and the Cross, the tenement contiguous to the Kirk and Tolbooth, the tenement of houses below the Brae, the stable, coach house, old office and court thereof, all in the years 1771, 72, 73 and 1774.

In 1775 demolished the new office and court thereof, Provost Campbell's, Arch. McLean's, Provost Duncanson's, Dugald Murray's, and John Colquoun's tenements, and all the office houses belonging to them in 1776.

The new bridge upon the water foot [Aray Bridge] finished in 1776; he built several large houses in the New town in 1774, 75 and 1776, a large barn and a large storehouse in the Maltland and several houses for accomodating tradesmen and labourers joined to the high wall of the garden, and stables for his work horses and labouring oxen, he also built a very large barn and stable at the forend and backside of the long row of houses in the ffisherland and is still carrying on and building houses of two stories and garrets and three stories and garrets for enlarging and beautifying the Burgh and making it regular and uniform, the old Town being now mostly demolished in 1776.'[39]*

From the next extant town rental after the Duke's illness we can see that his housing scheme was then (1783) practically complete. A number of merchants and other townsmen had built their own houses with compensation money from the Duke for the loss of their old property; in some cases, like Baillie Colquhoun's, the Duke granted a tack but himself built the house.[40] Apart from Neil McCallum's these were all in the front or northern half of Main Street, which is thus far from uniform in style and a great contrast to the southern (Arkland) half.

By far the largest and most elaborate private house was that of James Campbell of Silvercraigs, merchant and Provost, begun probably in 1773. Silvercraigs', adjoining Lachlan Campbell's two modest cottages on the north, is in height equivalent to the two ducally-built houses containing the temporary kirks, and its 63-foot frontage holds seven windows across with a central pend. It is further distinguished by dressed stone quoins and, besides the tall chimney-stacks at its gable ends, makes a feature of a wall-head chimney-gable containing a lunette. Intended to be completed in 1776, the house owing to its size and expense was not finished until 1780, and in applying for his tack to be postdated to 1781 Silvercraigs urged that his house was, 'he is safe to afirm, among the beste ever built on a Tack in Scotland, and wil one day or other, return the Family of Argyll from Fiftie to Sixtie Pound p Annum'.[41]*

While Silvercraigs' stands out as being remarkably large, and Lachlan Campbell's as especially small, the houses built by the Duke were on the whole regular in proportion and design. For example, the area between the new manse in Front Street and Silvercraigs' was built up as a uniform group from 1773, partly at least by John Marr. The house nearest Silvercraigs' was let to Baillie John Colquhoun as compensation for the loss of his house in the old town; the one next to it went to Patrick Brown, a mariner.[42] This little two-storeyed terrace with garrets, far lower than Silvercraigs', is regular in fenestration—though not monotonously so, the windows not being exactly spaced apart—and finished with hewn stone dressings; the regularity of frontage imparts urbanity to this end of the street in spite of the houses' modest dimensions.

On the opposite (west) side of Main Street mention may be made of the first

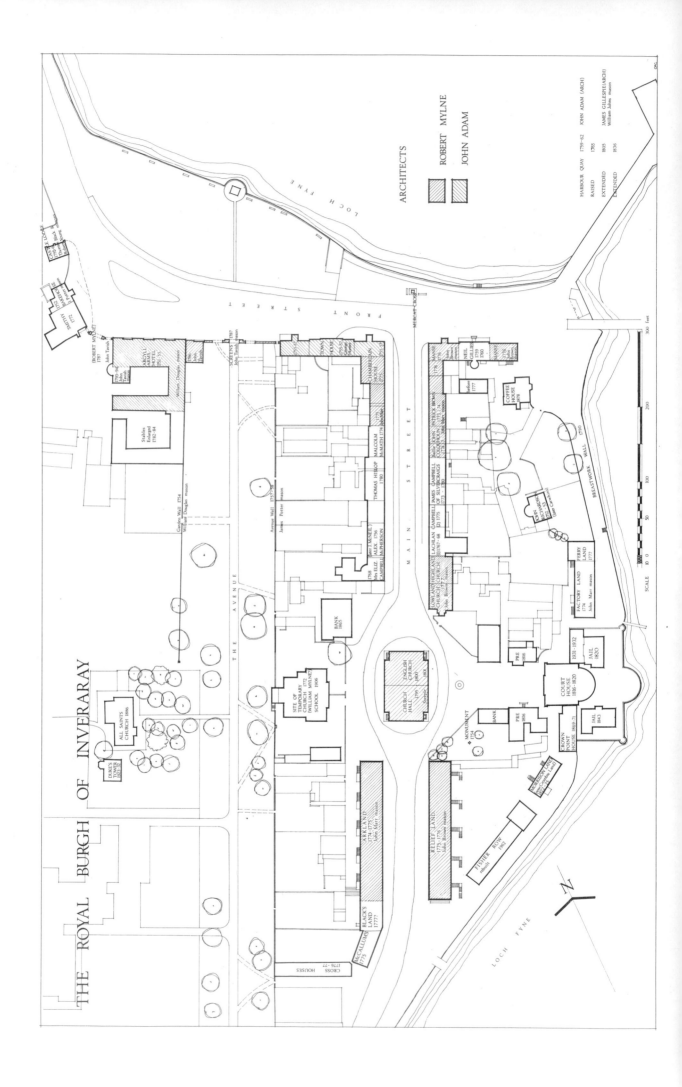

THE ROYAL BURGH OF INVERARAY

ARCHITECTS

ROBERT MYLNE
JOHN ADAM

HARBOUR QUAY 1759–62   JOHN ADAM (ARCH)
RAISED   1765   JAMES GILLESPIE (ARCH)
EXTENDED   1805   William Johns mason
EXTENDED   1836

LOCH FYNE

FRONT STREET

MAIN STREET

THE AVENUE

MERCAT CROSS

CASTLE LODGE

SMITH 1772

ROBERT MYLNE 1787

ARGYLL ARMS HOTEL

Stables Enlarged 1782–94

Garden Wall 1754
William Douglas mason

Avenue Wall
James Potter mason

ALL SAINTS CHURCH 1886

DUKE'S TOWER 1921–31

SITE OF TEMPORARY CHURCH (WILLIAM MYLNE) SCHOOL 1906

BANK 1865

ARKLAND 1774–1775
John Marr mason

BLACK'S LAND 1777?

McCALLUM'S 1775

CROSS HOUSES 1776–77

THOMAS HISLOP 1780

MALCOLM McMATH 1774

CHAMBERLAIN HOUSE 1775

TOWN HOUSE 1755–57

SCREENS 1787

ENGLISH CHURCH 1795

CHURCH HALL

MONUMENT 1754

RELIEF LAND 1775–1776
John Brown mason

FISHER ROW 1902

CHURCH 1800

LOWLAND HIGHLAND CHURCH CHURCH 1774

JOHN McANDRESS 1832

LACHLAN CAMPBELL 1767–68

JAMES CAMPBELL OF SILVERCRAIGS 1775

Bailie JOHN COLQUHOUN 1775

PATRICK BROWN 1773–74

MANSE 1776

NEIL GILLIES 1759 1760

MANSE 1776

COFFEE HOUSE 1878

FERRY LAND 1777

FACTORY LAND 1774
John Marr mason

PRE 1816

BANK

PRE 1816

ROBERTSON LAND

COURT HOUSE 1816–1820

CROWN POINT HOUSE 1869–71

JAIL 1843

JAIL 1820

1931–1932

BREASTWORK WALL 1790

LOCH FYNE

N

SCALE

300 feet

pair of houses, now shops, of three storeys and resembling Arkland in their upper
storey windows being placed just below the eaves; they were built by 1774 to the
Duke's order for Malcolm McMath, one of his masons. The one between them and
what was then the Chamberlain's pay office on the corner was also built to the
Duke's order, by John Marr in 1775.[43] Another tacksman's house was Thomas
Hislop's, immediately opposite Silvercraigs' and equal to it in frontage, completed
by 1780.[44]*

Baillie Colquhoun and others constantly plagued the Duke with petitions and
memorials about the state of their houses, length of tacks, or loss of gardens.
William Ross, a cordiner or shoemaker (whose house, built by the Duke in 1774,
was in 1816 to be demolished to make way for the new Court House) for four years
dragged out claims for the lack of an office house, valuation of his 'third lodging
flat', the inferior garden ground allotted him, and even damage to his furniture 'in
flitting from the old to the new town'.[45]

By 1783 Inveraray had seventeen tacksmen's houses, whose number then remained constant. The terms of the tacks ensured a minimum standard for the
houses in being stone-built, harled white or near-white, and slated instead of
thatched. The effect, for a Highland town of this period, was unusually regular.

'The houses are neat, commodious, and substantial,' comments Loch, 'and
covered with Easdale blue slate.'[46] In 1787 Mr Bailey notes:

> 'Inveraray has but one street, its length about half a mile, and that not filled up
> with houses . . . as intended by the Duke. The new houses are all built after the
> English fashion; and, like those of the New Town of Edinburgh, uniform and
> of the same height. The old cottages, which are still numerous, in the inter-
> mediate spaces, are gradually disappearing . . . At the further end a handsome
> Church is meditated, where the street will edge off each way, as at the Cathedral
> of St Pauls in London. This, if once accomplished, and the street, at the same
> time rendered compleat, will have a very pleasing effect.'[47]

Mr Bailey, one suspects, was so dazzled by his gracious reception at the castle that
his observations are occasionally confused. As he gives the town's length as half a
mile his reference to old cottages suggests the Gallowgate (where ruinous houses
were indeed removed); yet he speaks of the intended church as at the street's
'further end'. He may have supposed that small houses like Lachlan Campbell's
were also intended for 'extirpation' in favour of grander buildings.

Thomas Newte in 1785 gives the number of 'houses' as two hundred, a surprising figure until it is remembered that Newte, an Englishman, probably got his
facts from the Chamberlain or inn-keeper, who would reckon in terms of tenement
rooms or flats. The town's population, calculated about 1791 for Scotland's first
Statistical Account (published 1793), was 1,063.[48]* John Inglis, while impressed by
its solid, well-built houses and fine appearance from where it first comes into the
traveller's view at Stron Point, commented critically on the way further expansion
was cramped by the Duke's surrounding policies, and adds:

> 'Few of them have any garden, those that have are very small, a publick garden

85. Plan of Inveraray New Town
    Showing dates of building and original occupants of houses.

Front of houses

86. Mylne's final design for the
town front

is 2 miles off, to which they are oblidged to have recourse, and are but ill served.
. . . There is not as much ground about the town as would make [a burial
ground] unless it was in the sands below high water mark; . . . the whole town
could not procure or cutt a cart load of hay.'[49]

Although the town's Front Street had been enhanced by addition of two manses
to John Adam's fine set of buildings, as yet it remained with no unifying feature;
while as long as the church was still unbuilt the main street led, as it were, to
vacancy. It was for Robert Mylne in both cases to provide the finishing touch.

Hitherto Mylne's designs for the town had been purely functional, for not until
the 1780s was it complete enough to warrant adornment, although he made a tentative sketch of a town front as early as 1774, when very little new building had been
done. Not until 1783 does he record making a plan of the town (which has not survived), and in 1785, during his last and longest visit, he turned his attention seriously to completion of the front. The following are Mylne's diary entries for that
visit relevant to the town:

'Sept. 20 . . . Visited Inn – New Town – Maltland – and Cascade Bridge.

. . .

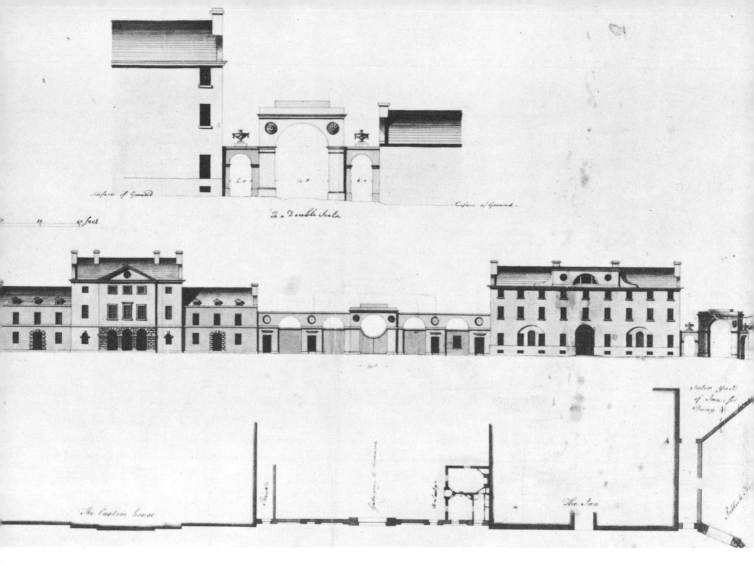

Sept. 23. At town – considering Entrance to Avenue and Gap, North Side of Inn, and Springhead, on entrance from Town and Lodge – arches over publick roads to carry private . . .

. . .

Sept. 25 . . . At Town, on Lodge and Crossings of roads . . .'

As a result of these inspections, on 11 December in London, Mylne 'Gave the Duke of Argyll a new drawing of a front for Inverary, with gateway at corner as an entrance'.[50] In February and March (1786) this was followed by a large working drawing, and 'a letter of answers, to Queries on Screen Wall – Lodge, and alterations of Inn at Inverary'.[51]*

Mylne's unifying plan for bridging the gaps between main street, avenue and Dalmally road, underwent several changes, and his final designs of 1788 and 1790 were not completely executed, probably because of the Duchess's death. His drawings show that at first he envisaged three-storeyed houses east of the main street (Gillies' and the manses), but the Duke ordered the manses lower. Mylne further proposed a pediment for Gillies' house similar to that on Adam's Town House. The inn too came in for changes – in the event not executed – with the alternative of a pediment and a new top feature of a 'thermal window' between roundels. Finally the arches themselves underwent several modifications, and an obelisk, decorative swags, and urns and sculptured roundels were all proposed and discarded.⁵²

The screens were built by John Tavish, starting in autumn 1786 with a small porter's lodge on the inn side of the beech avenue, followed early in 1787 by the avenue screen itself; last came the archway linking inn and smithy across the Dalmally road. 'For Building the Gateway betwixt the Inn and the Smiddy and Coping the said Gateway and the other Gateway on the other side of the Inn', Tavish received £42 2s 10d.⁵³

While Tavish was working on the second archway Mylne produced his design for a third: two variations on an elegant approach to the main street, with pedestrian gateways, cornices, parapets and urns.⁵⁴ Had the Duchess's fatal illness not happened at about this time, Inveraray might today have been presented with an awkward traffic problem; but aesthetically we must regret that the last proposed screen was never carried out.

However, the two-thirds of Mylne's design that was executed imparted a sophistication to Inveraray unrivalled in Highland towns, or indeed probably in any small town either side of the Border. The avenue is spanned by five arches, of which the outermost two have screen walls concealing small lodges which guard its entrances, with open lunettes above. The other three have wrought iron gates. The very slightly projecting central gateway is crowned by a cornice and dressed stone blocking courses, and in its spandrels are plain sunk roundels, harled as are the other surfaces. The remaining four spandrels are pierced by circular openings, that characteristic Mylne feature which echoes his Aray Bridge; below these are four square-headed doorways with detached cornices. The string-course below the adjoining Town House group's first-floor windows is continued across the screen, and forms a kind of vestigial 'capital' at the spring of the arches.

The design of the central arch, with its crowning courses and shallow roundels, is repeated west of the inn and given something of the air of a triumphal arch, flanked by much lower round-headed arches. With the screens' integration with the inn's Venetian-style windows and the Town House group's façade, the whole complex is so subtle that its ingenuity and imagination takes time to appreciate to the full.

'Hardly worth notice', observed the sportsman Colonel Thornton of the town in 1786, before the screens were built. Mr Bailey, soon after they were finished, enthusiastically admired the Great Inn's 'very elegant exterior ... so constructed as to resemble a Town Hall' (but perhaps he did mean the Town House?), and ennobled by the

> 'expanse of front which covers the whole town of Inveraray, and from the windows of the Castle, forms a compleat skreen against the port and quays ... As an entrance to a town it is quite magnificent, and may justly be accused of promising too much.'⁵⁵*

[37] The town front as executed

Other visitors were to echo this ambivalent judgment: some thought the town splendid, some inconsiderable, some pretentious. Some scarcely even noticed it. 'Neat, regular, and well built' was one characteristic minimum comment,[56] and at the other extreme a panegyric on its 'state and utility . . . the appearance of a palace with colonnades'.[57] In 1799 John Stoddart and his companion, the painter Nattes, while visually assailed by the whole grand composition 'bursting upon the eye at once, [which] excites no less admiration than surprise', were disappointed to find it prove so small a town; 'nor are the houses answerable, in point of accommodation, to their external appearance', or the large inn more than 'tolerable' compared with those of other towns.[58]* Mr George Douglas, on his way to the Hebrides in 1800, saw in Inveraray 'little beauty'; but as one wedded to the fashionable cult of the picturesque, he awarded high marks for its view from the quay, the group of castle, bridge, loch, hills and busy fishing-boats forming 'a masterly composition'.[59]

Masterly indeed, the Wordsworths found it to be:

'We seemed now to be on the edge of a very large, almost circular, lake, the town of Inverary before us, a line of white buildings on a low promontory right opposite, and close to the water's edge; the whole landscape a showy scene, and bursting upon us at once. A traveller who was riding by our side called out, "Can that be the Castle?" . . . The mistake is a natural one at that distance: it is so little like an ordinary town, from the mixture of regularity and irregularity in the buildings. With the expanse of water and pleasant mountains, the scattered boats and sloops, and those gathered together, it had a truly festive appearance . . . At the door of the inn, though certainly the buildings had not that delightful outside which they appeared to have at a distance, yet they looked very pleasant.'[60]

The Wordsworths, visiting at the very end of the Duke's life, were disappointed by the town's ill-kept streets; but within a decade of its building it was showing signs of dilapidation, and required much maintenance and restoration even before the Duchess's death. From 1787 the Duke more than once complained that

'The Tenants of the houses in the New Town neglect to keep their houses in repair – they must be Obliged to pay of yearly additional Rent equal to the expense I am at in keeping the Roofs skyelights &c of their houses in repair.'[61]

The Duke was further dissatisfied with his workmen. Tavish was dismissed soon after he had built the avenue archway,[62]* and as for labourers, many were 'so Old & infirm that they cannot possibly work equal to their present wages' and were pensioned off ('while they behave properly') at forty shillings a year, on condition that their wives and daughters spun for the factory. The Duke determined to import new 'under overseers' from the Lowlands, who would have more authority than local men, but Sonachan's despondent note, 'None yet found', shows this to have been more easily ordered than achieved.[63]

In 1789 the Duke ordered removal of 'Such of the Gallowgate houses as are insufficient' – possibly the shabby cottages that offended Mr Bailey – 'The Slates and every thing else usefull in them to be carefully preserved and laid by for other

[38] East side of Main Street, looking north,
    showing Silvercraigs' in centre

purposes'.[64] But by degrees vacant stances were again filled haphazardly with more cottages, houses, secession churches; and the 'Long Row', or Newton as it was soon called, ended with the uneven appearance it has today. For years the loch-side road was unsafe for carriages, as tides undermined the very walls, and since this was officially the town's responsibility the Duke's repeated requests for a protective breastwork were ignored as long as humanly possible. Only when, seeing the shore's dangerous erosion, he himself took charge (1782) was the bulwark leisurely begun, and in the autumn of 1785 he ordered its extension to the 'Long Row'. Similar passive resistance met the Duke's proposal to extend John Adam's quay.[65]

The Town House, over which the Duke had no jurisdiction, was fiercely criticized by the Sheriff and Commissioners of Supply; at a meeting in 1786 the Sheriff represented its stairs and entrance as dangerous and the prisons as insecure —witness the frequent escapes (with a little help from friends outside). On the recommendation of a special committee which included Sonachan and Silvercraigs a few slight improvements were made,[66] but not many years later John Adam's Town House and prison were voted completely out of date.

The great Inn too—which was later to undergo great changes to Mylne's design —early required improvements, carried out with characteristic indolence. Perhaps this was the fault of the new innkeeper, John Frazer, who in February 1787 received a lengthy ducal order to keep his fences, gates, windows, doors and stables in repair, with an exasperated rider that he could certainly keep no pigs unless they were safely penned 'and not allowed . . . tresspass upon my inclosures & run through the Town as they have been in use to do'.[67]*

Not surprisingly, perhaps, by 1791 Frazer had been superseded (by Alexander Marquis). It would be Frazer who snubbed Burns in 1787, inspiring his epigram on the inn's lack of hospitality. But the inn's service, then and later, was always patchy. Mr Bailey came only a month after Burns, and being a gentleman of substance received every comfort:

> 'I found here not only convenience but elegance. The furniture in some of the rooms was quite superb, and had it not been supplied from the Castle, could not have been purchased but at an inconvenient, and improper expense.'[68]

An earlier sufferer had been Jacob Pattison, the young academic of great promise who visited in 1780. His friend Lister, who because of a full house had to be boarded out, probably fared better than Pattison, who got the waiter's bed over the kitchen: first he was nearly suffocated by the huge fire below—'when I placed my hand upon the Floor it was like a maltkiln'; then, flinging open the window overlooking the stableyard in order to breathe, he was 'nearly destroyed by the gnats'. At last he slept soundly enough, but when the hostler called him at 6, 'I left my room with as much pleasure as St Laurence would have left his gridiron'. Pattison's views on the castle would have been worth hearing, and it is a pity that he decided not to visit it on a report that 'the inside did not altogether correspond' to its fine situation! His ideal revenge on an enemy henceforth, he resolved, would be to 'place him in the hot room at Inverary, & leave the window open'.[69]

The spinning industry inaugurated by Duke Archibald had lapsed after his death and by 1771 the chief, indeed only, industry in Inveraray was once again the herring fishery. The 5th Duke was eager not only to promote fisheries along the coasts but to support any other ventures (including, much later, the building of the Crinan Canal) to help Scotland's development, particularly in the Highlands. His own personal project was the Inveraray woollen factory, launched with the large workshop he built there in 1774:

> 'We hear that his Grace the Duke of Argyle is going to establish a maunfacture of woollen cloth in the town of Inverary . . . It were to be wished that the nobility and gentlemen of Scotland would follow the example of the patriotic Duke . . . and spend their money in encouraging industry and agriculture in their native country in place of squandering it away abroad in folly and dissipation. This laudable conduct would soon put a stop to the emigrations so frequent of late, and would also increase population, the true wealth of a country.'[70]

The patriotic Duke had made his first enquiries in 1771 as soon as he left Inveraray for London, applying to the Edinburgh Trustees for the Manufacturers, and also to the Society for the Promotion of Christian Knowledge, whose sponsors readily supported such schemes for the sake of the moral improvement expected from settling the poor into honest and educational employment.[71*]

The scene of the Duke's new woollen and carpet factory was the large upper-floor workroom built by John Marr, facing Loch Fyne at the east end of the new town; its ground-floor provided homes for its workmen. This plain rectangular building had an auspicious beginning, for at Inveraray, in the midst of good sheep country, a wide variety of wool could now be spun, product of the fresh breeds introduced by the Duke and his fellow-landowners.[72*] The factory's first output of coarse yarn for woollen cloth and blankets was so satisfactory that only a year later the backers were emboldened to more ambitious operations and built a larger workshop outside the town. While the gentlemen of Argyll were being invited to subscribe, Sonachan was requested to find 'a man of skill and substance' to run the new factory.[73]

> 'They are desirous of enlarging the plan,' ran Sonachan's advertisement on the front page of the *Edinburgh Evening Courant* of 15 November 1775, 'and of giving the necessary support to any person of skill that will become a partner and undertake the management of it . . . It seems particularly well adapted for furnishing coarse woollen cloths for the West Indies, and for America (when that trade is again opened) from its vicinity to Glasgow.
>
> Any person of good credit and character, willing to engage in this business, may commune or correspond with the Chamberlain of Argyle, at Inverary, or James Ferrier writer to the signet, at Edinburgh.'

William Inglis, a manufacturer from Lanark, soon presented himself. The subscribers had raised £700 capital, and the Duke provided the manufacturer with premises, utensils, a free house, garden and grass for a cow, £40 for his removal expenses and a salary of £100 a year. In return Inglis, with a nine-year contract dating from Whitsun 1776, must find six weavers, a dyer and a thrower. From a minimum supply of 400 stones of wool to be spun annually in Inveraray and neighbourhood, he was to produce 'Carpets coarse cloths Kendal Cottons or Stockings'.[74]

In this way was launched Clunary factory at Douglas Bridge, three miles down Loch Fyne towards Kenmore. The contractors, two masons named John Moodie and Robert Alexander (the latter eventually handing over to John Brown), between January 1777 and 1778 built a factory house with walls two feet thick and three-foot high gavels, an outer stair and a brick chimney-stack; with a fulling-mill, connected by a stair to the dye-house, a comb-shop, press house, weaving house, storehouse and office or 'writing-room', and the dwelling for Inglis and his family. Roads were laid, and ground levelled for a dye-field, and the Inveraray looms were dismantled and removed to Clunary. The outlay over two years on buildings was £331 11s 2d, and on the equipment £249 15s 8d.[75]

'And here the Woolen Manufactory
Is also in its useful infancy,'
declaimed James Maxwell in 1777. And at first all went well. David Loch, to whom Sonachan showed the 'carpet manufactory and spinning house' in May 1778, found employment booming, with over a hundred girls spinning flax alone. As some tasks could be performed by men, the numerous poor were thus kept in work, and (thought Loch) if only the Duke could use his influence towards a reduction in the price of coals, living in this part of the Highlands would be cheap and good. Altogether circumstances seemed to 'augur a prosperous and valuable future to the factory – a valuable and permanent acquisition to the internal commerce of this kingdom'.[76]

But difficulties had already appeared, for Inglis seems to have been a poor manager and unreliable in fulfilling orders, while his cloth proved of inferior quality. Through this he lost an order for uniforms for Lord Frederick's newly-raised Fencibles. Inglis and the local lairds, his backers, blamed one another for his losses, and the Duke had to come to the rescue by paying off the company's deficit and taking over its unsold stock. He and the other land-owners circulated patterns among their friends, and their servants were given liveries of Clunary cloth, blue with a red collar and turn-up.

Thus maintained, the factory struggled on; the local population rose, a school was opened in 1781 for the workmen's children, and in 1787 the Duke had to forbid the building of 'low mean hutts' by the roadside.[77] John Inglis (apparently no relation of the factory manager's) in 1784 commented on its thriving condition. Yet exactly a year later William Inglis failed, and handed over factory, machinery and equipment in a very run-down condition to two Glasgow woollen manufacturers, John Wood and John Parker, who signed a new contract with the Duke. In the same month (July 1785) Thomas Newte remarked on the new management which, he noted, had 'met with some success'.[78]

But in spite of improvements and repairs the remaining history of the woollen factory is one of misfortune. Wood and Parker soon found it 'inconvenient' to carry on, preferring to pay the defaulter's fine of £100 and escape. A pair of partners from Kilmarnock faring no better, for a time some of the workmen staved off unemployment by carrying on independently with the now worn equipment, till in about 1791 Archibald McNab, a Campbeltown dyer, brought fresh ideas to the industry.

One of its chronic difficulties was the shortage of spun yarn, and this McNab tried to remedy by the introduction of the spinning jenny.[79]* At the same time he persuaded the Duke that as failure had been due to 'the aversion of the woman of the country to the spining part of the business', Sonachan must be got to order 'the woman of every family Tenent Cottar & Labourer upon my Estate' to spin six stone of wool before Candlemas 1792. But when Sonachan came to list the women, at Kenmore all but two and at Achintibert all but one refused, while in Inveraray itself he had to mark many as 'dead', 'left the town', 'unable', 'doubtful', or even 'not to be trusted being dissipated'. A deputation of women who came to wait on him warned that this method had already been tried by McNab, and McNab was unreliable both with wool supplies and with pay.

McNab's version of the story was rather different; but labour difficulties and unbusinesslike management both contributed to failure. A partner brought up from Manchester complained that McNab fiddled accounts, fraudulently appropriated products, ran short of fuel and raw materials, and instead of making readily saleable goods like 'Blanketing, Negro Clothing, and Sailor Jacketing' went in for unpopular lines like 'Carpeting and coarse Hunter's Cloth'. McNab appealed for a renewal of the Duke's order for servants' liveries; but his attempt to clothe another Volunteer Corps ended in failure.[80]* Weavers threw up their jobs in disgust, looms stood idle, and in 1795 the country's 'great Stagnation of Trade' brought work to a stop.

According to the Reverend Paul Fraser in the first *Statistical Account of Scotland*, the shortage of spinners was due to the women's having to work cutting peat; which was due to the fuel shortage; which was due to the price of coal.[81] The price of coal, indeed, meant that the Clunary factory would always have to rely on water-power, but the high costs of production in so remote a part of the country, together with the restriction of markets during the war, completed the disasters. McNab gave up. He had several successors, including an Inveraray merchant Alexander Campbell who in 1803 tried to run the factory with a hired manager. The last contractors appear to have been Patrick and Alexander MacFarlane from Perth, but the former reported in 1809 that a heavy fall in wool prices, combined with 'Stagnation in the market for woolen goods', had 'effectually crushed his hopes'.

The 5th Duke of Argyll had unfailingly, and in the face of all obstacles, continued to back his persistently unsuccessful factory with cheap loans, provision of buildings, equipment and other facilities; but as in so many of his industrial and commercial ventures he offered the best possible conditions only to see the project come to grief.[82]* At Inveraray flax spinning and weaving still continued, but later visitors significantly cease to mention the Clunary factory, and instead comment on the town's lack of manufactures and the uncertainty of its herring industry. Today

only a group of ruinous buildings near the roadside at the Bridge of Douglas, looking less like a one-time factory than an abandoned farm, remains to commemorate
the 5th Duke's nobly-intentioned attempt to introduce the woollen industry to
Inveraray.

It has become so much the resort of travellers, of late, that any description is almost unnecessary.

The Travellers' Guide Through Scotland and its Islands, Edinburgh 1798

It will readily be believed that this noble seat and it's scenery, when beheld by the rude sons of Caledonia, in unequal comparison with their lowly huts and naked wilds, are regarded as a perfect elysium and the residence of a divinity.

Joseph Mawman *An Excursion to the Highlands of Scotland and the English Lakes,* privately printed 1805, Ch. 11

Hail, Inverary! here the muse would dwell;
Would range amid thy gardens, fields and groves;
Survey thy beauteous lakes and shady glens . . .
The grand and beauteous seat of Great Argyle.

James Cririe, DD, *Scottish Scenery, or Sketches in Verse,* London 1803

IX

Duke John, having lost his beloved wife when he was sixty-seven, lived to be eighty-three and died in 1806. Long before then the Western world had weathered a time of revolution and was entering the dawn of a modern era; ideas of freedom, philanthropy and expansion were in the air.

Even at Inveraray, a place now very different from the remote backwater it had been in 1743, the feeling of a new age is apparent. No longer inaccessible, it was in summer and autumn a regular resort of visitors from England and abroad, and had become an elegant, modern – if very small – provincial capital. By the 1790s, the once-weekly post by messenger from Dumbarton, which served the town when Duke Archibald first moved in, became a daily service linking it with the south, and its postmasters no longer automatically became bankrupt. Of its modern industries, the little linen factory still functioned in the town,[1]* the woollen factory at Douglas Bridge was running its halting course, and Henry Kendall's Argyll Furnace Company on Loch Fyne prospered under its latest director, John Lathom. Between July and January the long-established herring fishery with its hundreds of boats kept the town lively, and sometimes more than 20,000 barrels were cured in a season.

Yet the town was as poor as ever, for its revenue was so miserably small. And its inhabitants, according to the Reverend Paul Fraser, had declined in piety and become indifferent to the Sabbath – due perhaps to the free-thinking and loose habits of visitors – while the lower orders were 'too lavish in the use of spirits'. But he found them still 'high spirited, generous, and brave', and good soldier-material though orderly and peaceable by choice.[2]*

Their great landlord, the Duke, lived in these days increasingly at his castle, and as he grew older left it only to visit Rosneath, or to pass part of the winter in or near Edinburgh on business, where at least in 1799 and 1800 he stayed at Bellevue, a house in its own grounds round which Drummond Place was later built. In summer and autumn his children stayed with him at the castle. A rather malicious picture of the family at Inveraray during the melancholy summer after the Duchess's death is given by the Duke's niece Mrs Damer, in a letter to Mary Berry:

'. . . my uncle what people call *thinking* himself ill, that is, being so, for, otherwise, I am convinced, it is a subject no one thinks about. His spirits are low –

cause or consequence of the first : Lady Augusta, no doubt, dawdling away her time with that most *indifferent* sposo, and Lady Charlotte carving *some* name on *some* tree and lolling on the arm of a confidante . . .'³*

The Duke's old age was further clouded by the irresponsibility of his heir; and contemporary references to the marriages of his daughters suggest that they, too, caused anxiety. Both were great beauties and great outragers of convention. Lady Augusta eloped with Lieutenant Henry Clavering not long before her mother's death and by all accounts never ceased to regret it : her unhappiness was reflected in ill-health and the rapid decay of her celebrated looks. Lady Charlotte, fifteen years younger than her sister, in 1796 at Inveraray married respectably – if dully – her kinsman John Campbell of Shawfield, and bred a large family of boys and girls; the marriage was not unsuccessful even if her friends considered her thrown away on 'that great fellow, her husband'.⁴*

Year after year the whole family spent long periods at Inveraray, and year after year the two daughters appeared with more children. Lord Lorne, now in his thirties, as yet showed no sign of marrying : he was too involved with Harriet Wilson and others. The most responsible member of the family, Lord John, was quiet and scientifically-inclined like his father, like him too perhaps a trifle unexciting as a personality, but in later years the family's saviour from ruin.

The chief cause of this near-ruin was Lord Lorne, that 'hopeful young nobleman' who, towards the close of the century, displayed a reckless, spendthrift indulgence, so dissipating his charm and considerable talents as to cause his father, who took responsibility very seriously, great concern; for sheer laziness and idle abandon Lorne seemed likely to rival the Prince of Wales. He ran up debts which even by present-day standards were on a staggering scale, and the impressive Argyll rent-rolls suffered from the strain. In 1796 James Ferrier noted in casting up the annual accounts that £23,900 4s 1d had had to be borrowed over the year on Lord Lorne's behalf, and while they managed to settle his debts to the tune of £30,057 5s 5d, more than £3,000 still remained to pay. This was at a period when total building expenditure at Inveraray had sunk to between £700 and £800 a year. Ferrier opened a special account to deal with Lorne's debts, and in 1797, while a miserable £276 3s 8¾d was paid out for building Robert Mylne's new church, Lord Lorne's creditors swallowed up £2,466 5s 4d of the Argyll rents. Next year they took £2,641 13s 10d; so it continued.⁵*

'I have avoided hitherto reproaching you with your imprudence however distressing they have been to me, but the late information I have received of an additional debt of ten thousand bears so hard upon me that I cannot help complaining of your want of confidence in not acquainting me before of this unhappy affair. It remains now for you to give me your positive assurance that . . . you spend your time in such a manner & in such Company that I am secure in future from being plungd into despair by your misconduct. Consider the happiness of your Sisters & Brother will soon depend upon your being able to pay regularly the sums engaged for their maintenance & that they as well as myself must in the mean time suffer in seeing you forfeit your Character & the good Opinion of the World which no man is better qualified to possess with a little attention . . . adieu my still dearest George.'[6]

With the Duke's increasing age and financial and personal burdens, at the castle everything was now wearing out and needing repair, and little more than mainten-ance was kept up. The frequency with which orders were repeated shows the over-seers to have become slack and dilatory. In 1792 the Duke, tender to his family and dependants but brisk and military as an organizer, drew up a set of sharply-worded standing orders to prevent fraud and waste. The Chamberlain was to keep written records of piece-work, to approve all contracts personally, and to keep a book ac-counting for all articles required by the overseers – who were to report at the pay office for orders 'at least three times a week at a particular hour'.[7]* But before very long standards relapsed once more.

Among the few ornamental additions made to the castle during these years was a set of glass-fronted book-presses for the Duke's turret adjoining his dressing-room on the north front, made in 1795–6 by John Simpson (son of the John Simpson who in 1784 succeeded George Haswell as chief wright). They were finished and painted by James Bell, the carpenter who made the elm-wood chairs for the inn.[8]*

The designer of these exceedingly elegant cupboards was presumably Mylne, although no diary references to them occur. They are shaped to the curve of the turret wall, and so placed (like the much less elaborate pair in the tapestry drawing-room turret) to be seen at once by anyone entering the tiny room, on either side of the fireplace facing the door. Surmounting them are large oval medallions in the antique style, set in frames of garlands, and the silk-lined glass doors have elabor-ately fitted panes in interlacing circles and arcs and are framed by a carved frieze of acanthus leaves and vases.

The other new items were chimney-pieces, one of which has a rather un-expected history. In 1800, as the future of Bellevue was under discussion by the Edinburgh Council, the Duke of Argyll made an offer for this drawing-room item, observing that it looked sadly out of place there since the 'Tapestry and other rich Furniture which was once there . . . has been removed'. He offered in exchange either a suitable sum in cash, or 'a plain handsome one' of his own and £100. The Edinburgh committee cannily settled for £200 cash, probably reflecting that as Bellevue was now to be converted into a Customs House they could replace the fitting for far less.[9]*

As a result of this transaction Inveraray's tapestry-drawing-room received its present statuary chimney-piece, of two classical female figures in white marble, each leaning an elbow along the fireplace frame to hold the drapery forming its central ornament.

Inveraray castle was at this time more in need of maintenance than improve-ment, but the town, that pioneer example of planning evolved by the multiple efforts of Duke Archibald, the Adam family, Duke John and Robert Mylne, long remained like an unfinished arch lacking its keystone. Between 1795 and 1802, however, the long deferred building of Robert Mylne's church achieved the town's final integration into a planned whole.

The new double church was Mylne's last commission for Inveraray. Its building history was like that of all other major contributions to the town – halting and beset with complications; and it ended in stormy arguments and the eventual disruption of Mylne's relationship with the Duke.

> 'Sent the D. of Argyll a design for a double church at Inverary of the following drawings: a plan, elevation, 2 cross sections, and 1 long section, all Neatly washed, figured, etc. etc. – 25 [guineas].'

That was on 16 July 1792. The following May Mylne submitted an amended design, 'the former not being perfect', the charge 'Nothing – as it was an amendment'.[10]

Inveraray's whole central area, which had been little more than a building site for twenty years, was thoroughly uneven in surface, and after an abortive beginning at clearing it and quarrying, followed by a long delay – probably for financial reasons – the Duke in November 1794 ordered the site to be properly levelled and the debris thrown into 'the hole near the Highland church'. After a further delay due to severe winter weather, the church's foundation was at last laid in March 1795, the masons already engaged were joined by others diverted from restoring the Gothick dairy and other jobs, and on 1 May building began. The Duke's intention was to complete the church by 1799.[11]

At first the stone was quarried from Dalchenna and St Catherine's, and Robert Lemon cut the granite slabs for corner-stones and flags for founding the steeple and cross-wall, while Peter Gardner was employed for hewing finer pieces for doors, windows and columns. Easdale slates and crown glass from the Dumbarton Glass Company were ordered, the latter held up for some weeks by snowy weather, which prevented its being removed from the Rosneath boathouse where it was stored.

St Catherine's stone was declared unsuitable for the 'hewn work' and finishings, and from 1796 freestone from the Arran quarries now being worked for building the long-discussed Crinan Canal, was brought at six shillings a ton for the relatively modest project of Inveraray church. In the autumn of 1798 a further 360 tons of Arran stone were still required, ten times as much as small sloops like the *Smart* could carry in one cargo. When 1799 saw no further progress, the Duke's former mason John Tavish, now styling himself 'architect', was twice sent for from Kilmartin to survey the building and estimate its outstanding cost. The financial situation was eased by the Duke's selling some timber.

By then, as the Chamberlain Colonel Graham admitted, 'For some time past nothing has been done in the building way. So many difficulties have been experienced in procuring Materials'; but the Duke, who was spending the winter in Edinburgh, determined to use the money he had raised in 'finishing the Churches this spring. I mean only the Shell of them exclusive of plaistering – Stair – Loft – Seating, and Pulpit, which I think by your Estimate was to amount to £681 st.'

[39] Inveraray Castle, state drawing-room, detail of marble chimney-piece acquired from Bellevue, Edinburgh, in 1800

Colonel Graham advised putting the job out to contract as 'the Cheapest, as well as the Speediest way of executing that work', and rather than employ Tavish or Carmichael the Duke approved his recommendation of a Mr Bogle,[12]* whose 'connection with Seafaring people in Clyde' would help with the problem of transporting the Arran stone. However, much to the Chamberlain's annoyance Bogle proved unco-operative, pleading the distance involved and his fear of competition (which would presumably force him to lower his fees). The Duke forebore to 'court' Bogle which he foresaw would 'occasion his being extravagant in his demands'.

During the delay the Duke was greatly irritated by the disproportionate trouble taken over a very minor job – a new cottage for George Haswell's widow Margaret, on one of the old Gallowgate stances.

> 'Mrs Haswell's house is the most tedious operation I was ever concerned in. I now observe door ways slaping out, & walls building which were never intended at first, particularly the door which I think I expressly forbid.'

Colonel Graham's explanations were lengthy: the Fisherland door led to the only accessible water supply, the retaining wall would 'prevent the Soil of the Garden from tumbling down', and so forth. The Duke was not impressed.

> 'One man and a boy almost constantly employed at Mrs Haswels, occurs to me to be more than is necessary. . . . Get rid of that work as soon as possible.'

A month later he was annoyed to find that the plan of the church, long laid aside, had vanished. His trunk, the lumber room, the Rosneath house, were searched in vain, and Graham had to write to Mylne in London for another. Mylne sent up two plans, two elevations and a section of the roof, which in March (1800) was shown to yet another architect, Hugh Cairncross.[13]* The latter also made two visits to the site, and as a result of his survey and estimate the church, apart from its steeple, was finished that year.

The Duke had consulted Cairncross over Mylne's plans in Edinburgh, and proposed to the Chamberlain immediate quarrying for the spire, for

> 'if the point of the Steeple could be built of St Catherine Stone, & painted white like the front of the Inn, it would have a good effect from the Castle, Kilmaleu &c.'

Accordingly Lemon resumed quarrying, including forty-nine cartloads for columns; and two new contractors, the brothers William and Adam Russell, were found.[14]* The windows were glazed in 1801–2, and upholstery and fittings (the pulpit for the English church cost £20) installed. The Russell brothers' fees accounted for £450 of the church's total cost which, between its inception in 1793 and its completion amounted (excluding Mylne's fees) to some £1,685 – a mere fraction of what the Argyll estates had to find for Lorne's gambling debts in a single year.

Mylne's way of handling his double design was to place the two churches, English and Gaelic, back to back with identical façades, and his exterior gives no clue to the building's dual nature. The two churches, entered from the north and

[40] Inveraray Castle, the south drawing-room turret,
    showing the bookcases made in 1795–6

south fronts, had their pulpits placed against the central dividing partition, from which doorways gave access to the steeple stair.

The exterior, like most of Mylne's Inveraray designs, is a blend of the simple and the ingenious. In each harled side wall the tall pair of round-headed windows have little adornment beyond the complex pattern of their clear glass panes. The gable façades, however, Mylne treats in the manner of a pedimented portico, but only the end bays are open, where Tuscan columns with a fluted necking carry the angles. At the three centre bays, the body of the church projects into the portico, with only a suggestion of pilasters in the projecting white-harled panels which frame the three local blue-stone Venetian windows (whose side lights are blind) of the church's upper level. Below, the central square-headed doorway is framed by Tuscan columns in antis, and flanked by blind segmentally-arched windows in the harled outer bays. The entablature and pediment gable, of Arran stone ashlar, have the characteristic Mylne pierced circle – one being intended to hold the bell – draped by swags in shallow relief which have been left in block.

The steeple, focal point of the church as the church was focal point of the town, was a tall, solid octagonal drum with engaged columns, rising from a square base and supporting a plain entablature and high ribbed dome, with a slender tapering pinnacle above, in St Catherines stone, contrasting with the Arran stone used for the church's dressed surfaces. J. M. W. Turner, on a three-week tour of the Highlands, visited Inveraray probably in July 1801, and made numerous sketches about the town which he later worked up into paintings and engravings. He recorded the new church with its unfinished steeple still under scaffolding.[15]* The unfortunate removal of this tall drum, dome and pinnacle, in 1941, when it was found to be unsafe, robbed the church of much of its significance, and the failure to restore it has left Inveraray's appearance architecturally the poorer.

Mylne designed further decorative features for his church, the history of whose abandonment closes another era in the building of Inveraray. His earliest plan shows only three shallow steps to the church doors at either end, as today. The successive elaboration of ideas can be traced through the relevant entries in his diary during 1800 and 1801.[16]

7th March, 1800: Sent the Duke of Argyll copys of 2 plans and 2 elevations in lines, for Inverary Church, the former having been lost by the Mail Coach.

25th March: Wrote D. of Argyll, and sent a Section of the Roof of Inveraray Church . . .

8th June: Wrote the D. of Argyll, on Colonade's proposed to be added to Inverary Church. – 1.

19th July : – Wrote D. Argyll a long letter on Round porches to each side of Church at Inverary, and sent a Drawing (copy) of the Plan of the Town – Square – Church &c. – in lines.

1st Sept. : – Wrote the Duke of Argyll . . . and sent him a *Plan* of the town of In—y and of the Circular Porticos introduced therein. – 1.

87. Inveraray Church before the removal of the steeple in 1941

> 24th Sept. : – Sent D. of Argyll 2 Plans & 2 Elevations of the side of church at
> Inverary, in lines, with the Plan & Elevations of Portico's attached to the sides
> thereof, washed and neat – one design being for the circular Porch, my way. –
> the other square, the Duke's way.

A world of irritated disagreement is implied in the last unemotional phrases. The
argument continued into the following year, by which time the Duke had found an
ally in the newcomer Alexander Nasmyth, and Mylne now had two opponents to
convince.

The cause of all the argument was a pair of colonnades or porches intended as
covered market stances for the town centre – a highly decorative as well as practical
feature, which in Mylne's successive drawings may be seen to have increased in
complexity. The first plan shows a pair of stepped semicircular porticos, with five
grouped columns, in the centre of the church side-walls, the east one being the true
porch shielding two doors, while that on the west covered the tron or public weigh-

88. Inveraray from the south, 1801
    Showing the church steeple still unfinished.
    After a drawing by J.M.W.Turner.

bridge, a series of stepped seats, and a 'Porch for exposure of wares'. Three months later (September 1800) came the idea of extending these porticoes into balustraded colonnades the length of the church, and adding square open porches to the north and south entrances.[17] Mylne's following letters evidently defended his design against the Duke's mounting criticism, and he was obliged to produce alternative versions demonstrating his own and his patron's opposing preferences.

One of Nasmyth's large paintings of Inveraray taken from the loch (which includes the Gothick lighthouse he fancied for the extended quay) shows a very elaborate, almost pagoda-like version of the church steeple, and also lightly sketches in an outline of the proposed colonnades. In the end, however, neither the Duke's nor Mylne's idea was adopted, and no porticos, nor even small porches, were ever built. Here again the result is aesthetically a loss to the church's appearance and to the town itself; and the absence from the building of this finishing touch is a testimony to the collapse of relations between the Duke and Mylne.

From the spiritual to the corporeal. While Inveraray's double church was being built, a dung-pit conforming to the most advanced agricultural theories was constructed in the Gallowgate.

For some years the burgh magistrates had complained of Inveraray's slovenly appearance and ruled, without much success, that townspeople must empty no

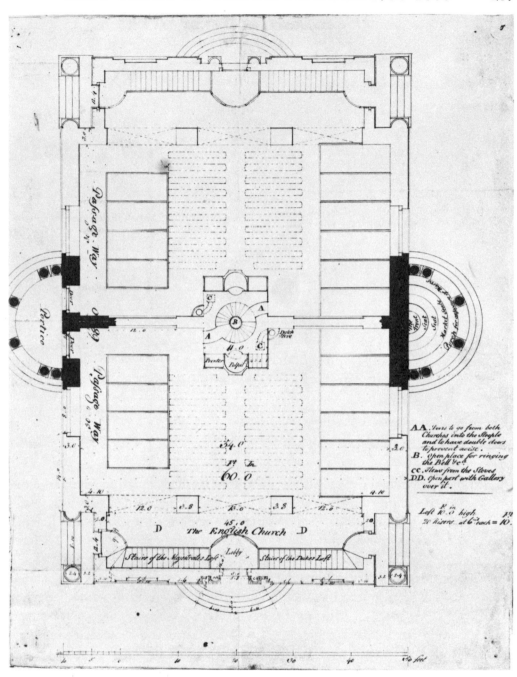

89. Inveraray Church
   Plan by Robert Mylne, showing the proposed semi-circular porticoes, 1800.

90. Inveraray Church before the removal of the steeple
    Looking east, showing: left, the George Hotel, with Ferry Land and
    Factory Land behind; right, the new Court House.

slops from their windows, leave off the 'indecent practice' of washing clothes in the
town well, and keep the fronts of their houses clear of 'any filth or nastiness whatever'; in return public middensteads were to be made for the 'filth'. The herring
fishers and salters were taken to task for throwing refuse from their boats about
the streets and shore, to the great 'Stinck and putrefaction' of the same.[18]

Cleaning and even paving never got very far, and pigs wandering at large added
a further unsavoury touch. In 1795 the Duke had the ground before the town
levelled and gravelled, and its sewers cleared. Of the town dung-pit, for which
Robert Lemon began quarrying in 1799, the Duke himself took charge in consultation with the Chamberlain. It was sited at the bottom of a slight slope down
which liquid from neighbouring stables and byres drained into its specially designed reservoir, 'paved with Stones bedded in Clay' and with a hinged cover. (A
second middenstead to take 'all the Dung & Ashes of the Towns' People' was
built by Donald McPhedran opposite Cross Houses.)

The result was no mere waste-heap for the casual shovelling of rubbish, but a
roofed construction supported on columns with a 25-yard ridge batten and fourteen air slits. But these modern improvements did not prevent the townspeople
from leaving dung and rubbish on the streets exactly as before.[19]*

[41] The Dalmally road screen by the Argyll Arms, showing the
addition to the inn (with bow window), 1793–4

In 1793–4 the inn had received an important addition (built by John Tavish at a cost of £455 2s 5½d) at the side facing the Dalmally road, with a bow running its full height. This provided a new dining-room and four more bedrooms, and the stables and coach-houses were also altered and a second courtyard added. To match the main building and every other house in the town, the extension was finished with Easdale slates and Dumbarton glass, and '2 Grates, 2 setts Fire Irons, 2 Steel Fenders' were brought from Burrow & Lawson's foundry for £6 1s 5d. An interesting detail is thirty-six elm-wood chairs for the new dining-room made by James Bell at three-and-sixpence each. Mylne's notebooks contain no references to the inn except in connexion with the screen wall, but he records inspecting it during his last visit to Inveraray (1785), and in May 1792 he waited on the Duke in London to discuss 'various pieces of business', one of them undoubtedly the church and another probably the inn. Certainly the Duke's order for the new additions (November 1792) refers to a plan.[20*]

The last improvement made during the 5th Duke's lifetime, extension of the quay and breastwork, was the town's own responsibility. John Adam's quay, finished in 1762, was only 100 feet long and provided anchorage for only two small vessels – wholly inadequate in a port which now served a herring fleet of 500 local boats and at least 100 others; while the many cargo ships could not put in at all but had to unload their supplies of building materials, meat and grain, and take on board the town's exports of wool and timber bark, by small rowing-boats.[21*] Although the Duke had no jurisdiction over the pier, in 1795 he ordered estimates for its extension and 'some ornamental building' at its end. Nasmyth's monumental lighthouse, designed for this, never materialized since even the quay, let alone any extras, proved so difficult and expensive to build.

In 1796 it was decided to apply for a grant to the Convention of Royal Burghs, but since nothing in Inveraray was ever achieved in a hurry, only in 1800 did the Convention agree to offer £200, provided the magistrates found £435. Towards this the Duke, the Commissioners of Supply and the Kirk Session each contributed £100, which with other small sums left them far short of the total; and time was passing. In 1805 they sought an estimate from William Johns, a mason, to restore the ruinous parts of the quay, build on a further 116 feet and rebuild the stairway parallel with the masonry. For all this, with a blue flag foundation, dressed Arran freestone facing and a granite causeway, Johns' estimate was £865. The total fund now raised was £681 11s 0d.

The magistrates were evidently doubtful about Johns' proposals and asked James Gillespie,[22*] 'an Architect of Eminence' from Edinburgh, who had occasionally visited Inveraray, to inspect the pier. Gillespie, on 17 May 1805, recommended strengthening the pier by laying its foundations level and horizontally stepped down, instead of following the beach's natural slope, and by securing certain courses and cross-walls with iron 'batts'.

The town council accepted Gillespie's advice, but Johns in a rage 'refused to receive the same accompanying his refusal with some strong expressions'.

[42] Main Street, looking south

Driven to subterfuge, the Town Clerk posted him the report under plain cover. A committee then examined Johns' work with great displeasure and ordered him, on pain of compulsion, to fulfil Gillespie's terms.

Next year when the job was finished Johns had his revenge. The Council still owed him more than £260 which he demanded from them with threats, and even served on them a Letter of Horning.[23]* The magistrates in a panic had to beg again from the Convention of Royal Burghs.

Eventually the money was raised, but only after long negotiation, and in a desperate effort to increase Inveraray's tiny revenue the magistrates ruled that every person who trafficked in merchandise must take out a burgess ticket – which netted the town the magnificent sum of two and a half guineas per applicant.

Lord Lorne, in addition to his gambling debts and his general extravagance as a gay young nobleman in London, was, in Scotland, indulging in some costly architectural follies. The proved artistic integrity and imagination of a Robert Mylne were not enough for this young man, who preferred the showier experiments of more newly fashionable architects.

At the time of his square-versus-circular porch controversy Mylne was also supervising repairs to Argyll House in London, and Lorne several times kept him dangling before admitting him to talk business on either subject. 'Waited on M. of Lorne – could not see him' is a not uncommon entry in Mylne's diary during 1801, when he had various schemes to discuss with the Marquess. One of these was for a 'Covered Way for Inveraray town, &c. at or near the Church', that is, the market portico scheme; but not until early June did Lorne spare time to admit him to a 'Long Consultation', and then turned down the idea, of which we hear no more.[24]*

For, besides indulging Nasmyth's fanciful proposals round and about Inveraray, the Marquess's chief interest was the improvement of Rosneath Castle. Since 1783 Mylne had produced a number of designs for Rosneath, chiefly a new wing and alterations to the first floor apartments.[25] Of these additions no details are known, since no drawings of the castle appear to survive subsequent to the sketches of Morris's and William Adam's improvements made for Duke Archibald half a century earlier. This much altered building was fated to cost the Argyll family a great deal of money, lost for ever when on 30 May 1802, at 6 o'clock in the evening, a fire broke out and in seven hours the best part of the fabric had been 'entirely consumed' – a loss estimated at £18,000. The amateur painter and philosopher James Denholm, visiting Rosneath from Glasgow soon afterwards, saw in it great possibilities as a fashionably romantic ruin:

'its lofty and embattled towers – its broken arches and windows contrasted with the many fine trees around; time was only wanting, to cover with its mosses and shrubs, the walls and crevices . . . to render it one of the finest and most picturesque ruins.'[26]

Lord Lorne had other ideas. Perhaps unconsciously following the methods of

91. Rosneath Castle
    Designed by Joseph Bonomi for the 6th Duke; begun in 1803,
    still unfinished in 1822, now demolished.

Duke Archibald, within a few months he had the ruins of the old house totally removed and was ready to erect a grandiose new palace of his own. But Robert Mylne,
the obvious man for the job, was dropped, and the architect Lorne consulted was
Nasmyth. Nasmyth's innings was brief, and once he had chosen the site and planned
the court of offices crowned by the 90-foot 'prospect' tower which was built first,[27]
he was cast aside in favour of a new, better-known protégé, who was a far more
formidable rival to Robert Mylne.

This was Joseph Bonomi, only five years Mylne's junior, an Italian who had
made his career in England at the suggestion of Robert and James Adam, with
whom at first he worked. Elected an A.R.A. in 1789, Bonomi became a favoured designer of country houses, and at this period his most recent products included
Laverstoke, near Whitchurch in Hampshire and Sandling House near Hythe (now
demolished).[28]

Bonomi's Rosneath was, in its own way, as original a design as Inveraray itself.
Although it had four floors, it created the impression of a long, low building, as its
base storey was below ground and its attic concealed behind the balustrade intended to surround it (though this was never completed). Externally it had two
noticeable peculiarities. First, a domeless drum surmounted the library bow on the
garden side, containing several rooms and a staircase. Secondly, the unorthodox
five-columned portico was a *porte-cochère*, entered by carriages from the side – as
the odd number of columns plainly demonstrated. The *porte-cochère* portico (after
the manner of Henry Holland's Carlton House of 1783) was a favourite theme
with Bonomi, who used it first at Longford Hall in Shropshire (1789–92) with four
columns, and then at Eastwell in Kent (1793–9) with five, to demonstrate as at

Rosneath that the portico was not to be entered frontally. This portico was balanced by another, with three free-standing columns, at either end of the house; and similarly on the library front, a central bow with six irregularly spaced columns was to be flanked by end porticoes with four : in fact the drums there were never erected. Again as at Eastwell Bonomi used a baroque Ionic capital. None of the columns supported a pediment, and this, with the absence of a dome, gave the house very horizontal, neo-classic lines, and a kind of ponderous gravity.

Internally, further oddities were to be found. A central passage 178 feet long traversed the entire house from end to end; and Bonomi not only contrived his staircases so ill that access to the main stair from the hall involved making two right turns, but he provided only a single service stair, at one end of the immense passage. Finally, in intention at least (for this too appears never to have been executed) he indulged his fondness for the 'covered way', designing one 156¾ feet long connecting the yard at the eastern end of the house with the water-side.

Rosneath was mostly built between the years 1803 and 1806, though several of the rooms were unfinished as late as 1822 (Bonomi having died in 1808), and the garden side never received its intended portico. To Thomas Telford, a near-contemporary, the house showed 'originality of genius, and a disposition to simplify truly laudable'; to Sir John Summerson in our own time, it displays like other designs of Bonomi's 'a marked insensibility'.[29]*

By 1803 the old Duke was suffering an attack of remorse over his difference of opinion with the ageing and intractable Mylne, and the 'Injury and Mortification done him'. He had deep misgivings over his son's new architectural associates, and while Lorne was deep in the planning of his latest scheme at Rosneath, sent him a series of cautionary letters. While admitting the charm of Nasmyth's preliminary sketches he warned him,

> 'I had no doubt but that you & he could make a pretty Picture of a house but this is only a skindeep merit, & I am convinced that old Mylne and your old Father could have made a more convenient & a more comfortable habitation.'

After a further warning (not his first) of the high cost of buildings whose benefits he himself was unlikely ever to enjoy the Duke continued,

> 'Two Houses of Expence & Taste are sufficient to ruin any Family. If you would display your taste, Here are capabilities ad infinitum, here they will be much more seen & resorted to.'

Rather significantly, the father expressed a strong preference for the 'Castellated Gothick Castle' over his modish son's innovation of 'your chaste Italian Casino'.

A couple of months later when Bonomi had become the favourite, the Duke after some slighting references to the Italian's Rosneath designs confessed,

> 'I am terrified every night with the Ghost of poor Mylne. For God's sake lay that perturbed Spirit. If you acquaint me that this is accomplished, Columns – Domes – Atticks &c. shall all rise as fast as you please.'

His letters continued full of regrets for the old architect and warnings against the new:

'. . . Your display of Taste, & Bonomis fame are Securd—but let me observe to you en passant that, Taste without Prudence & Œconomy, is a Mill stone about a Mans Neck, and therefore I hope you will not associate too much with Bonomi and Nasmith—You will find them expensive Pets—they will not consult your Pecuniary Interest as poor old Mylne us'd to do mine.'[30]

'Poor old Mylne', incidentally, was still far from a ghost, and although during his last years his physical powers, without succumbing to any positive disease, were much impaired, he lived until 1811. Nichols wrote in his *Literary Anecdotes*:

'He loved his profession but not the emoluments of it, and therefore, after all his distinguished employments, did not die rich. Those who knew him could not fail to respect his integrity, and admire his talents.'[31]

The 5th Duke of Argyll would no doubt have heartily endorsed these sentiments.

The grand tour of England and Scotland was now fast rivalling the Continent as part of a gentleman's education, and Inveraray, since its transformation in appearance and accessibility, was on the gentleman-tourist route. They came by chaise, by hired conveyance, on horseback and on foot, noblemen, poets, painters, scholars and citizens with their tutors, relatives and friends. Most came notebook and sketchbook in hand, and by the end of the century a few were composing Scotland's earliest actual guide-books. The discovery of Scotland from the 1780s onwards was comparable to the opening up of Greece in the 1950s and 1960s. In 1803 Dorothy Wordsworth, watching the splendid equipage of 'the renowned Miss Waughs of Carlisle' descending on Arrochar from the wilds, observed that

'twenty years ago, perhaps, such a sight had not been seen here except when the Duke of Argyle, or some other Highland chieftain, might chance to be going with his family to London or Edinburgh'.[32]

Those who had no personal introduction to Inveraray Castle and stayed at the inn found much to complain of behind that grand façade. The Reverend John Lettice, visiting in 1792, devoted three whole pages to its servants' deficiencies, their inability to answer bells and the long wait for breakfast. After a perfect carillon of bell-ringing in vain from every room he and his companion could only trace a waiter by tipping an hostler from the stable-yard.[33]* Another victim was the writer Robert Heron:

'The servants seemed to be too few for the extent of the inn, and not to have their proper posts and tasks, assigned them with a distribution sufficiently judicious. They did not always attend when called; but when they appeared, their anxiety to oblige, easily induced me to excuse their delay . . .'[34]*

So, too, John Stoddart in 1799, one of the minority who hid admiration behind self-conscious criticism. Perhaps travelling with the painter Nattes made him over-anxious not to seem impressed. Everything was slightly short of perfection: castle, town ('perhaps ostentatiously displayed'), houses (not 'answerable, in point of accommodation, to their external appearance'), and inn ('tolerable, but not greatly superior to what we had already met with').[35]

92. Main Street, Inveraray, looking north, in the 1930s
   Much as a visitor would have seen it in the early 19th century.

Indeed, the advent of the picturesque cult caused nearly every gentleman – or lady – to feel it necessary to pass aesthetic judgment, usually patronizing, and the younger the critic, of course, the more ruthless. For example, George Douglas, aged twenty-seven, in 1800 tempered the expected praises of Inveraray with a grudging qualification that 'on the whole, nature has done more than art, and the grounds are by no means judiciously laid out'.[36]*

Inveraray Castle, with its uncompromising fort-like shape and unmellowing newness – to this day it preserves a look of having been quarried and built only months ago – was a gift to the pompous and facetious. It was, complained James M'Nayr in 1797 in one of the first guide-books to the Highlands,

   'not suited to the grandeur of the surrounding scenery . . . somewhat gothick
   . . . and very much resembles a cruet frame, or carron grate, to which it has been
   compared by some modern travellers'.[37]

However, for its interior few had anything but praise – except where they objected to its grandeur.

   'Somewhat gothick . . .' More than one critic complained of the castle's bastard form.

   'In a Gothic edifice such as this is intended to represent, we look for the varied
   outline, the subordinate buildings, the courts, gateways, towers, whose forms
   give picturesqueness, and whose extent augments grandeur. Here is nothing of

all this. The house is a square mass ... the windows are large, unsuitable to the style of architecture, and there is not even a door-way correspondent to the magnitude of the building.'[38]

One visitor really believed the castle to be consciously modelled 'upon the plan of the mansions of some of the German nobility',[39] others (plagiarizing Pennant) compared its stone to that of the King of Denmark's palace in Copenhagen.[40] Yet these were hardly more fanciful than William Burrell, who forty years earlier had seen 'a strong resemblance to Solomon's Temple'.[41]

But being a natural goal for travellers Inveraray received abuse as well as praise, and it became memorable for many features : the unusual quality of the castle's building stone; the ingenuity of the Duke's drying-barns and originality of Mylne's farm buildings in Glenshira; the splendour of the inn, in spite of its poor service; the steep climb to Duniquaich for its unparalleled view over loch, town and castle; loch and shore crowded with herring-busses. Taking a wider view, it was remarkable for having a ducal castle totally rebuilt to order within living memory, in a style not only well in advance of its time but, to say the least, exotic in its surroundings; for being a pioneer example of a planned town, first designed a full generation before any other in the country; for being the scene of industrial and agricultural experiments, and finally, for being a welcome oasis of civilization in the still wild Highlands.

The old Duke's declining powers meant that, while to the end he kept strict watch over his farms and estates and wrote several times a week to his Rosneath factor, the indoor management, lacking a regular châtelaine, noticeably deteriorated. But the house was at many seasons as full as ever. Even in 1805, at the very end of the Duke's life, the establishment is shown to have comprised forty-five persons, and in April 1806, sixty. These, besides the Duke, consisted on this occasion of Lady Augusta with her family of six; Lord Lorne and his servant; Mrs Campbell (probably of Carrick) and servant; the Duke's physician Dr Stewart and servant; the housekeeper Mrs Lover, five housemaids, four kitchenmaids, four laundry-maids, six stable-boys, three upper servants (Ritchie, Marquis and Wilson), three footmen, the baker, the gamekeeper and second table boy. These constituted the 'family' : 'strangers' with their own servants were separately listed.[42*]

Among the most notable visitors during these years – some of them already mentioned – were the painters Joseph Farington in 1792[43] and J. M. W. Turner in 1801; statesmen or future statesmen included William Lamb, later Lord Melbourne, the young Henry Temple (in 1800) with his parents the 2nd Viscount and Lady Palmerston, and Lachlan MacQuarie, later Governor of New South Wales. Of writers and poets 'Monk' Lewis was a frequent visitor, and also Tom Sheridan (son of the dramatist), Thomas Campbell, who spent the summers of 1795 to 1797 at Colonel Graham's, adoring with effusion but little hope the lovely Caroline, daughter of the Reverend Paul Fraser;[44*] James Hogg, the Wordsworths, and Lady Louisa Stuart.

Those who stayed or were otherwise entertained at the castle were nowadays mostly the friends of the Duke's children, and gay parties of young people gathered there with the fecund Lady Charlotte, the sickly, disappointed Lady Augusta, the charming but thoughtless Lorne and his studious brother John. By all accounts they were a happy, devoted family and, whatever their failings, at home at Inveraray they appear their gayest and best.

Several of their visitors have left us entertaining glimpses of family life and hospitality at the castle in these lively days, and two young noblemen whose visits are fully recorded were Edward Adolphus Seymour, 11th Duke of Somerset, in 1795, and John Henry Manners, 5th Duke of Rutland, in 1797. Somerset, then twenty, was travelling with his tutor the Reverend J. H. Michell, who wrote up a very self-conscious account for publication; the Duke of Rutland published his own (anonymous) three-volume account of his complete British travels during 1795–7.[45]

Somerset's party arrived at Inveraray on the morning of 21 July 1795, and were intercepted at the new Garron Lodge by a servant sent by the Duke of Argyll and escorted to the castle through the beech avenue. Lord Stonefield (John Campbell, son to Sheriff Stonefield), with whom they had just been staying at Levenside, was here as another guest.

> 'Our reception into the splendid seat of this noble family still more interested us in its beauties, and our only regret was, that the gloom of the day precluded us from enjoying its external ornaments till the evening, when the Duke of Somerset was conducted through different parts of the park, by the amiable daughters of Argyll ... Some charming music by the ladies closed the evening's entertainment.'

Next morning after a late breakfast the young men walked to the Glenshira farm and drying-barns with Mr Campbell, another clergyman, whom they had met at Levenside; and were shown the conventional sights. It was the height of the herring season, always a curiosity to the visitor, and the last year's catch of the Clyde fleet had been estimated at £30,000, even higher than usual.

An elegant dinner followed, and Michell and Campbell then walked along the shore and enjoyed the spectacle of others, namely the fishermen, preparing for the toils of the night. Back at the castle,

> 'the noble ladies entertained us by dancing reels, in a style of ease and elegance which I never before saw, and increased our pleasure by playing on the organ ... which gratified me far beyond my expectations, when accompanied by the sweet voice of the amiable sisters. Some of the party were engaged in cards, a sad but necessary resource where some employment is requisite for the vacant mind.'

The sycophantic Mr Michell, in postures of adulation as Lady Augusta accompanied herself on the organ, was not the only clergyman who had scruples about cards. The Duke of Rutland in 1797 was accompanied by two clergymen, Mr King and Mr Culling Smith, and Mr King was made of sterner stuff. He required to be

93. Inveraray in 1824, from the slopes of Duniquaich
    Engraved after a drawing by John Clark.

actively deceived, and for him the organ performance was put on with deliberately
seductive effect :

> 'The fascinating melodies of Lady Charlotte Campbell [writes the Duke of Rut-
> land] were intended so to occupy the attention of our clerical tourists, that they
> were not to suspect that any other amusement but that derived from the "con-
> cord of sweet sounds" was going on in the house. The apothecary [Dr Alex-
> ander Stewart], who resided in the house with the Duke of Argyll, had some
> scruples relative to card-playing on the Sabbath, and he at first concealed him-
> self in the music party, but being hunted out, was compelled to make one of the
> performers at the green board.'

Rutland, moving like a royal progress from ducal house to ducal house with a carriage, a curricle, saddle horses and servants, had in Yorkshire gathered into his
train yet another young clergyman, Mr Hayes. Inveraray came between visits to
the Dukes of Atholl and Montrose, though at first they politely put up at the inn,
from which Rutland sent a note to Lord Lorne.

> 'We received an immediate invitation to the castle. At dinner, we met (besides
> the Duke of Argyll, Lord Lorne, Mr and Lady Charlotte Campbell, a family
> Physician, and Mr Graham, his Grace's agent), Lord and Lady Seaforth, the
> Dean of Litchfield (Dr Proby), and his family.'

It was September, and the large party was to celebrate Lorne's birthday. After
dinner there were bonfires and fireworks, and they all went down to the town where
Lorne was 'received with acclamations by the inhabitants, among the lower orders
of whom he distributed money'. The Dean and family left next day, so that Rutland

and his companions after one night at the inn were able to move up to the castle, and the young gentlemen went shooting with Lorne while the clergymen 'more placidly' viewed the scenery.

> 'After dinner we were entertained by some excellent catches and glees, from Lord Lorne and his sister, Lady Charlotte Campbell, in which they were assisted by the Duke himself. During the evening the two former sung duets from Italian operas, in a superior style of tone, taste, and execution.'

It was next day, Sunday – after a sight of the herring-boats, and a ride up Glenshira – that the little deception was practised so that the lay members could play cards. So content were the party that they accepted the Duke's pressing invitation to stay another day before going on to Buchanan Castle, and in a rare spell of fine weather in a bad autumn, went roebuck shooting on Duniquaich. 'Our evening concluded as usual, with music and duets, most charmingly performed', and next morning they regretfully departed to exchange 'this hospitable mansion' for dinner at Arrochar's 'solitary inn'.

At that same inn of Arrochar in 1796 the Honourable Mrs Murray, who had been staying with Colonel and Mrs Humphrey Graham, was stormbound in company with three German gentlemen who had been ascending Glen Croe on foot, while another traveller had his horse die of exposure in the glen.[46*] Four years later on another Highland jaunt Mrs Murray encountered the brother of one of the same Germans 'skipping among the rocks with hammers' beside Loch Lomond, with Dr John Leyden (a Scotsman, in spite of his name) and two more German students from Edinburgh University.[47] The gifted and versatile Leyden, then only twenty-five, was conducting this party on an energetic pedestrian tour of the Highlands looking for geological specimens, a favourite contemporary pursuit among scientifically-minded gentlemen. While at Inveraray that July (1800) they dined with the Duke, who was entertaining Sir John McGregor Murray, then bound for the Hebrides seeking evidence for Ossian's authenticity. They also met Sir William Hart,[48*] another frequent visitor at the Castle, who lent Leyden a manuscript journal of his own tour of the Crimea, but it proved to be merely a catalogue of what Hart had eaten, drunk and worn! At Lochgilphead a few days later Leyden's party had to give up their rooms to Robert Campbell of Asknish – who since Stonefield's retirement and death had been Sheriff of Argyll – but Asknish hospitably invited them to his own home, Loch Gair House, farther down Loch Fyne, where they met his family and other Inveraray Campbells.[49*]

An appreciative account of an evening at the castle in 1804 is left us by Lachlan MacQuarie, when as a forty-three-year-old widower on leave from India he had been revisiting his old home in Mull after many years' absence. Returning from there MacQuarie joined at Inveraray his cousin Miss Elizabeth Campbell, daughter of John Campbell of Airds, to whom he shortly became betrothed. After breakfasting at the inn, joined by the Reverend Paul Fraser, MacQuarie and his kinsman McLachlan of McLachlan called on Colonel Graham, who offered to escort them to wait on the Duke. 'His Grace, however, being rather indisposed could not be

94. Ruins of Mylne's Riding House in the Maltland
    Used as a private theatre by the Argyll family and burnt down in
    1817 (rebuilt 1897). From a drawing of 1825 by the Rev. John Skinner.

seen so early', but Lorne, Lord John and Shawfield (Lady Charlotte's husband)
came and conversed 'in a very frank and friendly manner'; and when they delivered
a dinner invitation from the Duke, MacQuarie at once deferred his departure from
Inveraray. He spent the few hours before dinner riding with Fraser through the
grounds, while his cousins, attended by his servant, visited the castle and park.

At six o'clock the gentlemen presented themselves at the castle and were received in the drawing-room by the Duke and his daughters. Dinner was served at
half-past, a fashionable hour probably introduced by Lorne; the party of fifteen
included, besides the family and the doctor, Mrs Campbell of Carrick,[50]* Colonel
Graham, 'Mr Sheridan Junr', and 'Mr Lewis'. Macquarie was delighted with the
occasion.

> 'The good old Duke eat and drank heartily, was very sociable, and attentive to
> everyone. – He sat at the head of his own Table, with one of his Daughters on
> each hand of him.
>
> Mr Sheridan sung two or three most excellent Songs after Dinner, and then
> the Duke left us to take his usual Evening's Ride in his Carriage accompanied
> by his favorite Daughter Lady Charlotte.'[51]*

Matthew Lewis, a great friend of Lorne and Tom Sheridan, had been a frequent
visitor at Inveraray since at least 1795. Like many profoundly unhappy persons
'The Monk' kept up an outward appearance of liveliness and fun. So long as the
family were there, his visits were notable for the musical evenings or night-long
billiard-matches with Tom Sheridan, rehearsals of amateur theatricals, and composing of rollicking flights of fancy which Matt Lewis incorporated into his weekly

Inveraray newsletter, *The Bugle*, to appear on Saturday's breakfast-table. But often Lewis passed weeks at the castle in deliberate solitude and melancholy, reading books and writing to his mother or Lady Charlotte, with whom he was rather negatively (so far as his ambivalent temperament allowed) in love; yet when surrounded by friends he was the mainspring of their gaiety.

Inveraray's theatricals were performed at Robert Mylne's riding-house in the Maltland, which witnessed many a high-flown speech and dramatic gesture even though the audience was pretty sparse:

> 'No shillings for entrance were dropt at the door,
> No voices applauding, bawl "Bravo!" and "Encore!"
> And our ardour for glory it surely must quench,
> To think that we play to three chairs and a bench.
> When Selim, the tyrant, presumed to rebuke,
> All he wish'd was obtaining a smile from the Duke;
> And when the Queen said the King's cruelty shock'd her,
> She hoped for some little applause from the Doctor.
> But our utmost ambition was stretch't to its tether,
> If the Duke and the Doctor cried "Bravo!" together . . .
> Captain Campbell gave Othman with strength and effect,
> Mr Trafford[52]* was graceful – Lord John was correct;
> Lord Lorne's easy air, when he got in a passion,
> Proved a tyrant must needs be a person of fashion . . .
> The worst (we are sorry to say, but it true is)
> Was the epilogue, written, we hear, by one Lewis;
> 'Twas terrible trash, but in justice we tell,
> It was thought to be *spoken* uncommonly well . . .
> But if in our play any merit is shown,
> I assure you, my friends, that the whole is my own . . .
> For when to rehearse the fifth act I was wishing,
> I was told Barbarossa was just gone a fishing.
> Out of tune, while Irene was straining her throat,
> That Othman was busy in building a boat . . .'

This epilogue to *Barbarossa* Lewis composed in 1797 to be spoken by Lady Charlotte.[53] Some of his verses for *The Bugle*, and many of his letters to the lady, clearly testify a subdued and probably unrequited passion. Long after he was dead Lady Charlotte, who did not scruple to publish private letters from her friends, noted maliciously in her memoirs that while Lewis had 'talents and good qualities', 'one of his mistakes was trying to be witty, for which nature had never designed him'.[54] William Lamb, too, in letters home from Inveraray, had written patronizingly of his friend Matt – permissible, perhaps, as a very young man's vanity; but at the reasons for Lady Charlotte's spiteful judgment in her old age we can only guess.

The Bugle was not only a collection of sentimental ballads. Facetious news and abuse of the house party, reams of satirical verses freely based on trivial domestic events, filled its handwritten columns. Whoever was deputed to be editor received the guests' contributions in a special box, and during his 'term of office' had full professional honours. Lewis launched this paper in the autumn of 1802, and when William Lamb shortly arrived 'The Monk' immediately appointed him editor of the forthcoming fourth issue.

That autumn's assembly was particularly gay and the house was even fuller than usual:

'Bed-rooms are in great request and William and Kinnaird being the last comers, are moved about from chamber to chamber . . . a formal complaint was lodged yesterday by a great Russian Count, that he only stept out for half an hour, and the first things which He saw lying on his bed when He came back, were a dozen pairs of Kinnaird's leather breeches.'

As a postscript to this report to Lamb's mother, Lady Melbourne, Lewis added that

'William's Newspaper has just appeared, in which He informs the Public that He is at length *stationary* in Lady Augusta's Dressing-room.'[55*]

Besides the Argyll family and Lewis's sister, the party also included the young Comte de Beaujolais, brother to the Duc d'Orléans, who had come with Lewis from the Duke of Atholl's, 'and we contrived to keep up such a continual riot, that I changed the name of Inverary to that of *Confusion Castle*, with universal approbation'.[56*] They acted *The Rivals*, and Lady Charlotte, although pregnant, played Julia (allowing for a worshipper's blindness) 'as well as ever I saw it performed'; William Campbell made 'a capital Sir Anthony' and Miss Lewis was Mrs Malaprop, with an ill-fitting wig whose hoped-for fate fascinated the audience far more than her acting. They also rehearsed *The Citizen* and *The Mock Doctor*, Lewis much chagrined because William Lamb 'obstinately refuses to be dressed as a shepherd with a wreath of roses and a bunch of cherry coloured ribbands ornamenting his hat'; they even tried 'a *walking* ballet' with a machine in which Miss Lewis was 'to fly up into the clouds in the character of the Queen of the Fairies', but the others privately thought the story – apparently composed by Lady Charlotte – so boring that they seized the first excuse they could to abandon it.[57]

Many years later another lady recalled what she had heard about 'the gay visitors of a former generation' and their private newspaper.

'At length, however, they became rather too personal, and were finally discontinued, on a gentleman becoming seriously offended, who, being afflicted with rather too long a nose, found a paragraph announcing the safe arrival of Mr R——'s nose, and that the rest of his person might be expected in a few hours.'[58]

By contrast in the autumn of 1803 the castle was 'tranquillity personified'. Lady Charlotte and her husband were in Edinburgh; Lorne was busy as Lord Lieutenant; Lord John was very subdued after escaping from 'the horrors of a French prison' where he had been interned by the Directoire Government. Lewis passed

two or three months at Inveraray 'reading furiously' and speculating whether
Bonaparte would invade Scotland and the roads round Edinburgh be 'broken up'
and closed.[59]

Lewis probably never knew that during August in this, to him, quiet summer
William and Dorothy Wordsworth came to Inveraray. Coleridge, who was with
them, had unfortunately become unwell and was forced to turn back at Arrochar.
Of the brother and sister's opinions of the little town and the Duke's parks we have
already read; but learning that the castle was only half a century old and contained
no important pictures, they dismissed it as too unromantic and

> 'did not think that what we should see would repay us for the trouble ... If there
> had been any reliques of the ancient costume of the castle of a Highland
> chieftain, we should have been sorry to have passed it'.[60]

So the Wordsworths and 'the little Monk' passed each other unknowingly by.
Such, too, was the case with James Hogg, whose visit early in June was probably a
little before Monk Lewis arrived. Hogg's description of his stay is perhaps the
liveliest of all, but it might have been even more hilarious had these two paradoxical, complex characters, the Monk and the Ettrick Shepherd, met and left a
description of one another.

James Hogg's rustic manners had led him, on his first introduction to formal
society, to commit gaffes which may have embarrassed his sophisticated friends
more than himself, but probably the more he saw of their rigid society the more
self-conscious he became. Unless he was deliberately exaggerating, his visit to
Inveraray Castle was a series of farcical mishaps.

Hogg, a Border countryman then thirty-three years old, travelled unassum-
ingly on foot dressed in black and wrapped in a stout shepherd's plaid, carrying a
staff, with his spare shirt and a couple of neckcloths in his pocket. This walking
tour in the West Highlands in the early summer of 1803 was one of several
which Hogg recorded in a series of letters to his friend and literary sponsor,
Walter Scott.[61]*

Scott had given James Hogg a letter of introduction to Colonel Campbell of
Shawfield, and having sent an inn servant to present this at the castle, Hogg was
astonished to receive in return the Colonel's compliments, 'naming the hour when
he would do himself the pleasure of waiting on me! Mark that, sir.'

Shawfield's 'unaffected simplicity of manners' soon put Hogg at ease in his own
company, but on the memorable visit to the castle which followed 'every hour during the time that I remained was marked by ... blunders and embarrassments'.
Shawfield first led the Shepherd through the house towards the south drawing-
room, announcing that he was about to present him to Lady Charlotte:

> ' "By no means," said I, "for heaven's sake. I would be extremely glad could I
> see her at a little distance, but you need never think that I will go in amongst
> them."
>
> " Distance!" exclaimed he. "You shall dine with her to-day and to-
> morrow." '

While Hogg was protesting himself overcome at the thought of meeting this celebrated beauty, Shawfield

> 'bolted into a circular room in one of the turrets, where her ladyship was sitting with some others, closely engaged with something, but I cannot tell what it was were I to die for it, and I am vexed to this hour that I had not noted what they were employed in when alone.'

Lady Charlotte received Hogg 'with the greatest familiarity and good humour' and did all she could to put the purple, tongue-tied poet at ease. But he seemed doomed to disaster.

> 'I would never have known that I was so ill had there not unluckily been a mirror placed up by my leg. Not knowing very well where to look, I looked into it. . . . My upper lip was curled up, my jaws were fallen down, my cheeks were all drawn up about my eyes . . . my face was extraordinary red, and my nose seemed a weight on it. On being caught in this dilemma I really could not contain myself, but burst out a-laughing. The ladies looked at one another, thinking I was laughing at them. However, to bring myself off, I repeated something that the Colonel was saying, and pretended to be laughing at it . . .
>
> This plaguey bluntness! shall I never get rid of it?'

The Duke was not well, so that the ordeal of meeting him was deferred until next day. On the whole Hogg 'got off better than could have been expected':

> 'The first time that we encountered was thus. I was returned from the top of Duniqueich, and just as I reached the castle gate, a coach drove up, out of which an old gentleman with a cocked hat, and a scarlet coat alighted. I thought him some old officer, and mounted the steps without minding him, but meeting on the flags Captain Campbell, with whom I had been in company before, I asked who these were. He said they were the Duke and Doctor Campbell . . .
>
> But he, who it seems had been enquiring who I was, relieved me by addressing me by name, and welcoming me to Inveraray.'

His host's cordiality overwhelmed the unworldly Hogg, especially when the Duke sat down to talk with him and remarked, with a smile, of his morning's sightseeing, 'I am sure that you have seen more than you are pleased with, and that you are even more pleased than edified.' He then excused himself to dress, leaving Hogg to look at books.

> 'I had not sat long when Colonel Campbell entered, who in a little time left me also, on the same pretence, that of *dressing for dinner*. I said he was well enough dressed; it was a silly thing that they could not put on clothes in the morning that would serve them during the day. He proved that that would never do, and went his way laughing.
>
> It was not long until the Duke rejoined me, all clad in black, as indeed all the gentlemen were who sat at table. I was always in the utmost perplexities, not knowing servants from masters. There were such numbers of them, and so superbly dressed, that I daresay I made my best bow to several of them. I remember in particular of having newly taken my seat at dinner, and observing

one behind me I thought he was a gentleman wanting a seat, and offered him mine.

I was so proud that although I did not know how to apply one third of the things that were at table, unless I called for a thing I would not take it when offered to me . . .

"What!" said the Colonel, "Lord, do ye eat your beef quite plain?"

"Perfectly plain, sir," said I, "saving a little salt, and so would you if you knew how much more wholesome it were." By great good fortune I was joined by several in this asservation [sic], which my extremity suggested.'

The Duke talked at length to Hogg as one farmer to another, and at his suggestion Hogg rode out next day with the farm overseer, 'on a fine brown hunting mare, as light as the wind'. But he did not care for his boastful escort, and the dislike was mutual. On the Duke's later asking for his opinion, Hogg with startling frankness said he could only imagine the overseer the worse for drink.

'That was impossible at this time of day,' answered the Duke, taken aback. 'You surely must be mistaken . . .'

'I certainly am not mistaken my lord,' persisted Hogg, 'for I look upon him as the worst specimen of your Grace's possessions that I have seen about all Inveraray.'

('Colonel Campbell was like to burst during this dialogue,' Hogg told Scott afterwards.) The Duke, not at all displeased, took him off to show him his 'workshops' and 'mechanics', and contrivances he had made himself. As for the Colonel, he insisted on showing Hogg everything from battlements to dog-kennels, walked him miles to point out the best views, and took a child-like pleasure in surprising him with the sight of Loch Dhu and Glenshira by intruding 'his huge bulk' in front of it and reciting poetry to divert Hogg's attention until the last minute. Worst embarrassment to the shepherd was being asked to criticize their miniature theatre in the Maltland, for, having published some opinions of the stage, he was reckoned an expert by his hosts, who spent a whole morning demonstrating the lighting and scenery.[62]*

'Forgive me if I knew what to say! I had often no other answer ready than scratching the crown of my head. I cursed in my heart the hour that I first put my observations on the stage on paper.'

All the same, when after a four-day stay Hogg finally left Inveraray he felt that he would like to stay for ever, although he was among those who saw in its superb scenery 'a sort of sameness' and preferred 'the artificial part . . . the elegant little town, the magnificent castle, the accurate taste and discernment . . .'

Some of his highest praise was for the Duke himself, the benevolent, unostentatious old aristocrat, who took such pleasure in his agricultural studies and improvements, 'of which the valley of Glenshira is a convincing proof'.

'His venerable age, the sweetness and simplicity of his manners, with the cheerful alacrity shewed by every member of the family to his easy commands, are really delightful. He is indeed, in the fullest sense of the word, a father to his country.'

[43] Inveraray, from the south, showing Newton Row
(old Gallowgate) on the far left

Yet it was noticeable to Hogg, as to most others at the close of the Duke's life, that his 'great age hath certainly impaired the faculties of his mind, as well as his body'.

A distant relation, Lady Louisa Stuart, has left us one of the last descriptions of the castle in the old Duke's time, in October 1804, about fifteen months after Hogg's visit. Lady Louisa, on a tour with her tiresome, capricious sister Lady Mary Lonsdale, came to Inveraray after an unenjoyable few days at Buchanan ('a dead flat') with the Montroses, he dull and pompous, she cold and reserved. Inveraray was very lively by contrast, but the household had lapsed into disorganization.

> 'I liked the people very much as well as the place; in every respect it was the reverse of Buchanan, and a little in the Castle Rack-rent style. The Duke is eighty-three and a charming old man, with all his faculties, but of course not very attentive to his household concerns, though very much so to his farm and estate. Lady Augusta is dejected and indolent and will not take the management of anything. Lady Charlotte is the younger sister and only a visitor, so feels she must not meddle. Therefore the servants do exactly what they think proper, and it is Confusion Castle with a witness, as nobody willingly troubles the good old Duke with complaints, and when his back is turned it is well if anybody will answer a bell or bring a single thing you want. The dinner is also abominably dressed, but nobody cares. Sometimes Lord Lorne goes into the kitchen and bustles to get the potatoes well boiled, but he relapses into indolence and the next day 'tis just the same.'[63]*

A melancholy decline from Inveraray's greatest days; and thanks to Lorne's improvidence many years were to pass before anything like its former splendour was restored. Yet even in the days of 'Castle Rackrent' or 'Confusion Castle' a stranger could write:

> 'It will readily be believed that this noble seat and it's scenery, when beheld by the rude sons of Caledonia, in unequal comparison with their lowly huts and naked wilds, are regarded as a perfect elysium and the residence of a divinity...
>
> Perhaps no man in the United Kingdom possesses so much personal influence as the benevolent Duke of Argyle.'[64]

[44] Inveraray, looking south from the Watch Tower on Duniquaich

W

Take a Duke of Argyle at the end of the eighteenth century, let him have his house in Grosvenor Square, his London liveries, and daughters glittering at St James's, and I think you will be satisfied with his present mansion in the Highlands, which seems to suit with the present times and its situation.

Dorothy Wordsworth, 'Recollections of a Tour made in Scotland in 1803', in *Journals of Dorothy Wordsworth* ed. E. de Selincourt, I, London 1941, p. 297

The more I examined the Structure, the more barbarous, & hideous does it appear. If it were situated in Middlesex, it would be considered so by all. But here on the Banks of a Loch in the Highlands, to wch. there is hardly any access from more civilized Portions of Scotland, this Castle rising up in the Desert, impresses with admiration.

Nathaniel Wraxall *Diary on my Tour into Scotland, in the Summer of 1813*, NLS MS 3108, 17 July 1813

There is very genteel society in Inverary. The castle itself is a complete importation, and disappointed me much; I expected a Highland residence, in place of which it is Bond Street or Brighton, both within and without . . .

David Wilkie to his brother, 21 August 1817; quoted in Allan Cunningham *The Life of Sir David Wilkie*, I, London 1843, p. 473

The edifice might be finer.

W. E. Gladstone, 17 August 1839. *The Gladstone Diaries*, ed. M. R. D. Foot, II, Oxford 1968, p. 621

X

For a long time before he died peacefully at home on 24 May 1806, the 5th Duke had endured heavy financial pressure. In spite of his rising rents, and the booming kelp industry – which for the past thirty years had rendered his island shores unprecedently profitable – the heavy outlay on Inveraray, Rosneath and his estates, together with the crippling effect of Lord Lorne's debts had forced him raise money by selling valuable farms. During this long war against Napoleon all land-owners were under strain, their estates run down and encumbered by debts, and buildings decaying, and many Highland lairds were entirely ruined. 'The dreary aspect of the times' affected the whole country, and the lot of tenants was often intolerable; it was hard enough to live, let alone pay their rents, and their insolvency was in turn reflected in landlords' inability to keep up the property.[1]*

At the end of the war in 1815 the situation was even worse: agricultural prices declined, the precarious kelp market collapsed, crops failed, and tenantry emigrated in thousands. The 5th Duke of Argyll did not live to see the full disasters which fell on his country, but within a generation most of his work had been undone and his visionary experiments and improvements became a memory. The removal of his restraining hand, coupled with the general economic stagnation, seemed to leave no obstacle in the way of his successor's running full tilt to ruin and dragging his estates after him; it was something of a miracle that this did not altogether happen.

Could the 6th Duke have combined his own undoubted talents with the responsible disposition of his brother John, Inveraray's catastrophic deterioration might have been mitigated. Duke George's weaknesses were such that even well-wishers like Lady Holland could not ignore:

'He is very handsome, well-made, and like a gentleman; his manner is remarkably simple and unaffected, and tho' his abilities are not of the most brilliant order, yet he does not appear in the least deficient. He has in his disposition an uncommon share of indifference, almost to apathy, and tho' in possession of every requisite for happiness, it does not appear that he enjoys anything.'[2]

Twenty years later Lady Holland's young son Henry Edward Fox recorded in his diary how his parents spoke of 'talent thrown away' in the person of 'the Duke of

Argyle, who with natural abilities and a good education has become insignificant, from nonchalance and indolence'.[3] Much that had happened in the intervening years justified this judgment.

At first the 6th Duke continued to stay every autumn at Inveraray, with his lively friends Monk Lewis, Tom Sheridan and others, and he was preoccupied with his white elephant of a mansion at Rosneath. In the autumn of 1806 Joseph Bonomi made a long visit, with an eye to 'improvements'. Eugenia Wynne, the bride of Lady Charlotte's brother-in-law Robert Campbell (of Shawfield), recounts the vivid impressions of her first visit to Inveraray that October. The Duke, himself ill at the time of his father's death, was now 'considerably recovered', but

> 'Lord John looks very ill, Bonomi . . . quarrels with Traffard [Humphrey Trafford Campbell] and is very entertaining – Mr Brownlow North whispers softly – Ly. Augusta Clavering does the honours of the house very well . . . was once lovely herself – but she is now crooked, has a bad Husband and bad health . . . The *ton* of the House is very pleasant, because every one is left at liberty to do as they please.'[4]

In the crowded autumn of 1807 we find a last glimpse of Monk Lewis at Inveraray, when from the moment of the Duke's arrival 'every nook of the castle has been occupied by visiters of all ranks, colours, and descriptions'.[5] They included the Marquesses of Ely and of Downshire, and Lord Holland with his tyrannical, egotistical lady – who astonished them by being uncharacteristically 'pleas'd with every thing, without wants, displeasure, or difficulties'.[6]* Then there were the Duke and Duchess of Bedford with their youngest son Lord John Russell: the fifteen-year-old schoolboy was delighted with Inveraray's beauties and the lively house-party.[7] Tom Sheridan brought his pretty, gentle wife Caroline Callander, with whom in 1805 he had made a run-away marriage. Lewis, thanks to plenty of company, seemed at his gayest, but complained of their excesses, for eating, drinking and games went an all night.

> 'We remain too long at table; so that, unavoidably, I eat and drink too much: and, dining, at 8, supping at 2, and going to bed at 4 in the morning, cannot possibly strengthen my nerves, my eyes, or my stomach . . .'[8]
>
> The other morning I happened to wake about six o'clock, and hearing the bill-balls in motion, I put on my dressing-gown, and went into the gallery, from whence, looking down into the great hall, I descried Tom Sheridan and Mr Chester (who had not been in bed all night) playing with great eagerness. Fortunately Tom was in the act of making a stroke on which the fate of the whole game depended; when I shouted to him over the balustrade, "Shame! shame! a married man!" on which he started back in fright, missed his stroke, and lost the game.'[9]

The Duke's birthday was celebrated with inevitable 'squibs and crackers and . . . diabolical noise', and 'all the blackguard children of the town . . . hallooing round the castle'.

'When the duke came into the breakfast-room just now, instead of wishing him

95. George William, 6th Duke of Argyll (1768–1839), as Marquess of Lorne
From a drawing by Henry Edridge, 1801.

"many happy returns of the day", I could not help telling him that "I wished to the Lord that he had never been born at all".'[10]

To Lady Bessborough Lewis painted a contrast between the insouciant Duke and Mr Henry Scott, 'so complete an *Angler* that every third word he pronounced is *fish*' : Scott's chief object was 'how much he could hurry with the *most* possible inconvenience to himself and every one else. The D. of A.'s aim was trying how much time he could lose with least possible satisfaction to himself or others.'[11]

Ducal indolence coupled with extravagance led quickly to disaster. 'Between Lady William Russell and the gaming table,' Lady Louisa Stuart had already re-marked, '. . . there will be an end of this fine place and of every comfort to the family.'[12]

Ever since 1789 Lady Louisa had thought it 'very provoking' that George had let slip the opportunity to marry Lord Jersey's daughter Lady Charlotte Villiers, so that she married the Duke of Bedford's brother instead. He then carried on a prolonged liaison with her while the husband, Lord William Russell, hovered un-obtrusively in the background. Lord William, noted Eugenia Campbell at a dinner-party in 1807 (Argyll was there too, of course) 'me parait un zéro dans sa maison'.[13] But Lady William died, and when Duke George eventually went to the altar in November 1810, it was with her beautiful younger sister Caroline, wife of Lord Paget, in a partner-exchanging extravaganza that involved a double divorce; so that his marriage created as much scandal as his former amours.[14]*

In 1811, then, we see this new Duchess established at Inveraray with her husband and lovely daughters, kindly receiving a party of visitors who arrived hungry, tired and dirty after sitting up all night in a hired Rothesay packet. They were Robert and Eugenia Campbell and Eugenia's sister Betsey : 'The Duke of Argyle is all attention to his Dutchess,' wrote Betsey, 'and they appear perfectly happy – but their marriage has something so revolting and extraordinary in it, that I cannot believe she ever can feel perfectly happy.'[15]*

This Inveraray party, typically gay and keeping the usual late hours, consisted chiefly of Argyll relations, but included also Lord and Lady Ponsonby, and Trafford Campbell from Loch Gair.

One negative quality shared by all these lively friends was, apparently, a total lack of interest in the appearance of the castle or its surroundings. Hardly a de-scriptive or critical word falls from their pens – yet Inveraray at this time showed horrifying signs of decay that the most light-hearted guest could hardly have over-looked. To early nineteenth-century eyes, of course, the 5th Duke's splendid de-coration of the castle appeared merely dated, and the late Duchess's 'old-fashioned ugly tapestry, and coloured prints', seemed 'in the very worst taste'. The French-American traveller Louis Simond, who pronounced these strictures in 1810, being an uninvolved outsider reflected dolefully on Inveraray's melancholy situation. Woods and parks, he observed, were now 'exhibiting a general appearance of neg-lect and *delabrement*', and although he saw hay being cut and the season was wet, the 'Gothic castles' in Glenshira were not even in use.[16]*

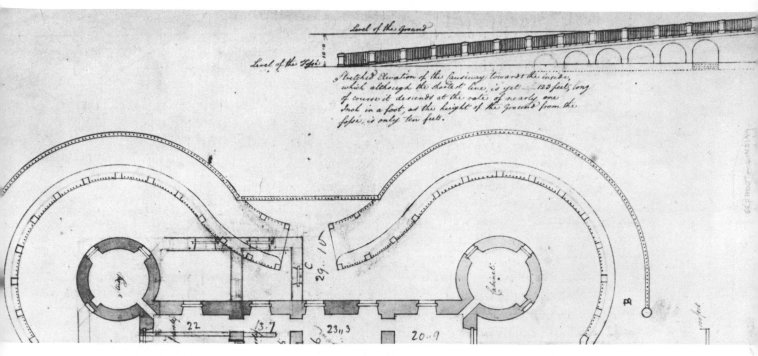

96. Proposed causeway to the fosse of Inveraray Castle
Detail of an unexecuted design by Joseph Bonomi, 1806.

Yet the 6th Duke was not wholly uninterested, and the three years after his father's death saw nearly £6,000 additional expenditure 'occasioned by the Great Repairs and alterations in the Castle'.[17] Of these no details are recorded; but Joseph Bonomi sketched some extravagantly trivial ideas which would have irritated and distressed the late Duke. These are dated at Bonomi's London offices in 1806 and 1807, when he was still working on Rosneath.[18]* Bonomi was the last architect who tried tinkering about with the fosse, with an abortive proposal for ramps or 'causeways' leading from ground-level to the base storey, so that carts could deliver to the kitchen quarters. (He had designed a similar scheme for Rosneath.) Another idea (1807) was a design for 'eight elegant Brass Brackets, supporting eight large Lamps to light the Great Vestibule from the bottom to the top', and an elaborate rearrangement of the armour in the great hall.

Less innocuous was Bonomi's scheme (1806), whose non-execution need cause no regrets, for 'two new Water-Closets to be erected over the two Brick Rooms, just half way to the Bed Chamber Story'. A neat little two-doored enclosure with a swinging circular window 'ventilating' directly on to the turn of the main stair, would have been no asset to Inveraray Castle. In the end, however, the poky, haphazardly placed water-closets of Duke Archibald's and the 5th Duke's installation remained unchanged until late in the nineteenth century.

The 6th Duke's mismanagement, paradoxically, gave rise to a last expiring flicker of town planning, in this place which had been a model of eighteenth-century design. By 1810 his financial affairs were in a critical state, and some months before his marriage a land agent, James Malcolm, was sent up from Grays Inn to make a complete survey of Inveraray. Malcolm's discoveries made him extremely unpopular with servants and tenantry, and not surprisingly, hostile accounts of him soon reached the Duke in London.

James Malcolm's 79-page report, offered on 30 May 1810, makes depressing reading. Discrepancies found in the accounts suggested ever-slackening control by old Colonel Graham and inevitable fraud by overseers. Pasture-land had deteriorated, parks were 'over run with Moss and Foggage full of Rushes or Sprits, and Sedge', fences decayed, and sheep had foot-rot. The Duke's sawyers (artisans 'well known in England [as] a most disatisfied set of men, always combining to raise their wages') had raised their pay by over-measuring their work – while the gardener's wages were plainly too low, for 'nothing opens the Door to fraud & peculation more than allowing Servants to receive perquisites'.

To restore Inveraray's prosperity Malcolm put forward an ingenious, up-to-date development plan : briefly, to turn the Fisherland into a model suburb of 46 houses, 'after the Plan of Mr Lorn Campbells at Rosneath, in pairs with a Small Garden in Front to the Shore and Gardens behind extending to the avenue'; and behind the avenue, paddocks for the houses. On 60-year leases the house rents would net £260 and the paddocks £140.

> 'I can find six Gentlemen who would engage to begin this summer as an Example . . . I have no doubt of being able to extend the Town of Inveraray in an handsome ornamental way by detached villas along the Shore for 5 or 6 Miles . . . As the Houses would be respectable in size and appearance, none but respectable people could inhabit them . . . It would be giving new Life to the Town of Inveraray.'[19]

But for this revolutionary idea no capital was available. The Duke's financial affairs were shortly put into the hands of a trustee, Charles Selkrig. The old estates of Castle Campbell and Dollar in Clackmannanshire, which the Argyll family had owned for generations, had to go, woods and cattle were sold, and household staff was drastically reduced. During these disastrous years the total assets raised to pay the Duke's debts were estimated at half a million, £400,000 of it in land, the rest in timber.[20] The total cost of building Inveraray by his more provident forebears had been just half that sum – £250,000.

Even when faced with near-ruin the Duke was as unrealistic as ever, seeking in vain some compromise by which he could live part-time at Inveraray and the unfinished Rosneath; while he added to his lawyer as a casual afterthought that he had forgotten, by the way, to mention the Duchess's personal debts of £2,000, and £200 owing for his box at Covent Garden . . . and – P.S. – urgent repayment to a friend of a £500 loan.[21]

When, therefore, Nathaniel Wraxall and his wife saw Inveraray in July 1813, the castle was unoccupied, tended only by two maidservants and a groom, and dismal to a degree. Wraxall was in any case disappointed by this 'famous Seat of Inverary, the Versailles of the Western Highlands . . . neither a Castle, a Palace, nor an

Abby, but a strange, barbarous Mixture of all three', and with 'no Pretension either to Taste, or to Architecture'.[22]* As for its unusual design, 'never was any thing more hideous or barbarous ... neither Grecian nor Gothic'. It was like the Castle of Giant Despair. Or a county gaol. Or a house of cards. Its public rooms were few, mean, and ill-provided with works of art. Wraxall's distaste so disturbed him that, with a kind of repelled fascination, before leaving next day he forced himself to visit the castle once more; but in vain. 'The more I examined the Structure, the more barbarous, & hideous does it appear.'

As for the town, long ago the Chamberlain had issued a warning that its houses were nearly uninhabitable, and the inn, thanks to the overseer Henderson's neglect, had decayed almost beyond repair.[23]*

'The inn is large, comfortless, ill furnished, dirty, & devoid of every thing which can render it agreable ... The Houses are dirty, mean, & not in the best Condition. As to the Church – Like most Scotch Churches it is a modern Building, haveing scarcely any Character of a Church, in *our* acceptation of the Term ... All the Windows are shut up with Shutters, except one, of which the Panes are broken. Indeed, the Windows are kept shut up, in order to prevent the Panes from being broken, as they assured me. The Building itself, like everything else here, is hardly in Repair, & wants to be whitewashed or beautified. ...

At present, every Part of the House, Grounds, & Park, exhibits Signs of Decay & Neglect. The Absence of the Duke, & his pecuniary Embarrassments, render Inverary silent & melancholy ... The Walks, Fences, Bridges, & other surrounding Buildings, are tending fast to Dilapidation or Ruin ... Nothing seems to be going on either of Business, or of Pleasure. There is a little Pier, but they have no Manufacture or Trade, except the Fishery for Herrings ... The People appear to be proud, indolent. & unemployed. It must however be owned that the Absence of the Duke of Argyle, & his present Situation, throw a Gloom over Inverary.'[24]*

Wraxall during his Scottish tour saw with amazement the first steam-boats, 'which go without Sails', plying on the Clyde between Glasgow and Greenock. Thanks to this remarkable invention Inveraray's prosperity was restored by external means, for the age of mass tourism now began.

Steam-boats met with immediate success, and in 1817 Lord Webb Seymour mentions no less than fourteen operating from Clydeside:

'In summer one of them leaves Glasgow for Inverary on Saturday, remains off there Sunday to gratify all the pleasuring folks with a view of the place, and returns to Glasgow with them on Monday ... The scheme answers so well, that, I am told, the crowd she brings to Inverary renders it difficult to procure a bed there at the time, or anything to eat.'[25]

This voyage of a little over a hundred miles might in stormy weather take more than fifteen hours; the fare was then ten-and-sixpence. On fine days it was lively enough

97. Inveraray, the Newton Row, formerly the Gallowgate

as a piper usually travelled on board, and a fiddler who played 'very ill' for the packed steerage crowds to dance strathspeys.[26]* By 1820 three steamers were serving Inveraray,[27]* and soon a set of alternative routes with complicated coach connexions gave a choice of three different approaches by water. A road cut through Hell's Glen, the pathless waste over which, many years earlier, Duke Archibald and his party had had to be guided on horseback, now connected Loch Fyne with Loch Goil, and a special coach met steamer passengers at Lochgoilhead to drive them over the pass to Saint Catherine's Ferry.[28]* Finally, the establishment of a regular coach service to Glasgow meant that Inveraray now had several means of access, and was within the orbit of any traveller.

As early as 1817 an apparent prosperity reappeared, and the thirty-two-year-old David Wilkie, on one of the early steamboat excursions, was at first impressed by Inveraray's grand, bustling Saturday appearance. So far, however, improvement was superficial: 'when the steamboat passengers are gone, it assumes the appearance of a forsaken Bridewell', and overnight 'dwindled into a little new-fashioned, modern upstart of a Scottish town'.[29]

But by degrees Inveraray ceased to be a mean, run-down community, and became 'very chearful and populous'.[30] Its walls newly whitewashed, it again appeared cosy and neat, even though Dorothy Wordsworth, on a return visit after nineteen years, still complained of its 'shabby finery' and 'inner impurities', and particularly of the Gallowgate's juxtaposition of fine new houses and filthy hovels. But the townspeople were all civil and articulate, although their pigs did still roam the streets; and on Sunday it blossomed into gaiety when the women appeared in red cloaks and clean white caps on their way to the kirk. Even the Duke and Duchess sometimes reappeared, and devoutly attended church; they also gave the cause of the town's new liveliness their official blessing – as well they might – by an occasional Sunday afternoon steamer trip up the loch.[31]

The inn was often so full that its grand ballroom in the new wing was turned into a tourist-dormitory, with beds 'erected on hard oak tables, & supported by chairs for want of better materials'.[32] The Chambers brothers' *Gazetteer* of 1832 noted:

'Till within the last 6 or 8 years Inveraray was a town rarely visited by strangers, on account of its inaccessibility. It is now daily visited every summer by scores of tourists . . . being now a chief rallying point in these excursions into the Western Highlands.'[33]

As for local industry, the woollen manufactory at Douglas Bridge having long failed, Inveraray's staple product was once again the herrings. Their shoaling up Loch Fyne had become erratic, but in season the fleet's nightly expedition was still a sight for visitors, and the morning dish of grilled herring gladdened their breakfast tables. A German visitor, Dr Spiker (librarian to the King of Prussia), observed in 1816 'several establishments for packing the herrings into casks, which announced themselves at a considerable distance by an effluvia that almost overpowered the olfactory nerves'.[34]* This new generation of travellers was more squeamish as well as more numerous.

The town also enjoyed the doubtful benefit of occasional entertainment by strolling players. Keats, on a walking-tour with Charles Armitage Brown in July 1818, witnessed an indifferent performance of an indifferent play, *The Stranger*, 'accompanied by a Bag-pipe'.

'There they went on . . . till the Curtain fell and then came the Bag-pipe. When Mrs Haller fainted down went the Curtain and out came the Bag-pipe – at the heart-rending, shoemending reconciliation the Piper blew amain.'[35]*

In 1822 Dorothy Wordsworth noted how the town had 'very much spread out behind', presumably by building in the tumbledown Gallowgate, and in new tenements raised on the south side of the town.[36]* One particular addition she remarked upon was the new Court House, the last of Inveraray's important buildings in its great tradition. Facing Mylne's church, in a small square created by the demolition of a few houses, this edifice had a characteristically vexed history of procrastination, litigation and financial disaster, laced with the usual element of farce. Also, as usual in Inveraray, several architects had a hand in its design.

Since the beginning of the nineteenth century an interest in philanthropy, and a modern desire for comfort and comparative hygiene, had rendered John Adam's Court House and gaol on Front Street out of date. The general feeling was that in Adam's handsome design 'convenience and usefulness seem to have been sacrificed to external appearance'.[37] The building's very prominence offended by its incongruity. 'The first house that arrested attention', writes David Wilkie, 'had three large doors, grated over, with people inside; this we found to be the county prison of Argyll.'[38] An Irish visitor in 1819 remarked disapprovingly on the local custom 'which allows the prisoners to walk in a grated piazza in front of their Cells, just in the line of the principal street, and exposing the miserable appearance of their apartments and furniture to shock the feelings of every passer bye'.[39]* Worse, this freedom which so displeased strangers, and the gaol's situation on the town front, positively invited escapes – usually in collusion with passing friends, for anyone could hatch a plot with a prisoner or slip a tool through the grating.

The building's fitness for purpose was indeed almost nil. Behind the respectable façade the cells were too few, confined, damp and unhealthy, while accommodation for the visiting judges was cramped and inconvenient.

> 'It might indeed have served . . . in the *darker age* when it was erected, but the present race of people in this country being incomparably more enlightened than their ancestors, and daily improving . . . it becomes adviseable to think of a building that will not only suit the present moment but that may be enlarged from time to time in proportion to the increasing wealth and crimes of the country.'[40]

But although for years the judges complained, and the Commissioners of Supply discussed it at meetings and even proposed a suitable new site, lack of money prevented immediate reform. Because of the burgh's minute income the capital cost would as ever fall on the county, namely the Argyll lairds, and opinion was divided on whether, to save the outlay on a new building and the cost of expropriating inhabitants of the suggested site, they might be able to tinker with the Adam gaol. To extend this would mean encroaching on the Chamberlain's house and garden, so for more than merely pious reasons Colonel Graham favoured building anew.

The Commissioners actually invited plans as early as 1807, and those submitted by Robert Reid of Edinburgh were approved. But disagreement on policy deferred the project, while prisoners continued to escape and judges to complain. Townspeople had to be pressed into serving as night-watchmen, until in 1811 the judges rebelled and Lord Boyle threatened to remove the courts from Inveraray altogether unless the poky, insecure, smelly old prison were abandoned.[41]*

The Commissioners therefore appointed a committee to obtain fresh plans and estimates. To authorize such a public building an Act of Parliament was necessary, and John Ferrier (James's son and successor), together with a Melrose lawyer, John Seton Karr, drew up the necessary petition, using the recent Cupar and Roxburgh Court House Acts as models. But, as supporters for the petition were apathetic, committee meetings were often short of a quorum; opponents, on the other hand, led by John Lamont of Lamont, strongly objected to the county's carrying the expense, and complained that Cupar gaol in the rich Kingdom of Fife had cost only £4000, whereas the poorer Inveraray was expected to raise £7000.[42]*

John and Archibald Ferrier re-examined Reid's drawings, and also invited plans from another Edinburgh architect, Richard Crichton. Of the latter no more is heard, and Reid's designs were considered unacceptable in their present form, for the committee next sought the advice of James Gillespie, as an architect they already knew and respected. (He had, too, designed the County Rooms at Cupar in 1810, and its gaol in 1813.)[43]*

Gillespie unhesitatingly dispelled any lingering thoughts of remodelling the

98. Proposed new Court House at Inveraray
    Elevation by Robert Reid, 1808.

existing building: 'I am decidedly of opinion that the old *must be abandoned*.' The proposed new site, abutting on to the foreshore east of the church, he thought infinitely preferable for its dry, healthier situation and relative remoteness, which would increase security and protect the town from 'indecent talk and intercourse which persons of some descriptions are disposed to hold to the annoyance of the Inhabitants and the Injury of their morals'. His estimate of £5,712 was little more than would be the cost of extending the Adam building.[44]*

It was Gillespie's adaptation of Reid's Court House plan that was eventually built, considered by John Campbell of Craignure, one of the most active committee members, as 'equally ornamental & contains a great deal more accommodation for the money'.

From this point onwards a series of fortuitous, often ridiculous circumstances seemed to conspire against the scheme's realization. In September 1813 Gillespie, on his way to show the plans to Lord John at the Dunbartonshire house, Ardincaple,[45]* and then to the Commissioners, was taken ill and the meeting was adjourned for six weeks; even then his assistant James Stevenson had to act as substitute. The committee, having persuaded most of the objectors, inadvertently

lost a whole Parliamentary session by omitting to display public notice of their intended petition; by a ludicrous accident they then very nearly lost the next session
as well. This time (at Seton Karr's urgent request) they had carefully observed all
the legal requirements, and at Michaelmas 1813 duly displayed the notice on the
front of John Adam's Court House.

This action proved almost disastrous. Protocol demanded display *on the mercat
cross*, and only after indignant protest from the gaoler who hung the notice, and a
hurried consultation of the burgh records, was it established that since the old
mercat cross was removed in 1776 along with the old town, by magistrates' decree
the Court House pillars officially *were* (for the purposes of public business) 'the
mercat cross'. A suitably ambiguous affidavit testifying to the notice's display was
compounded by Craignure and Ferrier, and the bill was at last sent to London for
its first reading on 25 March 1814. Apart from a hitch when Lord Walsingham, who
was to present it in committee, had a stroke, it then passed without difficulty and on
20 June received the Royal assent. As the burgh could raise no more than £50, the
Collector of Land Tax was authorized to levy £7000 on the county.

But more delay followed while Inveraray's new magistrates were elected (Craignure now became Provost and Sheriff Clerk), and the difficulty of finding contractors then meant that nearly two years passed before work actually began, in
spring 1816. The builders were William Lumsden and James Peddie, of 13 Charlotte Street, Leith, on a four-year contract for £5,850 2s 0d.[46*]

A series of mishaps now occurred recalling those of William Douglas with the
Great Inn and George Hunter with the old Court House. The budget was a tight
one, allowing for only one prison to serve both debtors and felons, but still expenses proved higher than expected. The most serious was due to an oversight of
Gillespie's assistant Stevenson, who had forgotten that a site abutting on the foreshore of a sea loch must be clear of high tide; the consequent raising of foundations
and floors, and building of protective bulwarks cost an extra £347.

The contractors meanwhile were quarrelling and work lagged; the Commissioners complained that their 'tardiness' increased expense, and when in 1820 the
building was at last ready, Peddie was bankrupt. His affairs in the creditors' hands,
he demanded another £1,000 and took the case to arbitration. The Commissioners
could not even meet their debts to the Duke and Gillespie, but luckily for them the
arbiter, Alexander Laing,[47*] after prolonged investigation awarded the plaintiffs
only the £347 for the boundary wall (June 1821).

All the resentment and frustration built into the new Court House resulted,
nevertheless, in a modern and convenient replacement for the old Tolbooth and a
very handsome addition to the town.

Gillespie's Court House, as built, resembled his Cupar County Rooms, but
retained many features of the Reid design, and hence has a distant affinity with
Robert Adam's original courtyard elevation of Edinburgh University. Reid's front
resembled his own west range of the Parliament House of the year before (1807),
which itself partly derived from the court elevation of the university, twenty years

[45] The Court House at Inveraray,
built to the design of James Gillespie, 1816–20

earlier again. All these façades are more interesting than Gillespie's adaptation and feature a rusticated ground-floor arcade with, above, a central loggia with free-standing columns in the Italian manner. The latter evidently did not commend itself to the Commissioners, and indeed is not noticeably practical for a Town House in the damp West Highlands climate. The arcaded ground floor, too, was probably vetoed in view of the criticism of that feature in the John Adam Court House.

Gillespie, therefore, while retaining the proportions of Reid's design, had to sacrifice its three-dimensional treatment, obtaining more limited contrasts from the ground-floor rustication, and the slight differences in plane of the central block and sides. Variety was also gained by a small central round-headed doorway flanked by lower square-headed windows, and arched windows in the outer bays. The upper floor is ashlar-faced with Tuscan pilasters, which are coupled in the advanced central bay to frame the Venetian window with which Gillespie replaced Reid's open loggia. Half-pilasters at the set-backs of the outer, recessed bays, and single pilasters at the angles complete the main floor's adornment; above, Gillespie retained the balustraded parapet, but enlarged and fluted its central panel for greater emphasis. Reid's panels above the main-floor windows – a feature he had used in his Perth Academy in 1803 – gave place to small windows, and another Reid feature which disappeared in Gillespie's adaptation was the key pattern at the spring of the ground-floor arches (unique in this group of related designs).

The court-room, on the first or main floor, is at the rear of the building with a deep bay, echoed in the high bulwark with corner 'bastions' built as protection against the tides (the costly and unexpected addition). Its judge's bench was decorated with 'appropriate pilasters and Cornice in the Doric order with the Kings arms in the Centre'. The prison had three-foot thick walls, in suitably primitive-looking 'strong coursed rubble work with rows of Headers at every 2nd course'.[48]*

Thereafter, little of architectural interest occurred in the town for many years, beyond the end of the Argyll Arms' monopoly in the 1820's when the two large houses formerly containing the temporary churches were converted to form the George Inn; and the destruction by lightning of the church steeple in 1837.[49]* A 'parochial library' established in 1832 met with little enthusiasm, a new water supply was piped to the town in 1836, and in 1841 the 7th Duke's Duchess established a school of industry, while an 'English' manse was built the same year, beyond what was by then called the Newton Row. Finally, the old town cross, long neglected, was by 1839 re-erected near the loch at the entrance to Front Street.[50]

Visitors who admired the town and surroundings liked the now unfashionable castle less and less. Dr John McCulloch, a geologist friend of Sir Walter Scott's, had criticized the square block, sunk in its fosse,

> 'as if, in succession, the three parts had been protruded, one out of the other, like a telescope, or . . . flown, no one knows whence, to alight on the top of this ponderous mass, itself pitched naked on a green lawn'.[51]

[46] Crown Point, looking north

99. The Mercat Cross, Inveraray
   Design, probably dating from the 1830s, for re-erection in the town

'The *cardhouse* of the Duke of Argyle,' writes another in 1840, '. . . a pitiable attempt at the grand . . . reminds one of those cockney pretences at castle-building which . . . may be seen on every road leading out of London.'[52] 'The castle is abominable', declared Lord Cockburn, the first of whose numerous attendances as circuit judge was in 1838; 'Inveraray to me is a scene of heavy dulness.'[53]*

In 1839 Duke George, revisiting Inveraray after some years' absence, suddenly died, leaving no legitimate children, although the father of numerous bastards. He was little lamented, except perhaps by those who piously reflected on his supposed remorse at the state to which he had reduced the family fortunes.

The unhappy marriage of his sister Augusta had ended in separation, and after living retired for some years at Rosneath she died in 1831. Lady Charlotte, who had lost her husband Colonel Campbell in 1809, made a second marriage in 1818 to the Reverend Edward Bury; she became a Lady-in-Waiting to the Princess of Wales, and achieved great contemporary fame as a novelist, dying at an advanced age in 1861.

Lord John–'a little, ugly but very agreable man'[54]*–was sixty-two when he succeeded his brother as 7th Duke, and during the eight years of his regime the family returned to Inveraray and the castle and estates to some extent revived. His family was, however, more at home at Rosneath and Ardincaple, where they were chiefly brought up.

This Duke John, fourth of that name, according to his son George was 'a mechanic, and not an agriculturist . . . an accomplished workman, making, with exquisite finish, various implements and articles'.[55] In these interests, and in a distaste for fashionable life, he resembled his father the 5th Duke.

His heir George, Lord Lorne, in 1844 married Lady Elizabeth Leveson-Gower, daughter of the Duke of Sutherland, and settled with his bride in London and at Rosneath. The young husband was noble in appearance, the wife a pretty, rosebud creature; both were earnest and devout. In their time, and through their example, an extraordinary change was to come over Inveraray until it became the very monument of heavy, nineteenth-century, outward respectability, and life at the castle was utterly transformed.

In 1847 the 8th Duke of Argyll, at twenty-four, inherited a still encumbered estate. This slight, yellow-haired young man, though he resembled Duke Archibald in nothing but the inherited Whig tradition, was the first successor since the latter's time to shine in politics: he became a member of every Liberal Cabinet between 1852 and 1881, notably as Secretary of State for India in Gladstone's government of 1868–74. Intellectual as well as pious, and deeply involved with church affairs, he was author of numerous books on the church, philosophy and politics. 'He is an

100. Inveraray Castle in 1821
    Engraved after the drawing by J. P. Neale.

extraordinary man,' noted Henry Crabb Robinson in 1851, 'being a Duke, a Scotch man, and a Presbyterian, and yet a very able man, and still young – an anomaly.'[56] To Lord Cockburn he seemed 'a very singular youth, studious, thoughtful, bene-volent, and ambitious'.[57] This loud-voiced peer, confident and unself-conscious in public but in private life gentle and modest, with his pleasing, almost beautiful features, seemed to epitomize the ideal of Victorian aristocracy; and sure enough he and his girlish, fairy-like Duchess with her flaxen hair and blue eyes, became close friends of Queen Victoria. The Queen's visit to the then barely occupied castle is one of the highlights of the Inveraray of her age.[58*]

The castle had again been left empty, even of servants, on the death of the 7th Duke, and that summer young Duke George was on a cruise with his father-in-law the Duke of Sutherland when he learned that the Queen – who was twenty-eight, four years older than himself – intended to visit Inveraray in the steamship *Fairy*.

The Queen was on her third visit to Scotland with Prince Albert, a voyage which took her from Osborne round the coast of Wales and the Isle of Man, by turns in the *Fairy* and the royal yacht *Victoria and Albert*, and escorted by four other steamers. The numerous party included the Queen's eldest children the Prince of Wales and the Princess Royal (aged five and six), and her half-brother Prince Charles of Leiningen. They were greeted enthusiastically on Clydeside, landed at Dumbarton, and steamed past Rosneath to Loch Long and the Kyles of Bute. But most of them were sea-sick, and next day (18 August) the Queen was lying down with a headache until within an hour of Inveraray.

Meanwhile the Duke of Argyll had had to hurry south from Portree to open up his castle. He convened the local lairds; his mother-in-law was luckily able to bring over staff, a field battery was mounted, marquees pitched, and at short notice decorations elaborate enough to merit the praise of the *Illustrated London News* were arranged.

On this bright, fresh day, with the clear green hills just tipped with clouds, Inveraray's surroundings were brilliantly colourful and the Queen was delighted with her well-nigh feudal reception 'in the true Highland fashion'. The fishing-fleet on the loch flew small pink ensigns, while the Marquess of Stafford's yacht, standing off the quay, was decked with flags. Ashore was equally gay, and the first part of the Queen's promenade along the pier had become 'a tastefully canopied walk' decorated with heather.

'It was constructed of pillars, festooned with evergreens and flowers, supporting a roof of white cloth fringed with blue, the floor of which was covered with scarlet cloth. From this covered gallery to the entrance to the Duke of Argyle's grounds, trees were planted on the side of the street next to the Loch, giving it somewhat the appearance of an avenue. A magnificent triumphal arch, grace-fully festooned with flowers and evergreens, and two galleries were also erected; the galleries being for the accommodation of the public . . . From the quay to the Duke's Gate, the Islay clansmen formed a living avenue, clad in their dark tartans, with broad red facings, and all the Highland accoutrements, including

101. Inveraray Castle, c. 1870
  Photograph showing the coloured glass windows in the
  Middle Tower, destroyed in the fire of 1877.

the formidable Lochaber axe. A body of the Duke's men, clad entirely in their
own tartans, without the red facings, also kept a portion of the ground. The
Highland Guard, including the Celtic Gentlemen, the clansmen of Islay, and
the tenantry of the Duke of Argyle, mustered from 300 to 500 strong.'[59]
A gun signalled the *Fairy*'s arrival, which was greeted by a cannonade as the royal
squadron anchored off the town, and the national anthem hailed the Queen as she
was rowed ashore, to be received by the Duke wearing the tartan, his Duchess ('dear
Lady Elizabeth Leveson Gower')[60] and members of her family. Leaning on
Argyll's arm the Queen and her train of royalty and nobility walked 'along the
arcade, the Celts giving the salute, the company making their obeisance, and the
people loudly cheering'. Her Majesty was gaily dressed:

> 'a blue and white striped silk dress, broadly fringed; a black damask silk *visite*,
> with a deep flounce, bracelets, and primrose gloves; white chip bonnet, trim-
> med with straw-coloured crape, and white marabout feathers, with dark green
> velvet feathers inside; and she carried a green parasol.'

Joined in the carriage by Prince Albert, the Duchess and her mother, Prince
Charles and the Duke, she received loyal addresses with 'the freedom of the burgh,
in a massive chased silver box, through Earl Grey, to Prince Albert'. Then (the
Queen records) they 'took a beautiful drive amongst magnificent trees, and along
a glen where we saw *Ben Sheerar*, &c.':

> 'The pipers walked before the carriage, and the Highlanders on either side, as
> we approached the house. Outside stood the Marquis of Lorn, just two years
> old, a dear, white, fat, fair little fellow with reddish hair, but very delicate

features, like both his father and mother; he is such a merry, independent little child. He had a black velvet dress and jacket, with a "sporran", scarf, and Highland bonnet.'[61]

The enchanted Queen 'took the little fellow by the hand and lifted him up, and kissed him'. She then determined to send for her own children from on board, who arrived

> 'amidst loud plaudits. The Prince of Wales was very plainly, but neatly dressed in nursery costume ... He lifted his little cap to the assemblage in acknowledgment of their cheers, but looked soft and delicate. The Princess Royal wore a pea-green silk Polka, a purple or brown dress trimmed with fringe, and a straw bonnet.'

After luncheon at the castle at two o'clock, 'the Highland gentlemen standing with halberds in the room',[62] the Queen received various people in the drawing-room, and stepped into the carriage again at three o'clock to return under escort to the quay. The more privileged went on board to take leave, and then the whole squadron steamed down the loch for Lochgilphead and the Crinan Canal. So ended the first visit by British royalty since Mary Queen of Scots.[63]*

Queen Victoria's second and much longer stay at Inveraray was as a widow, in 1875 : she was then mother-in-law to that dear little fellow who had so enchanted her as a child – Lord Lorne.

Life at Inveraray was now a model of Victorian rectitude. The Argylls' circle of friends included writers and poets as well as men in public life, and among their guests at Inveraray were Tennyson, Lord Macaulay and Harriet Beecher Stowe. This lady spent five days at the castle in 1856, with her sister and three of her grown-up children, and no description could demonstrate more effectively than hers the transformation that had taken place in the castle.

Mrs Beecher Stowe was on her second visit to Britain, and already famous for her publication of *Uncle Tom's Cabin*. Her account shows that the only feature of castle life in common with earlier generations was the freedom of its guests :

> 'We rise about half past eight. About half past nine we all meet in the dining-hall, where the servants are standing in a line down the one side, and a row of chairs for guests and visitors occupies the other. The duchess and her nine children, a perfectly beautiful little flock, sit together. The duke reads the Bible and a prayer, and pronounces the benediction. After that, breakfast is served – a very hearty, informal, cheerful meal – and after that come walks, or drives or fishing parties, till lunch time, and then more drives, or anything else : everybody, in short doing what he likes till half past seven, which is the dinner hour. After that we have coffee and tea in the evening.'[64]*

This ordered sobriety, and the visits of sober Victorian politicians and philanthropists like the Earl of Shaftesbury and John Bright were far removed from the days of Confusion Castle; or, before that, of Inveraray's bright morning of adventure, when this freakish, individualistic building, product of the ideas of three dukes and numerous architects, had slowly raised its gleaming walls and embattled towers above a sprawling village which was to see the country's first experiment in town planning.

But the greatest beauty of all is this . . . The closer the inspection, the more exalted your admiration; and the better acquaintance, the greater your esteem.

James Hogg *A Tour in the Highlands in 1803*, 1888, pp. 20 f.

EPILOGUE

INVERARAY CASTLE, as it appeared at the end of the eighteenth century and for the greater part of the nineteenth, was still externally the product of Roger Morris for the 3rd Duke of Argyll, and both its style and plan exerted a powerful influence on architecture and taste, with a line of houses indebted to it, directly or indirectly, for over seventy years.

Equally influential, within Scotland at least, was the 5th Duke's enrichment of his policies with ornamental buildings, in the manner already popular in England though until then little seen in his own country. Finally, while the Duke's industrial and agricultural innovations did not lastingly affect the Highland economy, planned towns and villages, which owed their origin to Duke Archibald's re-planning of Inveraray, survived and, in varying degrees, flourished. To this we owe late-eighteenth-century developments like Oban or Ullapool, founded by the British Fishery Society of which the 5th Duke was a leading member; while places like Newcastleton in Roxburghshire, built by the Duke of Buccleuch for hand-loom weavers in 1793, and Ardrossan and its harbour (1805, by the Earl of Eglin-toun), owed their foundation to families connected in some way with the Argylls. In this field Inveraray again was the pioneer, a generation earlier than the planned towns which followed.

The influence of Morris's design for Inveraray was almost immediate, showing as it did how a modern Palladian plan, familiar to both architects and clients, could without any sacrifice of convenience be given a convincingly castellated form. Following on the publication of Pennant's *Tour*, whose 1776 edition was the first to include the Moses Griffith view of the castle, Inveraray came to be widely illustrated.[1]* All the same, it is hardly surprising to find that those houses most directly derived from it were built by owners with some family connexion, or else designed by architects who either had worked at Inveraray or were influenced by other architects who had.

This was evident even during the lifetime of Duke Archibald, when Douglas Castle in Lanarkshire was begun in 1757, apparently to designs of the older Adam brothers. The imitation of Inveraray was doubtless intended as a compliment by the elderly Duke of Douglas, a political associate of Argyll's, who had recently married an ambitious young wife, and determined (it was said) to rebuild his castle as a copy of Inveraray but ten feet larger in all dimensions! This was supposedly the fulfilment of an old prophecy that whenever Douglas Castle should be destroyed it would rise again larger and more grand: the old castle was in fact burned down in 1758, the year *after* building the new one had begun.[2*] Douglas Castle was, however, according to the designs in *Vitruvius Scoticus*, intended to have a deep U-plan, of which only one jamb was built—and even that has since been demolished never to rise again. But in external detail, particularly the pointed windows—a feature not elsewhere employed in Scottish castellated houses before James Playfair's Melville Castle in 1786—the resemblance to Inveraray is close.[3*]

Robert Adam's own debt to Inveraray is an involved subject, and can be no more than touched upon here. Among his early designs, Wedderburn, of 1770, with mixed classical and Tudor motifs, resembles Inveraray only in having angle towers, and its garden façade has a central bow; while Caldwell (1771) is no more than a simple classical house with battlements and pepperpots. Oxenfoord (1780) has round towers but not at the angles. But in the wings of the landward front of Culzean (1777) Adam used round angle towers, setting the style for Pitfour (still building in 1794, though said to have been begun in 1784), whose rectangular main block has round angle towers similar in proportion to Inveraray's: the resemblance is otherwise slight, for it has a southern bow and square towers flanking the entrance. Dalquharran (1786) repeats this formula reversing the position of square and round towers. Both these houses have orthodox late classical plans, with central staircases lit by skylights. In his last houses, Seton (designed 1789) and Airthrey (designed 1791), where Adam abandons the basic rectangle in favour of advanced geometric planning, the debt to Inveraray is little more than generic.[4*] All these houses are in his own 'Roman castellated' manner, deriving rather from his Italian sketches than from native mediaeval architecture. The important series of houses descending from these, such as John Paterson's Monzie (another Campbell house) and Eglintoun, are extensions of the classical-type plan rather than Inveraray.

Adam's version of the castle-style was to have so much more immediate and powerful an influence in Scotland that the real crop of Inveraray derivatives did not appear until well after his death, partly no doubt as the result of the numerous descriptions and illustrations of the early nineteenth-century tourists, and the publication of *Vitruvius Scoticus* about 1810; and partly through the other houses descended from Inveraray (such as Melville or Kew) whose own influence was probably more direct.

By far the earliest example appears to be an English one: Fillingham Castle in Lincolnshire (*c.* 1760), where no immediate reason for the employment of the style is apparent. It has no central tower, but the square main block, excluding the north wing, in other respects echoes Inveraray, although with only two storeys and with rounded Gothick windows.[5]

In Scotland the only other eighteenth-century example was a kind of folly built

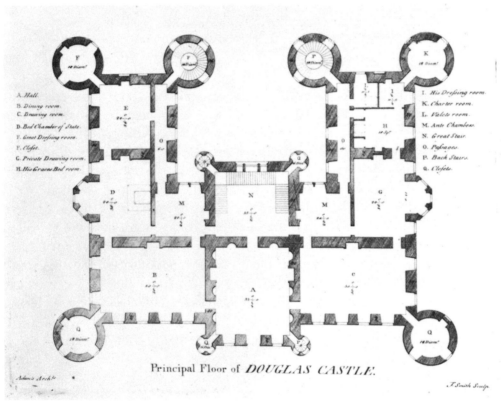

102. Douglas Castle, Lanarkshire
    Plan and elevation, probably by John and James Adam, from
    Vitruvius Scoticus. Begun in 1757, unfinished and now demolished.

103. Town House, Bo'ness
     Built about 1775 by the Duke of Hamilton, tower added in 1857.
     Lithograph shows the house before rebuilding in 1882; finally
     demolished in 1970. After a drawing by J. Heggie.

at Bo'ness (Borrowstouness) near Linlithgow, supposedly about 1778. According to local tradition, the 5th Duke of Argyll's stepson, the Duke of Hamilton, who was a fairly frequent visitor to Inveraray, presented this building to the people of Bo'ness as a Town House soon after his marriage to Elizabeth Burrell in 1778; although Pennant, who passed through the small place in 1769, already remarks that 'The town-house is built in the form of a castle'.

'The ground floor was intended for a prison, the second for a Court-room, and the attic story, for a school', writes the Reverend Robert Rennie in the *Statistical Account*. Joseph Farington sketched it in 1792: 'a large stone Inverary like building as a Town House at head of Harbour but it was never completed and is used as a granary.' Farington's drawing shows the unfinished turreted building with crenellated parapet, pointed windows and a central, chimney-like tower rising from a hipped roof which was also crenellated. 'If the original design were executed', Rennie reprovingly observed, 'the house would be highly useful and ornamental to the place.'[6*]

In the nineteenth century a square, ecclesiastical-looking tower was infelicitously tacked on, but during the 1880s mine-workings beneath the site caused the building's collapse. The ruins were later removed, the foundations more securely established, and the Victorian tower, though not the original building, was re-erected and survived until 1970. In its latter-day form no one unacquainted with the history of this architectural curiosity would have suspected its derivation from Inveraray.[7]

104. Kew Palace
    Begun in 1802, demolished by George IV.
    Engraved after a drawing by J. Grieg.

Inveraray's line of descent may now be said to divide and pass through Play-fair's Melville—similar in its block plan to its ancestor but with a central top-lit staircase like the Adam houses – which was itself to be the ancestor of, among others Taymouth and Stobo; and in England through Kew New Palace (begun 1802), prototype of such later houses as Eastnor. As we shall see, in the building of most of these houses there were strong personal reasons why either owner or architect harked back to the design of Inveraray.

The short-lived Kew Palace was begun by King George III, but abandoned, after heavy outlay, when he lost his sight and his reason, and eventually demolished by King George IV. Its main block, distinctly castellated with four round angle towers and also four smaller wall-turrets, followed Inveraray in having a tall central tower – though much smaller in proportion – and central stair. It is not impossible that the King himself determined the choice of style, since his early education had been in the hands of Duke Archibald's nephew the Earl of Bute, another great planner and landscaper. In his youth George III certainly showed talent as a draughtsman, and studied under Sir William Chambers (who incidentally was a later owner of Duke Archibald's house at Whitton); but the royal share in Kew's building probably amounted to little more than a proprietory supervision.[8]*

Smirke's Lowther Castle may next be considered, begun in 1806 for William Lowther, a cousin of Bute's son-in-law Sir James Lowther and created Earl of

105. Lowther Castle, Westmorland
    Designed by Robert Smirke and begun in 1806.
    Engraved after a drawing by J.P.Neale, 1819.

Lonsdale in 1807. This was Smirke's first important commission on returning from extensive foreign travels, and with Lowther Castle's success his career as an architect of public buildings rapidly followed. The castle's indebtedness to Inveraray is much obscured by wings and other additional features, especially at the entrance front which resembles the west end of a church; nevertheless the main block follows Inveraray's basic principle of square plan, crenellated corner towers and square central tower.[9]

The next two examples, both descending indirectly *via* the Melville design, are the work of Archibald and James Elliot: Stobo Castle in Peebles-shire (1805–11), and Taymouth in Perthshire (1806–10). Again the basic concept is obscured by wings and porches, and many points of detail differ, but their main blocks externally follow Inveraray as much as does Lowther. These two castles rise from ground level instead of being sunk in a fosse like Inveraray; nor, except in Taymouth's angle towers, are pointed windows employed, the main buildings having Tudor hood-moulds.

Stobo strongly resembles Inveraray on all elevations except the south, to which outbuildings and the stable block are attached, and its central tower, massive though lower in proportion, carries the chimney-flues like Inveraray's. But its central hall is lit from a dome, not from clerestory windows, and a raised central projection like an extra tower forms an addition on both north and south fronts. Texturally Stobo lacks Inveraray's smooth finish, being built of a more rugged 'random whinstone' with red sandstone dressings, less pleasing than the ashlar of its prototype's Creggans and St Catherines stone. Like Inveraray, the interior is strictly non-Gothick, but its plan is quite different; the hall contains the cantilevered and bifurcated grand staircase, with deep arcaded openings piercing the hall's upper-floor walls (in a kind of adaptation of the Inveraray idea), to form an integrated gallery.[10]

Simond, who saw Taymouth in September 1810, remarked that 'Lord Breadalbane is building a castle much in the plan of the Duke of Argyll's at Inveraray, but larger, and in a better style'.[11] Whether or not we agree with this aesthetic verdict, Stobo and Taymouth both afford us a hint of how Inveraray looked before the addition of its Victorian roof, dormers and conical turret caps. Taymouth as built was the result of several expensive changes both of mind and architect by the Earl, who had originally offered the redesigning of his castle to Robert Mylne. Mylne, after visiting it in 1789, produced drawings the following year for 'improving, adding to, and altering' the existing house. When building actually began, however, it was to a design not by Mylne but by John Paterson, of Edinburgh; but this was then demolished, and the present castle by the Elliot brothers was finally built.[12]* Although externally the Elliots' house has had various additions, the central block remains today almost unchanged. Even the local building stone used is similar to Inveraray's in colour and texture. The internal plan, however, is on the Stobo

106. Taymouth Castle, Perthshire, 1806–10
    Designed by Archibald and James Elliot.
    Engraved after a drawing by J.P.Neale, 1823.

model, with a central staircase of immense height lit by a great lantern tower which (surprisingly) was an afterthought during construction. The interior, after some hesitation, was at principal floor level made Gothick throughout, and was later much embellished.

Ashridge in Hertfordshire comes next in time, begun in 1808 for the 7th Earl of Bridgwater by James Wyatt, and completed by several other hands. Here there are no angle towers, but the chief rooms were grouped symmetrically round a vast central tower – rather like that at Taymouth – whose grand central staircase rose its full height. Once again the typical Inveraray or eighteenth-century model was followed in adapting a classical plan to a Gothick exterior and detail.[13]

Smirke followed his earlier Lowther by rebuilding the Herefordshire house of John Somers Cocks, Lord Somers, as Eastnor Castle in 1811, in a mainly neo-Norman version of the Inveraray model, although the immediate inspiration may well have been Kew. But, as at Inveraray, the effect achieved was a compact castle silhouette, from which its very low kitchen wing does not significantly detract. There is also a fosse, though less of a deliberate gesture than Inveraray's – which served the express purpose of sinking the kitchen offices out of sight : Eastnor's

107. Eastnor Castle, Herefordshire, 1811
    Designed by Robert Smirke. From a drawing by J. Buckler, 1820.

108. Blairquhan Castle, Ayrshire, 1820
    Designed by William Burn. Engraved after a drawing by J. P. Neale.

fosse does not completely encircle the house, and encloses a forecourt with a barbican lodge. It was, indeed, more a means of using the site's natural contours to picturesque advantage.

As at Inveraray, the hall is lit by a clerestory, but has one external wall on the earlier Blenheim principle, and it has only one grand staircase lit by a lantern in the ceiling on the east. The plan's most interesting feature is the way Smirke cleverly developed Morris's trick of making the angle towers almost disjoined: Smirke's (trefoil) towers are linked to the main block by narrow diagonal passages, thus further extending the frontage without enlarging the plan.[14] Smirke's detail is, of course, far more 'archaeological' than Morris's (the further mediaevalization of the interior came later) – a reminder that more accurate works than Batty Langley's *Gothic Architecture Improved* were now available; but superb though Eastnor's effect is, something of the pure, even naïve fantasy of Inveraray was lost in the process.

William Burn, who was a pupil of Smirke when Lowther was building and remained in touch with him, between 1818 and 1822 gothicized the Fletcher family's house at Saltoun; the then laird was another Andrew Fletcher, a grandson of Lord Milton's. Part of its old fifteenth/sixteenth-century tower was demolished to make way for a new high square tower raised above a central hall, of Inveraray type but without central stairs. Burn's main block, viewed from the east front from which the old castle behind is obscured, derives *via* Taymouth rather than directly from Inveraray, but with square corner towers, rectangular windows (pointed in the wing additions), and a loggia across the entrance.[15] At Blairquhan in Ayrshire,

109. The Lee, Lanarkshire, 1820
    Designed by James Gillespie.
    Engraved after a drawing by J.P. Neale, 1828.

designed in 1820, Burn retained the central lantern tower feature, but otherwise his design is derived from Tudor prototypes – with a carriage porch of Lowther derivation. In his next design, Carstairs (1821), all trace of Inveraray derivation disappears.

Mention must be made, finally, of James Gillespie. For Dunninald he produced, about 1818, a design so close to Saltoun that one suspects he must have had a sight of Burn's drawings. But in 1820, fresh from completion of Inveraray's new Court House, he designed the reconstruction of the Lee, creating even if on only one front of this Lanarkshire building an appearance startlingly like the original prototype.[16] This last Burn-Gillespie group revert to the original Inveraray principle of placing the central lantern over the hall, although the staircases in each case are treated differently.

In some of these buildings the reason for a derivation from Inveraray, in the years before Inveraray was widely known, is not far to seek – connexions with Lord Bute, for example, or passing on of the idea between architects. We may here add that Taymouth's owners, the Earls of Breadalbane, were a cadet branch of the Argyll Campbells, and in the 1730s the 2nd Earl had employed William Adam to remodel his sixteenth-century tower house, while his son the 3rd Earl filled the policies with ornamental buildings, some of them in the Gothick taste. In 1782 the title passed collaterally to John, son of Colin Campbell of Carwhin, so that this earl's first choice of architect, Robert Mylne, and final choice of style, Inveraray Gothick, is not surprising.

Eglintoun (1798) and Stobo were both built by members of the Montgomery family. The Earls of Eglintoun were connected by marriage both with the Argyll Campbells and with Lord Milton, who acted as guardian to the numerous children of Countess Susanna, widow of the 9th and mother of the 10th and 11th Earls. Eglintoun Castle was built for the 12th Earl – the same who later directed the construction of Ardrossan harbour and the Paisley Canal – by John Paterson, whose plan derives from those of Robert Adam, for whom he had worked. Stobo belonged to a distant connexion of the Eglintoun family, Sir James Montgomery, whose father had been a keen farmer and in 1763 bought the Whim (also in Peebles-shire) from the 4th Duke of Argyll, to whom its inheritor John Maule had by then returned it.[17]*

The houses here discussed are among the most obvious whose exteriors and plans Inveraray, directly or indirectly, influenced. In less obvious ways its influence was wider still, and as the Romantic movement spread Gothick was regarded as the only appropriate architectural style in which to execute the modern castles of rich or noble patrons, particularly where surrounding landscape was, or could be made to be, in harmony.

110. Inveraray Castle in the 1870s
    One of the last photographs taken before the fire of 1877.

Y

The Inveraray Castle we see today is the result of changes which have taken place over the past hundred years, the most obvious, and aesthetically the most regrettable, being the addition of its raised attic storey, conical turret roofs and tall chimney stacks. This was the work of Anthony Salvin after a catastrophic fire had burnt out the entire centre of the building, early in the morning of 12 October 1877. Within three hours the main tower roof, gallery and all the woodwork in the hall were destroyed, and the solid pieces of Baltic timber transported with such labour and expense more than a century earlier collapsed in ashes.

> 'Nothing remained from base to roof but a few smouldering beams near the top. The whole of the valuable decorations of the hall have been destroyed . . . The tapestries in the principal drawing-room are much injured by having been hurriedly torn down when that part of the building seemed in immediate danger.'[18]

The main body of the castle, and most of the furniture and portraits, were saved; and the Duke, remarking that it was fortunate they had another castle to go to, removed with his family to Rosneath while plans for restoring Inveraray were carried out.

Unfortunate though the resulting alterations may appear to us today, for the sake of Roger Morris's design we may be grateful that a far more ambitious alteration had not already destroyed the lines of the eighteenth-century house for ever. The Duke had earlier wished to enlarge and romanticize his castle in the Victorian-baronial manner, of which Salvin was one of the leading exponents, and had commissioned from him a set of elaborate designs with great growths of Franco-Scottish Renaissance stepped towers, strapwork and spires, enormously increasing the size of the Morris castle.[19]* In these Salvin showed considerable skill in imparting such an asymmetrical, late Victorian appearance to the formal Inveraray Castle; nevertheless, although one may regret that as an original Salvin design this ingenious transformation was never executed, the loss of the whole quality of a pioneer example of Georgian Gothick would have been far too high a price to pay.

After the fire in 1877, Salvin was asked to produce a much simpler scheme for the castle's immediate restoration. His change of the castle's silhouette was much modified, but its effect was still drastic by imposing high-pitched conical roofs on the corner towers, which detract from the central tower's importance. The latter, moreover, was further sunk behind the steep raised roof of the new top storey,[20]* which replaced Adam's poky attic floor and skylights. To accommodate this more spacious storey the wallhead battlements were removed, except round the towers, and heavy pedimented dormer windows substituted. This commission was one of Salvin's last works, for he was then seventy-eight years old, and in 1881 he died.

The cost of Inveraray's restoration was estimated at between £15,000 and £20,000, the castle then being insured for £106,000, £80,000 of which was for the fabric. The new roof was built under the protection of a hastily-raised temporary roof covering the burnt-out hall at the base of the battlements, and an old wooden model – probably Roger Morris's original model – was hunted out from the Malt-

[47] Inveraray Castle, the Victorian room. The portrait above the fireplace is of Princess Louise, Marchioness of Lorne

111. Proposed additions to Inveraray Castle
Elevation from the unexecuted designs by
Anthony Salvin in the 1870s.

land lumber-room to use as guide. St Catherine's quarry was reopened, as Creggans stone was thought inferior and more expensive to work. As shortage of water to fight the fire had aggravated the disaster, water pipes and hydrants—rather too late to be of use—were now built into the castle walls in neatly contrived cupboards, and connected from a circular reservoir (known today as the Moon Pond), which had been dug on the Black Hill in 1863.[21]*

In September 1879 the family were able to move back into the restored castle, but in May the previous year the Duchess Elizabeth had died.

Until the 8th Duke's time, the only alteration to the castle's exterior had been the lengthening of Morris's windows by Robert Mylne in the 1780s. The 8th Duke had early reglazed the main bedroom-floor windows with plate glass, and given the state drawing-room and dining-room windows astragals of a different pattern from Mylne's. He had also altered certain interiors, redecorating the private drawing-room and state bedroom (now the private dining-room) and installing rich plaster ceilings. Later, a bedroom was fitted up to form the present Brown Library, whose upper shelves are served by an open gallery, its wrought-iron railings elaborately adorned with interlaced A's and coronets, and the ducal galley.

The last of these alterations was for the use of Princess Louise, sixth of Queen Victoria's nine children, who married the twenty-six-year-old Marquess of Lorne in March 1871, and thus became the first English princess to make an officially approved marriage to a commoner for nearly 350 years.[22]*

For this ceremonial occasion the architect Sir Matthew Digby Wyatt designed an elaborate porch of iron and glass to cover the north front entrance bridge over

[48] Inveraray Castle, showing the turrets and upper storey
with raised roof, added in 1878

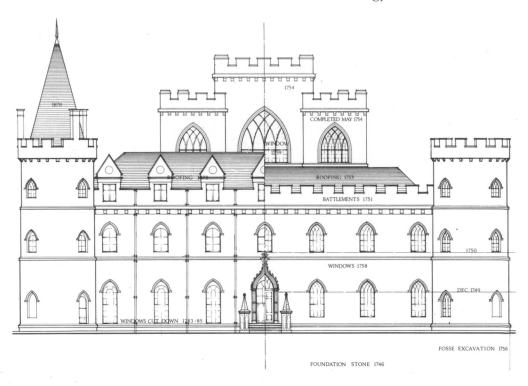

112. Inveraray Castle, south elevation
    Showing progress of construction and subsequent alterations.

the fosse, which consequently lost its squat obelisks. Digby Wyatt (1820–77) had collaborated in the building of Paddington Station, the experience of which this light glass and metal structure, with its sloping roof, reflects.

Among the Duke's earliest changes in the castle's surroundings was a re-landscaping of the gardens in 1848 by W. A. Nesfield, making a new approach along the riverside, and sweeping away a dense shrubbery of dark laurels – clipped so flat 'that you might almost drive a waggon over the surface'[23] – to create a formal garden of flower-beds on the castle's south side. As Nesfield was Salvin's father-in-law, he may well have been the means of introducing that architect to the Duke.

In the town, the most notable change was the building in the Fisherland in 1886 of a small Gothic Episcopalian church (architects Wardrop and Anderson), under the auspices of the then Duchess.[24]* This little church, innocuous enough, did not disturb the lines of the planned eighteenth-century town; but in 1923–32 the 10th Duke built alongside it a tall campanile which strikes an incongruous note, its alien appearance dominating the small Highland capital.[25]* Since 1941 the contrast has been the more obvious because in that year Robert Mylne's church steeple was found to be unsafe and was unfortunately removed; more unfortunately still, its stones were not kept, and because of the greatly increased cost of rebuilding, the steeple has never been replaced. Aesthetically this is a great loss both to town and church, which noticeably lacks its elegant finishing feature.

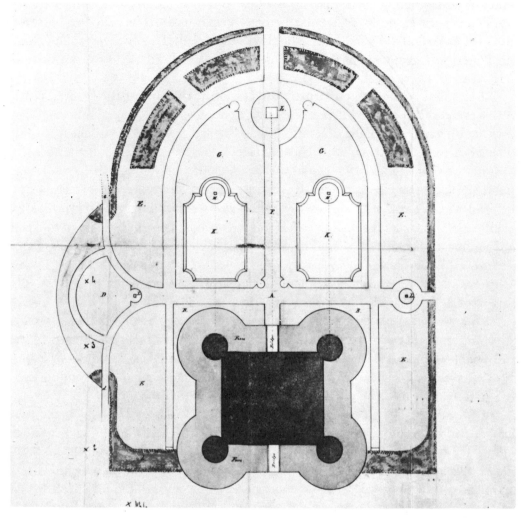

113. Garden layout for Inveraray Castle
    Design by W. A. Nesfield, 1848.

Another sad loss to the town has been the felling of the old beech avenue in the Fisherland, declared unsafe in 1951 as being over-mature, and on removal leaving only a few straggling trees to fringe the long meadow walk. (Recently, however, the new school has been responsible for some replanting.)

One feature which might well have altered Inveraray, but did not, was a railway, for when in 1897 the Callander and Oban Railway proposed to bring their line past the town, the ducal landlord strongly resisted this incursion into his domains along Loch Fyne.[26]* Some interesting sketches found at the castle show the proposed route running behind the Wintertown and Fisherland, as far away from the castle as the contours allowed; but it would not do, and no railway was brought nearer to Inveraray than Arrochar (21 miles) on one line, and Dalmally (16 miles) on the other.

The 8th Duke died in 1900; his son, the husband of Princess Louise and for some years Governor-General of Canada, died childless in 1914. The title then passed to his brother Archibald's son Neil, who died unmarried. The present (11th) Duke, Ian Douglas, a grandson of the 8th Duke's third son Lord Walter Campbell, inherited in 1949.

At the time of the present Duke's succession the effects of the second World War were very apparent in Inveraray. Loch Fyne, from the Kyles of Bute to Cairndow, had been a Combined Operations training area, with its HQ at the Victorian villa Tigh na Ruadh (now MacBride's Hotel), on the south side of the town.[27*] Although the castle, as residence of the Lord-Lieutenant of Argyll, was not commandeered, all the parks were used for army camps, and hundreds of nissen huts covered the valleys. The shores of Loch Fyne were thronged with the largest numbers of strangers that the place had known even in its palmiest days of tourism, and among the many VIPs who came to see the training operations were King George VI, King Haakon of Norway, and Generals Montgomery and Eisenhower. All these visits were highly confidential, and any reported in the press were disguised under the familiar location 'somewhere in Scotland'.

When the war ended Inveraray's parks were a wreck of camp debris – some of the concrete hut bases remain, hidden by undergrowth, to this day – the town was sadly neglected, and the castle in its latest phase of decay had dry rot and leaking roofs. It was at this stage of post-war conditions, when repairs were economically and practically prohibitive, that the 11th Duke inherited.

But by degrees the castle was restored, the parks cleared of the remains of camps, and thousands of new trees and shrubs were planted. The town presented a more daunting problem. Following the period when its style was unfashionable and it was dismissed as 'a typically dismal little Highland town', by the 1950s Inveraray was again recognized as an outstanding example of planned eighteenth-century building, and its restoration accepted as of great importance. But of 103 houses under consideration only 13 had bathrooms and only 22 indoor sanitation, and many roofs, joists, floors and partition walls were rotten. Without help, the Argyll Trustees would have been quite unable to carry out such a major work; and to ensure the town's conservation, at the Historic Buildings Council's suggestion they handed over the properties to the Ministry of Works at an agreed valuation. Ownership was now vested in the Town Council, with the Ministry as feu superiors.

Financially, the Council were as unable to maintain the town as their forebears had been in Duke Archibald's time, for by this time the population was only 503, and a penny on the rates would bring in no more than £16. The work was therefore carried out on grants from the Scottish Development Department and the Historic Buildings Council, and thanks to these and to the great interest taken, from the then Minister (Hugh Molson, now Lord Molson) downwards, between 1958 and 1963 a restoration of historic dimensions was executed.

The architects, who were Ian Lindsay and partners, brought a notable sympathy and sensitivity to their task. Some of the houses had to be completely gutted

114. Aerial view of Inveraray, looking north

but all external walls, street elevations and fenestration were retained; endless pains were taken to match the original harling, mixed with Irish limestone, and to renew the Easdale slates. Where modern features needed to be introduced (such as outside rear staircases) they were light and unobtrusive, and all external alterations were confined to the backs. Meanwhile inharmonious street lighting was redesigned, old and worn pavement renewed, and shop signs were carefully regulated.

Behind its eighteenth-century façade, Inveraray is now a modern town and a fine example of conservation. The light appearance of its white harling, replacing the drab grey which had taken over in the nineteenth century, re-creates elegance in a period which once again admires planned eighteenth-century building (though still too often allowing it to be destroyed). The crowds who now flock to the town far exceed even the throngs during the old circuit courts, or the week-end steamer hordes. No longer a hard day's journey away, Glasgow is now an easy drive of little over an hour and a half; no longer need a note be sent to the castle from the inn asking permission to visit, since it is officially open for half the year.

Had the 11th Duke not shown foresight and determination in his wish to restore the castle and the town as nearly as possible to their former beauties, posterity would have lost a valuable inheritance. But now much of the past splendour has been recaptured, and later accretion in the castle's interior removed. Every year tens of thousands come to this curious product of Vanbrugh's and Roger Morris's imagination with its late-Victorian addition, to admire the 5th Duke's splendidly decorated state-rooms, and to be shown Allan Ramsay's portrait of Duke Archibald, and those of his successors who in turn contributed to make Inveraray the place it is today.

GLOSSARY

bear = four-rowed barley

boll = grain measure used in Scotland, usually equivalent to 6 imperial bushels

buss = small two-masted vessel of the Dutch type, used in the herring fishery

cruive = (here) wicker salmon-trap

decreet arbitral = decision by arbiters

doer = legal agent

fail-dyke = wall built of turf sods

fall = land measure of 6 ells

feu = Scottish form of land or property tenure, where the vassal's annual payment in money or kind was originally made in lieu of military service

flit = to remove one's house or lodging

gab = (gob) mouth

gabart = kind of barge with sails; the word is possibly of French origin

gavel = gable

girnel = granary

grass-mail = rent paid for use of pasture

harl = rough-cast

horning, putting to the horn = declaring an outlaw by blasts of the horn at the mercat cross

land = tenement, group of households with a common entry

livering = unloading of cargo

lumb = chimney

merk = 13s 4d Scots (= 13⅓d sterling); see pound Scots

pend = (vaulted) passage-way for vehicles through a building

policies = gardens and pleasure-grounds of a mansion

pound Scots = at the time of the Union of 1707 worth 1s 8d sterling

set = (of property) let

tack = lease

tacksman = lessee: one holding a tack of land; in the traditional clan system, a kinsman of the chief with the right to sub-let; (later) a gentleman-farmer

writer = ordinary legal practitioner

ABBREVIATIONS

Manuscripts

Inv/ = Inveraray

AE, AEM = Argyll Estates, Argyll Estates Management

AECB = Argyll Estates Cash Book

C = Castle Building file

CA = Chamberlain's Accounts

CI = Chamberlain's Instructions

2DAC = 2nd Duke of Argyll's Accounts

5DA = 5th Duke of Argyll's Papers

EAC = Estate Accounts

EInst. = Estate Instructions

Inst. = Instructions

Jnl = Journal

KJ = Archibald Campbell of Knockbuy's Journal

LA = Ledger Accounts

Lindsay Howe = Papers formerly with Messrs Lindsay, Howe, WS

MLB = [Roger] Morris Letter Book

NPE = Newspaper Paragraphs relating to Elizabeth Duchess of Argyll

Q = Quarries file

RFD = Rental of Feu Duties

EBapR = Edinburgh Baptism Registers

HR = Heritors' Records

IBR = Inveraray Burgh Records

IPR = Inveraray Parish Records

Mylne = Robert Mylne diaries

NLS = National Library of Scotland

S = Saltoun MSS

SF = Stonefield MSS

SRO = Scottish Record Office

TCM = Town Council Minutes

Printed or photographic sources

Annals = James Cleland, *Annals of Glasgow*, I (1876)

CL = *Country Life*

DNB — *Dictionary of National Biography*

NMRS = National Monuments Record of Scotland

RCAHMS = Royal Commission on Ancient and Historical Monuments of Scotland

SDD = Scottish Development Department

SRS = Scottish Record Society

Publications of the Scottish Record Society, Edinburgh

AT = Commissariot Record of Argyll, Register of Testaments 1674–1800 (1902)

CB = Register of the Burgesses of the Burgh of the Canongate 1622–1733 (1951)

CM = Parish of Holyroodhouse or Canongate, Register of Marriages 1564–1800 (1915)

DB = Roll of Dumbarton Burgesses and Guild Brethren 1600–1846 (1937)

DUNT = Commissariot Record of Dunblane, Register of Testaments 1539–1800 (1903)

EA = Register of Edinburgh Apprentices (*a*) 1701–55 (1929), (*b*) 1756–1800 (1963)

EB = Roll of Edinburgh Burgesses and Guild Brethren (*a*) 1701–60 (1930), (*b*) 1761–1841 (1933)

ECP = Commissariot of Edinburgh, Consistorial Processes and Decreets 1658–1800 (1909)

EM = Register of Marriages for the Parish of Edinburgh (*a*) 1701–50 (1908), (*b*) 1751–1800 (1922)

ET = Commissariot Record of Edinburgh, Register of Testaments III, 1701–1800 (1899)

GB = The Burgesses and Guild Brethren of
Glasgow
(*a*) 1573–1750 (1925), (*b*) 1751–1846 (1935)
GT = Commissariot Record of Glasgow,
Register of Testaments 1547–1800 (1901)
RB = Index to the Register of Burials in the
Churchyard of Restalrig 1728–1854 (1908)
SCM = Monumental Inscriptions in St
Cuthbert's Churchyard, Edinburgh (older
portion) (1915)
ST = Commissariot Record of Stirling,
Register of Testaments 1607–1800 (1904)

Persons
Adam = John Adam
Argyll 3, etc. = 3rd, etc., Duke of Argyll
Asknish, Ask = Robert Campbell of Asknish
Cumming = Alexander Cumming, clockmaker

Douglas = William Douglas, mason
Ferrier = James Ferrier, WS
Fletcher = Andrew Fletcher younger
Graham = Col. Humphrey Graham,
Chamberlain of Argyll
Haswell = George Haswell, wright
Hunter = George Hunter, mason
Knockbuy = Archibald Campbell of
Knockbuy
Maule = John Maule of Inverkeillor
Milton = Andrew Fletcher, Lord Milton
Morris = Roger Morris
Mylne = Robert Mylne
Sonachan = Donald Campbell of Sonachan,
Chamberlain of Argyll
Stonefield = Archibald Campbell of
Stonefield, Sheriff of Argyll

1. MANUSCRIPTS

In spite of the formidable number of printed works referred to in the notes, the bulk of material on which this book is based is to be found only in hitherto unpublished manuscripts. Of these the most important were, of course, the Duke of Argyll's papers at Inveraray Castle, and for Part I of the book (1744–61) the Saltoun Papers, now in the National Library of Scotland. As neither of these large collections has yet been catalogued, references to the Inveraray MSS can only be exact in the case of bound records, and the Saltoun Papers are referred to by box numbers.

Other important collections consulted for Part I were the Bute MSS, in the possession of the Marquess of Bute, the Stonefield MSS (Scottish Record Office, Edinburgh), and the Campbell of Mamore MSS (National Library of Scotland).

For the architectural background to Part II (1771–1806), the most important manuscripts are Robert Mylne's own diaries, in the possession of Miss J. M. H. Mylne. The lack of more personal manuscripts for this period is to some extent made up by the number of journals, both published and unpublished, left by contemporary travellers. A select list of MSS quoted is given below.

Inveraray MSS (His Grace The Duke of Argyll, Inveraray Castle, Argyll)
Inveraray Burgh Records (Inveraray, Argyll)
Minutes of the Commissioners of Supply, Argyll

Part 1
Saltoun MSS (NLS)
Atholl MSS (His Grace The Duke of Atholl, Blair Castle, Perthshire)
Buccleuch MSS (SRO GD 224)
[Sir] William Burrell, MS Tour in Scotland (NLS MS 2911)
Bute MSS (The Most Noble The Marquess of Bute, Mountstuart, Isle of Bute)
Campbell of Mamore MSS (NLS MS 3733–6)
Campbell of Stonefield MSS (SRO GD 14)
Clerk of Penicuik MSS (SRO GD 18)
Coutts and Co. MSS (Strand, London WC2)
Glendoick MSS (NLS MS 3036)
Inveraray Parish Registers (New Register House, Edinburgh)
Inveraray Window Tax Returns (SRO E 204/1)
Laing MSS (University of Edinburgh)
Mrs Montagu Correspondence (BM Add. 40663)
Trustees to the Manufacturers, Letter Books (SRO NG 1)

Part 2
Robert Mylne, diaries (Miss J. M. H. Mylne, Great Amwell, Herts)
Heritors' Records (SRO HR)

MS journals of visitors
Jacob Pattison, 1780 (NLS MS 6322)
John Inglis, 1784 (SRO GD 1/46/16)
J. Bailey, 1787 (NLS MS 3294–5)
Mrs Thrale, 1789 (John Rylands Library, Ryl. Eng. MS 623)
Joseph Farington, 1792 (Edinburgh Public Library, 9 YDA. 1861.792, transcript from original in Royal Library, Windsor)
John Wood of Easter Fossaway, 1801 (NLS MS 3038)
Lachlan Macquarie, 1804 (Public Library of New South Wales, MS A 770)
Nathaniel Wraxall, 1813 (NLS MS 3108)
John Anderson, 1818 (NLS MS 2509)

2. PRINTED

Appropriate references to the printed works consulted are given in full in the following notes. There are, however, a number of important relevant works without whose background no-one embarking on a study of this nature could even begin. Besides the standard histories of Scotland, and the various *Statistical Accounts*, I may mention as obvious examples (some of which are referred to in the notes), Henry Hamilton's *Economic History of Scotland in the 18th Century* (Oxford 1963, vol. III of illustrated edition of G. M. Trevelyan's *English Social History* (London 1949–52), Henry Grey Graham's *Social Life of Scotland in the 18th Century* (London 1899), John Ramsay of Ochtertyre's *Scotland and Scotsmen in the 18th Century*, ed. Alexander Allardyce (Edinburgh 1888), Alexander Carlyle's *Autobiography*, ed. J. Hill Burton (Edinburgh 1910), Malcolm Gray's *The Highland Economy 1750–1850* (Edinburgh 1957), and the 8th Duke of Argyll's *Scotland as it was and as it is* (Edinburgh 1887). For bibliographical material, Sir Arthur Mitchell's *List of Travels and Tours in Scotland 1296–1900* (Edinburgh 1902), and its supplement; and Joan P. S. Ferguson's compilation, *Scottish Family Histories held in Scottish Libraries* (Edinburgh 1960).

On the more specialized aspect of Argyll, important works include the 8th Duke's *Autobiography and Memoirs*, edited by the Dowager Duchess (London 1906), and Eric Cregeen's edition of the *Argyll Estate Instructions, Mull, Morvern, Tiree, 1771–1805* (Scottish History Society 1964), with his illuminating introduction.

Finally, although it was not consulted for this book, as it appeared when the typescript was already complete and with the publishers, T. C. Smout's invaluable *History of the Scottish People 1560–1830* (London 1969) must be included; and I can only add that this list is intended to be selective, not exhaustive.

CHAPTER I

1.   Lady Louisa Stuart *Some Account of John Duke of Argyll and his Family*, written 1827 (privately printed 1863), reprinted in Introduction to *Letters and Journals of Lady Mary Coke*, I (privately printed, Edinburgh 1889).

2.   Balfour Paul *Scots Peerage*, I (1904).

3.   Historical MSS Commission *Report on the MSS of the Earl of Mar and Kellie* (H.M.S.O. 1904) p.303 (Earl of Mar, 29 October 1706). The obtaining of this peerage for his brother was a political manoeuvre by the 2nd Duke, who himself sat in the House of Lords by virtue of English titles as Baron of Chatham and Earl of Greenwich (later Duke of Greenwich, see p.5), and wished his family to qualify for a place among the sixteen representative Scottish peers established by the Act of Union. In all but one Parliament of Great Britain until his death, Ilay succeeded in being elected to the House of Lords. For his title he originally proposed to be 'Earl of Dundee', but the Marquess of Montrose objected to this assumption of one of his own clan's lapsed titles.

4.   For the careers of the two brothers see Balfour Paul *Scots Peerage*, I; Lady Louisa Stuart *Some Account*; William Coxe *Memoirs of the Life & Administration of Sir Robert Walpole, Earl of Orford*, I (London 1798) pp.235–6 and 610–15; Horace Walpole *Memoirs of the Reign of King George II*, ed. Lord Holland, I (London 1847) pp.275–8; Yale Edition of Horace Walpole's *Correspondence*, ed. W.S.Lewis and Warren Huntingford Smith, XV (Oxford 1952) pp.152–5; Robert Campbell *The Life of the Most Illustrious Prince John, Duke of Argyll & Greenwich* (London 1745). A modern account of the brothers' political influence by John M. Simpson in *Scotland in the Age of Improvement* ed. N. T. Phillipson and Rosalind Mitchison (Edinburgh 1970) pp. 47–72.

The 2nd Duke of Argyll's appointments and offices included Privy Councillor; High Commissioner to the Parliament of Scotland, 1705 (for the passing of the Union); a General commanding under Marlborough in the Low Countries, 1706–9; C. in C. in Spain, 1711; Governor of Minorca, 1712–17; C. in C. Scotland, 1712. In 1705 he was created Earl of Greenwich. He was dismissed from all his offices three times during his life, and resigned once: the first dismissal was in 1714, but he was reinstated by George I with the additional office of Groom of the Stole to the Prince of Wales. He commanded the Royal Army in Scotland in 1715–16, but was then again

dismissed and restored to favour only in 1719, becoming High Steward of the Household and Duke of Greenwich. From 1725–30 he was Master General of the Ordnance and in 1735 became a Field Marshal. Disagreement with Walpole's Government led to his further dismissal in 1740, but he was then briefly reinstated as C. in C. in 1742, on Walpole's fall, before finally resigning all his posts in political disillusionment.

5.   Lady Mary Campbell married in 1747 the dissolute Edward Viscount Coke, heir to the Earl of Leicester, a marriage which was an immediate and notorious failure, and which finally ended in a blaze of publicity. During the undignified family quarrels, Lady Mary sought the protection and assistance of her uncle, Duke Archibald.

6.   Lady Louisa Stuart *Some Account*.

7.   Horace Walpole *Notes of Conversations with Lady Suffolk* (Oxford 1924) pp.127–8. See also Bute MSS, Misc. Scottish Correspondence 1683–1763; Balfour Paul *Scots Peerage*, I. The story of the marriage is obscure and Lord Ilay, always reticent about his personal affairs, left very few references in his correspondence, and even fewer about Mrs Williams and their son.

8.   S31a and 400, letters of Lord Ilay to Lord Milton, 1739; Inv MSS, will of 3rd Duke of Argyll, 1760; S95 and 96, letters of Colonel William Williams and John Maule to Lord Milton, 1761.

9.   John Lord Hervey *Some Materials towards the Memoirs of the Reign of King George II*, ed. Romney Sedgwick, I (London 1931) p.295; Horace Walpole *Memoirs . . . of George II*, I, p.275.

10.   *The Autobiography of Dr Alexander Carlyle of Inveresk, 1722–1805*, ed. J.Hill Burton (Edinburgh 1910) p.398.

11.   S MSS, passim. See *Scotland and Scotsmen in the Eighteenth Century, from the MSS of John Ramsay, Esq., of Ochtertyre*, ed. Alexander Allardyce (Edinburgh 1888); G.Brunton and D.Haig *A Historical Account of the Senators of the College of Justice* (Edinburgh 1836); *First Statistical Account of Scotland*, X (1796) p.260 (Rev. Andrew Johnston); also Newcastle MSS, NE C 2222; [Elizabeth Halkett], Memoir of the Fletchers of Saltoun, Edinburgh University MSS La. III 364, ff. 44 f.

12.   S40, Maule to Milton, 22 October 1743. For the Argyll Street library see n.43, ch.II.

13.   Unsigned plans and elevations of the villa, formerly in the Bute Collection, are now in the Mellon Collection. Prints of villa and tower in possession of the Duke of Argyll at

Inveraray Castle; also in BM King's Maps
xxx. 21 (b) and (plan of grounds showing
elevations of buildings) Bodleian Library,
Gough Maps 18, fol. 5, Gen. Top. 62, 14a.
Unexecuted designs are in James Gibbs *Book of
Architecture* (1728) pls. 59–62, and the
elevation of the conservatory-house in
Ashmolean Museum, Gibbs Collection, iii, 90c.
See Penicuik MSS 2107, 2110 (1), Journals of
Sir John Clerk, 9 April 1727 and 20 May 1733.

14. s 43, 401, Argyll 3 to Milton, 29 October
and 3 December 1743, 15 February and 17
April 1744, etc. Walter Paterson (?1708–70)
is earlier recorded as working at Brunstane,
from where he sent seeds to Andrew Whyte or
Wight, then Lord Ilay's gardener at the Whim
(s 424, W. Paterson to A. Whyte, 5 April 1737).
See also ch. II n. 181. The Duke eventually
obtained Paterson for Inveraray by exchanging
him with James Halden, for Halden ended his
life as head gardener at Caroline Park
(Buccleuch MSS, SRO GD 224/168).

15. s 42, Maule to Milton, 3 March 1744.

16. s 40, 42, Maule to Milton, October–
November 1743 and 24 March 1744.

17. s 43, Argyll 3 to Milton, 20 March 1744.

18. Ibid., 3 April 1744.

19. s 401, Argyll 3 to Milton, 12 November
1743.

20. Ibid., 29 October 1743.

21. s 43, Argyll 3 to Milton, 19 June 1744.

22. Inv MSS. He was appointed by the second
Duke, apparently shortly before the death of
his half-brother James Campbell of Stonefield,
who had been in failing health for some time.
Until 1748 the hereditary Sheriffs of the
county were the Dukes of Argyll.

23. s 41, Stonefield to Lady Milton, 7 June
1744. Duke Archibald's mother, 1st Duchess of
Argyll, was Elizabeth Talmash, daughter to
Sir Lionel Talmash of Helmingham, Suffolk,
and Elizabeth, Countess of Dysart and Duchess
of Lauderdale. She married the 10th Earl and
1st Duke of Argyll (then Lord Lorne) in 1678,
but her husband parted from her long before
his death.

24. s 41, Stonefield to Milton, 25 February
1744.

25. s 41, Stonefield to Lady Milton, 7 June
1744. Duddingston House, a short distance
from Edinburgh to the east, was the 1st
Duchess's 'town' house, inherited from her
mother; and here the 3rd Duke, when Lord
Ilay, used often to stay on his Edinburgh visits.
After succeeding to the Dukedom he sold the
property to the Earl of Abercorn, for whom it

was in rebuilt 1763–8 by Sir William
Chambers.

26. s 43, Argyll 3 to Milton, 19 June 1744.

27. s 41, Stonefield to Lady Milton, 7 June
1744; to Milton, 5 July 1744.

28. s 41, Stonefield to Milton, 25 July 1744.

29. s 42, Maule to Milton, 28 June 1744. The
painting was presumably one of Allan Ramsay's
portraits of the Duke, as one was painted in
1744 and sent to Scotland.

30. Ibid., 16 June 1744.

31. s 43, Argyll 3 to Milton, 15 February 1744.

32. s 42, Maule to Milton, 16 June 1744.

33. s 402, 43, Argyll 3 to Milton, 31 May and
16 June 1744.

34. s 402 (2), Memorandum of things Ship'd
this 30th of June 1744. . . .

35. s 42, Maule to Milton, 30 June 1744.

36. Ibid., 14 June 1744.

37. Ibid., 28 June 1744.

38. Ibid., 3, 5 and 7 July 1744.

39. Ibid., 10 July 1744. In 1742 the 2nd Duke
of Argyll's eldest daughter Lady Caroline
Campbell married Francis, Earl of Dalkeith,
heir to the Duke of Buccleuch. Lord Dalkeith
died in 1751 before his father, and their second
son eventually succeeded to the dukedom;
Lady Dalkeith subsequently married Charles
Townshend.

40. s 14, Ld Ilay to George Middleton,
August 1729. THOMAS COCHRANE, a
great-grandson of the 1st Earl of Dundonald,
was MP for Renfrew 1722 and Commissioner
of Excise 1730–61; in 1758 he succeeded
collaterally to the earldom. In 1744 he married
as his second wife Jean, daughter of Archibald
Stuart of Torrence, and one of their thirteen
children became the celebrated Admiral
Cochrane.

41. s 15, Ilay to Milton, 1 September 1730.
For the early work on The Whim see s 399,
422; RCAHMS, *Peebles-shire*, II (1967) pp. 326–
31 and pls. 121, 122, 126. Roger Morris
sketched an 'Oval' for the Whim grounds in
October 1744, based on his inspection of the
estate in July (s 402).

42. s 43, Argyll 3 to Milton, 19 June 1744.

43. s 43, Milton to Gwyn Vaughan, scroll
letter [August 1744].

44. Ibid., and s 402 (2), accounts of John
Campbell, Deputy Chamberlain, 6 August–
28 September 1744.

45. Ibid. Sir John Shaw succeeded to the estate of Greenock in 1702, and held the barony of the town, which had been granted to his family in 1670 by Charles II. Energetic and progressive, Shaw was a great benefactor to local trade. See Sir James Marwick *The River Clyde and the Clyde Burghs* (Glasgow 1909) p. 171.

46. s 43, Milton to Gwyn Vaughan, scroll [August 1744].

47. The party's travelling expenses from Glasgow, including boat freights, customs dues, meals, tips and drinks for porters and boatmen at different stages, cost the Duke £41 7s 3½d sterling. s 402 (2), Deputy Chamberlain's Accounts 6 August–28 September 1744.

48. William Mackay Mackenzie *The Scottish Burghs* (Edinburgh 1949) p. 66; *New Statistical Account of Scotland*, VII (1845) pp. 34, 35.

49. Each half of the church was 54 feet long and 20 feet wide, the Lowland having the additional extension of a 'Duke's aisle' 16 feet by 11 ft 8 inches, and both kirks having a pair of lofts. In the Lowland Kirk the larger loft (approximately 12 × 9½ ft) was occupied by the magistrates (s 418, Measure of the 2 Kirks at Inveraray 1758). Until late in the 19th century the inhabitants were predominantly Gaelic-speaking.

50. SRO, Scottish Window Tax returns, vol. 7, Argyll North District, 1748–56.

51. Inv/18th-century leases.

52. The Hon. Lord Cameron, 'The Superior Courts' in *A Guide to the Scottish Legal System* (Edinburgh 1957) p. 27. SRO, Court Books of Western Circuit, 1748 ff.; Roll Book, Sheriff Court of Argyll.

53. The Circuit Courts last sat at Inveraray in the 1930s, and in 1954 were officially transferred to Oban (but have never yet sat there). The Admiralty Court was a separate body until 1830, when it was merged into the Court of Session.

54. Thomas Pennant *A Tour in Scotland 1769*, I (London 1790) pp. 238–9. The 'herring-buss' fleets were based on Clydeside ports, and in the season practically monopolized the West Coast herring fisheries until the early 19th century.

55. Inv/Memorial to the Duke of Argyll concerning the Houses in the Town of Inveraray, 4 October 1748.

56. Revenues consisted only of the local petty customs, and rent of Achinbreck common, bestowed on the town by the Argyll family.

Duke Archibald added a perpetual annuity of £20 (discontinued only in 1962). The total income at the time of the 1793 *Statistical Account* was £176, and of the 1845 *Statistical Account*, still only £186. (1793, V, p. 287 f.; 1845, VII, p. 35.)

57. Inv/Memoriall Anent the State of ye Highland paroch of Inveraray to the Manadgers of ye ffamily of Argyle, 1706.

58. Inv/Petition, the Burgh of Inveraray to the Manadgers of Argyll, 1709.

59. Inv/Petitions of Magistrates to the 2nd Duke of Argyll, the Duchess Dowager and Lord Ilay, 1718; 18th-century leases; Memorial of Archibald Campbell of Knockbuy and Captain James Campbell to 5th Duke of Argyll, 13 May 1775. See also IBR.

The bells were recast in 1728 by Robert Maxwell in Edinburgh, 'ane Exceeding lazy fellow' and 'too much given to his bottle'; the cost, £25, was borne by James Campbell of Stonefield, then Chamberlain. Above the burgh coat of arms is the inscription 'Ex benignitate spectatissimi viri Jacobi Campbell De Stonefield, justitiarii et vicecomitis delegati De Argyll. Robertus Maxwell me fecit Edinburgi anno 1728.' See Stonefield MSS, SRO GD 14/10/1, ff. 47, 61, James Campbell of Stonefield to George Gordon, WS, 4 and 17 January 1727/8; also James MacKechnie *Official Guide to Inveraray* (Aberdeen 1962) p. 12.

60. Even in 1968 a penny on the rates raised only £53 15s 5d. Inveraray's legal and economic significance is also discussed in chs. 2 and 3 of A. R. B. Haldane *Three Centuries of Scottish Posts* (Edinburgh 1971).

61. Campbell of Mamore MSS, NLS 3733/105, Gen. John Campbell to Maule, 20 January 1746.

62. Inv/Account of the Argyll family; printed in J. R. N. Macphail *Highland Papers*, II, Scottish History Society, 2nd Series, XII (Edinburgh 1916).

The old castle was built by Sir Colin Campbell, 1st Laird of Glenurchy, as tutor to his nephew Archibald, 1st Earl of Argyll, about the middle of the 15th century. See William Bowie *The Black Book of Taymouth* (Edinburgh, Bannatyne Club, 1855) pp. ii and 13; David MacGibbon & Thomas Ross *The Castellated and Domestic Architecture of Scotland*, V (Edinburgh 1892) p. 556.

Accounts for the building done in 1720–2 are preserved at Inveraray Castle, together with the unexecuted design for the additional wings. The latter is unsigned and undated, but McGill may be fairly confidently credited with the work as he was at Inveraray with the 2nd Duke in August 1720, and on 2nd August was admitted a burgess of the town along with his servant John Norman, his brother John the 'chirurgeon', Sir John Shaw, and the Duke himself with seven servants. The following year a number of the masons employed on the building were also admitted burgesses (IBR; see Index of Architects and Craftsmen; for the practice of admitting burgesses see ch.II, p.60).

ALEXANDER MCGILL, d. 1734, who began his career as a mason, is credited in *Vitruvius Scoticus* as being joint architect (with James Smith) of Yester House in East Lothian. His other important works include the building of New Greyfriars Church in Edinburgh (1722), and Donibristle House (1719–20) and chapel (1729) for the Earl of Moray. He also acted for Lords Ilay and Milton at Brunstane and the Whim, and for the Earl and Countess of Bute (sister and brother-in-law to the 2nd Duke of Argyll and Lord Ilay) in the building of Mountstuart (1716). The McGill brothers, architect and surgeon, were old friends of Ilay and Milton, and the medical services of John McGill were greatly valued. See John G. Dunbar *The Historic Architecture of Scotland* (London 1966) p.104.

63. s41, Stonefield to Milton, 25 February and 13 March 1744.

64. s401, Argyll 3 to Milton, 9 November 1743.

65. Inv/Wm Douglas, Report Concerning the Castle of Inverara, 19 January 1744 (in MLB). For William Douglas see Index of Architects and Craftsmen.

66. For Roger Morris's origins and career see Marie P. G. Draper *Marble Hill House and its Owners*, introduction and contributions on the architects, architecture and restoration of the house by W. A. Eden (London 1969). See also H. M. Colvin *Dictionary of English Architects* (London 1954), ad loc.; Saltoun MSS, letters from Col. John Campbell (later 4th Duke of Argyll) to Lord Milton, e.g. s22 (1734). *Vitruvius Britannicus*, IV (1767), pls.75–7, and John Newman *West Kent and the Weald*, Penguin Buildings of England Series (London 1969) pp.532–3, for Combe Bank. Laurence Whistler *The Imagination of Vanbrugh and his Fellow-Artists* (London 1954) pp.159 ff. for Eastbury (and see ch.II n.2). Marie P. G. Draper in *CL* (2 August 1962) for Wimbledon House. James Lees-Milne *Earls of Creation* (London 1962) pp.79–92, and Norwich Public Library, Hobart MSS 8862 (1724), for further on

Marble Hill. Coutts & Co. Ledgers 1727–9 ff. for Lord Ilay's payments to Roger Morris.

Signed and dated drawings in the Atholl MSS at Blair Atholl show that Roger Morris had in 1742 designed a small building for the Duke of Atholl's policies there: a rather heavy square structure, identical on all sides, each of which had an arched opening intended to hold a grille, and presumably intended as a hill-top viewpoint and eye-catcher; on one elevation the weather-vane is dated 1741. There is no relevant correspondence, however, to prove whether or not Morris had already visited Blair or other parts of Scotland before his visit to Inveraray in 1744.

67. The Lowlands too suffered freak hailstorms and winds, and John Maule, before rejoining the party, wrote from Edinburgh of the 'greatest rain accompanied wt thunder & hail yt ever was known, it lasted violently for about four hours' and destroyed the corn within a radius of two miles, s42, Maule to Milton, 14 August 1744; see also Ld Somerville to Milton, 14 and 20 August.

68. Papers in s29, 30, 399; also 435 (Milton's notebook of 1735 ff.); Stonefield MSS, SRO GD 14/10/3, f.252, Stonefield to Wm Smith, 8 September 1738.

69. s41, Wm Adam to Milton, 23 August 1744.

70. s42, Morris to Milton, 30 August 1744.

71. This remarkable manuscript was preserved by Lord Milton among his papers, where more than a century later it was discovered by Lady Caroline Fletcher and sent to the 8th Duke of Argyll with the suggestion that it 'might be of interest' to him.

CHAPTER II

1. The corners of Inveraray Castle happen to correspond very nearly with the cardinal points of the compass, but ever since the work was designed, the south-west front centred on the avenue has been known as the 'south' front, the south-east facing the loch as the 'east', and so on.

2. For the Eastbury plan see Colen Campbell *Vitruvius Britannicus*, III [1725], pl.16, and Laurence Whistler *The Imagination of Vanbrugh and his Fellow Artists* (London 1954) pp.156–60 and pls.72, 73. For Morris's completion of Eastbury, H. M. Colvin in *CL* (11 Feb. 1949) 317.

In general, cf. *Vitruvius Britannicus*, vols. I–III; James Gibbs *Book of Architecture* (1728); Sir John Summerson *Architecture in Britain 1530–1830* 4th edn (London 1963) chs. 18 and 20–22, and 'The Classical Country

House in 18th Century England' (Cantor Lectures) in *Journal of the Royal Society of Arts*, vol. cvii no. 5036 (July 1959); Christopher Hussey *English Country Houses, Early Georgian 1715–1760* (London, revised edn 1965); Kerry Downes *English Baroque Architecture* (London 1966); Bryan Little *James Gibbs* (London 1955).

The evidence for the Duke of Argyll's wishing Robert Adam to visit Eastbury is in a letter of Adam's dated 17 June 1758 (Penicuik MSS, SRO GD 18), quoted by John Fleming *Robert Adam and his Circle* (London 1962) p. 255.

3.   Mark Girouard discusses this group of houses, as well as Wollaton, in *Robert Smythson and the Architecture of the Elizabethan Era* (London 1966) pp. 64, 83–5, 88 ff., 93, 172; see also Summerson's *Architecture in Britain*, pp. 33–5.

4.   In this Lulworth resembles a design preserved in the library at Longleat, possibly by Smythson: Girouard, op. cit., pp. 86–7 and pls. 46, 47. It seems worth mentioning that Lulworth is within 25 miles of Eastbury, where Roger Morris was active for five years.

5.   H. M. Colvin and Maurice Craig *Architectural Drawings in the Library of Elton Hall by Sir John Vanbrugh and Sir Edward Lovett Pearce* (Edinburgh, Roxburghe Club 1964), no. 79, Pl. xxxvi (b).

6.   Ibid., nos. 138 and 139 (Pl. xxxv), and 120. Mention may here be made of Clearwell, near Coleford in Gloucestershire, whose discussion by Alistair Rowan (in *The Country Seat, Studies in the History of the British Country House, presented to Sir John Summerson on his 65th birthday*, ed. Howard Colvin and John Harris, London 1970, pp. 145–9) appeared when this book was already in the press. The architect of Clearwell is unknown, and there is no documentary evidence that it in any way influenced the style of Inveraray. Its owner was Thomas Wyndham, who died in 1753; in 1775 Francis Grose ascribed its date to 'about 40 years ago', so that in actual building (though not in original design) it apparently preceded Inveraray by about ten years.

In its earliest form Clearwell appears to have been basically an E-plan house, but with two massive square corner projections raised a further storey, giving the illusion of corner towers; its roof is castellated and its ground-floor windows are pointed Gothick. Although, therefore, it beats Inveraray to the post as a mansion built new with external Gothick features, it is not in the same line of descent; its plan is totally dissimilar and its dimensions are much smaller. Inveraray remains the pioneer 18th-century Gothick house of its size in Britain.

7.   Sold in Bute collection 23 May 1951, now in the possession of John Warren, Horsham; reproductions are in RIBA Prints and Drawings Library and in the National Monuments Record of Scotland. The attribution to Roger Morris was suggested by Mr John Harris.

8.   Inv/plan chest: 'Plans, Elevations and Sections of a House for the Duke of Argyll at Inveraray Designed in the Castle Stile, Defended with a Fossee and Covered Way, By his Graces most Obedient humble Servant Dugal Campbell', n.d.

9.   DUGAL CAMPBELL became Sub Engineer in the Civil Branch of the Office of Ordnance in 1734, and served as Engineer in Ordinary during the anti-Jacobite campaign in 1745–6, and in Flanders in 1746–7. In 1748 he became Subdirector, was promoted Major in 1757 and died at sea that September during the North American campaign. (Captain T. W. E. Conolly, R.E., *Roll of Officers of the Corps of Royal Engineers from 1660–1898*, Chatham 1898, Lists 2 & 3, no. 70; PRO, WO, 54, 207, p. 40; *Scots Magazine* and *Gentleman's Magazine* of November and October 1757. I am indebted to Dr Alistair Rowan for drawing my attention to these particulars.)

Campbell was also one of the engineers who surveyed the line of the new military road from Dumbarton to Inveraray in May 1744 (see ch. III, p. 122). It is noteworthy that Gibbs, Morris and Dugal Campbell all held posts with the Ordnance, where their careers were furthered by the 2nd Duke of Argyll; while earlier, Vanbrugh had been commissioned by the Duke of Marlborough to design Ordnance buildings.

10.   COLEN CAMPBELL (1676–1729), son of Donald Campbell of Boghole in Nairnshire, was related to the Campbells of Calder. His first house, Shawfield (1712), was appropriately designed for another Campbell, Daniel, the Glasgow MP. See G. L. M. Goodfellow in the *Architectural Review* (August 1966) 145–6 and *Burlington Magazine* (April 1969) 185–91; Howard E. Stutchbury *The Architecture of Colen Campbell* (Manchester 1967) pp. 77, 79, 80.

The 3rd Duke of Argyll's large collection of architectural books included, besides *Vitruvius Britannicus*, a Serlio (1663), a Palladio and Leoni's London edition of 1715, Scamozzi, Borromino, and Philibert de l'Orme; also William Kent's Inigo Jones designs (1727), Gibbs's *Book of Architecture*, Batty Langley, Robert Morris, Loggan's *Oxford* and

Cambridge, Britannia Illustrata (1707), Halfpenny's *Art of Sound Building* (1725), and many others. (*Catalogus Librorum ACDA* [*i.e.*, Archibaldi Campbell ducis Argatheliae], Glasgow 1758.)

The conjectural dates for Sudbrooke, some ten years earlier than hitherto supposed, are based partly on stylistic evidence, partly on payments made by the 2nd Duke to 'workmen' between 1712 and 1720 and one of £91 to James Gibbs in December 1719 (Coutts & Co., Ledgers ad loc.). The Duke purchased the Sudbrooke estate in 1714; he was out of favour at Court from 1716 to 1719, a period when he might be likely to devote himself to building and estate matters. Sudbrooke is discussed by Terence Friedman – to whose suggestions I am indebted – in his thesis *James Gibbs 1682–1754: the formation of his architectural style* (University of London 1971).

11.   s407A and MLB, Morris, Instructions of 6 November 1744.

12.   s403(1), Stonefield to Milton, 18 April 1745.

13.   MLB, Morris to Wm Adam, plan and instructions, 3 May 1745.

14.   Inv/1745.

15.   s44, Stonefield to Milton, 25 March and 12 June 1745; Sir James Fergusson *Argyll in the Forty Five* (London 1951) p.63. Arms were forbidden to the Scots even where their loyalty was not in question.

16.   s403(1), Stonefield to Milton, 29 July 1745; s44, John Campbell, Deputy Chamberlain, to Milton, 21 August 1745.

17.   Letters of Argyll 3, Maule, Milton and Stonefield in SF, SRO GD 14, and s44, 46, 403; s46, Morris to Milton, 1 August 1745; s46 and 403(2), Memorial Mr Adams about Roseneth, 7 August 1745.

18.   Letters of Sir John Cope, Maule, Milton and Stonefield in s44, 403 and SF, GD 14/26 ff.; s44, Col. John Campbell to Milton, 9 August 1745; Fergusson, op. cit., p. 14.

19.   SF, GD 14/27 & 28, Milton to Stonefield, 13 August 1745.

20.   John Heneage Jesse *Memoirs of the Pretenders and their Adherents* (London 1858) p.465, and Glendoick MSS, NLS 3036, f. 1.

21.   Jesse, op. cit., p.468, and NLS 3036, f.3; SF, GD 14.

22.   s46, Maule to Milton, 22 August et seq., 1745.

23.   Horace Walpole *Memoirs of the Reign of King George II*, ed. Lord Holland, I (London 1847) pp.275–8. See also HMC *Report on the Manuscripts of the Earl of Carlisle* (London 1897) p.200 (Robert Ord, MP, to Ld Carlisle, 29 August 1745); *A Series of Letters of the 1st Earl of Malmesbury, his family and friends, from 1745 to 1820*, ed. Earl of Malmesbury, I (London 1870) p.4 (Rev. Wm Harris to Mrs James Harris, 29 August 1745); William Coxe *Memoirs of the Administration of the Right Honourable Henry Pelham*, I (London 1829) pp.252 f.

24.   Fergusson, op. cit.

25.   So far it has not been possible to identify this character or her hostelry in Newcastle, where the Duke and his friends had always stayed whenever passing through the town. On 23 October 1747, John Maule reported to Lord Milton that she was 'broke', i.e., bankrupt (s66), and that is the last we hear of Mrs Hill.

26.   s46, Maule to Milton, 22–31 August, 5 September et seq., 1745.

27.   Ibid., 17 September 1745.

28.   Fergusson, op. cit., p.36; *The Cochrane Correspondence*, ed. James Dennistoun (Glasgow, Maitland Club, 1836) p.24 (Gen. John Campbell to Provost Cochrane, 25 October 1745); s46, Maule to Milton, 24 October 1745.

29.   SF, GD 14/42, Argyll 3 to Stonefield, 2 November 1745; s46, Maule to Milton, e.g. 29 October 1745.

30.   s46, Maule to Milton, 3 and 7 December 1745 et al.; see also, e.g., *Culloden Papers* (London 1815) and Yester MSS (NLS).

31.   s46, Maule to Milton, 10 December 1745.

32.   s44, letters of Stonefield to Milton; ibid., Peter Campbell to Milton, 22 December 1745; s46, Maule to Milton, 10 December 1745 et seq.; Fergusson, op. cit., pp.35, 40, 50, 58.

Stonefield was embarrassed by a warrant which the Duke, as Hereditary Sheriff of Argyll, had sent him, to arrest old Sir James Campbell of Achinbreck for trying to raise followers for the Prince among 'people of desperate circumstances'. Sir James was brought from his house on Loch Gare to the old castle at Inveraray, and Stonefield and his fellow deputy-Lieutenant and namesake, Archibald Campbell of Knockbuy, went through the aged gentleman's pockets for treasonable evidence. At the Duke's instructions Sir James was shortly taken under escort by sea to Dumbarton Castle, and was finally released as harmless on account of his age. (SF, GD 14/41, Argyll 3 to Stonefield, 31 October 1745; Fergusson, op. cit., p.43.)

33.   Inv/1745, 1746, accounts.

z

34. Campbell of Mamore MSS, NLS 3733/78, 3734/147, 3734/222, Gen. John Campbell to Argyll 3, 10 January 1746 et seq.; Fergusson, op. cit., p.139.

35. Mamore MSS, 3735; *The Lyon in Mourning*, ed. Henry Paton, I (Edinburgh 1896), p.162.

36. Mamore MSS, 3735/389 & 402, Stonefield to Gen. Campbell, 5 June, and to Col. John Campbell, 30 June 1746; S60, Archibald Campbell of Barnacarry to Stonefield, 15 July 1746.

37. S54, Maule to Milton, 20 March 1746; and for the trees, seeds, etc., idem, 18 February, 18 March 1746; SF, GD 14/76.

38. S54, Maule to Milton, 26 July and 9 September 1746.

39. MLB 9, Morris to Wm Adam, 19 June 1746.

40. SF, GD 14/99, Stonefield to Argyll 3, 13 July 1746. The letter is of some interest as showing the kind of task a working architect was expected to undertake. Stonefield added as an afterthought, 'There is one John Douglas at Edinr. next in Character to Mr Adams, he has built several houses but never so great a design as this–' For Douglas's work see Index of Architects and Craftsmen; and see Fleming, op.cit., pp.64–5, and 336.

41. S54, Maule to Milton, 26 July 1746.

42. S49, Wm Adam to Milton, 14 February 1746.

43. Mamore MSS, 3736/485, 486 & 508, Gen. Campbell to Argyll 3, ?20 September, Milton to Gen. Campbell, 20 September, Maule to Gen. Campbell, 14 October 1746; S54, Maule to Milton, 27 September 1746.

The library at Argyll House in Great Marlborough Street was 20 feet wide and 90 feet long, confirmed by plans now at Inveraray Castle. Lord Ilay added the room to his house in 1742, and the whole building was finally demolished in 1864 or 1865; the site is now covered by the London Palladium. (*Survey of London*, vol.31 (1963) pp.295–7; S38, Ilay to Milton, 8 July 1742.)

44. S54, Maule to Milton, 15 August 1746; Mamore MSS 3736/471, 486, 477, Milton to Gen. Campbell, 27 August and 20 September, Gen. Campbell to Argyll 3, 8 September 1746.

45. S404, Wm Adam, Memorial relating to the Foundation of the Castle of Inveraray; Mamore MSS 3736/508, Maule to Gen. Campbell, 14 October 1746; *Scots Magazine* (October 1746) 498. The adaptation is from Virgil, *Eclogue* i. 6: *O Meliboee, deus nobis haec otia fecit.* Doctor William King, Principal of St

Mary Hall, Oxford, severely condemned it as not only 'a very improper motto or inscription for a house' but 'very absurd; for when we borrow a verse from a Greek or Roman poet, and adapt it to a modern purpose . . . we should be careful to fit the words we insert to the measure of the verse. *Dux Cumbriae* will not stand in an hexameter . . . It is prose and poetry ill pieced.' (*Political and Literary Anecdotes of his own Times*, London 1818, p.84.)

46. S407, Memorial relating to the Deceast William Adam Architect his Journeys to Inveraray; S404 and copy with Morris's comments in MLB 12–19, Wm Adam, Memorial Relating to the Work at the Castle of Inverara, 29 September 1746.

47. MLB 10–11, Wm Adam to Argyll 3, 6 December 1746.

48. S407, Memorial relating to . . . William Adam, etc. (see n.46).

49. *New Statistical Account of Scotland*, VII (Edinburgh 1845) p.26. Similarly identified by, e.g., Robert Jameson *Mineralogy of the Scottish Isles*, I (Edinburgh 1800) pp.177–9.

50. MLB 10–11, Wm Adam to Argyll 3, 6 December 1746. Some shallow hollows beside a winding track among the plantations, with a few outcrops of rock, are all that is now visible of the old blue-stone quarry at Creggans, although until a few years ago remains of the quarriers' small house and stable still survived.

51. Bishop Richard Pococke *Tours in Scotland 1747, 1750, 1760*, Scottish History Society vol.I (Edinburgh 1887) p.67. Thomas Pennant *A Tour in Scotland, 1769* (London 1776) p.238. John Mawe *The Mineralogy of Derbyshire; with a description of the most interesting mines in the North of England, in Scotland, and in Wales* (London 1802) p.151.

52. MLB 20–3, Wm Adam to Morris, 7 March 1747, and sketch.

53. S46 and MLB 8 (copy), Morris to Milton, 1 August 1745. The original shows Morris's own individual spelling.

54. MLB 51, Memorial from William Adam, 1747; S407, Memorial relating to . . . William Adam, etc. (see n.46).

55. S63, Stonefield to Milton, 20 August 1747.

56. S66, Maule to Milton, 17 August and 3 September 1747; also S63, Stonefield to Milton, 20 and 29 August 1747. Walter Paterson remained head gardener at Inveraray until his death in 1770 (see ch.v).

57. s 63, Commr Colin Campbell to Milton, 1 October 1747. Colin Campbell, a Commissioner of Customs, was the younger brother of Sir James Campbell of Aberuchill (whose daughter Catherine in 1721 married George Drummond, six times Lord Provost of Edinburgh and a leading promoter of Edinburgh's New Town).

58. s 405, Argyll 3 to Milton, 10 September 1747; also Stonefield's of 29 August and Maule's of 3 September, loc. cit.

59. s 63, Robert Brisbane to—, 4 October 1747.

60. s 66, Maule to Milton, 3 September 1747.

61. IBR. In later years the captains of ships bringing timber cargoes were added to this number. The tide of new burgesses only slackened in the last years of the 3rd Duke's life; among the last of that period was John Wilkes, during his brief visit in 1758 (see p. 98).

62. s 63, Milton to Argyll 3, 29 August 1747; see also s 69, Adam to Milton, 3 November 1748.

63. s 63, Stonefield to Milton, 9 October 1747.

64. Ibid., 1 September 1747.

65. Ibid., 26 November 1747.

66. s 406(2), Milton to Maule, March 1748 (scroll letter); see also s 70A, Maule to Milton, 8 March 1748.

67. s 70A, Maule to Milton, 22 March 1748. ROBERT CAMPBELL OF ASKNISH (b. 1721), eldest son of Angus Campbell of Asknish, and later Sheriff of Argyll, was related on the female side to the Earl of Bute. On the 3rd Duke's death McMillan recommended him to Bute as 'one of those steady people, one may ride the water upon' (Bute MSS 700/1761, Alexr McMillan to Bute, 14 December 1761). In 1769 Asknish married Catherine, daughter of Mail Yates of Maghull, Lancashire; his son Humphrey Trafford Campbell was a great friend of the 5th Duke's family (see Ch.IX n.52 and Ch.X).

68. MLB 73–5, Wm Adam to Morris, 5 February 1748. s 406(1) & MLB 78–81, Contract to supply lime between William Adam and William Douglas, 29 January 1748. MLB 77, Contract between William Adam and John Innes, brickmaker of Canongate, 12 January 1748. Inv/1748, Wm Adam, Memorial concerning the works at Inveraray, March 1748.

69. s 69, Stonefield to Milton, 18 February 1748.

70. s 70A, Maule to Milton, 2 April 1748. Robert Lang, merchant, last Controller of Customs in Glasgow, died in 1766 (GT, 14 April 1766).

71. MLB 82, Morris to Wm Adam, 24 February 1748.

72. s 69, Wm Adam to Milton, 29 January 1748 (written in John Adam's hand).

73. RIBA collection L 12/2, notebook of John Adam, 1748; MLB 75, Wm Adam to Morris, 5 February 1748.

74. MLB 83, Morris to Wm Adam, 8 March 1748.

75. s 69, Milton to Argyll 3, July 1748 (scroll letter).

76. s 69, Robert Adam to Milton, 25 June 1748.

77. *Edinburgh Evening Courant* and *Caledonian Mercury*, 30 June 1748.

78. s 69, Harry Barclay to Milton, July 1748. HENRY BARCLAY (b. 1697) was the second son of Sir James Steuart of Goodtrees, Lord Advocate, and assumed the name and arms of John Barclay of Colairny, whose heiress Antonia he married in 1717. (Charles W. & Hubert F. Barclay *A History of the Barclay family*, privately printed, London 1924–34, II, pp. 339–40.)

79. s 69, Adam to Milton, 3 November 1748. Although at the time of William Adam's death John was the only son old enough to carry on the architectural practice, until comparatively recent years it was seriously supposed that he had little hand in it and merely managed the family's small estate. He was the only one of the four brothers to marry (July 1750); his wife was Jean Ramsay, daughter of a Kirkcaldy merchant, and from them are descended the present representatives of the Adam family.

80. s 71A & 73A, Fletcher to Milton, 8 November 1748 and 4 February 1749.

81. s 69, Milton to Argyll 3, July 1748 (scroll letter).

82. s 71A, Fletcher to Milton, 6 September 1748. JAMES STUART MACKENZIE (1719–1800) was the younger son of the 2nd Earl of Bute and Lady Anne Campbell (sister of the 2nd and 3rd Dukes of Argyll); he took the surname of his great-great-grandfather Sir George Mackenzie, whose property he inherited. Between 1741 and 1784 he represented various constituencies in Parliament, and in 1763, when his brother was Prime Minister, was made Keeper of the Privy Seal of Scotland. In 1749 he married his cousin Lady Elizabeth Campbell, second daughter of the 2nd Duke of Argyll; they had no children.

HENRY HOME (1696–1782), advocate, in 1752 became a Lord of Session with the title Lord Kames. He was a voluminous writer on law, author of *Elements of Criticism* (1763), and a keen agricultural improver. Among his friends was the blue-stocking Mrs Elizabeth Montagu.

83. s 69, Stonefield to Milton, 10 August 1748.

84. s 71A, Fletcher to Milton, 6 September 1748. ARTHUR DOBBS (1689–1765), an enthusiastic promoter of trade, was MP for Carrickfergus 1727–60, Engineer in Chief and Surveyor in Ireland 1730. After intensive study of the subject he made two unsuccessful voyages in search of a North-West passage to India and China, in 1741–2 and 1746. From 1754 he was Governor of N. Carolina.

85. Inv/Memorial Relating to the Works of Inveraray Castle, 8 September 1748 (Adam); Contract for supplying stones from Creggans Quarry, 12 September 1748, between John Adam and William Cowan, mason.

86. s 70A, Maule to Milton, 13 and 14 September 1748. Of the characters named among the season's visitors, JAMES TUDOR was one of the Commissioners of Customs; WILLIAM STEWART OF CASTLE STEWART was cousin to the 5th Earl of Galloway; DANIEL CAMPBELL OF SHAWFIELD (1670–1753), a son of Walter Campbell of Skipnish, had been MP of Glasgow at the time of the Malt Tax riots in 1725, and was owner of Shawfield, the Colen Campbell house wrecked by the mob; ALLAN RAMSAY, the portrait painter (1713–84), painted the Argyll brothers several times and appears to have been on a friendly personal footing with them.

By Succoth Maule probably means the Duke's lawyer ARCHIBALD CAMPBELL, WS (?1704–90), second son of William Campbell of Succoth and Under Keeper of the Privy Seal in Edinburgh (a post he had obtained at the recommendation of Lord Ilay and Lord Milton). He became Commissary of Glasgow in 1756, and Principal Clerk of Session 1770–85. He married Helen, daughter of John Wallace of Elderslie.

Of the two judges, SIR GILBERT ELLIOT OF MINTO, 2nd baronet (1693–1766), MP for Roxburghshire 1722–6, had been a Lord of Session, as Lord Minto, since 1726, and eventually (1763) became Lord Justice Clerk; CHARLES ERSKINE OF TINWALD (1680–1763) had been in 1707 the first Professor of Public Law at Edinburgh University, MP for Dumfriesshire 1722–41, succeeded Duncan Forbes as Lord Advocate 1737, and in 1744

became a Lord of Session as Lord Tinwald. He was Lord Milton's successor and Lord Minto's predecessor as Lord Justice Clerk, 1748–63.

87. *Edinburgh Evening Courant*, 22 September 1748.

88. John, Lord Campbell, *Lives of the Lord Chancellors and Keepers of the Great Seal of England*, v (London 1845–7) pp. 109–14. See Basil Williams *The Whig Supremacy, 1714–60* (Oxford 1962) pp. 282–3. A total of £152,237 was paid in compensation money to the dispossessed chiefs, of whom the Duke of Argyll, with £21,000, received by far the largest single share: of the others, the Earls of Eglintoun and Morton received £7000 each, the Duke of Queensberry £6000, the remainder considerably less. The total amount claimed was nearly four times that granted.

89. s 71A, Fletcher to Milton, 9 April and 15 September 1748.

90. For example, Walter Paterson was accused of collusion with Henry Roy, the Duke's smith, and James Gilmour, a mason and overseer, in selling drink in defiance of the Duke's prohibition. Paterson, in other respects still in high favour, maintained that he had been authorized, but the others 'promise to Quitt, whenever the Stock they had on hand & which they say was but a Small quantity . . . is consumed'. (Inv/Memorial concerning the Works at Inveraray, March 1748.)

Patrick Campbell's account of his escort of the Lovat trial witnesses is in his letters in s 405. For Henry Roy and James Gilmour, see Index of Architects and Craftsmen.

91. s 407(1), Memorial 2 October 1749; Inv/Chamberlains' commissions, 1748, in vol. on Argyll Estate Management, 18th century.

Three successive generations of Campbells of Danna (a branch of the Achinbreck Campbells) appear to have served as Sheriff Clerks of Argyll. John Campbell (1709–?70) also served as a Baillie of Inveraray. (AT, 5 July 1770) Donald Campbell of Airds (b. 1706) had been Morvern factor since 1732, with Archibald Campbell of Ballamore in charge of Mull, Coll and Tiree; the 1748 commissions appear to have been a reorganization.

92. s 70A, Maule to Milton, 27 September 1748.

93. s 69, Adam to Milton, 3 November 1748.

94. s 409, 410, 413. The Duke's movements in Scotland were generally reported in the *Edinburgh Evening Courant*, e.g. 10 August 1749, or 12 July 1750 (reporting that having arrived the previous evening at his lodging in Holyroodhouse, he was waited on by the

Provost and Magistrates, 'the Nobility, and other Persons of Distinction'). See also *Extracts from the records of the Burgh of Glasgow*, ed. Robert Renwick, VI (Glasgow 1911) 1739–59.

95. See Christopher Hussey on Inveraray Castle in *CL* (25 February 1944).

96. *Catalogus Librorum ACDA* (Glasgow 1758).

97. Coutts & Co., Ledger Accts of 3rd Duke of Argyll, Roger Morris and James Morris. At this time the Duke's banker was George Campbell, junior partner and successor of George Middleton (d. 1747), the Strand goldsmith who was banker to the Argyll Campbells for many years – as the present firm, Coutts & Company, still are.

98. Adam actually set off from Edinburgh on 13 December 1749, and was in London at least until the end of March 1750. s73A, Milton to Argyll 3, 12 December 1749; s74, Adam to Milton, 22 March 1750; s79, Fletcher to Milton, 9 December 1752.

99. s83, Fletcher to Milton, 28 March 1754, and enclosure, List of duties payable on deals from Norway (s412(3)); s85, Argyll 3 to Milton, 1 April 1756.

On 29 September 1756 the mason George Hunter, writing to beg the Duke's further interest in his son Robert Hunter (also a mason, then aged twenty-two), reminds him that Robert 'was two years at London with Mr Morris Your Grace's Architect through your Graces Intrest in the Drawing way and has been nigh two years in the Operative way since Under Your Grace' (s414(3)).

100. Penicuik MSS, SRO GD 18/4787, Robert Adam to Peggy Adam, 13 September 1755. The Adam sisters corresponded regularly with their brother while he was in Italy and passed on everything of personal and professional interest. The evidence for Robert Morris's death is an anonymous manuscript entry in a copy of his *Essay in Defence of Ancient Architecture* now in the RIBA library: 'The Author of this Book Died Novr ye 12th 1754 in ye fifty third year of His Age.' See John Fleming *Robert Adam and his Circle*, op. cit., p.341.

101. s412(1), Adam to Harry Barclay, 13 March 1754.

102. Penicuik MSS, GD 18/4745, Robert Adam to the Misses Adam, 21 September 1754.

103. Ibid. s426, receipt for £300 dated 25 September 1754, signed by John and James Adam.

104. Robert Adam loc. cit.

105. Drawings by Robert Adam in Adam collection at Blair Adam; drawings of Tombreac Dairy in Inveraray Plan Chest and Saltoun MSS.

106. s72, Major Thomas Cochrane to Maule, 21 March 1749.

107. Inv/Adam, Memorial Relating to the Works of Inveraray Castle, 14 September 1749; s407A, List of labourers employed [1749].

108. Adam Memorial of 14 September 1749, loc. cit.

109. s73A, Milton to Argyll 3, 12 December 1749, scroll letter.

110. MLB 28, and s407A, Adam, Memorandum relating to the Manner in which the Vents of Inveraray Castle are propos'd to be carried up, 11 September 1749. From the endorsement 'London' on the outside of this memorandum, John Adam probably took it with him to London to discuss with the Duke.

111. SF, SRO GD 14/30, Argyll 3 to [Stonefield], [?Aug.] 1745.

112. s44, Stonefield to Milton, 28 June 1745.

113. Inv/CA 1747 and Accts, 1750.

114. Adam Memorial of 14 September 1749, loc. cit.

115. s408(2), Geo. Hunter to Milton, 13 February 1750; s74, Knockbuy to Milton, 5 June 1750; Inv/Quarries.

116. s408(2), Adam to Milton, 5 September 1750; s74, Milton to Argyll 3, December 1750, scroll letter; s409(2), 1751 Inveraray accts (note of 12 October 1750: 'The overseer of Masson wages raised').

117. Inv/AEM, Instructions to Chamberlain, 23 October 1750; s408(2), Knockbuy to Milton, 11 March 1750; s78, Memorial relating to the Works of Inveraray Castle, 1751.

118. s409(2), Memorandum for My Lord Milton about Inveraray Castle 1751.

119. s409(2), Adam, Note of Timbers necessary for the Rooff & Joisting of Inveraray Castle, 10 October 1751, and superseded scantling dated 4 October 1751, by George Haswell.

120. s425, Whim accts; s72, Major Thomas Cochrane to Milton, 21 January 1749.

121. s78, Adam to Milton, 17 March 1752; s427, Milton, Inveraray Memos., 1753; s81, Fletcher to Milton, 27 January 1753.

In 1754 Graham also carried out plumbing repairs at Caroline Park (Buccleuch MSS, SRO GD 224/168). Graham, incidentally, had been a witness at the baptism of Robert Mylne's younger brother William at Edinburgh in February 1734 (SRO EBapR).

122. Strontian mines had been worked since at least the early 18th century and were now under contract to Alexander Telfer & Co. of Edinburgh. The mine overseers shipped the lead pigs to Campbeltown, where the Duke's factor had them transferred to another ship for delivery to Inveraray. A bar of lead weighed 8 stone, the price per stone varying between 2s 2d and 2s 5d; at London or Leith it was 2s 6d. The first Inveraray order was for 7000 bars. (Relevant papers in s411(1): Graham's memorandum on quantity required, orders from Edward Lothian to mines overseer John Paton, December 1752f., instructions for delivery, and receipts.) The mines, after changing hands several times, closed in the 19th century. Their managers included Captain Edward Burt, author of *Letters from a Gentleman in the North of Scotland* (London 1815), and the Quaker, Francis Place. A detailed list of the industrial buildings at Strontian set up by the York Buildings Company as they appeared in 1733 is given on a map of that date by Lieut. Alexander Bruce, entitled 'A Plan of Loch Sunart &c; become Famous by the Greatest National Improvement this Age has Produced', bound up with Sir Alexander Murray of Stanhope's *The True Interest of Great Britain, Ireland, and our Plantations* (London 1740).

123. Ardmaddy had once been occupied by Neil Campbell, brother to the 9th Earl of Argyll. COLIN CAMPBELL OF CARWHIN (1704–72), of a cadet branch of the Breadalbane Campbells, had served as a volunteer in the '45 and General Campbell thought him 'a very sencible pretty fellow'. In 1758 he married Elizabeth Campbell, Stonefield's daughter, and their eldest son succeeded to the earldom of Breadalbane. For a highly coloured anecdote on Carwhin's late marriage in order to secure the Breadalbane line, see Burke's *Vicissitudes of Families*, II (London 1869) pp. 38ff.

124. In that year (1845) Lord Breadalbane was providing slate without charge for the building of Free Churches throughout Scotland. The Argyll Campbells had retained the right of winning slates from Easdale since a contract signed in 1665 between the 9th Earl, his brother Lord Neil Campbell, and the then Earl of Breadalbane; in 1734, by a charter of resignation of the estate of Nether Lorne to Breadalbane, the 2nd Duke of Argyll still reserved this right to his family (copies in s412(2)).
See the various *Statistical Accounts of Scotland*: 1795, XIV, pp. 161–2; 1845, VII, Argyll, pp. 77–8; 1961, vol. 'Argyll', pp. 204–5;

also Robert Jameson *Mineralogy of the Scottish Isles*, I (Edinburgh 1800) pp. 194–6. Numerous travellers, including Pennant, describe the slate workings.

125. Inv/KJ 1752–6, entries on slate orders, 12 January, 2 & 22 February, 22 June and 3 August 1753. An even larger order had been made through Carwhin in December 1751, for slates for roofing the first houses built in Inveraray's new town–the cottages in the Fisherland meadow known as the Gallowgate (see ch.IV) (s78, John Campbell to Milton, 9 July 1752).

126. s410(3), Adam, Note of Stones necessary for the two Great Stairs of Inveraray Castle, 29 September 1752; Inv/1752.

127. s410(3), Carwhin to Milton, 6 November 1752; Inv/Journal (Cash Book) 1752–4; s78, James Campbell to Milton, 3 December 1752; s80, Knockbuy to Milton, 29 December 1753.

128. s78A, Lady Milton to Milton, 9 August 1752; s79, letters of Fletcher to Milton; s410(1), papers on *Princess Augusta* yacht and accts of travelling expenses.

129. s78A, Lady Milton to Milton, 9 August 1752; IBR ad loc.

130. s79, Alexander Lind to Milton, 22 September 1752.

131. Lady Milton to Milton. loc.cit.; s79, Stuart Mackenzie to Milton, 17 October 1752; s78, Corbyn Morris to Lady Milton, 26 September 1752.

132. SRO, Justiciary Minute Books, Western Circuit, ad loc.; s78, Milton to Gwyn Vaughan, 24 September and to Lord [Breadalbane], 30 September 1752 (scroll letters). Modern accounts of the trial are given by Sir James Fergusson in *The White Hind* (London 1963) pp. 133–79, who holds that it was conducted in strict probity; and Sir William MacArthur in the *The Appin Murder* (London 1960), who maintains that Stewart was condemned unjustly.

133. Milton to Vaughan. loc.cit. It was long supposed that the scene of the trial was the present 'Old Town House', but the foundation of that building was not laid until 1755, and in 1752 the new town of Inveraray virtually did not exist (see ch.IV).

134. s410(3), 410(2), Douglas to Milton, 28 October 1752, and his accounts for lime supplied to November 1752, attested by Adam. Douglas's running costs had risen considerably over the five years of his managing the lime kilns, due to an increase in the cost of freights, and also in the price of coals following the closure of several Clyde-side mines.

135. s 78, John Campbell, Deputy Chamberlain, to Fletcher, 2 February 1752.

136. Inv/Petition to Duke of Argyll by 15 masons, 12 September 1753; s 72A, Hunter to Adam, 14 March 1752; s 78, Asknish to Milton, 15 March, and Adam to Milton, March 1752.

137. s 78, Knockbuy to Milton, 25 March 1752; Inv/C, Asknish to Archibald Campbell, Chamberlain of Kintyre, 12 July 1752.

138. Inv/Journal (Cash Book) 1750–2; s 410, abstract of General Account, 1752.

139. s 411(1), Accts 1753; s 412(1) & (2), Accts 1754; Inv/Q. In quoting these figures shillings and pence have been ignored.

140. s 82 and 412(2), Asknish to Milton, 9 April and 28 November 1754; also s 80, Adam to Milton, 31 May 1753.

141. s 413(2), Memorandum 15 November 1755.

142. s 82, Argyll 3 to Milton, 21 March 1754.

143. s 82, Argyll to Milton, 7 February 1754. See also his letter of 28 February, loc. cit., and s 83, Fletcher to Milton, 23 February 1754.

144. s 413(1), comparative weekly accounts February/March 1755 and 1756; s 414(3), John Campbell, Dep. Chamberlain, to Asknish, 26 February 1756. The quotation is from *Aeneid* i. 118.

145. John Campbell to Asknish, loc. cit.

146. s 415, John Campbell to Asknish, 7 March 1756.

147. s 415, Asknish to Milton, 23 March 1756. The information about digging the fosse is contained in John Campbell's letter of 7 March, loc. cit. 'They' are the many tenants unable or reluctant to pay their annual rents to the Duke's factors, and 'Criefe' refers to the great Perthshire cattle fair or tryst (which in 1770 was removed to Falkirk).

148. Asknish to Milton, loc. cit.

149. s 414(3), weekly accounts, March/May 1756; s 415, letters of Asknish to Milton, 4–15 April 1756. Airds, who happened to have been the landlord of James Stewart of the Glen, had given evidence at the Appin Murder trial in September 1752. For the Argyll Furnace Company see ch. III, p. 136 and n. 42.

150. s 414(2), Instructions of 6 November 1756.

151. s 85, Alexr Forrester to Milton, 27 November 1756.

152. Inv/KJ 1752–6, 8 November 1756.

153. Robert Bathgate and his brother Andrew have a rather unhappy history at Inveraray. Robert (1718–58), who was trusting and honest, was backed by a 'Duke's party' including Patrick Campbell and John Richardson, who in 1755 advised Lord Milton to warn him 'not to be led by the nose & [be] less communicative'. He had two serious illnesses, one at home at Saltoun where he was buying sheep for the Duke, another at Inveraray, 'a bloody flux ane Epidemical desease in this Country and fatal to numbers'. But having narrowly escaped death he recovered, and the same Christmas in Edinburgh married George Hunter's daughter Betty. They settled in one of the Duke's new Gallowgate cottages adjoining the new town site at Inveraray, but Robert again fell ill, this time fatally, and died on 24 August 1758 within a fortnight of his fortieth birthday, leaving a young family.

His brother Andrew, who then came to take over his job, suffered even worse persecution from an upper-servants' clique. False complaints were lodged by the contractor for the Garden Bridge, David Frew, while Mrs Robinson the housekeeper, Alexander Cumming the clock-maker, and George Haswell the chief wright, ganged up against him. After the Duke's death in 1761 Andrew, with 'no frend in this place', appealed to Lord Milton, who had recommended him to the post, to find him a new one.

With this sad appeal the Bathgate brothers pass from the scene of Inveraray; but Andrew was not overlooked by Lord Milton, and was re-employed by him as a farm overseer at Saltoun. He died in 1782 at the age of sixty-six, and was buried in Easter Saltoun churchyard, where in 1807 his children erected a tombstone to his memory. (s 101; other accounts of the brothers' misfortunes, and the jealousy of fellow-servants, in s 413 ff.; Saltoun parish registers, SRO 419/1; stone in Easter Saltoun churchyard.)

154. Inv/KJ 1752–6, 2 February and 15 March 1753; s 411(1), report by Knockbuy, Hunter and Douglas, 1 February 1753, Milton to John Campbell, Chamberlain, 20 February 1753.

155. Inv/KJ 22 February 1753; s 81 and 412(2), Milton to Walter Paterson, 12 March 1753.

156. s 411(1), Asknish to Milton, 24 March 1753; s 81, John Paterson to Milton, 16 May 1753.

157. s 412(1), Knockbuy to Argyll 3, 10 March 1754.

158. s411(1), Adam, Memorial relating to the carrying on the Works of Inveraray Castle, 27 October 1753.

159. s412(1), Knockbuy to Argyll 3, 23 May 1754.

160. s84, Colin Campbell, Rosneath, to Milton, 11 June 1755; s84A, Fletcher to Milton, 10 June 1753.

161. s84A, Hunter to Milton, 12 May 1755; s84, Asknish to Milton, [?Sept.] 1755; s414(3), Hunter memorial to Argyll 3, 29 September 1756.

162. s413(2), John Paterson, account, 20 September 1755; s84A, John Paterson to Robert Brisbane, 28 August 1753; s414(3), Haswell, Note of necessaries for the Castle, 31 October 1756.

163. s85, Argyll 3 to Milton, 1 April 1756.

164. s415, Proposal by John Wardrop, 1756; s414(3), Hunter Memorial to Argyll 3, 29 September 1756, orders by Asknish, 10 November 1756; Inv/K J, 1756.

165. s84A, Hunter to Milton, 9 June 1755. The door referred to is the present front door of the castle, which then led directly into the long gallery on the north side.

166. s86, Hunter to Milton, 18 June 1756. The Roger Morris model of the castle was not involved in the site office fire, having been removed to the castle in 1753. (s411(1), Milton, Inveraray Memos. 1753.)

ROBERT MACKELL the millwright was possibly connected with the Meikle family of millwrights at Saltoun, a member of which may have removed to the Glasgow area and adopted a different spelling of the name. In letters and accounts his name appears as Meikle, Mickle, Mackle, Muckle, etc.; he himself spells his own name Mackell, and in Glasgow Council minutes it appears as McKell. The Duke of Argyll always refers to him as Meikle, no doubt through association with the Saltoun family.

James Meikle was the East Lothian millwright who in 1710 built the first barley mill in Scotland for Lord Milton's uncle, Andrew Fletcher of Saltoun; Meikle also went to Holland in 1715 to study milling machinery, in order to use his skills at Saltoun for Mrs Henry Fletcher (Lord Milton's mother). The earliest mention in the Saltoun MSS is to 'Mr McKal' and his brother in 1712 (s3), with references to work in Edinburgh and contracts in Glasgow. (Possibly the brother removed to Glasgow, and may have been Robert's father.) James Meikle was father to Andrew (1719–1811), inventor of the thrashing machine, who in the 1760s was associated with

Robert Mackell (see below).

Robert Mackell was established in Glasgow as a 'stranger millwright' at least by 1734, when he made a model for the city of an engine for slitting and chipping iron, and for rolling iron hoops. In 1744 the Duke of Argyll summoned him to Rosneath and Inveraray to make models of the machine mills he intended to set up when he launched new industries in the town (see ch.IV). Mackell later made and installed the milling machinery for the Whim and Rosneath (1749), and for Carlundon in Inveraray (1749–51). It may have been Mackell who made the copy of 'Marshal Saxe's House' for the Duke (see p.98 and n.208).

Mackell's later activities included a survey of the River Carron for Lord Napier in 1762, a year before John Smeaton's survey (1763–4) to determine a route for a Forth/Clyde canal; Mackell subsequently recommended cheaper alternatives to Smeaton's route. He and Andrew Meikle in 1768 patented a machine for dressing and cleaning grain, and Mackell is recorded during the 1770s as working on a scheme for deepening the River Clyde, and advising on an addition to old Glasgow Bridge.

I am indebted to Mr Richard Dell, City Archivist of Glasgow, for information on Mackell from Glasgow Corporation Minutes. For other information see s3, 4, 73, 343; W.C.Mackenzie *Andrew Fletcher of Saltoun, his life and times* (Edinburgh 1935) p.313; Henry Hamilton *An Economic History of Scotland in the 18th Century* (Oxford 1963) p.234; *Scots Magazine* xxix (1767) 129; Robert Mackell and James Watt *An account of the navigable canal proposed to be cut from the River Clyde to the River Carron, as surveyed by* (etc.) (London 1767); Patent Office, British Patent No. 896 (1768). For Andrew Meikle see entry in *DNB*. (See Index of Architects and Craftsmen.)

167. Inv/Inveraray Estate 1756–60 (accts); John Adam file, account for carving 'Obelisques upon the ends of the Bridges at the Castle of Inveraray', 31 October 1757. The total paid Templeton to that date was £33 5s 6d; a further £15 11s 3d was paid him in 1758 (Inv. Est. 1756–60). Adam made out his account in the name of Templeman, but elsewhere the name appears as Templeton and the carver himself signs 'Templetown'.

168. s414(3), Haswell, Notes of necessaries wanted for Castle, 30 September and 31 October 1756, and Memo. of 30 October 1756; Asknish, orders of 10 November 1756.

169. s87, Commissary James Campbell to Milton, 18 January and 5 March 1757; s88, Asknish and Walter Paterson to Milton, April 1757.

170. s416(3), [Adam, with Duke of Argyll's signature 7 November], Instructions by His Grace The Duke of Argyll for carrying on the several Branches of the Work at Inveraray Castle, 31 October 1757.

171. s416(3), G[eorge] H[unter?] to Asknish, Memorial on casemates, 1757.

172. s414(3), Haswell, Note of necessaries, etc., 31 October 1756, and John Graham, account, March 1756. For the comparable situation in English houses of that date see Laurence Wright *Clean and Decent* (London 1960) pp.103–4.

173. Wright, loc.cit. ALEXANDER CUMMING (?1732–1814), apparently the son of an Inverness-shire innkeeper, was discovered in 1750 by Sir Robert Gordon, who, impressed by his mechanical ingenuity and instinct for mathematics (self-taught), recommended him to Lord Milton. Milton kept him on board wages while, presumably, he was given some education, and by 1752 he was set up in Inveraray as a watch-maker. s75, Sir Robert Gordon to Milton, 2 July 1750; s409(3), 410(1), 426, receipts; IBR 5 October 1752 (burgesses admitted); and see Mary Cosh 'Clockmaker Extraordinary' in *CL* (12 June 1969). (See also p.106 and n.208, and Index of Architects and Craftsmen.)

The poet James Maxwell (see ch. VI, n.40), in describing with characteristic felicity the castle's 'large capacious vaults, unknown the number,/All arch'd above, for useful stores and lumber,' refers to the constant natural supply of water which served the water closets:

And there an aqueduct for ever springs,
Which to each room convenient water brings.

174. s87, Cumming to Milton, 28 August 1757, also 26 May 1757.

175. s74, Argyll 3 to Milton, 12 August 1750.

176. s84A, Fletcher to Milton, 3 May 1755 ('a four wheeld post Chaise').

177. s86A, ibid., 12 November (and 16 November) 1756; s84A, Lady Milton to Milton, 28 August 1755.

178. s84A, Fletcher to Milton, 7 August 1755. Inveraray Baptism Register, SRO, has the following entry:

'1754. A native of the East Indies, and servant to His Grace the Duke of Argyll, after having been instructed in the principles of Religion and particularly of the nature and end of baptism, and having made a publick profession of the faith was baptised by Mr Alexander Campbell, minister of Inveraray, this 23rd day of October 1754 years by the name of *William Campbell* before the witnesses Mr Lauchlan Campbell, minister of Ardnamurchan, Mr John Fallowsdale, Master of the Grammar School at Inveraray, Mr Dorret, Mr Cummin, John Morgan and [Angus] Sinclair servants to the Duke of Argyll.'

179. These were the requirements demanded for Dorret's successor, when he left the Duke's employment in the summer of 1755: s84A, Fletcher to Lady Milton, 8 May 1755. See also IBR, 17 September 1744 (burgesses admitted); s75, Fletcher to Milton, 9 September 1750; *A General Map of Scotland, etc.*, by James Dorret, Land Surveyor, Published by Act of Parliament April 1750 (BM Map Room, King's Collection XLVIII, 26); *Memoir relative to the construction of the Map of Scotland published by Aaron Arrowsmith, in the year 1807* (London [1809]) quoted in *Thomson's Atlas of Scotland* (Edinburgh 1832) Introd. p.iv. I am grateful to Mr D.G.Moir, Secretary of the Royal Scottish Geographical Society, for drawing my attention to the Arrowsmith reference.

180. s416(3), Commissary James Campbell to Argyll 3, 24 August 1757: 'My Son Archy Is about Compleating the Landscape of the Policy here, Your Grace Desired him to make out. . .' Dan Paterson had already produced, in 1756, a plan of the estate showing the stance of the new town (including Richardson's house), the Gallowgate, and a blank indicating the old town (see fig.54).

ARCHIBALD CAMPBELL (1739–91), Commissary Campbell's second son, became MP for the Stirling burghs in 1774 and again in 1789. Entering the army he served in India and America, and became Governor of Madras, a lieutenant-colonel, and (1785) a knight. He married in 1779 Allan Ramsay's daughter Amelia. He left his estate to his elder brother, Sir James Campbell, and is buried in Westminster Abbey. (*DNB*; Alastair Smart *The Life and Art of Allan Ramsay*, London 1952, pp.167, 219.)

DANIEL PATERSON (1739–1825) became an ensign in the 30th Foot in 1765 and eventually (1798), Lieutenant-Colonel. He was many years assistant to the QMG, and in 1812 was appointed Lieutenant Governor of Quebec; for some years before his death he lived in retirement near Windsor. (*DNB*)

Paterson's *New and Accurate Description of all the Direct and Principal Cross-Roads in Great Britain* (London 1771) included a list of places, routes from London, and judges' circuits; and *A Travelling Dictionary* (London 1772), tables of distances between the principal towns and cities in Great Britain.

181. s88A, Fletcher to Milton, 1 January and 3 May 1757; also s86A, 23 December 1756. Unlicenced trafficking in liquor (in England especially gin, in Scotland whisky) had long been a scandal which various forms of taxation and prohibition were unable to prevent, until public outcry in 1751 had resulted in an effective Act of Parliament against illicit sales. Enforcement of Acts always took longer to reach the Highlands.

The date of Walter Paterson's death is deducible from the Inveraray Window Tax Returns (SRO), vol.7, Argyll North District, 1769 and 1770.

182. s88A, Fletcher to Milton, 2 June 1757; s417(1), anon. letter to Argyll 3, January 1757, minutes of subsequent inquiry, 8–9 June 1757, and report of Archibald Campbell, WS, and Colin Campbell, Baillie of Rosneath, 30 June 1757. s418(1), Milton to Argyll 3, January 1758, scroll letter.

183. s88A, Fletcher to Milton, 6 August 1757, also 2 June 1757; s417(1), Argyll 3 to Milton, 11 June 1757.

184. Inv/Particular Papers, Commissions of Chamberlainry of Dugald McTavish of Dunardry, James Campbell, Commissary of the Isles, and Colin Campbell, Baillie of Rosneath, 11 November 1757.

185. Saltoun Plan Chest, plans and elevations of Rosneath Castle.

186. s86A, Fletcher to Lady Milton, 26 June 1756.

187. s88A, Fletcher to Milton, 24 May and 14 June 1757, and to Lady Milton, 11 August 1757; Lady Milton to Milton, from Rosneath, [?11], 18 and 24 September 1757; Molly Fletcher to Milton, from Rosneath, [September] 1757. s87, Colin Campbell, Baillie of Rosneath, to Lady Milton, 22 June 1757.

188. s88A, Lady Milton to Milton, September 1757; Molly Fletcher to Milton, 17 September 1757; s87, Sir James Colquhoun of Luss to Milton, 10 November 1757; *Edinburgh Evening Courant* (November 1757).

189. s420(3), payment of £50 to John Adam on account for Philip Robertson for plastering at Inveraray Castle, 14 March 1760. In 1758 the plasterers and their labourers were paid £326 4s 10d, and in 1759 £56 15s 11½d (s418(1), Asknish's accounts November 1757–November 1758, and s419(1), ibid. November 1758–November 1759).

190. s347, Estimate of Plaistring and Stuccowork To his Grace The Duke of Argyle . . . By Thos Clayton, Hamilton, 20 September 1756. Clayton's charges range from plain stucco ceilings at 6d a yard and plain cornices and mouldings at 6d a foot, to Ionic cornices (22d) and Corinthian (26d), and 'Ornaments' between 2s 6d and 5s, 'but is always Determined by Drawings'.

191. s416(3), Instructions by His Grace The Duke of Argyll for carrying on the several Branches of the Work at Inveraray Castle, 31 October 1757; Inv/C, Memorial relating to the Works Carrying on by His Grace the Duke of Argyll at Inveraray, 29 June 1761, item 8; Inv/Ledger 1754, account of John and James Adam, Architects, December 1757–October 1758. This is the first account (October 1758) to be presented in the names of John and James Adam (see n.192). James is known to have visited Inveraray at least in 1755 and 1756, and his name has been associated with the Garden Bridge (see ch. III, fig. 46 and n.47) (Penicuik MSS, SRO GD 18/4791 and 4826, Robert Adam to Betty Adam, 8 November 1755, and to James Adam, 4 December 1756).

The 'enrichment' of hall and chief rooms did not long survive, for they were altered for the 5th Duke by Robert Mylne (see ch.VI). The chimney-pieces referred to were then removed to Rosneath.

192. S416(3), John, Robert and James Adam's account for glass, 18 September 1757 (paid by Ld Milton at Brunstane 22 March 1758); account of John and James Adam, October 1758, loc. cit. (n.191); s417(1), Argyll 3 to Milton, 11 June 1757.

193. s418(1) and Inv/Ledger 1754, account of Robert Dewar, glazier, written and attested by John Adam, 1758; s416(3), John Adam, Estimate of One of the Large Sash Windows in the Middle Tower upon the top of the Castle of Inveraray, 31 October 1757; s418(3), John Paterson to Adam, 6 July 1758, his account 10 April 1758, and note of his time at Inveraray 1749–1757.

194. s90A, Fletcher to Milton, 22 February, 20 May, 22 June 1758; s418(1), Argyll 3 to Milton, 15 July 1758; s418(3), Haswell, note of timber required for middle tower, 12 October, and Memo. of 28 October 1758.

195. s419(2) and Inv/Inv. Est. 1756–60, and John Adam file: receipts of George Jamieson for November 1758–November 1759. Evidence for the son's work appears in a memorandum by Lord Milton on Asknish's Account (Nov. 1759): 'Carver has got to Acco. £36 10s. ?if his son is paid besides' (s419(1)).

196. s418(3), Adam to Milton, 1 November 1758.

197. s419(1), Adam to Argyll 3, 13 February 1759; s92, Hunter to Milton, 6 February 1759; s92A, Fletcher to Milton, and s91, Argyll to Milton, both of 10 March 1759; s93, Asknish to Milton, 14 April 1760.

According to the factor Dunardry the recipe for the paste was 'two thirds of White Lead and oyl and one third Smithy Culm'. George Hunter and John Brown, contractor for the Aray Bridge, both praised its efficacy. (s419(1), Dunardry to ?Adam, [Feb. 1759]). On 5 September a certain 'J.S.' submitted to Lord Milton a recipe of his own invention 'for curing the defects in Buildings by Rain or Damps', a liquid which he 'is positive will Cure the Complaints of the House of Inveraray', and better still, 'May be vastly Usefull Many ways such as leying over Window's Doors, Gaits, Rails, and every other woods Expos'd to Air & Raines', and if used in the making of partitions etc. 'will Effectually prevent their Oppenning or Sherinking afterwards & keep out air As no watter hote or Cold will lous or Carrie it off. And adhairs so Closs to the wood that the whole is as one solied pice. . .' (s347). Unfortunately his ingredients are not given, which suggests that Lord Milton did not follow up the offer. John Aitken, a mason who had worked for Lord Milton, 'Hearing of the Misfortune of the Grand House of Inverera', also offered advice (September 1759) on 'a cement so as to make the Joynts of the Ashler Impregnable against any Wethear frost not Excepted . . . This is a Liquod Composition and by opning the Joynts and beds Dove taill ways . . . and powring in the composte it hardnes in a Minute and Makes all as one Intire stone which I will adventure on the highest penalty to last for Many Centurys . . . at no Great Cost . . . P.S. a fool may give wise men a Counsel at Chance.' (s91).

198. s92A, Fletcher to Milton, 31 May 1759.

199. Penicuik MSS, SRO GD 18/4848, Robert Adam to James Adam, 17 June 1758. On 11 August he writes, 'The Duke . . . gave me a £20 note to give to my Italian. But I who am more needy than he gave him £5.5 of it & with the Rest paid £6 for the Frame & £3 for the Cloath, Colours &cᵃ & Twenty Shillings for a Frame to his small view of it', thus keeping 'near £5' for himself. 'Brunias is as Happy as a Prince & I have the Consolation to think my Time has not been thrown away in vain.' (Ibid.)

200. Atholl MSS, 73, I, Memo. book A 22: 25 and 30 September 1755.

201. *Autobiography of Dr Alexander Carlyle*, ch.VIII. JOHN HOME (1722–1808) had been minister at Athelstaneford, Haddingtonshire, since 1746, but in 1757 diplomatically resigned his living after his play *Douglas* was successfully repeated in London, where he had the Duke of Argyll's patronage. Home was a friend of Alexander Carlyle's, and was introduced to the Duke by Lord Milton.

202. *Autobiography of Dr Alexander Carlyle*, pp.397ff.; s90A, Lady Milton to Milton, from Rosneath, 13 September 1758; s89, Harry Barclay to Milton, 7 and 17 October 1758, Adam to Milton, 14 October 1758.

203. s92A, letters of Lady Milton and Molly Fletcher to Milton, 21–30 September 1759. Early in October 1759, Adam Smith, then thirty-six and Professor of Moral Philosophy at Glasgow University, spent an expensive two days at the Inveraray inn with the Hon. Thomas Fitzmaurice (brother to Lord Shelburne), vainly awaiting the Duke's arrival. In the end, disappointed, they had to leave without seeing him. Adam Smith was a younger cousin of the 2nd Duke's private secretary, William Smith. (Robert Scott *Adam Smith as Student and Professor*, Glasgow 1937.)

204. Horace Bleackley *The Story of a Beautiful Duchess* (London 1908); *Letters of Horace Walpole*, ed. Mrs Paget Toynbee (Oxford 1903–5) in vols.III and IV (XX, XXI of *The Yale Edition of Horace Walpole's Correspondence*, ed. W.S.Lewis, Oxford 1939ff.). Letters on the marriage settlement between the Duchess of Hamilton and Colonel John Campbell are in s419(1).

205. Sir William Burrell MS *Travels in Scotland* [1758], NLS 2911, pp.21 ff. WILLIAM BURRELL (1732–96), second son of Peter Burrell of Langley Park, Beckenham, Kent, studied law at St John's College, Cambridge and was called to the bar in 1760. He was a keen antiquarian, and elected an FRS. From 1768–74 he was MP for Haslemere, and in 1793 married Sophia, daughter of Sir Charles Raymond, to whose title he succeeded as 2nd baronet. (Burke *Peerage*.)

206. IBR. Their servants, William Beal and John Swan, were admitted burgess at the same time.

207. This tunnel, on the east side of the fosse, was carried a short distance, but Burrell was evidently anticipating, for there is no evidence that it was ever completed.

208. s86A, Fletcher to Milton, 21 October 1756; s414(3), Haswell, Note of necessaries for the castle, 31 October 1756. The original 'Marshal Saxe's travelling house' was in existence at least until 1780, when it was in

Hyde Park while the army was stationed there during the Gordon Riots. (Paul Sandby *The Virtuosi's Museum*, London 1778f., pl.94.)

In 1755 Lord Milton's second son, Henry, wrote to his sister from his regimental headquarters in Waterford, asking her to write to 'the young Lad [Cumming] . . . That makes Clocks & Watches for the Duke at Inverara; To make me a Moddel of Marshal Sax's House, By the scale of a Foot to an Inch, being 9 inches long'. The finished model was to be sent to Edinburgh for collection by Sergeant Grant, then recruiting in the Highlands. Henry Fletcher added, 'That Invention is not known here; but I believe their will be severall, after the moddle arrives.' (s84A, Capt. Henry Fletcher to Mally Fletcher, 12 March 1755.)

209.   Horace Bleackley *Life of John Wilkes* (London 1917) pp.47–8. Nearly twenty years later Wilkes related to Dr Johnson how he had joked with the Duke's clansmen that he was lucky to have pleased them, otherwise 'there is not a Campbell among you but would have been ready to bring John Wilkes's head to him in a charger. It would have been only "Off with his head! so much for *Aylesbury*".' (Boswell's *Life of Johnson*, ed. G.B. Hill, III, Oxford 1887, p. 75.) Wilkes too was admitted a burgess of Inveraray, on 5 October 1758, with his servant Mathew Wharam (IBR).

210.   *Autobiography of Dr Alexander Carlyle*, pp.344–5.

211.   Ibid., pp.397ff. ALEXANDER MCMILLAN of DUNMORE, WS ('Sandie M'Millan'), was Deputy-Keeper of the Signet 1726–42 and 1746–70, and a commissioner for the management of Lord Bute's estates. It was in McMillan's office that Asknish had worked as a junior before becoming the Duke's accountant. As a drinking companion McMillan was always popular, being (says Carlyle) 'loud and joyful, and made the wine flow like Bacchus himself'. (*The Society of Writers to H.M. Signet*, Edinburgh 1936, adloc.; Carlyle, op.cit., ch. XIII.)

212.   s418(1), Milton to Argyll 3, 13 May 1758, scroll letter; s89, Asknish to Milton, 4 June 1758; IBR, ad loc.

213.   John Campbell (of Stonefield) to Charles Townshend, 25 September 1759, in *Letters of Lady Mary Coke*, II (privately printed, Edinburgh 1889) p. 84, n.2. See also s91, idem to Milton, 25 August 1759 and Asknish to Milton, 19 and 23 August 1759; s92A, Fletcher to Milton, 16 August 1759. JOHN CAMPBELL, later Lord Stonefield (?1729–1801), Stonefield's eldest son, was at this time

Sheriff of Forfar; in 1763 he became a Lord of Session. In 1750 he had married Lady Grace Stuart, daughter to Lord Bute, and he and his wife were among the visitors to Inveraray in 1757 (see p.92), also during Dr Carlyle's stay in 1758 (Carlyle, loc.cit.).

214.   *Letters of Lady Mary Coke*, loc.cit. Similarly sumptuous provision was made in August 1760 for a three-day visit by the Earl (created Duke in 1766) and Countess of Northumberland. Asknish met them at Tarbet, and in spite of poor weather they 'seem'd much pleas'd with every thing they saw both here and on the road to it'–especially the voyage from Cairndow in the Argyll barge. (s93, Asknish to Milton, 23 August 1760.)

215.   s91, Asknish to Milton, 20 September 1759; Lord Lyttelton to Mrs Montagu, [?Aug.] 1759, in *Elizabeth Montagu . . . Correspondence from 1720 to 1761*, ed. Emily J.Climenson, II (London 1906) p.165. In her reply to Lord Lyttelton on 16 September, the lady condescendingly suggested that 'the Duke of Argyll was in very agreeable circumstances, while he was looking on his vast territory and the rude magnificences of nature, and at the same time attending to the conversation of a guest polished by all the fine arts of life, and adorned by every gentle virtue.' She continued: 'As King of the Goths I do not so much envy him; a cold climate, rude inhabitants, a soil uncultivated, and all the accomplishments of savage greatness may please surly and solitary pride, but I think his Grace of Argyle is much in the right to rule there by a viceroy, the greatest part of the year, and enjoy the comforts of being a subject of England for the rest.' (*Letters of Mrs Elizabeth Montagu*, ed. Matthew Montagu, IV, London 1813, pp.237–8.)

Before returning south, Lyttelton and his son dined in Edinburgh with the magistrates and corporation, 'and supped with the Duke of Argyll, who honoured me with his presence at the dinner, a distinction he never paid to any other than upon this occasion'. (*Elizabeth Montagu . . . Correspondence*, op.cit., Lyttelton to Mrs Montagu, 10 September 1759.)

216.   BM Add. 40663, Mrs Montagu to Mrs Robinson, 4 December 1766; Mrs Montagu to Mrs Carter, August 1766, in *Mrs Montagu, Queen of the Blues*, ed. Reginald Blunt, I London 1923) pp.146–7. Mrs Montagu tells both correspondents that 'the great Leviathan' has been seen in Loch Fyne; all she remarks of the castle is that 'His Grace's house has cost a great deal of money, but makes little figure, being surrounded by such immense objects'.

217. s91, Sir Alexander Dick to Milton,
27 October 1759; J. Bennett Nolan *Benjamin Franklin in Scotland and Ireland* (Pennsylvania 1938) which, however, does not mention the Inveraray visit; *Papers of Benjamin Franklin,* ed. Leonard W. Labaree & Whitfield J. Bell, Jr, VIII (New Haven 1961) p. 431. In Edinburgh Franklin had met friends and protégés of the Duke of Argyll including 'Jupiter' Carlyle and Dr William Cullen; he later received an honorary degree at St Andrews. Of his Inveraray visit no details unfortunately survive, but it is mentioned by Sir Alexander Dick of Prestonfield, with whom Franklin stayed on returning to Edinburgh.

Nor is anything known of what became of the 'Franklin Stove', an improved form of fireplace of which Franklin sent the Duke a specimen in 1748, though whether intended for Inveraray or for the Duke's London house is not stated. (*Papers of Benjamin Franklin,* op. cit., III, p. 327.) The Duke may have installed it in London and then had it copied, for in 1757 he writes to Lord Milton that he is sending 'by the first convoy 2 Grates of different sorts for encreasing heat & preventing smoak, I shall have them first deposited in the Abbey for inspection of friends, the Cast Iron can be better done at Newcastle than at London. the best of all is from Shropshire from whence it is sent to London.' (s417(1), 10 December 1757.)

During a later visit, in 1771, Benjamin Franklin stayed with David Hume, after the latter's own return from Inveraray where he made one of the 5th Duke and Duchess's grand initiatory house-party. (*Letters of David Hume,* ed. J. Y. T. Greig, III, Oxford 1932, no. 462) (See ch. VI, p. 193).

218. Henry Home *Elements of Criticism,* III (1762) p. 376 (reference is to the 1763 edition). Home was certainly at Inveraray in 1750, when his servant – though not, for some reason, himself – was admitted burgess on 10 September. (IBR)

219. s90A, letters of Molly and Francis Fletcher and Mrs Mary Hepburn (sister of Lord Milton) to Milton, 1758; s90A, Fletcher to Milton, 21 February and 16 December 1758, and to Capt. John Wedderburn, 7 December 1758.

Betty Wedderburn's daughter Elizabeth survived, and later, with her father, took the name Halkett when John Wedderburn succeeded to the baronetcy of Halkett of Pitfirran. She married M. Lally Tollendal.

As the Fletcher entry in Burke's *Landed Gentry* is inaccurate, and no information on the marriage of Andrew Fletcher younger appears to have been published, it seems worth recording here. In fact Andrew married twice, obviously in a much-needed attempt to secure an heir, for two of his younger brothers were already dead, the surviving two (Henry and John) were both unmarried and on active service, and by the end of 1764 Lord Milton's health and powers had irrecoverably declined.

The evidence is in (*a*) Saltoun parish registers (SRO); (*b*) Saltoun MSS 393, in a genealogy of the Fletcher family apparently compiled about 1780 for Henry Fletcher; (*c*) Edinburgh University MSS La. III. 364, a Memoir of the Fletchers of Saltoun written in or before 1785 by Elizabeth (Wedderburn) Halkett.

Andrew married, first (23 November 1764) Jean, daughter of Sir Robert Myreton of Gogar; on 22 May 1766 she gave birth to a daughter, Mary, but died at Moffat on 10 August following, and the child died at Saltoun on 15 of the same month. Secondly, in 1769 Andrew married Jean, daughter of the late Rev. Alexander Leask, former Minister of Clatt, Aberdeenshire, but they had no children.

On Andrew Fletcher's death in 1779, Saltoun passed to his brother General Henry Fletcher, who had already inherited Boquhan in Stirlingshire from their mother's cousin Mary Campbell (daughter of the youngest brother of the 1st Duke of Argyll), and was now known as Fletcher Campbell. When Henry inherited Saltoun the youngest surviving brother, General John Fletcher, himself inherited Boquhan and also took the name Campbell.

Andrew Fletcher was MP for the Haddington burghs from 1747–54 and again from 1754–61; from 1761–8 he sat for the county of Haddington. He was also, from 1751, Auditor of the Exchequer in Scotland, having been granted the reversion of that office in 1748 as part of the recompense for his father's services during the Forty-Five. After 1761, however, he appears to have made rare appearances in the Commons and to have lived chiefly at Saltoun, where he he was a keen 'improver' and follower in the steps of Duke Archibald.

220. s92A, 94A, letters of Lady Milton, Molly and Andrew Fletcher to Milton; s93, letters of John Maule.

221. s418(1), Argyll 3 to Milton, 5 August 1758; s90A, Fletcher to Milton, 16 December 1758 et al.; s92A, Lady Milton to Milton, 27 September 1759 et al.; s94A, Fletcher to Milton, 30 August and 7 September 1760.

222. s93, Asknish to Milton, 14 April 1760.

223. s419(1), Robert Dewar, account for lead windows, August 1759. s420(3), John Graham, plumber, account (1760) for installation of cisterns, 'poises' and brass cocks. The system appears to have been fairly elaborate. His bill for £150 7s 7d included 994 stone sheet lead @ 6d a stone for the office houses and casemates, and 263½ stone @ 9d for the 'Cesterons'. (See also n.225.)

224. s420(3), Milton to Argyll 3, 17 May 1760, and Duke's reply 29 May.

225. s420(3), Haswell, estimates for nails required, 27 December 1759 and 23 January 1760, prices quoted by Robert Scott at the Cock, Edinburgh, and James Wright, Saltmercat, Glasgow. Inv/Inv. Est. 1756–60: freight charges on slates, lead, timber, May–June 1760. The following all in s420(3): Adam, accounts for materials, December 1759–September 1760: £120 18s 1d for screws, nails, white lead etc. and carriage, and £395 3s 3d for total of 505 bars lead, including charges, commission and insurance; bills of lading for the lead, shipped by Haliday & Dunbar on the *Gerzey*, master Archibald Crawford, and the *Elizabeth*, master Robert Turner, from Liverpool for Greenock, 50 and 90 pigs respectively, 27 March and 27 May 1760. ('Gerzey' is probably an error for 'Grizzy', the spelling used in Adam's account.)

The remaining 365 bars, also ordered by Adam, were shipped from Liverpool in the *Prince of Wales*, Captain Gillies, and insured for £300–providentially as it turned out for it was lost off Kintyre, and Adam had to order a fresh supply, which arrived safely by the *Katie*. Lead from either Liverpool or Chester was considered reasonable in price and 'extremely good'. (s418(3), Adam to Milton, 1 November 1758; s419(1), Milton to Argyll 3, 28 December 1759, scroll letter; s93, Adam to Milton, 6 June 1760.) The insurance compensation, less 2 per cent conform to the policy, less ½ per cent brokerage and a further 1 per cent commission, was agreed by the merchants Fairholme & Malcolm on 11 January 1760, leaving £289 11s 10d to be placed to Adam's account. (s420(3))

Other smaller cargoes of lead were delivered at Inveraray in 1760. According to Adam's information, 11–12 tons were needed by the plumber for piping water into the house; a bar or pig weighed about 8 stone. (Adam to Milton, 1 November 1758, loc. cit.)

226. Richard Pococke *Tours in Scotland 1747, 1750, 1760* I, pp.64ff. Pococke (b. 1704), later Bishop of Meath, described his travels in letters to his sister. Asknish informed Lord Milton (s93, 8 June 1760) that 'the famous Traveller the Bishop of Ossory' had, during his two-day stay, 'made the Tour of the place'. For Alexander Cumming see n.173 and Index of Architects and Craftsmen.

227. The building of park walls and dykes began in 1750 with William Douglas at Tombreac. In addition to the kitchen garden wall, James Potter took on the Stable Park, Stronshira and others, while Douglas continued with Achinbreck, Kilbraid, etc. (Inv/Journal (Cash book) 1750–1 et seq.). The military road's extension towards Tyndrum began in 1757 when the Aray Bridge was also begun (see ch.III).

228. *Edinburgh Evening Courant*, 21 October 1758.

229. s41, Stonefield to Milton, 25 July 1744; s402(2), Donald McLean of Torloisk to his son, 19 July 1744; s401, scantling of timber salvaged from cargo of the *Maria Elizabeth* purchased at roup of 27 September 1744. See also Duncan MacTavish *Inveraray Papers* (Oban 1939) p.34.

Archibald Campbell of Ballamore was younger brother to Sir Duncan Campbell of Lochnell. Dugald, his second son, became MP for Argyll from 1754–61, and during the Seven Years' War commanded a battalion of Argyll Fencibles. He was a frequent visitor at the Duke of Argyll's house at Whitton; he married Christian, widow of David Campbell of Dunloskin (q.v., ch.IV, p.171). (Burke *Landed Gentry*.)

230. *Inveraray Papers* pp.27, 30–1.

231. s41, Stonefield to Milton, 15 October 1744; s43, Argyll 3 to Milton, 30 October 1744.

232. s407(1), Memorial by John Campbell, Chamberlain, 28 September 1749.

233. s41, Stonefield to Milton, 21 October 1744.

234. See p.46 of this chapter. Since no floors or joists were yet intended to be put in, as much scaffolding was required inside the building as out.

235. s44, Argyll 3 to Milton, 12 January 1745.

236. s44, Stonefield to Milton, 25 March 1745; Inv/CA 1743, item 21 (20 October 1744).

237. s46 and MLB, Morris to Milton, 1 August 1745.

238. Mamore MSS, NLS 3735/402, Stonefield to Col. John Campbell, 30 June 1746; and see Fergusson *Argyll in the Forty-Five*, p.222.

239. MLB 49–50, Abstract of Account August 1746–August 1747. A later memorandum, however (Inv/1748, Memorial concerning the Works at Inveraray, March 1748), shows that in March 1748 more than 50 tons still remained in Tiree, and means of bringing it to Inveraray were still being discussed.

240. s405(1) & MLB 47–8, Order to Capt. Peter Frelsen for a cargo of iron and timber, signed Roger Morris and William Adam, 7 September 1747.

241. s66, Maule to Milton, 30 April 1747 ('I can get time to say no more, they're roaring for me to play at Whisk; Legrand has wrote to Vaughan that there's a Danish ship stranded at Stranrawer wt timber on board, the Duke thinks some of it might be proper for his buildings . . .'). s72, Stonefield to Milton, 7 December 1749: Stonefield commissioned a John Ferguson to go up to Barra to examine the cargo, but Ferguson omitted to note the timber's dimensions, and in any case the local people who had salvaged the cargo had already been given the best pieces. Stonefield was vexed as the wreck was strictly Admiralty property and very little could now be made of it, while Ferguson's voyage, including the hire of a wherry, had cost £10 and 'it was a hazardous & troublesome Expedition this time of year'.

242. s64A, Memorial of Angus Fisher, merchant in Inveraray, October 1747, also his petition to grind malt for use of the workmen, and letter to Lady Milton, 10 October 1747.

243. Inv/C, Adam, Memorials relating to the Works of Inveraray Castle, 8 September 1748 and 14 September 1749; s73A, Milton to Argyll 3, 12 December 1749, scroll letter; s408(2), Hunter to Milton, 13 February 1750.

244. s74, James Campbell to Milton, 6 January 1750; s72, Charles & Robert Fall to Milton, 24 April 1749; s407(1), Knockbuy to Milton, 28 October 1749.

245. s72, Argyll to Milton, 23 November 1749.

246. s74, Archibald Campbell of Limecraigs, Baillie of Kintyre, to James Campbell at Inveraray, 1 January 1750; James Campbell to Milton, 6 January 1750. The Collector of Customs at Campbeltown sent James Campbell the further news that Bee [sic] had sold his cargo in December to James Agnew & Company, merchants in Larne, and that there was no question of the 'Leakiness or Insufficiency of the Ship'. (s74, Collr Thomas Fraser to James Campbell, 8 January 1749/50.)

247. s408(2), Knockbuy to Milton, 11 March 1750, and (s74) 26 March and 5 June 1750.

248. s76, James Campbell to Milton, 10 February 1751.

249. s74, Charles & Robert Fall to Milton, 10 May 1750.

250. s408(1), Allan Dreghorn, Glasgow, to Asknish, 20 August 1750; invoice of deals belonging to John Knox & Co.; Josiah Corthine, Port Glasgow, to [?Asknish], 22 August 1750. Allan Dreghorn (1706–64), to whom 'the Captain of the Danish Ship' had sold his cargo, was a Glasgow timber merchant, wright and architect; he was the designer of St Andrew's Church there (1739), and (with James Craig) of the Town Hall, later the Tontine building (1737–40). (Andor Gomme & David Walker *Architecture of Glasgow*, London 1968, pp.58–9, 271, and see Index of Architects and Craftsmen.) Josiah Corthine was Collector of Customs at Port Glasgow.

251. s409(2), Memorandum for My Lord Milton about Inveraray Castle 1751.

252. s409(2), Scantling of Timber for the Roof of the Castle of Inveraray, 4 October 1751, and Adam's amended note of 10 October 1751. (See p.75) The full text of the amended scantling is as follows:

40 peices	21 ft. long	13 ins. Sqr.
for principal Rafters		
4 Dos.	26	15
for Diagonals or Hips		
4 Dos.	36	15
for Diagonal tye beams		
30 Dos.	25	15
for the other tye beams		
6 Dos.	28	15
for do. over the Hall		
44 Dos.	14	12 by 18 in.
for King posts		
4 peices	26	15
for principal Girders over the Hall		
12 Dos.	22	15
for do. over the Parlours, Bedchambers, & Dressing rooms		
11 Dos.	23	15
for do. over the Gallery		
8 Dos.	19	15
for do. in the round Towers		

There will also be needed 300 Tons of Sqr. Timbers, of the ordinary lengths of Saw baulks, & to run from 10 to 14 Inches Sqr., for purloins, Springs, Hows, Spars; Rafters over the middle Tower & Staircases, Collar beams; Runtrees, Sleepers &c.

All the above timbers must be of the best upland red firr, as Square as possible, & free of Sapwood & Shakes.

2000 Dealls from 10 to 12 foot long, 1½ Ins thick, for Serking to the principal rooff, & the rooffs of the Towers; Also for putting under the Lead on the platforms, & in the Gutters.

Another list in James Campbell's hand, 'Note of Timber for the half of the Roofe of The Castle of Inveraray' s 409(2), ends: 'The Rest of the Ships Loading May be filled up With ffirr Timber of the Ordinary Lengths and to run from 10 to 14 Inch Square. NB . . . altho' Each of the above first five kinds of Timber should be a foot or two Longer than the above Dimensions It Matters not, since They all must be Solid Wood of the Dimensions above set down at least.'

253. s 416(3), James Campbell to Peter Frelsen, 30 November 1751 (covering letter for the scantling for half the roof timbers quoted above).

254. s 78 & 410(3), letters and instructions from William Fullarton, George Cheap (on behalf of, or dictated by, Lord Milton), and Richard Tod at Leith, ordering cargoes of Norway timber.

William Fullarton, 'a wealthy Ayrshire gentleman', died about 1770; his son William (1754–1808) became Government Commissioner for Trinidad. (*DNB*)

255. s 410(3), George Cheap to Milton, 2 March 1752, and Instructions to James Hay, 27 March 1752. The price list (ibid.) is as follows:

Long Sound in Norway
Red wood logs from 14 to 20 feet long from —to 14 inches square pr dozen 14½ RDs
Do from 20 to 30 feet long & from—

to—inches	pr Dozen	12
Deals		R^ds
16 feet long red wood		
· 2 inches thick at p hun^d		34
do. white wood		
2 do.	at	23
14 feet red wood		
2½ do.	at	37½
Do		
2 do.	at	30
Do white wood		
2 do.	at	21
12 feet red wood		
2½ do.	at	31
Do		
2 do.	at	25
Do		
1½ do.	at	19
Do white wood		
2 do.	at	19
10 feet red wood		
2 do.	at	22

14 Do Do		
3 do.	at	45
12 Do Do		
3 do.	at	37½
Single battons 10 to 16 feet long at		7½
halfe deals red wood	at	8½
Do. white wood	at	7

Dutys and all Charges in Norway will amount to about on[e] fourth of the first cost.

256. s 410(3), Letters from James Hay at Brevik and Frederikstad to Archibald Campbell younger of Succoth and George Cheap, 12 May and 24 May, and 20 June 1752; invoice of timber shipped on the *Anne Belle*, 8 July 1752; Richard Tod, Leith, to Milton, 29 July 1752. Tod belonged to a noted family of Edinburgh merchants the head of whom, William, was also a director of the British Linen Company.

257. s 410(3), Invoice of goods on board the *Betty*, in service of James Hay, Preston Pans, 10 May 1752; John Campbell, Chamberlain, to Milton, 21 May 1752. s 410(2), ibid., 16 June 1752.

258. s 410(3), Haswell to John Campbell, Chamberlain, 15 June 1752, and to John Paterson, wright at Queensferry, 16 June 1752.

259. s 410(3), Note on James Hay's bills by Ld Milton and Archibald Campbell, w.s., July 1752; s 79, Wm Hogg & Son, Edinburgh, to Milton, 1 August 1752; s 78, George Campbell, banker in The Strand, to Milton, 6 August 1752.

260. s 410(3) & 78, Account with James Hay for timber shipped on the *Betty* and the *Anne Belle*; s 410(3) & Inv/Jnl (Cash Book) 1750–2, invoice of timber shipped on the *Anne Belle*, 8 July, and account of duty paid at Inveraray; s 410(3), account of Richard Tod for timber for the inn, September 1752, and timber figure in abstract of general account, 1752.

A list of duties on Norway deals, supplied by James Morris in the spring of 1754, quotes the following (s 412(3)): 'Deales from Norway under 20 foot long and 3 Inches thick are Rated in the Book of Customs at five pounds p hundred, Six Score, and the Duty payable on them by British & in British Ships . . . £1 8s 7d. Firr Timber is rated at 12^s/6 p load of 50 foot, and the Duty Payable on it . . . [etc., as above] 3^s/7^d p Load.' Wainscot bore a duty per inch of 4½d.

Morris explained the method of computing the duty at 5 per cent less a small discount for prompt payment, plus various subsidies, and impost and a new duty. He added: 'The other duty called Aliens Duty is payable when the goods are Imported in a Foreign Ship which Duty is ¼ of the Rate and Comes to 1^s/3^d p C on Deales. There is also a Duty Payable by Foreign Ships to the City of London called Scavage', 1s 6d per cent on deals, 2s per load on timber. Further loading charges were 'Bill money 3ˢ/2ᵈ, Warrant 3/6, Landwaiter 21/-'.

261. s409, John McCulloch, Kirkcudbright, to James Campbell, 6 May, and James Campbell to Milton, 15 May 1751; s416(3), John McCulloch to James Campbell, 23 November 1751; s409(3), Thos & Richard Spencer & Co., Riga, to John Wilson & Son, Edinburgh, 2 January 1751 (with details of timber exported from Riga); s409(1), James Campbell to Milton, 27 December 1751.

262. s410(3), Wilson & Son, Edinburgh, to Milton, 29 August 1752.

263. s411(1), Note of Timbers wanting for Inveraray Castle, 19 June 1753, Fletcher to Robert Cormack, 23 June 1753; also s412(3), Adam's earlier note on timbers, 30 September 1752; s81, John Paterson to Milton, 16 May 1753.

264. s411(1), Milton to Robt Cormack, 23 June 1753; s410(2), Jas Spalding to Milton, 20 August 1753. Cormack had urgently requested the commission from Lord Milton on learning that he was importing cargoes for Inveraray, insisting that Russian timber was better value than Norwegian, dispraising the last cargo delivered for the Duke and claiming that 'Russ Logs is Squire Like adice' and up to 50 feet in length, 'and not a foot of a thousand blue wood but pure reid wood'. Cormack's own son appears to have been in business in Russia at the time. (s78, Robert Cormack to Robert Brisbane, 10 April 1752, and to Milton, 3 and 23 September 1752.)

265. s411(2), John Paterson, at Glasgow, to Haswell, 13 September 1753.

266. s411(2), Duncan Glassford at Bo'ness to John Paterson, 26 September 1753, John Paterson to Milton, 27 September 1753.

267. s412(2), Adam, note on timber, January 1754.

268. s412(2), Letters of Robert Cormack, January–February 1754 on his Inveraray timber commission; Adam, Note of Firr Planks wanting for Inveraray Castle, 20 February 1754.

269. s412(2), Asknish to Milton, 2 June 1754 (with invoice, 6 May, of goods shipped on *Hibernia* at risk of Edward Smith, and price list, 2 June), Robt Cormack to Milton, 3 June 1754.

270. s412(1), Asknish to Milton, 9 June 1754; s412(3), Ibid., 23 June; s426, Ibid., 7 July; s412(3), Robt Cormack to Asknish, 22 June 1754, and accts and valuation of timber cargoes, August 1754; s426, settled account with Robt Cormack, 27 August 1754.

271. s413(1), Adam, Memorial relating to the Timber on hand at Inveraray, and what is necessary to be provided, 27 October 1755; s85, Argyll 3 to Milton, 1 April 1756; s415, Adam to Milton, 17 June 1756; s427, freight of timber shipped on the *Margaret* of Leith, 1756.

272. s416(3), Instructions by His Grace of Argyll for . . . Inveraray Castle, 31 October 1757, Haswell, note on mahogany on Clydeside, 2 December 1757; s418(3), Haswell to Adam, 7 January 1758; s418(1), Milton to Argyll 3, January 1758, scroll letter; Inv/Ledger 1754, account of John and James Adam, December 1757–October 1758 (entry of December 1757).

273. s418(3), Haswell, note on mahogany required for middle tower windows, 12 October 1758; s418(3) & 90, Graham Strathearn to Milton, 24 October, 11 November and 1 December 1758.

274. s419(1), Milton to Argyll 3, 28 December 1759, scroll letter.

275. s420(3), Papers on cargo of iron and deals from Gothenburg on the *Young Tobias* (master Olaf Knutsen Bagge) and the *Concordia* (master Johan Berg), with instructions by George Carnegie, merchant in Gothenburg (May 1760), timber accounts, duty etc. JOHN WATSON (d. 1762), son of David Watson, also a lawyer, was from 1746 Substitute Keeper of the Signet. By this time (1760) he had been in bad health for some years, and his frequent letters to Lord Milton express daily expectation of death. (s88, 90, 92, 94 etc.) He made over his means to charity, by which the John Watson Institute in Belford Road, Edinburgh, was built and endowed. (*The Society of Writers to H.M. Signet*, ad loc.)

276. s420(3), Haswell to Milton, 28 November 1760.

CHAPTER III

1. Ane Descriptione of certaine pairts of the Highlands of Scotland, in *MacFarlane's Geographical Collections*, II (Scottish History Society 1907) p. 144.

2. Information supplied by Mr Angus Davidson, former Head Forester to the Argyll Estate. The date 1674 is given in a list of trees planted that year (Inv MSS), and 1661 from a ring count.

3. s 401, Maule to Milton, 19 November 1743.

4. s 401 & 43, Argyll 3 to Milton,
31 December 1743 and 19 January 1744.

5. s 402, ibid., April 1744.

6. Inv/Particular Papers, and CA 1743,
Survey of 'the Line of the New road from
Dunbarton to Inveraray, 1744'.

7. s 402, Argyll 3 to Milton, 31 May 1744.

8. s 43, ibid., 16 June 1744.

9. Sir Kenneth Mackenzie of Gairloch *General
Wade and his Roads*, Trans. Inverness
Scientific Soc. and Field Club (Inverness 1902)
v, 145–177, and *Military Roads*, ibid., pp. 364–
84. See also mins. of a meeting of
Commissioners of Supply of Argyll, 5–7 June
1745, in s 402, at which Colin Campbell of
Glenure, victim of the Appin Murder in 1752,
took the chair, and members included
Stonefield, Airds, Knockbuy, Dunardry,
Archibald Campbell of Barnacarry, Dugald
Clerk of Braleckan, and the then laird of
Asknish (Angus, father of Robert).

Colonel Edmund Martin, of Wolfe's
Regiment, then stationed at Fort William,
wrote to the Duke of Richmond on 17 September
1744; 'They are making a new road . . . on
ye D. of Argiles estate 50 miles, the Estimate
6000£, twill be of little use to any body but ye
Duke . . . .'; and again on 14 May 1745,
'They are making a piece of road here to please
one Great Man that he may drive easily to his
house (when he gets one) tis about 40 miles
where there is to be 17 bridges, *one* will cost
2 or 3000£, thro' a country all rock and Bogg,
where nobody will ever have occasion to pass
but he himself and that perhaps but once more
in his life if he does that'–a piece of cynicism
which proved ill-founded. (Charles Gordon
Lennox, Earl of March, *A Duke and his Friends*,
II, London 1911, pp. 460, 461.)

10. The whole of this account is taken from
an unsigned memorial, probably by Major
Caulfield, about the road from Dumbarton to
Argyll, February 1748, s 406(1). See also s 72,
Archibald Campbell, w.s. to Milton, 11 April
1749.

Many travellers were to describe the stone
erected at the head of the pass–which also
commemorated the work of Colonel Lascelles's
regiment–so placed as to command a view
back down the whole valley. In 1822 Dorothy
Wordsworth, on her second visit to the district,
records how on the steep ascent she looked in
vain for the road-side stone, because the line
'had been altered since I was last here [1803]
for the sake of an easier ascent. The old
track . . . was much overgrown with grass.'

(*Journals of Dorothy Wordsworth*, ed. E. de
Selincourt, II, London 1941, p. 362.) Today the
old zigzag ascent has long been closed, except
for motor trials, and the modern road rises
almost in a straight line along the side of the
valley.

11. Inv/Est. Management vol. III, Report
anent The Rent of Achintraw . . ., 1748.

12. s 63, Milton to Argyll 3, 29 August 1747,
scroll letter.

13. MLB 75, Wm Adam to Morris, 5 February
1748.

14. s 407A, Major Caulfield to Milton,
13 September 1749.

15. s 407A, Henry Fox to Gen. Churchill,
20 July 1749 (copy), Charles Collier to Major
Caulfield, July and 12 September 1749.

16. s 74, Argyll 3 to Milton, 12 August 1750.

17. Inv/Folio, Pedigrees. This is a slightly
different version of *Ane Accompt of the
Genealogie of the Campbells*, NLS Advocates'
Library MS 34.5.22, vol. III MS B, which was
published by J. R. N. Macphail in *Highland
Papers*, II, Scottish History Society, 2nd ser.
vol. 12 (Edinburgh 1916).

18. MLB 63 and Inv/CA 1747, Contract,
Douglas with Morris and Wm Adam,
2 October 1747.

19. MLB 70, 84, Morris to Douglas, 1 January
1747/8, and Douglas's reply, 8 March 1748.

20. Inv/C. This may have been the same
storm that blew the roof off 'Marshal Saxe's
house' (Inv/KJ 1752–6, under April/May
1753), after which it was repaired, but damaged
again in 1756 (see ch. II, p. 98).

The watch-tower on Duniquaich has been
struck by lightning several times since 1752,
most recently in 1958, when the estimate for
its repair was £1200–£1500.

21. Sir William Burrell MS *Travels in Scotland*,
1758, loc. cit.

22. J. Bailey MS *A Journey in Scotland*, 1787,
NLS 3294–5, II, 405 ff.

23. Inv/Acct Bk 1749, p. 48 (Douglas's
Account).

24. Act XXII Parliament of Scotland
XXVIII of June 1617, 19.

25. s 406(1), Estimate of the new miln
Design'd on the water of Aray by William
Douglas, 1748; s 73, Robert Mackell to Milton,
29 November 1749.

26. In the possession of Sir John Clerk of
Penicuik.

27. MLB 84, Douglas to Morris, 8 March 1748; Inv/Acct Bk 1749, loc. cit.

28. S15, Ilay to Milton, 17 December 1730.

29. e.g. S422, Memo. for the Whim, July 1733 ('to mark out the Countess').

30. Inv/Acct Bk 1749, loc. cit.

31. Ibid.

32. S409(2), Estimate of a Bridge propos'd above the Milln on the watter of Array, by William Douglas, 1751.

33. Inv/AEM 18th cent., vol.II: CI 7 November 1752, p.2; S413(2), Douglas, accts and letters December 1751 ff., Douglas to Milton 21 April 1755; S416(3), Hunter, report on bridge above the mill, 21 October 1757.

34. Inv/Ledger acct 1754; Jnl (Cash Bk) 1750–2. The boathouse is now ruinous. The Instructions to the Kintyre Chamberlain in 1752 include one to the effect that Mr Somers in Campbeltown is 'to build His Grace a float as the Duke directed him for supporting the Chinese float for the Duloch', but no other record appears of this attractive scheme.

35. S410(2), Proposalls to my Lord Miltoun by James Potter to Build the Kittchen Garden wall, 1752; S410(3), 411(1), 412(1) & (2), Abstracts of general accounts, 1752–4; S410(2), James Potter's accounts, 1755.

36. S407A, Gardener's Memorandum about Carrying on the Works, 30 September 1749; S410(2) & (3) et seq., abstracts of accounts 1752 ff.; S414(2), memoranda on roads, river and Fisherland, 1756 ff.; Inv/Jnl (Cash Bk), 1750–2, and KJ 1752–6.

37. Inv/KJ, 9 & 25 December 1752, 23 February 1753.

38. S84A, John Richardson to Milton, 14 June 1755.

39. S88, Walter Paterson to Milton, 23 March 1757. The storm was accompanied by an exceptionally high tide and caused serious damage in the West Highlands and islands. On the west coast of Mull the stones of the sea barricades were washed away and in parts of the island the waters met across the land; in Tiree the quay at Scarnish was destroyed. (S417(1), Donald Campbell, Chamberlain of Tiree, to Asknish, 3 April 1757.)
On the making of the salt water pond: Inv/Jnl (Cash Bk) 1750–2, Inv/C, Inst. 1753; Inv/Ledger 1754; Inv/Estate 1756–60; Inv/KJ, 1 January 1754, 10 February 1756. It was sometimes referred to as the 'Gallows Green pond'.

40. *Vitruvius Scoticus* (plates engraved in William and John Adam's lifetime), published Edinburgh ?1810, pl.74.

41. *Glasgow Courant*, 18 & 25 July 1748.

42. Drawing in S416(3), with Memorial for the builders of the bridge, 1 November 1757, and note by Haswell on wood required, 29 October 1757. Brown was at first accommodated in 'the Easter pavilion called the Sheriffs house'; later he and his men were moved to a row of houses in the lower town, which had been evacuated for demolition to make way for the new road and bridge. (S416(3) & 418(3), Inst. of October and November 1757.) For John Brown see Index of Architects and Craftsmen. I am indebted to Mr Richard Dell, Glasgow City Archivist, for information on the two master masons, John Brown I (d. 1773), builder of the first Aray Bridge, and John Brown II, builder of the second. For the latter see ch.VII, p.234 and n.23.
The firm of smelters were Henry Kendall and Company, of Ulverstone in Lancashire, who in 1753 had made a survey of the Duke's woods and conducted a lengthy correspondence with Lord Milton on setting up a furnace on Loch-Fyne-side. In 1754 Kendall established himself at Goatfield, formerly the house of the late Donald Clerk of Braleckan, and in 1755 the smelting furnace was built beside the loch eight miles south of Inveraray. It was lined with St Catherine's stone, as the best to withstand heat.
The ruined building now to be seen there, at the hamlet still known as Furnace, bears the date 1775. Eventually renamed the Duddon Company, the same firm (apparently) continued to smelt iron by Loch Fyne until 1813. (Henry Hamilton *An Economic History of Scotland in the Eighteenth Century*, Oxford 1963, p.192.) Correspondence dealing with Kendall's Argyll Furnace (which was also known as Craleckan) is in S412 ff.; the contract (October 1754) between the Duke and Kendall, and the 57-year tack granted, in S426; other relevant letters in S427(2), e.g. from Kendall in 1756, and the account for iron supplied to Inveraray, including for the castle stair, 1756–7.

43. S89, Commissary James Campbell to Milton, 15 July 1758; Inv/C, CA, 28 November 1758.

44. S414(3), Proposal by Thomas Brown, mason, October 1756. Thomas Brown had contracted with the Irvine magistrates in January 1748 to rebuild their bridge for £350 to a design similar to the old; the contract was completed in April 1753 (Sir James Marwick

The River Clyde and the Clyde Burghs, Glasgow 1909). Brown's proposal for the Deer Park bridge is the first we hear of a scheme to bridge the Garron Water where it runs from the Dhu Loch; but none was built there until 1785 (see ch.VII, p.243).

45. s418(3), Adam to Milton, 1 November 1758.

46. Inv/Est. 1756–60, accts; s419(1), Adam to Argyll 3, 13 February 1759, and Haswell, accts for putting up centres, 3 November 1759; s94, Hunter to Milton, 10 June 1760; Inv/Argyll 4, Inst. to Walter Paterson, 21 August 1761.

47. Inv/1756, Adam Memorial relating to the Works carrying on by His Grace the Duke of Argyll at Inveraray, 30 June 1761, item 26 (one of two items added the day following his long report dated 29 June). The papers provide evidence that the bridge was designed by John Adam, although *Vitruvius Scoticus* pl.74 assigns it to James.

48. Inv/AECB 1759–60; AEM 18th cent.; Inventory of Rentals, Tacks etc. delivered by Asknish to Sonachan; Inv. Accts 1767–72.

49. Drawings in Inveraray and Saltoun MSS. Accounts and instructions in Inv/KJ 24 November 1752, 30 June 1753; Jnl (Cash Bk) 1752–3; do. on the alterations and additions of 1758ff. in s418(3), Duke's Instructions, Minutes and Instructions November 1758, and Potter's accts October 1757–October 1758; s419(1), Memo. on Asknish's account, October 1759; s420(1), 'calculs' October 1760; s420(2), abstract of Asknish's accounts, 1759–60. Inv/Inveraray Estate 1756–60, accts; Inv/AECB 1759–60; Inv/AEM 18th cent. and AEM 1762–3; Inv/C, Adam Memorial relating to the works etc. 29 June 1761, item 23.

Extensions and alterations to the dairy were begun in 1758 and were still incomplete at the Duke's death; the little folly appears to have appealed to everyone's imagination, and several variants were sketched of a Gothick frontage, and one based on the Palladian villa style. It is now impossible to be certain which design was adopted, as the building finally fell down about 1880 and was totally removed.

50. Inv/Inveraray Estate 1756–60. According to the Dewar MSS at Inveraray Castle 'there never was such a thing' as a cherry orchard there, and although early 18th-century maps mark the ground as 'Cherry Garden', the name is said to be a corruption of the Gaelic *Pairce na Siriston* or *Siristach*, i.e. Colts' or Ponies' Park. The inhabitants of Inveraray had supposedly adopted a kind of 'half Gaelic half English' lingua franca from the Cromwellian soldiers billeted there in the 17th century, and such bastardized expressions would be especially likely to survive in topographical names. *Sirist* was a local form of the word used for the Tiree ponies which carried charcoal bags for the Braleckan iron smelters, but it is also the word for 'cherry'. The Dewar MSS further state that the park in front of the Court of Offices was enclosed to keep the ponies ridden by the Marquess of Lorne's children during the 4th Duke's time.

51. s419(1), Computation of Timber and Dealls necessary for the Buildings order'd by His Grace The Duke of Argyll, to be Executed at Inveraray in 1760; Inv/1756; s94, Hunter to Milton, 10 June 1760.

52. s420(2), Abstract of Asknish's accounts, 1759–60; Inv/C, Haswell's Not[e] of Glass wanted for the windows of the Court of offices in the Cherry Park 1761, Adam, Memorial 1761, loc. cit. (see n. 49).

53. Inv/AECB 1759–60 and AEM 18th cent.; Adam Memorial 1761, loc.cit.

54. Inv/Folio, Pedigrees (see n.17). The fountainhead below Duniquaich, which still provides the main water-supply, is now enclosed in a Victorian wooden Gothic house.

55. Richard Pococke, op.cit. (see ch.II, n.226). The 'old bridge' was the town bridge, at that time intended to be retained, and the third bridge was the Garden or Frew's Bridge. The well in the wood is Bealachanuaran, though 'Gothick' is hardly the appropriate word. Possibly Pococke was confusing its appearance with that of the 'Physic' or mineral well.

CHAPTER IV
1. The British Linen Company's charter, delayed by the Jacobite rising, received the King's signature on 5 July 1746. In 1765 the Company became the British Linen Bank. While the Duke of Argyll had the interest to promote Scottish industry, it was Lord Milton who provided most of the practical measures, and who had for many years supported the linen industry, a connexion inherited from his mother, Margaret Carnegie. The Fletchers grew flax at Saltoun, experimented in bleaching and dyeing yarn, and were the patrons of the noted Meikle family, builders of milling machinery. Lord Milton was in 1727 one of the first Trustees for the Improvement of Agriculture and Fisheries appointed for Scotland, and was President of the Board's Linen Committee, who opened Government-subsidized spinning

schools and installed Dutch and Picardy weavers as instructors in the Edinburgh area. (Charles A. Malcolm *The History of the British Linen Bank*, privately printed, Edinburgh 1950; W. C. Mackenzie *Fletcher of Saltoun*, Edinburgh 1935; papers in s350 et al.) (See also ch.II, n.166.)

2.   Campbeltown in the 1750s became the base for a whale-fishing company in which the Duke and Lord Milton had an interest. Extensive surveys (begun by William Adam) were also made in an attempt to revive old coal workings there. Neither venture succeeded for long. (s359, 75, 77, etc., including letters from Commodore George Walker, 1750 onwards; s407, Memorial on the Campbeltown Coal by Archibald Campbell, Chamberlain of Kintyre, 11 September 1749.)

An interesting early sequel in England to Duke Archibald's Inveraray is the village of Lowther, in Westmorland, built about 1765–73 and ascribed by Professor Pevsner to James Adam as probable architect (Nicholas Pevsner *Cumberland and Westmorland*, Penguin Buildings of England Series, London 1967, p.274 and pl.93). As the patron of this village was Sir James Lowther (later Earl of Lonsdale), son-in-law to Lord Bute, and as James Adam had been at Inveraray, the connexion seems clear; especially when we compare the alternation of higher and lower blocks at Lowther with John Adam's unexecuted design for Inveraray's main street. (See figs. 60 and 61.)

3.   s402.

4.   s41, John Anderson to Archibald Campbell, w.s., 21 July 1744; s402(2), Milton to Argyll 3, 25 October 1744, scroll letter.

5.   s402(2), Milton to Argyll 3, 13 November 1744, scroll letter.

6.   s403(2), Proposall, James Campbell Writer To His Grace the D of A, 3 September 1744.

7.   s63, Stonefield to Milton, 12 January 1747. Richardson also attended General Campbell on his Highland expeditions.

8.   s411(1), Tack of John Richardson's house, 29 October 1753. Later rentals show Richardson as paying 5s a year. The house is now known as Fern Point (after the old name of the headland on which the new town was built).

9.   s410(3), Memorial from Baillie Patrick (Peter) Campbell, 1752; s411(1), set of Dalchenna to Provost Duncanson and Baillie Peter Campbell 1753; Inv/AEM, 18th cent., CA

7 November 1752.

10.   Duncan MacTavish *Inveraray Papers*, p.52.

11.   Inv/C, CA October 1751. See also, e.g., s407A, Knockbuy to Milton, 28 October 1749; Inv/CA 1748, Jnl (Cash Bk) 1750–2, additions to rental 1751, and 1753 rental (AEM 18th cent.).

12.   Inv/AEM 18th cent., Inst., November 1760

13.   Inv/Plan Chest.

14.   Adam, Inveraray town plans of 3 September 1750, (i) s408(2), 'as at present lined out'; (ii), Inv/Plan Chest, 'as propos'd by His Grace'.

15.   s418(3), Grant of land for John Richardson's second house, 20 November 1758, refers to 'Mr Adams plan 1758'; similarly in the Duke's Instructions, November 1758 (ibid.) a much scored-out note concerning a garden for the schoolmaster Robert Dobson, mentions 'the division behind the Town house upon Mr Adams last plan in 1758', (the following words cancelled) 'in which the Church is in the Midle'. s418(1), 419(1), for James Potter's house plans for new town.

16.   Inv/C, Inst. 1753: 'I desyre that the sward be taken off the streets in the New Town & the earth carried off by the Gardiner.' Instructions were usually issued in October or November towards the end of the Duke's visit, and not executed or begun (unless otherwise specified) until the following spring.

17.   Inv/18th cent. leases, Tack of Alexander McPherson's house, November 1756.

18.   s83, Proposal of James Whyte to build 3 houses in new town, October 1755; s413(1), Alexander McPherson to Milton, 1 December 1755; tack of McPherson's house (see n.17).

19.   s72, Stonefield to Milton, 6 December 1749.

20.   s69, ibid., 31 March 1748.

21.   s72, ibid., 12 October 1749. Stonefield's elder half-brother James appears to have lived until 1731, although unable to continue in office because of his deteriorating health. The impression given of James in the brothers' letter book (SF MSS SRO GD 14/10/1–3) is of a shrewd, intelligent, humane and warm-hearted man; that of Archibald is similar, though with more of a tinge of the canny business-man.

The post of Deputy Collector of Cess had eventually passed (August 1746) to the lawyer James Campbell, and in May 1748 to Archibald Campbell of Knockbuy. (s407, James Campbell to Argyll 3, 23 April 1748.)

22. s408(2), John Campbell (late Deputy Chamberlain) to Argyll 3, 31 August 1750.

23. s75, Fletcher to Milton, 9 June 1750.

24. s76, Argyll 3 to Milton, 21 February 1751; s77, Fletcher to Milton, 23 February 1751.

25. Inv/Ledger 1754; Works at Inveraray 1750; Jnl (Cash Bk) 1750–2.

26. s410(3), Timber needed for the inn, 23 March 1752; s410(2), Douglas's receipt of timber from Richard Tod, 1 September 1752.

27. s410(2) and (3), Douglas to Milton, 28 October 1752, and accounts and other papers concerning his work, 1751, 1752.

28. s411(1), Milton to John Campbell, Deputy Chamberlain, 20 February 1753.

29. s412(1), Baillie Peter Campbell to Milton, 28 February 1754.

30. s412(2) & (3), Slate acct, 17 September 1754 (signed by Douglas); note on timber, 25 October 1754.

31. *Glasgow Courant*, 7 April 1755 (see n.46).

32. s412(2), Instructions to Douglas [1754]; s406(3), Haswell to Hunter, 26 December 1754.

33. s413(2), Adam, Reparations Propos'd to be made at the New Inn, 9 October 1755; Account of work done on inn by George Hunter, 1755–6.

34. s85, Argyll 3 to Milton, 1 April 1756.

35. s85, Baillie Peter Campbell to Milton, 14 February 1756.

36. Inv/Ledger 1754; s413(2), Douglas's account, 1755, and Reparations Propos'd to be made at the New Inn, 9 October 1755.

37. s413(1), Asknish to Milton, 16 March 1755; s414(1), list of necessaries supplied for Inn by the Duke, 14 October 1756.

38. s84A, Henry Kendall to Milton, 1 June 1755.

39. James Boswell's father, Lord Auchinleck, who with Lord Kilkerran was among the first circuit judges to stay at 'the Dukes new Inn', wrote of it approvingly to Lord Loudoun, that it 'woud in another place be called a palace and had every thing good' (Bute MSS, Loudoun papers, 26 September 1755).

In 1756 the Duke ordered that, before the next spring circuit, 'the old houses standing before the Inn & the Town house should be erased & the old Stones put in baskets made use of for the new harbor'. The timber was to be reserved for the Duke's own use. (s414,

Duke's Inst., 6 November 1756, and Milton's Memo book.)

40. s74, Stonefield to Milton, 10 October 1750.

41. IBR. In 1750 the burgh's income was £68 7s 0¾, in 1751 £81 4s 7d, and in 1753, £96 18s 2d (ibid.). The thirds of a penny sometimes found in Scottish accounts are the result of rendering pounds Scots or merks into sterling.

42. s412(1), Stonefield to Milton, 6 May 1754; Minutes of Commissioners of Supply, 21 May 1754.

43. s412(2), Contract for building Inveraray Town House between George Hunter and Donald Campbell of Airds, and estimate of expense, 25 October 1754.

44. s412(2), Slate account, 1754; Hunter, Memorial to Duke of Argyll, 1754.

45. s413(1), John Campbell, Chamberlain, to Milton, 23 February 1755.

46. *Glasgow Courant*, 7 April 1755. One might hazard a guess that the author was Stonefield, or possibly James Campbell. The account is reprinted, incomplete and with some inaccuracies, in Peter Macintyre *Inveraray, Its Scenery and Associations* (Glasgow 1923) pp.49–52.

The Masonic Lodge at Inveraray had been constituted in 1747 with Captain Duncan Campbell of Inverawe as Master, John Campbell, Sheriff Clerk, as Senior Warden, Dr John McNab as Junior Warden and David Gibson, tailor in Inveraray, as Treasurer. Its original members included the Provosts John Campbell and Alexander Duncanson, Dugald MacTavish of Dunardry, Archibald Campbell of Ormsary, the then Chamberlain John Campbell, James Campbell the lawyer, Angus Fisher, and Walter Paterson. The Charter of Constitution is preserved, but unfortunately no minutes survive before 1780, so the masonic account of this historic occasion of 1755 has been lost. (*History of Inveraray Masonic Lodge*, compiled by Bro. John Johnstone, 1909.)

47. s84A, Hunter to Milton, 12 May & 9 June 1755.

48. s413(2), 414(3), 416(3), Town House accounts, 1755, 1756, 1757; Inv/Ledger 1754; Minutes of Commrs of Supply, 17 May 1758.

49. s418(3), Adam to Milton, 1 November 1758, and Duke's Instructions, November 1758.

50. s416(3), 418(3), Duke's Instructions, 22 November 1757 and November 1758; s418(1), Stonefield to Milton, 18 January 1758, Milton

to Argyll 3, January 1758, scroll letter;
s418(3), memorial, Inveraray magistrates to
Milton, 1758; s92, Provost John Richardson
to Milton, 15 October 1759; IBR 1756–60.
Dobson's predecessor was the trouble-maker
John Fallowsdale, a 'Student of Philosophy'
who had been appointed usher to the grammar
school in 1736 and whom the Duke had wished
to remove as early as 1748; but although the
magistrates were equally anxious to be rid of
him Fallowsdale had had to continue for some
years because of the difficulty of finding a
successor. The chief obstacle was probably the
small salary – £36 a year in 1741, and although
various means were tried to augment it, not
until Dobson was engaged did the Duke
'graciously condescend' to contribute
something. In 1759 the town agreed to raise
£51 3s 4d towards Dobson's salary, which was
further increased by a quarterly levy from the
scholars (e.g. 5s for Greek and Latin, 3s for
English, etc.). Inveraray also possessed a
second school known as the English school.
(IBR)

51. s92, Hunter to Milton, 20 January 1758;
s420(3), ibid., 20 October 1759.

52. Minutes of Commrs of Supply, 30 April
1759.

53. s420(3), Hunter to John Duncanson,
21 June 1759.

54. s420(3), Hunter to Milton, 20 October
1759; Minutes of Commrs of Supply, 30 April
1761. Evidently Hunter did not entirely lose
the Duke's favour, for he continued to send
official progress reports until the Duke's
death. When Andrew Bathgate took over his
dead brother Robert's job, Hunter, Robert's
father-in-law, removed from his Gallowgate
cottage to make way for Andrew, and was
allowed to live with his widowed daughter and
grandchildren in the east wing of the old
castle. (Inv/CI 1760, nos.11, 57)

After the Duke's death Hunter returned to
Edinburgh, and in 1768–71 is recorded as
carrying out repairs at Caroline Park, which
was then in the possession of Duke Archibald's
niece Caroline, Baroness Greenwich. In 1765
he was admitted a burgess of Edinburgh, and
appears to have died in 1787. (Buccleuch MSS,
SRO GD 224/168; EB; ET. See also Index of
Architects and Craftsmen.)

55. The porch on the east house was built in
1783; the date of the other is unknown.
(Inv/CI 1782, December)

56. s418(3), Adam to Milton, 1 November
1758, and his estimate 'for Building a Circlear
Church in the New Town of Inverary',
13 November 1758.

57. s89, Hunter to Milton, November 1758
('Mr Adam wou'd not made any Application
to your Lordship in this Afear if he had not
heard that James Eweing is on the
Carpat . . .'). Ewing is named as of Greenock
in the Duke's Instructions of 25 October 1757
(s416(3)); for his work as mason at Rosneath
Castle, see s82, Colin Campbell to Argyll 3,
21 August 1754, and accounts in s418(2) (and
see Index of Architects and Craftsmen).

58. Inv/Estate 1756–60; s418(3), James
Potter's accts, October 1757–October 1758;
s419(1), abstract of annual accounts,
November 1759, and Adam to Milton,
13 February 1759; s92, Hunter to Milton,
20 January 1759.

59. Ian G.Lindsay *The Scottish Parish Kirk*
(Edinburgh 1960) p.60; Dunbar *The Historic
Architecture of Scotland*, p.166.

60. s418(3), Rev. Patrick Campbell to
Argyll 3, 24 October 1758.

61. s92, Provost John Richardson to Milton,
29 May 1759; s420(2), receipt, 26 October
1760, for payments towards 'carrying on their
new Harbour'; Inv/AEM, vol.II, Payments &
allowances in Argyll Collection for 1761.

62. IBR, and see n.39.

63. s414.

64. s414(2), Duke's Instructions, 6 November
1756; s418(3), minutes to the Duke,
November 1758.

65. s83, Draft of tack for James Whyte,
October 1755. For the building of McPherson's
house, s413(1) & 415, Alexander McPherson
to Milton, 1 December 1755 and 15 October
1756; Inv/18th cent. leases 1701–70, tack of
McPherson's house.

66. s413(1), 415, 88, John Richardson to
Milton, 9 October 1755, 3 November 1756,
24 February 1757.

67. s414(2), ibid., 31 October 1756; s418(3),
ibid. to Argyll 3, 18 October 1758, with Duke's
reply 20 November 1758.

68. Inv/18th cent. leases 1701–70, tack of
Neil Gillies's house, and renewal of tack 1828.

69. s72, David Campbell of Dunloskin to
Milton, 24 September and 31 October 1749,
and memorandum from the Justices of the
Peace of Argyll, Michaelmas 1750; s408(2),
Wm Tod to Milton, 6 October 1750.

70. s76, James Campbell to Milton, 10
February and 27 December 1751; s409, ibid.,
30 November 1751; s409, CI [Nov.] 1751.

71. s79, Milton to Fletcher, 9 April 1752,
scroll letter.

72. s78, James Campbell to Milton, 16 February 1752; s79, John Smith at Buchanan to James Campbell, 11 February 1752.

73. s80, James Campbell to Milton, 12 April 1753.

74. s411, 'Andswers' for James Campbell against Baillie Peter Campbell, 24 September 1753.

75. s413(1), James Campbell to Milton, 23 March 1755; Letter-books of the Trustees to the Manufacturers, SRO N.G. 1/1, vol. 6, 19. The Commissaryship was the office of judge in a Commissary (Admiralty) Court, fallen vacant by the death of Dugald Clerk of Braleckan. In 1755 the appointment took Campbell and Airds on an extensive tour of inspection in Mull, Morvern and Lismore, securing the Duke's woods from predators. (s413(1), James Campbell to Milton, 23 March 1755.)

76. Inv/KJ 22 February 1753; s411(2), James Potter's accts 1753. Inv/1753, possessors of houses in the Gallowgate, 11 September 1753.

77. s416(3), Houses in the Fisherland [i.e. Gallowgate], [1757], and Memorials on Dugald Murray's tenement (now James Campbell's) 1757; s87, Baillie Peter Campbell to Milton, 28 May 1757; s90, Dunardry to Milton, 26 February 1758.

78. Letter-books of Trustees to Manufacturers, loc. cit., vol. 6, 236.

79. Inv/Inst. November 1760, no. 57.

80. Inv/C and 1756, Adam, Memorial relating to the Works . . ., 29 and 30 June 1761, item 25.

CHAPTER V
1. s96, 96A, Letters of Maule and Fletcher to Milton, February 1761.

2. s421, Argyll 3 to Milton, 21 March 1761. The Duke's Edinburgh candidate was the English barrister Alexander Forrester (see ch.II, p. 83), but opposition to this foreign intrusion was so violent that Lord Milton advised the Duke that it would be prudent to withdraw him, after the Provost had been warned of 'the bad Consequences of chuseing any, but a Citizen, & . . . the Provost was afraid of the most disagreeable Tumults and Disorders' (s421, Milton to Argyll 3, 28 March 1761, scroll letter). To prevent their rival then carrying the election, the Duke's friends with his consent hurriedly substituted John Lind, a former Provost, for Forrester, and by means of fairly considerable political maneouvring the unexceptionable Lind was elected. This was finally settled barely ten days before the Duke's death.

3. s95, Milton to Asknish, March 1761, and s421, ibid. to Argyll 3, 4 April 1761, scroll letters.

4. s96, Maule to Milton, 15 April 1761. 'ye Dr & Colonel Williams' were Doctor Charles Stuart and the Duke's son Colonel William Williams; Mr William Campbell was the youngest son of the Duke's heir General Campbell. The Mr Coutts here mentioned would be James, third son of the founder of Scotland's first banking house: he had come to London and entered into partnership with George Middleton's brother-in-law and successor George Campbell, and was himself now head of the firm following Campbell's recent death.
   Maule's letter, evidently written in great haste and agitation, is full of omissions and words added between the lines.

5. s96, Maule to Milton, 16 April 1761.

6. Ibid. The Duke's Scottish estates were of course entailed, and their disposal was the subject of a separate document, apparently held by Lord Milton. The Duke left a week's wages to each of his London servants (including his Whitton gardener, Daniel Croft), 'excepting my cook, whose wages are too high'. (Inv/Will of 3rd Duke of Argyll; and quoted in *The Gentleman's Magazine* and *The Scots Magazine*, May 1761.)

7. s96, Maule to Milton, 16 April 1761.

8. ibid.

9. Ibid., 25 April 1761.

10. Ibid. Colonel Williams, who had been serving in Germany, in 1760 had obtained leave on health grounds, and was, through his father's application to Lord Bute, granted the Governorship of Jersey. His father's sudden death prevented his taking up the post, for his mother's own bad health and advanced age obliged him to cancel the appointment in order to look after their financial affairs. (Bute MSS 492/1761, Col. William Williams to Ld Bute, 29 July 1761.)

11. s96, Maule to Milton, 25 April 1761. Lord Bute had succeeded to the earldom in 1723 at the age of ten, and having been much favoured by the late Prince Frederick of Wales was now favoured still more by his son, who on becoming King in 1760 created him a Privy Councillor and gave him high Court offices. On 25 March 1761 – little more than three weeks before the Duke of Argyll's death – Bute was appointed Secretary of State.
   Bute's dutiful expressions of grief for his uncle arose from friendly feelings of very recent date, for until the end of 1760 the two

had been estranged for about three years, during which Bute and his brother Stuart Mackenzie complained bitterly of Argyll's stranglehold on Scottish affairs, and wished him well out of the way. Soon after the new King's accession, however, a reconciliation was arranged, to the great satisfaction of the Duke and his friends; from then until his death all was harmony between him and Lord Bute. (Bute MSS, 1760, and Fletcher letters in s 96A; and see J.M. Simpson in *Scotland in the Age of Improvement*, p. 63.)

12. s 96, Col. Williams to Milton, 30 May 1761.

13. s 421, Papers on Duke's funeral arrangements. *Edinburgh Evening Courant*, 16–23 May 1761.

14. s 421, Argyll 4 to Milton, 12 May 1761.

15. s 95, A Character of His Grace Archibald Duke of Argyle 1761 (unsigned), by the Reverend Patrick Cuming. Cuming (1695–1776) was Professor of Church History at Edinburgh University, and three times Moderator of the Assembly; the Duke had often consulted him about church patronage. In substance, much of what Cuming writes here is on the lines of the entry in Sir Robert Douglas of Glenbervie's *Peerage of Scotland*, first published in 1764 (basis of the Balfour Paul *Peerage*).

Alexander Forrester wrote of Cuming's draft to Lord Milton on 14 November 1761 that while he approved of it in parts, 'others must receive great alterations. There are mistakes in fact which must be rectify'd. Upon my shewing it a day or two after you gave it to me, to our friend Baron Maule, he produced a printed sheet of an intended Peerage of Scotland, done, I think he said, by one Douglas, with a character of his Grace somewhat similar to; but more accurate than this,' and Forrester offered to devote his Christmas holidays to compiling a 'pretty compleat one' from the two versions. (s 95A) The resulting account, we may presume, was what Douglas published in 1764. Cuming's draft omits the note on the Duke's marriage printed in the *Peerage*, but includes more on Inveraray and on the Duke's character.

16. Inv/C, Adam, Memorial relating to the Works . . ., 29 June 1761, items 23, 24.

17. Inv/C, Instructions for George Haswell Concerning the Wright Works at Inveraray, 24 August 1761.

18. *Vitruvius Britannicus*, IV, pls. 75–7; H.M. Colvin *Dictionary of English Architects*, ad loc. In 1775–7 Robert Adam designed alterations for Combe Bank for Lord Frederick Campbell, which appear to have remained unexecuted. Mrs Damer, staying there in 1803, wrote to Mary Berry, 'This house, as you know with everything that is ornamental and pretty, has little of comfort, and the cold of it is beyond imagination.' (28 January 1803: *The Berry Papers*, ed. Lewis Melville, London 1914, p. 222.)

19. The Lornes' first child was a daughter, Augusta, born in March 1760; the first son, also named George, was born in February 1763 and died at Rosneath in July 1764. The younger children were Charlotte, born in February 1775, and John, born 1777. The Duchess also had three children by her first husband the Duke of Hamilton. (See ch. VI) (Horace Bleackley *The Story of a Beautiful Duchess*, op. cit., pp. 131, 141, 149, 160.)

20. Inv/Articles Agreed upon, 1762, between 4th Duke of Argyll and Lord Lorne; Lorne to Argyll 4, January 1767.

21. Inv/RFD, 1768, State of Augmentations upon Feu duties.

22. *Scotland and Scotsmen in the Eighteenth Century*, I, 90; and s 101, etc.

23. *Private Papers of James Boswell from Malahide Castle*, compiled by Frederick A. Pottle (privately printed 1928–30) XII (6 November and 6 December 1776); *Boswell: The Ominous Years 1774–76*, ed. Charles Ryskamp & Frederick A. Pottle (London 1963) pp. 108, 139, 266. The 3rd Duke bequeathed the Whim to Baron Maule, who very quickly found the bequest an embarrassment and re-disposed of it to the 4th Duke, by whom it was then sold.

24. s 420(3), Mrs Betty Campbell to Archd Campbell, W.S., 10 November 1760; SRO Inveraray Window Tax returns, 1769–71; Inv/AECB 1759–60. Sonachan (d. 1808) was appointed by the 4th Duke, at first apparently as assistant to James Campbell (Inv).

25. IBR. Richardson is first named as Provost in 1759.

26. Henry Scott *Fasti Ecclesiae Scoticanae*, IV, Synods of Argyll, Perth and Stirling (Edinburgh 1923) p. 11; SRO Inveraray Window Tax returns, 1769–70; Inv/AEM, vol. II, Deductions from rental 1763–8. See ch. IV, p. 168.

27. s 401, Argyll 3 to Milton, 27 October 1743.

28. *Memoir and Correspondence of Susan Ferrier*, ed. J.A. Doyle, 1898. JAMES FERRIER (1744–1829), third son of John Ferrier of Kirkland, Renfrewshire, in 1767 married

Helen, daughter of Robert Coutts, of
Montrose; from 1802–26 he was Principal
Clerk of Session. His eldest son John
(1771–1852), who started his career as his
father's apprentice, later became Deputy
Keeper of the Great Seal. James Ferrier is,
however, chiefly known as the father of the
novelist Susan Ferrier (1782–1854), youngest
of his ten children, who frequently visited
Inveraray with her father and there became
friendly with the 5th Duke's niece Miss
Clavering. The latter collaborated in a small
way with Susan Ferrier's first novel, *Marriage*,
written in 1810 though not published until
1818. (Sir Walter Scott thought highly of her
books – with whose authorship he was for a
time popularly credited.)

29.   Pennant *Tour in Scotland 1769*, p. 238.
Pennant's criticisms, which applied strictly to
a time when Inveraray was looking its worst,
were unfortunately accepted by many later
writers as gospel. His travel books deservedly
became such classics that lazier followers in his
footsteps, even after several decades, often
repeated his descriptions unedited and without
acknowledgment, to fill the gaps in their own
observations: in this way a glaring misreading
by one writer of 80 for 18 bedchambers at
Inveraray was itself frequently repeated in
early 19th-century guide-books. Pennant's
aesthetic judgment of the castle was also
repeated almost unaltered, or facetiously
improved on, and the myth was established
that old Inveraray had always been a miserable
slum.

CHAPTER VI

1.   Details of the 5th Duke of Argyll's career
from Balfour Paul *Scots Peerage*.

2.   The Gunning sisters and their marriages
are the subjects of anecdotes by most diarists
and letter-writers of the period – notably, of
course, Horace Walpole. Among the stories of
Lady Coventry is that of her refusing, in Paris,
an invitation to Madame de Pompadour's
reception because it was the hour for her
music-master; while at Court in London,
prattling away to the ageing King George II,
she cheerfully remarked that the one ceremony
she really longed to see was a coronation. The
two sisters' fame was even commemorated in
novels of the day. Mrs Charlotte Lennox in
The Female Quixote, published in 1752 (ed.
Margaret Dalziel, Oxford 1970, pp. 148–9),
vividly describes Maria Gunning's inane
behaviour at the play with mannerisms (and a
pet squirrel) that captivated her gallants.
Elizabeth Gunning eventually became mother
to four Dukes, as her two sons by the Duke of

Argyll both (though long after her own death)
inherited the title.

For the Douglas Cause see, e.g., *Boswell in
Search of a Wife*, ed. Frank Brady & Frederick
A. Pottle (London 1957), A. Francis Steuart *The
Douglas Cause* (Glasgow 1909), and Bleackley
The Story of a Beautiful Duchess. In this
protracted lawsuit claim was laid on behalf of
Elizabeth Gunning's son George, Duke of
Hamilton, to the estates of the Duke of
Douglas, on the grounds that the two sons of
Douglas's sister Lady Jane Stewart, were not
genuinely hers but had been passed off as her
own by subterfuge. The judgment, originally
given in favour of the Duke of Hamilton, was
later reversed.

3.   A note in Robert Mylne's diary for 24
March 1764, that he 'gave 2 outlines for
tapestry to Marquis of Lorn [i.e. the future 5th
Duke]' may refer to
temporary installation of these tapestries at the
Clachan, Rosneath. For the Duchess's
looking-glasses, Inv/Gen. Inst. 1788 (Inst. to
Wrights, Oct. 1788, p. 500).

4.   A significant item of freight charges of £10
for pictures in September 1768 suggests that
furnishing of the castle had already begun.
(Inv/Accts 1767–72).

5.   Inv/NPE: *Edinburgh Advertiser*, June 1771.

6.   Daniel Wray, FRS, FSA, letter of 15
October 1771, quoted by John Nichols
*Illustrations of the Literary History of the 18th
Century*, I (London 1817) pp. 141–2.

7.   GENERAL THE HON. HENRY SEYMOUR
CONWAY (1721–95), was younger brother to
the Earl of Hertford and a cousin of Horace
Walpole's. He had early entered the army, but
was also a Member of Parliament almost
uninterruptedly from 1741–84 (at this period
for Thetford). In 1745 he had been ADC to
the Duke of Cumberland and was present at
Culloden and other battles. In 1757 he was
appointed a Groom of the Bedchamber, but
dismissed from his court and army
appointments during the Wilkes case; in 1765,
however, when King George III was forced to
accept Rockingham's administration, Conway
became a Secretary of State at Cumberland's
order, resigning in 1768. In 1759 he became a
Lieutenant General, and in October 1770 was
given command of the Royal Regiment of
Guards. (*DNB*)

Conway in 1747 had married the widowed
Lady Ailesbury, daughter of General John
Campbell (later 4th Duke of Argyll), by whom
he had one daughter Anne, who became Mrs
Damer. His portrait by Gainsborough hangs in
the saloon at Inveraray Castle.

LORD STANLEY, Lady Betty's husband, later succeeded to the earldom of Derby. LADY BETTY was also a great friend of Hume's. Henry Mackenzie relates that one Sunday at Inveraray Hume, notoriously a sceptic and atheist, agreed to go with Lady Betty to church. 'The sermon was on the subject of unreasonable scepticism. "That's at you, Mr Hume," said his fair companion. At the close of his discourse the Minister said, "And now, my friends, I will address a few words to the chief of sinners." – "That's to your Ladyship," said Mr Hume.' (Henry Mackenzie *Anecdotes and Egotisms*, Oxford 1927, p.97)

WILLIAM MURE (1718–76) was eldest son of William Mure of Caldwell in Ayr and Renfrewshire. After studying law at Edinburgh and Leyden, from 1741–61 he was MP for Renfrewshire and in 1761 became a Baron of the Exchequer, but his great interest was in agricultural improvements. He was a friend of Lord Bute, through whom he eventually became influential in Scottish local affairs. His wife was Anne Graham, daughter of the judge Lord Easdale. (*DNB*)

8. Baron William Mure to David Hume, 4 September 1775; *Letters of David Hume*, p.362.

9. Boswell had passed six days at Inveraray in 1771, with his father Lord Auchinleck on the Western Circuit. At that time he admired the 'magnificent seat' with 'all the highland wild grandeur, and a vast addition from art', and wrote 'a pretty good description of it', which has unfortunately disappeared. (Boswell to John Johnston, 22 May 1771, Yale edn of the *Correspondence of James Boswell and John Johnstone of Grange*, ed. F. A. Pottle et al., London 1966, p.264 and n.)

The whole passage of Johnson and Boswell's visit in 1773, too long to quote here in full, is well worth reading: Boswell's *Journal of a Tour to the Hebrides with Samuel Johnson, Ll.D., 1773*, ed. F. A. Pottle & Charles H. Bennett (London 1963) pp.348, 351–7, 359. See also *Letters of Samuel Johnson*, ed. R. W. Chapman (Oxford 1952) I, 377 and II, 214 (letters 332–6 and 552); *Private Papers of James Boswell . . .*, XIII (23 September 1777).

10. Donald Campbell of Airds died eighteen months later at his own house, on 6 May 1775 (*Edinburgh Evening Courant*).

11. ANNE MCVICAR (1755–1838) later married a young minister and, as Mrs Grant of Laggan, became a noted authoress after the turn of the 19th century. This account, from her *Letters from the Mountains* (London 1807), is based on her Inveraray letters of April 1773.

12. In 1776 the Reverend William Gilpin admired some mezzotints in the west corner (now the Library) turret, whose varnish and colour was 'all the work of the present duchess of Argyle', by a newly invented method 'sold, under promise of secrecy, to many ladies'. (*Observations relative chiefly to Picturesque Beauty*, London 1779). A review in *The Topographer*, I, 1789, p.294, also admires the 'small pictures . . . which are in so mellow a style as to strike one with the belief of their being fine old paintings'. This small round room consequently became known as the 'Print Turret', and above its present bookshelves many of the mezzotints still form part of the wall decoration.

13. Mylne 1764 and 1765.

14. Ian G. Lindsay *Georgian Edinburgh* (Edinburgh 1948) pp.12, 21; A. J. Youngson *The Making of Classical Edinburgh, 1750–1840* (Edinburgh 1966) pp.62–3.

15. Inv/5DA Corresp. and Accounts, Acct of Wm Mylne 1770–2.

16. These and the following particulars are all in Inv/CI 1771 ff. pp.151, 154 (February and December 1771).

17. Traces of this staircase, removed at a much later date, may still be seen on the turret wall – below the Duchess's 'prints'.

18. Colvin *Dict. of British Architects* ad loc. The celebrated Almack's Assembly Rooms were built 'with great haste' between May 1764 and February 1765; Mylne also designed, or advised on, a bow window for another of Almack's properties in Pall Mall which may well have inspired the famous later bows at White's and Boodle's.

Robert Mylne's commissions for William Almack probably resulted from his work for Lord Lorne (alternatively, it may even have been Almack who first introduced Mylne to Lorne), for the family of Almack's wife, Elizabeth Cullen, had old connexions with the 5th Duke and Duchess of Hamilton (parents of Elizabeth Gunning's first husband). Elizabeth Cullen's father had been the Duke of Hamilton's factor, her brother Dr William Cullen was his physician before the Duke's death in 1743, and Elizabeth herself is reputed to have been the Duchess's waiting-maid before marrying Almack and settling in London by 1746.

Almack was probably of Yorkshire origin, and the tempting story that he was a Scot named McCaul or Mackal who reversed his name because of English prejudice, appears to be unfounded. (Robert Kerr *Memoirs of the Life of William Smellie*, I, Edinburgh 1811, pp. 436–7, repeated by Lady Russell *Three Generations of Fascinating Women*, London 1905, p. 129.)

According to one version, Lord Lorne put up the capital for the Assembly Rooms which Robert Mylne was designing in 1764. Mylne's diary for January 1765 mentions business for Almack on dates when he also dealt with Lorne about the latter's stables.

(*Survey of London* XXIX, pt I (London 1960) pp. 304–7, 327, 329; Dr John Thomson *An Account of the Life, Lectures and Writings of William Cullen, M.B.* (Edinburgh 1832) pp. 1, 11, 17, 22 and 544 ff.; Rev. Charles Rogers *Familiar Illustrations of Scottish Life* (London 1866) pp. 112–13; *DNB*; Mylne 1764 and 1765).

19. John Nichols *Literary Anecdotes of the 18th Century*, IX (London 1815) p. 233.

20. Mylne August–September 1772.

21. *Scots Magazine*, October 1772. Thomas Pennant, during a second visit to Inveraray on 14 August that year, had remarked on this fine bridge, 'built at the expence of Government': it was destroyed little over three weeks after he saw it. His *Tour of Scotland and Voyage to the Hebrides* II (1776) includes two illustrations showing the bridge immediately before its destruction, one a full-page view from the loch, the other a title-page vignette. Both clearly show that by then only one of the mock turrets still retained its crenellations.

22. Mylne September 1772.

23. Ibid., and Rev. Robert Scott Mylne *The Master Masons to the Crown of Scotland* (Edinburgh 1893) p. 276.

24. See Ada K. Longfield 'The Manufacture of Raised Stucco or Papier Maché Papers in Ireland', *J. Royal Antiq. Soc. of Ireland* 78 (1948) 55–62, and (as Ada K. Leask) 'Papier maché, its use as raised paper stucco', *The Papermaker*, 32, no. 2 (1963) (Hercules Powder Co., Wilmington, Del., U.S.A.). It was used by Horace Walpole in the Holbein Chamber at Strawberry Hill, and by Lady Luxborough at her house, Barrells, near Wootten Wawen. See Mrs Delany *Autobiography and Correspondence*, II (London 1861) p. 532; *Letters written by the late Rt Hon. Lady Luxborough to William Shenstone, Esq.* (London 1775) pp. 299–300; Margaret Jourdain *English Interior Decoration 1500–1830* (London 1950). Henry Clay in Birmingham patented his method in 1772, after which the process became very commercialized and moved out of its experimental phase. It is possible that the Inveraray ceiling was a product of this kind. For the method used in the 19th

century see Charles F. Bielefeld *On the Use of the Improved Papier Maché in Furniture* (London ?1840).

25. Inv/CI (to Geo. Haswell, p. 157), 1 December 1772.

26. Ibid., pp. 162, 187, November 1773 and 1782; and to Chamberlain, 13 December 1782. CA 1773–4, f. 18; CA 1774–75 and 1781–2.

The following advertisement appeared in the *Edinburgh Advertiser* on 2 June, 1775:

M. DUPASQUIER GILDER
from PARIS
(Lately employed by his Grace the Duke of Argyll in finishing INVERARY HOUSE, which Work has been universally admired) GILDS and BURNISHES, in the neatest manner, all sorts of HOUSEHOLD FURNITURE, AND PICTURE FRAMES.

Noblemen and Gentlemen who incline to favour this Artist, are requested to send their orders to him, at Messrs. *Home* and *Cleghorn's*, Coach builders, Prince's Street, New Town, Edinburgh.

Although the transition from gilder to sculptor may seem improbable, there seems a reasonable case for identifying this Dupasquier with the sculptor Antoine Léonard du Pasquier (1748–?1831)–who exhibited in the Paris Salon under both forms of the surname–born in Paris and a student under Charles Bridan. He won prizes in 1773 and 1776, then is recorded as studying in Rome until 1779, after which he conveniently disappears until 1791 when he is known to have exhibited in Paris. Later sculptures included a bas-relief of battle scenes round the base of the Colonne Vendôme, a statue for the Pont de la Concorde, and another of the celebrated naval captain Réné Duguay-Trouin, in the Cour d'Honneur at Versailles.

Apart from the awkward year 1773 when du Pasquier was winning a prize in Paris and Dupasquier was working at Inveraray, no positive evidence seems to contradict this possible identification, and Dupasquier's work in Scotland might account for the sculptor's 'lost' years. The other available evidence is the record of the marriage in Edinburgh, 15 July 1778, of Leonard Dupasquier, 'carver and gilder' of Old Kirk parish, to Margaret Anderson, daughter of a smith at Alloa. This would not conflict with a period of (non-continuous) study at Rome until 1779. A marriage is also recorded, in Edinburgh in 1787, of a Mary Dupasquier, daughter of John Bernard du Pasquier, merchant in Burgundy: who may or may not have been also Léonard's father (or possibly uncle). It is worth noting that the Edinburgh newspaper advertisement above refers to the gilder as 'from Paris'. (EM; Stanislas Lami *Dictionnaire des Sculpteurs de l'Ecole Française*, I, 18th cent. (Paris 1910); E. Bénézit *Dictionnaire antique et documentaire des peintres, sculpteurs, dessinateurs et graveurs*, VI (Paris 1966); Thieme-Becker *Allgemeines Lexikon der Bildenden Künstler*, XXVI, Leipzig 1932.)

27.   The records are surprisingly silent about the final disappearance of the old tower and pavilion, but the Chamberlain's Accounts 1773/4 show that from the beginning of 1774 the old town and its church were actually being removed, and the Chamberlain's Instructions dated October 1775 show demolition in full swing. Mary Ann Hanway, visiting in August 1775, refers to new building but says nothing of any old, which might imply that there was already little or none to be seen (*A Journey to the Highlands of Scotland*, ?1776). Gilpin (op. cit.) similarly says nothing of the old castle. (See p. 232 and ch. VIII p. 264 and n. 39.)

28.   Mylne 1772 (memo.), 1 May 1773, 27 September 1775; Inv/CI 31 October 1775; CA 1776/7 and 1777/8. For the 'covered way', Mylne 27 August 1776. The original 'covered way' on the east side, mentioned by William Burrell in the 1750s (see ch. II, p. 98 and n. 207), was begun as an underground passage to the old town for the use of carts, but it was excavated for no more than some twenty yards. In 1779 a new water closet was ordered to be made in the vault from which this abandoned exit opened. (Inv/CI 1779, to Haswell, p. 176.)

29.   During his visit in August 1776 the Duke presented Mylne with a portrait of the Duchess, which remained in his family for over 100 years and was returned to the 8th Duke by his descendant R. W. Mylne in 1888. (Rev. Robert Scott Mylne op. cit. p. 275.)

30.   Mylne 3 April 1777; Inv/CI 1782 and 1783 to Haswell (pp. 187, 190), 7 October 1784 to Sonachan and to wrights (p. 192), 29 October 1785 to wrights (p. 194).

31.   The Duchess's second son and youngest child by the Duke of Argyll was John Douglas (later 7th Duke), born in London in November 1777. See ch. V, n. 19.

32.   *Edinburgh Evening Courant*, 24 May 1775; *Edinburgh Advertiser* May–August 1775; *Memoirs of Sir James Campbell of Ardkinglas* (London 1832).

33.   Inv/Arch. Campbell [of Succoth]'s Accounts 1767–78 (for June 1777). On 5 April 1778 the 8th Duke of Hamilton married Miss Elizabeth Burrell, sister of William Burrell, and the newly-married pair left for Scotland towards the end of June. According to one report the Duke of Argyll also went to Scotland that summer, but if so he certainly did not go as far as Inveraray.

34.   Inv/1765–1812, Argyll 5 to [Arch. Campbell of Succoth], 18 June 1778.

35.   Inv/5 DA, Donald Campbell of Sonachan (Chamberlain) to Argyll 5, 5 July 1778.

36.   Ibid., 18 September 1778. LORD FREDERICK CAMPBELL (1729–1816), 4th son of the 4th Duke of Argyll, was MP for the Glasgow Burghs 1761–80 and for Argyll 1780–99. In 1765 he became a Privy Councillor and from 1768 until the end of his life was Lord Clerk Register of Scotland, in which capacity he laid the foundation stone of Robert Adam's Register House in Edinburgh in 1774, and was also responsible for recovering from England some valuable Scottish Parliament records. He married Mary Meredith, divorced wife of the notorious Earl Ferrers who was hanged in 1760 for the murder of his steward. A natural daughter Mary married, in 1778 at Ardincaple (their house near Rosneath), Donald Campbell of Barbreck. Lady Frederick was accidentally burned to death at Combe Bank on 24 July 1807. (Balfour Paul *Scots Peerage*.)

37.   [Mary Ann Hanway], op. cit.

38.   Rev. William Gilpin, op. cit.

39.   David Loch *Essays on the Trade, Commerce, Manufactures, and Fisheries of Scotland*, II (Edinburgh 1778) pp. 219 ff. The Crinan Canal was begun in 1793 by a private company and opened in 1801. DAVID LOCH, who died in Edinburgh less than two years after this visit to Inveraray, was a native of Over Carnbie in Fife and was bred to the sea, but became a prosperous merchant and ship-owner at Leith and claimed to be the first merchant in Scotland to send his ships to Archangel, and to Havana. A pioneer in many ventures, he traded extensively with Europe and America (which he visited), and in the 1770s published numerous letters and essays on commerce and the expansion of industry, particularly wool. See his *Curious and Entertaining Letters concerning the Trade and Manufactures of Scotland* (Edinburgh 1774) and *Essays*. (Subscribers to the latter publication included the Duke of Argyll (6 copies), Lord Frederick Campbell (5 copies), the Duke's lawyer James Ferrier, Baron John Maule, James Boswell, Dr William Cullen, and Robert Fall, of Dunbar (2 copies).)

40.　JAMES MAXWELL (?1720-1800), born near Paisley, was a rather unfortunate character who worked as clerk and usher, married in England but was left by his wife when he returned to Scotland and set up his own school. Later he became a parish school-master and Session Clerk in or near Campbeltown (when, no doubt, he made this visit to Inveraray), but he returned to Paisley in penury in 1782 with arrears of salary owing, for which he repeatedly applied in vain. He was reduced to menial jobs, and in his last years, troubled by illness, gained a livelihood selling pamphlets and his own verses in the street, or

　　. . . sometimes in making rhyme
For Gentlemen whoe'er would me employ.
Maxwell's publications, mostly printed at his own expense in Paisley, included a metrical version of the psalms (1776), followed between 1785 and 1796 by numerous poems on topical or religious subjects. In 1785 he wrote a verse account of Paisley which recalls the Inveraray epic, and in 1795, in his 76th year, 'A Brief Narration, or some remarks on the Life of James Maxwell, a Poet, written by himself' (in verse, of course), from which the above information is extracted. See also Robert Brown *Paisley Poets*, I (Glasgow 1889) pp. 14-26. The full title of Maxwell's Inveraray poem, published in Glasgow in 1777, is *A Descriptive Poem on His Grace the Duke of Argyle's Noble Palace at Inveraray: as also Some Description of the New Town of Inveraray, in 1777. To which is added, An Appendix, with farther Observations taken at a second Visit.*

41.　Paterson's immediate successor as gardener, in 1770, had been John McNure, to whom the earliest Chamberlain's Instructions of the 5th Duke (1771) are addressed.

42.　In 1787 Stebbing Shaw and his friend were also shown the view from the leads, ascending from the top of the east turret. (See n.69).

43.　Inv/CI 1779, 1780, to Haswell (pp.175, 176, 178). In 1789-90 an Edinburgh plumber installed two further w.c.s, one 'the Closet below the Stair near my [i.e. the Duke's] Turret, the other in one of the Closets up Stair lighted from the Stair where the Coals are now kept.' The ground-floor w.c. adjoined the kitchen, and was evidently reached by the turret stair built in 1780; the 'up Stair' (i.e. main floor) one was in the lobby opening off the west stair-case hall. They are shown in Bonomi's plans of 1806. Their plumbing and lead cost £44 3s 7d. (Inv/Gen. Inst. 1788, pp.5, 13; CA 1789/90.)

44.　Mylne 6 September, 2 and 5 November 1780; Robert S.Mylne, op.cit. p.277.

45.　Mylne 7 September and 5 November 1780; Colvin *Dictionary of Architects*, ad loc. No evidence has to date been found of any relationship between the two Claytons, but the dates and the fact that both worked for Dukes of Argyll make it a plausible deduction. It would evidently be the later Clayton who worked at Sir Lawrence Dundas's house in St Andrew's Square, Edinburgh. For information about the two Claytons and Richard Lawrence (see next note) I am indebted to Mr Geoffrey Beard.

46.　Robert S.Mylne, loc.cit. 'Mr Lawrence' is probably Richard Lawrence, a carver, fl.1764-83, who worked at Somerset House and Fulton Manor, Berks.

47.　Inv/CI, 19 December, 1783, and to Haswell, 1783 (p.190). The windows of the main floor rooms were replaced in the 19th century, and such glazing-bars as exist (e.g. in the state dining-room and drawing-room) date from that time.

48.　See n.30.

49.　Inv/CI, to wrights 29 October 1787 (p.198).

50.　Mylne 1783, 1785.

51.　Mylne's first visit to Rosneath was as early as 1769, three years before he even set foot in Inveraray; but not until 1783, when he spent a day surveying the house, does he appear to have undertaken any alterations. In 1785 he visited Rosneath both before and after going to Inveraray. None of his numerous plans for the castle have, apparently, survived, but between 1783 and 1787 his diary lists consider-able alterations, including addition of a turreted NE wing, changes in 'the back, front and Plan of first floor', and improvements to the offices. In 1790 he sent the Duke further designs, in 1792 plans for a double cottage, and after a long gap, in 1801 plans for bath and water pipes at Rosneath, and '2 plates of looking glass'. At that time the Duke was living entirely in Scotland, and Mylne appears not to have seen him after 1796, but to have conducted business with Lord Lorne, who more often kept the architect waiting than admitted him to a consultation. (Mylne, ad loc.)

52.　Inv/CI 1783, to Haswell (pp.189-90). In 1778 Haswell, referred to as 'architect, of Inveraray', had been invited to design Castlehill Church at Campbeltown, and it was built 1779-80 to his design, by the mason and contractor John Brown who built several of the tenements in Inveraray new town (see ch. VIII). (SRO HR 67/1, Campbeltown Heritors' Minute Book 1778–1821, 1, 8 f., 22.) On Haswell's death his widow was paid a pension of £15 a year (Inv/CA).

53. Inglis MSS, SRO GD 1/46/16, Diary of John Inglis, farmer in Holm, 1784.

54. Barthélemy Faujas de Saint-Fond *A Journey through England and Scotland to the Hebrides in 1784* (English translation revised and edited by Sir Archibald Geikie) (Glasgow 1907). FAUJAS DE ST FOND (1741–1819) had been educated in the law, but was always more interested in natural history, and became attached to the Musée d'Histoire Naturelle in Paris. Later he was appointed Royal Commissioner of Mines, and finally a Professor of Geology. His interests included zoology, botany and mineralogy, and among other works he published a treatise on ballooning and a work on extinct French volcanoes. He travelled extensively in England, where he met other scientists. (An account of his life is given in Sir Archibald Geikie's edition of the *Journey*.)

55. Col. Thomas Thornton *A Sporting Tour through the Northern Parts of England, and great part of the Highlands of Scotland* (London 1804).

56. Thomas Newte *Prospects and Observations on a Tour in England and Scotland* (London 1791) (first published 1788 under the title *A Tour in England and Scotland in 1785, by an English Gentleman*, with the pseudonym William Thomson).

57. NLS 3294–5, J. Bailey *A Journey in Scotland*, 2 vols.

58. Inv/CA 1781/2.

59. Bailey, loc. cit. All this, together with the central tower roof, and the organ, perished in the fire of 1877. See Epilogue.

60. Inv/CI 1783, to Haswell (p. 189). In 1806 the 6th Duke commissioned Joseph Bonomi to devise a new arrangement for the arms (designs preserved at the castle), but his layout was not adopted. They were last rearranged in 1953 by direction of the present Duke, in principle restoring the original appearance, but with the addition of fan-shapes and quarter-circles. All the military colours were lost in the fire of 1877.

61. John Walker *An Economic History of the Hebrides and Highlands* (Edinburgh 1808) p. 379.

62. Inv/CA 1781/2.

63. Boswell's *Tour to the Hebrides*, p. 355. The gentleman referred to was Adam Livingstone, MP for Argyll.

64. Mr Bailey refers to use of a turret room as the family breakfast room.

65. Inv/CA 1781/2, which gives £98 15s as the payment for the four main rooms and £25 7s 11d for the turret. The remaining £184 1s 2d is for unspecified work over the year.

66. These tapestries were probably ordered by the Duke and Duchess during a visit to Paris soon after their marriage, and would have taken some years to weave. They were hung in August or September 1787, the probable date of Mr Bailey's visit, when he observed that 'a person from the Cambresis was occupied in affixing . . . a most delicious new tapestry, the subject shepherdesses with their flocks, and the colours so vivid and well-mixed, that I thought it little inferior to the most exquisite painting'.
Miss Edith Standen of the Metropolitan Museum, New York, has now dated the Beauvais tapestries to 1785, and describes them as almost certainly 'the only set of eighteenth-century Beauvais tapestries that remains in the room for which it was made'. This information came to our attention when the book was in proof.

67. I am indebted to Mr Edward Croft-Murray for suggestions on the style of these rooms. The Ashburnham decorations appear to be identical with, and probably were transferred from, the salon whose walls were designed by Charles-Louis Clérisseau and executed by Etienne de Lavallee in 1777, for the Hôtel Grimod de La Reynière near the Place de la Concorde. See Edward Croft-Murray's article in *Apollo* LXVIII (1963) 377–83; John Harris 'English Rooms in American Museums', *CL* (8 June 1961) 1329; Margaret Jourdain *English Decoration and Furniture of the later XVIIIth Century, 1760–1820* (London 1923) p. 74.

68. Inv/Gen. Inst. 1788, Inst. to Wrights October 1788 (p. 500). The painting over 'the Tope of the Glass' was replaced in the 19th century by a panel, 'The Dancers', by George Richmond, RA (1809–96), said to have been executed while the artist was on a visit to the castle.

69. Stebbing Shaw *A Tour in 1787, from London, to the Western Highlands of Scotland* (London 1788) p. 158. STEBBING SHAW (1762–1802), topographer, was the son of a Derbyshire clergyman of the same name to whose living he succeeded in 1799. Educated

at Cambridge, on taking orders he became tutor to the son of Robert Burdett, of Ealing, with whom he travelled to the Highlands. His anonymously published journal of this tour received little notice, but that of a tour to the west of England in 1788 proved successful, and he later collaborated on a careful series, *The Topographer*. In 1795 he became an FSA. Before his death he was cataloguing manuscripts for the British Museum, and was said to have had a mental breakdown from over-work. (*DNB*)

70.   Inv/Gen. Accts 1783/4 (Guinand); CA 1786/7, 1787/8, 1789/90, 5DA Accts 1788/9, CI October 1787, to Sonachan (Girardy); CI 1782, to Haswell (p.187); 13 December 1782, 7 October 1784, 29 October 1785 and October 1787, to Sonachan; CA 1781/2, 1785/6, 1786/7, 1787/8, and Gen. Accts 1783/4 (Dupasquier).

71.   *Royal Academy of Arts, Dictionary of Contributions*, ed. Algernon Graves, II (London (1905) ad loc.; Bénézit *Dictionnaire*, III and IV; Thieme-Becker *Lexikon*, vols. X, XIII, XIV, ad loc. The *Archives de l'Art français* (Nouvelle période), vol. IX (Paris 1915), mention a Jean-François Guinand living in Rue du Regard, Paris as 'reçu en 1765' at the Académie de S. Luc; and a Guinand, possibly the same, as living in Rue S. Placide (pp.317, 360). The *Procès-verbaux* of the Académie Royale de Peinture et de Sculpture, Guiffrey-Berthélemy's List of the Pensionnaires at the Académie de France à Rome, and Bellier de La Chavignerie's *Dictionnaire Général des Artistes de l'École Française* (Paris 1882), have no relevant information. Further, these artists have resisted the combined knowledge of Mr Francis Watson, Mr Edward Croft-Murray, the Service d'Etude et de Documentation at the Musée du Louvre, Mme Bouleau-Rabaud at the Ecole Nationale Supérieure des Beaux-Arts, Mme Guerin at the Musée des Arts Décoratifs, the Bibliothèque Nationale (Cabinet des Estampes), and Mr Charles Sterling of the Musée du Louvre–to all of whom my thanks are due for their help. Future documentary discoveries may bring some further information to light, but until then our knowledge of these *petits-maîtres* remains almost entirely hypothetical.

72.   Inv/5DA Accts 1788/9.

73.   Inv/CI 29 October 1785, to Sonachan (looking-glasses); CA 1781/2 (doors), and 1786/7, 1788/9 (upholsterer and weaver). Among other artists and craftsmen employed in a minor capacity were William McEwen or

McHain, probably a house painter (see p.211), from Glasgow, 1784–6; Alexander Christie, (probably house) painter, 1783 (paid £16 6s); Archibald Shaw, marble cutter, 'for marble by Mr Haswell for Dining Room', 1784; and James Hutchison, plasterer, paid £7 10s in August 1782. (Inv/CI 7 October 1784, 29 October 1785, to Sonachan; CA 1781/2, 1785/6; Gen. Accts 1783/4.)

74.   Inv/CI 1782, to Haswell (p.186), 7 January 1787, to wrights (pp.196, 199); CA 1781/2, 1786/7, 1787/8, 1788/9; Gen. Inst. 1783/4.

75.   Inv/Inventory and Valuation (1960) by Knight, Frank & Rutley; Anthony Coleridge 'English Furniture in the Duke of Argyll's Collection at Inveraray Castle' in *The Connoisseur* (March 1965) 154–61.

76.   John Knox *A View of the British Empire, more Especially Scotland* (London 1785) p.597.

77.   *The Life and Works of Robert Burns*, ed. Robert Chambers, II (Edinburgh 1851) p.97; *Letters of Robert Burns*, ed. J. de Lancey Ferguson, I (Oxford 1931) p.98. Burns wrote to John Richmond on 7 July, 'I have lately been rambling over by Dumbarton and Inverary and running a drunken race on the side of Loch Lomond with a wild Highlandman. . .' (Ibid., I, p.101). Both fell off their horses, and Burns was (he said) covered with bruises.

78.   The party included the Earl of Breadalbane (the Society's Vice-President) and his brother the Hon. Colin Campbell, Sir Adam Fergusson of Kilkerran, George Dempster the noted agriculturist, Isaac Hawkins Browne, and Professor Thorkelin, a distinguished Icelandic antiquarian who was keeper of public archives at Copenhagen. The British Fishery Society was founded largely at the instigation of Dempster, who also planned this voyage and invited Thorkelin to visit the country. The Duke of Argyll, who accompanied the travellers on the first part of the voyage, had been elected President of the new Highlands and Agricultural Society of Scotland in 1785. (*The Bee, or Literary Weekly Intelligencer*, vols. 8 and 9, 1792; *Letters of George Dempster to Adam Fergusson, 1756–1813*, ed. James Fergusson, Studies in Modern History, (London, 1934.)

79.   Inv/Gen. Inst., October 1788, to wrights (p.500).

80.   Boswell *Tour to the Hebrides* p.353.

81.   Diary of John Inglis, MS cit.; Col. T. Thornton *A Sporting Tour*.

82. NLS 1080, *A Travelling Journal*, 1789. The neglect complained of was due, however, not to the Duke's 'depravity' but to the Duchess's failing health, which distracted him from estate business. (See p. 226.)

83. Newte, loc. cit., Faujas de St Fond, loc. cit.

84. For evidence of Lord Herbert's visit see *Pembroke Papers, 1780–94*, ed. Lord Herbert (London 1950) (Ld Pembroke to Ld Herbert, 26 July and 12 August 1781). Lord Pembroke himself passed through Inveraray once more in 1782 on his way to review troops in Belfast (*Morrison Collection* v, 117, Ld Pembroke to Ld Carmarthen, 20 July 1782). For Burke and Windham, see *Diary of the Rt Hon. William Windham*, ed. Mrs Henry Baring (London 1866) pp. 61 f. Burke and Windham reached an inn ten miles from Inveraray (presumably Cairndow) at dinner-time on 4 September 1785, where they received a message from the Duke inviting them to breakfast next morning. They rode about the grounds at Inveraray seeing the usual sights. Among those staying were Lord Lorne, Lady Augusta, Lady Derby (the Duchess's daughter by the Duke of Hamilton), 'a painter who seemed to be an Englishman', and others. Burke's complimentary letter of form to the Duchess written after leaving is included in *Intimate Society Letters of the 18th Century*, ed. John 9th Duke of Argyll, I (London 1910) p. 214.

A description of Raspe's exploits in the West Highlands and Islands is given in John Carswell's *The Prospector* (privately printed 1950).

85. Thrale MSS, John Rylands Library, Ryl. Eng. MS. 623, Mrs Thrale's Journey to Scotland 1789, f. 13v. Samuel Rogers, then aged 26, preceded the Piozzis at Inveraray by a few days, during a horseback tour alone except for his servant. On his way south he called on the Piozzis at the Saracen's Head in Glasgow before they set off for Argyll. (P. W. Clayden *The Early Life of Samuel Rogers*, London 1887, pp. 100–1, 103.)

86. Faujas de St Fond, op. cit. Lady Augusta's skill was often praised not only as a pianist but in playing the organ built by Alexander Cumming. Other contemporary accounts mention regular visits to the castle by the Duke's sister Caroline Countess of Ailesbury and her second husband, General Seymour Conway; the two Argyll daughters, Augusta and Charlotte, and the Countess of Derby (never with her husband – the marriage eventually broke up with a scandal). Of St Fond's own party, WILLIAM THORNTON (1759–1828) was a versatile and ingenious young man of Quaker forebears who was born in Tortola, Virgin Islands. He studied medicine under Dr Cullen at Edinburgh University (1781–4), but had taken his degree at Aberdeen shortly before this tour. Later he went to the United States and in 1788 became an American citizen, spending some years in Philadelphia. He was talented as a painter and had a taste for amateur architecture, winning a competition with his design for the fine Philadelphia Library building (1789–90, demol. 1880), while his other designs included some rather unpractical plans for the Capitol building in Washington. He wrote widely on numerous subjects, particularly inventions, and indeed would have been a man after Duke Archibald's own heart. From 1802 until his death Thornton was Superintendent of the Patent Office in Washington. (*Dictionary of American Biography*, London 1936, vol. XVIII.)

Charles Greville, who with his uncle Sir William Hamilton had made an unsuccessful attempt to reach Staffa in rough weather shortly before St Fond and his party visited it, identifies St Fond's somewhat improbably named 'M. de Mecies' as Mr Massie, 'a young English gentleman fond of chemistry at Oxford' and delicate in health. (Charles Greville to Sir William Hamilton, [October 1784], in Alfred Morrison *The Hamilton and Nelson Papers*, I, privately printed 1893, p. 91.)

87. ROBERT MCQUEEN, LORD BRAXFIELD (1722–99), Lord Justice Clerk, was renowned alike for his vigorous ability and his coarse wit. He was the original of Stevenson's *Weir of Hermiston*. Lord Cockburn – who, however, had not known him personally – regarded this 'giant of the Bench' as some kind of ogre. 'His very name makes people start yet. Strong built and dark, with rough eyebrows, powerful eyes, threatening lips, and a low growling voice, he was like a formidable blacksmith. His accent and his dialect were exaggerated Scotch; his language, like his thoughts, short, strong, and conclusive.' (*Memorials of his Time*, Edinburgh 1856, p. 113.)

St Fond does not name Lord Braxfield; evidence of his attending the autumn circuit court in 1784 is in *Edinburgh Evening Courant*, 22 September 1784. There were no cases for trial at Inveraray.

88. Col. T. Thornton, op. cit., pp. 244 f.; see also Michael Brander *Soho for the Colonel* (London 1961).

89. J. Bailey, MS cit.

90.   NLS 6322, Jacob Pattison, MD *A Tour Through part of the Highlands of Scotland*, 1780, entry for 11th August. JACOB PATTISON, of Witham, Essex, who died in 1782 at the age of 23, studied at Edinburgh University, where he was simultaneously President of the Royal Medical, Physical and Speculative Societies.

91.   Mrs Grant of Laggan, op.cit.

92.   John Knox, op.cit. Knox (?1720–91) also established fisheries in north-east Scotland. (*Dictionary of Eminent Scotsmen*.)

93.   Horace Walpole, whose anecdotes are sometimes unreliable as well as obscure, suggests that this resignation was provoked by the Duchess's 'insolence' and familiarity towards the Queen. He also implies that, if not actually mistress of George III, she 'had long aimed at' that honour, and that her English barony was granted as a result of the friendship. (Walpole *Last Journals*, II, London 1910, pp.202–3.)

94.   Joseph Cradock *Literary and Miscellaneous Memoirs*, I (London 1828) p.252.

95.   Gen. Seymour Conway to Horace Walpole, 23 December 1790, in *Supplement to the Letters of Horace Walpole*, ed. Paget Toynbee, III (Oxford 1918–25) pp.301–2.

96.   Inv/NPE: *Caledonian Mercury*, 13 January 1791.

97.   Ibid: *Edinburgh Evening Courant*, 15 January 1791.

98.   Horace Walpole to Sir David Dalrymple, 25 February 1759, *Letters*, ed. Paget Toynbee, IV (Oxford 1905) p.245.

99.   Inv/Gen. Inst., August 1789, to Sonachan (p.9); CI 1783, to Haswell (p.190); 5DA Accts 1788/9 (April 1789).

CHAPTER VII
The chief sources for the material in this chapter are two manuscript volumes of Instructions among the Inveraray papers: Instructions to the Chamberlain 1771–87 (including instructions to the gardener, farm overseer and wrights); General Instructions, for the period 1788 onwards. (Both have been frequently cited in Chapter VI.) Except where otherwise stated, the information in this chapter is to be found in one or other of these volumes.

1.   Jacob Pattison, *A Tour* etc., MS cit.

2.   Thomas Pennant, *Tour 1769*, p.238.

3.   Inv/5DA correspondence and accounts.

4.   Mrs Grant of Laggan, op.cit.

5.   During the 1960s, when the present Duke restored the Court of Offices, converting part of it into Chamberlain's offices and a Muniment Room, it was discovered that some of the interior walls, doors and rebates were built of Cock of Arran stone. As this was the stone partly used for the old castle and the 2nd Duke's 'pavilion' of 1720–1, the inference is that in completing the Cherry Park court in the 1770s the old stones from such portions of the old buildings as were already demolished were re-used.

6.   Inv/Adam, Memorial relating to the works . . ., 29 June 1761; AEM 18th cent.; AECB 1759/60; and see Bishop Pococke op.cit., p.64.

7.   John Inglis diary, MS cit. Inv/CA 1775/6, and CI.

8.   Clayden *Early Life of Samuel Rogers*, loc.cit. Inv/CA 1775/6, and CI.

9.   Inv/CA 1774/5, and CI.

10.   Mylne 6 May 1774.

11.   *The Bee, or Literary Weekly Intelligencer*, 9 (1792) 93.

12.   Richard Joseph Sulivan *Observations made during a Tour through different parts of England, Scotland and Wales in 1778* (London 1780; reprinted 1807 in vol.III of William Mavor's *British Tourists, or Traveller's Pocket Companion*, pp.120f.).

13.   Inv/Accts 1772 etc.

14.   Inv/CA 1773/4, and CI. In addition to their pay the labourers received a special whisky allowance: for example George Haswell's men working on the cascades and river bank were allowed three bottles per ten men (at one shilling a bottle, or 2s 4d a pint), and Dugald McKellar and 25 men at the river in 1778, for pay between 8d and 1s 2d a day (1s 4d for Dugald), received a whisky allowance of £2 5s 1d. (Accounts 1772, etc.) In 1787 the Duke, significantly, felt obliged to order 'no more than one glass of whisquie to be given each man employed at any extraordinary Jobb after hours, and even that rarely when its necessary they should work after hours, let them be paid in money'.

15.   Inv/5DA corresp., Sonachan to Argyll 5, 8 and 18 September 1778.

16.   Thrale MSS, loc.cit.

17.   'Recollections of a Tour made in Scotland (A.D. 1803)' in *Journals of Dorothy Wordsworth*, ed. E.de Selincourt, I (London 1941) p.297.

18.   Inv/CA 1774, 1775/6, and 5DA corresp.

19. Inv/CA 1775/6.

20. Mylne 8 & 10 September 1772.

21. Ibid., 30 April & 24 May 1773.

22. Ibid., 1772, 1775, 1776; Colvin *Dictionary of English Architects*, ad loc.

23. Mylne MSS, and R.S.Mylne, op.cit., p.276 (where, however, the date is incorrectly given as January). It seemed natural to assume that the John Browns who built bridges and tenements for Inveraray were identical, but the published Glasgow *Register of Testaments* shows that John Brown, 'late Baillie of Dumbarton', was dead by 1773. Another John Brown, who was Master of Work at Glasgow in the 1770s and 1780s, appears to have been the builder of the second Aray Bridge and of Inveraray's later tenements (Relief Land, Cross Houses and Ferry Land) (see ch.VIII, p.260). This mason might well have been son to the other, though there is no evidence for it. His last recorded commissions are in Kintyre: superintending the building of Southend Church, and of the Town House spire and Castlehill Church at Campbeltown (1778–80). (See ch.III, n.42, and Index of Architects and Craftsmen.)

24. Mylne 25 August 1776.

25. Mylne's diary shows that he visited Perth immediately before going to Inveraray in 1772.

26. Mylne 14 March & 6 May 1774. 6 December 1775.

27. R.S.Mylne, loc.cit.

28. Mylne 9 February 1776; plans and elevations of Kilbryde dairy in Inveraray plan chest. Much later, in November 1792, the Duke ordered the building at Kilbryde of 'a good house . . . of dry stone with a glass window in the Front and another in the East Gavell at the Gateway on the march of Auchnagoul'. It served as a lodge.

29. Inv/CA 1775/6.

30. Henry Skrine *Three Successive Tours in the North of England, to the Lakes, and great part of Scotland*, 2nd edn (London 1813) p.46.

31. Mylne 1776.

32. Inv/Report by James Ferrier 1777/8. The Duke was, too, involved in a prolonged and expensive lawsuit with the Macleans concerning the lands of Brolas in Mull, and in 1783 judgment was finally given against him.

33. Inv/5DA corresp.

34. David Loch, loc.cit.

35. Inv/Accts & Rentals 17th–19th cent.

36. Mylne December 1785, February–April 1786.

37. Ibid., 5 November 1780, 5 March & 30 April 1781, 5 February 1782.

38. See (among numerous other descriptions) Robert Heron *Observations made in a Journey through the Western Counties of Scotland in the Autumn of 1792*, I (Perth 1793), pp.306 ff.

39. Inv/Gen. Accts 1783.

40. J.Bailey, MS cit., II, 405 ff. See also the Rev.J.Lettice *Letters on a Tour through Various Parts of Scotland in the Year 1792* (London 1794), entry of 6 September. The reference to slate from Cowal is another of Bailey's inaccuracies, for all Inveraray's slates were brought from the Easdale quarries.

41. Dorothy Wordsworth, loc.cit.

42. John Inglis diary, MS cit.

43. John Knox, loc.cit. Mylne also advised on restoration of the Bealachanuaran well, and the landscaping of its approach. When completed this made a very attractive walk or drive, as far as Esachosan where another fine avenue led to a waterfall. Another favourite excursion was down the loch to the Water of Douglas to see the supposedly Roman bridge, and the new woollen factory nearby. (See ch.VIII.)

44. Thrale MSS, loc.cit., f.13r.

45. Mylne September 1785, and CI.

46. Mylne 15 January 1777, and R.S.Mylne, op.cit., p.277.

47. Mylne September 1783; R.S.Mylne, op.cit., p.278.

48. Inv/1776–1808.

49. Ibid., and CI.

50. Mylne 20 September 1785 ff., and Inv/CI.

51. The Hon. Mrs Sarah Murray (of Kensington) *A Companion and Useful Guide to the Beauties of Scotland, to the Lakes of Westmorland, Cumberland and Lancashire*, etc., I (London 1799) pp.358 f.

52. Mylne 21 September 1785 and 4 April 1786.

53. Ibid., 10 November 1785.

54. Inv/CA 1785.

55. Inv/Misc. 1760–1800, Patrick McVicar to James Ferrier 17 August 1802.

56. See, e.g., James Maxwell *Descriptive Poem*, op.cit., Appendix.

57. PATRICK MCKELLAR (1717–78), architectural and military engineer, served in Minorca for some years, where he completed the defences of Port Mahon, and twice served

in America, including under Wolfe at the siege of Quebec. He also restored military works in Scotland, and died a colonel. The *DNB* refers to him as of an 'old Scottish family'; unfortunately the Inveraray and Glenaray parish registers are missing for the years 1714–18, but among the Inveraray MSS (Rental of feu duties, 1768) is a note of 'Colonel Mackellar' holding the house in old Inveraray set to his father John MacKellar in 1741.

In 1750, when on leave from Minorca, he revisited Scotland, bringing recommendations from his senior officers to George Drummond, then third time Provost of Edinburgh, who sent him on to Inveraray with a personal introduction to Lord Milton:

'He left the Countrey, a good many years ago, and was taken into the service under the board of Ordnance, by the late Duke of Argyll, and, under His Grace's patronage, and by his own merite, has risen to the rank of an Engineer.'

Drummond begged Lord Milton to introduce him to Duke Archibald 'as a Gentleman of Established reputation & caracter' and 'Thoroughly attached, To the Duke and to his family'. (s74 George Drummond to Milton, October 1750).

McKellar evidently impressed Duke Archibald, for on returning to Minorca he was made Engineer in Ordinary and completed the defences of Port Mahon, until recalled in 1754 to serve in America.

In 1767 the Hon. William Hervey, youngest son of John, Lord Hervey and Molly Lepel, during his first visit to Inveraray made an expedition with Asknish to Maam farm, birthplace of McKellar, whom he had known on service in America. (*Journals of the Hon. William Hervey from 1755 to 1814*, ed. S. H. A. Hervey; Suffolk Green Books No. XIV, Bury S. Edmunds 1906, p. 207.) For McKellar's service under Wolfe (when he was Chief Engineer to the Expeditionary Force) see Christopher Hibbert *Wolfe at Quebec* (London 1959) p. 36, etc.

58. James Maxwell, op. cit.

59. Mylne 9 July 1784, 5 July 1785.

60. Inv/CA 1785, 1789, 1791; 5DA Accts 1788/9; Estate Acct. 1792; also CI and Gen. Insts.

61. Mrs Murray, op. cit.

62. Brian Connell *Portrait of a Whig Peer* (London 1957) p. 429.

63. NLS 3038, John Wood of Easter Fossaway, MS *Journal of a Jaunt to the Island of Mull in the month of October 1801.*

64. Inv/Gen. Accts 1798/9, and Gen. Insts. Rev. John Smith *General View of the Agriculture of the County of Argyll, with observations on the means of its improvement* (Edinburgh 1798) pp. 14 f. The author, who was one of the ministers at Campbeltown, in this book illustrates Glenshira barn with the engraving by Robert Scott, commissioned by the Duke in 1797 (Inv/James Ferrier's accts).

65. James Robson *General View of the Agriculture in the County of Argyll and Western Part of Inverness shire* (London 1794) p. 31.

66. In 1793 an attempt was made to adapt the Elrickmore barn, but its walls were found too frail to stand a new tiled roof. A new barn was therefore ordered on the same site, with a loft and internal 'mid-wall' after the fashion of the others.

67. *Journals of the Hon. William Hervey*, p. 403.

68. Inv/Misc. 1760–1800, and Gen. Insts.

69. Inv/'Inveraray first half 18th Cent.': Report of the Intended Road through Glen Shira to Tyndrum (n.d., but enclosed in paper watermarked 1794 and endorsed '1796').

70. *First Statistical Account of Scotland*, V, Inveraray pp. 287 ff., by the Rev. Paul Fraser, minister of Inveraray.

71 Thrale MSS, loc. cit.

72. John Knox, op. cit., p. 597; *Gazetteer of Scotland* (Dundee 1803) ad loc.

73. *Journals of the Hon. William Hervey*, loc. cit.

74. James Robson, op. cit.

75. George Langlands was employed by the 5th Duke in making farm plans and advising on agricultural improvements, particularly in Kintyre, where he rented one of the Duke's farms. The Achnagoul proposal not materializing, the settlement retains to this day its traditional appearance; the last Munro tenant of many generations died not very long ago. The neighbouring farm settlement of Auchindrain has during the 1960s been turned into a museum, and the late 18th- and early 19th-century buildings are being preserved.

76. Robert Heron, op. cit.

77. James Robson, op. cit.

78. *First Statistical Account*, loc. cit.

79. Colonel Humphrey Graham (Chamberlain of Argyll), 'Husbandry in the neighbourhood of Inveraray', in Appendix to James Robson, op. cit.

80. *First Statistical Account*, loc. cit. The figure refers to the whole of Glenaray.

81. Inv/CA 1795/6, and Gen. Insts.

82. *Wood's Town Atlas* (Edinburgh 1818–28), plan of Inveraray Estates by J. Wood, Surveyor (printed at Edinburgh by A. Forrester, 1825). Inv/AE Accts 1796, 1797.

83. Inv/Gen. Accts 1798/9, and Gen. Insts.

84. Inv/Accts 1800/1; Gen. Accts (Rosneath Letter-book) 1799 etc.; Household & Estates Acct 1802.

85. Inv/Household & Estates Acct 1802. See also T. Garnett *Observations on a Tour through the Highlands and part of the Western Isles of Scotland*, I (London 1800).

86. Inv/Alexr Nasmyth to Argyll 5, 7 November 1801. The cradle chimney, also known by various other names such as the 'hanging chimney', was very common in the West Highlands, and may still be seen to-day in western Ireland and the Isle of Man. It consisted of a wooden core resting on a beam above the fireplace, woven round with wattle and covered with mud and dung, and formed the central construction of the cottage. ALEXANDER NASMYTH (1758–1840) started his career apprenticed to a coach-maker. His skill in the decoration of coach-panels brought him to the notice of Allan Ramsay, who took him into his studio to work on the backgrounds of portraits. Once established as a painter in his own right, Nasmyth's talent for landscape improvement and the altering of houses brought him more varied commissions, and the Duke of Atholl consulted him on the scenery of his lands round Dunkeld. Nasmyth also designed St Bernard's Well by the Water of Leith at Edinburgh (1789). At the time when he was at Inveraray his 'reforming' political opinions had led to a falling-off in his portrait commissions and he was turning more to landscape work. (*Autobiography of James Nasmyth*, ed. Samuel Smiles (London & Edinburgh 1883); Alastair Smart *The Life and Art of Allan Ramsay*, op. cit., pp. 122–3.)

87. 'Journal of Jessy Allan, wife of John Harden, 1801–1811', ed. William Park, in *Book of the Old Edinburgh Club*, XXX (Edinburgh 1959) p. 73.

88. A large view of the town by Nasmyth formerly at Inveraray Castle shows that this huge erection was proposed for the end of the town quay (see ch. IX, p. 289). The derivation of detail from the style of the castle is obvious.
     James Denholm, of the 'Drawing and Painting Academy' in Argyle Street, Glasgow, mentions seeing at the castle in 1802 a view of Inveraray from Loch Fyne, 'very warm and rich', and another of a waterfall near the town, both by Nasmyth. (James Denholm *A Tour to the Principal Scotch and English Lakes*, Glasgow 1804, pp. 67 ff.)

CHAPTER VIII

1. This painting, now at Inveraray Castle, from its evident date must, however, be the work not of Lord Eldin but of his father John Clerk of Eldin (1728–1812). The latter was seventh son to Baron Sir John Clerk of Penicuik, and brother-in-law to John and Robert Adam. From about 1758 onwards John Clerk made a number of views and sketches, and from these, towards the end of his life, he made 80–90 etchings. These were published in 1825 and 1855 by the Bannatyne Club, Edinburgh.

2. Inv/RFD 1768; 18th cent. leases 1701–70; Ledger III (tacks), tack of Lachlan Campbell's house 1768. Colin Campbell of Bragleenmore, one of a cadet branch of the Lochnell Campbells, had been Chamberlain to the 2nd Duke of Argyll before James Campbell of Stonefield. The Campbell monument is dated 1754, but no record apparently exists of the occasion or of the donor. Nor is it known whether it was originally placed in its present position or in the old town. James Maxwell saw it in the present position (now the Bank gardens) in 1777, though it was then presumably not concealed by a wall. The monument commemorates a number of Campbells killed at Inveraray in 1685 for complicity in the Earl of Argyll's rebellion against King James VII and II. The inscription runs:

SACRUM MEMORIAE COLINI, FRATRIS GERMANI GUALTERI CAMPBELL de SKIPNESS, qui inter alios Evangelicae Religionis et Libertatis Populi tenaces, injustae occubuit neci, anno Dni MDCLXXXV.
     Scilicet adversis probitas exercita rebus tristi tempore, habet laudis materiam.
On the other side:
     Avo dudum mortuo,/sed adhuc bene memorando,/Pietatis ergo Duncanus Campbell/posuit, anno Dni MDCCLIV./ Prospera lux oritur/Linguis animisque favete.
The following English rendering was made by the late Mr H. D. Smith of Inveraray:
     'Sacred to the Memory of Colin, brother-germane of Walter Campbell of Skipness, who, among others tenacious of Evangelical Religion and the Liberty of the People, yielded to an unjust death, in the

year of Our Lord 1685. His probity, though tried by adverse circumstances in a sad time, has good ground for praise.'
'To his Grandfather, now long dead, but still to be well remembered; from a loving regard, Duncan Campbell has erected [this Monument] in the year of our Lord 1754. "The favouring light arises, Help ye with tongues and minds".'
(Peter Macintyre *Inveraray, Its Scenery and Associations*, Glasgow 1923, pp. 20–1.)

3.   The Reverend Patrick Campbell (*c.* 1700–73) was succeeded as minister in 1774 by his son Archibald, who retained the 'free house & a good garden in the Gallogate', with a fee from the Duke in lieu of a manse. The 'Lowland Minister', the Rev. John Macaulay, who was incumbent between 1765 and 1774, was still occupying his old manse, presumably in the old town (see ch.v, p.185). (*Fasti Eccl. Scoticanae*, IV, loc. cit; Inv/CA 1777/8, AEM vol.II, RFD 1768, and 18th Cent. file (assignation of tack of Dalchenna 1768.)

4.   Inv/1767–72; IBR, 1770.

5.   Inv/RFD 1768 (changes for 1771, 1772), CA 1773/4, CI 1771 p.7.

6.   Inv/CI 1771 pp. 11, 155.

7.   Ibid. p. 155 (no. 20).

8.   Ibid (no. 16). David Loch (1778) describes the church as 'large'. For the later history of the building and site see n.30.

9.   Inv/5DA corresp. and accts, acct of William Mylne 1770–72.

10.   Ibid., and CI 1772 p. 30. The bell hanging on a tree was remarked by John Inglis (MS cit.; see p.263).

11.   Mylne 14 March 1774. Mylne's diary references for his first visit are only to castle and Aray bridge, but he could and probably did see the town on 9 September, for which he makes no diary entry at all.

12.   Inv/1756 ff., acct. of 1764–6. The slaughter-house was one of the buildings demolished in 1816 to make way for the new Court House.

13.   Inv/CA 1773/4, CI 1771 p.10, December 1772 p.12. It was John Marr who built the steeple of Banff Tolbooth in 1764–7, to the design of 'Mr Adams' (probably John), and who at the same period was either clerk of works or superintending architect at Cullen House under John Adam's direction. (Banff TCM; *Annals of Banff*, I, p. 311; Seafield MSS, SRO 982/I, 1197, 1725.)

14.   Inv/AEM 18th cent., Rentals 1774, 1776. The insurance policy, however (see p.261), refers to only five dwellings below the factory.

15.   Inv/CA 1777/8 (roofing 'the house at the end of the factory', December 1777).

16.   Ibid., and CI 1774 p.45.

17.   Inv/CA 1773/4.

18.   Inv/CI 31 October 1775 p.51. This stipulation may have been dictated by the insurance company, bearing in mind that when the first insurance policy was taken out only Arkland had been built. See p.261.

19.   Ibid., and 5 November 1776 p.64; CA 1775/6.

20.   Inv/AEM 18th Cent., Rental 1775. For Neil McCallum see Index of Architects and Craftsmen. About 1830 McCallum's was renamed Broomfield's Land after a later owner, and is to-day known as MacKenzie's. (William Broomfield's tack actually dated from 1826.) (Inv/Rentals 1828, 1833; Ledger of tacks.)

21.   Inv/CI 5 November 1776 p.62; CA 1776/7. The south-most group of Cross Houses has been gutted and converted into a garage.

22.   Inv/Accts & Rentals 17th-19th cent. The Edinburgh Friendly Society was founded in 1767. The Inveraray policy is signed by the directors Andrew Steuart Junior, James Stodart and Hary Guthrie, and countersigned by Christ. Moubray, cashier. Concurrently with this policy ran another with the Sun Fire Office in London, in identical terms for the castle and furnishings only, no. 365,305 dated 14 February 1776. Its premium was initially £7; in 1785 the premiums on both policies were substantially increased.

23.   Inv/CI 5 November 1776 p.64.

24.   Inv/AEM 18th cent., Rentals 1769–71; CI December 1771 pp.1, 8, 11; CI December 1772 p.27; CI December 1773 pp.36, 42, etc.; rentals and tacks.

25.   Inv/CI 31 October 1775 pp.51, 58, 59, 60, 61. The new manses were occupied by the Rev. Archibald Campbell, son of the Rev. Peter or Patrick Campbell who had died in 1773, and the Rev. Alexander McTavish, who was presented by the Duke in 1774 in succession to the Rev. John Macaulay. (*Fasti Eccl. Scot.*, loc. cit.) The attic dormers to both houses are a subsequent addition, as are the porch of the former (now the Temperance Hotel), and the enlarged ground-floor windows of the latter (converted into a shop).

26.   Inv/CA 1776/7.

27. Mylne 1776.

28. Inv/CI 13 December 1782 p.98; John Inglis Diary, MS cit.

29. See p.257. In 1775 Lachlan Campbell's had received an even smaller addition on its north side, but the size was dictated by the position of Silvercraigs' house, which was then already building. By virtue of his addition Lachlan Campbell obtained a seven-year extension to his tack. (Inv/Ledger of tacks.)

30. Evidence of the old building's conversion into a school appears at least by 1809. The 1848 rental shows on the site a 'school of industry', a 'parochial' school and the grammar school. In 1907 the building was demolished to make way for what has now in turn become the 'old' school-house–for that too was given up when a new school was built on the far side of the avenue in 1962. (Inv/Ledger III, petition of John McNiven, 1809; Rental 1848.)

31. Inv/CA 1773/4, 1774/5, 1775/6, 1776/7, 1777/8.

32. Ibid., and CI 6 November 1778 p.71.

33. James Maxwell, op. cit. See n.24.

34. Inv/CI December 1771 p.8.

35. Ibid. 31 October 1775 p.50.

36. Mrs Grant of Laggan, loc. cit.

37. Rev. William Gilpin, loc. cit.

38. David Loch, loc. cit.

39. J.R.N.Macphail Highland Papers, II, loc.cit. (see ch.III n.17). One version of this manuscript is preserved at Inveraray, and appears to have been transcribed from originals by 'Dr McLeod of Campsie for Lady Charlotte Bury' (that is, the 5th Duke's younger daughter).

40. Inv/Ledger of tacks, Rental 1783.

41. Permission to build was given by the Duke in December 1772. Silvercraigs' (now Macintyre's, and divided into two) originally paid a five shilling rent. The tack allowed him to sub-let only to 'the better sort of Inhabitants such as can afford to pay a rent of £10 Sterling yearly or more but not to the lower class of inhabitants who would destroy the house and have fit accommodations provided for them in other parts of the Town'–i.e. in Arkland or Relief Land. When Silvercraigs' old house, which he had inherited from his father Baillie John Campbell, was condemned in 1772 along with others in the old town, he was allowed to carry away the materials, valued at £42 4s, and compensation of £130. (Inv/18th Cent. Leases 1701–70.)

42. Inv/18th cent. Leases 1701–70 (Patrick Brown proposal of 1772), Ledger of tacks (John Colquhoun 1773), CI November 1773 and October 1774 pp.161, 164, CA 1773/4.

43. Inv/CI 1773, 1774 pp.42, 45; CA 1773/4; AEM 18th cent., Rental 1774 (Augmentations since Martinmas 1773).

44. Inv/18th cent. Leases 1701–70 (Thomas Hislop's tack). The house was inherited by Hislop's son Dugald, Surveyor of the Customs, who in 1814 paid 200 guineas for a new lease; in the 1848 Rental the house is named Hislop's Land.

45. Inv/CA 1773/4; 18th cent. Leases 1701–70, William Ross's claim 1779.

46. David Loch, loc. cit.

47. J.Bailey, MS cit.

48. Thomas Newte, loc. cit; First Statistical Account, loc. cit. At the date of the Account the population of the whole parish (Glenaray) was 1,832, a great fall from the 2,751 estimated in 1755, when Duke Archibald's works had brought many outsiders into the area. (See ch.VII n.80.)

49. John Inglis Diary, MS cit.

50. Mylne 26 September 1783, September and 11 December 1785.

51. Ibid., 1786. Mylne was then at the height of his work for the Duke, as he was also busy with plans for the alterations to Rosneath, and was advising on property in London.

52. Inv/plan chest, Mylne drawings.

53. Inv/CA 1786/7; 1776–1806 file, John Tavish receipt 1787.

54. Mylne 1788, 1790.

55. Col. T.Thornton, loc.cit.; J.Bailey, MS cit. At that time the view from castle to town was uninterrupted, as the ground had been so recently cleared and was still bare of planting.

56. James McNayr A Guide from Glasgow to some of the most remarkable Scenes in the Highlands of Scotland (Glasgow 1797) p.146.

57. [Rev. J.H.Michell] The Tour of the Duke of Somerset through parts of England, Wales and Scotland in the year 1795 (London 1845) pp.86f.

58. John Stoddart Remarks on Local Scenery and Manners in Scotland during the Years 1799 and 1800, I (London 1801) p.257. SIR JOHN STODDART (1773–1856), journalist and advocate, was brother-in-law to William Hazlitt. From 1803–7 he was King's and Admiralty advocate in Malta, and later on returning to London became a Times leader-writer and a newspaper editor (when he was

known as 'Dr Slop'). From 1826–40 he was
Chief Justice of Malta, and was knighted by
King George IV. During the last years of his
life he carried out research in etymology.
(*DNB*)

JOHN CLAUDE NATTES (?1765–1822),
topographical draughtsman and water-
colourist, worked in Britain and France, and
exhibited at the Royal Academy. He published
numerous illustrated topographical works,
including *Scotia Depicta* (1804), and engravings
of his drawings appeared in such works as
The Copperplate Magazine and *The Beauties of
England and Wales.*

59.　George L. A. Douglas *Tour in the
Hebrides in 1800*, ed. John A. Fairley
(Aberdeen 1927), entry for 31 July.

60.　*Journals of Dorothy Wordsworth*, I, 294.

61.　Inv/CI 30 October 1787 p. 139.

62.　Ibid. p. 141. Tavish, who appears to have
lived at Kilmartin (between Lochgilphead and
Loch Awe), was employed on commission,
and reappears regularly between 1788 and
1805, e.g. for the building of Maam 'circle'
(1788–90) and the extensions to the inn
(1793–4). See ch. IX and Index to Architects
and Craftsmen.

63.　Ibid. 29 October 1785 and 7 February
1787, pp. 122, 129.

64.　Inv/Gen. Insts. 17 August 1789 p. 10.

65.　Inv/CI 13 December 1782 pp. 101, 103,
104; 29 October 1785 pp. 118, 120.

66.　Minutes of Commissioners of Supply,
1 May 1786.

67.　Inv/CI 7 February 1787 p. 136. The first
major alterations to the inn, ordered in 1782–4,
were division of its 'great room' by a movable
partition, and enlargement of the stables.
(Ibid. December 1781, December 1782,
December 1783, October 1784, pp. 93, 99, 106,
113.)

68.　J. Bailey MS cit.

69.　Jacob Pattison MS cit.

70.　*Edinburgh Advertiser*, 3 January 1775,
afterwards printed with slight alteration in
the *Scots Magazine* of that month.

71.　Inv/CI December 1771 p. 2. David Loch,
in a letter dated 9 January 1775 to the
Caledonian Mercury, remarks, 'It is with the
greatest pleasure I perceive, that his Grace the
Duke of Argyle, my Lord Gardenston, and many
other worthy gentlemen in Scotland, are now
patronizing its staple, the Woollen Manufacture.' (David Loch *Letters Concerning the
Trade and Manufactures of Scotland*, Edinburgh
1775, p. 7.)

72.　The *Edinburgh Evening Courant* on 4
December 1775, in repeating the advertisement
for a manager for the factory, observes:
'The late Duke of Argyl introduced
into this country a breed of large English
Sheep about 10 or 12 years ago, and the present
Duke lately purchased a different breed from
Mr Cully in Northumberland, so that variety
of fine wool may be expected.'

73.　Inv/CI 31 October 1775 p. 52.

74.　Except where otherwise indicated,
information on the Clunary factory is derived
from a box file on the subject among the
Inveraray MSS. It is discussed by Eric Cregeen
in his Introduction to the *Argyll Estate
Instructions* (see ch. X n. 1).

75.　Inv/CA 1775/6, 1776/7, 1777/8; Accts
1772 f.

76.　James Maxwell, op. cit; David Loch
Essays etc., II, 219.

77.　Inv/CA 1781/2; CI 30 October 1787
p. 140.

78.　Thomas Newte, loc. cit.

79.　James Ferrier, when visiting David Dale's
wool factory near Kilpatrick in November
1791, remarked that Dale's spinners had given
up 'the large wheel, erected at great expence,
and betaken themselves to the jennys, such as
McNab has got at Clunary'. (Inv/Ferrier to
Argyll 5, 9 November 1791.)

80.　In July 1794 Ferrier, acting as the Duke's
commissioner, ordered from McNab a quantity
of blue, white and scarlet cloth for a Volunteer
Corps that was to be raised. McNab had the
material spun, woven and dyed, but a severe
drought which then set in prevented him (he
claimed) from having it milled or wauked in
time, and so the order was lost. The material,
being unsuitable for other purposes, was left
on his hands. (See n. 74.)

81.　*First Statistical Account*, loc. cit.

82.　For example, the Ross of Mull fishery
experiment, which failed in about 1790.

CHAPTER IX
1.　*First Statistical Account*, op. cit., pp. 287 ff.
The linen factory is referred to by Richard
Ayton as late as 1813 (in *A Voyage round Great
Britain*, III, London 1818, pp. 27–9).

2.　*First Statistical Account*, loc. cit. Only four
other royal burghs had a lower income. The
following is an example of Inveraray's town
accounts, for the year ending May 1814
(Inv/Report of Committee appointed to
examine into state of gaols, Appendix):

Income, £136 6s 1d – Annuity from the Duke, £20; Petty Customs, £36; rent of Town Common and S. Catherine's ferry, each £21 5s; school funds, £37 16s 1d.

Expenditure, £112 15s 7d – including interest on loans for building pier, £13 1s 2d; school salaries: Grammar School master £31 12s 8d, English School master, £14 4s, mistress of the boarding school, £4; etc.

The £20 annuity introduced by Duke Archibald continued to be paid until 1962.

3. The Hon. Mrs Damer to Mary Berry, 9 July 1791, in *The Berry Papers* (*1763–1852*), ed. Lewis Melville (London 1914) p. 50. Mrs Damer was Anne, daughter of the 5th Duke's sister Lady Caroline Campbell by her second husband, General Seymour Conway. For Bellevue see n. 9.

4. Lady Louisa Stuart to Lady Portarlington, 5 October 1804, in *Gleanings from an Old Portfolio*, ed. Mrs Godfrey Clark (privately printed, Edinburgh 1898). Lady Augusta had fleetingly engaged the affections of the Prince of Wales. 'Coeval with his passion for Perdita,' writes Wraxall, 'was his attachment to Lady Augusta Campbell, the "Ophelia" of the court of George III . . . Her youth, her rank, and her face, which was very charming, though not intelligent, compensated for the defects of her shape and figure; but she possessed neither accomplishments nor mental qualifications to retain her "Hamlet" in bondage . . . The Prince soon transferred his affections to Lady Melbourne.' (Reminiscences of Royal and Noble Personages, in *Historical and Posthumous Memoirs of Sir Nathaniel William Wraxall 1772–84*, ed. Henry B. Wheatley, v, London 1884, pp. 369–70).

5. Inv/James Ferrier's accts 1795/6. His annual accounts between 1786 and 1795 show that only in three years did outlay on the castle exceed £800. See also Inv/AE accts 1796, 1797, 1799/1800.

6. Inv/5DA corresp., Argyll 5 to Lorne, 11 December 1798.

7. Inv/Gen. Insts. 20 November 1792 p. 38 (general orders). These instructions may have coincided with the appointment that year of the new Chamberlain Colonel Humphrey Graham, an able man of agreeable personality who succeeded to the post on Sonachan's death. The Duke became a Field Marshal in 1796, though by then he had given up active service.

8. Inv/Gen. Insts. 29 Oct. 1795 p. 514 (to House Carpenters); Day Book 1795 (April). Simpson is here referred to as 'Junior'. The elder Simpson appears to have come to Inveraray from 'the Low Country' in 1789, and the next year returned to fetch his family. (Gen. Inst., and CA 1789/90). In the interim the chief wright was probably Hugh Alexander. See Index of Architects and Craftsmen.

These shelves were removed to the south (drawing-room) turret by the present Duke, when the north corner rooms were converted into butler's pantries and service rooms.

9. James Brown, creator of George Square in Edinburgh, was the architect of Bellevue, which was built soon after 1766 on the site of an earlier house owned by Lord Provost George Drummond (who had died in that year). At the time of the Duke of Argyll's tenancy its owner was the Marquess of Titchfield – heir to the Duke of Portland – who in 1800 decided to sell it to the city of Edinburgh for use as a Customs Office. The house, forming a focal point for the streets later built in that part of the New Town, faced east along London Street. It was demolished in 1844 when the tunnelling of the Edinburgh, Perth and Dundee Railway underneath caused subsidence. Lord Cockburn has an interesting comment on civic Philistinism at the time of Bellevue's sale:

'No part of the home scenery of Edinburgh was more beautiful than Bellevue . . . and a luxurious house it was. The whole place waved with wood, and was diversified by undulations of surface, and adorned by seats and bowers and summer houses . . . We clung long to the hope that, though the city might in time surround [it], Bellevue . . . might be spared. But in 1802 Bellevue was sold. The magistrates, I believe, bought it; and the whole trees were instantly cut down . . . the mere beauty of the town was no more thought of at that time by anybody than electric telegraphs and railways.' (*Memorials*, pp. 171–2.)

At the time of the sale Alexander Gowan & Sons, a firm at Abbey Hill, Edinburgh, offered to make the Duke, for £103, an 'exactly similar' copy of the carved fireplace, except that its figures would have 'a dead polish (instead of a shining one like the other parts of the marble), which is now reckon'd a great improvement in Marble Carving, as the shining polish must in it's process take off the *Sharpness* . . .' The Duke, however, mistrusting the thought of a copy, refused the offer. (Transactions and correspondence are in Edinburgh TCM, vol. 134 pp. 198/9, and Misc. papers, Bundle 34; also partly transcribed in Boog Watson MSS, Edinburgh Room of Edinburgh Public Library, vol. 9, p. 336. I am grateful to Miss Helen Armet and Mr W. H. Makey, the former and present Burgh Archivists, and to the staff of the Edinburgh Room for their help in tracing this information.)

In 1803 George Campbell, of Glasgow, was paid 30 shillings for 'marble ornaments' for 'the Drawing room Chimney piece', presumably that in the south corner drawing-room. (Inv/Accounts 1804.)

10.   Mylne 16 July 1792, 13 May 1793.

11.   All the information which follows on the building of the church is to be found in the Inveraray MSS: Gen. Insts. November 1793, November 1794, December 1798, October 1799 pp. 44, 46, 49, 52, 227, 234, 509, 510, 515; EAC 1792/3, 1797/8; CA 1794/5, 1795/6, 1799/1800, 1800/1, 1803, 1804; AE Accts 1796/7; Gen. Accts 1798/9; Rosneath Accts 1798/9, p. 36; James Ferrier's Accts 1799/1800; Particular Papers 1796; Household & Estate Accts 1801/2; 5DA corresp.: Graham to Argyll 5, 23 October 1798; Inv. Letter Bk 1799/1800 (letters between Duke and Chamberlain).

12.   Michael Carmichael was architect of the church at Colonsay (1802). A Michael Bogle, timber merchant, was partner to Allan Dreghorn (see p. 367, n. 250) until the latter's death in 1764, after which he continued in business as Bogle & Scott. However, his name disappears from the Glasgow street directory in 1799, and since the correspondence between the Duke and the Chamberlain makes it clear that 'Bogle' had written to the Rosneath Chamberlain in late January or early February 1800, this particular Bogle may have been a son to Michael. (*Glasgow Journal* 24 July 1766; Glasgow street directories. Inv/Letter Book 1799/1800, Graham to Argyll 5, 4 January and 11 February 1800, Argyll 5 to Graham, 7 January and 13 February 1800. Information on Michael Bogle kindly supplied by Mr Black of the Mitchell Library, Glasgow.)

13.   Mylne 7 and 25 March 1800. Hugh Cairncross in 1806 built a large classical house at Ardgowan, Renfrewshire, for the Shaw Stewart family, and (1807) nos. 12–32 Gayfield Square, Edinburgh. (Information from Mr David Walker.) In 1801 he was paid £25 5s 5d 'for measuring & valuing the work in the finishing of the English & Gaelic Churches at Inveraray, making a description thereof &

reporting the expence including travelling Charges &c March & June 1800' (Inv/Accts 1800/1.

14.   Adam Russell also carried out alterations and additions, including a staircase, new windows, a lodge and stables, for the house of Captain Archibald Campbell (who became Chamberlain in 1810) at Inveraray, in 1801–2. There are also numerous accounts for work at 'the Chamberlain's house', i.e. Colonel Graham's, and there is some ambiguity over whether this was in fact the same house and leased by one gentleman to the other. (Inv/Accts 1800/1, Household & Estate Accts 1802.) In 1798–9 Russell had submitted designs for the New Highland Church at Campbeltown, when he is referred to as 'of Edinburgh' (SRO HR 67/1, Campbeltown HR Minute Bks 1788–1821, pp. 28 ff.). Adam and Thomas Russell, of Edinburgh, had been Robert Adam's contractors at Seton Castle (1789), and built Airthrey to his design without superintendance (1791). (John Fleming in *CL*, 23 & 30 May 1968.)

15.   A. J. Finberg *A Complete Inventory of the Drawings of the Turner Bequest* (H.M.S.O. 1909). Finberg's *Life of J. M. W. Turner* (Oxford 1939) p. 73, shows that Turner left Edinburgh on 18 July 1801 and made a three-week tour including Dumbarton, Luss, Arrochar, Inveraray and Dalmally before turning eastwards (when he also visited Taymouth).

16.   Mylne 1800, 1801.

17.   Architectural drawings at Inveraray Castle, plan chest.

18.   IBR 8 January 1783, 12 August 1795.

19.   Inv/Gen. Insts. 29 October 1795, December 1798, 11 October 1799 pp. 47, 49, 52; 5DA corresp.: Graham to Argyll 5, 21 May 1799; Gen. Accts 1800, 1801. The Gallowgate dung-pit was beside the Gallowgate stables, on the stance of the demolished cottage of Archibald Campbell, a carter.

In 1803 Dorothy Wordsworth was distressed to find the well-built town 'a doleful example of Scotch filth . . . the windows and door-steads were as dirty as in a dirty by-street of a large town, making a most unpleasant contrast with the comely face of the buildings towards the water'. (loc. cit.) In 1818 the streets were so filthy that a typhus epidemic broke out and Lord John Campbell set up a fever hospital in an estate cottage in Esachosan. The town water supply was often polluted through defective pipes from the spring-head. Yet after the epidemic the streets were as bad as ever, and wandering cows strayed even into the houses. (IBR, 1814–19.)

20. Inv/Gen. Insts. 20 November 1792 p.41; EA 1792/3, 1793/4; CA 1794/5; Day Book 1794, 1795. Mylne 20 & 23 September 1785, 1 May 1792. A fire in the 1950s unfortunately . . destroyed the inn's internal fittings, together with the roof, which had to be replaced.

21. IBR, 22 December 1806 (Memorial to Convention of Royal Burghs). The same records provide most of the information on the building of the quay: 11 October & 22 December 1800, 27 April 1801, 23 March 1803, April–June 1805, 24 August 1805, and 1806. Inv/Gen. Insts. 29 October 1795 p.46. On the breastwork, Inv/CA 1795/6, 1797/8, 1799/1800, Gen. Accts 1798/9. The pier was further extended in 1836 at a cost of £1200, of which £800 was provided by the fishery board, and the remainder by the (7th) Duke and the town. (*New Statistical Account*, VII, Edinburgh 1845.)
    One of the 5th Duke's last philanthropic acts for his townspeople was to compensate for the shortage of common ground by fencing an area for kitchen gardens, between the Kilmalew burial ground and the salmon draught near Garron Bridge. These allotments, and the cabins built on them, appear to have remained in use for many years. (Inv/Gen. Insts. 11 October 1799 p.53; Gen. Accts 1798/9. See also 'A Cosmopolite' *The Sportsman in Ireland etc.*, II, London 1840, p.176.)

22. Later known as Gillespie Graham (c. 1777–1855). He became a noted exponent of the castellated style in houses, doubtless influenced by his knowledge of Inveraray (see Epilogue, p.336); his other designs included Moray Place in Edinburgh (1822) and Haddington Town House (1830) (John Dunbar, op. cit.; Ian G. Lindsay *Georgian Edinburgh*, Edinburgh 1948). He also rebuilt Achnacarry House for Cameron of Lochiel, near the site of the old one burnt by the Duke of Cumberland in 1746: by an odd coincidence James Hogg met him there in June 1803 soon after leaving Inveraray (see pp.302 ff.). Referring to him mistakenly as 'John', Hogg calls the architect 'a respectable young man, possessed of much professional knowledge' (James Hogg *A Tour in the Highlands in 1803* reprinted from *The Scottish Review*, Alexander Gardner 1888, p.41). Gillespie is said to have started life humbly as a working joiner in Dunblane, but Hogg's account implies that he was related to Thomas Gillespie, who had removed from the south of Scotland to the Fort William area in the 1780s and became a wealthy

sheep breeder. See Index of Architects and Craftsmen.

23. A Letter of Horning was a writ to pay a debt: a debtor not paying within the stated time was 'put to the horn', that is denounced as a 'rebel' at the mercat cross by blasts on the official messenger's horn, and his goods were impounded. Baillie Peter Campbell was put to the horn by John Fallowsdale during Inveraray's numerous town feuds in the 1750s.

24. Mylne, February–June 1801. On 13 June 1801 – a date when his diary shows he again 'waited on Lord Lorne', presumably without success – Mylne wrote to the Duke about their consultation ten days earlier, when they 'had full time to discuss the business of Porticos or Collonades, round, or anyways attached, to the Church at Inveraray.
    'I hope his Lordship will write Your Grace, as he was requested, to take some time, to Consider of the result of our Conference; and the ideas which arose out of the Question.'
This letter is, however, the last word extant on the subject. (Inv/18th cent., box file.)

25. See ch. VI, n.51.

26. James Denholm, op. cit., p.82.

27. Ibid.

28. H. M. Colvin *Dictionary of British Architects*, ad loc.; Sir John Summerson *Architecture in Britain*, pp.271–2.

29. Wyatt Papworth 'Memoir of Joseph Bonomi, Architect and A.R.A.' in *TRIBA, Session 1868–9* (London 1869) pp.123–4; Thomas Telford 'Essay on Civil Architecture' in *Edinburgh Encyclopaedia*, ed. Sir David Brewster (Edinburgh 1830) VI, p.651, XIX, p.181 (plan); Sir John Summerson, loc. cit. Rosneath was later occupied by Princess Louise, wife of the 9th Duke of Argyll; it was finally demolished in 1962.

30. Inv/5th–7th Dukes file: Argyll 5 to Lorne, 14 January, 10 March and 24 April 1803.

31. John Nichols *Literary Anecdotes of the Eighteenth Century* (London 1812 f.) IX (1815) p.233. See also Joseph Farington's *Diary*, ed. James Greig, VI (London 1922) pp.271–2.

32. *Journals of Dorothy Wordsworth*, I, p.289.

33. Rev. J. Lettice, op. cit. JOHN LETTICE (1737–1832), son of a clergyman, became a Fellow of Sidney Sussex College, Cambridge, and at the time of his Scottish tour was Rector of Peasmarsh. He published various works, and was subsequently tutor to the Beckford family, and chaplain to the Duke of Hamilton. (*DNB*)

34. Robert Heron, op. cit. ROBERT HERON (1764–1807), a precocious though superficial student of law and medical jurisprudence, and an unscholarly historian, was a native of New Galloway. He was author of an inaccurate Scottish history and an unsuccessful play, and eventually died in a debtor's prison. (*DNB*; also *Life and Times of Henry Lord Brougham*, written by himself, I, Edinburgh 1871, p. 91 and App. XI).

To the less worldly Wordsworths, Inveraray's inn, although it received them well, appeared 'over-rich in waiters and large rooms to be exactly to our taste, though quite in harmony with the neighbourhood'. (*Journals of Dorothy Wordsworth*, I, p. 295).

35. John Stoddart, loc. cit.

36. George L. A. Douglas, loc. cit. GEORGE DOUGLAS (1773–1847), was second son of John Douglas of Tilquhillie, Kincardineshire, and Hannah, daughter of Sir George Colquhoun. He was admitted advocate in 1796 and in 1812 became Sheriff Depute of Kincardine. He lived for most of his life at 75 Queen Street, Edinburgh. (Ibid.)

37. James McNayr, loc. cit.

38. John Stoddart, loc. cit.

39. T. Garnett, FRS *Observations on a Tour through the Highlands and part of the Western Isles of Scotland*, I (London 1800) pp. 76 f.

40. e.g. *The Travellers' Guide through Scotland and its Islands* (Edinburgh 1798), and *Scotland Described* (Edinburgh 1799) p. 279. The original comparison is in Pennant's *Tour* of 1769, loc. cit.

41. William Burrell, MS cit.

42. The second table boy waited on the upper servants. These figures are taken from 'Meat Returns' rendered during the Napoleonic Wars, preserved among the Inveraray MSS (November and December 1805, and March and April 1806).

43. Joseph Farington, Diary July 1792, typed transcript in Edinburgh Public Library (9YDA 1861. 792) from original in the Royal Library at Windsor.

44. William Beattie *Life and Letters of Thomas Campbell*, I (London 1849) pp. 160–4. Thomas Campbell was a nephew of Robert Campbell of Kirnan, the biographer (1744) of the 2nd Duke of Argyll. (Ibid., I, pp. 4–6).

45. [Rev. J. H. Michell] *Tour of the Duke of Somerset*, op. cit.; John Henry Manners, 5th Duke of Rutland *Journal of a Tour to the Northern Parts of Great Britain*, II (privately printed, London 1813) pp. 224 ff.

46. The Hon. Mrs Murray, loc. cit. SARAH MURRAY (1744–1811) had been married to Mr George Aust since 1786, but wrote under her name by her first marriage (to the Hon. William Murray, brother to the Earl of Dunmore). (*DNB*) During her Inveraray stay she pays tribute to 'the good temper and never-ceasing cheerfulness of Mrs Haswell', who from the context appears to have been employed by the Grahams.

47. Ibid., II (1803).

48. SIR WILLIAM HART was a Knight of the Illustrious Order of Saint Stanislaus in Poland, and died at Inveraray Castle on 24 October 1804, aged 63; he was buried in Kilmalew graveyard. From Leyden's account, and a fleeting reference by James Hogg in 1803, he appears to have been regarded as a rather comically tiresome character. (James Hogg, loc. cit.; obituary notices in *Scots Magazine* and *Gentleman's Magazine*, November 1804; gravestone at Kilmalew.)

49. Dr John Leyden *Journal of a Tour in the Highlands and Western Islands of Scotland in 1800*, ed. James Sinton (Edinburgh 1903). The anecdote about Sir William Hart is also described in a letter from Leyden to Thomas Brown, 25th [July] 1800, preserved among his correspondence, NLS 3380, f.31. JOHN LEYDEN (1775–1811), born at Denholm in Roxburghshire, was educated for the church at Edinburgh University, dabbled in poetry and helped Walter Scott with his collection of Border Ballads, took up medicine and went to Madras, and finally studied oriental languages, becoming a professor at Bengal College. He died of fever when only thirty-six, on a trip to Java with Lord Minto. (Joseph Irving *Book of Eminent Scotsmen*, Paisley 1811, and *DNB*.)

Asknish, formerly accountant and financial agent to Duke Archibald, had in 1769 married Miss Yates, daughter of a Lancashire gentleman. He became Sheriff Depute of Argyll on Stonefield's retirement in 1776. It was presumably in his capacity as Sheriff that he needed to occupy the inn rooms at Lochgilphead at the time of Dr Leyden's visit.

50. The Campbells of Carrick were connected with the Argylls through the marriage of Jean, one of the numerous sisters of the 4th Duke, to John Campbell of Carrick. The lady here referred to appears to have stayed at Inveraray a good deal, but otherwise lived at Holyroodhouse—then the home of a number of French émigrés—where in 1806 Robert and Eugenia Campbell (Shawfield's younger brother and his wife) called on 'Mrs Campbell Carrie who

has appartements there—She is an O.M.—but was chere amie to Lord Frederic Campbell and scandal says she had a daughter by him'. (*The Wynne Diaries 1789–1820*, ed. Anne Fremantle, Oxford 1952, p. 477, entry of 4 November 1806.)

51. MS Journal of Lachlan Macquarie, 28 and 29 August 1804, Public Library of New South Wales, MS A 770 (from a micro-film extract kindly provided by the library); partly quoted in M. H. Ellis *Lachlan Macquarie* (London & Sydney 1947). LACHLAN MACQUARIE (1761–1824), son of a poor tacksman of Ulva, was on his mother's side nephew to his chief, Murdoch Maclaine of Lochbuy. From 1787 he served in the army in India. His second wife, whom he married in 1807, was Elizabeth Campbell, a niece of Stonefield's daughter Mrs Elizabeth Campbell of Carwhin, and in 1808 she travelled with MacQuarie and his regiment (the 73rd) on his appointment as Governor of New South Wales. During the disintegration of the Argyll estates under the 6th Duke MacQuarie added to the lands he had already acquired in Mull. On his death the 6th Duke was among those who sent their carriages to follow MacQuarie's funeral cortège. (M. H. Ellis, op. cit.)

52. 'Captain Campbell' was probably William, son of the 5th Duke's younger brother Lord William Campbell: father and son both served in the Navy. 'Mr Trafford' was Humphrey Trafford Campbell (1770–1818), Asknish's eldest son, who was a frequent visitor at Inveraray. He married in 1799 Elizabeth, daughter of John Williams of Ruthyn, Denbigh. (See also ch. x)

53. Quoted in *Life and Correspondence of M. G. Lewis*, ed. Margaret Harries, I (London 1839) pp. 197–9.

54. Lady Charlotte Bury *Diary illustrative of the Times of George IV*, II (London 1838) p. 103f., note; in the later edition (*Diary of a Lady-in-Waiting*, ed. A. F. Stuart, I, London 1908, p. 289f.), the spiteful note has been omitted.

55. *In Whig Society, 1775–1818*, ed. Mabell, Countess of Airlie (London 1921) pp. 65, 67, Matthew Lewis to Lady Melbourne, [October 1802]. CHARLES KINNAIRD (1780–1826), MP for Leominster 1802–6, succeeded his father as 8th Baron Kinnaird in 1805 and from 1806–7 was a Scottish Representative Peer. On 8 May 1806 he married Lady Olivia Fitzgerald, daughter of the Duke of Leinster. (Burke *Peerage*.)

56. *Memoirs, Journal and Correspondence of Thomas Moore*, ed. Ld John Russell, VIII (London 1856) pp. 43ff. (Matthew Lewis to Thomas Moore, 19 November 1802). LOUIS CHARLES, COMTE DE BEAUJOLAIS and his other brother, Duc de Montpensier, had both been imprisoned for some years in their boyhood during the Revolution, and later went to America. 'A very pretty, lively, pleasant young man', according to Lady Jerningham, Beaujolais and his brother 'speak English as if they had been born here'. Beaujolais died of tuberculosis in Malta in 1808. (See, e.g., *The Jerningham Letters*, ed. Egerton Castle, I, London 1896, and *Memoirs of the Comtesse de Boigne, 1781–1814*, London 1907, p. 117.)

57. *In Whig Society*, loc. cit.

58. Catherine Sinclair, *Scotland and the Scotch—or, The Western Circuit* (Edinburgh 1840) p. 85.

59. *Memoirs . . . of Thomas Moore*, loc. cit., Matthew Lewis to Thomas Moore, 9 November 1803.

60. *Journals of Dorothy Wordsworth*, loc. cit.

61. The following account is taken from Hogg's *Tour in the Highlands in 1803*, loc. cit., pp. 20–34. Scott's own apparent failure to visit Inveraray is a great gap in its history. He had, however, a strong historical interest in the place, and besides his picture of the 2nd Duke in *The Heart of Midlothian*, he gives a vivid though entirely imaginary description of the old castle in *A Legend of Montrose*. In 1810 Scott was to make a voyage to Mull, Iona and Staffa, apparently *not* taking in Inveraray, when he wrote to Lady Abercorn on 30 September of the care shown by Macdonald of Staffa for his clansmen: 'I wish I could say so of the [6th] Duke of Argyle but his isles are in a wretched state. That of Iona in particular . . . is now in a most deplorable condition. . . .' (*Letters of Sir Walter Scott*, II, London 1932, p. 377.)

62. According to Hogg the theatre's interior design and fittings were Colonel Campbell's own work.

63. *Gleanings from an Old Portfolio*, III, pp. 130–2. LADY LOUISA STUART (1757–1851), youngest daughter of the 3rd Earl of Bute, was a great-niece of Duke Archibald, through his sister Anne who had married the 2nd Earl. She died unmarried in her 94th year, having lived a retired life, and although she had a considerable talent for writing, few of her friends or even her sisters were allowed to know of it; during her life-time she allowed publication of only one work, an introduction

to a life of her grandmother, Lady Mary Wortley Montagu. At the time of Lady Louisa's visit to Inveraray Lady Charlotte was again pregnant, and expecting her next child the following month.

64.　Joseph Mawman, op. cit., ch. II.

CHAPTER X

1.　200 Argyll properties existing in the middle of the 18th century were reduced by insolvency to 156 in 1800. For a valuable picture of the state of the Highlands in the latter part of the 18th century, with particular reference to Argyll and its islands, see Eric R. Cregeen's Introduction to *Argyll Estate Instructions* (*Mull, Morvern, Tiree*) (Edinburgh, Scottish History Society 1964.)

2.　*The Journal of Elizabeth Lady Holland*, ed. The Earl of Ilchester, I (London 1908) p. 233 (entry of 25 March 1799).

3.　*Journal of the Hon. Henry Edward Fox, 1818–30*, ed. The Earl of Ilchester (London 1923) p. 34 (entry of 23 July 1820).

4.　*The Wynne Diaries, 1789–1820*, p. 474 (Eugenia [Wynne] Campbell, 10 October 1806).

5.　*Life and Correspondence of M. G. Lewis*, II, pp. 4 ff.

6.　*Private Correspondence of Lord Granville Leveson Gower, 1781–1821*, ed. Castalia Countess Granville, II (London 1917) p. 287 (Lady Bessborough to Lord Granville, 1 October 1807). LADY HOLLAND, born Elizabeth Vassall, had been formerly the wife of Sir Godfrey Webster, who divorced her for her adultery with Lord Holland (1797). Although she was domineering and even notoriously rude, her beauty and vivacity as a hostess made the Holland House circle renowned for brilliance.

7.　Spencer Walpole *Life of Lord John Russell*, I (London 1889) p. 32.

8.　*Life and Correspondence of M. G. Lewis*, loc. cit.

9.　Percy Fitzgerald *Lives of the Sheridans*, II (London 1886) pp. 324–6.

10.　*Life and Correspondence of M. G. Lewis*, loc. cit.

11.　*Private Correspondence of Lord Granville Leveson Gower*, loc. cit.

12.　*Gleanings from an Old Portfolio*, loc. cit. (1804).

13.　*The Wynne Diaries*, p. 482 (Eugenia Campbell, 1 May 1807).

14.　HENRY, LORD PAGET (1768–1854), eldest son of the Earl of Uxbridge, was created Marquess of Anglesey in 1815, after losing a leg at Waterloo. In 1809 he had been party to the divorce of Lady Charlotte Wellesley, whom he was able to marry once his own marriage was dissolved. See *Diaries of Sylvester Douglas* (*Lord Glenbervie*), ed. Francis Bickley, II (London 1928) pp. 73–4, 104; Louis Simond *Journal of a Tour and Residence in Great Britain during the years 1810 and 1811 by a French Traveller*, II (Edinburgh 1815) pp. 44–6; *Memoirs of the Comtesse de Boigne* (London 1907) p. 150; *Private Correspondence of Lord Granville Leveson Gower*, II, pp. 366, 428 and n.

15.　*The Wynne Diaries*, p. 504 (Betsey [Wynne] Fremantle, 18 September 1811). EUGENIA AND BETSEY WYNNE, daughters of Richard Wynne, of Swanbourne, had in girlhood lived chiefly on the Continent with their family. Betsey married Captain (later Admiral Sir) Thomas Fremantle.

16.　Louis Simond, op. cit., I, p. 297 (30 August 1810). In 1812 a Mr Thermuthis Collinson, visiting with his relatives, did not even bother to view the interior of this 'modern building of inelegant appearance', being told that there was nothing worth attention apart from these tapestries and 'a moderately good collection of paintings'. (Thermuthis Collinson, of Cleadon, MS *Tour through some of the Southern and Western Counties of Scotland*, BM Add. 36454, 9 October 1812.)

17.　Inv/Note on CA, 1806, Ledger.

18.　Details of Bonomi's designs, and the drawings, are in Inv/Bonomi-Rosneath file, and plan chest. Bonomi's office was at 76 Great Titchfield Street. The 6th Duke was as unbusinesslike with him as he had been with Robert Mylne, and never troubled to answer his letters. The non-execution of Bonomi's plans at Inveraray was almost certainly due to lack of money: a warning from the Chamberlain took the form of a comparative statement of expenditure on buildings (chiefly repairs and alterations at the castle), in 1806 totalling £1129 5s 6d, in 1807 £2505 17s 3d, and 1808 £2254 10s 10½d. (Inv/CA 1806, and Bonomi-Rosneath file.)

19.　Inv/Report by James Malcolm, Land Agent, 1810.

20.　John Parker Lawson *An Enlarged Gazetteer of Scotland*, II (1841) p. 64; Catherine Sinclair *Scotland and the Scotch* p. 60 (who gives the figure for land sales as £300,000).

21. Inv/1765–1812; Argyll 6 to [James Ferrier], 13 December 1811.

22. Rosneath, on the other hand, even though half-finished, appeared to Wraxall 'beautiful, elegant, & delicious'.

23. Henderson, who is heavily criticized in Malcolm's report, was probably the overseer 'H.—' to whom James Hogg took such objection in 1803.

24. Nathaniel Wraxall MS *Diary of my Tour into Scotland, in the Summer of 1813*, NLS 3108, vol. II (15–17 July 1813). Between 1815 and 1819 the then Chamberlain, Captain Archibald Campbell, regularly reported to Selkrig on this sad state of affairs, for which of course the country's economic stagnation was partly responsible. The town's run-down condition rendered the cost of repairs prohibitive, and a further charge soon fell on the Duke, of rehousing tenants expropriated when the new Court House was built. In 1818 Captain Campbell did succeed in renewing the Castle's extensive lead roofs, now badly leaking, at a cost of £254: the job took two men 48 days. (Inv/Particular Papers: tenants' petition 1816, and letter, D. R. McCallum to Capt. Archd Campbell, 3 February 1818.)

25. *Correspondence of Two Brothers: Edward Adolphus, 11th Duke of Somerset, and his brother Lord Webb Seymour*, ed. Lady Guendolen Ramsden (London 1906) (Ld Webb Seymour to Duchess of Somerset, 2 December 1817).

26. John Anderson, MS *Sketch of a ramble through the Highlands of Scotland in the summer of 1818*, NLS 2509 (22–23 July 1818); Allan Cunningham *The Life of Sir David Wilkie*, I (London 1843) p. 473f. In 1817 David Wilkie found himself voyaging with a party of about 200 sheep shearers going from the Hebrides to the Lowlands harvests at a special rate of two shillings a head–to them a sum so great that from Inveraray a number of them 'had chosen to walk'.

27. The *Argyle*, 78 tons (built 1815), *Neptune*, 82 tons (1816), and *Inveraray Castle*, 112 tons (1819). The publication in 1820 of Lumsden & Sons' *Steamboat Companion* shows Scotland launched as a tourist country in the modern sense.

28. *An Account of the Principal Pleasure Tours in Scotland*, 2nd ed. (Edinburgh 1821) p. 47. Several 19th-century travellers describe the coach-drive over Hell's Glen. In mid-Victorian times the coachman John Campbell, who was also the St Catherine's inn-keeper, was a renowned local 'character' and raconteur. He would relate how he had carried Lord

Palmerston, Alfred Tennyson, and the minor poet Martin Tupper. (Tennyson, long a great friend of the 8th Duke and Duchess, stayed at the castle in 1857.) *The Tourist's Guide-Book* of 1878 refers to the 'large, well-appointed coach' serving Lochgoilhead and St Catherine's, whence the steamer *Fairy* sailed for Inveraray. An anonymous visitor from Dover in 1856 describes the coachman Campbell as 'a man of extraordinary natural abilities . . . he kept us in a roar of Laughter by relating anecdotes told with the most inimitable houmour' [sic]. (NLS 9233, p. 105; see also Alexander Smith *A Summer in Skye*, London 1865, pp. 68–72.)

29. Allan Cunningham *Life of Sir David Wilkie*, loc. cit.

30. Mrs Selwyn *Journal of Excursions through the most interesting parts of England, Wales and Scotland during the summers and autumns of 1819 [to] 1823*, privately printed, London [?1824].

31. 'Journal of my Second Tour to Scotland', in *Journals of Dorothy Wordsworth*, II, pp. 369–75.

32. John Anderson *Sketch of a ramble etc.*, MS cit.

33. Robert & William Chambers *The Gazetteer of Scotland* (Edinburgh 1832), pp. 577–8.

34. Dr S. H. Spiker *Travels through England, Wales and Scotland, in the year 1816* (translated from the German) (London 1820) pp. 208 f. About the end of the 19th century the herrings disappeared, probably because of changes in the loch's water temperature, and because plankton was no longer found in it; today they are again fished in Loch Fyne, though no nearer Inveraray than Tarbert.

35. *The Letters of John Keats*, ed. Maurice Buxton Forman (Oxford 1952) pp. 186–7 (Keats to Tom Keats, 17 July 1818). Keats says that this play was acted in the barn. As the Maltland riding-house where the castle's family theatricals used to be performed was burnt out in 1817, these public performances may well have been held in the great Fisherland barn.

36. James Peddie, one of the contractors for the new Court House, obtained permission to build private houses of 42′6″ frontage in vacant Gallowgate stances; one elevation, dated 27 December 1817, is preserved at Inveraray Castle. After Peddie's bankruptcy a partly-built house was taken over and completed before 1822 by a lawyer, Duncan Paterson; it is now known as the Old

Rectory. A similar house was built two doors along. Dorothy Wordsworth's contrast of solidity and squalor very likely refers to one of these houses. (Inv/Lindsay Howe papers, Boxes 24 and 33A, and see p.314.)

Duncan Paterson (b. 1765) was, incidentally, a son of the 3rd Duke's gardener Walter Paterson by his second wife Agnes Campbell. In 1839, being heavily encumbered with debt, he made over to trustees his Gallowgate house and adjoining property which he had acquired, and on the latter ground a Secession church was built in 1842. Duncan Paterson had a son Walter Campbell Paterson, who died in or before 1842. (Inv/Lindsay Howe papers, Box 24/1, p.105, 1–35, and p.111, 1 & 2 index.)

Between 1822 and 1825 Inveraray's last tenement row was built by Charles Morrison, fish-curer (tack-holder of McPherson's former house in Main Street), 'betwixt the range of houses called the Releif and the Sea'. The original tack ran for 76 years (i.e. 4 × 19 years instead of the usual 3); the row is still known as Crombie's Land after Alexander Crombie, the plasterer to whom it was first set. The celebrated writer Neil Monro was born there in 1864 – the year in which Crombie died. (Inv/ledger of tacks; Rentals 1826.)

37.   Inv/Lindsay Howe papers, Box 33A, Graham to Ferrier, 11 April 1807.

38.   Allan Cunningham *Life of Sir David Wilkie*, loc.cit.

39.   *Notes of a Visit to the Hebrides and Walking Excursion through the Highlands in July and August 1819*, anon. MS by an Irishman probably living in Greenock, NLS 6336 (August 1819).

Robert Southey, who also visited Inveraray in 1819, with Thomas Telford, remarks disparagingly on the 'unaccountable liking of both Scots and English for "*jails-ornées*".' (Robert Southey *Journal of a Tour in Scotland in 1819*, ed. C.H.Herford, London 1929, p.240.)

40.   Graham to Ferrier, loc.cit.

41.   IBR, 14 October 1811; Minutes of Commissioners of Supply, 15 October 1811. In 1806, after the burgh officials had been blamed for negligence, Robert Napier, smith, was paid £162 11s 2d for strengthening the gaol; the Duke contributed £91 for new railings. (Inv/CA 1806, and Lindsay Howe papers, 33A.)

ROBERT REID (1776–1856) became the last Master of the King's Works for Scotland before the office was abolished in 1840. His chief works to date had been Edinburgh's 'second New Town' scheme with Sibbald in 1802, Marshall Place in Perth (1801), and Logierait Manse (1804). His re-fronting of the Edinburgh Parliament House dates from 1807, which accounts for the similarity of the Inveraray Court House façade to the east and west ranges of the Parliament House. (I am indebted to Mr David Walker for information on Reid; see also Ian G.Lindsay *Georgian Edinburgh*; A.J.Youngson *The Making of Classical Edinburgh*, pp.133–4, etc.) (See Index of Architects and Craftsmen.)

Although the Commissioners were ready to consider plans by 1807, Reid himself appears not to have visited Inveraray until 1808, when Ferrier reported to the Commissioners (20 October 1808) that Reid had 'lately come to Inveraray to see the present building and ground behind it and also such other areas as the Duke of Argyll had consented to give for a building, if that shall be thought necessary'. He then returned to Edinburgh to draw up his plans. The latter were still under discussion early in 1812, at the time when Crichton (see n.43) was invited to submit an alternative design. (Minutes of Commissioners of Supply, 2, 5 and 10 March 1812; Inv/Lindsay Howe Papers, 33A.)

42.   The Duke was titular head of the committee, but its effective chairman was Lord John, who was MP for the county. Other members included Trafford Campbell and the lairds of Stonefield, Sonachan and Ederline.

The remainder of this section is based chiefly on information found in IBR 1811–20, and Inv/Lindsay Howe papers, 33A. The plans and elevations by Robert Reid are in Inveraray Castle plan chest. Other information is derived from IBR 12 August 1776; Minutes of Commissioners of Supply, October 1820, 1 May and 25 July 1821; Home Office Letter No.84420 (at Chief Architect's Office, Dept of Health for Scotland); Report of Committee of House of Commons respecting providing of Jails, 1818, p.40.

43.   No Court House plans by Crichton have been discovered. RICHARD CRICHTON (1771–1817) worked chiefly on private houses. His principal works were Rossie Castle, Angus (1800); Gask (1801), a house somewhat in Robert Adam's style for Laurence Oliphant; and (with R. and R. Dickson) the Gothick Abercairny (from 1803, demol. 1960). (Information from Mr David Walker; and John Dunbar *The Historic Architecture of Scotland*, pp.120, 128.)

44. The value of the new site was calculated at £285 2s 6d more than the old, a sum payable to the Duke. Among properties which had to be demolished was the tenement known as William Ross's, one of the earliest (1774) built in the 5th Duke's time (see ch.VIII, p.267 and n.45).

45. Lord John Campbell inherited Ardincaple from his uncle Lord Frederick Campbell in 1816; but had earlier frequently occupied it while in Scotland.

46. The balance of the £7000 went on the difference in site value, architects' fees and legal and other expenses. A James Peddie, possibly this same contractor or his son, designed South Leith Poorshouse in 1851. (Information from Miss K. Cruft.)

47. ALEXANDER LAING, of Edinburgh, is first heard of as a mason (1774), and Archers' Hall in Edinburgh appears to be his earliest recorded work (1776). His designs include Huntly (1805) and Peterhead (1806) Parish Churches, and a large addition to the old castle of Darnaway in Moray (1812). He was known at Inveraray, having inspected and measured Mylne's church in January 1806; at the time of the Court House arbitration he was also acting as arbiter in the protracted case of Aberdour Manse in Aberdeenshire (1814–22). (Gordon Castle Muniments; pamphlet on Aberdour Manse proceedings, 1823; Edinburgh street directories; EB; Inv/Executors' Account of Estate, 1806.) (See also Index of Architects and Craftsmen.)
   The architect John Paterson (see Epilogue, pp.328, 337) was appointed alternative arbiter, should Laing not have been available. In 1818 Peddie tried unsuccessfully to use Laing and Paterson to put pressure on the Commissioners to settle his claims. (Inv/Lindsay Howe papers, 33A, Contract of Peddie and Lumsden 1816, Campbell of Craignure to James Gillespie, 6 July 1818.)

48. The second gaol at the rear was added only in 1843, and in 1869–71 the unobtrusive Police Station (Crown Point House) was built at the south side, concealed by the houses in the small square. The Court House remained in decreasing use in the present century, but after the Circuit's official transfer to Oban was still used for minor courts. Later the Post Office occupied part of the ground floor, but since 1963 even that has been removed, and the future of this fine building remains in doubt.

49. Roof and clock were also badly damaged, 'the stones falling in all directions, some being thrown to an immense distance'. An eye-witness described 'the noise of the tottering steeple, the huge stones bursting from it and falling thick as the leaves of autumn around. . . .' The Argyll estates, which were by then restored to greater stability, contributed £500 to its repair, the balance coming from the Hercules Insurance Company (£734 10s). (Christina Brooks Stewart *The Loiterer in Argyllshire*, Edinburgh 1848, Letter I; Inv/Lindsay Howe papers, Box 21, no.11A.)

50. Inv/Town Rentals 1828, 1833, 1834, 1848; Cash Book 1841/2; Lindsay Howe papers, Box 21A, no.11A (for church repairs 1837–8). Also Robert & William Chambers op.cit. (1832); MS *Travel Journal* (1833) of Henry Crabb Robinson, in Dr Williams' Library, Gordon Square, W.C. 1; *New Statistical Account of Scotland*, VII (Edinburgh 1845). For the cross, NLS 8926, 8927, *Tour* of Mr Clement Mansfield Ingleby, and Miss Taylor's *Journal* (both 1842).

51. Dr John McCulloch *The Highlands and Western Isles of Scotland, in letters to Sir Walter Scott, Bart*, I (London 1824) p.256 f.

52. *The Sportsman in Ireland, etc.*, II, p.176.

53. Henry Cockburn *Circuit Journeys* (Edinburgh 1889) 22–23 April 1843. Cockburn's first visit to Inveraray appears to have been in 1808 as a young Advocate Depute. (*Journals 1831–34*, I, Edinburgh 1874, p.267.)

54. *The Wynne Diaries*, p.454 (Eugenia Campbell, 11 June 1806). All Lord John's children were by his second wife Joan Glassel, daughter and heiress of John Glassel of Longniddry, Midlothian; she died at Rosneath in 1828. Lord John, then twice a widower, was remarried in 1831 to Mrs Anne Colquhoun, daughter of John Cunningham of Craigends and widow of Dr George Cunningham Monteath.

55. George, 8th Duke of Argyll *Scotland as it was and as it is*, II (Edinburgh 1887) p.174.

56. *Diary, Reminiscences and Correspondence of Henry Crabb Robinson, barrister-at-law*, ed. Thomas Sadler, II (London 1872) p.330.

57. Henry Cockburn *Journals 1831–34*, II, p.276.

58. Inveraray had already had two royal visits in the 19th century. In 1832 came the heir apparent to the deposed King Charles X of France, the twelve-year-old Comte de Chambord, known as Henri V. The exiled French royal family had been given the hospitality of Holyroodhouse. The boy evidently found Inveraray both unromantic and discomfiting and 'sortait mécontent . . . pour le noble Henri, la journée était

malheureuse': in the castle he saw weapons taken from the French in 1745, while outside was a cannon captured from François I! (M. d'Hardivillier *Souvenirs des Highlands, Voyage a la Suite de Henri V en 1832*, Paris 1835.)

A happier visit was that of King Frederick Augustus of Saxony in 1844, during his extended tour of Italy, France and Britain and following a splendid royal entertainment to him and the Czar of Russia at Windsor Castle. Inveraray Castle was empty, but the weather was Germanically romantic, the castle Anglo-Gothically splendid, the Argyll Arms elegant and the herrings delicious. (Dr C. G. Carus [trans. S. C. Davison] *The King of Saxony's Journey through England and Scotland in the year 1844*, London 1846, p. 288.)

59. Except where otherwise stated, the account of this visit is taken from the *Illustrated London News* for 28 August 1847, p. 133.

60. Queen Victoria *Leaves from the Journal of Our Life in the Highlands* (London 1877) p. 52.

61. Ibid.

62. Ibid.

63. In July 1563 Mary, Queen of Scots was the guest of the 5th Earl of Argyll at old Inveraray Castle, with members of her government including the Earl of Moray and Chancellor William Maitland. Among the festivities were a deer drive in Glenshira, when the Queen is said to have brought down a stag with her crossbow at Elrig, and games held in what is now the Stable Park. On departure the royal entourage went by road to Creggans and from there by ferry to Strachur.

64. H. B. Stowe to Professor Stowe, 6 September 1856, in Charles E. Stowe *Life of Harriet Beecher Stowe, Compiled from her Letters and Journals* (London 1889) pp. 270 ff. About a week before going to Inveraray Mrs Beecher Stowe had 'just the very pleasantest little interview with the Queen that ever was . . . just an accidental, done-on-purpose meeting at a railway station, while on the way to Scotland'. The Queen delightedly pointed out Mrs Stowe's party to Prince Albert, and accepted copies of her new book *Dred* which she and the Prince were soon busily reading. Mrs Stowe thought the Queen 'a real nice little body with exceedingly pleasant, kindly manners'. (Charles E. Stowe, loc. cit.)

EPILOGUE
1. The Moses Griffith view, taken from the south side of the castle, actually appeared in 1774 in *Additions to the Quarto Edition* of the 1769 *Tour*, published in London. It was included in subsequent editions. His view of the castle from the loch, showing part of the old tower and the old town, appeared in volume II of Pennant's 1772 *Tour in Scotland*. Garret's view, in Newte's *Tour of England and Scotland* (1791) was also published in Newte's earlier, anonymous edition (1788). Accurate plans and elevations of Inveraray were published in *Vitruvius Scoticus*, which did not appear until about 1810, although its plates were published in some form considerably earlier, during Robert Adam's lifetime. For example, we know that 'Adam's' (sic) *Plans of Public Buildings and Gentlemen's Seats in Scotland* was among the books owned by James Craig, planner of Edinburgh New Town, in November 1785. (Youngson, op. cit., Appendix p. 295, n. 6)

2. Sir William Fraser *The Douglas Book*, II (Edinburgh 1885) pp. 469 ff. and 597–8; *Douglas Peerage*, ed. Balfour Paul, ad loc.; John Fleming 'Robert Adam's Castle Style' in *CL*, 23 May 1968. For the burning of Douglas Castle in December 1758, s 89, Milton to Argyll 3, 18 December 1758. Pennant, who describes the new building, an 'imperfect pile' with three round towers and Gothic windows, in his 1772 *Tour* (1790 ed., I, pp. 132–3), quotes the inscription on its foundation stone as dated 1757, which means that the Duke of Douglas had started building anew while his old castle was still standing. (See also n. 3.)

3. Plans and elevations in *Vitruvius Scoticus*, pls. 135, 136; and see Dunbar, op. cit., pp. 125, 126. The *Vitruvius Scoticus* plans presumably represent the original intentions of 1757, though the single jamb formed a complete mansion in itself down to the time of demolition. Dr Alan A. Tait recently discovered unsigned plans, which may be attributed to the older Adam brothers, for the castle as first proposed, which was to be built on to the remains of the original castle. These plans confirm the evidence of the engravings (and of course the Pennant description) that the house had an 'Inveraray' character from the start. The interior was later altered by James Playfair, and Dr Tait has also discovered unexecuted Playfair drawings (1791) for extending the building and remodelling the exterior. The castle's external alterations were not in fact made until the 19th century.

4. Most of the houses mentioned here are discussed by John Dunbar, op. cit., pp. 125–6. Wedderburn (modified by James Nisbet), also discussed by Alistair Rowan in *The Country Seat*, op. cit., pp. 174–6. See also A. R. Bolton's

Topographical Index to the Collection of Adam Drawings in vol.II of *The Architecture of Robert and James Adam* (London 1922) (which does not include Wedderburn or Pitfour).

5. N. Pevsner and John Harris *Lincolnshire* (Penguin Buildings of England Series 1964) ad loc.; photographs in National Buildings Record.

6. Pennant *Tour 1769*, p.264; *First Statistical Account* (1796) XVIII, p.429; Joseph Farington Notebook No.3 (1792), MS cit. Rennie, compiling his contribution to the *Statistical Account* in 1795, says that the building was erected 'about 20 years ago'.

7. Thomas Salmon *Borrowstounness and District* (Edinburgh 1913) p.244 and Appendix II, p.451. I am indebted to Miss J. Cameron and Miss Grant of the Bo'ness Public Library for information on the history of this building.

8. Antony Dale *James Wyatt* (Oxford 1956) pp.186–9; illustration in *The Surrey Tourist, or Excursions through Surrey* (London 1819). John Evans, in *An Excursion to Windsor* (London 1817)–a series of letters supposedly dated 1810–writes that 'the beginnings of a *new Palace* may be seen near Kew, close to the river side . . . It has by no means a pleasant external appearance; and the interior apartments are, it is said, on a particularly small scale. No progress has been made in the building since his Majesty's illness; and it may therefore for years remain unfinished. The situation is damp and low; indeed, the foundations of the edifice must be occasionally inundated.' (p.76.) Evans further tells us in *Richmond and its Vicinity* (Richmond 1824) p.227, that the palace had been built 'even to the turning of the arches' before it was abandoned.

9. Colvin *Dictionary of English Architects* p.545; illustration in Neale's *Seats*, V.

10. RCAHMS *Peebles-shire* (1967) I, p.44, II, pp.308ff., and plates 82–5.

11. Mylne 1789, 1790. Alistair Rowan 'Taymouth Castle, Perthshire', *CL*, 8 and 15 October 1964, and unpublished thesis on *The Castle Style in English Architecture*.

12. John Paterson (d. 1832) was clerk of works to Adam and Charles Russell at Robert Adam's Seton Castle in 1789–91 (see ch.IX, n.14). (Fleming loc. cit.; Dunbar, op. cit., pp.120, 126, 127.) Archibald Elliot later adapted the Inveraray style in part of his design for Jedburgh gaol (1823), a much smaller building using a central circular tower in place of the high square tower (Dunbar, p.207).

13. Antony Dale, op. cit., pp.166–9.

14. Alistair Rowan 'Eastnor Castle, Herefordshire' in *CL* 7–21 March 1968.

15. Saltoun MSS, plan chest: plans and elevations.

16. Alistair Rowan, unpublished thesis, op. cit.

17. RCAHMS *Peebles-shire*, II, p.327, and Inv/Lindsay Howe papers. The Eglintoun family were under great obligations to the 3rd Duke of Argyll and to Lord Milton. Lady Milton (a Kinloch of Gilmerton) was full cousin to Susanna Kennedy, third wife to the 9th Earl and one of the most beautiful and remarkable women of her time. An aunt to both these ladies earlier married James, a younger brother of the 1st Duke of Argyll. See Sir William Fraser *Memorials of the Montgomeries, Earls of Eglintoun* (Edinburgh 1859); *DNB* for Sir James Montgomery; Saltoun MSS, letters from Susanna, Countess of Eglintoun to Ld Milton.

18. *The Architect*, 20 October 1877, p.218.

19. Drawings in the Sir Banister Fletcher Library Drawings Collection in RIBA Library W8/23 1–5. ANTHONY SALVIN (1799–1881), an FSA as early as 1824 and a near-founder member (from 1836) of the RIBA, bridged the gap between the age of Turner, Nash and the elder Pugin, all of whom he had known, and the high Victorian architects like Butterfield and Gilbert Scott. His early houses include Mamhead in Devon (1827–33), Scotney, Kent (1835–43), and the Tudor Revival Harlaxton in Lincolnshire (1831–8); among his later are Peckforton (1844–50) and Thoresby, and his restorations of Windsor and Warwick Castles, both in the 1860s. See Christopher Hussey *English Country Houses, Late Georgian, 1800–1840* (London 1958); *Building News*, 23 December 1881, p.818; and (for Peckforton) Mark Girouard in *CL* 29 July 1965.

The 8th Duke of Argyll's payments made to Salvin in 1878/9 were £247, and in 1879/80, £630 6s 0d. (Coutts & Co., ledgers ad loc., ff.563, 562.)

20. Apparently this was done at the Duke and Duchess's choice. The Duchess writes to her son Lord Lorne in November 1877, of Salvin's first drawings, 'we do not think the roof high pitched enough'. (Inveraray MSS)

21. Inv/Victorian Letter-books, vols. 9, 10. The old model must have proved too battered to use, for in February 1878 £10 2s 4d was paid for a new one. Neither has survived.

22.　The precedent was the marriage of King Henry VIII's sister to the Duke of Suffolk in 1515. On Princess Louise's wedding-day a local woman was recorded as having remarked, 'My, will the Queen no' be a proud woman this day, getting her daughter married to the Marquess!' (John Maclean *Royal Visits to Inveraray*, privately printed 1933.)

　　The fitting up of the Brown Library was executed by William Alexander & Sons, joiners of Ayr, for £253 2s 7d, and the ornamental railing to its gallery was made by Walter Macfarlane & Co., Glasgow, for £86 14s. The fireplace, of Kintyre marble, was made and installed by Galbraith & Winton, marble cutters, of Glasgow, for £63 8s. (Inv/Cash Bk 1869–73, October–November 1871.)

23.　Catherine Sinclair *Scotland and the Scotch*, pp. 60 f. The Nesfield sketches are preserved at Inveraray Castle.

24.　Hew Montgomerie Wardrop (1856–87), and Sir Robert Rowand Anderson (1834–1921).

25.　The tower was built as a war memorial to all Campbells who fell in the 1914–18 war; it contains a fine peal of ten bells.

26.　During the Select Committee inquiry in the House of Commons, the Duke of Argyll observed that he had no objection to extending the railway to Campbeltown, so long as it did not come near Loch Fyne. 'Do you know that there is another distinguished residence within sight of two railways – Windsor Castle?' asked Mr Littler. The Duke replied uncompromisingly, 'I do not.' (*The Scotsman*, 1 April 1897.)

27.　Another of these Victorian villas, Rudha-na-Craig, was built in 1863 by James Cunningham Grahame, Sheriff-Substitute of Argyll from 1860–7 and father of Kenneth Grahame, who lived there for a short time in his infancy. (Peter Green *Kenneth Grahame, 1859–1932*, London 1959, pp. 10–13, 29–30; and Inv/Lindsay Howe papers.)

The following index comprises all names that could be traced of masons, carpenters and joiners, plasterers, painters, slaters, smiths and other craftsmen recorded as working at Inveraray (and in some cases Rosneath) between approximately 1720 and 1820. All architects known to have any connexion with Inveraray are included up to the present day, with the exception of the four main architects William and John Adam, Roger Morris and Robert Mylne, whose work there is fully covered in the main index.

The evidence has been collated with information available (particularly if hitherto unpublished) on work known to be by these craftsmen in other places. The description attached to the name (e.g. 'BUCHANAN, Robert, carpenter in Greenock') is taken wherever possible from documentary evidence. Certain apparently trifling items have been noted where they seem to provide proof of work on any Inveraray buildings, whether in policies, town or castle. As far as possible the list has been checked with the Scottish Record Society's published records of marriages, burgess-ships, apprenticeships, testaments, etc., with the Edinburgh baptism records and Inveraray parish records at Register House, and with the Burgh Minute Books at the Town Clerk's office at Inveraray.

Names mentioned in this book (marked with an asterisk) are given appropriate page and note references in italics. Names or information not so noted are given abbreviated source references (see list of abbreviations, p. 345).

Names in sub-entries set in italics (usually followed by details of burgess-ships, marriages, etc.) indicate that identification with the particular craftsman in the main entry is doubtful because of the commonness of the name. Where the name occurs so frequently in records (e.g. John Campbell, James Miller) that identification is very tentative or the information is mutually exclusive, the name in italics *precedes* the date of the item instead of vice versa as normally.

In checking and compiling this index I have been particularly indebted to Kitty Cruft, of the National Monuments Record of Scotland, to John Dunbar and to David Walker.

ADAM,* James, architect, 1732–94
1757, first mention of in Inveraray accounts, as partner to John and Robert Adam, and (1758) to John Adam. *p. 362, nn. 191, 192*
?1757, jointly credited with John Adam with design for Douglas Castle, Lanark, earliest derivative of Inveraray. *p. 327*
1758, credited in *Vitruvius Scoticus* with design of Garden Bridge, Inveraray. *p. 372, n. 47*
1765–73, probable architect of Lowther village, Westmorland, influenced by John Adam's designs for Inveraray town. *p. 373, n. 2*

ADAM,* Robert, architect. 1728–92
1748, June, informs Ld Milton of William Adam's death. *p. 63*
1748, 1754, with John Adam in Inveraray before his travels in Italy. *p. 70*
1752, possible influence of, on John Adam's designs for Inveraray, e.g. for Tombreac dairy. *p. 140*
1770 f., debt to style of Inveraray Castle, in designs for, e.g. Wedderburn, Caldwell, Oxenfoord, Culzean, Pitfour, Dalquharran, Seton, Airthrey. *p. 328*

AITKEN, James, wright in Glasgow
1722, 16 May, admitted burgess of Inveraray: IBR

AITKEN, John, wright in Glasgow
1722, 16 May, admitted burgess of Inveraray: IBR

AITKEN,* John, mason in Lugton, Dalkeith
?son to John Aitken, mason at Bridge End, Dalkeith, and Margaret Hastie, both d. by 1733: Testament of Margaret Hastie, 20 June 1733, ET
works for Lords Milton and Somerville for 25 years from c. 1735: Aitken to Sir John Dalrymple, April 1760, s 93
1736–?40, employed at Whim, builds doorways, frieze and cornice, bridges, garden wall and coping: Whim accts, s 423, 424
1739 f., in charge of quarriers at Whim: s 404
1745, ? August, inspects lime quarries, head of Loch Fyne: Inv/1745
1746, proposed as builder of bridge in garden, Inveraray: Milton to Stonefield, ?18 August 1746, SF, SRO GD 14/31
?1750s, works at Gilmerton for David Kinloch (payment still outstanding 1763): Aitken to Milton, 15 February 1763, s 99
1751–3, on recommendation of Lords Milton and Somerville works at Dalkeith Palace for Duke of Buccleuch (repairs to palace, houses, mills, dykes etc.), under John Adam's direction: Aitken to Dalrymple, loc. cit.
1754, gives dimensions for chimneys and oven of St Catherine's stone for Inveraray: s 347
1759, recommends a cement to protect Inveraray Castle against weather. *p. 363, n. 197*
1763, recommended to Mr Kay, overseer to Lord Abercorn, for decorative carving (capitals etc.) at Duddington House: Aitken to Milton, 15 February 1763, s 99
1764, works for Milton at ? Brunstane; applies for work at Stuart Mackenzie's

'Grand house in the north': Aitken to Milton, 25 May 1764, s100

AITKEN [AITKIN, AIKEN], Thomas, brickmaker in Dalkeith
employed by Lord Milton before 1750
1750, sent to Inveraray at Duke of Argyll's expense (presumably on Ld Milton's recommendation) to try local clays for brick-making; recommends Loch Gair clay: Letters of Andrew Fletcher (20 January, 5 December), Knockbuy (7 March 1750), and Aitken (26 May 1750), to Milton, s72, 74, 75, 408(3). Apparently leaves Inveraray without building draw-kiln (built by William Douglas, q.v.): G. Hunter report, 29 October 1755, s413(2)

ALEXANDER,* Hugh, wright
Hugh Alexander, journeyman wright, New Kirk p., m. Mary, dau. to George Drummond, sailor in N. Leith, 24 December 1769: EM
Hugh Alexander, wright, Canongate p., m. Agnes McAllan, 10 June 1770: CM
1782f., with John Johnstone makes mahogany doors for main rooms at Inveraray Castle. *p.219*
1784f., ?succeeds George Haswell as chief wright to 5th Duke of Argyll. *p.393, n.8*
1785f., executes part alterations to Kilbryde dairy, Inveraray: Inv/CI 1785
1787, advises on leading of large windows, Inveraray Castle: Inv/Inst. 1787
1788, renews 7 windows at great inn, Inveraray: Inv/Gen. Inst. 1788

ALEXANDER,* Robert, mason
1777, contractor (with John Moodie) for Clunary wool factory, Inveraray; hands over to John Brown. *p.274*

ALEXANDER,* William, & Sons, joiners in Ayr
1871, fit up Brown Library and other works in Inveraray Castle; fit up stables in north side of Cherry Park court. *p.404, n.22*

ALLAN, Charles, mason
c.1747f., working at Inveraray; loses possessions in masons' 'guildhall' fire of March 1752: Inv/AEM

ALLAN, John, painter, ? and wright
John Allan, journeyman wright, New Greyfriars p., m. Helen, dau. to James Scot, thatcher in Hawick, 5 January 1766: EM
John Allan, wright and slater, admitted burgess and gild brother of Glasgow, 9 February 1797 by purchase: GB
John Allan, wright, St Andrew p., m. Mary, dau. to James Hamilton, painter in Canongate, 26 December 1799: EM
1788, paid to account £9 8s 4½d for painting at Inveraray Castle: Inv/CA 1787/8

ANDERSON, Andrew, wright
1732, 10 October, admitted burgess of Inveraray: IBR
1742, 18 August, *Andrew Anderson*, wright, admitted burgess of Edinburgh as apprentice to Henry Antonius, wright and burgess: EB

ANDERSON, David, mason in Ayr
1722, 10 July, admitted burgess of Inveraray: IBR

ANDERSON, James, mason in Inveraray
?eldest son to William Anderson, maltman, and as such admitted burgess and gild brother of Glasgow, 7 August 1755: GB
James Anderson, journeyman mason, Tron Kirk p., Edinburgh, m. Jean, dau. to dec. John Guild, quarrier in Blackford, 27 March 1768: EM
c.1747f., working at Inveraray; loses possessions in masons' 'guildhall' fire of March 1752: Inv/AEM
1756, tenders for running St Catherine's quarry as successor to William Paull: s414(2), 415
1757, November, successfully tenders against John Wardrop to build Achnagoul and Barvrack dykes, Inveraray: s89
1758–60, builds dykes at Inveraray: Kilbryde, Achingoul, Barvrack, Cruit, Bealachanuaran (1758–9); Garron, Duniquaich, Kilbryde, Balintyre (1760): s418(1), 419(1), 420(2); Inv/EAc, Inst., CB 1759/60
1762f., builds walls, maintains dykes at Inveraray: Inv/AECB, Ask. Inventory of Rentals
1764f., repair of Town quay (1764–8) and Tolbooth (1766–8 and 1772–4), Inveraray: IBR
1768f., living in Deacon Thomson's former house, Inveraray; his house demolished (1776): Inv/RFD, AE Rentals

ANDERSON,* Sir Robert Rowand, architect. 1834–1921
1886, with H.M. Wardrop designs Inveraray Episcopal Church. *p. 340*

ARNOT, John, mason
c.1747f., working at Inveraray; loses possessions in masons' 'guildhall' fire of March 1752: Inv/AEM
1758, 19 November, John Arnot, mason in New Kirk p., m. Elisabeth, dau. to dec. David Gullen, farmer in Donssington, Prestonpans: EM

ARTHUR, James, mason
1752, October/November, hewing stone for Clerk's house, Inveraray new town, under James Potter: s410(2), 411(2)

AXLIE, Thomas, bricklayer
1745, July f., building vents and oven for
bakehouse, Inveraray old town: Inv/1745

BELL, Angus, quarrier
1754, quarrying for Tombreac dyke,
Inveraray, under William Douglas younger:
s412(2)

BELL, Archibald, and partners, masons
1776, casting foundations of wauk mill,
Bridge of Douglas, Inveraray: Inv/CA 1775/6
1795-6, R.W. Master of Inveraray Masonic
Lodge: *Inveraray Masonic Lodge* (1909)

BELL,* James, wright
1781, James Bell, wright, New Kirk p., m.
Elizabeth, dau. to John Adams, wright in
Stirlingshire, 18 May: EM
1794, makes 3 doz. elm chairs for Inveraray,
inn. *pp. 281, 289*
1795-6, finishes and paints John Simpson's
book-presses for Duke's turret, Inveraray
Castle. *p. 281*
1795, makes scaffolding and trestles (with
Donald McArthur) for building Inveraray
church: Inv/Day Bk
1796, erects church scaffolding and prepares
beams for Inveraray church roof: Inv/Day Bk

BELL, John, sawyer
1816-28, mentioned, living in Arkland,
Inveraray: 1833-48 mentioned as living in
Relief Land; 1848 referred to as 'retired':
Inv/Rentals 1816, 1828, 1833, 1848

BELL, Malcolm, quarrier
1754, quarrying for Tombreac dyke,
Inveraray, under William Douglas younger:
s412(2)

BLACK, James mason in Inveraray
1748, January, mentioned in court case,
Inveraray: s406(1)
1760, ?under-overseer, working at St
Catherine's quarry: Inv/Q accts

BLACK,* Thomas, mason from Monzie
1795-6, builds Wintertown Gate lodge,
Inveraray, with Robert Young. *p. 252*
1796, one of 8 masons building Inveraray
church; returns home November: Inv/AE
accts 1796f.

BOGG* [BOOG], Maitland, carver and
gilder in Edinburgh
(The name is Flemish, a variant of Boog,
Boag or Bogue.)
1783, 21 February, Maitland Boog, carver
and gilder, Old Greyfriars p., m. Mary, dau.
to James Liddell, farmer in Borthwick:
EM
1788-9, gilds girandoles in south saloon,
Inveraray Castle. *p. 219*
James Boog or Bog, son to Maitland, is
apprenticed to Deacon Alexander Clerk,
painter, for 6 years, 4 April 1782: EA

James Bogue, carver and gilder (possibly
grandson to Maitland), is admitted burgess
of Edinburgh, 25 May 1807, as apprentice
to John Caitcheon, gilder: EB

BOGLE*, Michael, timber merchant and
contractor. d. ?1799
? younger son to Robert Bogle of
Shettleston, merchant; partner to Allan
Dreghorn (d. 1764) (q.v.), thence trading
as Bogle & Scott. *p. 394, n. 12.*
1757, 8 July, admitted burgess and gild
brother of Glasgow: GB
1800, 'Mr Bogle', possibly son to above, refuses 5th Duke of Argyll's offer to contract
for completion of Inveraray church. *p. 283*

BONOMI*, Joseph, ARA, architect. 1739-
1808
76 Great Titchfield Street, London
1803-6, designs Rosneath Castle for Lord
Lorne; left unfinished. *pp. 291-2*
1806, alterations to Inveraray Castle include probable removal of entresols and
rearrangement of arms. *pp. 197, 311, p. 383,
n. 60.;* unexecuted proposals include fosse
causeways, stair water-closets, bracket lan-
terns for hall. *p. 311*

BOWER,* Mr——, wood carver in London
1781-2, carves trusses for drawing-room and
dining-room doors, Inveraray Castle, to
Robert Mylne's design. *p. 211*

BROOKS, John, surveyor
probably schoolmaster at Inveraray
said to have drawn plans of Inveraray harbour, etc. for Duke of Argyll, n.d.: Inv/
Ledger III, tack of Morrison's house (1822)
1815, surveys new Court House site and
draws plan showing buildings marked for
demolition; makes sections of levels from
quay, to determine foundation depth:
Inv/Lindsay Howe 33A
1822, makes plans for Morrison's new house
(i.e. Crombie's Land): Inv/Ledger III,
tack of Morrison's house (1822)

BROWN, Donald, ?mason and quarrier
1776, demolishes houses in old town,
Inveraray: Inv/CA 1773/4
1777, with partners, quarrying flags at
Bridge of Douglas for Inveraray houses:
Inv/CA 1777/8
1782-3, with 24 men filling up course of
River Shira and levelling ground: Inv/accts
1772f.

BROWN, James, wright
James Brown executes work in 1743 for
Duke of Argyll's laboratory at the Whim:
s428, Robt Brisbane acct books
3 *James Browns*, wrights, are named as
Edinburgh burgesses between 1745 and
1797; in Glasgow a *James Brown* is admitted
burgess 20 September, 1787 through his

Shaw Stewart family. *p.394, n.13*
1807, designs 12–32 Gayfield Square, Edinburgh. *p.394, n.13*

CAIRNS, Robert, mason
*c.*1747f., working at Inveraray; loses possessions in masons' 'guildhall' fire of March 1752: Inv/AEM

CALDER,* James, mason
3 *James Calders*, masons, recorded as marrying in Edinburgh 1736–50: (*a*) of S.S.W. p., to Margaret Ross, 6 June 1736; (*b*) of New Kirk, p., to Margaret Methven, svt to Mr Falconer, advocate, 27 May 1744; (*c*) journeyman mason of New Kirk p., to Isobel, dau. to dec. Daniel Ferrier, merchant, 10 June 1750: EM
James Calder, journeyman mason, admitted burgess of Edinburgh 28 November 1750, in right of his wife Isobel Ferrier: EB
John Calder, son to *James*, late mason in Queensferry, is apprenticed to Walter Scott, merchant, 11 June 1766: EA
1746, memorial to, from William Adam, on laying foundation of Inveraray Castle: s404
1747f., principal mason at Inveraray Castle, under foreman George Hunter. *p. 73*
1747, 29 September, admitted burgess of Inveraray (with George Hunter): IBR

CAMERON, Duncan, causeway layer
1772, 28 March, sent to Inveraray by William Mylne: Inv/5DA
Duncan Cameron, journeyman mason, Old Kirk p., m. Janet, dau. to Donald Cameron, tenant in Currie, Fortingall, 16 October 1788: EM

CAMPBELL,* Alexander, mason
before 1752, under-grieve at Ardmaddy marble quarries, Argyll. *p.76*
known to William Douglas, mason: Carwhin to Milton, 6 November 1752, s410
1752, December, at Campbell of Carwhin's recommendation inspects Tombreac marble quarry, Inveraray. *p.76*
1754, in charge at Tombreac marble quarry: Inv/Q

CAMPBELL,* Colen, architect. 1676–1729
dedicates designs in *Vitruvius Britannicus* to 2nd Duke of Argyll and Earl of Ilay, including 'New Design for the Duke of Argyll' (unexecuted) with high central feature. *p.45*

CAMPBELL, Colin, wright
1764–6, 1770–2, payments to, by Inveraray Burgh Council for work (?repairing Tolbooth): IBR

CAMPBELL, Donald, mason
1785, co-builder with John Tavish of Dhu Loch Bridge, Inveraray: Inv/plan chest, sections dated 10 August 1785

CAMPBELL,* Dugal, military engineer.
d.1757
1734–57, Engineer in Office of Ordnance; promoted Major 1757. *p.45*
1739f., Clerk of Works to Board of Ordnance with house in Tower of London (while Roger Morris is Carpenter to the Board, and William Adam its mason in Scotland): PRO, WO 54, 207, p.40
1742, 24 September, admitted burgess of Edinburgh gratis, for services as H.M. Engineer for Northern district: EB
1744, with Mr Brereton, engineer at Fort Augustus, surveys line of military road Dumbarton/Inveraray. *p.352, n.9*
?1744, designs (unexecuted) for a castle for 3rd Duke of Argyll. *p.45*
1745–6, serves in Scotland during Jacobite rising; 1746–7 serves in Flanders; 1757 at Louisburg; dies at sea between Halifax/New York. *p.352, n.9*

CAMPBELL, Duncan, wright
1751f., mentioned, living in Gallowgate, Inveraray: Inv/1753
1757, now discharged from Duke of Argyll's service: s416(3)

CAMPBELL, Mr George, joiner in Edinburgh. d.?1768
1730, 24 June, George Campbell, wright, admitted burgess and gild brother of Edinburgh by right of father George Campbell, merchant, B. & G.B.: EB
1734, 20 September, admitted burgess of Inveraray: IBR
1768, 6 April, testament of George Campbell, house-carpenter in Edinburgh: ET

CAMPBELL,* George, marble carver in Edinburgh
1803, carves chimney-piece ornaments for south corner drawing-room, Inveraray Castle. *p.394, n.9*

CAMPBELL, James, wright in Inveraray
1732, 10 October, admitted burgess of Inveraray: IBR
1738, 30 August, *James Campbell*, wright, admitted burgess and gild brother of Glasgow as eldest living son to dec. William Campbell, wright, B. & G.B.: GB

CAMPBELL, John, alias McIVER, see McIVER

CAMPBELL, John, slater in Inveraray
?identifiable with John Campbell, slater in 'Down' (Doune), admitted burgess of Inveraray 11 October 1742: IBR
1752, slating houses in Gallowgate, Inveraray new town: Inv/Jnls 1750/2
1753f., referred to as living in Gallowgate, Inveraray: Inv/1753, RFD; s416(3)
1752–4, slating and mending houses in

Inveraray; sent to Easdale for slates
(1753): Inv/Jnls 1752/4
1756, slating casemate roofs, Inveraray
Castle: s415
1758, slating turret and outbuildings,
Rosneath Castle: s418(2)
1764–6, 1770–2, payments to, for work for
Inveraray Burgh Council: IBR
1770, pointing and slating old tower,
Cherry Park court of offices, and town
houses, Inveraray: Inv/AECB 1759/60
1774, do. at Ross's house, Colquhoun's
house and Inveraray factory; 'stripping'
old Inveraray church and houses; repairs
to Inveraray inn, manse, and Argyll burial
place at Kilmun: Inv/CA 1773/4
1776, slating Arkland, ministers' office
houses, and Highland church, Inveraray:
Inv/CA 1775/6, 1776/7
1777–8, slating Ferry Land, harling Cross
Houses, Inveraray: Inv/CA 1777/8

CAMPBELL, John, wright in Inveraray
John Campbell, wright in Dumbarton,
admitted burgess and gild brother of
Dumbarton by right of father (wright, B.
& G.B. 1730), 29 September 1757: DB
John Campbell, wright, New North p., m.
Janet Troup, relict of James Savenger,
Officer of Excise, 15 February 1761: EM
John Campbell, wright, admitted burgess
and gild brother of Glasgow by purchase,
1778: GB
1772–3, given house in Gallowgate, Inveraray (his former house in old town demolished 1776): Inv/AE
1773, employed on addition to Chamberlain's house, Inveraray: Inv/CA 1773/4
1774, wright work for Inveraray factory and
addition to John Roy's house: Inv/CA
1773/4
1775, makes windows for wool factory at
Bridge of Douglas, Inveraray: Inv/CA
1774/5
1776, wright work for Rev. Alexander
McTavish's manse, Inveraray: Inv/CA
1775/6

CARLAW, George, marble cutter
1790–1, cuts marble from quarry for fireplaces, ?for Inveraray Castle: Inv/CA
1790/1

CARMICHAEL,* Michael, architect
1799, considered by 5th Duke of Argyll for
completion of Robert Mylne's church,
Inveraray. *p.283*
1800, builds wall across castle kitchen
garden, Inveraray, and sunk fence alongside, for £253 10s 3½d: Inv/accts 1800/1,
and see *p.251*
1802, designs Colonsay church. *p.394, n.12*

CATION [CAUTION], David, mason and
carver
1731, 22 May, admitted burgess of Inveraray as apprentice to William Douglas,
mason and carver (q.v.): IBR
1740, executes sculpture of Town House
(later Tontine building), Glasgow:
Glasgow TCM, 22 September 1741
1742, 6 October, admitted burgess of Glasgow, as wright and carver, gratis, by act of
Council 4 October: GB

CHAPMAN, James, mason
1752, October/November, hewing stone for
Clerk's house, Inveraray new town, under
James Potter: s410(2), 411(2)

CHAPMAN, William, mason in Inveraray
1723, 10 October, admitted burgess of
Inveraray: IBR

CHRISTIE,* Alexander, (?house) painter
son to David Christie, gardener: EA
1777, 8 October, apprenticed to George
Farquhar, painter in Edinburgh, for 6
years: EA
1783, employed in painting at Inveraray
Castle; paid to acct £16 6s. *p.384, n.73*
1785, 2 April, Alexander Christie, painter,
Tolbooth p., m. Miss Euphemia, dau. to
William Ballantyne, merchant in America:
EM

CHRISTIE,* Mr——, mason
1748–9, master mason under John Adam's
supervision, at Garron military bridge, Loch
Fyne. *p.125*
1749, October, to advise with George
Hunter (q.v.) on building of Garden
Bridge, Inveraray: Memo. by John Campbell,
late Chamberlain, s407(1)

CHRISTY, Peter, gilder
1801, employed at Inveraray Castle: Inv/
accts 1800/1

CLARK see CLERK

CLAYTON,* John, plasterer and stuccoist
?son to Thomas Clayton (q.v.)
1781–2, probably executes (in London)
entablatures and friezes for drawing- and
dining-rooms, Inveraray Castle; letter to,
from Robert Mylne (5 November 1780);
visits Inveraray to instal said plaster-work,
also in vestibule and dining-room turret.
pp.210–11, 215
1788, 3 September, Elizabeth, dau. to John
Claiton, plasterer, m. Rev. Mr Reston,
minister of Biggar: CM

CLAYTON,* Thomas, plasterer in Hamilton
works under Adam brothers at Hopetoun
and Dumfries; employed by Duke of Atholl
at Blair Castle
1756, sends detailed estimate of stucco-work
to Duke of Argyll (possibly works at
Inveraray 1757?). *p.93*

CLERK, John, mason
1783, *John Clark,* mason in Edinburgh,
institutes Process of Scandal against John
Kay, portioner in Crosscauseway: ECP
no.787
1787, 9 August, *John Clark,* mason in
Extended Royalty, admitted burgess of
Edinburgh: EB
1805, builds porter's lodge at Horse Park,
Inveraray, for £23 14s 10d: Inv/CA 1805
CLERK, Malcolm, hammerman in Inveraray
1732, 10 October, admitted burgess of
Inveraray: IBR
COCKBURN, Mr [?Andrew], ?stone
carver
1781, 9 October, *Andrew Cockburn,*
journeyman mason, New Greyfriars p., m.
Mary, dau. to Duncan McDuff, farmer at
Muthill, Perthshire: EM
?1782, Mr Cockburn consulted by Robert
Mylne over principal bedchamber chimney-
piece, Inveraray Castle: Inv/Plan chest,
drawing of do., n.d.
CORSS, David, wright in Glasgow
1721, supplies garden and quarry tools for
Inveraray for 2nd Duke of Argyll:
Inv/2 DAc. 1720/1
CORSSAR,* John, wright and glazier in
Inveraray
m. Christine Wood before 1741
1737, 10 October, admitted burgess of
Inveraray: IBR
1739–43, principal wright to 2nd Duke of
Argyll at Inveraray: memorial, s413(2)
1743f., retained by 3rd Duke for outside
wright work, but wages and privileges
reduced: s413(2)
1746, wright work for slaughter-house and
flesh market, Inveraray old town, and for
old Inveraray Castle offices; applies with
William Thomson (q.v.) to make sash
windows for new castle: Inv/1746; Memorial
1 December, s404
1748, erects gibbet at Fisherland Point,
Inveraray: Inv/CA 1748
1749, with William Douglas values new
houses in Inveraray: Inv/accts 1749.
Petitions for rise in wages: s407A(1)
?1750–56, overseer of outside wright work
(i.e. excluding castle) at Inveraray:
Memorial, s413(2)
1751, with William Douglas surveys Tarbert
Castle and estimates repairs: Inv/Particular
Papers
1753, to paint ducal barge and fittings, including coat of arms: Inv/Jnl 1752–6
1756, sides with Commissary James
Campbell and John Fallowsdale in feud
against Robert Bathgate, overseer. *p.90*
1756, leaves or dismissed Duke's service

with his men; succeeded as outside overseer by George Haswell (q.v.): Milton
memos., s413(2); Haswell to Milton,
October 1759, s419(1)
COWAN,* William, undertaker and quarry
overseer. d.1751
1748, 12 September, contracts with John
Adam to work Creggans quarry, Inveraray.
p.66
1750, gives up through ill-health. *p.73*
1751, spring, dies; succeeded by James
Potter (q.v.): Inv/accts 1750/2
possibly father to William Cowan, who is
apprenticed (as son of the late William
Cowan, mason in Loanhead), to Francis
Marshall, merchant in Edinburgh, 1767: EA
CRANSTOUN, Andrew, wright
1753, living in Gallowgate, Inveraray:
Inv/1753
CRAWFORD, Donald, dyke builder
1754, building dyke in Tombreac park,
Inveraray: s412(2)
CRICHTON,* Richard, architect in Edinburgh. 1771–1817
son to James Crichton, mason
1797, 11 May, admitted burgess of Edinburgh, as mason: EB
architect of Rossie Castle, Angus (1800),
Gask (1801), Abercairny (with R. & R.
Dickson) (1803f.), Balbirnie addition,
Fife (1815) *p.400, n.43*
1808–10, designs Stirling Court House and
prison: RCAHMS *Stirlingshire,* II, p.293
1812, invited to submit designs for Inveraray Court House and prison. *p. 316*
monument to family, in St Cuthbert's
churchyard, Edinburgh: SCM no.78
CROMBIE,* Alexander, plasterer. d.1864
1793, 8 May, *Alexander Crombie,* wright,
Old Greyfriars p., Edinburgh, m. Bethia,
dau. to John Dyce, merchant of Aberdeen: EM
1820, mentioned, living in Arkland, Inveraray: Inv/Rental
1826, acquires tack of newly-built Morrison's Land, thence known as Crombie's
Land, Inveraray (still there 1833). *p.400,
n.36*
grave-stone at Kilmalew, Inveraray
CUMMING,* Alexander, clock-maker.
?1732–1814
1751f., employed at Inveraray on board
wages: Inv/Jnl 1750/2
1752, 5 October, admitted burgess of
Inveraray: IBR
1755, commissioned by Capt. Henry Fletcher
to copy model of 'Marshal Saxe's house'.
p.364, n.208
1756, restores instruments damaged by sea-
water in stranded ship, for Duke of Argyll:
R.Lang to Milton, 28 January 1756, s415

1757, builds organ in Inveraray Castle, assisted by brother John (q.v.). *p.88*
1760, elected to Inveraray Burgh Council: IBR
1761, draws ground-floor plan of Inveraray Castle: Inv/Ask. Inventory
1763f., working as clock-maker in London under patronage of Earl of Bute *et al.*; makes barometric clocks for King George III (1765), self (1766) and Sir James Lowther (1775); patents water-closet (1775); makes machine organ for Ld Bute (1780s); hon. freeman of Worshipful Company of Clockmakers (1781); FRS of Edinburgh (1783); author of *Elements of Clock and Watch Work* (1766) etc.: *CL* 12 June 1969, pp.1528ff., and see standard works on clock-makers

CUMMING,* John, painter, brother to Alexander
1757, assists Alexander Cumming (?as painter) in fitting up organ, Inveraray Castle. *p.88*

CUNNINGHAM, David, smith at Maltland, Inveraray
1783, mentioned in connexion with Maltland smithy, Inveraray: Inv/Inst. 1783
1787, Whitsun, removed; succeeded by Robert Napier (q.v.): Inv/1760–1800

CUNNINGHAME, Robert, mason
*c.*1747f., working at Inveraray; loses possessions in masons' 'guildhall' fire of March 1752: Inv/AEM

CURRIE, William, plumber
1770, payments to, for plumbing, ?town water supply, Inveraray: Inv/AECB 1759/60

DAWSON, John, wright
1755, 20 August, *John Dawson*, carver, admitted burgess of Edinburgh: EB
1778, wright work for Bridge of Douglas factory, Inveraray: Inv/Accts 1772f.

DEOR [DEWAR], Neil, smith. d. by 1828
1816, mentioned, assistant to Robert Napier (q.v.), living in Cross Houses, Inveraray; dead by 1828: Inv/Rental

DEOR [DEWAR], Peter, wright and cooper. d. by 1828
1775, given house in Maltland, Inveraray: Inv/AEM
1777, wright work in new town houses, Inveraray: Inv/CA 1777/8
1816, mentioned, living free in Maltland; dead by 1828: Inv/Rentals

DEWAR,* Robert, glazier in Edinburgh. ? 1721–98
son to John Dewar, merchant in Dalkeith: EA
1731, 15 December, apprenticed to George Wight, glazier in Edinburgh: EA

1739, 5 December, admitted burgess of Edinburgh (as apprentice): EB
1753, 28 September, admitted gild brother of Edinburgh (as apprentice): EB
1758, glazes windows at Inveraray Castle; probably recommended by John Paterson, of Queensferry (q.v.). *pp.93–4*
1759, glazes castle middle tower windows with coloured panes. *p.105*
1756–83, 5 apprentices successively recorded as bound to him: EA
2 children of *Robert Dewar* buried Restalrig churchyard, Edinburgh, 1763, 1765; also their father Robert Dewar, of Abbeyhill, buried 10 December 1798, aged 77: RB

DOLLAR, Alexander, mason in Stirling
*c.*1710, works at Stirling Town House: *Stirling Nat.Hist. & Arch. Soc.Recs.* (1889/90) p.36
1721, 3 May, admitted burgess of Inveraray: IBR; in charge of alterations to 'old apartment', Inveraray Castle: Inv/AE accts 1706f; paid £167 for mason work at Inveraray; works on door of 'Lodging' (June): Inv/2DAC 1720/1.

DOLLAR, John, master mason to 2nd Duke of Argyll
1729, 20 May, admitted burgess and gild brother of Inveraray: IBR
1737, John Dollar, mason in Stirling, mentioned: *Stirling Recs.* (1889) p.239

DOUGLAS,* John, architect in Edinburgh and Leith. d.1778
probably one of Douglas family of masons in E. Lothian: John Douglas younger, mason, works at Yester 1663; John Douglas, mason, burgess of Haddington 1677, works at Thirlestane (1677) and Lethington for Ld Lauderdale; John Douglas, mason, at Belton 1703, works at Yester for Ld Tweeddale: inf. from John Dunbar and David Walker
1733, advises Ld Aberdeen at Haddo: Penicuik MSS, SRO GD 18
1735, design for Glasserton, Wigton (but John Baxter's design adopted): Penicuik MSS, SRO GD 18
1736, design for converting Blair Castle into symmetrical 'William Adam type' mansion: Blair Castle, plan chest
1737–8, alterations to Abercairny
1745, 21 August, admitted burgess of Edinburgh: EB
1746, July, recommended by Stonefield, as second choice to William Adam, for clerk of works or 'Intendant General' at Inveraray Castle: Stonefield to Argyll 3, 13 July 1746, SF, SRO GD 14/99 and *p. 354, n.40*
1754–7, designs St Salvator's Quadrangle, St Andrews, north side; living in Leith

brother Robert, merchant: GB
1737–40, designs Town Hall (later Tontine building), Glasgow, with James Craig. *p.367, n.250*
1739, designs St Andrew's Church, Glasgow. *p.367, n.250*
1750, buys timber cargo of the 'Danish Captain' (i.e. Captain Bee?) and offers for sale for use at Inveraray Castle. *p.367, n.250*

DRUMMOND, James, mason
*c.*1747f., working at Inveraray; loses possessions in masons' 'guildhall' fire of March 1752: Inv/AEM
1757, 3 December, James Drumond, journeyman mason, Canongate p., m. Isobell, dau. to dec. Daniel Forbas, wright in Perth: CM

DUFF, John, surveyor and/or mason in Edinburgh
1794, 30 July, *John Duff*, mason in Tron Kirk p., Edinburgh, m. Janet, dau. to Robert Dick, Excise Officer in Blairgowrie: EM
?1820, surveys and reports on additional retaining wall for new Court House, Inveraray: Inv/Lindsay Howe 33A, Lumsden & Peddie claim of 20 December 1820
1821, witness on above, in arbitration case conducted by Alexander Laing (q.v.): Inv/Lindsay Howe, 33A, Decreet arbitral of 11 June 1821

DUNCAN, James, wright
1784, 23 April, *James Duncan*, carpenter, St Giles p., Edinburgh, m. Margaret, dau. to Alexander Johnston, cooper in Leith: EM
1796, prepares beams for building church roof, Inveraray: Inv/Day Bk

DUNCAN, John, mason
1752, October–November, hewing stone for Clerk's house, Inveraray new town, under James Potter: s410(2), 411(2)
1766, 5 June, *John Duncan*, journeyman mason, Canongate p., m. Helen, dau. to dec. Charles Robertson, labourer: CM

DUPASQUIER,* Leonard, gilder, of Paris
?son of John Bernard Du Pasquier, merchant in Burgundy: whose dau. Mary Dupasquier (?sister to Leonard) m. William Roy, watchmaker, 27 April 1787: EM
conjectural identification of, with Antoine-Léonard du Pasquier, sculptor (1748–?1831). *p.380, n.26*
1771–5, gilds picture-frames at Inveraray Castle; 'finishing' house interior. *p.200*
1775, in business as gilder in Edinburgh. *p.380, n.26*
1778, 15 July, Leonard Dupasquier, carver and gilder, Old Kirk p., m. Margaret, dau. to John Anderson, smith at Alloa. *p.380, n.26*
1782–7, employed seasonally as gilder at

Inveraray Castle, mainly on furniture. *pp.200, 202, 218, 219*

DUTHIE, James, mason in Stirling. d. ?1740
1723, 11 January, admitted burgess of Inveraray: IBR
1740, 24 July, testament of James Duthie, mason in Dunblane: DUN T

EWING,* James, mason in Greenock. d. ?1773
1754–8, mason to 3rd Duke of Argyll, at Rosneath; employed on Roger Morris's alterations to castle. *p.375, n.57*
1754, advises Colin Campbell, Rosneath bailie, on timber cargo for Rosneath Castle: Colin Campbell to Argyll 3, 21 August 1754, s82
1758, applies for contract to build Inveraray new church. *p.165*
1773, 20 August, and 1774, 1 October, testament of James Ewing, late mason in Greenock: GT

FERGUSON, Colin, carpenter
1768–70, employed by Inveraray Burgh Council: IBR

FERGUSON, Duncan, quarrier
1725, 19 October, admitted burgess of Inveraray: IBR

FERGUSON, & partners, thatchers and ?wrights
*c.*1774, thatching 'the big house' at Kenmore, Inveraray: Inv/CA 1773/4
1796, *Duncan Ferguson*, wright, admitted burgess and gild brother of Glasgow: GB

FERRIER, Robert, smith
1721, April–July, smith work for Duke of Argyll's quarriers and masons: Inv/2DAc.

FINLAY, John, plasterer in Glasgow. d. ?1725
1721, plasterwork and whitening 'old office' and castle, Inveraray: Inv/2DAc.
3 May, admitted burgess of Inveraray: IBR
1725, 15 June, testament of John Finlay, plasterer in Glasgow: GT

FLEMING, James, smith
1773, payment to, for white iron supplied in 1772, on behalf of George Haswell: Inv/CA 1773/4
1779, manufactures iron used by John Roy (q.v.) for Inveraray Castle railing: Inv/CA 1778/9

FORSYTH, Thomas, mason, from Ayrshire
1796, comes to Inveraray after working on Crinan Canal; one of 8 masons building Inveraray church (September/November); returns to Ayrshire November: Inv/AE accts 1796, 1797
1815, 25 September, Thomas Forsyth, mason, admitted burgess and gild brother of Glasgow by purchase: GB

FREW,* David, mason and undertaker in Edinburgh. d. ?1764
1759–61, builds Garden or Frew's Bridge, Inveraray, to order of John Adam; total payments recorded £752. *pp.138, 140*
1763, 9 January, David Frew, mason, Lady Yester's p., m. Katherine Home, relict of Alexander Bew, smith in Colmure: EM
1764, 22 September, testament of David Frew, mason in Edinburgh: ET
?father to George Frew, quarrier, who marries in Edinburgh 1793: EM

GALBRAITH & WINTON,* marble cutters in Glasgow
1871, make and instal mantel-piece of Kintyre marble for Brown Library, Inveraray Castle. *p.404, n.22*

GALLOWAY [GALLWAY], Alexander, wright
Alexander Galloway, turner, New Greyfriars p., m. Mary, dau. to dec. John Scott, smith in Galashiels, 11 April 1762
Alexander Galloway, turner, Tolbooth p., m. Elizabeth Murray, widow of James Stronach, merchant in Thurso, 12 May 1776: EM
1769f., given rent-free house at Inveraray; when old house demolished given Maltland house (1775): Inv/AE, CA 1773/4
1774, roofing and joisting 'great shade', Maltland, Inveraray: Inv/CA 1773/4
1776, wright work for Clunary (Bridge of Douglas) factory, Inveraray: Inv/CA 1775/6

GARDNER,* Peter, mason and stone-cutter
1788, makes 10 pairs whinstone gate-posts (of Tombreac stone), for Inveraray policies; dresses stone for seats: Inv/CI 1789f.
*c.*1788–90, makes 'embrasures' for Maam circle, Glenshira, Inveraray. *p.247*
1795, hews stone for doors, windows and columns for Robert Mylne's church, Inveraray. *p.282*
1795–6, cuts stones for foundation of Maam stack, Inveraray: Inv/CI 1789f.
*c.*1796, makes granite gate-posts for Wintertown Lodge gate, Inveraray. *p.252*
before 1796 living in Maltland, Inveraray; 1816–33 living in Cross Houses, Inveraray: Inv/Rentals 1795/6, 1828, 1833

GARNER, John, mason
1752, October/November, hewing stone for Clerk's house, Inveraray, under James Potter: s410(2), 411(2)

GARRAFF,——, gilder
1800, paid £35 12s for unspecified work at Inveraray: Inv/LA 1799/1800

GILLACE [GILLIES], Archibald, quarrier
1760, in charge of quarriers at Maltland stables, Inveraray: Inv/Q accts

GILLESPIE* (GRAHAM), James, architect. 1776–1855
1803, rebuilds Achnacarry for Cameron of Lochiel. *p.395, n.22*
1805, advises Inveraray Burgh Council on alterations to town quay, completed to his recommendations by William Johns (q.v.) *p.289*
1810, designs Cupar County Rooms and (1813) Gaol. *p.316*
1812, advises rebuilding of Inveraray Gaol. *pp.316–17*
1813, adapts Robert Reid's design for Inveraray Court House (building begun 1816). *pp.317ff.*
1818, designs Dunninald, closely resembling William Burn's Saltoun Hall: debt to Inveraray. *p.336*
1820, designs The Lee: debt to Inveraray. *p.336*
1822, designs Moray Estate, Edinburgh. *p.395, n.22*
1830, designs Haddington Town House, *p.395, n.22*

GILMOUR,* James, mason
1748f., with William Paull joint undertaker at Creggans quarry; builds forge and huts for quarriers there, and improves quay: Inv/1748, accts 1750/2, Jnl 1750f; censured for illegal sale of drink at Inveraray with Walter Paterson and Henry Roy (q.v.). *p.356, n.90*
?1749f., building houses in Gallowgate, Inveraray (1751–2 with James Potter, q.v.); building 7 ft wall dividing Gallowgate from ducal enclosures; allowed rent-free house there. *p.149* and s410(3)
1751, ordered to build Chamberlain's house, Inveraray under George Hunter's supervision, according to plan: Inv/AEM
1752, foreman of quarriers for castle garden wall, Inveraray: Inv/Jnl 1750/2

Le GIRARD* [GERARD, GERARDY, GIRARDY], Irrouard, painter. fl.1784–9
born Paris; member of Acad. de Peinture, Paris; exhibitor (1784) at Royal Academy, London. *pp.216, 218–19*
1786–9, paints arabesques in dining-room, Inveraray Castle (with Guinon, q.v.); paints window-casings and 3 overdoors in drawing-room. *pp.216, 218–19*

GOWAN & Sons,* Alexander, marble cutters, at Abbey Hill, Edinburgh
?son to Alexander Gowan, mason in N.E. p., who m. Mary, dau. to dec. George Martin, merchant in Jedburgh, 22 June 1755 and d. ?1777: Testament of Alexander Gowan,

architect in Edinburgh, 1 October 1777,
ET, EM; ?brother to William Gowan, sculptor, who d. 25 January 1828 aged 62
1800, offer to make for Duke of Argyll exact
replica of marble drawing-room fireplace at
Bellevue (Edinburgh), for Inveraray Castle.
p.393, n.9

GRAHAM,* James Gillespie,
see GILLESPIE

GRAHAM,* John, plumber in Edinburgh
character: ill-natured and contentious. *p.76*
1734, February, witness at baptism of
William Mylne (q.v.) in Edinburgh.
p.357, n.121
1742, 6 December, admitted burgess of
Edinburgh: EB
1744, 1749, employed at the Whim; 1749
employed by Ld Milton at ?Saltoun
bleachfield. *p.75*
1749, April, recommended to be King's
plumber, for skill and cheapness: Maj.
Cochrane to Milton, 8 April 1749, s 72
1751, commissioned to direct fixing of
gutters, and rain-water pipes at Inveraray
Castle. *pp.75–6*
1752–4, casts sheet lead for battlements, and
leads roof, Inveraray Castle: Ask. to Milton
28 November 1754, s 412(2), and s 427 accts
1754, plumbing repairs at Caroline Park:
Buccleuch MSS, SRO GD 224/168, Ron.
Dunbar's acct bk p. 10
1754–5, casts lead for and leads roof of
Rosneath Castle: s 414(1), s 427 accts.
1756–60, plumbing of water-closets,
Inveraray Castle. *p.366, n.223*
1760, further plumbing at Rosneath Castle,
and Ld Milton's Canongate house: s 420(3)
accts

GRAHAM, William, mason in Crieff
1796, comes to Inveraray after working on
Crinan Canal; one of 8 masons building
Inveraray church (September/November);
returns to Crieff November: Inv/AE accts
1796, 1797

GREIG,* David, assistant overseer
1786, new thatched house provided for in
Glenshira farm court, Inveraray: Inv/Inst.
1785
1793, unsuccessful attempt to alter Elrickmore, barn, Glenshira. *p.248*
?1798, attempts to bank River Shira
criticized by 5th Duke of Argyll. *p.248*
1801, in charge of men re-channelling
River Shira: Inv/accts, Rental

GUINAND or GUINON,* [?Jean-
François], painter, d. ?1787
possibly of Acad. de S.Luc, Paris, *p.218*
1784–7, paints dining-room ceiling and ovals
at Inveraray Castle; dies at work before
August 1787. *p.218*

HALL, David, mason in Inveraray
1723, 10 October, admitted burgess of
Inveraray: IBR

HALLY, George, slater or wright
1796, August, erects 38-ft plaster cornice in
Inveraray inn: Inv/Gen.accts 1798
1816–33, referred to as 'slater', living in
Arkland, Inveraray: Inv/Rentals 1816,
1828, 1833

HALLY, Robert, slater in Auchterarder
1786, as visiting Brother to Inveraray
Masonic Lodge, offers free services to slate
new lodge (never built): *Hist.Inv.Mas.
Lodge* (1909)
1788–1834, living rent free in Arkland,
Inveraray (1834 ref. to as 'old', i.e. ?re-
tired): Inv/Rentals 1788ff.
1794, July, slating new stables and 'little
house' at Inn, Inveraray: Inv/EAC. 1793/4
1803, harls Hexagon summer-house,
Inveraray: Inv/accts 1804

HALLY, Simeon, slater
?brother to above
1782, slates schoolmaster's house, Glenaray:
Inv/CA 1781/2

HARDLAY, John, brickmaker
assistant to Thomas Aitkin (q.v.)
1750, accompanies Thomas Aitkin to
Inveraray and Lochgare to make bricks for
Duke of Argyll: 1756 accts, s 427

HART, Alexander, mason in Stirling
1723, 11 January, admitted burgess of
Inveraray: IBR

HART, Alexander, mason in Inveraray.
d. by 1816
1774, 'Hart and partner' execute mason-
work of Baillie John Colquhoun's house,
Inveraray: Inv/CA 1773/4
1775, demolition of his house in old town,
Inveraray: Inv/AEM
1777, paves Mrs Campbell of Duntroon's
house, causeways minister's office house,
Inveraray: Inv/CA 1776/7
1784–5, hews stone to complete Tombreac
dairy, Inveraray: Inv/Inst. 1784
1787–8, temporarily replaces John Tavish
for town mason-work at Inveraray; repairs
inn passage pavement (1788); living in
Arkland, Inveraray: Inv/CI 1787, Gen.
Inst.1787, 1788, Rental 1788
1790, with Sonachan and John Simpson
inspects condition of Ladyfield: Inv/Gen.
Inst. 1790
1796, one of 8 masons building church,
Inveraray: Inv/Particular Papers
1801, one of masons building new town
houses, Inveraray: Inv/accts 1800/1
1816, his widow named as living in Factory
Houses, Inveraray: Inv/Rental 1816

HART, John, mason in Inveraray. d. ?1744
  1723, 10 October, admitted burgess of
  Inveraray: I B R
  1744, 20 September (also 23 December
  1747, 30 January 1750), Testament
  (Glasgow) of *John Hart*, mason in Paisley: G T
HASWELL,* George, Duke of Argyll's
  wright at Inveraray. ? 1726–84
  marries in or after 1756
  1750f., as chief wright to Duke of Argyll,
  supplies Inveraray Castle masons with
  scaffolding; controls timber supply to works,
  draws up scantling of roof timbers for castle,
  corresponds on, with John Paterson, wright
  of Queensferry (q.v.), receives timber
  cargoes at Inveraray. *pp. 75, 94, 112, 114–15,
  116*
  1751, 17 May, admitted burgess of Inveraray
  as chief wright to Duke: I B R
  1753, estimates wright work for Patrick
  Campbell's house at Dalchenna, Inveraray:
  s411(2). Examines and repairs 'Marshal
  Saxe's house' (finally destroyed 1756: see
  p.98): Inv/K J
  1754, making furniture and fireplaces for
  new inn, Inveraray. *pp. 156, 157*
  1755f., joinery for new Town House,
  Inveraray. *p. 162*
  1756, succeeds John Corssar (q.v.) in charge
  of wright outworks, Inveraray: s413(2)
  1756–7, reports on timber and windows
  outstanding for Inveraray Castle: s413(2).
  Buys mahogany in Glasgow for castle
  doors and windows, and flooring deals from
  John Adam, Edinburgh, p. *118*
  joinery for dining-room and other rooms,
  Inveraray Castle; draws sections of rooms
  for wrights. *p.93* and Inv/plan chest
  1757, advises on timber requirements for
  Aray Bridge, Inveraray: s416(3)
  1758, orders mahogany for middle tower
  windows, Inveraray Castle. *p.119*
  1759–60, orders timber for, and prepares to
  roof, Cherry Park court of offices, Inveraray;
  makes centres for Garden Bridge: s419(1),
  s94, and see *p.138*
  1761f., remains in charge of wrights on 3rd
  Duke's death; completes minor wright-work
  outstanding, to John Adam's order. *p.182*
  1771, in charge of outworks for 5th Duke,
  including finishing Cherry Park, castle's
  main rooms and entresols, dividing long
  gallery, 'baying' windows and preparing
  room for plasterer: Inv/Inst. 1771, and see
  p.197
  1772, re-erects lofts and seats from old
  Inveraray church in new temporary church,
  p.258; wright work for Fisherland barn and
  new town houses (Ross's, Chamberlain's),
  Inveraray; in castle, finishing chief bedrooms,

preparing attics for chief servants; stair in
library turret; main stair-case door to
entresol: Inv/CI 1771
1773, finishes Cherry Park court of offices
and Maltland coach-house; prepares Inveraray
Castle dining-room: Inv/CI
1773–4, roofs and joists Maltland shade and
sawmill, finishes Cherry Park stable and
windows; completes securing of River Aray
breastwork and cascades (taking over from
Michael Waterstone, gardener): Inv/CI,
CA1773/4
1774, prepares Inveraray Castle principal
bedroom for gilder; makes shelves for
Duchess's turret closet: Inv/CI
1775–6, re-uses stones of mineral well for
building manses, Inveraray new town. *p.233*
1775, to alter castle attic rooms to Robert
Mylne's plan: Inv/CI
1775–9, miscellaneous: in charge of wright
work in new town, Inveraray; advises on
supports for wool factory floor, Bridge of
Douglas; fits up Fisherland stable, Maltland
shade and forge; fells timber for new Aray
Bridge; widens Aray channel, extending
breastwork between old and new bridges:
Inv/CI
1778, submits plans for new church at
Castlehill, Campbeltown (referred to as
'architect'). *p.382, n.52*
1780–1, consulted by Robert Mylne on
Maltland plans: Mylne 3 November 1780,
March/April 1781
1780, directs work on Wintertown lodge
gates, floating plank bridge, River Aray
stepping-stones; in charge of erecting
Duchess's turret stair, new north front door,
and installation of new w.c.'s, Inveraray
Castle: Inv/CI
1781, prepares pillars for pigeon-house
'temple' conversion (unexecuted): Inv/CI
December 1780
1782, paves great hall, Inveraray Castle;
continues with Maltland, garden cascades:
Inv/CI
1783, orders timber from Glasgow for castle
window-casings; ordered to make new
drawing-room window, set up arms in great
hall, make turret room floor, Inveraray
Castle, *p.212*; finishes dining-room and
chimney-piece, finishes great hall, Inveraray
Castle: Inv/CI
1784, advises on making metal window-
frames, alters drawing-room turret windows,
erects arms in hall, Inveraray Castle; erects
'pins' for sheaves, Maltland riding-house:
Inv/CI
1784, 24 March, death of. *p.212*
annual wages £39: Inv/CA, passim

HIGGINS, Andrew, wright
1751f., living in Gallowgate, Inveraray:
Inv/1753
HOGG, James, mason
c. 1747f., working at Inveraray; loses
possessions in masons' 'guildhall' fire of
March 1752: Inv/AEM
HORSEBURGH, Robert, mason and quarry
overseer
c. 1747f., working at Inveraray, loses
possessions in masons' 'guildhall' fire of
March 1752: Inv/AEM
1757, overseer at St Catherine's quarry;
checks James Anderson's (q.v.) measurement
of output: Jas Campbell to Milton, 5 March
1757, s87
1757, 16 January, Robert Horsburgh, mason,
Old Greyfriars p., m. Joan, dau. to dec.
John McCulloch, dyer: EM
HOWIESON, Alexander, mason
c. 1747f., working at Inveraray, loses
possessions in masons' 'guildhall' fire of
March 1752: Inv/AEM
HUME, Thomas, architect in Inveraray
1824, with John Simpson (Duke of Argyll's
house carpenter) inspects Robert Napier's
fitting up of debtors' prison, Inveraray:
Inv/Lindsay Howe 33A
HUNTER,* George, mason and overseer to
Duke of Argyll. d. ? 1787
mason in Edinburgh by 1733; marries
Margaret Robertson before 1733: SRO
EBapR; marriage of daughter Betty to
Robert Bathgate, farm overseer (1754);
takes her as widow with family, into own
house (1758); allowed to live in wing of
old Inveraray Castle (1760). p.359. n.153,
p.375, n.54
1747, 29 September, admitted burgess of
Inveraray: IBR
1747–61, overseer of works and deputy to
John Adam at Inveraray Castle; renders
progress reports. pp.72, 73
1748–9, specifies scaffolding timber required
from Glasgow; orders local timber for
girders, Inveraray Castle: Inv/1748, Wm
Adam memo. 10 October 1748; Milton
notes, s418(3)
1750, advises on purchase of timber cargo,
p.112; rise in wages for, secured by John
Adam, p.73; recruits masons in Edinburgh,
advises on quarry overseer. p.73
1751, ordered to oversee James Gilmour's
building of Chamberlain's house, Inveraray
new town: Inv/AEM; G. Hunter memorial,
s78
1752, reports to John Adam on masons'
'guildhall' fire; Adam's advice to, on
restoration: corresp. Hunter/Adam, March
1752, s72A, 78

1752, to build John Graham's raglings into
battlements, Inveraray Castle: Adam to
Milton, 17 March 1752, s78; advises on slates
required: John Campbell to Milton, 9 July
1752, s78
1752f., directs marble quarrying (through
James Stirling) at Tombreac for Inveraray
Castle stair; plan for quarriers' house at
Tombreac: Inv/1753, and p.76
1753, February, settlement of dispute on
division of St Catherine's quarry workings
between Hunter and Wm Douglas: progress
report of 1 February 1753, s411(1), and
Inv/KJ 1752/6
1754, calculates slates required for roof and
extension, Rosneath Castle: Adam to
Hunter, 8 October 1754, s82
1755, mason work for Patrick Campbell's
house at Dalchenna, Inveraray; roofs
pigeon house: s413(1) and (2); building
bridge over fosse, Inveraray Castle. p.86
1755–8, undertaker for Town House and 2
adjoining houses, Inveraray, to John Adam's
designs. pp.158ff.
1756, employing 62 masons: John Campbell
to Milton, 26 February 1756, s414(3)
1757, resumes unauthorized quarrying at St
Catherine's on Loch Fyne: Argyll 3 to
Milton, 24 February 1757, s87
1758, John Adam proposes as undertaker for
new church, Inveraray (unexecuted). p.165
1758–9, ordering timber for and making
additional schoolhouse windows (adjoining
Town House), Inveraray. pp.163–4
1759f., in charge of quarrying for Cherry
Park offices; overseer of building do. (1760).
p.141
1760, builds great hall chimneys, Inveraray
Castle; builds Maltland stable: report
10 June 1760, s94
1761, builds houses in new town, Inveraray:
Inv/AECB
1765, admitted burgess of Edinburgh: EB
1768–71, mason for repairs at Caroline Park
for Lady Greenwich. p.375, n.54
1787, 19 December, testament of George
Hunter, mason in Edinburgh: ET
HUNTER, Robert, mason in Arran
1721, employed on repairs and alterations to
'old apartment', Inveraray Castle: Inv/AE
accts
1722, 3 April, admitted burgess of Inveraray:
IBR
HUNTER,* Robert, mason. b. 9 November
1733
son to George Hunter (q.v.): SRO EBapR
c. 1752–4, studies draughtsmanship under
? James Morris in London; subsequently
employed as mason by Duke of Argyll at
Inveraray. p.357, n.99

1756, Duke of Argyll's interest sought for, by George Hunter. *p.357, n.99*
1761, employed in building new town houses, Inveraray: Inv/AECB

HUNTER, William, wright in Inveraray
1747, 20 September, William Hunter, journeyman wright, N.E.p. (Edinburgh), m. Mary, dau. to dec. Archibald Campbell, mariner in Inveraray: EM
1753f., living in Gallowgate, Inveraray: Inv/CA 1758

HUTCHISON,* James, plasterer
1782, employed as plasterer at Inveraray Castle. *p.384, n.73*

HUTTON, Thomas, wright in Alloa. d. ?1748
1734, 3 November, Thomas Hutton, wright in Alloa, m. Mary, dau. to dec. Charles Stewart, merchant in Edinburgh: EM
1745, submits estimate to Ld Milton for piece work and journeyman work (?for Inveraray): s403(2)
1748, 29 July, testament of Thomas Hutton, merchant and wright in Alloa: ST

INNES, John, brick-maker, of Carlisle. d. ?1774
working in Canongate, Edinburgh, by 1744
1744, 3 November, John Innes, bricklayer (*sic*), m. Mary Waters: CM
1747, experiments in making bricks from Loch Gair clay; submits tender for water-bricks: MLB66, Wm Adam to R. Morris, 22 December 1747
1748, contracts with Duke of Argyll to make 50,000 each of water and stock bricks with Argyll clay, at 12s 6d and 16s per 1000, providing own coal: MLB66, 73, 77, R.Morris/Wm Adam correspondence, 1 January & 5 February 1748
1774, 22 June, testament of John Innes, at Brickfield, Edinburgh: ET
1786, 5 April, John Innes, ?son to above, of Bruckfield (*sic*), College Kirk p., m. Miss Anne, dau. to David Skae, merchant: EM

JACQUES,* Mr——, ?wood carver, of London
1781–2, executes 'artificial ornaments' for drawing- and dining-rooms, Inveraray Castle, to Robert Mylne's design. *p.211*

JAMIESON,* George, and son, wood carvers in Glasgow
1758–9, carve chimney-pieces for great hall, dining- and dressing-rooms, and pedestal for Alexander Cumming's organ, Inveraray Castle. *p.95*
1758, mahogany sought from, for upper floor windows of Inveraray Castle: G.Haswell memo, 12 & 28 October 1758, s418(3),

Gr. Strathearn to Milton, 1 Dec. 1758, s90

JOHNS,* William, mason
1805–6, extends town quay, Inveraray; completes under James Gillespie's supervision. *pp.289–90*

JOHNSTON, Alexander, mason at Inveraray
1759f., living in Gallowgate, Inveraray: Inv/AEM
1768–72, payments to, for work for Inveraray Burgh Council: IBR

JOHNSTON, John, plain plasterer
1755, plasters kitchen flues, vent and oven, Inveraray Castle: s413(2)

JOHNSTONE,* John, wright
John Johnstone, journeyman wright, Old Greyfriars p., m. Agnes, dau. to dec. Hugh Angus, gentleman's servant, 9 October 1763: EM
John Johnston, wright in Nicholson Street, Edinburgh, has a son James apprenticed 1797 to Alexander Thomson, confectioner: EA
John Johnston, wright of Jock's Lodge, Edinburgh, buried at Restalrig 10 August 1804 aged 49; his widow Mary Stewart d. 30 April 1837 aged 77: RB
1782f., makes mahogany doors for main rooms of Inveraray Castle, with Hugh Alexander. *p.219*

KER, William, dyke builder
1754, building dyke at Tombreac park, Inveraray: s412(2) accts

KERN, David, mason in Ayr
1722, 10 July, admitted burgess of Inveraray: IBR

KERR, Andrew, joiner in Stirling
1721, 1 August, admitted burgess of Inveraray: IBR

KING, James, wright
1782, wright work for schoolmaster's house, Glenaray: Inv/CA1781/2

KING, Thomas, wright in Kilmichael Glassary
1728, 12 September, admitted burgess of Inveraray: IBR

KIRK, Andrew, mason
*c.*1747f., working at Inveraray; loses possessions in masons' 'guildhall' fire of March 1752: Inv/AEM

LAING,* Alexander, mason and architect in Edinburgh. d. ? 1824
marries (1) Charlotte, dau. to James Polson, Esq., advocate, 1772; (2) Margaret, dau. to dec. George Turnbull, WS, 1786; (3) Beatrix, dau. to dec. Rev. John Currie, 1789: EM
builder of Archer's Hall, Edinburgh (1776): contractor for South Bridge, Edinburgh

(1786–8): Youngson *Classical Edinburgh* p.112; designs (*inter alia*) Inverness Tolbooth steeple (1789), Dysart parish church (1802), Huntly parish church (1805), Peterhead parish church (1806), Darnaway Castle, Moray (1802–12): NMRS
1782, admitted burgess of Edinburgh, as mason: EB
1806, January, inspects and measures Robert Mylne's church, Inveraray. *p.401, n.47*
1814–22, arbiter in Aberdour Manse case, Aberdeenshire. *p.401, n.47*
1820, arbiter in Inveraray New Court House case; then living at 6 Gayfield Square, Edinburgh, *p.318*

LANGLANDS,* George, land surveyor
1792, proposes model village at Achnagoul, near Inveraray. *p.250*
1790s, draws up farm plans for 5th Duke. *p.250*
1798–9, surveys farms at Kelislade, Argyll: Inv/Gen. accts 1798/9

LAWRENCE,* Richard, carver. fl.1764–83
works at Somerset House and at Fulton Manor, Berks
1781–2, probably carves ornaments for drawing- and dining-rooms, Inveraray Castle, for Robert Mylne. *p.211*

LE GIRARDY,* Irrouard, see GIRARDY

LEE, Andrew, quarrier
1726, 10 October, admitted burgess of Inveraray: IBR

LEMON,* Robert, mason and quarrier
1795, cuts flagstones and granite corner-stones for Inveraray church, *p.282*; quarries stone for inn additions, Inveraray: Inv/CA 1794/5
1798–9, quarries and builds middensteads, Inveraray new town; digs and paves Maam dung-pit, Inveraray. *pp.248, 288*
1799, July, with Dugald McKellar hews and paves with flags Chamberlain's back court, Inveraray; repairs Carlundon Mill, Inveraray: Inv/Gen. accts 1798
1799–1800, quarries and builds breastwork south of new town, Inveraray: Inv/Gen. accts 1798
1800, quarries stone for church steeple, Inveraray, *p.282*; works Fisherland flagstone quarry and rubble-stone quarry for new houses, Inveraray: Inv/Gen. accts 1800
1802, quarries stone for breastwork at Hexagon (Carlundon), Inveraray: Inv/accts 1804
1816–33, living rent free at Cross Houses, Inveraray: Inv/Rental 1816ff.
Robert Alexander Lemon, wright, ?son to above, living at Factory Houses 1828–33: Inv/Rental

LESLIE or LESSLY,* William, stone quarrier
1783, quarries and dresses stone for corbels and belt of Dhu Loch Bridge, Inveraray; quarries at Bealachanuaran for Inveraray town breastwork: Inv/Gen. accts 1783
1785–6, blasts rock at Bridge of Douglas, Inveraray, to make room for factory machinery; quarries flags for do.: Inv/Factory.
1787–8, quarries stone in Glenshira for Maam barn, Inveraray. *p.247*
1788, dresses marble quarry stones for seats: Inv/Gen. Inst. 1788

LINDSAY,* Ian G. (1906–66) & Partners, architects in Edinburgh
1958–63, restores Inveraray town for Ministry of Works. *pp.342–3*

LIVINGSTON, John, mason in Inveraray
1732, 10 October, admitted burgess of Inveraray: IBR

LUMSDEN,* William, & PEDDIE,* James (q.v.), building contractors, 13 Charlotte Street, Leith
William Lumsden, joiner, St Andrew Kirk p., Edinburgh, m. Helen, dau. to dec.—— Bathgate, of Craigiehall, Linlithgow, 25 March 1793: EM
William Lumsden, wright, do., m. Margaret, dau. to William McKenzie, flesher, 28 August 1795: EM
William Lumsden, wright, admitted burgess of Edinburgh 1 April 1803: EM
1807–8, Mr Lumsden, carpenter to 6th Duke of Argyll, tests Joseph Bonomi's 'patent' windows and instals in Duke's bedroom at Inveraray Castle and Rosneath: Inv/Bonomi
1816f., Lumsden & Peddie contractors to build Inveraray new Court House. *p.318*

McALESTER, James, mason in Alway (? = Alloa)
1725, 3 June, admitted burgess of Inveraray: IBR

McALISTER, James, mason, ?same as above m. Ann McLean
1744–5, demolishing old tower, Inveraray Castle, with party of soldiers: Inv/1745
1748, wife charged, with others, with trespass and wood-stealing: IBR

McALISTER, Archibald, mason. b. ?1724
1748, January, mentioned, witness in court case, Inveraray: S406(1)

McARTHUR, Angus, sawyer
1788–1833, mentioned, living in Arkland, Inveraray: Inv/Rentals

McARTHUR,* Charles, mason and quarrier
1773, mentioned, demolition of his house in old town, Inveraray: Inv/Rental
1796–7, with Duncan McNuir builds and

thatches lodge at end of Deer Park (Dhu Loch), Inveraray. *p. 252*

McARTHUR, Donald, wright
1794, with John Simpson, finishes mouldings, architraves etc. for ground floor doors and windows of inn additions, Inveraray: Inv/EAC 1793/4
1795, with James Bell makes scaffolding and trestles for new church, Inveraray: Inv/Day Book
1796, preparing beams for church roof, Inveraray: Inv/Day Book

McARTHUR, Duncan, sawyer
1788, living in Relief Land, with Alexander McDougall: Inv/Rental

McARTHUR, John, ?sawyer or ?gardener
John McArthur, gardener, admitted burgess and gild brother of Glasgow, 22 August 1776, as eldest living son to dec. James McArthur, gardener: GB
1777, demolishing house, Inveraray old town, and levelling ground, with 13 men: Inv/accts 1772
1788, *John McArthur*, sawyer, mentioned, living in Arkland, Inveraray: Inv/Rental

McAULAY, Archibald, wright and overseer, Master of Works to 2nd Duke of Argyll. d. 1732
sometime of Doncaster; m. Anne Hatton (still alive 1753)
1710, 19 July, *Archibald McAulay*, bailie of Dumbarton, admitted burgess and gild brother of Edinburgh gratis for services: EB
*c.*1728, comes to Edinburgh from Doncaster, apparently at Duke of Argyll's order; thence to Inveraray: Petition of Arch. McAulay younger 1753, S411(1)
1729, 29 September, admitted burgess of Inveraray as overseer to Duke of Argyll's works (together with his nephew Richard, son to Alexander McAulay, merchant in Huddersfield): IBR

McAULAY, Archibald, younger, wright and glazier
son to above; apprenticed wright after father's death; journeyman wright *c.*1748–53: Petition of Arch. McAulay 1753, S411(1)
1764–6, payments to, for repairing old Town House, Inveraray: IBR
1771, mentioned, demolition of his house in old town, Inveraray: Inv/AEM
1788, mentioned, living free in Maltland, Inveraray: Inv/Rental

McBAIN, Dugald, quarrier
1754, quarrying stone for Tombreac dyke, Inveraray, under William Douglas younger: S412(2)

McCALLUM, Donald Roy, wright in Inveraray. d. ?1773
1755 m. Katherine McCallum, of Inveraray: IPR
1756, dismissed Duke of Argyll's service but still at Inveraray
1761, mentioned as possessing rent-free house, Town Head, Inveraray old town, which is demolished 1771; widow mentioned 1773 still living in his new house: anon. letter January 1756, S417(1); Inv/AEM

McCALLUM, D.R., plumber in Greenock
1814, plan and estimate for town water supply for Inveraray, thought too high, referred to committee: IBR

McCALLUM, John, elder, mason
1777, 17 November, *John McCallum*, marble cutter, College Kirk p., Edinburgh, m. Margaret, dau. to William Clark, farmer in Wick: EM
1796, September f., one of 8 masons named as building Inveraray church: Inv/Particular Papers

McCALLUM, John, younger, mason
1796, September f., one of 8 masons named as building Inveraray church: Inv/Particular Papers

McCALLUM,* Neil, wright to 5th Duke of Argyll. b. after 1739; d. by 1816
?son to Neil McCallum, mason in Inveraray (admitted burgess of Inveraray, 1723) and Katherine Leach: IBR; IPR; Inv/1748, Rental 1749
1760, m. Mary Sinclair, of Glenaray: IPR; living in High Street, Inveraray old town: Inv/RFD
1773, his garden in Inveraray new town mentioned; ordered to remove from old house by Whitsun 1774: Inv/tacks ledger, Inst. December 1772
1775, as tacksman, builds own house (now Mackenzie's Land), Inveraray new town. *p. 261*
1787, makes inventory of equipment at Bridge of Douglas wool factory, Inveraray: Inv/Factory
1816, his house occupied by 'heirs': Inv/Rental

McCONNIE,——, plasterer
1772, makes stucco cornice mould for William Mylne, ?for Inveraray Castle: Inv/5DA

McDOUGALL, John, wright
1775, mentioned, living 'below the Factory' at Inveraray: Inv/AEM

McDOUGALL, Peter, wright
1816, mentioned, living in Factory Houses, Inveraray: Inv/Rental

mentioned: pensioner, employed as Cromalt gate-house keeper; his widow Margaret Bell still pensioned 1790: Inv/Particular Papers

McKICHAR, John, quarrier
1754, quarrying for Tombreac dyke, under William Douglas younger: s412(2)

McLACHLAN, Andrew, mason and quarrier
1759, employed as mason at St Catherine's quarry: Inv/Q

McMASTER, Donald, ?mason
1763–4, paid by Inveraray Burgh Council for repairs to town quay: IBR

McMASTER, John, quarrier
1754, quarrying for Tombreac dyke, under William Douglas younger: s412(2)

McMATH, Donald, mason
?1794, executes mason rubblework to wall behind Chamberlain's stable, Inveraray: Inv/CA 1797/8

McMATH, James, wright
1816, named as living in Arkland; his mother living in Relief Land, Inveraray: Inv/Rental

McMATH,* Malcolm, mason to Duke of Argyll. d. ?1779
?successor to William Douglas; named among original masons employed by George Hunter c.1747f.; applies for school-mistress's house (1752); house destroyed by flood (?1756); living rent free as Duke's mason in Laigh Street, Inveraray old town (1768): memorials s416(3), 417(2); memorial of Catherine Wright s410(3); Inv/RFD
1763–8, mentioned as Duke's mason in rentals: Inv/Ask. inventory
1774, first pair of houses on main street west side, Inveraray new town, built for, to Duke's order; old house demolished (1775). p.267
1779, testament of Malcolm McMath, 15 March: AT

McMILLAN, William, smith
1749, tenders to Ld Milton for smith work at Inveraray or quarries; employed at Creggans quarry under James Gilmour and William Cowan (q.v.); in winter applies for smithy in town: s407A
1750, applies for free house in Inveraray when Cowan deprives him of house at quarry; apparently granted: s408(2) and Inv/Rental 1749

McNAB, Duncan, smith in Inveraray
1749, living rent free in Inveraray as 'country smith' (as distinct from Henry Roy, Duke of Argyll's smith, q.v.): Inv/CA 1748

McNAUGHTON, Alexander, mason in Inveraray
c.1721, February, paid for making vent in apartment above stables, Inveraray Castle: Inv/2DAC.

McNEILAGE, Archibald, wright in Inveraray
1723, 10 October, admitted burgess of Inveraray: IBR
1743, October, paid by Inveraray Burgh Council for work on town well windlass with (?son) Donald McNeilage: IBR
1760, his house in Inveraray ?old town mentioned: Inv/Inst. 1760

McNEILAGE, Donald, wright in Inveraray ?son to above
1743, October, paid by Inveraray Burgh Council for work on town well windlass with Archibald McNeilage: IBR
1749, mentioned, living at Town Head, old Inveraray; his house converted to a guildhall (1759); Inv/accts 1749, AE1759/61

McNICOL, Archibald, wright
1788, mentioned, living with brother in Relief Land, Inveraray: Inv/Rental

McNICOL, Donald, and partners, quarriers
1773–4, quarrying stones for great shade, Fisherland barn, Inveraray: Inv/CA1773/4
1778, quarrying stones for Garron Bridge porter's lodge, Inveraray: Inv/CA1777/8

McNICOL, Nicol, quarrier
1754, quarrying for Tombreac dyke, under William Douglas younger: s412(2)

McNIVEN, Duncan, wright
1772–3, employed at Inveraray: given house in Maltland: Inv/AEM

McNIVEN, John, wright
1795, August, makes scaffolding and trestles for church, Inveraray: Inv/Day Book; December, renews doors of schoolmaster's house: Inv/Gen. Inst. p.514
1796, prepares beams for church roof: Inv/Gen. Inst., p.514
1799, with James Bell, roofs new house in Newton, Inveraray, and makes 5 windows: Inv/Gen. accts 1798
1801, with wrights making doors and floors for Capt. Archibald Campbell's house, Inveraray (under Adam Russell, q.v.): Inv/Hshld & Est. accts 1802
mentioned: using shed adjoining old (temporary) church, Inveraray, given stance in Newton (Gallowgate) when church converted to school (1809), allowed to rebuild (1817): Inv/Ledger III, petn.; living in Gallowgate, Inveraray (1816), permission given 1818 to build own house to plan (identified in 1848 rental as 4th door in Newton Row); subsequently named as a tacksman at 1s. p. year: Inv/Rental 1816ff. and Ledger III

McNOCKARD, Angus Roy, wright in Inveraray
1723, 10 October, admitted burgess of Inveraray: IBR

1730, 13 May, nominated a birlieman (i.e. arbiter) in local dispute: IBR

McNUIR,* Duncan, mason in Inveraray; formerly in Barbreck. d. by 1813
1773, given half of Alexander McIntyre's house in Gallowgate, Inveraray; also land adjoining for a house (1778), in place of house he built in old town: Inv/AEM and Lindsay Howe papers
1796–7, with Charles McArthur builds and thatches Gothick lodge in Deer Park (Dhu Loch), Inveraray. *p. 252*
1813, his Gallowgate house inherited by son Duncan, messenger (who d. 1819), then by daughter Ann (m. Archibald Monro), who cedes property (1819 and 1827) to Duncan Paterson, w.s., son of Walter Paterson: Inv/Lindsay Howe papers, and see *p. 400, n. 36*

McPHEA, ——, & WHITE, ——, see WHITE

McPHEDERAN,* Donald, mason
1774 (as labourer), levelling bank above old smithy, Inveraray: Inv/accts 1772f.
1775, allowed rent-free house at Park Head, Inveraray: Inv/AEM
1786, builds new road-line near Dhu Loch, Inveraray: Inv/Inst. 1787
1797, builds dairy and outhouse at Dalchenna, Inveraray: repairs road and bulwark towards Creganacorrach; makes road through Stuckagoy farm, Glenshira: Inv/AEM
1798, rebuilds 179 yds of Newton Point breastwork, Inveraray: Inv/CA 1797/8
1799, builds cottages at Carlundon mill and Kilbryde bridge, Inveraray. *p. 252*
1800, builds middenstead opposite Cross Houses, Inveraray. *p. 288*
1800–2, builds Balantyre lodges, Inveraray. *p. 252*
1802, rebuilds byre at Dalchenna, Inveraray: Inv/Hshld accts 1802
1803, thatches Hexagon summerhouse at Carlundon (built by John Tavish, q.v.). *p. 252*

McPHERSON, Duncan, wright
1747, 29 September, admitted burgess of Inveraray: IBR

McPHERSON, John, wright
1815, 18 August, *John McPherson*, wright, admitted burgess and gild brother of Glasgow as serving apprentice with Messrs Cleland & Jack, wrights, B. & G.B.: GB
1816–28, named as living in Relief Land, Inveraray: Inv/Rental

McTUCKER, John, quarrier
1788, named as living in Arkland, Inveraray: Inv/Rental

McVICAR, Angus, ?mason
1806, April–May, with John Munro and others builds Bridge of Douglas schoolhouse: Inv/CA 1805/6

McVICAR, John, and partners, quarriers
1768, as 'John McVicar & Co.' quarrying limestone: Inv/18th c.
1773, in charge of demolition and ground levelling near Inveraray Castle: Inv/accts 1772f.
1776, with 'partners' casting foundation of River Aray breastwork: Inv/CA 1775/6

McVICAR, Neil, and partners, ?masons at Kenmore
1774, in charge of making dam sluice for Carlundon saw-mill, Inveraray: Inv/CA 1773/4
1796–7, quarries St Catherines stone for Inveraray church: Inv/AE accts 1796/7

MAIN, Edward, mason
c. 1747f., working at Inveraray; loses possessions in masons' 'guildhall' fire of March 1752: Inv/AEM

MALCOLM,* James, land agent, of Gray's Inn
1810, surveys Inveraray estates; proposes model suburb for Inveraray south end with 46 semi-detached houses and gardens and 5–6 miles of detached villas. *p. 312*

MARR,* John, mason from Cullen
1764–7, builds Banff Tolbooth steeple to ?John Adam's design; clerk of works at Cullen House. *p. 390, n. 13*
1772, removes from Cullen to Inveraray as mason pieceworker. *p. 260*
1772, with George Haswell values materials of Campbell of Silvercraigs' house, Inveraray old town: Inv/18th c. leases
1773–4, demolishes old town houses, old church and steeple, Inveraray. *p. 260*
1773, builds part of shade, stable and dunghill at Fisherland barn, Inveraray: Inv/CA 1773/4
1774, builds wool factory, Inveraray. *pp. 260, 273*
1773–5, builds main-street houses, Inveraray new town, e.g. Baillie John Colquhoun's and Patrick Brown's (1773), house next Chamberlain's pay office (1775). *p. 267*
1774–5, builds Arkland, Inveraray, by contract. *p. 260*
1774, builds sunk fence in Fisherland; hews coping for fosse, Inveraray Castle: Inv/Inst. 1774, CA 1773/4
1776, builds divisions in Relief Land, Inveraray: Inv/CA 1775/6
1825, 6 July, John Marr, mason, ? son to above, admitted burgess and gild brother of Glasgow by purchase: GB

MARSHALL, [?William], plumber.
?1746–1826
William Marshall, plumber, New Kirk p.,
Edinburgh, m. Isobel, dau. to dec. William
Murdoch, miller in Thornhill, 1 September
1771: EM
William Marshall, Esq., plumber in Edinburgh, d. at Portobello 29 June 1826 aged
80 years; his 'social qualities . . .
rendered him an agreeable companion' and
'high moral principles . . . endeared
him to the heart'. His wife Isabella (sic)
d. 1 May 1822 aged 74, his son John
d. 24 October 1810 aged 32; also a dau.:
SCM no. 439
1807, Marshall and Ritchie report on work
done at Inveraray: Inv/Bonomi

MARTIN, Thomas, mason
1752, October–November, hewing stone for
Clerk's house, Inveraray new town, under
James Potter: s410(2), 411(2)

MATHIE, Thomas, mason
1752, October–November, hewing stone for
Clerk's house, Inveraray new town, under
James Potter: s410(2), 411(2)

MATHIE,* William, wright and carver.
d. ?1765
1733, 29 August, William Mathie, son to
Capt. Thomas Mathie, merchant in Cocken-
zie, apprenticed to Alexander Peden
[= Peters], wright in Edinburgh: EA
1757–8, employed by Adam Brothers;
finishes chimney-piece to their design for
Inveraray Castle. *p.93*
1760, as wright, apprentice to Alexander
Peters, admitted burgess of Edinburgh:
EB
1765, 15 February, testament of William
Mathie, carver in Edinburgh: ET

MAXWELL,* Robert, bell-founder in
Edinburgh
son to James Maxwell, merchant and
burgess: EB
1700, 25 December, admitted burgess of
Edinburgh by right of father: EB
1714, 25 November, m. Elizabeth, dau. to
dec. James Douglass in Spittall hall: EM
1728, recasts bells of Inveraray old church
(removed to new town 1772), paid for by
James Campbell of Stonefield; described
as drunken and lazy. *p.258*, and *p.350,
n.59*
1729, founds bell for Bothkennar church
(now at Fallin): *Stirlingshire* I
(RCAHMS 1963) p.150

MEIKLE,* James, mill-wright
father to Andrew Meikle (1719–1811);
works for Fletcher family at Saltoun;
possible relationship of, to Robert Mackell
(q.v.). *p.360, n.166*

1748, February, to make scale model of a
mill model ('these two years a making')
intended by Duke of Argyll for Marshal
Belleisle: Argyll 3 to Milton, 25 February
1748, s69; 6 October, admitted burgess of
Inveraray as Duke of Argyll's joiner: IBR

MEIKLE,* Robert, see MACKELL

MELDRUM, John, mason in Inveraray
1749, mentioned, given house (with John
Reid) at Bridge End, Inveraray old town
(demolished 1752): Inv/Rental 1749, CA
1748f.

MILLER, Daniel, wright in Glasgow
1740, 24 January, admitted burgess of
Glasgow gratis, by act of Council 22 October
1739: GB
1744, makes furniture (6 elm chairs,
mahogany chest of drawers, quadrille table,
etc.) for old Inveraray Castle: CA, s402(2)
1745, makes 12 ash chairs for Rosneath or
Inveraray: memo. Colin Campbell, s403(1);
Robert Mackell's mill models left in packing-
cases at his Glasgow workshop: s403(1)

MILLER & Co., James, contractors in
?Glasgow
James Millar, merchant of Glasgow, m.
Miss Elizabeth, dau. to dec. Rev. John
Christie, min. at Carnwath, 13 April 1799:
EM
James Millar, wright, admitted burgess and
gild brother of Glasgow, 31 August 1815,
as younger living son to William Millar,
B. & G.B.: GB
1803, demolishing old Rosneath Castle after
fire: Inv/Ros.accts

MILLER, John, wright and glazier
?son to John Millar, glazier, who is admitted
burgess of Canongate 2 September 1682
by right of wife Bessie (dau. to
Patrick Alexander, baxter, burgess), and
who ?remarries 8 May 1697 Margaret, dau.
to Adam Reid in Torryburne: CB, CM
1717, 23 May, admitted burgess of Canongate as apprentice to John Miller, glazier:
CB
1720, glazes Duke's aisle, old Inveraray
church; glazing and wright work (including furniture) at old Inveraray Castle:
Inv/2DAC.

MILLNER [MILLER], John, mason in
Inveraray
John Miller, master mason, builds William
Allan's tenemant, Fore Street, Stirling,
1732; Deacon of Incorporation of Mechan-
icks in Stirling 1736, 1739: *Stirling Recs.*
(1889), pp. 222, 234, 520; mentioned 1737,
1739: Ibid. pp. 239, 247; process of
(?trouble-maker): Ibid. pp. 247, 250, 360

John Miller, mason, New Kirk p., Edinburgh, m. Ann, dau. to Geo. Smeel, cordiner in Jedburgh, 20 July 1735: EM
John Miller, journeyman mason, S.S.W. p., Edinburgh, m. Margaret Davis, indweller in do., 5 November 1738; apparently d. by 1750 (see next item): EM
John Miller, mason in Leith (?same as above), testament of, 28 August 1749: ET
1723, 10 October, admitted burgess of Inveraray: IBR
MILLER, Mathew, wright in Newport, Glasgow
1728, 12 September, admitted burgess of Inveraray: IBR
MILLER, William, mason
1801, named among masons building houses in new town, Inveraray: Inv/Gen.Accts 1800/1
MOCHRIE, John, dyke builder
1754, building dyke in Tombreac park, Inveraray: s412(2)
MONRO, ——, mason
1760, mentioned, living in part of old Inveraray Castle east wing: Inv/AE 1759/61
MONRO [MUNRO], John, blacksmith in Inveraray
1721, makes ironwork for Duke's kitchen at Inveraray: Inv/2DAC
1723, 10 October, admitted burgess of Inveraray: IBR
MOODIE,* John, mason
1752, 5 July, John Moodie, journeyman mason, m. Jean, dau. to dec. John Campbell, merchant (poulterer): EM
1758, 10 May, admitted burgess of Edinburgh by right of wife: EB
1777–8, contractor with Robert Alexander for Clunary wool factory, Bridge of Douglas, Inveraray. *p.274*
MORISON, David, mason in Doune. d. ?1761
1725, 3 June, admitted burgess of Inveraray: IBR
1761, 12 May, testament of *David Morrison*, journeyman mason and residenter in Portsburgh, Edinburgh: ET
MORRISON, [MORISON], Donald, ?thatcher
1806, with John Munro thatches Bridge of Douglas schoolhouse, Inveraray, for £3 7s 6d: Inv/CA 1805/6
MORISON, Dugald, mason
1799, builds new town gardens fence, between Kilmalew and salmon draught, Inveraray: Inv/Gen.accts 1798
MORISON, William, ?mason
William Morison, journeyman mason in Edinburgh, m. Margaret Dow, indweller of Canongate, 19 November 1756: CM

1776, laying main street drainage channel, Inveraray new town: Inv/CA 1775/6
MORRIS,* James, son to Roger Morris
1749, inherits father's business. *p.68*
1752, advises on piecing of timbers for Inveraray Castle. *p.68*
1754, advises Ld Milton on duties on deals. *p.368, n.260*
1756, advises on window sashes for Inveraray Castle; recommends London glass. *pp.86, 118*
MUCKLE,* Thomas, mason
1777, builds part of Cross Houses and manses' office houses, Inveraray new town, under John Brown, (q.v.). *p.261*
MUNN, Samuel, wright
1773, fits up stable in Fisherland barn, Inveraray: Inv/CA 1773/4
1774, makes corn-drying frames for do.; roofs Ross's house, Inveraray new town: Inv/CA 1773/4
MUNRO, Duncan, sawyer
m. Mary Stewart, change-keeper in Inveraray
1756, 18 October, wife applies (?unsuccessfully) for drink-selling licence: IBR
1757, although 'turned away for roguery', occupies Peter Campbell's former house in Inveraray until evicted: anon. letter, January 1757, s417(1); Jas Campbell to Milton, 24 August, s416(1)
MUNRO, John, ?mason or sawyer
1806, April-May, with others building and thatching Bridge of Douglas schoolhouse, Inveraray (building £21, thatching £3 7s 6d): Inv/CA 1805/6
1816, John Munro, sawyer, named as living in Cross Houses; 1828–34, living at Maltland, Inveraray: Inv/Rental
MUSKAT, Alexander, ?plumber
1782, erects lead 'rigging' at schoolmaster's house, Glenaray: Inv/CA 1782
MYLNE,* William, architect, 1734–90
younger son to Deacon Thomas Mylne; practising in Edinburgh with his brother Robert; designs North Bridge there (1765) *p.196*
1758, 12 April, admitted burgess of Edinburgh, as mason and architect, by right of father: EB
1770, March, 10-day visit to Inveraray; plans alteration and extension to Cherry Park court of offices. *pp.196, 230*
1771, August, 7-day visit to Inveraray; supervises preparation of main rooms for plastering; reverses castle front; 'bays' drawing-room windows. *pp.196–7*
?1771, work attributed to, at Inveraray Castle: building of turret stairs, and creation of servants' rooms (*a*) off east hall,

(*b*) by altering John Adam's attic layout,
(*c*) by making entresols, *p.197*; December,
plans for church, court of offices and bridge
for Inveraray (including ?temporary church
in new town, and ?Cherry Park), *p.230*
1772, July, 8-day visit to Inveraray;
?supervises outbuildings (see 1771),
advises on Fisherland barn, directs George
Haswell, *pp.230, 258*; stucco cornice made
for, by McConnie (q.v.); sends Duncan
Cameron, causeway layer (q.v.) to
Inveraray: Inv/5 D A

NAPIER,* Robert, smith to 5th & 6th
Dukes of Argyll; formerly in Old Kilpatrick
1787, replaces David Cunningham (q.v.)
as Duke's smith; removal expenses paid,
given rent-free quarters and smithy
(Maltland): Inv/Misc.1760/1800 and Rental
1799, 27 December, admitted burgess and
gild brother of Glasgow (as 'hammerman')
by purchase: G B
1806, makes ironwork to secure Inveraray
gaol at £162 11s 2d. *p.400, n.41*
1808, 8 December, to repair iron gate of
Bealachanuaran well, Inveraray: I B R
1814, 13 March, tender for piping water to
Inveraray town considered too high: I B R
1824, fits up top flat of new Court House,
Inveraray, as debtors' prison: Inv/Lindsay
Howe 33 A
1816–33, named in rentals as living at
smithy, Inveraray: Inv/Rental
(Some of the later entries may refer to
Napier's younger son Robert, smith,
admitted burgess and gild brother of
Glasgow 1807: G B)
NAPIER, William, smith
son or grandson to above
1822, named as living in flat of Old Town
House, Inveraray: Inv/Rental
1827, 30 March, William Napier, hammerman, admitted burgess and gild brother of
Glasgow as younger living son to Robert
Napier, smith: G B
(Alexander Napier, ?son to William Napier,
named as living at Inveraray smithy 1848:
Inv/Rental)
NASMYTH,* Alexander, painter and architect. 1758–1840
1799–1800, payments to, for unspecified
work at or for Inveraray: Inv/L A
1800–2, annual visits to Inveraray. *pp.252–3*
1801, designs 'Beehive' cottage, probably
designs Hexagon and Cromalt lodge,
Inveraray, *pp.252–3*; unexecuted designs
for Gothick lighthouse for Inveraray pier,
and 'ruined castles' for Stron Point and
Duniquaich, *p.254*; opposes Robert Mylne's

scheme for market stances at Inveraray
church, *p.285*
1802, fixes site of new castle at Rosneath;
designs its court of offices and a tower.
p.291
NEILSON, Charles, joiner in Stirling
1721, 1 August, admitted burgess of
Inveraray: I B R
NIMMO, Alexander, Duke of Argyll's wright
(?wheelwright) at Inveraray
m. Ann Reid by 1748: I P R
1747–9, mentioned, memorials of instructions for: s 407(1), Inv/Particular Papers
1749, Duke's dissatisfaction with ('very ill
used by that fellow Nimmo'); superseded
by John Paterson (q.v.): Argyll 3 to Milton,
9 November 1749, s 407(1)
NISBET, William, mason
*c.*1747f., working at Inveraray; loses possessions in masons' 'guildhall' fire of March
1752: Inv/A E M
NISBETT, Deacon James, wright in Glasgow
1710, 31 August, admitted burgess and gild
brother, master, of Glasgow, as serving
apprentice with dec. John Nesbitt (?father),
wright, B. & G.B., and after his death with
Francis Stevenson, wright, B. & G.B.
(q.v.); gratis, 'for his services at the late
accidental fire in the Gallowgate' (Glasgow), by act of Council of date: G B
1738, Deacon of Incorporation of Wrights,
Glasgow: *Annals*
1742, supplies timber for Dugald Murray's
tenement near mercat cross, Inveraray
old town: memorial August 1747, s 405(1)
NORRIE, James, elder, painter. 1684–1757
father to James Norrie younger (1711–36)
and Robert Norrie (d.1766); family firm
continues till 1845: Ellis Waterhouse
Painting in Britain 1530–1790 (1953)
p.117
1708, admitted burgess of Edinburgh:
E B
1732–40, commissioned for painting at
Whim and Brunstane for Lds Ilay and
Milton: s 399, s 424 accts
1746, paints and mounts military colours
with ducal arms and supporters for Duke
of Argyll: Inv/1746
1750–3, 'Norrie & Co.' paint vestibule,
dining-room, Duke's bedroom and pavilion
room at Whim; Norrie paints crests on
Duke's chaise: Maule to Milton, 21 April
1750, s 75, 409, 411(2) and 425 accts
1754, painting at Mertoun, Berwickshire:
Polwarth M S S 132
1757, painting at Blair Castle, including
pictures for dining-room: Blair M S S
40.11137

OAT, John, slater
1753, mentioned, living in Gallowgate, Inveraray: Inv/1753

ORR, James, ?mason
1773–4, working at Kenmore, Inveraray, building dykes, repairing thatch, harling shore houses: Inv/CA 1773/4

PAPWORTH,* John, plasterer. 1750–99
Master Plasterer to Office of Works
1780, September, agrees with Robert Mylne on execution of ceiling moulds for Inveraray Castle: Mylne 7 September 1780
1781, executes moulds (in London) for drawing- and dining-rooms, Inveraray Castle. *pp. 210–11*

PATERSON,* John, wright in Queensferry. d. ?1776 or 1777
possibly grandfather to John Paterson, architect (d. 1832)
family: son John b. to John Paterson, wright to Mr Adams, and his wife Mary Young, 4 June 1738: SRO EBapR; James, son to John Paterson, wright at Hopetoun, apprenticed to James Herriot, wright in Edinburgh, 5 June 1751: EA
1736–8, employed by Ld Ilay at Whim (including making library windows) and later at Holyroodhouse, *p. 84* and s423, s399
1750f., visits Inveraray to take charge of part of wright work, replacing Alexander Nimmo (q.v.): letters of Argyll 3 and Milton, November 1749, Fletcher, January 1750, Walter Paterson, February 1750, s407(1), s75
1751f., employed at Hopetoun House: Hopetoun MSS
1752, corresponds with George Haswell on Inveraray Castle roof timbers. *p. 115*
1753, 27 March, admitted burgess of Inveraray as 'principal joiner' to Duke of Argyll: IBR
1753, at Inveraray, makes tower roofs and garret skylights for castle, *p. 84*; unsuccessful search for timber for castle roof from Forth and Clydeside firms (e.g. Duncan Glassford in Bo'ness, Greenfield in Dalkeith). *pp. 116–17*
?1754, at Queensferry, makes 13 windows for Inveraray Town House front, and 12 for 2 adjoining house fronts. *pp. 86, 162*
1755, at Queensferry, makes window-frames for Inveraray Castle and Cherry Park court of offices. *p. 86*
1757, at Queensferry, makes fittings for Alexander Cumming's organ at Inveraray Castle, *p. 88*; at Queensferry, makes doors and windows for 'great dining-room' at Inveraray Castle: Alexr Cumming to Milton,

28 August 1757, s87; probably recommends Robert Dewar, glazier (q.v.), *p. 93*; charges considered expensive, *p. 94*
1760, process of scandal by John Paterson, wright of Queensferry, against James Ferguson, wright, and William Duncan, weaver, both of Queensferry: ECP no. 471
1777, 15 January, testament of John Paterson, wright in Hopetoun: ET

PATERSON,* John, architect. d. 1832
? descendant of above; debt to Inveraray, in designs for Monzie (1785–90), Eglintoun (1798). *pp. 328, 337*
1797, design for Taymouth Castle, Perthshire, begun but demolished 1805. *p. 333*
1816, appointed 2nd arbiter (vice Alexander Laing, q.v.) in Inveraray Court House case. *p. 401, n. 47*
1818, attempt by James Peddie (q.v.) to threaten Commissioners of Supply through. *p. 401, n. 47*

PAULL,* Deacon William, mason and quarry overseer. d. ?1790
2nd son to William Paull (burgess of Glasgow 1718 and Deacon of Incorporation 1733, 1745, 1749) and Jean Kerr (dau. to James Kerr, mason and burgess of Glasgow): *Annals*, GB
1748, goes to Inveraray from 'Low Country' as joint overseer at Creggans quarry with James Gilmour (q.v.): Wm Adam memo., Inv/1748
1751, trials and estimate for working St Catherine's quarry on Loch Fyne: s409(1); 19 September, admitted burgess and gild brother of Glasgow (with his elder brother James, mason): GB
c.1752–6, works St Catherine's quarry for Inveraray Castle; supplies stone for Richardson's house, Inveraray new town (1753); estimate for rebuilding St Catherine's kiln after fire (1755): Inv/Q; Inv. memos., s411; s413(2)
1756, March, dismissed by John Adam for fraud. *pp. 83, 84*
1767 and 1777, Deacon of Incorporation of Masons, Glasgow: *Annals*
1790, 25 May, testament of William Paul, late Deacon of Masons in Glasgow: GT

PEDDIE,* James, building contractor, 13 Charlotte Street, Leith
1816–20, contractor with William Lumsden (q.v.) to build Inveraray new Court House. *p. 318*
1817, designs and begins building 2 large houses in Gallowgate (Newton Row), Inveraray ('Old Rectory' and companion house). *p. 399, n. 36*
1820, bankrupt; takes Court House case to arbitration. *p. 318*

1851, *James Peddie*, ?son to above, designs
South Leith Poorshouse. *p.401, n.46*

PETTIGREW, Gavin, wright in Glasgow.
d. ?1779
1742, 25 August, admitted burgess and gild
brother of Glasgow as apprentice to James
Nisbett, wright, B. & G.B. (q.v.): GB
1744, makes furniture for Duke of Argyll's
(old) house at Inveraray: 2 mahogany
dining-tables, 10 'Common ash Chairs',
6 Virginia walnut chairs at 12s. each:
s402(2), CA
1779, 13 February and 18 June, testament
of Gavin Pettigrew, wright in Glasgow: GT

PHILP, George, mason
1752, October-November, hewing stone for
Clerk's house, Inveraray new town, under
James Potter: s410(2), s411(2)

POTTER,* James, mason in Inveraray
m. Jean Campbell before 1756: IPR
?1749f., builds Gallowgate houses,
Inveraray (partly with James Gilmour,
q.v.). *pp.148–9*
1751, succeeds William Cowan (q.v.)
as part undertaker at Creggans quarry,
Inveraray; makes gates for Garron and
Stronshira bridges: Inv/1751, Jnl 1750/2,
accts 1750/2
1751–2, builds Dhu Loch boathouse,
Inveraray, *p.134*
1752, takes over lime supply contract for
Inveraray works from William Douglas
(q.v.). *pp.78, 154*
1752, builds Clerk's house, new town bakehouse and oven, and wrights' shade,
Inveraray: Inv/accts, Jnl 1750/2, s410(2)
and (3), s411(2);
1753, cuts stone for high tower windows,
Inveraray Castle, *p.84*; builds two houses
at Dalchenna, Inveraray, *p.148*; builds
'factory' or weaver's house in Gallowgate,
Inveraray, *p.172*
1752f., overseer for building dykes and
estate bridges, Inveraray (including two-
arched bridges, Glenshira (1753), Cromalt
bridge (1754–5)): *pp.106, 134*, and Inv/
KJ 1752/4, s411(2) accts.
1752–?7, builds Stronshira park wall,
Inveraray: Inv/KJ; J. Campbell to
Milton, 7 March 1756, s415
1752–7, builds kitchen garden wall for
Inveraray Castle. *p.134*
1755, 4 July, admitted burgess of Inveraray:
IBR
1757, contracts to run St Catherine's
quarry: s87, s416(3); builds avenue wall
(Inveraray new town boundary), *p.168*;
removes from Garron to a Gallowgate house,
improved by self, *p.171* and s416(3)
1758, supplies St Catherine's stone for

(unexecuted) church at Inveraray, and for
paving dairy milk-house: s418(3)
1758–9, in financial difficulties, unable to
pay quarriers; continues in charge of outworks, and of stone and lime supply
to works till at least 1760. *p.165*
1758–62, quarries for and builds Inveraray
quay by contract, to John Adam's design.
p.168
1759, refits Inveraray Castle windows damaged by weather: A. Cumming to Lady Milton, 8 February 1759, s91
1758, 1759, designs for houses (unexecuted)
for Inveraray new town. *p.151*

?RALLY, Hugh, brick-maker at Rosneath
1750–3, output at Rosneath brickfield,
gross 650,000 at 12s per 1000 prime cost:
s411(2) accts

RAMSAY, James, slater in ?Edinburgh.
d. ?1797
son to James Ramsay, slater in Haddington,
and Margaret Carmichael, servant to James
Sim (= Syme), slater and burgess (q.v.);
James Ramsay elder m. 12 December 1718:
EM
(Either of the following marriages may relate to another James Ramsay, son to
Alexander Ramsay, slater, apprenticed to
Simon Andrew, slater, 1747 and burgess of
Edinburgh 1754: EA, EB)
James Ramsay, slater, N.N. Kirk p., m.
Janet, dau. to dec. John Hutton, sailor in
Bo'ness, 17 April 1743: EM
James Ramsay, slater, m. Christian, dau. to
dec. Thomas Stirling, farmer in Newburgh,
27 January 1754: EM
employed by James Syme (q.v.)
1753, slates Inveraray Castle roof, and
mineral well: Inv/Jnl 1752/4, s411(2)
and s426 accts
1797, 21 November, testament of *James
Ramsay*, slater in Edinburgh: ET

REID, John, mason in Inveraray. d. ?1773
1749, mentioned, given house at Bridge
End, Inveraray, with John Meldrum, which
is demolished 1752: Inv/rental 1749, CA
1748f.
1773, 19 February, testament of *John Reid*,
mason in Greenock: GT

REID, John, wright in Glasgow
1775, paid for making 18 windows for new
town, Inveraray: Inv/CA 1774/5; admitted
burgess and gild brother of Glasgow by
purchase: GB
John Reid, wright, admitted burgess and
gild brother of Glasgow as eldest son to
William Reid, wright, B. & G.B., 11 August
1757: GB

REID,* Robert, architect in Edinburgh. 1776–1856
son to Alexander Reid, architect and burgess of Edinburgh: E B
last Master of the King's Works for Scotland (1809–40). *p. 400, n. 41*
1793, 26 January, Robert Reid, land surveyor in St Andrew p., Edinburgh, m. Miss Catherine, dau. to dec. Baillie William Fisher of Inveraray: E M
1802f., work in Edinburgh: with William Sibbald designs 2nd New Town (1802); refronts Parliament House (1807). *p. 400, n. 41*
1807, 18 August, admitted burgess of Edinburgh: E B
1808, plans and elevations for new Court House, Inveraray (unexecuted; later adapted by James Gillespie, q.v.), echoing his Parliament House front. *pp. 316, 318–19*

REOACH, George, mason
1752, October-November, hewing stone for Clerk's house, Inveraray new town, under James Potter: s 410(2), 411(2)

RHIND, [RIND], Martin, mason
*c.*1816–20, employed in building new Court House, Inveraray; levels street opposite building and repairs damage caused to adjoining house: Inv/Lindsay Howe 33A, Lumsden & Peddie's acct 1820

RICHARDSON,* William, smith in Edinburgh. d. ?1794
?grandson to Thomas Richardson, Bo'ness, and son to William Richardson (who is apprenticed to William Broun, locksmith in Edinburgh, 1708, and m. Margaret, dau. to dec. Nicol Gibson, smith, 17 August 1716); Smith to the Mint: E A, E M
William Richardson, smith, S.S.E.p., Edinburgh, m. Jane Kincaid, widow of Thomas Mercer, Commissary Clerk, 22 April 1739: E M
William Richardson junior, smith in Edinburgh, eldest son to William Richardson senior etc., decreet in process of Declarator of marriage against, by spouse Barbara Nairn, dau. to John Nairn, glover in Banff, 20 August 1741: E C P no. 329
1744, makes ironwork for Whim: locks, fenders, jack pulleys, laboratory chimneys; and for Duke of Argyll's lodging, Holyroodhouse: Inv/1744, s 402(1), 404
1745, 5 June, admitted burgess of Edinburgh in right of his father William Richardson, smith, burgess: E B
1745, work on kitchen chimneys, old Inveraray Castle: S403(2)
1754–6, supplies ironwork for Inveraray: hinges, to George Haswell (1754), locks and bands for old castle kitchen (1754–6):

s 416(3) accts; W. Richardson to G. Haswell, 13 September 1754, s 83
1755, supplies fire-irons for new inn, Inveraray. *p. 157*
1759, commissioned to make grates and fenders for new Inveraray Castle, including for dining-room, dressing-room, bedrooms: memo. 30 June 1759, s 419(1), Milton to Argyll 3, 17 May 1760, s 420(3)
1771, ordered to finish 2 polished grates for Inveraray Castle: Inv/CI February, 1771
2 *William Richardsons,* smiths in Edinburgh, either possibly son to above, married in Edinburgh, 1777, 1794: E M
1794, 3 October, and 23 January 1795, testament of William Richardson, smith in Edinburgh: E T

RICHMOND,* George, R.A. 1809–96
executes painted panel above drawing-room chimney-piece, Inveraray Castle, n.d. *p. 383, n. 68*

RIND, William, mason
1816–28, mentioned as living in Arkland, Inveraray: Inv/Rental

RITCHIE, ——, ?mason at Rosneath
Edinburgh marriages show *James* (1758), *John* (1767), journeyman masons, *William* (1768) and *Thomas* Ritchie (1774), masons: E M
John Ritchie, sometime mason in Edinburgh, now in Paisley, m. Margaret, dau. to dec. Robert Halliburton, late bottle-maker in Glasgow, 12 March 1786; process of Declarator of marriage against, 1788, by Margaret Leslie in Edinburgh, alleging marriage on 1 November 1785: E C P no. 896
Thomas Ritchie, mason in Canongate: dau. Elizabeth m. Robert Kemp, mason, 1 April 1794: C M
1806, 'attending to the stone and brick work at Rosneath'; ordered by Joseph Bonomi to alter main stairs at Inveraray Castle for installation of w.c.'s: Inv/plan chest, Bonomi plans
1807, reports on Joseph Bonomi's work at Inveraray; with John Simpson (q.v.) estimates for Bonomi's fosse causeways at £986 4s: Inv/Bonomi; H. Graham to Argyll 6, 5 February 1807, Inv/1806 file

ROBERTSON, ——, mason
*c.*1816–20, employed in building new Court House, Inveraray; with Martin Rhind (q.v.) levels street opposite building: Inv/Lindsay Howe 33A, Lumsden & Peddie's acct 1820

ROBERTSON, David, locksmith, d. ?1793
?son to David Robertson, of Brunton: E B
?King's smith: E T
1734, apprenticed to George Old or Ald, locksmith: E A

1747, locksmith, admitted burgess of Edinburgh as apprentice to above: E B
1754, 24 November, David Robertson, smith, S.E.p., m. Penelope, dau. to Henry Robertson, factor to Earl of Dumfries at Crangrie, Clackmannan: E M
1759, supplies locks and other ironwork for Inveraray Castle: s 419(1), acct of 12 February 1759
1793, 24 May, testament of David Robertson, King's smith, residing at Head of Cowgate, Edinburgh: E T

ROBERTSON [ROBINSON], John, slater, in Inveraray
1751, 30 September, admitted burgess of Inveraray: I B R; slates old castle roof, stable and other offices, Inveraray: Inv/Jnl 1750/2, 1751 file
1752, harls Gallowgate houses, Inveraray: Inv/Jnl 1750/2
1753–4, payments to, unspecified: Inv/Jnl 1752/4

ROBERTSON,* Philip, plasterer
c.1758–60, working at Inveraray Castle; paid by John Adam £108. p.93

ROBINSON, John see ROBERTSON

ROSS, Francis, wright in Glasgow
1707, 18 September, Francis Ross, wright, admitted burgess and gild brother of Glasgow as serving apprentice to dec. James Luke, wright, B. & G.B.; gratis, 'for his good service at the late accidental fire at the cross at the head of the Gallowgate' (Glasgow), by act of Council 16 September: G B
1721, employed in rebuilding 2nd Duke of Argyll's office houses at Inveraray: Inv/ 2 D Ac; 3 May, admitted burgess of Inveraray: I B R

ROSS, John, watchmaker in Inveraray. d. by 1816
1766, mends Inveraray town clock: Inv/A E C B 1759/60
1773, cleans a clock at Inveraray Castle: Inv/C A 1773/4
1778–9, repairs Inveraray Castle clocks: Inv/C A 1778/9
1788–96, named as living in Laigh house next McCallum's, Inveraray; widow in same house 1816: Inv/Rental

ROY,* Henry, Duke of Argyll's smith at Inveraray. d.1770
m. Elizabeth Campbell, Inveraray, before 1740
1743, mentioned as smith in Inveraray (21 May): I B R
1745, named as smith to Duke of Argyll: Inv/1745; supplies ironwork to Inveraray Castle and works. p.79
1746, smith-work for 'new office' and

'hospital', Inveraray: Inv/1746
1748, paid for ironwork for armoury, 'new tower' model room, old Inveraray Castle: Inv/C A
1748f., on regular piece-work, supplying own coals: M L B 73, 76, W. Adam to R. Morris, 5 February 1748
1754, suspected of negligence and fraud. p.80
1757–8, makes stair and gallery railing for Inveraray Castle: Inv/Adam accts 1757/8, Ledger 1754; memo. October 1757, s 416(3)
1757–9, supplies additional ironwork for new Town House, Inveraray. p.163
1764, paid for additional ironwork for gaol cells, Inveraray: Mins. of Commrs of Supply
miscellaneous: sells drink without licence, subsequently authorized to keep public house (1748): Inv/Memo. on works, and Inst. 1748. Rent-free house at Bridge End mentioned (1749, 1768): Inv/C A 1748f., R F D. Inveraray Petty Customs and Anchorage dues set to (1755, 1758): I B R
1770, death of; succeeded in post by son John (q.v.). pp.184, 258

ROY,* John, Duke of Argyll's smith at Inveraray. 1747–?1788
son to Henry Roy; m. Jean Campbell 1770: I P R
1771f., succeeds father as Duke of Argyll's smith; removes from Bridge End, Inveraray, to new smithy at Wintertown Gate (built 1772). p.258, and see Inv/Inst. December 1771, s R O Window Tax returns, E 204/1
1770–4, payments to, for ironwork for Inveraray gaol: I B R
1776, makes ironwork for Clunary wool factory, Bridge of Douglas, Inveraray: Inv/C A 1775/6
1777–8, makes iron railing to surround Inveraray Castle: Inv/Inst. October 1775, C A 1777/8
1788, 7 May, testament of John Roy, smith in Greenock: G T

RUSSELL,* Adam
1789, 12 October, Adam Russell, builder, St Andrew p., Edinburgh, m. Beatrice, dau. to George Blake, farmer at New Barns, Haddingtonshire: E M
1798–9, designs New Highland Church, Campbeltown, p.394, n.14
1801–2, executes alterations to Capt. Archibald Campbell (later Chamberlain)'s house, Inveraray. p.394, n.14

RUSSELL,* Adam and Thomas, architects and building contractors in Edinburgh
1789, contractors for Robert Adam at Seton Castle. p.394, n.14
1791, build Airthrey to Robert Adam's design. p.394, n.14

SMITH, William, mason. d. ?1786
c.1747f., working at Inveraray; loses
possessions in masons' 'guildhall' fire of
March 1752: Inv/AEM
William Smith, journeyman mason, m.
Susan, dau. to Alexander Gills, shoemaker
in Lanark, 13 June 1767: CM
William Smith, mason in Edinburgh, has a
son George apprenticed to John Lockhart,
white ironsmith in Edinburgh, 13 January
1785: EA
William Smith, architect, buried Calton
cemetery, Edinburgh, 1786; inscription
'S.M.Gul. Smith—Architectoris 1786':
NMRS

SOMMERS, John, carpenter in Campbeltown
1751, 25 June, admitted burgess of
Inveraray: IBR

SPENCE, David, mason
1758, tenders for building sunk fences,
Inveraray (Wester Creggans/Bridge of
Douglas, Cruit/Stronmagachan gate):
s418(2)
1777, 13 July, David Spence, mason, m.
Katharine, dau. to dec. Andrew Hart,
farmer at Inverkeithing: EM

SPENCE, Robert, mason in Inveraray
?son or grandson to Robert Spence, mason
admitted burgess of Glasgow 18 February
1675: GB
1723, 10 October, admitted burgess of
Inveraray: IBR
1754, estimate accepted to build
Stuckscarden dyke, Inveraray: Inv/KJ
1752/7, s412(1)
?1755–60, dyke-building at Inveraray,
Stuckscarden/Maam, Dalchenna, Elrigbeg
and Kilblaan (taken over from James Potter,
q.v.), Achinbreck, Kilmun, Balantyre, Inn/
Wintertown, Old Town Common, Maltland park, Black Hill/Esachosan, etc.:
s414(2) and (3), 416(3), 418(2), 419(2)
1760, makes and paves drain to new town
well, Inveraray: s420(2)

STEVENSON, Francis, Deacon of Incorporation of Wrights in Glasgow 1713, 1721,
1730
?son to Francis Steinstoune, wright (burgess
of Glasgow 1675 as son to dec. John
Steinstoune, wright and burgess): GB
1721, executes wright work and repairs at
'old office house' and 'new office',
Inveraray: IBR; 3 May, admitted burgess of
Inveraray: IBR

STEVENSON, Francis, younger, ?wright
in Glasgow
grandson to the above
1721, 3 May, admitted burgess of Inveraray
with his grandfather and others, while

employed in rebuilding 2nd Duke's office
houses, Inveraray: IBR

STEVENSON,* James, surveyor and architect in Edinburgh
assistant to James Gillespie (q.v.)
1813, acts as substitute adviser on Inveraray
Court House during illness of James
Gillespie, *p. 317*; values old Court House and
new site, Inveraray; miscalculation in
foundation level, *p. 318*

STEVENSON, Thomas, wright in Glasgow
1744, August, makes floors for Duke of
Argyll's lodging, Inveraray: s402(2) accts

STEWART, Duncan, mason
1788, named as living in Relief Land,
Inveraray: Inv/Rental
1803, 10 March, *Duncan Stewart*, mason at
Drunkie, admitted burgess and gild brother
of Glasgow by purchase: GB

STEWART, James, mason
James Stewart, mason, Canongate p., m.
Jean, dau. to William Frasser, labourer,
28 May 1792: CM
James Stewart, mason, admitted burgess and
gild brother of Glasgow by purchase, 8
February 1823: GB
c.1816–20, foreman of works in building
new Court House, Inveraray: Inv/Lindsay
Howe 33A, Decreet Arbitral 11 June 1821

STEWART, Robert, mason
1801, one of masons building houses in
new town, Inveraray: Inv/Gen.Accts 1800/1

STIRLING, James, mason
1748, estimate for building dyke in Stronshira, Inveraray, regarded by Duke of Argyll
as 'extraordinary'(high): Fletcher to Milton,
23 February 1748, s71A, s406(1)
1752, to work new Tombreac quarry under
George Hunter's direction: Inv/CI 1752

STOBIE, William, mason in Doune
1725, 3 June, admitted burgess of Inveraray:
IBR

STODARD,* [STOTHARD], William,
from Arrochar
1785, called to Inveraray to direct building
of ice-house. *p. 244*

STRANG, Andrew, quarrier to Duke of
Argyll
1731, 27 September, admitted burgess of
Inveraray: IBR

STRATHEARN,* Graham, Duke of Argyll's
wright at Rosneath
m. Robina Craufurd: GB; ?father to John
Strathearn, 'wright in the Abby', Canongate,
who m. 9 May 1795 Flora, dau. to Hugh
McDougall in Inveraray, and who in 1800
(as 'journeyman wright in Kilmarnock')
institutes process of Adherence against the
said Flora, sometime servant in Broomhill,
Lanarks: CM; ECP XXV. 91 no.1174

1758, secures cargo of mahogany from Glasgow, for Inveraray Castle middle tower windows, and for Rosneath. *p. 119*

*c.*1762f., in charge of building materials at Rosneath: Inv/4DA & Ld Lorne, articles 1762

1770, 23 August, admitted burgess and gild brother of Glasgow as husband of Robina, dau. to dec. Francis Craufurd, wright and burgess: GB

1772, his house in Inveraray old town demolished: Inv/accts 1772f.

1773–6, payments to, for work at Inveraray: Inv/CA 1773/4, 1775/6

1778, erects crop-drying 'pins' in Fisherland barn, Inveraray: Inv/CA 1777/8

n.d., designs ornamental gates for Inveraray estate: Saltoun plan chest

SUTHERLAND, [?Alexander], & partners, wrights

1774, working at saw mill (?Carlundon), Inveraray: Inv/CA 1773/4

1775, *Alexander Sutherland*'s house, Inveraray old town, demolished: Inv/AEM

SYME, James, 'free slater in Edinburgh' son to James Syme, slater and burgess of Canongate, who m. 1700 Elizabeth, dau. to Hendrie Frazer, herald painter, and d. ?1741 (testament 17 February 1741 of James Syme, sometime deacon-convener of Trades of Edinburgh). The elder Syme is presumably the one who worked at Inversnaid Barracks 1718f.: CM; ET; *Stirlingshire* (RCAHMS 1963) II p. 273

1732, admitted burgess of Edinburgh as son to James Syme, slater in Edinburgh: EB

1741, James Syme elder and younger named as slaters to Board of Ordnance on Scottish establishment (during period when William Adam was King's Mason): PRO WO 54, 207, p. 37

1753, slating roof of Inveraray Castle with James Ramsay (q.v.) and 2 others; slating mineral well: s411(2), 426, 427, accts

TAVISH,* John, mason and architect (at Kilmartin 1788f.)

1781–2, builds Maltland shades and riding-house to Robert Mylne's design. *p. 240*

1783, estimate for Dhu Loch bridge, Inveraray; builds bridge 1785–7. *p. 243*

1786, builds avenue lodge by Great Inn, and town front screens, Inveraray, to Robert Mylne's designs, *p. 270*; builds 3 bridges on new road at Old Town Common, and workmen's houses at Maam, Inveraray: Inv/CA 1785/6

?1787, repairs Inveraray quay at £4 2s (pd February 1788): Inv/CA 1787/8

1788, occupying 2 rooms in Arkland, Inveraray: Inv/Rental; temporarily dismissed in spring, *p. 271*; sent for from Kilmartin for advice when Dhu Loch bridge in danger: Inv/CA 1787/8

1788, ?October-1790, executes mason-work of Maam 'circle' (barn), Inveraray. *p. 247*

1793, builds Garron Lodge doors and windows, and 2 workmen's houses and 4 byres in Pony Park, Inveraray: Inv/EA 1792 and Gen. accts

1793–4, builds rear extension and bow window to Great Inn, Inveraray. *p. 289, p. 392, n. 62*

1798, builds bridge at Stuckagoy, Glenshira. *p. 248*

1799, 1800, tenders for completion of Robert Mylne's church, Inveraray (summoned from Kilmartin, as 'architect'), *p. 282; p. 392, n.62*; proposed by Col. Graham for building new garden wall with Michael Carmichael (q.v.): Inv/Ltr Book 1799/1800

1802, mason work for new house at New Town Point, Inveraray: Inv/Accts 1802

1802–3, builds Hexagon summerhouse, and two houses opposite Carlundon, Inveraray. *p. 252*, and Inv/Hshld accts

1803, builds bridge on road from new kiln to Tombreac quarry, Inveraray: Inv/Accts 1804

1805, builds lime-kiln coal-house at £43 17s 4d: Inv/CA 1805

TAYLOR, Henry, mason and builder in Falkirk

1810, contractor (with William Black, wright) to build Falkirk church to design by James Gillespie (Graham); completed 1811: SRO Falkirk HR

1813–4, erects town steeple, Falkirk, designed by David Hamilton: Johnston *The Falkirk Steeple* (Falkirk Rotary Club)

*c.*1818, recommended by James Gillespie as Inspector (Clerk of Works) for new Court House, Inveraray; renders progress reports to Commissioners of Supply: Inv/Lindsay Howe 33A

1820, July, reports completion of outstanding items in Inveraray Court House contract: Inv/Lindsay Howe 33A

1821, interviewed by Alexander Laing in Court House arbitration case: Inv/Lindsay Howe 33A

TEMPLETON,* [TEMPLETOWN], William, stone-carver

1756–8, carves obelisks for fosse bridges, Inveraray Castle. *p. 86*

1760, mentioned, employed at Inveraray Castle as mason: Inv/Q accts

James Veitch, glazier (?father or son), S.W.
p., Edinburgh, m. Isobel, dau. to Alexander
Greive, farmer in Keillie, Traquair, 5 May
1734: EM
c.1734–54, recorded as working for Ld Morton and his son, also for Ld Hopetoun, John
Dickson, MP, and 3rd Duke at Abbey
lodging, Holyroodhouse. Known to John
Paterson, wright of Queensferry (q.v.):
Memorial 1754, s83
1749, admitted burgess of Edinburgh: EB
1754, applies to Ld Milton on strength of
above, (a) for post of King's glazier, (b)
for employment at Inveraray: Memorial
1754, s83
1756, glazes front windows of Town House
and 2 adjoining houses, Inveraray. p.162
1762, 12 June, testament of James Veitch,
glazier in Edinburgh: ET

WAINS, William, quarrier to Duke of Argyll
1731, 27 September, admitted burgess of
Inveraray: IBR
WARDROP,* Hew Montgomerie, architect.
1856–87
1886, with Sir R. Rowand Anderson (q.v.),
designs Episcopal Church, Inveraray. p.310
WARDROP,* Deacon John, mason in Glasgow. d. ?1767
1755, 4 July, admitted burgess of Inveraray:
IBR
1756–8, contractor for digging out fosse
and casemates, Inveraray Castle. p.86
1757, excavates fosse for building servants'
privies, Inveraray Castle. p.87
1758, tenders for building Achnagoul and
Barvrack dykes, in competition with James
Anderson (q.v.). Referred to as George
Hunter's foreman: s89
1762, 27 May, admitted burgess and gild
brother of Glasgow by purchase: GB
1763, 1764, Deacon of Incorporation of
Masons, Glasgow: Annals
1767, 24 December, and 11 November 1768,
testament of John Wardrop, mason in Glasgow: GT
WARDROP, John, wright in Glasgow
son to John Wardrop, wright (who served
apprenticeship with David Stevenson,
wright and burgess, and became burgess of
Glasgow 1724, Deacon, 1736): GB
1751, 13 September, John Wardrop younger,
wright, admitted burgess and gild brother
of Glasgow as serving apprentice with his
father: GB
1757, buys Duke of Argyll's fallen timber at
Inveraray, from John Richardson, merchant
(later Provost) of Inveraray: s414(2)

WATSON, J[ohn?], ?slater in Edinburgh.
d. ?1798
1755, at John Adam's request checks James
Syme's account for slating at Inveraray:
s413(2)
1798, 18 May, testament of John Watson,
slater in Edinburgh: ET
WELLS, Andrew, interior decorator and
leaded glass craftsman. 8 Newton Terrace,
Glasgow, d.1902
brother to Willie Wells, painter of the
Glasgow School; in business 1869; 1897
amalgamated with J. & W. Guthrie
(estab. 1852); recorded as decorating St
Andrew's Halls, New Club, and churches
of St Andrew's parish, Hillhead Established,
Belhaven and Camphill in Glasgow;
Cairndhu at Helensburgh, Ardincaple,
Skipness and Kelburne; n.d., all before
1886: The Bailie, Glasgow 1886
?1875 (?or 1871), decorated 'Library and
Royal Apartments', Inveraray Castle:
The Bailie (information from Frank
Christie of Guthrie & Wells, via David
and Averil Walker)
WELSH, Thomas, glazier in Edinburgh
1758, makes 'broads' for tower windows,
Inveraray Castle; prepares panes for
glazier: Inv/Ledger 1754, Adam Bros accts
1757/8
WHITE, ——, & McPHEA, ——, partners,
quarriers
1773–4, quarrying stone for shade at Fisherland barn, Inveraray: Inv/CA 1773/4
1755, 18 June, John White, son to John
Adam's clerk Alexander White, apprenticed
to Thomas Mylne (father to Robert and
William Mylne), mason in Edinburgh: EA
WHITEHEAD, James, plasterer
1744, 25 November, James Whitehead,
journeyman wright, S.S.E. p., m. Margaret
Ireland, servant to John Gibson, merchant:
EM
1757, paid £42 8s. for unspecified plaster-
work at Inveraray: abstract accts, s416(3)
1773–80, unspecified plasterwork at Barns
House, Peebles-shire: SRO Burnet of
Barns MSS, Box 17 Bundle 40
Robert Whitehead, son to above, apprenticed to John Murdoch, watchmaker in
Edinburgh (1770); James Whitehead,
plasterer in Troup (?another son), m. Janet
Simpson, widow of Robert Galbraith,
bricklayer (11 May 1786): EA, EM
WHYTE,* James, house-wright
1755, obtains 140-ft frontage site in main
street of Inveraray new town; unexecuted
due to financial difficulties; part-site of
Alexander McPherson's house, built
1756. p.151

GENERAL INDEX

Names of persons about whom further information is given in the Index of Architects and Craftsmen (pp. 405ff.) are followed by *. Page numbers in italic refer to text illustrations.

Morris, Roger, association with – *cont.*
Ilay, 29–31; choice as architect for Inveraray, 29; first visit to Inveraray, 12, 16,
18, 26, 31–2; payments, 68; prevention
of visit by the Forty-five, 48; visit of 1747,
58, 60–1, 70, 125; *see also under* work
elsewhere); 4th Duke (as Colonel Campbell), 31, 62; Howard, Mrs Henrietta, 30,
40; Marlborough, Duchess of, 31, 41;
Pembroke, Earl of, 30, 40; Milton, Lord,
32; Vanbrugh, Sir John, 30–1, 37, 40–1
bridges, survey of sites for, 60
Castle: bedrooms, 36; building supervision,
56; chimneys, instructions for, 72; design
and plans (criticism by Clerk of Eldin, 34;
derivations of, 35–40; description, 35–45,
36, *43*, 52, *58*, *59*, 338; excavation plan,
46; foundation plan, 31, 52; Gothick
elements, 35–7, 41; influence on other
buildings, 327–37; model, 60, 73, 109,
338–9, 360 n.166, 403 n.21; Palladian
elements, 36–7, 43, *43*, 45; survey of site,
31; working plans, 32); drawing-rooms,
36; fosse, 35, 36, 45; hall, 36, 37; long
gallery, 36, *36*, 196–7; staircases, 35, 36,
37, 38, *85*; storeys, number of, 35; timber,
instructions for, 58, 60, 72, 75, 107, 108–9,
110; windows, 35, 36–7, 203
dovecot, 127–8, *131*, 237, 238, pls. 8, 14
Duniquaich watch-tower, 127, 128, *129*, 130,
131, pl. 7
Garron Bridge, 62, 125, *126*, *137*, 200,
pls. 5, 6
military road, inspection of, 61, 125
physic or mineral well, 127, 140, 143, 233,
262
work elsewhere: Blair Atholl, building for
policies, 351 n.66; Blenheim Palace, 30,
40; Combe Bank, 31, *31*, 62, 182; Eastbury, 31, 37, 40, 41, 352 n.4; Marble Hill,
30; Rosneath, 32, 61, 67, *91*, 92, 290;
Whim, sketch for 'Oval', 349 n.41;
Whitton Place, villa attributed to, 10, 31–2,
45; Wilton, 30
Morrison, Charles, house at Inveraray, 400 n.36
Morrison, George, QMG of the Forces, 90
Morton, Robert Douglas, 12th Earl of, 356 n.88
Morvern, 19, 46
Deputy Chamberlains of, 19, 48, 67, 376 n.75
see also Campbell of Airds, Donald
Moubray, Christopher, Edinburgh Friendly
Insurance Society, 390 n.22
Mount Edgcumbe, Devon, 38, 40
Mountstuart, Bute, 101, 351 n.62
Muckle,* Thomas, mason, 261
Mull, 19, 46, 107, 112, 298, 371 n.39, 376 n.75,
387 n.32, 397 n.51
Deputy Chamberlain of, 67; *see also* Camp-
bell of Ballamore, Archibald
Ross of Mull fishery, 392 n.82

Munro family, 388 n.75
Munro, Neil, 399–400 n.75
Mure, Anne, née Graham, wife of Baron Mure,
193, 379 n.7
Mure of Caldwell, Baron William, 193, 205,
379 n.7
Murray, Dugald, house in old town, 265
Murray, Sir John McGregor, 298
Murray, Hon. Mrs Sarah, wife of Hon. William
Murray, visit to Inveraray, 243, 248, 256,
298, 396 n.46
Musselburgh Links, troop reviews on, 191, 193,
203
Mylne, Maria, daughter of Robert Mylne,
drawing by, *198*
Mylne, Mary, wife of Robert Mylne, 199
Mylne, Robert: parentage, 106; study in Rome
and St Luke's Academy award, 106, 184;
attitude of Robert Adam to, 106, 184;
reputation, 196, 198; character and independence, 199, 293; elected FRS, 198;
Surveyor to Canterbury Cathedral and
New River Company, 198; marriage and
family, 199; fees, 203, 208, 236; last years,
292–3; death, 293; portrait, *198*
and 5th Duke: association with, 184, 196,
199, 212, 282, 284–6, 289, 382 n.51, 391
n.51; disagreement with, 199, 282, 285–6,
292; Duke's appreciation of, 199, 237,
292–3; portrait of Duchess presented by,
237, 381 n.29
and 6th Duke, as Lord Lorne, 199, 290, 291,
382 n.51
Aray Bridge, pls. 25, 26, 35: design, 233,
234–6, *235*; inspection and rebuilding of,
200, 234–6; spandrel opening, 235–6, 270
architectural style: architectural features
employed by, 235–6, 263, 269–70, 284;
use of Gothick style, 244, 247–8
barns: Fisherland (New Town), 230–1, 236;
Maam (Glenshira), 231, 247–8, pls. 29, 30;
Maltland, 231, 240, *240*, 241
Bealachanuaran springhead: advice on
restoration, 269, 387 n.43; landscaping of
surroundings, 244, 387 n.43
bridges, inspection after storm, 199–200, 234
Castle: arms, arrangement of, 212, 213;
book-presses, 281; ceilings, 200, 208, 211,
215, 216, pl. 19; chimney-piece, alteration
to, 212; 'covered way', proposal for fosse,
203; dining-room, section of, *210*; doors,
design for, 208, *209*; fosse, post-and-chain
fence for, 203; interior, transformation of,
199, 200, 208–16, 362 n.191; saloon
garden door, 211, 212; survey, 199;
windows (astragals, 203; circular tops,
200, *201*, 203, 215, *217*; lowered to floor-
level, 200, *201*, *202*, 203, 211, 339)
church: as focal point, 149, 259, 267, 268,
282; building materials, 283–4; colonnades

plasterwork and stucco, 200, 211, 215
  cost of, 211, 215, 362 nn.189, 190
Playfair, James, architect, 328, 331, 402 n.3
plumbers
  cost of, 75–6, 105
  employed at Castle, 75
  plumbing at Castle, 75–6, 87–8, 366 n.223
  water-closets, 87–8, 208, 311, 382 n.43
  water-pipes, 105, 339, 382 n.51
Pococke, Bishop Richard, visit to Inveraray,
  57, 105–6, 143, 366 n.226
Police Station, *see* Crown Point House
policies
  Balantyre plantations, 252
  Bealachanuaran springhead, *see* Bealachanu-
    aran
  'belvedere', proposed, *see* Duniquaich
  Black Hill, 46, 127, 130, 258, 339
  cascades, 134, 199, 208, 233, 386 n.14
  Deer Park, 137, 236, 243, 244, 372 n.44
  2nd Duke's additions, 26, *29*, 121
  3rd Duke's improvements, 10, 61, 121–43,
    205, 229
  5th Duke's improvements, 203, 229–54
  6th Duke's neglect of, 313
  excursions round, 60, 128, 194, 239, 296,
    387 n.43
  extent, 242
  farm buildings, *see* Fisherland, Glenshira,
    Maltland
  influence in Scotland, 327
  landscaping, 205, 225, 340, *341*
  lawns, 87, 228, 232
  Oak walk, 127, 128, 137
  park walls and dykes, 76, 79, 81, 106, 134,
    136, 143, 232, 366 n.227
  plans: *c.* 1722, *28*, *29*; 1756, *89*, *155*; 1757,
    142
  river course, 160
  roads: bridges (small), 134, 199, 242;
    crossings, 244, 269; Deer Park, 243; Duni-
    quaich, 128, 221; Esachosan, 238, 239,
    387 n.43; estate, 134, 238, 239; Garron
    Lodge entrance, 236–7; Mylne's planning
    of, 237, 244; public, through parks, 122;
    Wintertown, 73, 160
  visitors' comments: general, 229, 250; Gilpin,
    J., 205; Inglis, J., 242; Loch, D., 238;
    Pattison, J., 229; Pennant, T., 229;
    Pococke, R., 105; Thrale, Mrs, 242
  woodlands, 61, 242, 250
  see also avenues, bridges, cottages, dairy,
    dovecot, Duniquaich, Hexagon, parks,
    physic well, Salt Water Pond
Pollion, Shiel of, 250
Pond, Salt Water (Gallows Green Pond)
  building and stocking of, 134–5, *135*, 160,
    371 n.39
  3rd Duke's interest in, 134
  effect of military bridge on, 135, 233

infilling of, 233
Ponsonby, John William, Baron, later 4th Earl
  of Bessborough, 310
population
  Glenaray, 251, 391 n.48
  Glenshira, 245
  new town, 267, 342
porte-cochère, Bonomi's use of, 291
Porteous Riots, 5
Portincaple, Dunbartonshire, 65
Portland, 3rd Duke of, William Henry
  Cavendish-Bentinck, 198, 393 n.9
Portland, 4th Duke of, *see* Titchfield, Marquess
  of
Port Mahon, Minorca, 387–8 n.57
Port Sonachan, Loch Awe, 229
Post Office
  at Inveraray, 401 n.48
  postal service to Inveraray, 279
Potter,* James, mason and overseer
  bridges, estate, 106, 134
  Castle tower, stone-cutting for, 84
  Dalchenna houses, 148
  Dhu Loch boathouse, 134
  kitchen garden wall, 134, 366 n.227
  lime supply contract, 78, 154
  new town: avenue wall, 168; Gallowgate
    (houses, 148–9; weaver's house or 'factory'
    172); houses, unexecuted designs for, 151,
    373 n.15; quay, 168
  park walls and dykes, 106, 134, 366 n.227
  personal: financial difficulties, 165; living in
    Gallowgate, 171
Prestonpans
  Battle of, 49
  Customs officers, 60, 113
Princess Augusta yacht, 67, 76, 86
Proby, Rev. Baptist, Dean of Lichfield (father-
  in-law of Lord Seaforth), visit to Inveraray,
  297
Pujolas, Henry, major-domo to 3rd Duke, 179

quarriers
  accommodation for, 57
  cost of, 79
  labourers, 46
  number employed, 79, 81, 154
  payment of, 165
  slackness, 67, 80
quarries
  Arran, 282
  Carlundon (rubble), 128, 242
  Creggans, 56, 57, 62, 66, 73, 75, 127, 136,
    354 n.50
  Dumbarton, 260, 263
  Easdale (slate), 76, 387 n.40
  Fisherland: flags, 252; rubble, 136, 154, 165,
    169, 230
  Glenshira, 247
  Greenock, 48

ACKNOWLEDGMENTS

The publishers would like to thank the following individuals and institutions for permission to reproduce illustrations:

His Grace The Duke of Argyll, for figs. 1, 7, 8, 9, 12, 19, 21, 23, 24, 26, 30–2, 34, 40, 41, 43, 45, 49, 52, 53*b*, 54, 55, 64, 65, 69–72, 74–6, 78–81, 83, 86, 89, 95–6, 98, 110, 113

His Grace The Duke of Atholl, for fig. 3

The Rt Hon. The Lord Middleton, for fig. 14

Capt. J. T. T. Fletcher of Saltoun, for figs. 2, 10 (411.2), 27 (418.1), 33 (Plan Chest), 39, 42 (417.1), 44 (394), 47 (417.1), 48 (411.1), 50 (417.1), 51 (402), 53*a* (408.2), 56 (417.1), 57 (411.2), 58 (Plan Chest), 60 (418.2), 62 (408.2)

Capt. Charles Adam, for figs. 22, 25

Sir Ilay Campbell of Succoth, for fig. 20

Capt. P. L. Mackie Campbell, for fig. 4

Mary Cosh, for figs. 28, 29, 67, 68

R. Scott Morton, Esq., for fig. 92

John Warren, Esq., for fig. 18

Aerofilms and Aero Pictorial Ltd, for fig. 114

Bo'ness Burgh Council, for fig. 103

British Museum, for figs. 5 (Top. xlix.31.1.a), 35, 38, 93, 94 (Add. 33687 f.175)

Country Life, for figs. 87, 107

Courtauld Institute, for figs. 15, 18

Department of the Environment, for fig. 90

Inveraray Grammar School, for fig. 84

Messrs Ian Lindsay & Partners, for figs. 85, 112

National Library of Scotland, for figs. 11, 13, 16, 36, 37, 46, 59, 77, 82, 88, 100, 102, 104, 105, 106, 108, 109, and Dorret's Map

National Monuments Record of Scotland, for figs. 18, 73, 91, 101

Penguin Books Ltd, for fig. 61

Royal Institute of British Architects, for figs. 17, 111

Scottish National Galleries, for figs. 6, 63, 66

Scottish Record Office, for fig. 99

Thompson of Edinburgh, for fig. 97

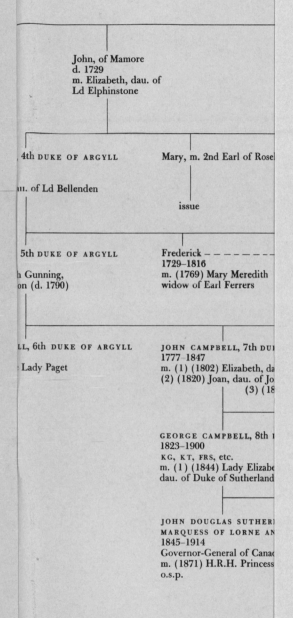

John, of Mamore
d. 1729
m. Elizabeth, dau. of
Ld Elphinstone

, 4th DUKE OF ARGYLL

ui. of Ld Bellenden

Mary, m. 2nd Earl of Rose

issue

, 5th DUKE OF ARGYLL

h Gunning,
on (d. 1790)

Frederick — — — — — —
1729–1816
m. (1769) Mary Meredith
widow of Earl Ferrers

LL, 6th DUKE OF ARGYLL

: Lady Paget

JOHN CAMPBELL, 7th DUI
1777–1847
m. (1) (1802) Elizabeth, da
(2) (1820) Joan, dau. of Jo
(3) (18

GEORGE CAMPBELL, 8th I
1823–1900
KG, KT, FRS, etc.
m. (1) (1844) Lady Elizabe
dau. of Duke of Sutherland

JOHN DOUGLAS SUTHERI
MARQUESS OF LORNE AN
1845–1914
Governor-General of Canac
m. (1871) H.R.H. Princess
o.s.p.